权威 · 前沿 · 原创

皮书系列为

“十二五”“十三五”国家重点图书出版规划项目

BLUE BOOK OF HENAN

Annual Report on Development of Henan

(2017)

Editor-in-chief / Wei Yiming Zhang Zhancang

Vice Editor / Zhou Li Yuan Kaisheng Wang Chengzhe

社会科学文献出版社
SOCIAL SCIENCES ACADEMIC PRESS (CHINA)

图书在版编目(CIP)数据

河南发展报告. 2017：英文 / 魏一明，张占仓主编
. -- 北京：社会科学文献出版社，2018.1
（河南蓝皮书）
ISBN 978-7-5201-1963-4

Ⅰ. ①河… Ⅱ. ①魏… ②张… Ⅲ. ①区域经济发展
－研究报告－河南－2017－英文 ②社会发展－研究报告－
河南－2017－英文 Ⅳ. ①F127.61

中国版本图书馆CIP数据核字（2017）第312882号

河南蓝皮书
Annual Report on Development of Henan（2017）

主　　编 / 魏一明　张占仓
副 主 编 / 周　立　袁凯声　王承哲

出 版 人 / 谢寿光
项目统筹 / 任文武
责任编辑 / 张丽丽

出　　版 / 社会科学文献出版社 · 区域与发展出版中心（010）59367143
地址：北京市北三环中路甲29号院华龙大厦 邮编：100029
网址：www.ssap.com.cn
发　　行 / 市场营销中心（010）59367081　59367018
印　　装 / 北京季蜂印刷有限公司

规　　格 / 开 本：787mm×1092mm 1/16
印 张：26.25　字 数：506千字
版　　次 / 2018年1月第1版　2018年1月第1次印刷
书　　号 / ISBN 978-7-5201-1963-4
定　　价 / 98.00元

Introduction of Major Editors

Wei Yiming, male, born in Luoyang, Henan Province, Party Secretary of Henan Academy of Social Sciences, has published more than ten articles in *Chinese Social Sciences Weekly*, *Henan Daily*, *Journal of the Chinese People's Political Consultative Conference*, *Chinese United Front*, *Zhongzhou United Front* and other newspapers and periodicals, and has edited the *Think-tank in the Central Plains Series, Study of Construction of Safe Henan,* as well as other works.

Zhang Zhancang, male, born in Yanshi, Henan Province, Ph.D, Dean and researcher of Henan Academy of Social Sciences, and supervisor of Ph.D candidates, is an outstanding expert in Henan Province, an academic (technical) leader in Henan Province, and has been awarded the title of mid-aged national experts with remarkable contributions. He is a recipient of the State Council special allowance, and is Vice President of China's Association of Regional Economy. The primary focus of his studies is economic geography. He has earned 14 second-place and five third–place in the Henan Prize for Progress in Science and Technology, and he has published more than 130 academic papers. Additionally, he has served as editor or associate editor on 25 other publications.

Preface

As the world's largest province with more than 100 million people, Henan has made great progress in its opening-up affairs in recent years. During the Twelfth Five-Year Plan, the average annual increase rate of both imports and exports was 32.9%. In 2016, the total imports and exports of the province reached 471.47 billion and ranked the first place in the central and western regions of the country. Henan has becoming one of the most active provinces in the open economy under China's new normal, and the traditional hinterland is becoming the forefront of reform and opening-up. At present, Henan has entered into the new era of development of mutual openness with numbers of global enterprises from the inside and numbers of world's top 500 companies from the outside. Under the new historical situation, it is an objective need to encourage the world know better about Henan, understand it and take further cooperation with it. In order to implement the strategic plan of "turning Henan into the inland openness center", expand its international influence in opening-up intercourse, and exhibit its aspects of open, developing and profound to the world, Henan Academy of Social Sciences organized professors in relevant areas writing the book of *Annual Report on Development of Henan (2017)*, and it was republished by Social Sciences Academic Press. This book mainly consists of 12 special reports about Henan, including the fields of opening-up, economy, industry, finance, technological innovation, tourism, urban, agriculture and rural area, society, culture, rule of law, and Zhongyuan Bank Co., Ltd. This book analyzed the development trend and hotspot issues of the fields above happened from 2012 to 2016 with more than 500 thousand words, which presents a full and accurate literature for the foreign business and academia know well about the past 5 years' development and the future trends of Henan. Through this book, the English-speaking countries will realize that Henan is a great place with real and sustainable development, with energy and vitality, with important contribution to Chinese history, with openness and inclusiveness and responsibility. This is the origin point of this book and is the earnest desire of us.

The compilation and publication of *Annual Report on Development of Henan (2017)* has gained lots of concerns and supports from the provincial government and the community. Thanks for the long time concern, support and help. Additionally, Luoyang Institute of Science and Technology has made great effort in translation, which contribute a lot for the publication. Here, we would like to express our sincere gratitude to the translation team!

After the first publication of *Annual Report on Development of Henan (2016)* in 2016, this book is the second one, there must be some improprieties in it, and welcome any comment and suggestion from the readers both at home and abroad.

CONTENTS

B.1 Report on Opening-up and Development of Henan Province

Zhang Zhancang[*]

Abstract: As a traditional inland province, Henan province constructed an international hub of Zhengzhou airport in the Twelfth Five-Year Plan, which provided the ability of source supplies, thereby increasing production, enabling an increase of both imports and exports of 32.9%, and creating a new model of "opening-up by air". With an innovated Regional Development Mode, fully integrated into the "The Belt and Road Initiative", Henan Province promoted the strategic goal of a development platform for inland provinces, which has subsequently served as a strategic direction for further development.

Our studies suggest that in order to achieve this strategic goal, we must consistently promote the Central Plains provinces to become the forefront of open development, building a new two-way open system, consistently promoting the open economic development program, and focusing on five strategic initiatives: ①We must embrace the national "The Belt and Road Initiative"; ②Promote the advantages gained by the Zhengzhou airport development; ③Support the construction of Zhengzhou National Central City; ④Accelerate open innovation; ⑤Actively explore and develop the "economic hub", a free trade area. Henan province is moving to

* Zhang Zhancang, Henan Academy of Social Sciences.

the forefront of open development and striving to build an inland opening-up height.

KeyWords: The Belt and Road Initiative; Zhengzhou Airport; Opening-up by Air; Inland Opening-up Height; Open Economy

As the inland district of the country, Henan province was once China's political, economic and cultural center, and has made great contributions to the 5000-year civilization of the Chinese nation. However, since the Northern Song Dynasty, with tremendous changes in the political and economic territory of the country, Henan province has gradually faded as a significant contributor to the Chinese economy.

Navigable Chinese areas have exploited the lower shipping costs (1/20th of road transportation) to export to the world, aiding the rapid development of these areas.

However, inland areas have been unable to participate, expand, and develop in the new economic areas. Since the reform and opening-up in 1978, China has benefited exponentially in world trade. China's GDP in 2010 reached 5.7 trillion US dollars, surpassing Japan. China became the world's second largest economy. In 2016, China's GDP reached 11.2 trillion US dollars, accounting for 14.83% of the global share.

Henan is a large inland province without a coastal navigable port in the traditional sense. The province is fully aware of the need to develop a portal to the international markets.

Since the middle of the 1990s, the open development has been the main strategy for the province's development, and Henan province has explored the opportunities of opening to the outside world. In recent years, gradually seeking to open up the new model of development and achieving remarkable results, Henan province is progressing towards the forefront of open development in China.

I Create a New Model of "Opening-Up by Air"

1. Development Ideas Continue to Evolve

In October 2007, in order to speed up the construction of Zhengzhou

International Air Hub, Henan Provincial Party Committee and the Provincial Government approved the establishment of Zhengzhou Airport Economy Zone.

In March 2010, Henan province launched an unprecedented scale of development strategy study. And gradually Henan province focused on the Central Plains Economic Zone.

In October 2010, the State Council approved the establishment of Zhengzhou Airport Economy Zone in Zhengzhou Airport.

In November 2010, the Eleventh Session of the CPC Henan Provincial Committee at its eighth meeting examined and approved the outline of the construction of the Central Plains Economic Zone (Trial Implementation) which formally entered "the Twelfth Five-Year Plan" in Henan.

In March 2011, the Eleventh National People's Congress formally introduced the outline of the construction of the Central Plains Economic Zone in Henan into the national "Twelfth Five-Year Plan". In September 2011, the issue of *The State Council Guidance on Supporting the Construction of the Central Plains Economic Zone in Henan Province* (issued by [2011] No. 32) marked the rise of the Central Plains Economic Zone as a national strategy.

In November 2012, the State Council approved *The Plan of Central Plains Economic Zone (2012 - 2020)*. In the fifth section of Chapter 10, it is proposed that the construction of Zhengzhou Airport Economy Zone should have Zhengzhou airport as the main body, the Economy Zone and related industrial parks as the carrier, the comprehensive transport hub as the basis, the development of air cargo as a breakthrough, and strengthen the policy support, deepen the reform and innovation, and actively undertake domestic and foreign industry transfer, vigorously develop air logistics, air-preferred high-end manufacturing and modern service industry, and promote e-commerce pilot programmes for cross-border trade, and construct distribution centers for global products shopped online, and upgrade industrial structure and development mode, and strive to complete the country's major airports economic gathering areas by 2020 and serve as an ecological, smart, harmonious and livable modern air city, the new opening-up height among central and western regions, and the core growth area in the Central Plains Economic Zone. In March 2013, the State Council approved the development plan for the Zhengzhou Airport Economy Zone (2013-2025). Henan began to explore new ways to promote the opening and development of the inland areas by relying on the construction of the international air hub.

The establishment of the Zhengzhou Airport Economy Zone indicates to seek opening-up by air. The approval of the development plan is the international development dividends brought by the State Council for the Central Plains, against the background that in 2011 international air freight volume exceeded 1% of the total global freight, and air economy meets a special historical opportunity of rapid development. In accordance with the requirements of the State Council, Henan is devoted to the construction of Zhengzhou Airport Economy Zone, exploring and experimenting boldly, inviting foreign business and investment, and attracting wealth and talents, which has speeded the construction and completely changed the difficult situation of Henan's open economy since the 1978 reform and opening-up.

2. The Construction of International Air Hub has Achieved Remarkable Results

As the first of its kind approved by the State Council, Zhengzhou airport freight growth rate ranked first among the nation's major airports in 2013 and 2014, and passenger growth rate ranked the first among the nation's major airports in 2014. The rapid growth of passenger and freight transportation made the hub play a significant role in promoting the economic and social development of the region. In September 2014, when the ICAO air cargo development forum was held in Zhengzhou, Bernard, Chairman of the ICAO board of directors, said that Zhengzhou Airport was the fastest in freight growing around the world. In 2014, its international and regional cargo throughput increased by 82%, accounting for 55% of the total cargo, and exceeding domestic cargo volume; and cargo volume by cargo carriers played a leading role. By the end of 2015, the number of crossing-border entry-exit passengers at Zhengzhou Airport had exceeded 1.2 million. The crossing-border entry-exit volume maintained an average annual growth rate of 50% for eight consecutive years, ranking high among other domestic airports. UPS, FedEx, China Southern Airlines, China Eastern Airlines and other cargo airlines settled in Zhengzhou Airport. Zhengzhou Airport opened the international freight routes, accounting for about 90% of the central region, becoming the only approved area in the central region to carry out international express exports.

On June 27, 2014, "Zhengzhou - Luxemburg" "Double Hub" international freight line opened operation, and Zhengzhou Airport embraced its first international cargo airline: Cargolux International Airline, and by the end of 2014, its cargo traffic exceeded 10 thousand tons. By November 23, 2015, Cargolux International Airline had completed 438 flights, with 50 thousand tons of cargo, and by the end of 2015, the cargo volume exceeded 60 thousand tons. On June 15, 2016, at the 2016 Air Cargo China held in Shanghai, and delegates from Cargolux International Airline announced that in less than two years of launching the "Zhengzhou-Luxemburg" line, the cargo volume exceeded 100 thousand tons. It was only seven months since Cargolux International Airline announced in November 2015 that the cargo volume between the two hubs exceeded 50 thousand tons. The rapid cargo growth in Zhengzhou Airport exerted great influence upon the price of air cargo between China and Europe, so "Zhengzhou price" has became an important index of the international air cargo price between China and Europe. Cooperation with high-end international companies like Cargolux International Airline further promoted development of the Zhengzhou international air hub. The opening and efficient operation of Zhengzhou-Luxemburg "double hub" freight line accelerated the integration of the Zhengzhou international hub into the global transportation network, and it became a striking "Air Silk Road" between China and Europe. In 2015, the total import and export volume of Zhengzhou Airport Economy Zone was 48.33 billion US dollars, accounting for about 85% of Zhengzhou, and 67.4% of Henan province, and it has become a veritable inland opening-up height. As the second-phase project of Zhengzhou Airport put into use at the end of 2015, its passenger and cargo transport capacity has been significantly improved.

By the end of 2016, there were 41 passenger airlines operating in Zhengzhou Airport, including 32 domestic and 9 international ones; there were 186 passenger routes, including 25 international and regional routes; and there were 86 navigable cities, including 19 international and regional cities. Zhengzhou Airport opened all 34 international all-cargo routes and ranked first in China's interior, which formed a network covering major global economies. The cargo airlines, cargo flights and navigable cities operating in Zhengzhou Airport ranked fourth among the world's large airports, and Zhengzhou Airport had 15 destinations among the world's top 20 cargo hub airports. In 2016,

Zhengzhou Airport passenger throughput reached 20.76 million, an increase of 20%, ranking the fifteenth among domestic airports; cargo throughput reached 457 thousand tons, an increase of 13.4%, ranking the seventh in the country, the first in the central region, and the volume of passenger and freight transport reached a record high. From 2010 to 2016, the volume of cargo transportation in Zhengzhou Xinzheng International Airport increased rapidly from 85.8 thousand tons to 45.7 million tons, which made it to be China's seventh largest air cargo hub (Table 1). Zhengzhou Airport completed the international passenger and cargo handling capacity of 1.265 million travelers and 875,100 tons, an increase of 5.69% and 20.93% respectively, continuing the rapid expansion of international business.

Table 1 The development of passenger and cargo transport in Zhengzhou airport since 2011

Particular year	Cargo throughput (million tons)	Cargo throughput growth rate (%)	Passenger throughput (10000 persons)	Passenger throughput growth rate (%)
2011	10.3	19.8	1015	16.5
2012	15.1	46.6	1167	15.0
2013	25.6	69.5	1314	12.6
2014	37.0	44.5	1581	20.3
2015	40.3	8.9	1730	9.4
2016	45.7	13.4	2076	20.0

Note: The data in this table is collected by author.

On June 14, 2017, Chinese President Xi Jinping met Luxemburg Prime Minister Bettel in the Great Hall of the People and pointed out that the two countries should improve the quality of bilateral pragmatic cooperation, expand the advantages, tap potential, make the traditional areas of financial cooperation bigger and stronger, accelerate new cooperation growth points in air transportation, high-tech and green economy, and achieve a higher level of mutual benefits. The two sides should expand financial and production capacity cooperation within the "the Belt and Road Initiative" framework. China would support the construction of Zhengzhou-Luxemburg "Air Silk Road" and strengthen exchanges, such as culture, education and sports, and further facilitate personnel exchanges. Xi Jinping's keynote speech pointed out the direction for the construction of Zhengzhou international air hub, which will promote the construction to a new height.

3. The Construction of the Open Port is in Full Swing

In recent years, through continuous efforts, Zhengzhou has approved eight types of designated ports for imported edible aquatic animal, iced aquatic products, fruits, automobile, meat, Australian live cattle, food, and postal transport. Zhengzhou now has eight of the ten types of functional ports designated by the state, and the other two designated ports for imported flowers and plants, and medicine are under construction. Zhengzhou air-railway "double hub port" construction has made steady progress, and CR Express (Zhengzhou) has maintained its advanced level. 58.8 thousand tons of meat were imported in 2016, worth about $120 million, ranking the first in the national inland port; by the end of November, 7000 tons of fruit had been imported, equaling the import sum of 2014 and 2015; the volume of mail reached 10.298 million units, up 113%. The domestic and overseas double-hub and multi-point pattern is forming, "the East West" coverage continues to expand, and there is a network reaching 112 cities in 22 countries throughout EU, Russia and Central Asia. With further improvement and a greater role of the designated ports, and with more international air freight routes opened in Zhengzhou, the CR express (Zhengzhou) will further shorten the operational cycle. The Air Silk Road relying on the Zhengzhou airport international hub and the Land Silk Road relying on the CR express (Zhengzhou) together will play a more active role in promoting the open economy in Henan province.

Table 2 Operation performance growth of the CR express (Zhengzhou)

Time	Outgoing (column)	Return (column)	The total number (column)	Growth of the total number (column)	The value of cargo (100 million$)	Growth of cargo's value (%)	Cargo weight (10000 tons)	Growth of cargo weight (%)
2013	13	0	13		0.5		0.89	
2014	78	9	87	569.2	4.3	760.0	3.62	306.7
2015	97	59	156	79.3	7.14	66.0	6.35	75.4
2016	137	114	251	60.9	12.67	77.5	12.86	102.5

Note: The data in this table is collated by author.

4. Advantages of Cross-border E-commerce Highlights

On November 27, 2015, the Zhengzhou cross-border trade e-commerce service pilot was officially accepted by the state. The business volume of Zhengzhou pilot was the sum of the rest of the country's six pilots, and tax amount, the number of enterprises and other comprehensive indicators also ranked first in the country. The business volume of Zhengzhou pilot at an remarkable rate of development, the work was far ahead of other cities in the country. The Acceptance group gave congratulations, "The Zhengzhou pilot project is of strong innovation, is the most mature replicated nationwide model." These achievements have come from policy, mechanism, mode of innovation and leading the way. Zhengzhou pioneered the cross-border e-commerce bonded clearance mode of "e-commerce + bonded center + parcel bonded supervision in the national (customs code 1210)"; cross-border e-commerce policy, trade norms along with the development and innovation of logistics and industry were remarkable, a number of indicators in the leading position among the pilot cities. In January 2016, China (Zhengzhou) cross-border e-commerce Comprehensive Experimental Zone was approved. In May, its construction mobilization meeting was held in Zhengzhou, meaning that the zone entered into full construction phase, with the completion of the cross-border e-commerce service platform of services across the province. On December 16, 2016, China (Henan) international trade "single window" (2016 Edition) has run on the line, realized "goods declaration in seconds" and "customs clearance in seconds", laid the foundation for technology and management to accelerate cross-border e-commerce, and created excellent performance with 500 customs declaration forms cleared up in seconds. The continuous and rapid development of e-commerce builds up a new platform that provides new opportunities for our province to adapt to the new normal of China's economy, expands the opening-up and cooperation, fully integrates into the Belt and Road Initiative, and participates in the international division of labor. At the end of 2016, the volume of business exceeded 80 million, ranking first in the country. Amongst them, the import volume (53,522,200) was up 18.89% year on year; the export volume (29,380,08) was up 488.07% year on year. The government of Henan levied tariffs of 632 million yuan, up 440.17%; it levied land taxes of 163 million yuan, up 66.33%. Particularly, the rapid rise of export volume has opened up a new and efficient way and enlarged the quotient in international market for Henan's various export products.

5. Open Economy Development has Created A New Model

Airport peripheral industry appeared and developed rapidly in the Zhengzhou Airport Economy Zone. Because of the strong development of high-end manufacturing, the whole industrial chain has been formed that includes mobile phone R&D, machine manufacturing, parts manufacturing, software development, product design and mobile phone sales. It also has introduced and gathered 159 smart mobile phone production or supporting enterprises, such as Foxconn, Cool, Tianyu, Skyworth and others. In 2016, 258 million smart phones were produced, accounting for 18.97% of the global supply of 1.360 billion becoming one of the most intelligent terminal production bases in the world. The development of Airport Express Service Industry continued to be rapid. Zhengzhou became the first city approved to send international air express package directly to New York, Moscow, London and other 13 international cities, guaranteeing "next-day delivery". Zhengzhou Airport Economy Zone has become one of the 10 pilots of "maintenance for self-producing domestically-sold goods ", and has opened Truck-Airline or Customs Supervision Truck. It opened the first express supervision center in the central area, and approved to carry out bonded goods transfer pilot, in addition to opening the "Truck-Airline" for 13 major cities, including Beijing, Shanghai, Chongqing.

Led by Zhengzhou Airport, the total import and export volume of Henan totaled $US 283.2 billion during the "Twelfth Five-Year Plan" period, which was nearly four times the $US 71.4 billion during the "Eleventh Five-Year Plan" period, with an average annual growth of 32.9%. In 2015, the total import and export volume was over 460 billion yuan, and became the highest value for the six central provinces. It increased by 15.3% compared with the same period of the previous year, and the growth rate ranked the third in the country—22.3% higher than the national average growth rate, and became the new bright spot of the national opening-up height under the new normal of economic development. In 2016, the total import and export volume of Henan reached 471.47 billion yuan, up 2.6% compared with the same period of the previous year, ranking the first in the central and western regions of the country, while the total import and export volume of the whole country fell by 0.9% in the same period. The proportion of total imports and exports in the Henan province has risen significantly by 1.94% (Table 3), and compared with the long-term stagnation in the past of about 0.60%, and the development progress was encouraging, and the advantages of open development initially appeared in the central region (Table 4).

Table 3 The annual growth of import and export volume in China and Henan since 2006

Unit: $100 million, %

Particular year	2006	2007	2008	2009	2010	2011	2012	2013	2014	2015	2016
China	17604	21762	25633	22075	29740	36419	38671	41589	43015	39530	39174
Henan	98	128	175	134	178	326	518	600	650	740	760
Percentage	0.56	0.59	0.68	0.61	0.60	0.90	1.34	1.44	1.51	1.87	1.94

Notes: The data in this table is taken from *Statistical Yearbook of China (2016)* and *Statistical Yearbook of Henan (2016)*. Data for 2016 is taken from the Statistical Bulletin.

Table 4 The growth of total import and export volume in six provinces of China's central region in 2016

Unit: $100 million, %

Province	Henan	Shanxi	Hubei	Anhui	Hunan	Jiangxi	Total
Total	4714.7	1099	2600.1	2818.0	1782.2	2643.9	15657.9
Growth	2.6	20.5	-8.3	-7.2	-2.1	0.6	0.1
Nationwide	1.94	0.5	1.1	1.16	0.7	1.1	6.4

Note: The data in this table is collected by author from data published by the provinces.

This study summarizes the special process of exploring and developing the open economy in Henan province. It is a unique regional development model of "opening-up by air" given that Henan is not a coastal or border province. The model is closely related to the fact that the world is entering an era of network and navigation. In today's world, the impact of network and air transport on the allocation of resources is increasing. However, the impact of marine transportation on resource allocation has been significantly weakened in the industrial era. Therefore, under the influence of the Internet and air transport, the theory of regional development is facing important opportunities for innovation. Henan's exploration, with its 100 million people, has demonstrated that inland areas with cyber source configuration and international air hub advantages have the potential to become the new hot spot of new regional development. This is the era of the network economy. The important innovation tendency of regional development theory has changed the pattern of the global regional development in the past. This model of regional development has important reference value for the opening-up and development of inland areas in the world.

II The Main Idea to Build An Inland Opening-up Height

Faced with the new changes, new features and new trends of two overall situations at home and abroad, the Communist Party of China (CPC) headed by General Secretary Xi Jinping, has put forward a new concept of opening-up, and enriched new ideas for opening-up. General Secretary Xi Jinping pointed out that "the history of mankind development is in the opening-up process; and the development of any nation cannot only rely on the strength of this nation. Only with an open community, can the economic and cultural relations with the outside be maintained, can this nation be developed, and the fact is the law of the history." The next few years is a period to finish building a moderately prosperous society in all respects, and it is also a critical period of comprehensively deepening reform. Only by further opening-up can we continue to explore and develop new space, to enhance the position and function of Henan in the global industrial, value, and information chain, and to create new advantages for development. According to the reality of Henan opening-up and the basic characteristics of Henan province, and according to the strategic plan of the Tenth Congress of the Provincial Party Committee, we believe that the main idea to build an inland opening-up height is to adhere to the "three unswervingly".

1. Unswervingly Promote the Central Plains to become the Forefront of Open Development

Since the reform and opening-up in 1978, the national coastal and border areas have achieved sustained and rapid economic and social development. However, since Henan was located inland and there is no direct opening-up channel, its open economy has been developing at a sluggish pace, with the total import and export volume accounting for only 0.60% of the national total, and this is not commensurate with the province's economic aggregate ranking fifth in the country. Therefore, a scientific and feasible way of opening-up has always been sought after by the Provincial Party Committee and Provincial Government, as well as the people of Henan province. In the "Twelfth Five-Year Plan" period, we seized the opportunity of the State Council approving the construction of Zhengzhou Airport Economy Zone, and especially the construction of Zhengzhou international air hub opened the way for us to the outside world, so the province has been opening up and developing at a faster pace, and the level of foreign capital utilization has rapidly improved. In 2016, Henan directly utilized foreign capital of $17 billion—a year-on-year increase of 5.6%, accounting for 12.9% of the country's proportion (Table 5), and opening-up has become the new impetus to the development of local economy.

In the further development of Henan province, we still need to unswervingly promote the central plains into the frontier of opening-up, as General Secretary Xi Jinping stresses that "only in an open and exchange relationship, can we keep the economic and cultural communication with the outside"; to establish more diplomatic relations with the world; to learn the advanced experience and management ideas from developed countries; and let our development advantages, especially those in the high-end equipment manufacturing industry to go out, which will form a more open development pattern. The overall opening-up and overall deepening of internal reform have mutually promoted each other, which jointly promoted the rapid growth of Henan's economy in the past 40 years since the reform and opening-up, and proved the great momentum of opening-up and the irreversible development trend of the reform and opening-up. We must adhere to this experience of success, practice it well, and continue to create a new pattern of opening-up, to add new forces to the province's economic and social development, and to enhance the strategic position of Henan in China's opening-up scheme.

Table 5 The growth of FDI in China and Henan since 2006

Unit: 100 million US dollars, %

Year	2006	2007	2008	2009	2010	2011	2012	2013	2014	2015	2016
China	671	783	953	918	1088	1177	1133	1187	1197	1263	1315
Henan	18	31	40	48	62	101	121	135	149	161	170
Percentage (%)	2.7	4.0	4.2	5.2	5.7	8.6	10.7	11.4	12.5	12.7	12.9

Notes: The data in this table is taken from *Statistical Yearbook of China (2016)* and *Statistical Yearbook of Henan (2016)*. Data for 2016 is taken from the statistical bulletin.

2. Unswervingly Build A New System of Two-way Opening-up

Under the new situation, opening-up is no longer simply the process of introducing capital, technology, talents and other factors of production, but an overall integration of economic internationalization with industrialization, urbanization, informatization and marketization. The simple industry opening-up in the past is to be turned into a two-way opening-up of multi-level, wide-ranging and comprehensive introducing and going out of the economic development, scientific and technological exchanges, education resources sharing, city interaction, and social integration. Henan should conform to this development tendency and speed up the construction of an all-round new system of two–way opening-up. With economic development as the main line, efforts should be made to increase scientific and technological exchanges and introduce more talented people. With the opportunity provided by Provincial Party Committee and provincial government to promote cooperation with the University of Chinese Academy of Sciences and the UCLA, breakthroughs in higher education cooperation have been achieved. Henan will jointly set up high-level universities with famous universities in the United States, and Britain, Russia and other countries where higher education has been well developed, to enable more young students to gain top-class education at home, which can make up for the shortage of higher education resources, and cultivate and reserve local talents for economic and social development in the long run. At the same time, Henan will increase policy support and incentives to make good use of "the Belt and Road Initiative" opportunities, to promote cities and counties to go out, to actively carry out international cooperation of production capacity, and to share development opportunities, fully promoting opening-up in all aspects of the whole society, and releasing more energy of opening-up development.

3. Unswervingly Improve the Development Level of Open Economy

During the "12th Five-Year Plan" period, the construction of Henan's inland open economy highland yielded initial success, greatly enhancing the confidence in further building an inland open economy highland. According to the deployment of the 10th Party Congress of the Provincial Party Committee, to further opening-up and development, we should pay attention to the positive guiding role of governments at all levels, and at the same time pay more attention to the great role of opening the market and allocating resources, and make good use of those open development platforms such as China (Henan) free trade zone, Zhengzhou Xinzheng comprehensive free trade zone, Nanyang Wolong comprehensive free trade zone, Zhengzhou open comprehensive bonded area, Shangqiu bonded logistics center, Zhengzhou Airport Economy Zone, Zheng-Luo-Xin National Independent Innovation Demonstration Area and National comprehensive test area of big data. We will actively promote further development of the "Land Silk Road"—China-Europe Railway Express (Zhengzhou), the "Air Silk Road"—Zhengzhou-Luxemburg freight routes, "Online Silk Road" —cross-border e-commerce and the "3D Silk Road" that has integrated the sea, land, air and the Internet. We will attach great importance on new Internet-related concepts, models, formats, technologies, and trends. We will participate in international economic and technological cooperation and competition in larger scopes, at higher levels and in wider fields, to build a new high level of open economy. In particular, we will accelerate the development of a new economy closely related to the Internet, providing new supports for the transformation of economy and society, and for the development of the whole province.

III Strategic Measures to Build Inland Opening-up Heights

Since the 2008 global financial crisis, globalization has entered a new stage of transformation development. China, excellent in global governance and promoting global inclusive development, has had an increasing influence. In 2014, the informal meeting of APEC leaders was hosted in Beijing; in 2016, the G20 summit was held in Hangzhou; in 2017, "the Belt and Road Initiative" International Cooperation Forum was held in Beijing, and exerted great influence. Chinese style, concept, scheme, culture, and wisdom have become the important thought leading global development. Over the past 30 years, China's reform and opening-up had been dominated by global goods exchanges and is now upgraded to a new stage of open-mindedness. Further speeding up open-mindedness and opening-up are the historical trend of future development. According to the new pattern of opening-up development at home and abroad, we believe, in order to become the forefront of open development, and to construct inland opening-up heights, in the future Henan province should be guided by the concept of win-win cooperation which was repeatedly stressed by President Xi Jinping, supported by interconnection and interworking, taking the structural supply reforms as the main line, given full play to the advantages that Henan is the birthplace of inclusive culture in the Central Plains culture, and should seek greater two-way opening and cooperation space with greater inclusiveness. We will focus on the following five strategic initiatives:

1. Involved Deeper into the Belt and Road Initiative

We will take the unique advantages of Henan culture, location, industry and market, get involved deeper into the Belt and Road Initiative, comprehensively promote the multi-field open cooperation with relevant countries, and strengthen the strategic supporting role of the Central Plains in the Belt and Road Initiative. According to the vision of the Belt and Road Initiative, we will push forward the action plan for the Belt and Road Initiative construction in Henan. Along the route of the Belt and Road Initiative, we will select about 10 countries that industry and trade are complementary to those of Henan, and carry out in-depth exchanges and cooperation. A number of major investment projects with these countries will be chosen, tracked and promoted, opening up a new prospect in the Belt and Road Initiative. Recently, we have suggested concentrating on Henan Britain in-depth cooperation and exchanges, and then have researched and have exchanged the experience and practice of British cultural and have creatived entrepreneurship, financial services, R&D and high technology industry, smart city construction, air city construction, the new industrial park construction, rural construction, social governance, and higher education, and have taken the initiative to send government, education, entrepreneurs and business delegations to Britain for in-depth consultation and negotiation. The scientific and feasible ways of comprehensive cooperation between the two sides will be explored. We should make use of Brexit and Britain's policy of not setting limit to freight routes. Under these circumstances, we should open up Zhengzhou-Heathrow freight routes as soon as possible. Seizing the historical golden age of the Sino-British cooperation will improve the status of Zhengzhou Airport as an international air hub. We will further increase the infrastructure interoperability, given full play to the leading role of Zhengzhou international air hub, especially given priority to cargo development and make full use of the special chance when President Xi Jinping put forward that China would support the construction of Zhengzhou-Luxemburg Air Silk Road. To further expand the Zhengzhou-Luxemburg double-hub freight routes, we will build Henan into the core area of the central Air Silk Road. We should seek to open up similar routes in Southeast Asian countries like Vietnam, India, Pakistan, and Cambodia that have rigorous economic activities. We will gradually build air channels in the major cities along the Belt and Road with a greater impact, more lines and a wider range, so as to enhance the construction level of Air Silk Road for our opening-up, not only to stimulate our high-end industry, but also to accelerate the going out of advantage industries and products. The operation level of China-Europe Railway Express (Zhengzhou) will be enhanced. Based on the current preliminary operation of six expresses per week, we need to create conditions, strengthen international cooperation with Poland and Luxemburg in particular, and then open more expresses as soon as possible. We will accelerate the construction of Zhengzhou international inland port, and strengthen cooperation with Qingdao, Tianjin, Shanghai and other ports. We will actively joint the construction of the China-Mongolia-Russia, China-Pakistan Economic Corridors, and gain access to the sea and to the border, so as to form a more influential Land Silk Road. We are going to comprehensively promote the Online Silk Road—China (Zhengzhou) Cross-border E-commerce Comprehensive Pilot Zone. The sustained and rapid development of ecommerce builds a new platform and opportunities for expanding opening-up and cooperation, integrating into the Belt and Road Initiative, and participating in the international division of labor, which is beneficial to speed up Henan transforming from a province with limited opening-up in the past to the opening-up frontier under the new normal. The efficiency of cross-border e-commerce is very high, while the Central Plains region, with Zhengzhou as the center, has a very large population density, and has been a place of business, commercial competition and mode innovation since ancient times. When cross-border e-commerce becomes a new driving force for global business, Zhengzhou's commercial advantage is once again highlighted. In the future, with further innovation of cross-border e-commerce mode and operation mode, promoting Henan's open economy through the Online Silk Road will embrace promising prospects. At the same time, we should strengthen cultural exchanges, take advantage of Henan's profound cultural resources, cultural tourism resources and rich natural advantages, actively promoting rich and colorful cultural exchanges and tourism cooperation with countries along the Belt and Road, and expanding the opening-up scale of the tourism industry. We should make full use of the chance that the Belt and Road Initiative International Cooperation Forum was held in Beijing in May 2017. Based on comprehensive communication, we can cooperate with countries along the Belt and Road in many major projects, and speed up the comprehensive integration into the Belt and Road Initiative.

2. Further Enhance the Opening-up and Development Advantages of Zhengzhou Airport

Zhengzhou Airport Economy Zone is the largest open brand of airport industry in the province, which adheres to the construction of a large hub, the development of logistics, cultivating big industry, shaping the metropolis, expanding its international and regional influence, and gathering resources. We will speed up the integration and network of civil airport, railway, and highway, build a modern integrated transport hub which will contain the air hub as the main body, and include transportation highways, intercity railway, high-speed railway, city rail transportation, public transportation and others. We need to focus on the efforts to promote the construction of an international logistics center, an international airport, highway, railway freight stations and ports, develop strategic cooperation with domestic and international air freight enterprises, accelerate the construction of air logistics parks, improve the allocation of transport, warehousing and distribution, information service, distribution processing and other functions, and form a system of domestic and foreign interconnected multi-modal transport of a modern international logistics center. We should strengthen the industry support, further enlarge and develop the production base of electronic information industry of intelligent terminal R&D and production, actively develop high-end industry, air maintenance, bio medicine, and precision machinery, and form a modern industrial base led by the airport economy. We will play a leading role in Zhengzhou Airport Economy Zone through government and business interaction, and promote coordinated development of the airport economy and the regional economy in Henan at all levels.

3. Support the Construction of A National Central City in Zhengzhou

Zhengzhou will be built as a national central city with innovative vitality, cultural charm, and ecological wisdom, open and inclusive. It has the historical requirement of leading the development of the Central Plains, supporting the rise of the central region and serving the overall situation of the whole country. And it is the objective requirement to create an important node city along the Belt and Road. What's more, it is an important support for building a higher level of opening-up and cooperation platform and enhancing the strategic position of Zhengzhou and the province's opening-up. We will focus on the five core tasks:

Firstly, we will consolidate the industrial base, and comprehensively enhance the overall economic strength. We will strengthen the advanced manufacturing cluster, raise the level of service development, and accelerate the development of new economy. Based on the Chinese (Zhengzhou) Comprehensive Experimental Zone of cross-border e-commerce, we will build a complete cross-border e-commerce industrial chain and ecosystem, construct a number of cross-border supplier parks, warehousing and logistics centers, overseas warehouses, fully support cross-border business, create a global online shopping bulk distribution center, and enhance Zhengzhou's popularity in global business.

Secondly, we should stress reform and innovation, and speed up the development of new kinetic energy. We will further promote the transformation of government functions, deepen the reform, and raise the opening-up level of the Zhengzhou market and the level of investment and trade facilitation. We should reform, optimize and innovate the policy system, build a policy system of inclusive innovation, and create relaxing atmosphere for innovation. We will pool innovative resources, and actively build first-class universities, first-class disciplines, and invite domestic and foreign universities and national research institutes to establish branch offices, and to construct a key national center of science and education. And we will create an innovative development platform, promote the Zheng-Luo-Xin Innovation Demonstration Zone pilot policy, and accelerate the construction of double bases.

Thirdly, we will give full attention to regional advantages and build a comprehensive transportation and logistics center. Efforts will be made to strengthen the role of the air hub, and to consolidate and to upgrade the national railway hub, and to build a multimodal international logistics center.

Fourthly, we will adhere to internal and external linkages to build an inland opening-up economic highland. We will make great efforts to improve the node city along the Belt and Road, to build a two-way open platform, and to vigorously develop the port economy.

Finally, we will highlight humanities and build a modern international metropolis. It is necessary to speed up the opening, to integrate development of Xinxiang, Jiaozuo, and Xuchang, to build efficient convergence infrastructure, to keep ecological security, to share multiple public service system, and to create a special modern metropolis in the central plains. We should strictly protect the ecological system, optimize production, life, ecological space layout, and create beautiful living environment. We need to consciously and actively develop the ancient capital culture, Kung Fu culture, root culture, and Confucianism, Buddhism and Taoism, to enhance cohesion, integration, and communication, and to build an international cultural metropolis. In order to spread the open and inclusive ideas to the world, we will promote the Songshan forum, the Central Plains think tank forum and other influences to create a platform for dialogue and exchanges between Chinese and world civilizations. By optimizing the spatial layout of urban and rural areas, we will promote the overall development of urban and rural areas.

4. Speed Up Opening-up Innovation

Technological innovation is an important component of opening-up. The current innovation resources are being integrated into an international cluster-like knowledge network. Future technological development requires more international exchanges and integration between scientific and technological circles and the industry. We must promote the opening-up of science and technology and speed up opening-up innovation and actively integrate into the global industrial system. We need to make full use of strategic opportunities to support the construction of Zheng-Luo-Xin Innovation Demonstration Zone, to build innovative platform support system, to improve the province's high-tech zone, to economic development zone and industrial agglomeration zone, to establish international cooperation bases for science and technology, jointly-built laboratories, and to support more qualified enterprises to arrange overseas R&D branches. We should actively develop the intermediary service system. We will introduce a number of internationally renowned intermediaries for the patent risk investment business. The science and technology service industry in Zheng-Luo-Xin Innovation Demonstration Zone will build the province's science and technology parks into open co-operative core carriers. We encourage innovation of enterprises with foreign companies to jointly develop and share key intellectual property.

We should improve the transformation system of scientific and technological achievements, learn from the "Internet + technology market" model, carry out the province's major industrial technology research projects, and accept scientists, investors, and bid. We will actively support public space construction, build a number of low-cost, convenient, full-element, open-style public space, guide, motivate more young people to join the entrepreneurial action, encourage entrepreneurial passion and seek the driving force and innovation for industrial structure upgrading. We will improve personnel security system, increase support efforts, introduce a number of leading technology talents, high-level foreign talents, young scientific and technological innovative talents, speed up the promotion of students entrepreneurship parks, academics and other personnel carrier construction, innovation and scientific research personnel flow mechanism, and arouse within the talents a sense of identification and belonging with Henan, so that more outstanding young talents will come to the Central Plains for entrepreneurship, and innovation.

5. Actively Explore the "Hub Economy", A Symbol of the Free Trade Area

The free trade area is a comprehensive multi-purpose special economic zone, which has preferential tax and special customs regulatory policies as the main means, and its main purpose is to promote trade and facilitate investment. In August 2016, the CPC Central Committee and the State Council decided to set up a free trade pilot zone for China (Henan). Its strategic positioning to build a modern three-dimensional transport and logistics system, and build a modern transport hub for "the Belt and Road Initiative". This strategic positioning is in line with the special advantages of Henan as the China's and even Asia's transport hub since the beginning of the 20th century, which is of great significance to its opening-up, providing new supports for further developing "hub economy". On April 1, 2017, the free trade zone was put into operation, and a list of 180 reform tasks and 479 provincial management rights were put forward. A negative list was introduced for permission of foreign investment. Kaifeng has carried out the innovative system of "22 certificates into 1", which received high praise from Premier Li Keqiang, and the system has been extended to the whole province. By the end of June, 6038 enterprises have been added to the free trade zone, with a registered capital of 93.83 billion yuan. Advantages for open development of the free trade zone are increasingly emerging, which will further boost Henan's open economy. Developing "hub economy" has been written in the 2017 Henan provincial government work report. The province, taking comprehensive transport hub cities like Zhengzhou as nodes, improve modern functions of the hub, make good use of logistics and the hub to further boost industry development and cultivate high-speed rail and airport industries, and vigorously develop the hub economy. Modern three-dimensional transport and logistics systems are two keys to build Henan's "hub position", and policy innovation is of utmost importance for the active development of the free trade zone. Therefore, it is necessary to carry out policy innovation, to put forward new tactics, ideas and benefits, to facilitate investment and trade, to meet actual needs of the international hub economy, to gather large-scale industries related to the hub economy, to form an influential industry cluster, and to further push the province to the opening-up forefront.

IV Conclusion

In today's world, the idea of globalization and anti-globalization is always a heated debate; the historical trend of opening-up and development is irresistible, but the way of opening-up is constantly innovating. A higher level of globalization 3.0 era has come, led by China's "the Belt and Road Initiative". China's unique concept of opening-up and inclusive development has been recognized by more countries and nations in the world. The world has indeed become a community with a common future. The extent of opening-up will determine the extent of development. Under the new conditions of China's leading global development and opening-up, Henan, with the largest economy in central and western China, should follow the evolving trend, boosted by the Belt and Road Initiative. The focus of national opening-up and development has shifted to the central and western regions. Henan should give full opportunities for regional development model innovation, brought by a new era of the internet and navigation, carry out innovation, dare to take responsibility, have the courage to break through, speed up the opening-up policy, strive to be at the top, and activate people at the grassroots level. Through a large number of specific innovations, Henan has transformed from a traditional inland province into the forefront of opening-up and development, and has haken practical measures to build an inland opening-up height. Open-mindedness and inclusiveness will become the internal driving force to turn Henan province from a province with a large economy into one with a strong economy, play a greater role in building a prosperous, democratic, civilized, harmonious, and beautiful Henan, and enable the Central Plains to exceed in building a moderately prosperous society in all aspects and realizing the Chinese dream of the great rejuvenation of the Chinese nation.

B.2 Report on Economic Development of Henan Province

Research Team of Henan Academy of Social Sciences

Abstract: Since the 18th CPC National Congress in 2012, Henan province insists on maintaining stability in the general work guideline, led by new development concept, and takes the initiative to adapt to the new normal of economic development in order to focus on the "Four Cards". As a result, there is a sustainable increase in economic strength. The effort to optimize the industrial structure is paying off. People's livelihood has been further improved. A number of national strategies have been implemented. The open economy is developing actively. As a whole, great achievements have been made in economic and social development. At present, confronted with the complicated economic situation at home and abroad, Henan province will continue to deepen the structural reforms on the supply side, to stimulate actively domestic demand, to make great efforts to expand the opening to the outside world, to promote the new urbanization step by step, and to improve the living conditions of the residents in order to achieve sustainable economic and social development. Henan is stepping from a big province to a strong one in economy.

Keywords: Henan Province; Structural Reform on Supply Side; Seeking Advancement in Stability; Innovation Driven

Since the 18th CPC National Congress in 2012, the Central Committee of the Communist Party of China with Comrade Xi Jinping at its core grasps the two overall situations of China and the international community to promote the overall planning of the "Five in One" and to properly put forward "The Four-Pronged Comprehensive Strategy" to adhere to new development concept, in order to promote the structural reform on the supply side as the main line, to firmly push forward the reform, and to properly respond to risk challenges. Henan province fully implements the policies of the 18th CPC National Congress and all the plenary sessions, thoroughly implements the gist of the important speeches of General Secretary Xi Jinping, including those given when he was investigating and directing Henan's work. With the new development concept serving as a lead, Henan province takes the lead in adapting to the new normal in economic development, to focus on the "Four Cards", and to carry out the "Four battles" to maintain a stable and healthy development of the province's economy and society.

I The Basic Trend of Henan's Economic Operation in the Past Five Years

Since the 18th CPC National Congress in 2012, Henan province, facing the complex external situation and the heavy tasks for reform, development and keeping stable, sticks to the general work guideline of seeking advancement in stability, focusing on the rising of Central China, enhanced living standards of the people, and the revitalization and prosperity of Henan province, which goes upwards in seizing the opportunity, and makes its way in the transformation and overcoming difficulty. In the past five years, the economic strength has been greatly increased. The economic structure has been continuously optimized. People's living standards have been steadily improved. A large number of national strategies have been put into effect, and great achievements have been made in economic and social development.

1. Economic Strength has been Greatly Improved

Since the 18th CPC National Congress, Henan province adheres to the overall tone of seeking advancement in stability. Keeping growth steady and adjusting the structure is regarded as a main task of economic work to put forward the stable and healthy development of economy. Thus, economic strength has been greatly improved. The economic growth rate continues to be higher than the national average, and the main economic indicators maintaine steady growth. In 2016, Henan achieved regional GDP of 4.016001 trillion yuan, ranking the fifth in the country, with a year-on-year increase of 8.1%. The economic growth rate remains higher than the national average by more than 1 percentage point over the years (Figure 1). Especially in 2015 and 2016, the GDP growth in China entered the era of 6%, while the GDP growth in Henan province still maintained the state of more than 8% so that the status of Henan province in the overall development of the country has been promoted steadily. In the first half of 2017, GDP in Henan province increased by 8.2%, higher than the national average growth rate by 1.3 percentage points, thus maintaining obvious advantages in terms of regional development. The level of financial revenue has improved sustainably, and the general public budget revenue of Henan province reached 315.343 billion yuan, with a year-on-year increase of 8%, and an increase of more than 50% compared with 2012. Investment in fixed assets has been increasing rapidly. In 2016, the total investment in fixed assets in Henan province reached 3.975393 trillion yuan, with a year-on-year increase of 11.5%, and an increase of more than 85% compared with 2012.The average annual growth rate remains at the level of two digits. Consumption has been steadily increasing. In 2016, the total retail sales of social consumer goods in Henan province reached 1.761835 trillion yuan, with a year-on-year increase of 11.9%, and an increase of 61.4% compared with 2012. Financial institutions balance of foreign currency deposits has grown rapidly, reaching 5.397763 trillion yuan in 2016, with a year-on-year increase of 13.3%, and an increase of 68.8% compared with 2012. Grain production remains stable, and grain output was 60.671 million tons in 2015, which made important contributions to ensuring national food security. In 2016, affected by the decrease of the corn and the other autumn planting areas, grain production was 59.466 tons, decreasing by 2% compared with the previous year. Despite of this, the year still witnessed one of the highest annual grain output. Over the five years, Henan province, as a major economic province of the central region, has maintained an above-average

economic development, and has laid an important foundation for stable and rapid development of the national economy. Now it is marching on to a powerful economic province.

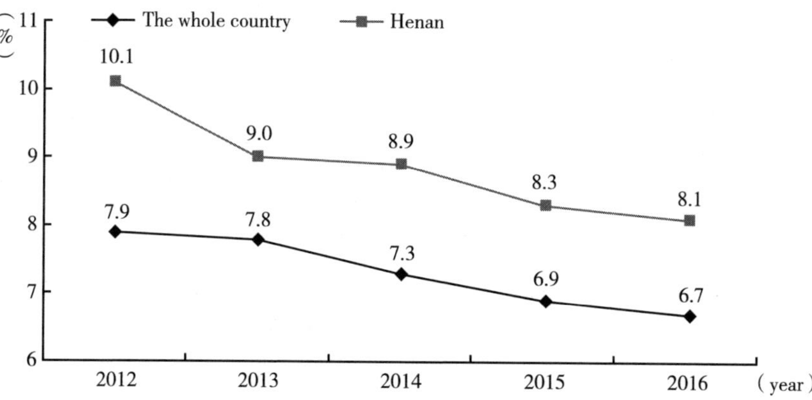

Figure 1 GDP growth in China and Henan in 2012-2016

2. The Gradual Optimization of Economic Structure

Henan province adheres to structural adjustment while maintaining development. The adjustment of economic structure and industrial transformation and upgrading have always been the priority of economic work. Over the five years, the economic structure has been optimized continuously, ensuring steady and healthy development in economy and society. In 2016, Henan province achieved an added value of 428.636 billion yuan in the primary sector, with a year-on-year increase of 4.2%; 1.905544 trillion yuan in the secondary sector, with a year-on-year increase of 7.5%; 1.681827 trillion yuan in the tertiary sector, with a year-on-year increase of 9.9%; the three industrial structure ratios reached 10.7:47.4:41.9 (Figure 2). Over the five years, while keeping the primary, second sectors developing steadily, Henan province also push forward the rapid development of the tertiary sector.The added value of the tertiary sector is accounting for an even-higher proportion in regional GDP, with an increase of 11 percentage points compared with 2012. This shows the rapid pace of industrial structure optimization. By conforming to this trend in development of China's national economy, Henan province has become one of the most active areas in terms of economic development in the country.

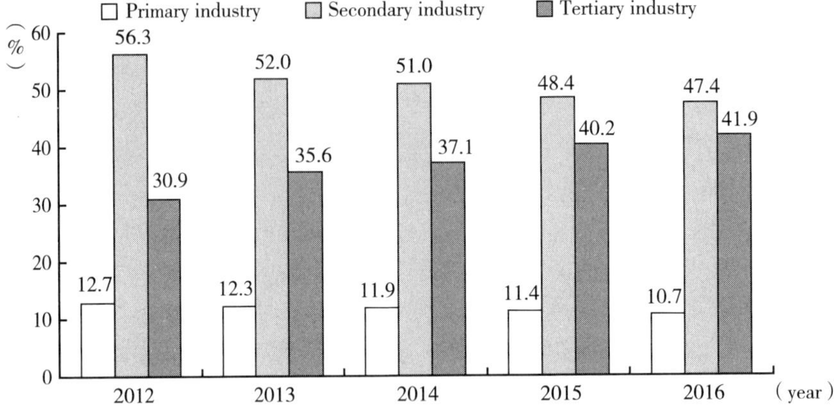

Figure 2 Change in the proportion of three industrial structures in Henan province from 2012 to 2016

The new urbanization has been steadily promoted and the urban and rural areas have taken on a new look. In 2016, the permanent residents in Henan province reached 95.3242 million. Among them, the permanent residents in urban areas reached 46.2322 million, with urbanization rate reaching 48.5%, with an increase of 1.65% compared with the end of 2015 (Figure 3). From 2012 to 2016, the urbanization rate of the resident population in Henan province maintained an annual increase of 1.5 percentage points. With the rural pepole moving to cities, farmers' income level got improved. The urban and rural consumption levels continued to be improved. The integration of urban and rural areas developed rapidly. At the same time, the urban agglomeration in the Central Plains has become an urban agglomeration claiming precedence in development in the national strategy. Zhengzhou has been included in the list of national central cities to be built, and its influence at home and abroad is getting bigger.

Significant progress has been made in the transformation and upgrading of the industry. In recent years, Henan province adheres to the construction of a strong province in advanced manufacturing. The high-growth industry increased by 10.6% in Henan province in 2016.The high-tech industry grew by 15.5%.The high-growth manufacturing has been making a greater contribution to the industrial growth above designated size. The equipment manufacturing industry, and food processing industry have become trillion-scale industries.

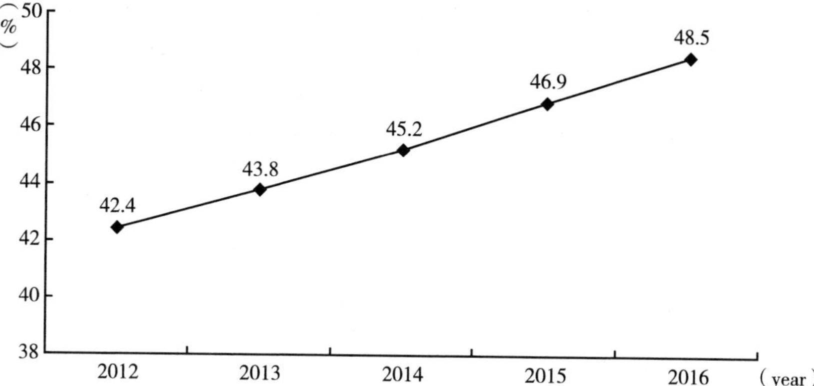

Figure 3 Change of urbanization rate in Henan province from 2012 to 2016

The automobile, electronics, new energy and other industries have developed rapidly. The world's major production base of intelligent terminals will be completed basically. Industrial agglomeration areas, central business districts and featured commercial districts downtown areas have become the key to economic transformation and growth. The high-growth services develop rapidly. "Financial Power of Yu" is rising at a high speed. In 2016, the added value of financial industry in Henan province accounted for 5.6% of the province's GDP, and it has become a new pillar industry. Tourism, express delivery, e-commerce, health services, pension services also develop rapidly in Henan province.

3. The Development Foundation has been Steadily Solidified

Over the past five years, Henan province has focused on the long term and consolidated steadily its foundation. The development carriers have been growing continuously, and a number of national strategies have been implemented. Zhengzhou-Luoyang-Xinxiang National Innovation Demonstration Area, the national big data comprehensive pilot zone, China (Zhengzhou) cross-border e-commerce comprehensive pilot area, and China (Henan) free trade zone have been approved in succession, since the Core Area of Grain Production and the Central Plains Economic Zone were approved. Central China city group has become a key one cultivated and developed by the nation. Zhengzhou has been approved as a prospective national core city. The implementation of a new batch of national strategic plans provides the support in policy innovation and development for Henan province, which elevates the status of Henan province in the overall situation of the whole country. The superposition effect of national strategies continues to increase. The status of modern integrated transportation hub has been consolidated. Air cargo hub construction has made significant progress. With the construction and operation of the second phase project, Zhengzhou Airport ranks the top of large airports in China in terms of the ability to handle passengers and cargo. The high-speed railway network in the shape of the Chinese character " 米 " is under construction at a high speed. Zhengzhou-Europe international railway freight trains have been opened and realized an normalized operation. The highway network connects all the cities and counties of the province. Zhengzhou Metro is under further construction. At the end of 2016, the province's railway mileage reached 5466 km, and the highway traffic mileage reached 6448 km. The international air freight network, the "two-hour traffic circle" connecting the surrounding capital cities, and the "one-hour traffic circle" connecting cities within the province is being formed. A modern, comprehensive and efficient system of multimodal transportation has taken a preliminary shape. The modernization infrastructure system is improving day by day. The country's first UHV AC and DC hybrid power grid has been built. The investment in the rural power grid continues to increase. Zhengzhou has become a direct joint of the state Internet, and takes the lead in realizing access to fixed broadband more than 50 megabytes. The first stage of the middle-route part of the Water Diversion Project from South to North has been completed in Henan province, and is under smooth operation. The reservoirs are reinforced by getting rid of risks. Long rivers, medium-sized and small rivers are cleared up. Big and medium-sized irrigation districts continue to be built. The project of water storage from Yellow River has been carried out smoothly. The construction of high-standard farmlands has been steadily pushed forward. With the implementation of national strategies in Henan province, its influence as a comprehensive transportation hub has been enhanced, and the infrastructure system keeps improving, which further highlights Henan's regional competitive advantage.

4. Promoting in-Depth Reform and Opening-up

Since the 18th National Congress of the CPC, Henan province has tried to solve the problems and to keep its vitality by reform and opening up, and has made great efforts to build an inland open city on the background of comprehensively deepening reform. With the deepening of the reform, the progress of the reform concerning key areas and key links is obvious. The reform of the structure on the supply side is on the way. Resolving overcapacity in the coal and steel industry is the focus. The policies concerning the treatment of workers and debt disposal are implemented earnestly. The work of transferring the social function of state-owned enterprises has been pushed forward. The administrative examination and approval procedures have been greatly simplified. The commercial system reform has been carried out in an all-round way. The system of "twenty-two certificates in one" in the pilot area of China (Henan) free trade is affirmed by the Central Committee. The reform of rural areas and state-owned enterprises is accelerating. The pricing mechanism for resource products is perfecting. The cooperation model between government and social capital is promoted extensively. All the urban and rural residents get access to serious diseases insurance. Reforms in transportation and law enforcement rank at the top of the country. Reforms in taxation, finance, medicine and health, education, science and technology and the system of province-governed county (city) are all advancing steadily. The new system of open economy is being formed at an accelerated rate. In 2016, the total volume of import and export in Henan province reached 471.470 billion yuan, ranking the first place in the Central and Western regions (Figure 4). In the past five years, under the special circumstances of the increasing uncertainty in the international macroeconomic environment, the steady growth in import and export has been maintained, an increase of 44.6% compared with 2012. Cooperation with the countries along the "Belt and Road" is enhanced in a pragmatic way. Zhengzhou Airport Economy Zone plays an increasingly important role in leading development. The international aviation logistics center takes its shape. The Zhengzhou-Luxemburg Aerial Silk Road is approved by the Central Committee. The comprehensive index of pilot e-commerce services for cross-border trade in Zhengzhou and the operation level of the Central Europe-Zhengzhou train ranks the top of the country. The system of comprehensive bonded zone and customs clearance mechanism has been improved. The number of functional ports ranks the first place in the inland provinces. A large number of leading and base enterprises have been introduced. Significant events such as the fourteenth meeting of the Shanghai cooperation organization, and the meeting with heads of government (prime minister) have been successfully held in Henan province. The opening-up of Henan province to the outside world has achieved a historic leap.

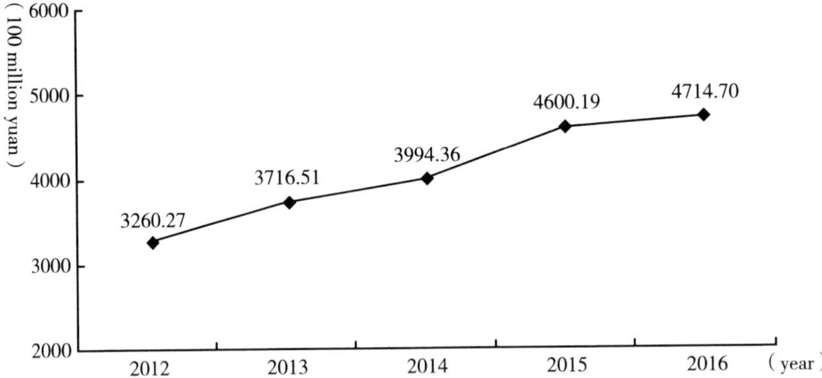

Figure 4 Change of foreign trade volume of import and export in Henan province from 2012 to 2016

5. Development Momentum Gradually Released

Since the 18th CPC National Congress, with China's economy entering into the new normal, Henan province has adhered to the new development concept, and takes the initiative to adapt to and to lead the new normal. The new advantages in development continue to accumulate. The new development momentum is gradually released. Scientific and technological innovation ability continues to increase. In 2016, the number of domestic invention patents in Henan province was 6811, ranking thirteenth in the country. By the end of 2016, there were 62005 effective invention patents in Henan province, reaching 6.33 invention patents per 10000 population. Zhengzhou-Luoyang-Xinxiang National Innovation Demonstration Zone is approved. The number of R&D (Reseach and Development) centers at the national level has doubled. Core technology such as communication with the help of the visible light, hard rock shield, new energy buses, and UHV power transmission equipment has made a great breakthrough. The construction of the National Technology Transfer Center (Zhengzhou) has been approved. The National Patent Examination Cooperation Center (Henan) has been established. Henan Food Crops Collaborative Innovation Center is among the first batch of national centers of its kind. Henan has become a pilot province of enhancing intellectual property rights. The kinetic energy of innovation-driven development is continuously strengthened. The atmosphere of "mass entrepreneurship and innovation" is becoming increasingly strong. In 2016, 991 thousand market entities were set up in Henan province, an increase of 20.7% year-on-year. Among them, 246 thousand enterprises were newly established, increasing by 29.8% year-on-year. In other words, 674 new enterprises were registered every day. By the end of 2016, the total number of market entities in Henan province reached 4.27 million, ranking the sixth in the country and the first in the six central provinces. The new economy takes on a vigorous development. In 2016, the investment in information transmission, software and information technology service in Henan province increased by 47.8%, 34.1 points higher than the investment growth rate in Henan province; in the same year, Henan's e-commerce transactions reached 1.0033 trillion yuan, an increase of 30%. Among them, cross-border e-commerce transactions reached $11.15 billion, twice as much as the amount of the previous year. The "1210 customs clearance supervision mode" applied to Zhengzhou's cross-border e-commerce is the first one in the country, known as one of the most efficient modes of supervision service.

6. People's Living Standard Steadily Improved

Over the past five years, Henan province has attached great importance to people's livelihood and carried out a series of measures to improve people's livelihood. Expenditure on people's livelihood has increased significantly. In 2016, per capita disposable income of the urban residents reached 27233 yuan while per capita net income of the rural residents reached 11697 yuan, basically realizing the goal of synchronizing income growth of the residents and economic development. The ratio of urban income to rural income was 2.72 in 2012 and fell to 2.33 in 2016. In the past five years, more than 7 million urban people have been employed while more than 4 million rural laborers have been moving to the cities to be employed. The gross enrollment rate of three-year pre-school education increases by about 30 percentage points. The balanced development of compulsory education has made new achievements. The gross enrollment rate of high school education reaches over 90%. The admission rate of the National College Entrance Examination increases by 14 percentage points. The higher education has developed rapidly. Vocational education ranks the top of the country. The resources of medical care continue to expand.High quality medical institutions such as Central China Fuwai Cardiovascular Hospital continue to be introduced. The health level of residents has increased significantly. The average life expectancy reaches 75.6 years. The coverage of social welfare is expanding continuously and the quality has increased significantly. The basic endowment insurance system for both the urban and the rural residents is basically established. The percentage of residents covered by basic insurance is higher than the national average. The percentage of people covered by basic medical insurance stays above 95%. The basic living allowances for urban and rural residents have been sustainably improved. 1.45 million indemnificatory apartments have been built. The system of housing security combining physical security with monetary subsidies has basically been established. 49 thousand kilometers of new rural roads have been built or rebuilt. The problem of low voltage has been solved for 4.40 million rural population. 1.03 million rural dilapidated houses has been repaired. The problem of safe drinking water for 32.4 million rural residents and school teachers and students has been solved. 6.77 million poor people in the rural areas get out of poverty. The project of moving into newly-built houses for residents around the Yellow River is carried out in a well-ordered way. A number of local residents take delight in moving into newly-built houses. The three major projects of blue sky, clean water and rural hygiene have been implemented in depth. The major project of energy conservation and emission reduction has achieved objectives regulated by the nation. The construction of ecological environment has made remarkable progress.

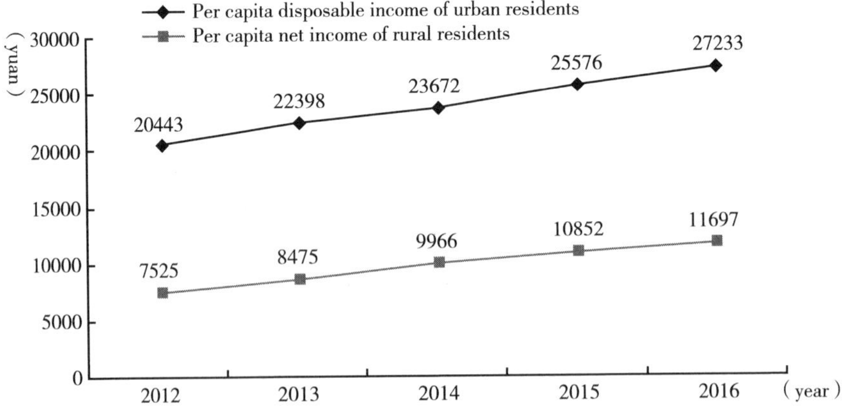

Figure 5 Change of per capita income of urban and rural areas in Henan province from 2012 to 2016

II The Overall Trend of Economic Development in Henan Province

Over the past five years, the international economy has been under slow recovery from risk and from crisis. The downward pressure on the domestic economy continues to increase. Adjusting structure and steadifying growth has become the theme of economic development in Henan province. Looking forward to the future, the economic situation at home and abroad is still very complex. The favorable conditions and constraints appear at the same time. The economic operation of Henan province is in the process of seeking new balance. The tenth Congress of CPC in Henan province put forward the overall policy of adjusting structure, steadifying growth, seeking development and preventing risk, put forward the goal of building a strong economic province, and draw a clear blueprint for the overall development of Henan province in the future. In this background, Henan will implement a series of strategic measures to adjust the structure, steadify growth and promote reform. Henan's economy will remain one of the relatively active areas of the national economic development.

1. Favorable Conditions

(1) Structural Reform on the Supply Side Continues to Have Influence

Since the third Plenary Session of the 18th CPC Central Committee, the central government has comprehensively deepened the reform, and has made a major breakthrough in the reform of key fields such as fiscal and taxation system, market system, and government functions. On this basis, to deal with the downward pressure on the economy, the Central Community implemented structural reform on the supply side focusing on de-capacity, de-stocking, deleveraging, cost reduction and improvement of weak links. As far as Henan is concerned, on the basis of the completion of many major reform tasks in the previous year, reform in key fields such as the system of investment and finance, pricing, etc. is the focus of the year 2016. Decentralization, delegation of power and services optimization are being further developed. In the next few years, the Henan Provincial Party Committees and government will introduce additional major initiatives concerning structural reform on the supply side to deal with "zombie enterprises" properly, to help enterprises reduce costs, to reduce real estate inventory, and to prevent financial risks. These reform initiatives have a positive effect on enhancing the kinetic energy of economic growth, providing effective support for the economic development of Henan province this year.

(2) New Urbanization Continues to Advance

Urbanization not only has the biggest potential of expanding domestic demand, but also highlights many problems in economic and social development. The national government has issued the new urbanization plan. The path to development of national urbanization in the future, the main objectives and strategic tasks are made clear. Meanwhile, the plan also provides new opportunities for effectively expanding domestic demand, reforming the land system, and promoting the transformation of economic development. At present, Henan province has a population of about 100 million, but the urbanization rate of the resident population is only 48.5%, nearly 10 percentage points lower than the national average of 57.35%. It is expected that the resident population urbanization rate in Henan province will reach 56% by 2020. Therefore, new urbanization is an arduous task to be finished. Accelerating the the process of new urbanization is beneficial to the increase of farmers' income, transformation and upgrading of consumption and the integrated development of urban and rural areas. It is of great significance for Henan province in that it can expand domestic demand and maintain economic growth. At the same time, the rural area comprehensive reform initiatives by the state government aims to deal with issues such as the rural land, collective ownership, household registration and social welfare. These initiatives have cleared up the system and policy barriers to promoting new urbanization of Henan province, and also provided a great opportunity to promote the coordinated development of urban and rural areas and various regions in Henan province.

(3) Participation in "The Belt and Road Initiative" has Apparent Effect

In recent years, the state government actively has promoted the "Belt and Road Initiatives", strengthening communication and promoting pragmatic cooperation with countries along the "Belt and Road". Led by this national strategy, Henan province – through Zhengzhou and Luoyang in particular– has actively participated in the construction of Silk Road Economic Belt. Sino-EU trains (Zhengzhou-Europe), the Land Silk Road, have been in operation since 2013. In 2016, 251 trains were in operation, achieving the goal of three trains going and three trains returning per week. From 2017 on, the frequency was "four going four returning" at the beginning of the year, and then became "five going five returning" in May, "six going six returning" in July, and "seven going six returning" in August. The freight volume and value both rank the top of all the Sino-EU trains. On 21st August, 2017, the Sino-EU trains (Zhengzhou) first opened the railway line Zhengzhou - Munich, expanding business scope to southern Germany and southern Europe (France, Italy, Spain, etc.) and Central Europe (Austria, Hungary, Czech, etc.). In September, the Sino-European trains (Zhengzhou) achieved a weekly running frequency of "eight going six returning". Zhengzhou-Luxemburg freight route-the Air Silk Route was opened in 2014, when the freight volume exceeded 10 thousand tons. In 2015, the freight volume exceeded 50 thousand tons. In 2016, the freight volume exceeded 100 thousand tons. "Zhengzhou price" has been formed in European air cargo markets, thus becoming a benchmark of Sino-EU air cargo market. In June, 2017, President Xi Jinping, when meeting Bethel, Prime Minister of Luxemburg in Beijing, pointed out that bilateral cooperation concerning finance and capacity, etc. should be deepened within the framework of the "Belt and Road", and China supports the construction of the Air Silk Route of Zhengzhou-Luxemburg. Thus, Zhengzhou was raised to a new strategic height in the national initiative. In August, the provincial Party committees and government formulated and issued the Special Planning for Constructing "Zhengzhou- Luxemburg" Air Silk Route (2017-2025) and the Scheme for Constructing the Air Silk Route of "Zhengzhou-Luxemburg". Because of this, the construction of the Air Silk Route of Zhengzhou-Luxemburg has entered a new stage. The "Online Silk Road" of Zhengzhou, namely the cross-border e-commerce, was approved in 2012. The business volume on a single day exceeded 1 million orders in March, 2015. It passed the acceptance inspection by the national authorities in November, 2015. In the first batch of 7 national pilot cities, the business volume created by the computer "single window" business model innovated by Zhengzhou accounted for more than 50% of the total, and the model was replicated and promoted in other cities. From the beginning of 2016, China (Zhengzhou) Cross- Border E-Commerce Comprehensive Experimentation Area was approved. The number of the pilot cities increased to 13. At the end of the year, the import and export orders of cross-border e-commerce reached 82.903 million, and the trading volume reached 6.4 billion yuan, with a year-on-year increase of more than 65%, keeping a leading position in the pilot cities and comprehensive experimentation areas in the country.

The "Multi-Dimensional Silk Road" integrating the sea, the land and the

air and the Internet, brings red wine, cosmetics and other goods to China by various means so that foreign products are stocked in the bonded warehouse for consumers to purchase via computers or smart terminals. The goods can be delivered to terminal customers through express delivery after the customs have checked them, which really offers convenience and benefits to consumers. Through participating in the "Belt and Road Initiatives", Henan province, located in inland, has created a new situation in development, which is characterized by the four "Roads" of sea, land, air and network. On April 1, 2017, the construrction of China (Henan) Free Trade Zone was initiated. This means that the development of open economy in Henan province will reach a new height, and the construction of open inland will be accelerated. The conditions of opening-up to the outside world become better. The open development will form a new support for economic development in Henan province.

(4) The Effect of Strengthening Foundation is More Obvious

In recent years, in response to the economic downturn, the provincial Party committees and government have implemented strategic initiatives of structural adjustment, steadifying growth and strengthening foundation. The developing force has undergone a significant change. The six high growth industries, such as electronic information, automobiles and parts, equipment manufacturing, etc. will gradually replace the resource-based industries to become the main support for the economic development in Henan province. The ability to prevent risk and steadily growth in economy of Henan province is becoming increasingly strong. The construction of the comprehensive economic experimentation area of Zhengzhou airport continues to upgrade. It has become a new engine and a growth pole to drive the province's economy to develop. The high-speed railway network with the shape of the Chinese character " 米 " have basically formed. The construction of comprehensive transportation hub continues to speed up. The Air Silk Route of "Zhengzhou- Luxemburg" is supported by the central government. Zhengzhou-Luoyang-Xinxiang National Innovation Demonstration Zone has been approved. The number of R&D centers at the state level is rapidly growing. The innovation-driven economic development is taking shape. The construction of infrastructure in information, transportation, irrigation and water conservancy, etc. is developing rapidly. The project of "Upgrading the Quality of One Hundred Cities" speeds up the integrated development of urban and rural areas. To achieve the goal of an all-round well-off society, the whole province spares no effort in the cause of poverty alleviation. In the next few years, with the implementation of these policies and significant projects, the georgraphical resource and industrial advantages of Henan province will be more prominent and the ability to deal with risks will be further enhanced. The "stabilizer" for the sustainable economic development in Henan province will be formed.

2. Constraints

(1) The Rise of Protectionism in International Trade

At present, the recovery in the world economy is still fragile. The international trade and investment are in the doldrums. The unstable and uncertain factors in the international economic environment are increasing. The American President Trump adopts isolationism in foreign trade, which is likely to trigger a global wave of protectionism for trade. In the future, China may confront more severe trade barriers and more anti-dumping investigations. Under the circumstances of the global economic downturn, the Federal Reserve has started the interest rate hike cycle, and the uncertainty in monetary policy has increased. In addition, "Brexit" will likely trigger dramatic changes in the global political and economic structure. These uncertainties will cause a severe impact on China's import and export in the future. For Henan, the uncertainty of the international environment will increase the difficulty of product in export. The export-oriented economic development will be affected to some degree.

(2) China's Economic Growth is Slowing Down

In 2014, the central government made the strategic judgment that China's economy has entered into the new normal. The shift in growth from a high speed to a medium-high speed has become the consensus of development. The economic growth in Henan province is inevitably slowing down. At the same time, the state continues to push forward the reform on supply side in steel, coal and other overcapacity fields, as well as in chemical, nonferrous metals, rare earth and other industries. In this background, the coal and iron and steel in Henan province will continue to bear greater pressure. Meanwhile, electrolytic aluminum, chemical and other industries will be greatly impacted. With the further implementation of "de-capacity", the resource industry in Henan will be further impacted, which will be a burden of economic growth. At the same time, the real estate market is operating at a high price. The uncertainty continues to increase. The inactivity of real estate market will seriously restrict the investment in fixed assets, and the development of many relevant industries such as the iron and steel, building materials, household appliances, decorative materials, etc., which has become constrains on the economic growth of Henan province.

(3) The Constraints to Factors and Enviroment have a Tendency of Tightness

The first is the insufficient supply of construction land. In recent years, with the acceleration of the pace of construction in the city, the framework of the city is widened gradually. A large number of suitable construction lands are needed. With business and investment being introducted and industry being transformed in-depth, many industrial projects also need a lot of lands. At present, the land resources in Henan province are rare, so the ability to carry out the projects is weak. It is difficult to take over good projects with high technology and good market prospects, which is a major factor restricting the economic development in this year. The second is the shortage of talents. At present, with the rapid development of high growth manufacturing and high-tech industries, there is a shortage of talents with professional knowledge of technology and mechanics, especially talents with high-level skills. Meanwhile, with the downward pressure on economy increasing, enterprises are faced with the dual pressures of decline in product prices and increase in labor cost. The phenomenon of being difficult to enroll workers and to be able to afford the workers is highlighted. The third is that the force of protecting environment to support economic growth is clearly insufficient. The proportion of steel, chemical, nonferrous metals and other industries of high consumption for energy and high pollution in Henan province is relatively large; crude, low, heavy and high-consumption products account for a large part, and pollution emission is intense. With the Central Government reinforcing accountability for the protection of environment, there will be some pressure on the economic growth of Henan province.

3. The Outlook of Henan Economic Trend

At present, the macro environment faced by Henan's economy is still not very favorable. The reform on structure has a long way to go. Structural problems, which have accumulated for a long period, are difficult to be completely solved in the short term. The situation of overcapacity remains difficult to ease in the short term. Insufficient external demand is difficult to change in the short term. Tightening of market liquidity and differentiation of real estate market will continue to exist. The difficulties faced by some industries and enterprises continue to grow. The difficulties confronted by the operation of Henan economy are complex and long-term. At the same time, we should also notice that the transformation of the new and old industries and the kinetic energy of development in Henan is in a critical period of continuity, and the positive factors and emerging forces are accumulating. In 2017, the reform and opening-up should be deepened in all the aspects. Administration streamlining and power delegating should be reinforced. Efforts should be focused on promoting mass entrepreneurship and innovation. Reform and innovation as "double engines" should drive economic development to actively deal with the impact brought by disadvantages, and make economy maintain steady and rapid development. In the medium and long term, Henan province is at a stage of accelerating new urbanization and new industrialization. Its potential in market demand is huge. The location, transportation, resources, policies and other advantages are further highlighted. The development carriers, open platforms, infrastructure and other strategic supporting conditions are becoming more and more perfect. The "three zones and one group", which consists of the three zones of Zhengzhou Airport Economy Zone, Zhengzhou-Luoyang-Xinxiang National Innovation Demonstration Area, and China' (Henan) Free Trade Experimentation Zone, and the group of cities of Central China will provide an important support for rapid and steady economic development in Henan province. In the future, the economy in Henan province will be able to keep the developing speed above the national average. New urbanization will be pushed steadily forward. The economic structure will continue to optimize. The pace of transformation and upgrading of industries will be sped up. The inland open economy will leap to a new stage. As far as the year 2017 is concerned, with the effect of macro policies becoming more obvious, the economic operation will initially stabilize and may rebound, and the annual GDP growth rate is expected to reach more than 8.2%.

III Three Measures to Promote Henan Province to Seek Advancement in Stability in Economy

The year of 2017 is not only a year in which the 19th National Congress of the CPC will be held, but also the first year of commencing comprehensively constructing Henan province into a strong one in economy according to the plan drawn up at the tenth Provincial Party Congress. We should conscientiously implement all the decisions made at the Central Economic Work Conference and the tenth provincial Party Congress. We should actively adapt to the new normal in economic development. We should promote the deepening of the structural reform on the supply side, regarding the new development concept as the guideline. We should focus on making the most of the advantages to play the "Four Cards". At the same time, we should promote steady growth, adjust structure, promote transformation, prevent risks, benefit the people's livelihood and maintain stability, to ensure the healthy and rapid development of economy and society. We should step forward with energy in a new journey of making Central China wealthier and more excellent in all the respects.

1. Deepen the Structural Reform on the Supply Side

Regarding promoting the structural reform on the supply side as a main line, we should add effective supply to operation system in the economy and society by means of innovation in system. We should reduce the invalid supply, and effectively improve the structure of factors supply, to provide a new development momentum for economic and social development in Henan province, and to lay a foundation in terms of factors of production for the province's transformation and upgrading. We should attach equal importance to both the total volume and optimization of the structure. The integration of industrialization and informationization, of manufacturing and service industries, and of new technology and new industry, should be promoted. A new industrial system with reasonable structure, clear hierarchy, and strong competitive power should be built. We should upgrade overall technical capacity and production levels of the manufacturing industry in Henan province, and eaernestly implement the *Made in China 2025 Henan Action Plan*. The production mode of intelligent manufacturing should be vigorously promoted. A number of significant projects with great stimulating effects, strong driving ability and high technology should be planned and promoted. The task of "three off, one down, and one up" should be properly accomplished. The overcapacity in coal, iron and steel industry should be reduced. We should promote the integrated development of the industries of manufacturing and services. The modes of flexible manufacturing, product customization and personalized manufacturing should be explored.

Transformation and upgrading of manufacturing industry towards intelligence, digital, network and service should be accelerated to lift the added value of the manufacturing industry. The modern service industries should be developed. Service industries such as cultural tourism, modern logistics, and new business and trade should be promoted. In the meantime, more support should be given to medical care, health services, elderly care, and education. We should also highlight the leading and supporting roles of the "Internet plus" and e-commerce to form many kinds of new commercial service patterns with both online and offline interactions and the combination of virtual and real entity.

2. Implementing Innovation-driven Development Strategies

The strategies of innovation-driven development and promoting the development of the province with talents should be further implemented by getting rid of institutional obstacles and perfecting the conditions for mass entrepreneurship and innovation. The economic system and development mode with innovation as the main leading and supporting factor should be formed at a higher speed. With the construction of Zhengzhou-Luoyang-Xinxiang National Innovation Demonstration Zone as the main focus, depending on innovation of policies, gathering talents and technology innovation, we promote innovation in system, in business, in model, and in technology. We should support all kinds of talents to dedicate their wisdom to entrepreneurship and innovation. Especially, we should create conditions to support young talents to stand out, offering them the opportunity to realize their dreams of the Central China and to realize the value of their life in the historical process of the rise of Central China. The high-tech enterprises, strategic emerging industries and new R&D institutions should be vigorously cultivated. The research and industrialization of the innovation fruits should be constantly promoted. Public entrepreneurship and innovation should be vigorously promoted. Support for the mass E&I platforms, crowdsourcing, crowd support, crowdfunding should be enhanced. We should guide powerful enterprises and research institutes to form an alliance concerning production, learning and research and support well-known universities and research institutions at home and abroad to set up branches and bases for transformation of scientific and technological achievements in Henan. The space for network economy should be expanded. In accordance with the "Internet plus initiative", we should promote deep integration of the Internet into economy and society, promote the prosperity of new technologies, new models and new patterns, and foster new economy in order to occupy the highground of development in the future.

3. Boosting Domestic Demand by Strengthening the Base and Expanding Consumption

Henan province should make full use of the oppotunity of investment. Based on resource endowments and its own advantages, Henan province should increase the investment in services for producers, and high-speed railway network, city infrastructure and highways. Henan province should speed up the progress of new and slow projects, and improve the operation rate of projects which has not yet started and the completion rate of investment in the project which has already started. According to the requirements of constructing a strong province in four aspects and protecting environment and coping with pollution, Henan province should plan actively to do several major projects concerning important infrastructure, major industries, livelihood and welfare, environmental protection and the like to help investment in Henan province grow in a continuous way. Henan province should encourage and guide persnal investment to play a major role by flowing into high growth manufacturing industries with good prospects. Henan province should play the basic role of consumption, including actively cultivating new consumption points, making great efforts to develop e-commerce and E-trade, and promoting the development of health care, pension services, sports and tourism. In addition, Henan province should continue to promote housing consumption, to support the demands of independent and improving-type housing, and to promote the healthy development of real estate industry. Henan province should accelerate the development of green industry, and strive to build an industrial structure with high technology, low consumption in resources, and less environmental pollution to greatly reduce consumption in energy, water and land, and to promote efficient use and recycling of resources.

4. Making Great Efforts to Build an Open Inland City

With the construction of China (Henan) Free Trade Zone as a central task, the construction of open platforms and ports with different kinds of functions should be strengthened. Through more open trade policy and financial policy, more and more industries will be attracted to enter the province, and more trade will be attracted to develop in the zone. The strong flow of things, people and capital at home and abroad is expected to gather in the zone to drive the development of industry and economy in Henan province. Henan province should fully integrate into the "Belt and Road Initiative", continue to optimize the environment for opening-up, construct a new system of opening-up, and improve the mechanism of ensuring government trustworthiness so that business and investment attraction will mainly rely on quality service instead of favorable policies. Based on the construction of "Silk Roads"of land, air and online, Henan province should plan to carry out international cooperation and exchanges more extensively with the countries along the "Belt and Road" to achieve mutual benefit and win-win in a new wave of globalization. Henan province should make full use of the opportunities for policy innovation given by the state, making great efforts to expand new space for international cooperation and accelerating the construction of infrastructure. A new growth point in economy should be created by combining the construction of comprehensive transportation hub with the FTZ platform. In this way, it will be possible to allocate resources more efficiently around the globe. At the same time, Henan province should make full use of its own advantages of historical and cultural resources, especially the rich and inclusive culture, to build a multicultural mechanism for in-depth exchange with European and Asian countries, to attract more and more young people to Henan province for entrepreneurship and innovation, and to help Henan province step forward from an inland province to an open and vigorous one.

5. Promoting New Urbanization in a Well-Organized Way

Taking the scheme of the urban agglomeration in Central China as an opportunity, Henan province should try to improve the quality of urbanization. With the goal of turning itself into a National Center City in mind, Henan province should build Zhengzhou into a modern international integrated transportation hub, an open city in Central and Western China, and a major base of advanced manufacturing industry and modern service industry. Efforts should be made to construct Luoyang as the sub-center city, to promote the integration of Zhengzhou and Kaifeng and the integrated development of Zhengzhou, Xinxiang, Jiaozuo and Xuchang on the basis of interconnected infrastructure, and to promote the agglomeration of production factors in Zhengzhou metropolitan area. Efforts should also be made to develop the economy of the counties. According to the inherent resources of specific counties, new types of industries should be developed and new modes should be practiced. Meanwhile, more importance should be attached to endogenous economic growth so that county economy can participate in city economy in a wider range and at higher level. According to the plan of "Quality Enhancement of 100 Cities" put forward by the Provincial Party Committee and Government, the level of infrastructure in 106 counties will be greatly improved to benefit the local people, with water running through the city, with trees shadowing the city, with culture making the city civilized, and with industry making the city prosperous. Henan province should seize the historic opportunity to build towns with their own characteristics, which will retain the traditional cultural memory and allow local residents to enjoy the green mountains and to clean rivers or the historical culture from the countryside. With the help of the system reform, especially through streamlining of administration and delegation of power, Henan province should promote the factors to flow orderly to establish a unified and open market system with orderly competition. The cross-region mobility of production factors such as labor force, capital, talents, information, resources and even services will be realized by getting rid of various institutional barriers to the free flow of production factors. Rural population working in the city should be turned into urban residents so that they can equally enjoy education, employment services, social welfare, medical care, affordable housing and other aspects of public services. Greater efforts should be made to alleviate poverty, and the task of poverty alleviation should be given top priority to economic and social development. Specific measures may include training of skills, regional cooperation and development, financial support, infrastructure docking and so on.

6. Improving People's Well-being and Promoting Harmony and Stability

Henan province should combine the improvement of people's livelihood with the enhancement of the economic power and social vitality. Following the requirements of "holding the bottom line, highlighting key points, improving the system, and guiding public opinions", Henan province should promote the equal share of basic public services, focus on improving the efficiency in the use of fiscal funds for people's livelihood, and make great efforts to launch a number of new initiatives of both short-term and long-term benefits in finance, health care, social welfare and other areas. We should strengthen the work related to employment and social welfare, implement effectively various services and policies concerning the employment and entrepreneurship, strengthen the training on vocational skills, properly deal with the employment of key groups, and promote entrepreneurship as a means of employment. Livelihood projects such as building affordable housing and renovating shanty towns must be conducted earnestly. Greater support should be given to rigid housing demand and demand on improving housing. We should also meet the demand on housing of those who move from countryside to city by encouraging them to buy houses in cities, monetary compensation for resettlement, and housing provident fund accumulation. We should vigorously develop the rental housing market to promote the smooth operation of the real estate industry. For special groups such as young newly-employed college students, policies and moves more suitable for the needs of these groups should be introduced in order to effectively solve their housing problems. Henan province makes great efforts to do the job getting out of poverty. Various means of poverty alleviation such as training, employment, industry helping and enterpreneurship should be used to help people out of poverty and prevent them from returning to poverty, so that the people in Henan province better share the fruits of reform and development.

References

[1] Jin Bei. The New Trend of Development of Chinese Regional Economy in the New Era of Globalization[J]. *Regional Economic Review*, 2017(01).

[2] Fan Hengshan. Practice and Trend of the National Strategy of Regional Development[J]. *Regional Economic Review*, 2017(01).

[3] Li Wei. Several Important Issues in the Current Economic Operation [N]. *China Economic Times*,2017-2-20.

[4] "Blue Book on Henan Economy" Research Group of Henan Academy of Social Sciences. To Achieve Steady Growth in the Battle of Structural Reform on the Supply Side[J]. *Academic Journal of Zhongzhou*, 2016(08).

[5] Lian Weiliang. Leading the New Norm of the Economic Development in Promoting the Structural Reform on the Supply Side[J].*Truth*,2017(12).

[6] Zhang Zhancang. Draw the Grand Blueprint that Makes the Central China More Colorful[N]. *Henan daily*, 2016-11-11 (Theoretical Edition).

[7] Yuan Kaisheng etc.. Strive to Play "Four Cards", Let the Central China Become More Colorful[N]. *Henan Daily*,2016-12-22 (Theoretical Edition).

[8] Zhang Zhancang. Economic Trend of Henan and Countermeasures under the New Norm[N]. *Henan Daily*, 2016-10-19(Theoretical Edition).

[9] Gu JIanquan. The Research on the New Pattern of Construction of "1+1+3" Regional Development in Henan[J]. *Regional Economic Review*, 2016(05).

[10] Zhang Zhancang. Henan Moves from Inland Hinterland to Frontier with the Characteristics of Opening-up and Development[J]. *Henan Science*, 2017(02).

[11] Zhang Zhancang. Building an Architecture of "Three Districts and One Group" for Building a Powerful Economic Province[N]. *Henan Daily*, 2017-4-28.

[12] Gong Jinxing, Ma Yuefeng. to Play "Four Cards", to Make Henan More Colorful[N]. *People's Daily*, 2017-6-3(01 Edition).

[13] Gao Xuan. To Train New Kinetic Energy, to Find Three Force Points [N]. *Economic Daily*, 2017-7-14(014 Edition).

[14] Peng Junjie. Regional Exploration and Countermeasures for Building a Powerful Economic Province in Henan [N].*Henan Daily*, 2017-4-27 ((Theoretical Edition).

[15] Wang Dan. Free Trade Zone Makes Henan Conform to the World in Depth — Interview with Du Mingjun, Researcher of Institute of Economics, Provincial Academy of Social Sciences[N].*Henan Daily*,2017-2-22.

[16] Zhang Zhancang. The Scientific Connotation and Strategic Measures of Building a Powerful Economic Province in Henan[J].*Henan Social Science*, 2017(07).

[17] "Henan Economic Blue Book" Research Group, Henan Academy of Social Sciences. To Continue to Promote Economic Stability in Henan for the Better Development—Analysis of the Economy Operation and the Trend in the First Half of 2017 in Henan[J]. *Academic Journal of Zhongzhou*, 2017(08).

[18] Wan Shiwei. To Promote Optimization and Upgrading of the Industrial Structure, to Improve Benefit of Supply Quality[N]. *Henan Daily*, 2017-3-22 (Theoretical Edition).

B.3

Report on the Industrial Development of Henan Province

Research Team of the Industrial Economic Institute, Henan Social Sciences Academy

Abstract: Since 2012, Henan has seized the national strategic opportunities, pushed forward the structural reform on the supply side, accelerated the transformation of kinetic energy, and maintained steady development in industry. Over the past year, the overall situation of the industrial economy of Henan became slower in stabilization and better in recovery. The structure on the supply side is optimized and the profit growth rate rises steadily, coupled with the accelerated advanced manufacturing mode and the remarkable steady industrial growth, which all together supports the steady and rapid economic development in Henan. In 2017, because of the deepening of the transformation and development and the structural reform of the manufacturing industry on the supply side in Henan, Henan's industry will continue to maintain stable growth rate, and it is expected that with the continued optimization of the industrial product structure, the added value of above-designated-size industries will be increased by about 8.0% and five leading industries and the high-tech industry will continue to maintain rapid growth.

Keywords: Industry of Henan Province; Made in China 2025 Initiative; Industrial Transformation and Upgrading; Structural Reform on the Supply Side; Advanced Manufacturing Province

I Analysis of the Industrial Economic Performance of Henan Province

Since 2012, facing the complicated environment globally and domestically, including the world economic downturn, the unfavorable growth of global trade, the superimposed Three Periods and downward pressure in domestic economy, Henan has seized national strategic opportunities to promote the structural reform on the supply side, treating industrial growth as a prominent task. Henan vigorously implemented the steady, industrial growth of structural adjustment efforts to increase the efficiency of activities and paid more attention to upgrading the technical level, strengthening the manufacturing capacity, adjusting the industrial structure, and optimizing a long industrial chain, in order to promote the steady growth of industrial production and structure optimization.

1. The Overall Trend

(1) The Industrial Economy of Henan Province Maintained Stable Performance

In 2016, Henan's total industrial added value reached 1 trillion and 683 billion 74 million yuan, an increase by 7.5%, compared with the previous year. Since 2012, Henan's industrial added value grew steadily, with sustained growth rate in stabilization, higher than the national growth rate of industry.

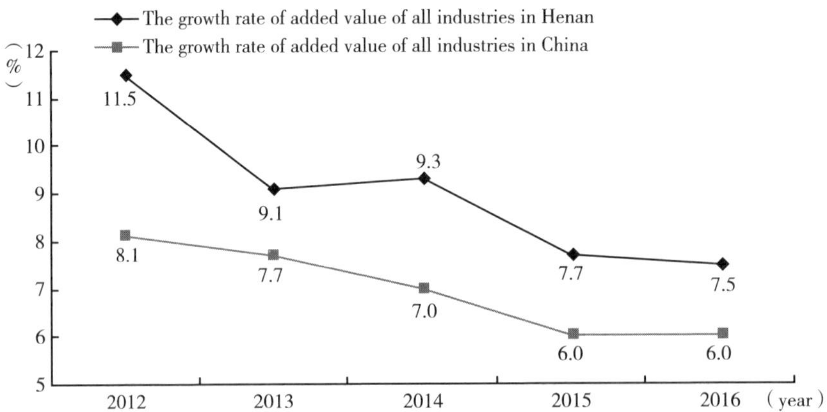

Figure 1 Comparison of the growth rate of added value of all industries between Henan province and the whole country

Data source: Henan Bureau of Statistics.

In 2016, the added value of above-designated-size industries of Henan increased by 8.0%, 0.6 percentage points lower than the previous year, but the number is still 2 percentage points higher than the national average value. As is shown in Figure 2, every month, the overall situation of the generally stable industrial economy is slow in stabilization and better in recovery. In particular, the monthly growth rate increases continually in the second half of the year, with the growth rate in December reaching 8.2% and a noticeable effect stimulated by steady growth in industry. In 2017, Henan's industry has continued to maintain the good trend of the previous year. In June, the industrial added value of above-designated-size industries increased by 8.5%, compared with the same period of 2016, and from January to June, the industrial added value of above-designated-size industries of the whole province increased by 8.2%, with a better growth momentum coming.

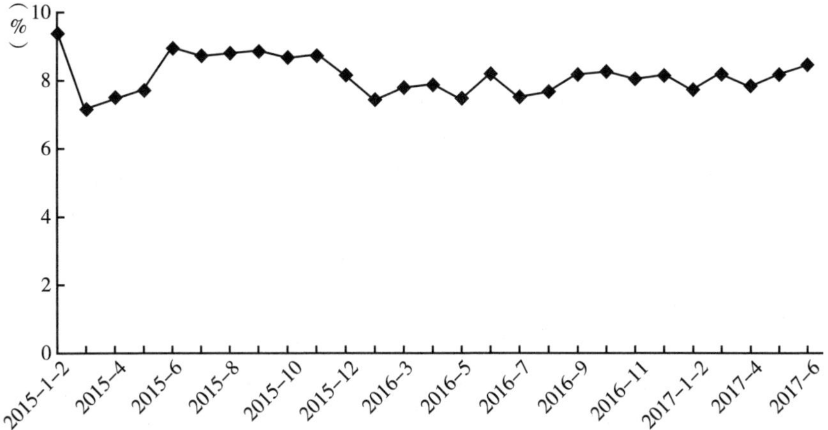

Figure 2 Comparison of year-on-year growth of the added value of above-designated-size industries between Henan province and the whole country

Data source: Henan Bureau of Statistics.

Nationally speaking, in 2016, the growth rate of the added value of above-designated-size industries ranked seventh of the country and third of the central region. As is shown in Figure 3, compared with other four large industrial provinces domestically, in 2016, the cumulative growth rate of the provincial

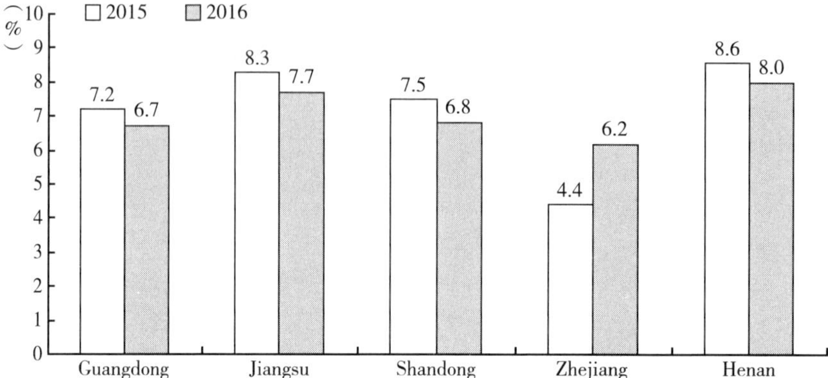

Figure 3 Comparison of the growth rate of the added value of above-designated-size industries in five large industrial provinces

Data source: The data of 2015 are from *China Statistical Yearbook in 2016* and the data of 2016 are from *The Bulletin of the National Economic and Social Development* respectively.

industry still ranked first. Compared with the growth rate of 2015, in 2016, the four provinces except for Zhejiang (Zhejiang rebounded sharply by 2 percentage points) are all showing a downward trend.

(2) The Obvious Optimization of the Industrial Product Structure

Since 2012, Henan has pushed forward the structural reform on the supply side in the manufacturing industry, improved the overall quality and competitiveness of industry, and paid more attention to the optimization of the industrial product structure. The proportion of high growth manufacturing has been significantly improved, and the proportion of traditional industry and high energy-consuming industries has continued to decline, while the added value of high-tech industry maintains rapid growth, much higher than the growth rate of the total industrial added value (Figure 4).

Five major manufacturing industries, equipment, food, new materials, electronic information and automobiles, have made rapid progress. In 2016, the growth rate of electronic information, automobiles and equipment was 15.4%, 14.7% and 12.7% respectively, far higher than the average level of the provincial industry. New material industry has found its way both in supply and demand. And in our field study, it is recognized that, with the rapid development of consuming electronics and new energy vehicles in

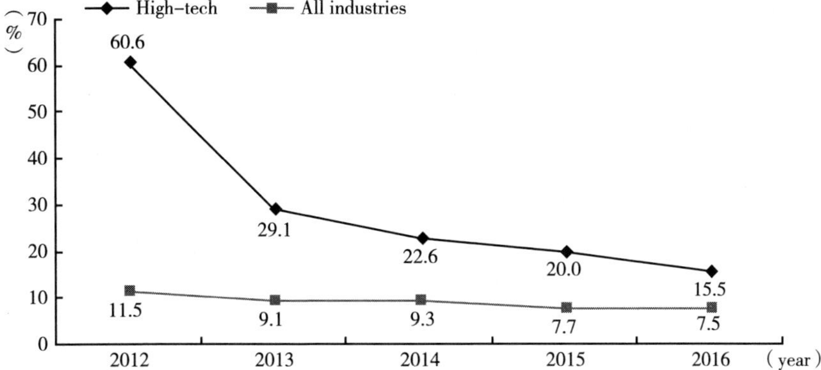

Figure 4 The growth rate of the added value of high-tech industry compared with all other industries

Data source: Henan Bureau of Statistics.

the downstream, the orders of aluminium foil, copper foil, alloy, materials, polymer materials, battery materials and other material industries in the upstream have been placed again and again, showing great willingness of expansion.

According to the analysis of the product structure, the enterprises from Henan have paid more and more attention to the investment in R&D and development for new products during the past years. Manufacturing products also quicken their pace to the mid-to-high end market significantly. In 2016, mobile communications handsets, metal cutting machine tools, SUVs and other products have achieved a year-on-year growth of 30.3%, 27.2% and 25.8% respectively. The production quantity of cement, flat glass, iron, steel, alumina and other products declined in varying degrees, which shows the good outcome of cutting excessive industrial capacity. In recent years, many enterprises with advantages show their willingness to a new reforming project, with a number of high value-added industrial projects put into practice and achieving great success, such as the high precision aluminium program of Zhong Fu Aluminium and the special robot program of CITIC Heavy Industry, both of which are finished and in operation, with the share of mid-to-high end market continuing to increase. In December 2016, the Ministry of Industry and Information Technology of the People's Republic of China announced the first batch of 60 individual champion demonstration enterprises, among which two projects from Henan (CITIC Heavy Industry's mineral grinding machine and YTO Group Corporation's large tractor) were selected.

(3) The Economic Effectiveness of Enterprises Keeps Getting Better

Since 2012, the economic effectiveness of Henan's industrial enterprises has been continually improving. In 2016, Henan's above-designated-size industrial enterprises showed a total profit of 517.44 billion yuan, a year-on-year by 6.4%, 6.5 percentage points higher than that of the previous year. The enterprise effect has been improved, changing the phenomenon of negative growth in 2015. From 2012 to 2016, the growth rate of above-designated-size industrial enterprises of Henan province has risen by 6.5%. In 2016, the total profit was 517.414 billion yuan, up 28.8% from 4016.39 billion yuan in 2012.

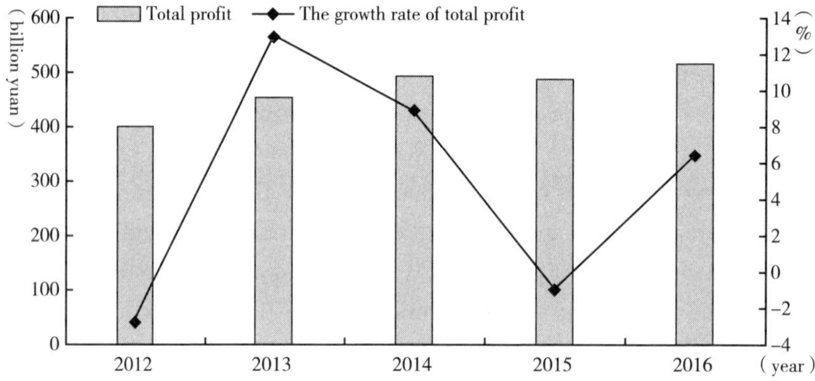

Figure 5 The total profit and growth rate of above-designated-size industrial enterprises of Henan province

Data source: Henan Bureau of Statistics.

As shown in Figure 6, from the angle of every month, profit growth increases steadily, compared with the negative growth in 2015, indicating that the profitability of industrial enterprises continues to be strengthened, contributing to the increasingly better and better producing and operating status.

However, on the whole, the profitability of industrial enterprises in Henan is still weaker than that of other provinces, and the growth rate of

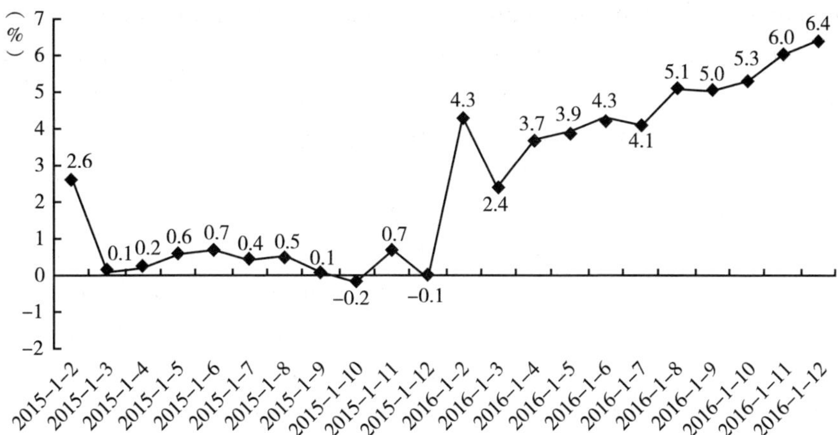

Figure 6 Month-on-month cumulative growth of the total profit of above-designated-size industrial enterprises in Henan province

Data source: Henan Bureau of Statistics.

the profits of above-designated-size industrial enterprises is 2.1 percentage points less than the national average growth rate. From the angle of profit margin, in 2016, the profit margin of main business is 6.53%, 0.16 percentage points less than that of 2015.According to the analysis of product structure, the profits of high-growth manufacturing increased by 6.4%, while the profits of traditional pillar industry increased by 7.6%, and the profit growth is mainly driven by traditional industries, with the year-on-year growth of metallurgical industry increasing by 28.1%.According to the research, it is also found that the producing management of electrolytic aluminium, iron and steel industry has become better since 2016, mainly benefitting from the fact that the price of raw materials has been more suitable since 2016, but the price of raw materials of energy fluctuated recently, which shows that the sustainability of the recovery of traditional industry should have more attention paid to it. In 2016, the electronic information industry, which had great support for the adjustment of Henan's industrial structure years ago, showed a loss of -7.0%, which was much less than the growth rate of 23.5% of the previous year.

(4) The Advanced Manufacturing Pattern Achieved Gradual Penetration

In recent years, under the pressure of demand pull, policy support and environmental protection, the advanced manufacturing pattern has found its way into various industries, with the expanding enthusiasm of transforming to automation, intellectualization and environment-friendliness. Since the implementation of Made in China 2025, policy support from governments at all levels has significantly expanded. For example, on February 26, 2016, the provincial government issued Henan Action Plan for Made in China 2025, which proposed the development of the advanced manufacturing pattern such as intelligent manufacturing, service-oriented manufacturing, collaborative manufacturing and cloud manufacturing etc.. And in December 2016, Henan also issued "The implementing Plan for the Deepening Integration between Manufacturing and Internet of Henan", which proposed the construction of different and characteristic pilot projects for intelligent manufacturing, service-oriented manufacturing, service customization, internet collaborative manufacturing and other brand-new manufacturing pattern. In the list of pilot projects for intelligent manufacturing in 2016 published by the Ministry of Industry and Information Technology of the People's Republic of China (MIIT), Yutong's pilot project "intelligent manufacturing of bus" found its place. In June 2016, there are four pilot projects of Henan in the list of "comprehensive standardization for intelligent manufacturing and application of new models in 2016" published by MIIT, including CITIC Heavy's "intelligent manufacturing factory for specialized robots", YTO Group Corporation's "a new application model of intelligent manufacturing for a new wheeled tractor", Xinxiang Aviation Industry Corp's "the digital workshop for key parts of aviation", Zhengzhou Institute of Abrasive Grinding's "new intelligent manufacturing model for super hard material grinding tools with high performance".

In March 2016, there were 10 intelligent manufacturing pilot projects approved by the provincial government, including "the new energy bus factory" declared by Zhengzhou Yutong Bus Co., Ltd, Henan Jiyuan Iron and Steel (Group) Co., Ltd., "the third assembly plant" declared Chinese YTO Group Corporation, "power lithium battery production line" declared by China Airlines Lithium (Luoyang) Co., LTD., "the electro - hydraulic base" declared by CITIC Heavy Machinery Co., LTD., "Yuchuan smelting plant" declared by Henan Yuguang Gold & Lead Group Co., Ltd., Henan Shunda Chemical Technology Co., Ltd., "Low voltage power distribution equipment in Smart Grid" by Henan Senyuan Electric Co., Ltd., "the cylinder liner factory" declared by ZYNP Group Co., Ltd. and "Chinese nutritious meal factory for an annual output of 500

thousand tons per year" declared by Henan Dayong Industrial Co., Ltd.. The innovative and entrepreneurial base designed for the integration between the manufacturing industry and the Internet is actively set up across the province, includes Henan Internet Industry Association, Intelligent Manufacturing Industry Promotion Union, CIO Union, Virtual Reality Industry Alliance. And different new manufacturing modes are being developed, including service-oriented manufacturing by CITIC Heavy, intelligent manufacturing by Yutong Bus, customized manufacturing by Daxin Cabinet, and platform-oriented transformation by Zhongpin Group.

(5) The Continual Reduction of Investment Growth in Industry

In the past years, the growth rate of investment in industry keeps decreasing, and in 2016, industrial investment grew by 8.9%, 4.8 percentage points lower than that of all investment in fixed asset and 1.8 percentage points than that of the same period of the previous year (10.7%). The growth rate of investment in industry keeps decreasing in the past four years, from 21% in 2012 gradually down to 8.9% in 2016.

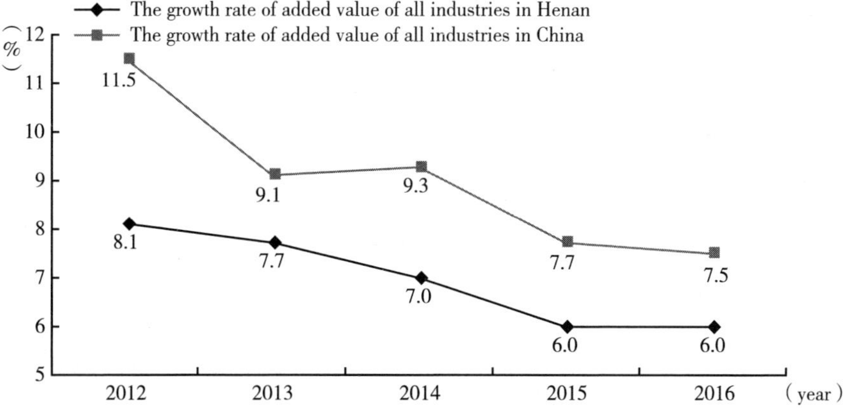

Figure 7 The growth rate of industrial investment of Henan from 2012 to 2016

Data source: Henan Bureau of Statistics.

The investment structure has deteriorated; in recent years, the situation that the growth rate of investment in high-growth manufacturing is higher than traditional pillar industries and power consumption industries has changed (Figure 8). In 2016, the investment in high-growth manufacturing grew by 7.5%, 1.4 percentage points lower than that of the traditional pillar industries and 5 percentage points lower than that of the power consumption industries, respectively. In particular, the cumulative growth of the investment in six greatest power consumption industries increased to 12.5%, much higher than that of the same period of the previous year, the growth rate of which is just 8.9%.

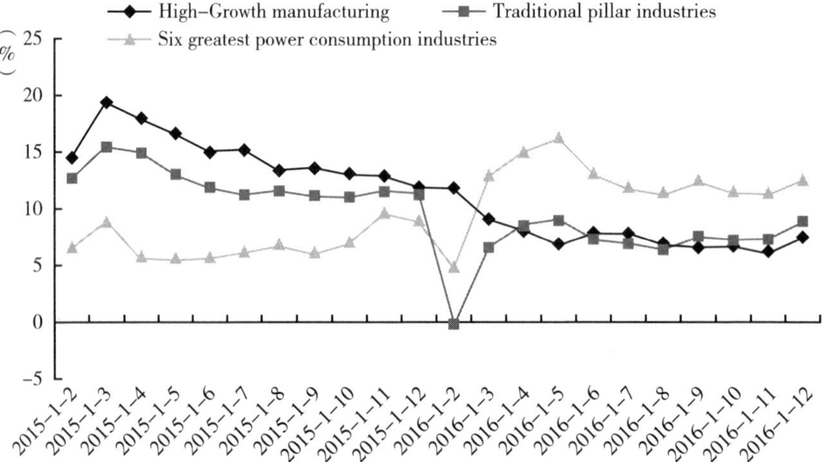

Figure 8 The comparison among the cumulative rate of investment in fixed assets of different industries in Henan

Data source: Henan Bureau of Statistics.

In particular, the growth rate of the investment in electronic information, automobile industry and equipment, which played an important role in the upgrading of Henan's industrial structure before, has decreased sharply, with the growth rate growing by -2.1%, 1.7% and 9.4%, respectively, in 2016, compared with that of the same period of the year before, with the growth rate being 9.8%, 21.2% and 17.8% respectively. To some degree, the present investment structure decides the future industrial structure, so it is necessary that more and more attention is required to be paid to the deteriorating tendency of the industrial investment structure of Henan. In recent years, one of the highlights of Henan investment structure is the rapid and continual growth rate of the investment in information transmission, computer services and software, with the substantial growth rate being 47.8% in 2016, which serves as a strong support for Henan's IT-based industrial transformation and upgrading.

2. Issues Remained

In combination with comprehensive review of the 2016 Henan industrial operations and the situation we found in the communication with entrepreneurs and government staff in our research, great attention should be paid to the following issues existing in the present industrial development of Henan.

(1) The Issues about the Reducing Efficiency of Traditional Development Mode because of the Logical Changing of Industrial Growth

At present, the inherent logic of industrial growth in China is undergoing a fundamental change, and it is a general trend to change from the investment-based industrial development mode to the innovation-based one. Before the international financial crisis, owing to the great gap between China and developed countries, many industries had potential to make great progress, so a consensus was easy to be reached about what industry the investment was supposed to be put into, and the investment is the main force to promote the development of industry, in which the government played an important role. Because of the surplus of traditional industries and the undersupply of new products and new industries, it is necessary to optimize the supply structure to form an innovation-based development mode. That it is called "innovation-based" doesn't mean no investment is needed, because it is necessary to invest in new technology, new equipment, new infrastructure and public services in order to develop the "Four New Economies", which means the economy powered by new technology, new industry, new business pattern and new mode. In our research, local government administration and industrial investment sector generally said that the recent investment and industrial investment efficiency reduced obviously, which shows that, in our opinion, there exists a huge difference between the developing environmental requirements of "Four New Economy" and that of traditional industries. Therefore, great attention is required to be paid to the theoretical changing of the industrial development mode from the focus on hard construction to the focus on soft environmental construction, to create a suitable industrial ecology for innovation.

(2) The Shortage and Loss of High-level Talents in the Context of New Industrial Revolution

The elite are the key support for industrial transformation and upgrading. The new round of industry and technology revolution is in the ascendant, with the rapid penetration of intelligent manufacturing and the accelerating integration between the internet and manufacturing etc., all of which is driven by the technical elites. From the research, we find that the number of senior technical personnel in fields such as intelligent manufacturing, industrial robots, the Internet and other industries, is obviously insufficient. The loss of high-level talent is serious. For example, some enterprises said that with the preferential policies of coastal areas, most of their technical employees resigned. In recent years, the economically developed regions, such as Zhejiang, Jiangsu, Fujian, Guangdong and other places, have provided large-scale investment in the development of innovative and intelligent manufacturing. They introduce a series of preferential policies to attract a large number of talents they need for the development of advanced manufacturing.

(3) The Unwillingness of Investment with the Conversion from Old Energy to New Energy

Henan's industries have undergone the key period of the conversion from old energy to new energy, so the innovation-based development requires high-quality investment. Most of Henan's enterprises are in the upper reaches of the industrial chain, so they are not familiar with the field of the terminal high-end products. In communication with entrepreneurs, we find that, in the context of the widespread surplus and fewer opportunities of traditional industries, some entrepreneurs show their unwillingness to invest in new industries. In particular, some enterprises have been becoming afraid of investing in the upgrading and intellectualization of traditional industries, after the failure of the pre-production of new technology in which they are interested, which is one of the most important reasons why private investment fell sharply in recent years. According to the data released by the Financial Survey and Statistics Department of the People's Bank of China, on the whole, the confidence index of entrepreneurs has shown a downward trend since 2014, indicating that enterprises are not very optimistic about the future.

(4) The Financing Difficulties Private Enterprises have to Face because of the Separation of Finance from the Real Economy

In recent years, due to the serious problem that the finance breaks away from the real economy and the capital always tends to go into state-owned enterprises and government financing platform, private enterprises' financing difficulties have been becoming more and more severe, especially for the manufacturing industry. In the survey, we realize that, although Henan has introduced "some policy measures to optimize enterprise financing services", the influence of these measures is not as effective as we expected, because the financial institutions still carry on credit crunch on private enterprises widely. Since 2016, the proportion of industrial loans out of all loan balances of financial institutions has declined as a whole, down from 22.4% in February to 19.9% in November, a decrease of 2.5 percentage points. At present, with the general decrease of industrial profit margin, if new projects are launched, the profits are not even enough to repay the interest of loans, so the high cost of capital makes private enterprises very cautious in their investment. At present, enterprises are at a critical stage of transformation and upgrading, and new technologies, new equipment and new products need financial support, so the risk of enterprises' capital chain rupture needs attention.

Ⅱ Prospective and Environmental Analysis of Henan Industrial Development Trends for 2017

1. Environmental Analysis of Henan Industrial Development

(1) Supporting Conditions

Firstly, with the national strategic platform support, Henan is the home of 12 national strategic planning and platforms, including "the core area of food production", "Central Plains Economic Zone", "Zhengzhou Airport Economic Comprehensive Experimentation Area", "Central Plains City Group", "Zheng-Luo-Xin National Innovation Demonstration Area", "China (Zhengzhou) International Electronic Commerce Comprehensive Experimental Zone", "China (Henan) Free Trade Zone" and "National Dig Data Comprehensive Experimental Zone", among which there are five National Platforms landing in Henan (Table 1) in 2016, and Zheng-Luo-Xin National Innovation Demonstration Area of Made in China 2025 will be also approved. With the superimposed effect and the multiplication effect generated by the coordination of these national strategic planning, Henan's industries will benefit from the dividend policy released by the multiple positive coupling policy, which will give the Henan's industries a golden time for entrepreneurship and innovation. At present, Henan's industries are at the stage of shifting from "quantity" to "quality" and from "big" to "strong", so the implementation of these strategic plannings will help achieve the goal of

Central China Rising and accelerate the transformation and upgrading of Henan's industries.

Table 1 Henan's national strategic planning platforms in 2016

NO.	Time	Name	Approval department
1	January 6, 2016	China (Zhengzhou) International Electronic Commerce Comprehensive Experimental Zone	The State Council
2	April 5, 2016	Zheng-Luo-Xin National Innovation Demonstration Area	The State Council
3	August, 2016	China (Henan) Free Trade Zone	Party Central Committee and State Council
4	October 8, 2016	National Dig Data Comprehensive Experimental Zone	NDRC, MIIT and CAC
5	December 28, 2016	Urban Agglomeration Development Planning of Central China	The State Council
6	May 24, 2017	Zheng-Luo-Xin National Demonstration City Group of Made in China 2025	Ministry of Industry and Information Technology

Data source: Prepared according to the related statistics.

Secondly, Henan's industries will benefit from both national and local policy support. In 2017, the Ministry of Industry and Information Technology of the People's Republic of China will revise and perfect the provincial guide of "Made in China 2025", encouraging the differential development of regions and the rational distribution of productive forces in key industries, deepening city (city group) pilot demonstration, and starting the outstanding promotion plan of new national industrialization demonstration base to determine the first batch list of "Made in China 2025" pilot demonstration base for the outstanding promotion. These measures described above will form a collaborative network development pattern in which the central government, the provincial government, the pilot cities and the industrial bases will work together, hand in hand. In addition, in order to cooperate with the implementation of the "Made in China 2025", the Ministry of Finance will adopt some tax credit policies, including the R&D costs plus pre-tax deductions and the accelerated depreciation of fixed assets. As well, the Ministry of Finance will provide more policy support for the promotion and application of the firstly applied main equipment and the insurance premiums for the first application of new materials and key components should be included in the scope of compensation. In order to speed up the implementation of

Henan's "Made in China 2025", Henan promulgated "Henan's Committee of Industry and IT's Notice about the Publication of Industrial Transformation and Upgrading (Made in China 2025) Key Projects in 2016", "Henan's Special Action Guide about the Development of Service-oriented Manufacturing (2017-2020)" and other documents. At the end of 2016, the 10th Party Congress of Henan proposed that great attention should be paid to the construction of advanced manufacturing industry and introduced a series of policies and measures. In 2017, Henan's Committee of Industry and IT took measures to promote a new round of large-scale technical transformation, facilitating the implementation of "Ten, Hundred and Thousand" technical demonstration projects, which means that the provincial government will provide more support for 10 manufacturing innovation center projects, 100 large-and-medium-sized enterprises' pilot projects of "start-ups and innovation" and 1000 technical renovation projects focusing on developing new products, in order to make the investment growth of technical renovation reach more than 20%. In order to further the integration of banks and enterprises, production and marketing, employment and industry-university-research cooperation, the implementation of "Baiqianwan Growth Plan" is put forward, which means that, firstly, the government will provide a entrepreneurship training for hundreds of outstanding entrepreneurs, and secondly, the implementation of "Billions of Capital Powering Advanced Manufacturing Province Construction" is proposed, and in the end, the government will encourage thousands of officials to help thousands of enterprises. We will integrate the industrial chain to create industrial clusters, striving to achieve more than 16 industrial clusters with production value of over 100 billion yuan.

Thirdly, the internet economy plays a great role in the development of Henan's industries. In 2016, the development of Henan's information and telecommunications made great achievements. For example, the total number of internet users exceeded 80 million, of which 4G users accounted for more than 50%, and the population of broadband users with the bandwidth more than 50Mbps (megabits per second) was the largest in the country. In addition, Zhengzhou Internet Dedicated Channel was launched, with the explosive growth of IPTV, networking and other internet-based businesses, which will provide more and more internet support for the development of Henan's industries. On October 8, The National Development and Reform Commission, Ministry of Industry and Information Technology and Cyberspace Administration of China together sent the notice, which approved Henan's application of building National Dig Data Comprehensive Experimental Zone. Henan has become one of the second provinces with the official approval to build National Dig Data Comprehensive Experimental Zone after Guizhou. The national major IoT applied pilot projects goes well. On the one hand, a relatively complete industrial chain has been formed and a number of industry backbone enterprises with strong competitiveness in the country has emerged. On the other hand, Henan has issued the "Guiding Opinions on Promoting the Open Cooperation of Big Data and Cloud Computing", the "Action Plan of Internet Plus" and other systematic policy measures, which all together forms a good social atmosphere and environment for development. The integration of informatization and industrialization in 14 key industries is being furthered continually, including electronic information, equipment manufacturing, automobile and its parts, food, biomedicine, energy saving and environmental protection etc. Among industrial enterprises above designated size, the coverage rate of Enterprise Resource Planning, Manufacturing Execution System, Product Lifecycle Management System, Supply Chain Management System and the employment of CNC equipment has reached 47%, 26%, 20%, 20%, 42%, respectively. From 2014 to 2016, there are 52 enterprises have been identified as the national implementing standard pilot enterprises in the integration management system of informatization and industrialization.

Finally, Henan's industries possess regional advantages. With strategic location advantages, Henan is located in the centre of Central China. And the implementation of the "Belt and Road" strategy will greatly enhance the economic impact of the New Eurasian Continental Bridge on the world. As the core area of inland strategic hinterland and New Eurasian Continental Bridge, Henan will seize the opportunity to expand the space for the development of manufacturing, by strengthening the cooperation with countries along the BELT, in industries, technology and marketing. China-Europe Train (Zhengzhou) has covered 3/4 provinces of China (autonomous regions and municipalities directly under the central government), which will benefit the whole province. The goods from other provinces accounts for 80% of the total freight volume in Zhengzhou. On the one hand, With Zhengzhou as the center of the domestic hub, China-Europe Train (Zhengzhou) will work together with the coastal ports in the east to promote the economic exchange with Asia Pacific countries and regions, including South Korea, Japan, Taiwan, Hong Kong and other countries and regions. On the other hand, in the west, with Hamburg as the hub and some European and central Asian cities as the two-level Collection and Distribution Centre (Paris, Milan, Prague, Warsaw, Malaszewicze, Brest, Alma-Ata and Zamyn-Uud), the trade network will cover 112 cities across 22 countries in EU, Russia and Central Asia (Figure 6). Based on the strategic leap-forward development of Zhengzhou - Luxemburg's "double hub", Zhengzhou Airport Economy Zone has launched other passenger and cargo flights which will benefit the countries along the B&R, to develop multimodal transportation and facilitate the construction of opening economic corridor, linking East and West, North and South, which will make Zhengzhou the important opening inland port and the International Aviation Logistics Center providing support for the construction of the Silk Road Economic Belt.

(2) Constraints

Firstly, the shortage of high-end talents can impede the development of Henan. At present, compared with the situation of Wuhan, Xi'an, Chengdu and other cities, the accumulation of high-end production factors in Henan is insufficient, the number of high-end innovation and entrepreneurship talents is relatively less and more and more high-end talents in manufacturing have left in recent years. In the research, entrepreneurs believe that we are at the stage of promoting new product development and industrial transformation, but the lack of technical personnel is serious.

Secondly, the lack of capital also should be taken into consideration. Because the enterprise is at a critical stage of transformation and upgrading, new investment is essential for new technology, new operational types of industries and new projects. However, the lack of investment is a commonly serious problem among enterprises in Henan, due to the excessive dependence on bank loans and the low proportion of direct financing, leading to a great financing gap. In 2016, the corporate bonds within Henan is 37.9 billion yuan and the domestic stock financing of non-financial institutions is 39.3 million yuan, which together accounts for only 11.32% of total social financing scale increment (682.4 billion yuan), 11.65 percentage points lower than the national average (22.97%), not only at the bottom of the top five provinces as far as economic aggregate is concerned, but also at the bottom of the six provinces of central China (Table 2).

Table 2 Statistical table of regional social financing scale increment in 2016

	Scale increment of social financing (100 million yuan)	Corporate bonds (100 million yuan)	Domestic stock financing of non-financial institutions (100 million yuan)	Proportion (%)
Guangdong	21155	3715	2313	28.49
Jiangsu	16758	3626	1232	28.98
Zhejiang	7485	1270	1294	34.25
Shandong	8312	1531	446	23.79
Henan	6824	379	393	11.32
Hubei	5911	829	416	21.07
Hunan	4437	1228	249	33.29
Anhui	6284	353	372	11.54
Jiangxi	3876	421	185	15.65
Shanxi	1831	361	122	26.38

Data source: Website of the People's Bank of China.

Thirdly, environmental protection also needs attention. With the large population, Henan is also a big agricultural province, so the amount of agricultural ammonia emission is rather large and the problem of crop residue burning is relatively serious in the north of China. Meanwhile, as a major industrial province, in 2016, the proportion of coal accounted for more than 70% of the total primary energy, and the emission of pollutants from gas enterprises was very heavy. Surrounded by the mountains from three sides, the terrain of Henan is not conducive to the diffusion of pollutants. Among the 338 prefecture-level air quality rankings, except for Xinyang, Zhoukou and Hebi, the other 15 municipalities are all within the list of the 50 worst cities, as far as PM10 is concerned. Air pollution control has been listed as one of the four major battles, and the environmental problem will generate great impact on the development of Henan's industries.

2. Development Trend Prospection

This year is the first year of the construction of an advanced manufacturing province. Accompanied by the comprehensively implementation of the transformation and development battle and the deepening of the structural reform on the supply side in our province, Henan's industry will continue to maintain stable growth as a whole, without big fluctuations, and it is expected that with the continued optimization of the industrial product structure, the added value of industries above a designated scale will be increased by about 8.0%. With the decreasing growth of traditional industries, five leading industries are expected to maintain rapid growth, including equipment manufacturing, food manufacturing, new materials manufacturing, electronics manufacturing and automobile manufacturing, which shows that structural transformation and kinetic energy conversion have made great progress.

Compared with other advanced manufacturing, the structural reform on the supply side of the traditional industries, such as steel, chemicals, nonferrous metals, coal and other traditional industries, will still be a hot potato for months to come. In addition, some enterprises will disappear in the merging and reorganization of industries, or even go bankrupt. Five leading industries, including equipment manufacturing, food manufacturing, new materials manufacturing, electronics manufacturing and automobile manufacturing, will continue to maintain stable growth. With the clearly increasing service-orientated level of the high-end and intelligent equipment manufacturing, the production of metal materials, chemical materials and cutting-edge new materials, with characteristics as light-weight, alloying and specialization, has made great progress. With the increasing rapid growth of the high-tech industry, the "Four New Economy", which means the economy powered by new technology, new industry, new business pattern and new mode, has boomed. A new generation of information technology, including Mobile Internet, IoT, Cloud Computing and Big Data Technology, has been widely used in the industrial economy, which will accelerate the economic development powered by the "Four New Economy".

III Strategic Measures Taken to Promote the Transformation and Upgrading of Henan's Industries

1. Focus on the Transformation and Development Battle based on the "Four Modernizations"

According to the standards of industrial transformation and upgrading, such as premiumisation, environment-friendliness and intellectualization, the transformation and development battle is supposed to adhere to the combination between typical projects and comprehensive development, the combination between the short-term breakthrough and long-term transformation and the combination between adaptation and forward-looking cultivation, to accelerate the harmoniously integrated development of traditional industries and emerging industries. In addition, based on the research on the different situations of industries, different transformation strategies should be made in accordance with the present situations of industries, to achieve major breakthroughs and promote the transformation and upgrading of Henan's industries. As far as the development of industries is concerned, measures are supposed to be taken to solve the problem of lack of innovation and capital among enterprises now, so, based on the manufacturing innovation center, a batch of new R&D institutions are essential for the formation of innovation platform. And at the same time, a number of industrial development funds will be set up at the provincial level, which will guide the establishment of special industrial development funds in various regions, to expand the financing channels for enterprises and solve the difficulties of transformation and development.

2. Focus on the New Momentum and New Advantages of the Five-Major Manufacturing

At present, the industrial competition presents a new pattern, and a regional industrial upgrading needs to identify the best combination of the forefront of industrial development and local comparative advantages, which is the key factor of the core competitiveness. The industry chain of five major manufacturing industries, such as equipment, food, materials, IT and automobiles, is related to a really wide range of industries, so the development of new technology, new mode and new formats in this five industries is relatively active. Henan has a comparative advantage in some areas. The development of five major manufacturing industries, including equipment manufacturing, food manufacturing, materials manufacturing, information manufacturing and automobile manufacturing, will play an important role in the transformation and upgrading of 4 traditional industries, including metallurgy, building materials, chemicals and textile, and the development and expansion of 4 emerging industries, including intelligent manufacturing equipment, bio-medicine, energy conservation and environment protection and new energy equipment and new generation of information technology, to accelerate the formation and development of new energy and new competitive advantage. Based on the further study of strategies and the formulation of five manufacturing special action plan, more attention should be given to the advantage analysis of traditional industries and emerging industries. Benefiting from the integrated development of traditional industries and emerging industries, the transformation and upgrading of industries has to focus on the following aspects: the development of equipment from traditional mode to high-end and intelligent equipment; the development of autos from traditional mode to energy-saving and new energy vehicles; the development of food manufacturing from traditional development mode to medium and high-end products; the development of materials manufacturing from traditional mode to the field of new materials and the increasing growth of information industry, to turn the upstream advantage into the terminal advantage, traditional advantage into emerging advantages, scientific research resources advantage into industrial competitive advantage and human resources advantages into high-quality talents advantage, which will, in the end, promote the upgrading of all the industries of Henan.

3. The Cultivation of High-end Development Carrier based on Zheng-Luo-Xin

Benefiting from the platform of scientific and technological innovation center in the Midwest of China, including Zheng-Luo-Xin City Group and Zheng-Luo-Xin National Innovation Demonstration Area, Henan will become the leading Integrated Carrier and the Growth Pole that will led the innovation-driven development of Henan. With the advantages of high-level innovation platform, Henan's industries have the chance to get into the national research network, further to benefit from the global innovation resources, which all together will promote the cooperation of Henan's enterprises with global R&D elements. As well, Henan's enterprises can integrate the global innovation resources through mergers and acquisitions of foreign research institutions and the joint research center. The provincial government will provide encouragement and support for the investment in the construction of High-tech Business Incubator and University Science and Technology Park, and encourage all kinds of incubation carrier to implement the market-oriented operation by using the public potential. And a number of Internet-based new incubator platforms will promote the sharing of technology, development, marketing and resources and improve the open innovation ecosystem, which will provide strong scientific and technological support for the transformation and upgrading of Henan's industries. Zheng-Luo-Xin National Innovation Demonstration Area will provide Henan's industries with a good opportunity to undertake the over-sized and large-scale industrial projects so as to take part in the national key projects. With the implementation of "Made in China 2025", Henan's industries can make full use of the technologies and advantages in industries as materials manufacturing, power equipment, new energy bus, modern agricultural machinery, information security and other fields, so that they can actively undertake national major technological and industrial projects which China are planning to carry out, to achieve great success in some areas and benefit the transformation and upgrading of Henan's industries. In addition, given that, in the face of a new round of technological revolution and the industrial revolution, large enterprise groups will also adjust their domestic strategic planning to adapt to the development tendency, Henan's industries can actively grasp the chance to cooperate with multinational enterprises and domestic enterprises, with the in-depth study of enterprise strategic planning, in order to take part in the strategic planning of large enterprise groups.

4. Focus on the Weaknesses of Henan's Industries

When working hard to achieve success in high-end market, Henan's manufacturing industries should focus on overcoming their weaknesses by solving the problems they face. Firstly, the development of high-end producer services, such as industrial design and creativity, industrial software, information services, technology services and other producer services, will provide value-added services for the manufacturing industries' restructuring and upgrading and improve the added value of industrial products. Secondly, more attention should be paid to the added services of manufacturing to accelerate the development of producer services. Most of Henan's industries are just responsible for weak links, such as manufacturing and products, and have no advantages in system integration, solutions providing, package deal and other industrial links with relatively high added value, which is an important cause of low profitability. So, Henan's industries will provide general contracting services, such as the package deal of outfit and other services providing, to foster a number of comprehensive solutions provider and encourage manufacturing enterprises to provide a full range of integrated services to customers with the help of Internet and big data platform. Thirdly, it is believed that the cultivation of famous brands will be awfully beneficial for the transformation and upgrading of Henan's industries, especially the existence of a number of influential brands globally and domestically, which will strengthen industrial integration in the province and crack down on counterfeiting misdeeds harmful for the development of regional brands. Fourthly, in order to strengthen the comprehensive assembly capacity of core components and achieve strong industrial foundation engineering, more attention are supposed to be paid to fostering a number of competitive enterprises with the capacity of core components assembly, with the help of Henan's industrial chain advantage, to promote the transformation of small-and-medium enterprises from single product supply to modular supply, which will help the enterprises with advantages get into the supply chain system of global well-known enterprises, and then, with the help of Zhengzhou's integrated transportation system, a global supply chain base will appear. Finally, with the help of China's Medium- and Long-Term Talent Development Plan and Provincial Hundred Talents Program, great measures are taken to attract high-level talents to the innovation and entrepreneurship of Henan, such as the construction of "big craftsman" studio and skillful masters' studio, and in addition, Henan will foster 100 science and technology innovation team and the 1000 Chief Technologists of different industries.

5. The Deeply Integration of Informatization and Industrialization Focusing on Intelligent Manufacturing

Benefiting from the integrated development between manufacturing and Internet, Henan's industries can grasp the global intelligent manufacturing development opportunities to deepen the implementation of the integrated development plan of manufacturing and Internet. For example, measures will be taken to cultivate 50 smart factories and 100 intelligent workshops in equipment, food, chemicals, automobile, metallurgy, building materials, clothing and other industries every year and to promote industrial robots, CNC machine tools and other intelligent equipment and products in welding, handling, packaging and other production links. Henan will continue to take measures to meet the standards of national management system standards for the integration of manufacturing and Internet, and improve the level of industries' network informatization and the management and operation efficiency. More support will be provided for the development of leading enterprises focusing on providing intelligent manufacturing solutions. For example, Machinery Industry Sixth Design Institute Co. Ltd. is expert in the designing and constructing of intelligent plants. In June, 2016, Ministry of Industry and Information Technology of the People's Republic of China announced the New Model Applied Projects of Comprehensive Standards of Intelligent Manufacturing of 2016, among which the company won the bidding "Intelligent Plant Construction Standard Guide for Research and Experimental Verification Platform". At present, the smart factory laboratory has been built. Henan can rely on the company to create a manufacturing innovation center with national influence, which will provide support for the transformation of Henan enterprises— intellectualization and network using.

6. Focus on New Product Development and Intensify Technological Transformation

Traditional industries have great potential for transformation and upgrading, and focus on the development of new products, Henan will accelerate the technological transformation of traditional industries. Given the demand of high-end products, such as smart equipment, new materials and green products, measures will be taken to ensure the annual implementation of "Ten, Hundred and Thousand" Technical Upgrading Demonstration Projects by turns, and to guide enterprises to adopt new technology, new technique, new equipment and new materials, to support the implementation of more large-scale technical transformation of a higher level and improve the technological transformation investment's proportion in industrial investment, output ratio of new products and resources and energy utilization rate. With the implementation of the New Product Cultivation Plan and the perfection of the first-time support policy in the adoption of major technical equipment (set), new materials and new software, Henan will expand the scope of product identification of first (set) major technical equipment and foster thousands of new products with features of high technology, high added value, to improve product hierarchy and product quality.

References

[1] Chen Hui. 2017 Henan Started the Transformation and Development Battle and Developed into A Strong Province with Advanced Manufacturing [N]. *Henan Daily*, January 10, 2017.

[2] Chen Yimiao and Zhang Zhenyu. Six Measures to Develop Advanced Manufacturing Industry [N]. *China Industry Daily*, March 4, 2015.

[3] Cui Zhijian. the Rapid Development of Henan Large and Medium-Sized Industrial Enterprises in Mass Entrepreneurship and Innovation [N]. *Guangming Daily*, February 9, 2017.

[4] Fan Xia. 2016 Henan Industrial Economic Data: Profit Growth Rate of Industries Above Designated Size Over 6.4% [N]. *Henan daily*, February 7, 2016.

[5] Feng Qiyu. This Year's Industrial Transformation Focuses on Improving Quality and Efficiency [N]. *Economic Daily*, January 4, 2016.

[6] Huang Qunhui. With the Industry Down, The Promotion of Manufacturing Capacity Should Be Noticed [N]. *People's Daily*, December 2, 2015.

[7] Huang Qunhui and Jun Jun. Core Competence, Functional Orientation and Development Strategy of China's Manufacturing Industry — Review *(Made in China 2025)* [J]. *Chinese Industrial Economy*, Sixth of 2015.

[8] Li Lianshui. *Research Report on the Development of China's Manufacturing Industry 2015* [M]. Peking University Press, 2016.

[9] Li Jingjing, Miao Changhong and Ye Xinyue. Analysis of The Multi-Scale Evolution Mechanism of The Core Periphery Structure of Regional Economy — Taking Henan Province as An Example [J]. *Economic Geography*, tenth of 2016.

[10] Li Zhengxin. The Enlightenment Of "German Industry 4" On Industrial Upgrading of Henan [J]. *Regional Economic Review*, second of 2015.

[11] Liu Yumei and Wang Dan. A Journey to Upgrading the Quality and Efficiency of Henan Industry [N]. *Henan daily*, April 20, 2015.

[12] Miao Wei. Grasp the Trend, Seize the Opportunity, to Promote China's Manufacturing Industry from Big to Strong [J]. *China Industrial Review*, seventh of 2015.

[13] Sun Yeqing. The Point of View of the Transformation and Upgrading of "Made in China"[N]. *People's Daily*, March 10, 2016.

[14] Wang Li and Chen Ying. Henan's Force in Supply Side Reform [J]. *Decision-Making Exploration*, ninth of 2016.

[15] Wang Zheng. The Stability, Growth, Difficulty of Industrial Added Value Over 6% [N]. *People's Daily*, July 26, 2016.

[16] Wang Zhaoping. Innovation Drives Henan To Speed Up the Construction of Advanced Manufacturing Province [N]. *China Industry Daily*, 2016-12-26.

[17] Zhao Qian. Analysis of The Optimization and Upgrading of Industrial Structure and Construction of Industrial Competitiveness in Henan Province [J]. *Innovation and Technology*, fifth of 2016.

[18] Institute of Industrial Economics, Chinese Academy of Social Sciences. *Report of China Industrial Development (2016)* [M]. Economic Management Press, 2016.

[19] Institute of Quantitative and Technical Economics, Chinese Academy of Social Sciences. *Industry Sentiment Index Report of the Four Quarter Of 2016* [R]. January, 2017.

B.4

Report on Financial Development of Henan Province

Henan Provincial Academy of Social Sciences Research Group[*]

Abstract: Since the 18th National Congress of the CPC, Henan has insisted steady development and deepened innovative reform in its financial industry to enhance its financial strength and institutions. Overall, it has significantly improved the ability to serve the real economy, made breakthroughs in the financial poverty alleviation, and constantly fostered innovations in the financial reform. Looking ahead the complicated economic situation at home and abroad, Henan is facing coexisted opportunities and challenges in its financial development. In the next few years, Henan should give more financial support for key areas, accelerate the development of multi-level capital market, stimulate financial innovation for weak parts, deepen financial reform, highlight regulation and supervision, and strengthen risk prevention, so that Henan's financial industry can maintain healthy and constant development.

Keywords: Henan Financial Institutions; Supply-side Structural Reform; Financial Innovation; Henan Province

---

* Group leader: Zhang Zhancang; Group members: Wan Shiwei, Zhao Ran, Wu Wenchao, Wang Fang, Shi Tao.

I The Basic Development Trend of Henan's Financial Industry in the Past Five Years

In the past five years, Henan's financial industry has actively adapted itself to the new norm, conscientiously implemented the national financial policy, adhered to innovative development and stable operation, made efforts to promote supply-side structural reform and to serve the real economy. As a result, Henan's financial institutions have risen rapidly and financial industry entered a new stage.

1. Further Enhancement of the Financial Development

The added value of the financial sector has improved steadily. In the past five years, the added value of Henan's financial sector has increased from 101.36 billion yuan in 2012 to 225.37 billion yuan in 2016, with an average annual growth of 22.4% and an average annual increase of 31 billion yuan. At the same time, its proportion in GDP has risen from 3.4% in 2012 to 5.6% in 2016, with an increase of 2.2 points. In 2016 particularly, Henan's financial industry added value has a higher growth rate of 3.7% than Henan's GDP, ranking the first among the six central provinces and the eighth around the country. Obviously, the financial industry has become a pillar industry in Henan's development.

The scale of banking institutions has expanded gradually. In the past five years, the total assets of banks increased from 3918.61 billion yuan in 2012 to 6960.2 billion yuan in 2016, with an average annual growth of 15.5% and an average annual increase of 760.4 billion yuan. The size of the banks' foreign and domestic deposits increased from 3197.04 billion yuan in 2012 to 5497.97 billion yuan in 2016, with an average annual growth of 14.5% and an average annual increase of 575.23 billion yuan. The scale of foreign and domestic currency loans increased from 2030.17 billion yuan in 2012 to 3713.96 billion yuan in 2016, with an average annual growth of 16.3% and an average annual increase of 420.95 billion yuan. At the same time, the loan to deposit ratio increased from 63.5% in 2012 to 67.6% in 2016, with an increase of 4.1 points. In 2016 particularly, the bank's foreign and domestic currency deposits growth rate and loan growth rate were respectively 2.6 and 4 points higher than the national average, and the

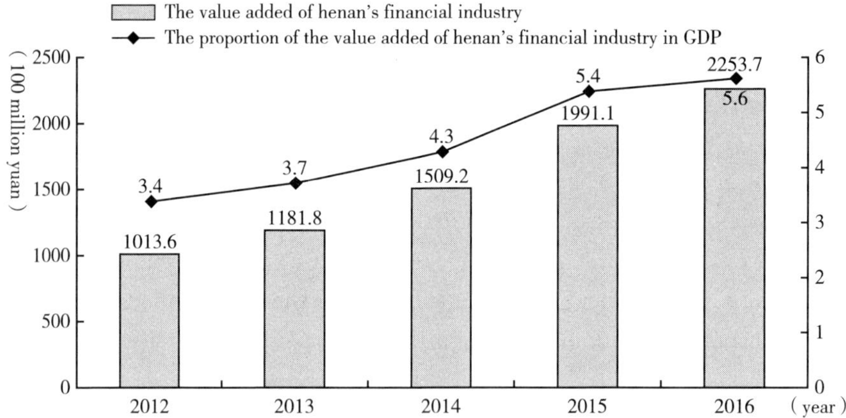

Figure 1 Trends in value added of Henan's financial industry and its proportion in GDP from 2012 to 2016

Note: Without special instructions, the data are from the statistical yearbook of the People's Bank of China, the Statistical Yearbook of Henan province, the statistical bulletin of the Henan provincial government and the financial development report of Henan province (2017, 2016 and 2015), similarly hereinafter.

balance ranked the ninth and eleventh in the country respectively. The bank's net profit rose from 49.59 billion yuan in 2012 to 66.86 billion yuan in 2016, with an average annual growth of 8.4% and an average annual increase of 4.32 billion yuan, showing great enhancement in competitive strength.

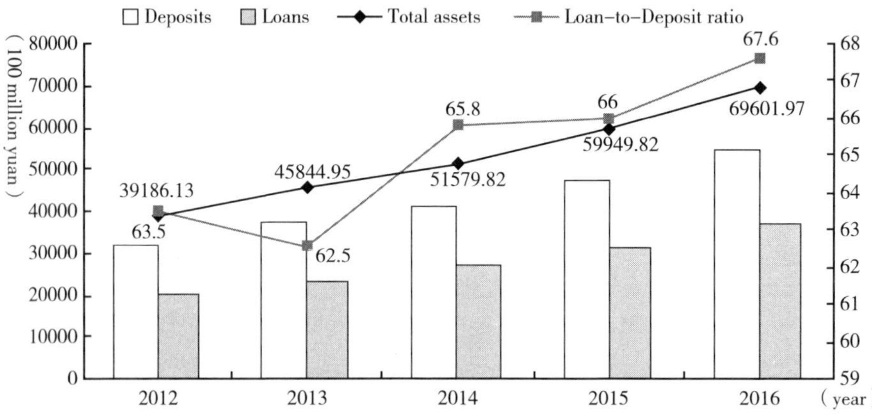

Figure 2 Trends in total assets, deposits and loans and their ratios of Henan's banking industry from 2012 to 2016

The depth of insurance and the rate of economic securitization have maintained steady growth. In the past five years, the income of insurance increased from 84.11 billion yuan in 2012 to 155.52 billion yuan in 2016, with an average annual growth of 16.8% and an average annual increase of 17.85 billion yuan. The insurance depth rose from 2.8% in 2012 to 3.9% in 2016, with an increase of 1.1 points. The total market value of the securities increased from 246.07 billion yuan in 2012 to 871.48 billion yuan in 2016, with an average annual growth of 54.7% and an average annual increase of 156.35 billion yuan. The rate of economic securitization increased significantly by 13.4% from 8.3% in 2012 to 21.7% in 2016.

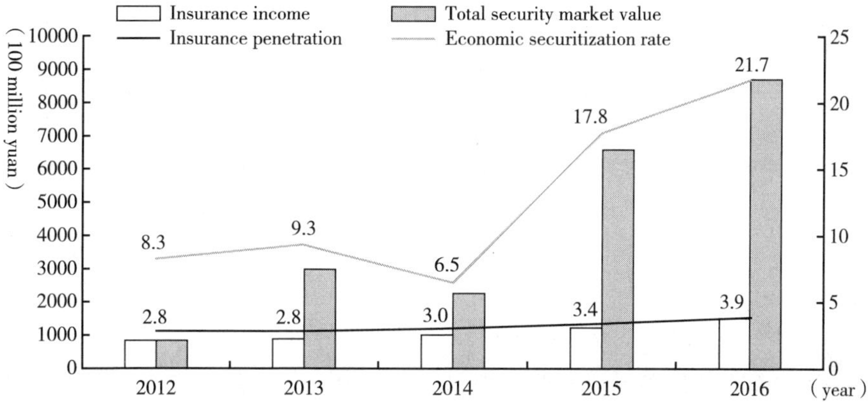

Figure 3 Trends in insurance income, total security market value, insurance penetration and economic securitization rate of the securities industry in Henan province from 2012 to 2016

2. Significant Increase of the Financial Service Capability to the Real Economy

The scale of social financing continued to expand. In the past five years, Henan's social financing increased from 475.6 billion yuan in 2012 to 682.36 billion yuan in 2016, with an average annual growth of 10.6% and an average annual increase of 51.69 billion yuan. In 2016 particularly, such scale reached 682.36 billion yuan with an increase of 18.5%, ranking the seventh in the country, compared with ranking the fifth in 2015. For the three consecutive years since 2014, Henan has ranked the first among the six provinces in Central China in social financing scale,

54 billion yuan, 91.27 billion yuan, 238.69 billion yuan, 294.78 billion yuan, 499.3 billion yuan higher than Anhui, Hubei, Hunan, Jiangxi, Shanxi, respectively in 2016 particularly.

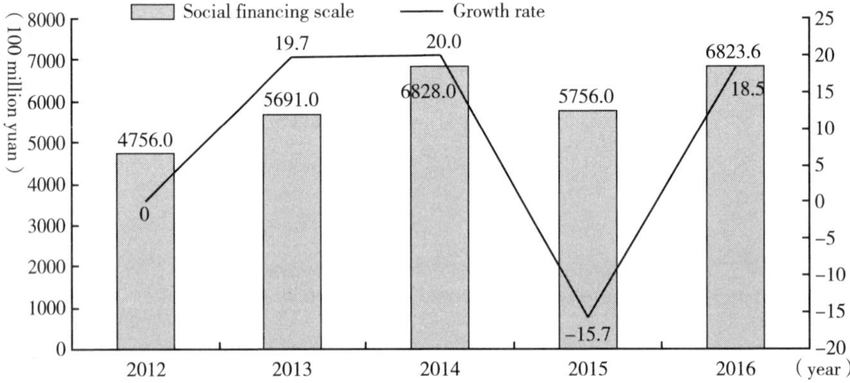

Figure 4 Trends in scale of social financing in Henan province and its growth from 2012 to 2016

Serving Henan's major development strategy. In the past five years, the new-added loans to "The Belt and Road" and the six national strategies increased from 144.9 billion yuan in 2014 to 266.13 billion yuan in 2016, with an average annual increase of 60.61 billion yuan. The new-added loans to the infrastructure and urbanization increased from 73.47 billion yuan in 2014 to 122.28 billion yuan in 2016, with an average annual increase of 24.41 billion yuan. The loans to affordable housing projects rose from 67.2 billion yuan in 2014 to 173.25 billion yuan in 2016, with an average annual increase of 53.02 billion yuan. In 2016 particularly, the new-added loans to the strategic emerging industries, six high growth industries, and the loan of "going out" and "mass entrepreneurship and innovation" increased by 29.3 billion yuan. In the insurance industry, the scale of export credit insurance in "The Belt and Road" increased from $3.72 billion in 2015 to $4.2 billion in 2016, with an average annual increase of $480 million and an average annual increase of 12.9%. The coverage of credit insurance in Henan's general trade also increased from 29.6% in 2015 to 32.8% in 2016, with an increase of 9 points. In 2016 particularly, Henan's new insurance funds reached 25.34 billion yuan in the application scale amd 40.8 billion yuan through the docking investment in the investment scale.

Serving Henan's supply-side structural reform. In 2016 alone, Henan reduced 610-million-yuan loan in the steel industry and 1.71-billion-yuan new-added loan in the coal industry for the purpose of production de-capacity, increased 58.38 billion yuan and 224.44 billion yuan respectively in the new-added loans of the housing projects and personal housing for the purpose of destocking. In terms of deleveraging, the Agricultural Development Bank and China Development Bank issued 50.09-billion-yuan special funds, while China Construction Bank reached 35-billion-yuan market share of debt to equity swap. In terms of cost reduction, Henan's banking industry has reducted benefits of 3.14 billion yuan, and the insurance industry has reformed commercial auto insurance to lower the comprehensive cost. As for the weak areas, the new-added households of small and micro loans witnessed a year-on-year increase of 49 thousand, and the ratio to obtain loans reached 97.5%, 0.9 point higher than the same period of the last year.

Serving the loaning and financing of agriculture related and small and micro enterprises. In the past five years, the scale of agricultural related loans increased from 829.81 billion yuan in 2012 to 1499.03 billion yuan in 2016, with an average annual growth of 15.98% and an average annual increase of 167.306 billion yuan. The size of small and micro loans increased from 356.7 billion yuan in 2012 to 1034.69 billion yuan in 2016, with an average annual growth of 32.44% and an average annual increase of 169.497 billion yuan. In 2016 alone, Henan's insurance institutions offered 1.82 billion yuan for small and micro businesses, guarantee institutions offered 1.25 billion yuan for agribusiness, small loan companies provided 10.67 billion yuan and 5.49 billion yuan respectively for small and micro businesses as well as agribusiness.

3. Rapid Rise of "Henan Financial Institutions"

In the past five years, Henan Provincial committee and government have attached great importance to the development of Henan's financial industry, and effectively built "Henan financial institutions" through many strategies such as "introduction" and "self-cultivation". The past five years witnessed not only the rapid outbreak of Henan's financial industry, but also the rapid emergence of Henan "financial institutions ".

"Introducing investment into Henan" and "new Henan phenomenon" won the good reputation. In the past, the financial industry was a weak part of Henan's social and economic development, and the lack of financial subjects was even weaker. Initially there existed only major state-owned commercial banks such as Industrial and Commercial Bank of China, Agricultural Bank of China, Bank of China and China Construction Bank. Then Guangdong Development Bank settled branch in 1995. Later CITIC Bank (1998), China Everbright Bank (2000), Shanghai Pudong Development Bank (2001), China Merchants Bank (2002), Industrial Bank (2004), the Zhengzhou branch of China Minsheng Bank (2008), Huaxia Bank (2011), Ping An Bank (2012), Evergrowing Bank (2016) and the Bank of Bohai (2016) in succession. At the same time, HSBC, Standard Chartered Bank, Bank of East Asia, as well as a large number of securities, insurance and other financial institutions have also settled in Henan. With the opening of Zhejiang Merchants Bank in 2017, it marked a breakthrough in Henan's "introducing investment into Henan" and Henan became the sixth province with 12 national joint stock commercial banks in China. Henan's six national strategies, from Central Henan Urban Agglomeration to the Zhengzhou National Central City, effectively supported the development of the Henan Financial institutions, and created a "new Henan phenomenon" in the financial industry.

The "Henan Financial institutions" rose rapidly. The first stage was the initial stage starting from 2014 to 2015. Zhongyuan Bank became the first provincial legal person bank and the only local legal person broker that listed Central China Securities in Hongkong to bridge provincial and overseas capital markets. The establishment of BOL Financial Leasing Co.,Ltd. has filled the gap of non-financial and non-banking financial institutions in the province. The second stage was the rising stage starting from 2015 to 2016. With securities, insurance, funds, trusts and other branches assembled fast and effectively, Zhongyuan Airport Industry Investment Fund Management Company Limited, Zhongyuan Agricultural Insurance Co.,Ltd., Tianrui Group Finance Co.,Ltd., Central China Equity Exchange, Zhongyuan Asset Management Co.,Ltd., Zhengzhou Bank have been listed in succession, making the financial industry more comprehensive to become a pillar industry in Henan province. The third stage was the stage of overall development starting from 2016 to 2017.With the enhancement of the strength, Henan Shuanghui Group Finance Co.,Ltd., Henan Agricultural Credit Guarantee Company Limited, Henan Zhongyuan Financial Holding Company Limited, Henan Agricultural Financial Leasing Co.,Ltd., Henan Zhongyuan Consumer Finance Co.,Ltd., Zhongyuan Capital Investment and Management Co.,Ltd., Zhongyuan Financial Asset Trading Center Co.,Ltd., Zhongyuan Aviation Financial Leasing Co.,Ltd., Zhongyuan Business Factoring Company Limited were established in succession, and the "Henan Financial Institutions" gradually stepped up in the market in the province, making up the gaps in Henan's financial segmentation, and entering the overall stage of development.

4. New Breakthroughs on Accurate Financial Poverty Alleviation

Breakthroughs have been made in the banking system of three-dimensional financial precision poverty alleviation. In December 2016, the State Council formally approved the general plan of Lankao Inclusive Financial Pilot Zone construction as China's first national inclusive financial reform pilot area to explore the inclusive financial Lankao Model. Lankao Model refers to the government-led, Bank-supported and enterprise-driven financial poverty alleviation, with government securities as collateral, the bank enlarged several times of the government bond to actively support poor households and poor enterprise at preferential rates. By changing poverty alleviation from blood-made type poverty alleviation instead of a blood transfusion type, Henan has explored the inclusive financial development model that can be copied and be promoted in poor areas. In 2016, according to the requirements on "*Implementation Plan to Promote the Construction of the Rural Financial Reform Pilot Area of Central Plains Economic Zone in Henan Province(2015-2020)*", a comprehensive rural financial reform pilot area construction in the Central Plains Economic Zone was launched that made up the implementation plan and the supporting system of credit information centre construction in Lankao County, and formed the initial formation of the credit information sharing mechanism for Lankao model. At the same time, the "Lushi Model" (provincial financial zone), "Guangshan Model" (the county model, Bank of China), "five in one Model" (the county model, the Agricultural Bank of China) were also gradually set up, forming the national and provincial and county financial precise poverty alleviation model system. By the end of 2016, the amount of financial aid for the poor in Henan reached 57.71 billion yuan. Among them, the individual precise poverty alleviation loans amounted to 10.06 billion yuan, the industry precise poverty alleviation loans amounted to 40.78 billion yuan, the project precise poverty alleviation loans amounted to 6.88 billion yuan, the loans of the population out of poverty amounted to 10.26 billion yuan, and 1.763 million people were brought to build files as poor population, accounting for 30.1% of the poverty population in Henan.

The insurance company continued to explore innovative poverty alleviation pilot. For example, Zhongyuan Agricultural Insurance implemented "zero risk out of poverty" comprehensive protection project in Lankao, designed agricultural insurance, agricultural accident and health accident insurance and other 16 kinds of insurances for the risks of leading enterprises and poor households, and provided 8.4 billion yuan insurance for poor people. Such model has been extended to Guangshan, Xin County and other places. China Life Insurance in Tanghe piloted poverty exclusive micro insurance portfolio, making efforts to solve the risks of poverty diseases and poverty alleviation loans. Jiaozuo introduced health poverty alleviation project, and formed a new health insurance scheme that featured "government-supported, professionally operated, precisely guaranteed as well as convenient and efficient". PICC in Lushi County piloted "government financial insurance" model that use insurance funds as a direct financing to implement the "blood made" rather than "blood transfusion" poverty alleviation.

New breakthroughs have been made in poverty alleviation in the capital market. Firmly grasping the favourable conditions of *Suggestions of China Securities Regulatory Commission on the Role of the Capital Market to Serve the Country's Anti-poverty Strategy ([2016]19)*, Henan capital market made innovations for precision poverty alleviation. First, new breakthroughs were made in the guidance of listing and trading for companies. In 2016, 3 registered counselling enterprises in Henan's poverty county were added, and one more enterprise was being checked in the meeting, 5 enterprises registered in poor counties raised 22.86 billion yuan through IPO funds, 1 enterprise achieved bonds of 600 million yuan, 11 new three board enterprises in poor counties raised 970 million yuan, and 271 enterprises in impoverished county made formally listed and started trading in Central China Equity Exchange. Second, the industry poverty alleviation funds were constantly established. In 2016 alone, Muyuan Food Stuff Co.,Ltd. led the establishment of 5 billion yuan scale "Anti-poverty Industry Fund by Jiaotong of China Securities", Bank of Communications established a 7 billion yuan scale of "the Construction and Development Fund for Poverty Alleviation of Commercial Development by Bank of Communications in Shangqiu", and the Bank of Communications and the Xinyang People's government jointly established a 6.8 billion yuan scale of "the Equity Investment Fund for the Revitalization of Dabie Old Revolutionary Base Areas in Xinyang".

5. Frequent Highlights on Financial Reform and Innovation

New breakthroughs were made in the reform of rural credit cooperatives and rural commercial firms. In the past five years, the number of institutions dropped

from 124 in 2012 to 81 in 2016, with an average annual decrease of 11.At the same time, capital was enriched and shareholder structure was optimized to set up rural commercial banks, and the number of rural commercial firms and institutions increased from 19 in 2012 to 59 in 2016, with an average annual increase of 10. By the end of 2016, the total rural commercial bank institutions in Henan reached 75 (including the number of chips), accounting for 54% of the province's agricultural organization number, effectively to resolve the rural cooperative organization development risk, and to establish a modern bank foundation. By the end of 2016, the capital adequacy ratio and provision coverage ratio of agricultural cooperatives in Henan had increased to 10.2% and 97.5% respectively, with a year-on-year up of 2.6% and 27.3% respectively.

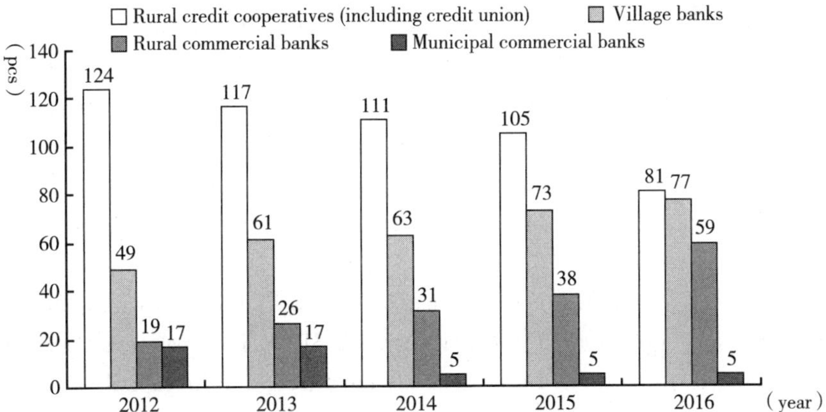

Figure 5 Trends in the number of major municipal commercial banks, rural credit cooperatives and other institutions in Henan province from 2012 to 2016

The comprehensive strength of urban commercial banks has increased significantly. In the past five years, the number of the province's city commercial banks decreased from 17 in 2012 to 5 in 2015, with an annual reduction of 3. Through the integration of financial resources, a series of region boutique banks were gradually formed revolving Zhongyuan Bank, Zhengzhou Bank and Luoyang Bank as the core. Since the establishment in 2014, Zhongyuan Bank increased its asset from 209.4 billion yuan in 2014 to 433.07 billion yuan in 2016, and its net profit rose from 2.54 billion yuan in 2014 to 3.36 billion yuan in 2016, with an average annual growth of 111.84 billion yuan and 410 million yuan respectively.

With its comprehensive strength was rising, Zhongyuan Bank ranked from the 225th in 2015 to the 210th in 2016 in global capital level, as well as the ninth in the city firms of mainland China in 2016. Zhengzhou Bank was listed in Hongkong in 2015, with its asset size increased from 203.7 billion yuan in 2014 to 366.15 billion yuan in 2016, and its net profit rose from 2.46 billion yuan in 2014 to 4.05 billion yuan in 2016, with an average annual growth of 81.22 billion yuan and 790 million yuan respectively. Committed to creating "Boutique Citizens Bank", "Business Logistics Bank", "SME Financing Expert", it was recognized as one of the city's "bellwethers". In global ranking, its capital level ranked from the 571st in 2012 to the 338th in 2016, with an average annual increase of 58; its asset size ranked from 612nd in 2012 to 327th in 2016, with an average annual increase of 71. Besides, it has been the world's top 1000 finalists for 7 consecutive years and the world's top 500 finalists for 3 consecutive years, and the comprehensive strength ranked forty-ninth among the mainland bank institutions in 2016. In 2016, Zhengzhou Bank showed strong development momentum and comprehensive competition, with 1.64% of the rate of return on assets that ranked the 203rd in the global banking industry, 26.49% of the cost income ratio that ranked the 158th in the global banking sector, 24.88% of the rate of return on capital that ranked the 89th in the global banking industry. Luoyang Bank increased its assets from 117.27billion yuan in 2014 to 183.08 billion yuan in 2016, and its net profit rose from 1.66 billion yuan in 2014 to 2.28 billion yuan in 2016, with an average annual growth of 32.9 billion yuan and 310 million yuan respectively. The comprehensive strength has been gradually enhanced, and its capital level in the global ranking rose by 73 from 501st in 2015 to 432nd in 2016. Since 2012, it has been entitled "China's top 500 service enterprises" for 5 consecutive years.

Table 1 The development situation of banks including Zhongyuan Bank from 2014 to 2016

Unit: 100 million yuan

Year	Zhongyuan Bank			Zhengzhou Bank			Luoyang Bank		
	net profit	capital scale	rank	net profit	capital scale	rank	net profit	capital scale	rank
2014	25.4	2094.0	--	24.6	2037	480	16.6	1172.7	--
2015	30.5	3012.6	225	33.6	2656.2	440	26.1	1563.0	501
2016	33.6	4330.7	210	40.5	3661.5	338	22.8	1830.8	432

Notes: The ranking refers to the world ranking of the "tier one capital" in the world bank top 1000 in *The Banker*, and the net profit and asset size data are from the bank financial annual reports (2016, 2015, and 2014).

The rural banks were constructed with high standard, and rural financial facilities were covered in the whole. In the past five years, the number of rural banking institutions in Henan province increased from 49 in 2012 to 77 in 2016, with an average annual increase of 7. In 2016, it has covered 88 provinces and cities, with a covering rate of 82%, ranking the first in China. The rapid development of rural banks has also made breakthroughs in rural financial infrastructure in the province to achieve full coverage. By the end of 2016, the province's financial payment network had covered 100% township level in rural areas, and the establishment of various bank branches reached 7704, covering 100% of township level financial payment network, and the system joined 100% in interbank payment of The People's Bank of China. The financial services terminal made a 100% coverage of administrative villages, and 16 thousand units of ATM terminals were put in rural areas and 304 thousand units of POS terminals, and it implemented 100% of the financial infrastructure in the province's administrative villages. In addition, the province's agricultural aid business transaction has been ranked the first in the nation for 2 consecutive years, and the special service transaction of bank cards for migrant workers has been ranked the first in the nation for 9 consecutive years.

6. Significant Increase on the Ability to Control Financial Risks

Financial institutions' ability to resist risks continued to increase and the overall credit risk was under control. In the past five years, the non-performing loan rate rose from 2.9% in 2012 to 2.19% in 2016, with a rise of 0.71 point. But in 2016, the rate of non-performing loans decreased down by 0.2 point over the same period in 2015, and the overall rate of non-performing loans decreased slowly; the provision coverage ratio declined from 188.21% in 2012 to 109.8% in 2016, and the capital adequacy ratio dropped from 13.3% in 2012 to 12% in 2016. The liquidity preference of corporate bodies continued to increase and the ability to compensate for risks steadily increased. The ability of local legal institutions gradually increased, and the proportion of liquidity risk of legal institutions reached 59.6% in 2016, and the capital adequacy ratio reached 12%, with an increase of 0.37 point compared with 2015, and local corporate financial institutions had a better liquidity; the provision coverage rate reached 119.07%, with an increase of 30.97% over 2015; the excess reserve rate of urban commercial banks, rural cooperative financial institutions and rural banks reached 6.6%, 8.8%, and 5%, respectively, and the risk compensation ability increased.

The illegal fund-raising and other major regional financial security incidents were struck hard. In the past five years, the Henan Provincial Finance Office, the Provincial Public Security Bureau, Zhengzhou Central Sub-branch of People's Bank of China, Henan Banking Regulatory Bureau and other departments continued to increase the illegal fund-raising and other major cases disposal efforts, reaching remarkable results. First, the legal protection mechanism for illegal fund-raising has been gradually established. Since 2012, the relevant departments of the provincial government has successively promulgated the notice on "*the Supervision System of Henan Province on Combating and Disposal of Illegal Fund-raising Work, " (2012)*, "*Notice of Henan Province on the Process of Disposal of Illegal Fund-raising Work " (No. 7 [2012] of Henan's Leading Group for the Disposal of Illegal Fund-raising)*, "*Notice of the Office of the People's Government of Henan Province on Issuing Accountability Measures for the Combating and Disposal of Illegal Fund-raising Work in Henan Province" (No. 113 [2012] of the Office of the People's Government of Henan Province), "Opinions of the Office of the People's Government of Henan Province on Further Improving the Prevention, Combating and Disposal of Illegal Fund-raising Work" (No. 22 [2015] of the Office of the People's Government of Henan Province), "Notice of the People's Government of Henan Province on the Implementation of the Spirit of No 59 Document in 2015 of the State Council to Further Improve the Prevention and Disposal of Illegal Fund-raising Work" (No. 70 [2015] of the People's Government of Henan Province), "Guiding Opinions of the Applicable Legal Issues on the Handling of Illegal Fund-raising Criminal Cases"(2016), "Notice of the Office of the People's Government of Henan Province on Issuing the Reward Interim Measures for Illegal fund raisings in Henan Province"(No. 215 [2016] of the Office of the People's Government of Henan Province)* and other documents, and gradually established the legal guarantee system of the disposal of illegal fund raisings. Second, the warning of illegal fund-raising risk reaped outstanding results. In the past five years, the Financial Office of Henan Province in conjunction with the Provincial Public Security Department and other relevant departments have established the monitoring and early warning system of the province's illegal fund raising to identify, warn and combat against acts of illegal fund raising, in the year of 2016 alone,1668 enterprises were found through the cumulative risk investigation, and 319 enterprises have successfully resolved, 422 enterprises were registered as a way of disposal, and 927 enterprises remained the risk enterprises, with a decrease of 135 compared with that in 2015. Throughout the year, the number of illegal fund-raising cases in the province, the amount involved, and the number of participants decreased by 50%, 41.87% and 58.92% respectively, compared with the same period last year. The disposal of the cold cases reached a major breakthrough, with a transferred completion rate of the new cases of 93.19%, a pending completion rate of 94.45%, a recovery of the loss of the illegal fund-raising cases of 650 million yuan, to restore the previous economic loss of 2.23 billion yuan, and the number of new cases decreased from 1st to 5th in China, and the combat and disposal of illegal fund-raising work in the province ranked 2nd in the nation for 2 consecutive years. Third, the internet financial restructuring remediation gained outstanding results. In 2016 alone, more than 10400 people were mobilized to check the risk investigation of 59818 institutions, and 288 institutions were found to have carried out financial activities online, 7169 institutions engaged in financial activities offline, and 377 institutions were investigated as the illegal fund-raising cases. At the same time, we analyzed the complaint situation of illegal fund raisings regularly for early deployment, and to cope with them properly. Focused on major sensitive period of stability control work, strengthened intelligence warning, made detailed stability control measures, and the instability issues caused by illegal fund-raising did not occur in the province.

II The Outlook for the General Trend of the Current Financial Development in Henan Province

In the past five years, the international economy has recovered slowly from the risk and crisis, and China's economy has entered a new normal state. The pace of financial market reform and innovation has been quickened, and the integration of finance and technology has become an irresistible force. Henan's financial industry has developed rapidly in the process of building a high growth service industry. The role of finance in the regional economy is constantly increasing, and the Henan Financial institutions are growing rapidly. In the future, the development pace of domestic and international financial markets will continue to accelerate, and the risks and opportunities will coexist in the development. Facing favorable conditions and unfavorable factors, the financial sector in Henan province is expected to accelerate the reform and innovation in serving the real economy and to provide strong support for the high growth of service industry and economy construction in Henan province.

1. Favourable Conditions

(1) The Accelerating Pace of Development and Innovation in China's Financial Industry

With the steady development of China's financial industry, the reform of the financial market system and the pace of development and innovation have become one of the characteristics of the development of China's financial industry. The bank's balance sheets maintain growth, the support for the economic transformation and upgrading increases, the level of financial services for the weak areas improves, and the developmental financial institutions, policy banks, and large commercial banks continue to promote reform. The securities and futures industry market has developed steadily, the supervision has been strengthened, and the basic system construction has been further improved. The insurance industry has shown a rapid overall development trend, the scale of assets has been expanding, the premium income has increased rapidly, the reform has been carried out further, and the service and social capacity have been enhanced. The participants in the financial market have been further enriched, the market system has been firmly promoted, and remarkable progress has been made in opening up to the outside world. The scale of money market transaction continues to expand, and the elasticity of interest rate has increased. Foreign exchange market transactions continue to be active; the pace of internationalization of the RMB continues to accelerate. The volume of bonds, shares and futures have increased rapidly. The financial infrastructure construction has made new progress, payment, clearing and settlement system have continuous improvement, and the financial laws and regulations constantly improve, the development of the credit market and the construction of social credit system continue to promote, and the macro prudential policy framework constantly improve. The steady and healthy development of China's financial market and the deepening of the reform of the financial system have provided a good macro environment for the development of Henan's financial industry.

(2) The Investing and Financing Needs of Henan's Economic Development

In 2016, 4016.001billion yuan GDP were achieved in Henan province, ranked 5th in the country, with a year on year increase of 8.1%, and the economic growth has maintained more than 1% for many years higher than the national average, and the revenue of about 100 million of the resident population increased with economic growth. The rapid development of regional economy will inevitably lead to the growth of investment and financing requirements. Specifically, Henan province has accelerated new urbanization in recent years. Urbanization rate of the resident population for many years has maintained more than 1%, bringing infrastructure construction and real estate investment growth.

Urbanization transferred from the agricultural population brings consumption growth, and the upgrading of the consumption and financial needs increase after income increasing. These changes bring a lot of financial service needs such as investment and financing, financial transactions, etc., providing a vast market potential for business growth of the Henan financial industry. At the same time, in the macro background of China economy entering a new norm, the pace of economic structure adjustment and industrial upgrading accelerates, so does the development of emerging industries such as technical innovation, green development, cultural consumption as the representative, meanwhile, it also brings a lot of credit and investment demand, and financial institutions such as banking, securities, and trust especially the fund industry and the risk investment funds are facing rapid development opportunities.

(3) The Opportunities for Innovation Brought by National Strategy Superposition

In the past five years, Henan has focused on the long-term development and has constantly schemed its development blueprint, and the national strategy has concentrated on Henan province. Zhengzhou Airport Economic Zone, Zheng-Luo-Xin National Innovation Demonstration Area, the National Data Comprehensive Experimental Zone, China(Zhengzhou) Cross-border E-commerce Comprehensive Test Area, China(Henan) Free Trade Test Zone, Lankao Inclusive Financial Reform Pilot Area have been approved in succession, and Central Henan Urban Agglomeration has become the national focus on fostering the development of the city group. The landing of a new batch of national strategic plans gave Henan province the space for the implementation of reform and innovation in a number of pilot areas such as regional development, comprehensive transportation hub construction, technological innovation, investment and financing system, and opening up, etc.. Under such a great opportunity, Henan's financial industry is also faced with historical opportunities for development and innovation. Around Zhengzhou Airport Economic Zone, supply chain finance, aviation finance, business factoring and other aspects of business will be developed centering on Zheng-Luo-Xin National Innovation Demonstration Area, plus science and technology, finance, venture capital, industry investment and so on. Around China (Zhengzhou) Cross-border E-commerce Comprehensive Test Area and China (Henan) Free Trade Test Zone, financial sectors will be opened up to attract foreign financial institutions in bonded delivery, cross-border settlement, the import and export insurance and other areas of business. Lankao Inclusive Financial Reform Pilot Area will be taken as an example to innovate the agricultural and rural financial services, and develop the rural financial system. Taking advantage of the major opportunities of the national strategy and actively deepening financial reform and innovation will be conducive to Henan's financial sector in the forefront of the country in some areas.

(4) Continuous Optimizing of Henan's Financial Industry Development Environment

In recent years, Henan accelerated the construction of high growth services province, vigorously supported the development of the financial industry, enriched quantity, scale and kinds of financial institutions in Henan, enlarged the Henan Financial institutions, and constantly optimized the financial environment in Henan. Financial strength continued to grow. In 2016, the added value of Henan's financial industry was 225.367 billion yuan, accounting for 5.6% of the province's GDP, while in 2010, the proportion was only 3.2%. The deposit and loan balance of Henan Financial institutions reached 5497.97 billion yuan, and 3713.96 billion yuan respectively, and the deposit and loan ratio reached 67.6%, the size and ratio of deposit and loan have significantly improved compared to the past, the scale and efficiency of Henan's financial industry improved significantly, and it has become a new pillar industry in Henan province. Henan Financial institutions developed rapidly. Zhongyuan Bank, Zhongyuan Agricultural Insurance Co.,Ltd., BOL Financial Leasing Co.,Ltd. and Zhongyuan Asset Management Co.,Ltd. were established. Zhongyuan Bank, Zhengzhou Bank and Central China Securities have been listed, and the size, type and management level of the Henan Financial institutions have reached a new level. Nongovernmental financial institutions developed rapidly. In 2016, Henan had 328 financing guarantee institutions, with the registered capital of 44.073 billion yuan, to provide 82.193 billion yuan of new-added security for 22.8 thousand small and medium-sized enterprises and "agriculture, rural areas and farmers" in the whole year. After several years of rapid development, the financial industry in Henan has abundant strength, and the market size, market participants and market competitiveness have greatly improved, which lay a good foundation for the further development of reform and innovation.

(5) Historical Opportunities Brought about by the New Economic Model

At present, the new economic model is developing rapidly. The integration of the financial industry with network technology and information technology has become not only a hot spot of development, but also a strong impact on the development of the financial industry. With the rapid development of the Internet economy, the integration of the retail industry with the Internet, logistics, supply chain and finance has led to rapid changes in the development of these industries. E-commerce enterprises have gradually developed the management channels in the financial field, at the same time, with the advantages of information technology and data, online transactions, mobile payment, Internet banking and other services began to develop. The transition of traditional financial institutions accelerated rapidly, and the combination of online and offline was implemented, and Internet companies continued to integrate. Crowd-funding, Internet transactions, mobile payments and other new financial transaction model developed rapidly, sharing economy rose rapidly, and the business model innovation in the new economy promoted rapid change in the financial industry. Innovation and change bring opportunities. For Henan's financial industry, the acceleration of financial innovation is the opportunity for Henan's financial development to catch-up and overtake around the curve. Along with the landing of National Data Comprehensive Experimentation Area, China (Zhengzhou) Cross-border E-commerce Comprehensive Experimentation Area, Lankao Inclusive Financial Reform Pilot Area in Henan, Henan's financial industry has the environment and opportunities for innovative development, and is expected to achieve leapfrog development in innovation.

2. Adverse Factors

(1) Increasing Uncertainty of International Economic and Financial Market

At present, the foundation of the world economic recovery is still fragile. The international economic and financial situation is still complex and severe, and there are many outstanding contradictions and problems. With the incidents of the British voting to leave the European Union and the American president-elect Donald Trump taking office as symbols, global protectionism, anti-globalization and populism are rising, and the complexity, instability and uncertainty of the international economy will be further highlighted. The new U.S. government trade policy exists uncertainty, and the market is generally expected that the new government will take "tax and infrastructure" expansionary fiscal policy, which helps to promote economic growth in the United States and boost global demand, but the financial and debt burden may exacerbate problems. Expansionary fiscal policy may push up inflation, leading to faster pace of the Fed to raise interest rates than expected, and for some emerging market economies with large scale of foreign debts, high economic vulnerability and limited policy space, the pressure of currency devaluation and capital outflow may increase. Some European countries have a lower level of profitability in the banking sector and a high level of non-performing loans, which may have a negative impact on investment. The geopolitical conflicts broke out and the risk factors accelerated. The European refugee crisis and the rise of terrorism may lead to a multi-point outbreak of geopolitical conflicts, and the risk factors and uncertainties are accelerating. The complicated external situation may bring "black swan" to the financial market at any time, which adds uncertainty to the financial development of China and Henan province.

(2) Potential Risks Brought out by the Downward Pressure on the Domestic Economy

From the domestic point of view, the basis of economic and financial stability is still not solid, the downward pressure on the economy is still large, the regional and industry trends continue to differentiate, and the challenges and risks cannot be underestimated. The problem of high non-performing assets in China's banking sector has not been resolved, the capital adequacy ratio has declined, and the profit growth has slowed down. Non-financial enterprises leverage rate rises, some enterprises rely on the mode of "borrowing new to pay for the old", and even "borrowing new to pay for the interest" to maintain business, and the turnover efficiency of new-added financing is low. Some zombie enterprises with no-competitive products, unsustainable finance, debts exceeding assets take up credit resources, and reduce the efficiency of the use of funds. In some areas, the situation of malicious escaping and abandoning debts occurs. Some banking financial institutions still lack in corporate governance and internal control, and problems such as risk management and compliance management still exist. Major cases have occurred from time to time and the crime field have spread from the traditional deposit and loan business to interbank business, off-balance sheet activities and other fields. The risk of real estate market increases, new-added lending resources are too concentrated on the real estate field, and there are bubbles in some areas. Although the off balance sheet business of commercial banks is developing rapidly, business management is still relatively weak, and internal and external risks may have cross infections. Internet banking and illegal fund-raising risks would remain exposed. Under such circumstances, Henan's financial industry should maintain rapid development and hold the bottom line to resist the regional financial risks, and the responsibilities and pressures will be heavy.

(3) The Weak Foundation of Henan's Financial Development

Although the financial industry of Henan has experienced rapid development, the scale and level of the Henan Financial institutions have improved rapidly, yet the foundation is still relatively weak. First, the Henan Financial institutions are still in the initial stage of development, and the competitiveness is not strong in the country. Zhongyuan Bank has just set up in 2015, Central China Securities, Zhongyuan Trust, Bridge Trust and other enterprises belong to the middle level of the industry across the country. Enterprises such as Zhongyuan Agricultural Insurance Co., Ltd., Zhongyuan Asset Management Co., Ltd., BOL Financial Leasing Co., Ltd. are in the early stage of the formation and development, and the future task of the financial development of Henan Financial institutions is relatively heavy. Second, the development environment of the financial industry is still not excellent. The construction of social credit system is not perfect. The financial demands of the residents are strong while the financial knowledge is relatively weak. The risk of private financial institutions still cannot be ignored. The fact that the regional financial development environment is not good will have certain constraints for the financial development of Henan. Third, the rural financial institutions are few and the financial system is weak. As a big food province, a big agricultural province, Henan has a large population in rural areas, and the task of agricultural development is heavy. Rural financial institutions are still few and the financial system is underdeveloped. The tasks of the authentic right and land transaction on property rights and management rights of rural, and forest land are heavy, and the financing channels are relatively narrow, becoming one of the difficult problems of Henan financial development.

3. The Outlook for Henan's Financial Trend

At present, Henan is in a period of rapid urbanization and a new type of industrialization. The economic and social development is in a steady and healthy process, and the pace of economic restructuring and industrial transformation and upgrading has been accelerating. At the same time, China's financial market is experiencing a rapid development and change, the relationship between financial institutions is increasingly deepening, the integration of finance and Internet information technology is deepening, the pace of innovation of the financial products and services continues to accelerate, the internationalization of the RMB continues to promote, and the stock market will soon launch a registration system. With the rapid development of Henan's financial industry for many years, the scale and efficiency of the financial industry have improved rapidly, and the strength of Henan Financial institutions has been continuously enhanced. In the future, the financial industry in Henan will firmly establish the development concept of innovation, coordination, being green, opening-up and sharing, center on the principal work of developing economy in Henan, serve the construction of "three areas and one group", play well "four cards", promote the deepening of the reform of the financial market and financial institutions in Henan, move forward the innovation of financial products and services, constantly improve the financial system, and hold the bottom line to resist the regional financial risks, so as to provide financing guarantee for the economic and social development.

Ⅲ Suggestions on the Healthy Development of Henan's Financial Industry

To promote the rapid and healthy development of financial industry in Henan, we must continue to deepen financial reform, promote financial innovation, improve the financial system, prevent financial risks, and play a supporting role in the development of the real economy, in order to lay a solid foundation for the overall well-off and the colourful Central Plains.

1. Increase Financial Support for Key Areas and Strengthen Financial Security

First, we should increase credit input to key engineering and projects. Around the planning of major strategy and industrial development in Henan, we should increase the financial support for the key projects such as advanced manufacturing, strategic emerging industries, modern service industry, circular economy, energy saving and environment protecting areas, etc., guiding to promote the transformation and adjustment of key areas and industries. Second, we should focus on the construction of "three areas and one group" and increase financial support. Around accelerating the construction of Zheng-Luo-Xin National Innovation Demonstration Area, we should focus on setting up branches and networks with science and technology, expand the scale of intangible assets pledged loans such as intellectual property hypothecated loan, and try to carry out the pilot of linkage between investment and loan; around China (Henan) Free Trade Test Area, we should actively carry out the innovative cross-border RMB business and foreign currency offshore business pilot, to carry out the cross-border two-way use of investment and financing of insurance funds; and around the construction of Zhengzhou Airport Economic Zone, we should make up the supporting plan of specialized credit, set up other plans such as the plans of infrastructure investment of insurance funds, real estate investment plans and projects, asset investment plans, etc.; in addition, around the construction of Central Henan Urban Agglomeration, we should make efforts to increase the support for major projects such as public transport, city parking lot, city underground pipe gallery construction, sewage and garbage disposal, affordable housing construction, shantytowns transformation, etc. Third, we should actively connect "The Belt and Road" construction. "The Belt and Road" initiative is not only oriented along the countries and regions, but also for the domestic related areas and cities. As the "The Belt and Road" initiative continues, the economic development pattern of China and other related nations and regions will have significant and profound changes, emerging a large number of new financial services needs in the infrastructure, the docking of production and capacity, foreign trade, cross-border finance and other aspects, etc. We should take the initiative to seize the opportunity for development, and actively organize the special docking of provincial financial institutions and foreign financial institutions, strengthen the coordination in and out of the system, and vigorously expand the financing mode such as trade financing, overseas loan under domestic guarantee, overseas mergers and acquisitions, overseas bonds, etc..

2. Accelerate Multi-level Capital Market and Expand Direct Financing Scale

The direct financing of enterprises through the capital market is an important form of financing in the modern market economy. We should further tap the financing potential and expand the scale of direct financing. First, we should actively promote the listing and trade of enterprises. We should intensify the cultivation of the reserved listed companies, classify and organize the training on how to be listed in domestic and foreign market, make regular supervision and guidance, strengthen dynamic management of the reserved enterprise library, especially from the strategic emerging industries and major industry transformation, screen and support excellent enterprises with strength and good growth for listing and financing, establish the Easy Access for enterprises to be listed, comprehensively utilize administrative means such as finance, taxation, land, industry and commerce, etc., to accelerate the cultivation of listed enterprises. Second, we should strive to improve the quality of listed companies. Listing of a company is the first step of the effective use of capital market, and it needs a further effective management of the market capitalization, and to continuously inject good assets to the listed companies, to enhance the value and liquidity of the enterprise assets, to enhance the financing capacity of enterprises, realizing the maximization of enterprise value. We should encourage the refinancing of listed companies, through the ways of public offering, private offering, allotment and equity pledge financing, etc., to improve the efficiency and level of using the capital market allocation of resources. Third, we should attach great importance to bond financing and expand the financing scale of the bond market. We should increase the efforts of financing publicity and promotion of the bond market, guide enterprise to make flexible choices of multi-bond-financing tools for financing such as corporate bonds, company bonds, convertible bonds, perpetual bonds, medium-term notes, and short-term financing bonds, etc., through the inter-bank market, exchange market, regional equity transaction market and overseas market, to reduce the cost of financing. Fourth, we must improve government financing capacity. We should give full play to the role of all kinds of financing platform, support the market transformation of all levels of governmental investment and finance companies, issue special bonds such as city underground pipe gallery building, city parking lot construction, the incubation of mass entrepreneurship and innovation, green bonds, pension industry, and strategic emerging industries, etc. Fifth, we must accelerate the construction of various elements market. We will accelerate the development of the market for capital, land, human resources, property rights transactions, technology transactions and intermediary services, etc. and build a high-level factor market system. We must accelerate the construction of Central China Equity Exchange, conduct equity pledge financing, and actively apply for the new three board recommended pilot qualifications; we will accelerate the construction of Zhongyuan Financial Asset Trading Center, study and formulate"*Measures of Henan Province on the Supervision and Administration of the Equity Trading Places*", and make good supervision of the equity trading places.

3. Strengthen Financial Innovation in Weak Parts and Focus on Inclusive Finance Development

We should strengthen the innovation of the financial organization, financial products and service mode, and increase efforts to protect financial services focusing on mass entrepreneurship and innovation, small and micro businesses, issues of agriculture, rural areas and farmers, poverty alleviation and other weak links. First, we should strengthen credit support for small and micro enterprises. We should strengthen policy guidance, encourage financial institutions to increase efforts to support small and micro businesses, organize the special inspection on difficult financing and expensive financing for the banks related to small and micro businesses and private enterprises in Henan, carry out special action plans of financial support for small and micro businesses, vigorously promote the "finance-tax link" business model, expand the size of the hypothecated loan of intellectual property rights and accounts receivable, etc., to meet tailored needs of the development of financial products and services for small and micro businesses. Second, we must continue to promote rural financial innovation. In Henan province, we should actively promote security innovation, circular credit and other eight kinds of effective innovation models, and actively and steadily carry out the collateral loan pilot of rural land management rights and housing property rights of farmers; and in view of the new agricultural operators such as big family, family farms and farmers' professional cooperatives, we should carry out financial cultivation in an all-round way. Third, we should increase support for tackling poverty. We should strictly implement policies related to the state's small interest poverty alleviation loans and ensure that the individual poor production and operation household should be loaned; and also, we should actively promote the companies in poverty-stricken areas to raise funds through listing and bonds, support the listed company to initiate the establishment of poverty alleviation industry fund, and for those enterprises with strong power on poverty alleviation and development, we can launch innovative unsecured and uncovered credit loans. Fourth, we should support the development of small financial institutions. We will relax market access, decentralize approval authority, and support the development of small financial institutions such as village banks, credit cooperatives, micro credit, consumer finance, financial leasing, etc. And also, we should further increase and improve financial supply, improve the quality of financial services and the efficiency of supply, with its advantages of "grassroots finance", to better meet the market demand for funds for the market entity such as small and micro businesses, individual operators, farmers, etc.. Fifth, we should strengthen financial support for vulnerable groups. Efforts will be made to increase support for migrant workers' entrepreneurship and employment and youth entrepreneurship loans, and to strengthen barrier-free financial services for the disabled and the elderly. We should also expand the coverage of rural and village financial services, improve the availability of financial services, and continue to promote the construction of Lankao Inclusive Financial Reform Pilot Area.

4. Continue to Deepen Financial Reform and Strengthen Henan Financial Institutions Steadily

First, efforts should be made to improve the organizational system of the Henan Financial institutions. We should speed up the establishment of private banks and legal person life insurance companies around the regional characteristics of "Henan Financial institutions". And also, we should promote large enterprise groups to organize financial companies, promote local financial institutions to set up financial leasing companies, and guide the financial institutions to speed up the extension of branches into provincial cities and economically developed counties; We should make a comprehensive review of all kinds of financial licenses, study the establishment of property insurance companies, health insurance companies, mutual insurance companies, auto finance companies and other multi category and innovative financial subjects, so as to continuously expand the "Henan Financial institutions" team, enrich financial industry and financial industry chain, and ensure the brand continues to grow. Second, we must continue to deepen reform. We should speed up the work of reforming rural credit cooperatives to agricultural enterprises, speed up the reform of county level rural credit cooperatives and the reform of the rural credit cooperatives in cities and towns, and strive to complete the task of setting up rural commercial banks by the end of 2017; and we should promote Zhongyuan Asset Management Co., Ltd. to promote business around the bill factoring trading, supply chain finance, factoring asset securitization and other aspects, to form new profit growth point; and also, we should support Zhongyuan Trust, Bridge Trust to carry out asset management business and asset securitization in industry fund; accelerate the launch of urea and other new varieties of futures in Zhengzhou Commodity Exchange, and pilot sugar options as soon as possible. Third, we should promote the development of financial service products. We will actively introduce and promote financial innovative products at home and abroad, and encourage financial institutions to accelerate the innovation of aviation finance, logistics and supply chain finance, trade financing and leasing, green finance, inclusive finance and other products, and we will strengthen strategic cooperation between bank and enterprise, securities and banks, bank-insurance, trust companies and banks, and other multi-financial institutions, and jointly develop integrated financial products. Fourth, we should continue to implement the project of introducing investment into Henan. We will further strengthen the construction of Zhengdong New District Financial Agglomeration Core Functional Area, and accelerate the construction of financial infrastructure, especially to improve the financial background services, data services, and product research and development centers. We will strengthen the carrying capacity, agglomeration, innovation, radiation function of Zhengdong New District Financial Agglomeration Core Functional Area, to provide driving force of the financial industry agglomeration for the emergence of the "Henan Financial institutions". Besides, we will support qualified local financial institutions to establish regional headquarters, village bank headquarters, and product R&D center, the background service center and other institutions in Zhengdong New District Financial Agglomeration Core Functional Area.

5. Attach Importance to Normative Supervision and Enhance the Overall Strength of the Security Industry

First, we must improve the guarantee industry system and standardize business activities. We should pay attention to make the most of governmental financing guarantee institutions, focus on the provincial, municipal and county financial investment guarantee institutions, integrate security resources, focus on policy support, to make them bigger and stronger, and become the main force to serve the small and micro enterprises and "agriculture, rural areas and farmers" in Henan, playing a leading role in the demonstration, and supporting the development of the whole industry. We should support the participation of social funds in the guarantee system so as to expand the number and scale of guarantee institutions and promote the coordinated development of policy guarantee institutions and private guarantee institutions. We should guide guarantee institutions to strengthen internal management, standardize business practices, and improve risk control capabilities and security capabilities. Second, we should improve the risk sharing and compensation mechanism of guarantee institutions. Because the financing guarantee is a high-risk intermediary behavior, we must spread risks through re-guarantee, co-guarantee, proportional guarantee and other ways, to enhance the ability of guarantee institutions to resist risks. We should further improve the re-guarantee mechanism, in accordance with the principle of the government leading, professional management and market operation, to accelerate the formation of the Central Plains re-guarantee corporation, and to give full play to its "stabilizer" role of transferring policy guidance and guiding the industry standard management, and defusing the industry risk. We will implement the financial policy of the central government to support the establishment of the agricultural credit guarantee system, and take the provincial agricultural credit guarantee corporation as the leading factor to speed up the full coverage of the agricultural credit operations in the 30 major agricultural counties of the province. We should establish a risk sharing mechanism for government, bank and guarantee corporation, study the establishment of the governmental financing guarantee fund, and promote the establishment of the joint participation, mutual benefit and risk sharing mechanism and a sustainable mode of cooperation for government, bank and guarantee corporation; and we should increase the risk compensation investment for financial guarantee institutions, taking the provincial re-guarantee institutions as a platform and re-guarantee business as a link, to promote the cooperation between financing guarantee institutions and banking financial institutions. Third, we must establish a sound regulatory system. In accordance with the principle of prudent supervision, we should establish and improve a series of industry regulatory systems, such as overall planning of the industry, establishment, alteration and withdrawal of institutions, standardization of the operation of the company, strengthening of routine supervision, and effective prevention and control of risks, etc.; and we must strengthen the credit management of the financing guarantee institutions, establish business credit information publicity system, accelerate the construction of credit information publicity system of financing guarantee institutions, strengthen the credit supervision and social supervision, to promote the healthy and rapid development of the industry.

6. Strengthen Risk Prevention and Prevent Systemic Financial Risk

First, we should strengthen the daily monitoring and warning of financial risks. The financial institutions should strengthen the monitoring and early warning of the suspicious fund flow, make macro prudential assessments, strengthen risk study and judgments, and give timely warning tips; and we should strengthen the prudent management of financial institutions, and attach great importance to and do well in the financial risk prevention of "de-capacity, de-stocking, deleveraging", to maximize the ability to slow down the contradiction between de-production capacity and financial bond protection. Second, we must do a good job in preventing, combating and disposing of illegal fund-raising. We must continue to further promote the prevention of illegal fund-raising campaign, make full use of television, radio, newspapers, internet, public transport facilities and other carriers to vigorously promote the risks and hazards of illegal fund-raising, organize the investigation and clean-up activities of the advertisement, news and information that are alleged illegal fund-raising, enhancing the publicity and effectiveness of the propaganda; and we must make overall arrangements of special rectification work for unstable issues of illegal fund raising, increase the intensity of cold case disposal, accelerate the new case handling process, and promote illegal fund-raising cases to continue to decline, to ensure the overall stability. Third, we must strengthen the clean-up and remediation for the Internet financial risks. We must make a clean-up remediation for the Internet financial institutions, form a list of Internet financial institutions, and implement classified disposals in accordance with their illegal actions. For the institutions holding financial business license, if they are compliance management, but the risk is greater, we must do promptly rectification and strengthen risk control; and for illegal operations, business should be suspended according to the law, and be asked for a rectification within a prescribed time limit; if the business is extremely non-standard and intends to evade supervision, it shall resolutely be banned in accordance with the law; and for the serious illegal act of suspected malicious fraud, we should crack them down in accordance with the law. Fourth, we must do a good job of petition stability. We must do a good job of policy interpretation, counselling and persuasion to go home for petitioners, coordinate disposal of mass incidents and emergencies caused by illegal fund raising. We must investigate unstable factors in depth, grasp the dynamic information, open channels of dialogue, respond to the demands of the masses timely, guide to solve problems through legal channels, and do a good job in conflict disposal, to ensure stable financial order and social stability.

References

[1] Analysis Group on Financial Stability of People's Bank of China. *Report on Financial Stability of China (2017)* [M]. China Financial Publishing House, July,2017.

[2] Institute of International Finance of Bank of China. *Report on Global Economic and Financial Outlook*[R]. December,2016.

[3] Institute of International Finance Research of Bank of China. *Report on Economic and*

Financial Outlook of China [R]. December,2016.

[4] Statistics Bureau of Henan Province. *Henan Statistical Yearbook (2016)* [M]. Henan Statistics Bureau website, http://www.ha.stats.gov.cn/.

[5] Statistics Bureau of Henan Province. *Statistical Bulletin on National Economic and Social Development of Henan Province in 2016*[R]. Henan Statistics Bureau website, http://www.ha.stats.gov.cn/.

[6] Henan Daily. To Tackle Difficulty in the Process of Reform and to Sail Forward in front of Challenges[N]. *Henan Daily*, June 27, 2017.

[7] Zhou Xiaochuan. Hot and Difficulty Issues on the Reform of "13th Five-Year" Financial System [J]. *Chinese Economic and Trade Guide Magazine*, Tenth of 2016.

[8] Zhang Zhancang. The Scientific Connotation and Strategic Measures on Building a Powerful Economic Province in Henan [J]. *Social Science in Henan Province,* July, 2017.

[9] Zhang Zhancang. Painting the Grand Blueprint that Let the Central Plains be More Brilliant[N]. *Henan Daily*, November 11, 2016.

[10] Zhang Zhancang. The International Environment and the Strategic Expectation of China's "13th Five-Year" Planning and Development[J]. *Journal of Zhongzhou*, November, 2015.

[11] Wang Fang. Research on the Innovation and Development of Science and Technology Finance under the New Economic Background [J]. *Journal of Hubei University of Economics,* Sixth of 2016.

[12] Wang Fang. Performance Evaluation and Countermeasure Suggestion on the Conjunction of Science and Technology and Finance in Henan Province [J]. *Financial Theory and Practice*, Twelfth of 2016.

[13] Pan Weihong. Comparative Analysis on the Level of Financial Development in Henan [J]. *Contemporary Economy*, Second of 2016.

[14] Shi Tao. Regional Practice and Enlightenment on Tackling the Entrepreneurial Financing Difficulties of Small and Micro Technology Enterprises in Henan [J]. *The Second Half of June*, 2017.

[15] Zhao Ran. Deepening Financial Reform and Serving the Real Economy[N]. *Henan Daily*, August 2, 2017.

B.5
Report on the Innovation-driven Development of Science and Technology of Henan Province

Yuan Jinxing[*]

Abstract: The past five years has witnessed both challenges and great achievements. Since the 18th CPC National Congress in 2012, Henan has been conscientiously implementing the major decisions made by the central government of pursuing the innovation-driven development strategy; thus, the development of science and technology in Henan province has been significantly promoted. The grand blueprint of economic and social transformation driven by innovation is coming into reality on the Central Plains, making innovation the primary driving force of the strategy "building a moderately prosperous society in all respects and a more outstanding Henan province". In the new developmental period, the conditions in Henan, in China and in the world are all undergoing profound changes, hence there are new situations, opportunities, demands and challenges for the innovation-driven development of science and technology in Henan. In the future, Henan should continue to put innovation at the core of the overall development, to give full play to the key leading role of scientific and technological innovation, as well as to create a new model of scientific and technological innovation in the central

---

*

and western regions of China, providing more powerful support for building an economically stronger province and promoting the Central Plains to give more outstanding performance in the realization of the Chinese Dream of national rejuvenation.

Keywords: Scientific and Technological Innovation; Innovation-driven Strategy; A New Model of Scientific and Technological Innovation in the Central and Western Regions of China; Henan Province

The advancement in science and technology brings prosperity and strength for a nation. To make China prosperous and strong and achieve the national rejuvenation, science and technology need to be vigorously developed. The 18th CPC National Congress has put forward the strategy of innovation-driven development strategy to boost innovation in science and technology, which must occupy a central place in China's development and serve as the support for improving social productivity and comprehensive national strength. Over the past five years, under the strong leadership of the Central Committee of the Communist Party of China (CPC) with Comrade Xi Jinping at its core, and the sound leadership of the CPC Henan Provincial Committee and provincial government, the province has been thoroughly implementing the innovation-driven development strategy by planning a strategic, global and long-term system for scientific and technological innovation, and by launching a series of groundbreaking and long-rang strategies, thus creating a new situation for the development of science and technology. The future situations at home and abroad will still be complicated, and Henan will confront many difficulties as well as challenges in its development. The important thesis that "Innovation is the primary driving force for development" put forward by the central government must be adhered to. More than 100 million people living on the Central Plains are striving to make more accomplishments in the prospects of a beautiful life, by creating a new model of scientific and technological innovation in the central and western regions of China, comprehensively enhancing the innovation capacity with scientific and technological innovation as the primary driving force and accelerating the revitalization of Henan as a stronger and more prosperous province, so as to make the Central Plains more outstanding in realizing the Chinese Dream of national rejuvenation.

I The Significant Progress in the Innovation-driven Development of Science and Technology in Henan since the 18th CPC National Congress

Since the 18th CPC National Congress in 2012, the Central Committee of the Communist Party of China with Comrade Xi Jinping at its core has been putting great emphasis on scientific and technological innovation and made the decision to fully implement the strategy of innovation-driven development, which has pointed out the direction and provided the guideline for scientific and technological innovation in Henan. General Secretary Xi Jinping has explicitly required Henan to make extensive use of four strategies ("Four Cards") including promoting innovation-driven development mainly by establishing an innovation system during his investigation in 2014. By ensuring the core position of scientific and technological innovation in the economic and social development, Henan has fully implemented the strategic plan outlined by the central government. The province continues to accelerate the implementation of innovation-driven development strategy, resulting in significantly enhanced innovation ability, breakthroughs in certain areas and key technologies in some pillar industries, as well as a series of scientific and technological progress with great influence nationwide. The capacity of scientific and technological innovation, which serves as a driving force for the economic and social development, has been further enhanced, therefore the fastest improvement has been made in Henan in this period. More fruitful achievements than ever have been made in innovation, making this the greatest contribution to the economic and social development. Important strides have been made in creating a new model of scientific and technological innovation in the central and western regions of China.

1. The Remarkable Improvement in Regional Capacity for Innovation

Henan has consistently viewed the increasing capacity for innovation as the core objective to implement the innovation-driven development strategy. Various measures have been taken to gradually establish a market-oriented and government-guided system of scientific and technological innovation with enterprises as the mainstay. The system, with Henan characteristics suitable for the provincial situation, is based on the cooperation of the government, enterprises, institutions of higher learning, scientific research institutes, financial institutions and intermediary agencies of science and technology. Hence, the regional capacity for innovation has been consistently improved.

Over the past five years, the province has put a total of 258 major scientific and technological projects into practice, with a total investment of 30.54 billion yuan (US$ 4.64 billion) and new sales income of 73.5 billion yuan (US$ 11.16 billion). The development of strategic emerging industries such as high-end equipment manufacturing, electronic information, new energy, materials, energy vehicles, biological medicine as well as energy conservation and environmental protection have been promoted.The transformation and upgrading of equipment manufacturing, chemical industry, agriculture and other traditional industries have been accelerated. A number of new- and high-tech industries with technological and market advantages have been formed. In the innovation of agricultural science and technology, the plan of supporting the core area of crop production with science and technology has been put into practice and the seed-breeding of new varieties of major crops has been further improved. The number of new varieties (types) has reached more than 400, achieving an all-round upgrade for wheat, corn and other leading food crops, thereby making a significant contribution to the annual increase of crop production in the province. To enhance people's livelihood from scientific and technological aspect, projects have been launched to provide scientific and technological support for the poor areas and for improving people's living standard, to conserve energy and reduce emissions, and to bring the air pollution under control.There has also been the remote medical technology, known as one of the "Top Ten Projects for People's Well-Being in Henan". New breakthroughs have been made in technological innovation in various areas such as biological vaccines, new drugs, and recycling of solid waste and construction waste. Henan has established 13 national sustainable development experimental areas and 17 provincial ones. The living standard has been continuously improved as a result of the progress made in science and technology.

Henan's investment in research and development has reached 49 billion yuan (US $ 7.44 billion) in 2016, 1.6 times greater than that in 2012. In the past five years, Pingdingshan and Jiaozuo High-tech Zones were officially approved as the national high-tech zones, making the total of the national zones reach seven

in the province, and the number rank first in central and western China. At the same time, according to the latest National High-tech Zone Evaluation (trial) released by the Ministry of Science and Technology, the comprehensive ranking of all the national high-tech zones in Henan has been enhanced. Zhengzhou and Luoyang rank 16th and 20th respectively among over 100 high-tech zones in China; Henan has moved up by 5 notches in the national list of the index of regional comprehensive progress in science and technology. At the same time, the number of high-tech enterprises in Henan has reached 1,664, 2.2 times as many as the number in 2012, while the number of small and medium high-tech enterprises has exceeded 15,000.

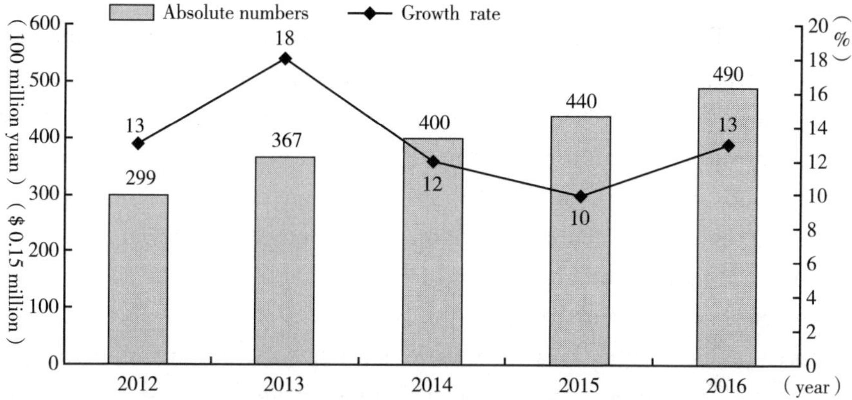

Figure 1 Investment in R&D and its growth rate in Henan from 2012 to 2016

2. The Model Effect of Zheng-Luo-Xin National Innovation Demonstration Area

The establishment of national innovation demonstration zones is a strategic move to pursue the concept of innovation-driven development, to implement the strategy of innovation-driven development, as well as to drive the construction of a scientifically and technologically powerful nation. The whole province has coordinated its efforts to build Zheng-Luo-Xin National Innovation Demonstration Area, by setting up a steering group with the governor of Henan province as the group leader and establishing a working mechanism for coordination among departments and cooperation between the provinces and cities. On April 5th 2016, the State Council issued the paper "The Approval of Zheng-Luo-Xin High-tech Zone Constructing National Innovation Demonstration Area". On May 27th 2016, Zheng-Luo-Xin National Innovation Demonstration Area was officially founded. The upgrading of three former national high-tech zones (Zhengzhou, Luoyang and Xinxiang) to become national innovation demonstration zones has become a national strategy, adding more power to the innovation-driven development in Henan. The CPC Henan Provincial Committee and Henan provincial government has issued "Implementation Plan for the Construction of Zheng-Luo-Xin National Innovation Demonstration Area"along with the "Development Plan for Zheng-Luo-Xin National Innovation Demonstration Area (2016-2025)", and implemented the "1+N" policy system which is mainly based on "Opinions on Accelerating the Construction of Zheng-Luo-Xin National Innovation Demonstration Area". More than 30 groundbreaking, proactive and practical policies have been proposed, from the perspectives of stimulating the vitality of the innovators, promoting open innovation, gathering talents at home and abroad, innovating the management system of science and technology, and optimizing the entrepreneurial environment for innovation. Special funds from the provincial finance and guiding fund for the transformation of scientific and technological achievements made in the Area has been set up, which supports the development of the Area from various aspects. At present, the Area as a model begins to demonstrate its role. The added value of high-tech industries in the cities where the Area is situated accounts for nearly one third of that of the whole province; the value of technical contract transactions accounts for more than 90% of that of the province. There are more than 90 national innovation platforms in the Area, accounting for over 60% of the province's total. The number of high-tech enterprises accounts for 55% of the province's total. The driving force of the Area in the innovation-driven development in the province is proving invaluable.

3. The Marked Enhancement in the Enterprises' Function as Major Innovators

Enterprises are the main body of market competition, as well as the engine and the driving force of innovation. Over the past five years, Henan has been carrying out a series of fruitful work centering on strengthening various enterprises' dominant role in innovation. The internal driving force of scientific and technological innovation for enterprises has been continuously strengthened, which has gradually turned the enterprises into the main participants of research and development investment, technological innovation, and innovation achievement application. Enterprises have been playing an increasingly significant role in implementing the strategy of innovation-driven development in Henan.

Over the past five years, Henan has been improving the long-term incentive mechanism of research and development investment of enterprises. The document "Management of Special Fund for Market Entities in Government-guided Technological Innovation" has been formulated and implemented, highlighting the market orientation and enterprise entities. Research and development investment by enterprises has accounted for more than 85% of that of the whole venture. Innovative enterprises have been developed with significant effort. There are 30 newly-developed leading innovative enterprises, 1,664 high-tech enterprises, 294 model enterprises in technological innovation including energy conservation and emission reduction, and over 15,000 small and medium high-tech enterprises. A development system of innovative enterprise clusters is gradually forming, led by the leading enterprises in innovation, followed up by high-tech enterprises, and supported by small and medium high-tech enterprises.

Over the past five years, efforts have been consistently intensified to build research and development platforms in enterprises which include large and medium enterprises with provincial-level research and development. 87.2% of provincial-level and above research and development platforms in the province have been set up in enterprises. Enterprises have been encouraged to become the mainstay of technological research and development, and achievement transformation. Through projects such as the implementation of major science and technology projects, high-tech industrialization, a number of leading innovative enterprises have emerged, for example, Citic Heavy Industries, China Railway Engineering Equipment Group Co., Ltd. (CREG), Xuji Group Corporation, Zhengzhou Yutong Group Co., Ltd.. Four national strategic alliances and 88 provincial ones of industrial technology innovation led by the enterprises in Henan have been established, with 73.5% of the research and development personnel in the province coming from the various enterprises.

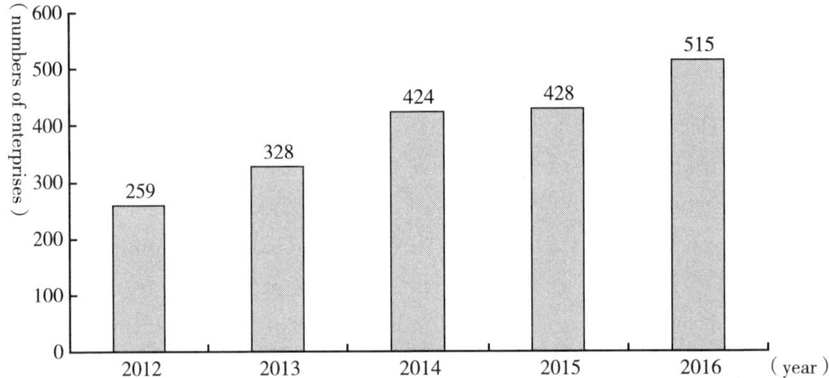

Figure 2 Numbers of provincial innovative (pilot) enterprises in Henan from 2012 to 2016

4. The Emergence of Many Achievements in Scientific and Technological Innovation

As Henan's innovation capacity is being remarkably enhanced, a significant number of innovation achievements have been achieved, promoting some advantageous fields in the province to reach the advanced level at home and resulting in breakthroughs in certain areas, a series of scientific and technological progress with appreciable influence nationwide and key technology in some pillar industries. The capacity for scientific and technological innovation as a driver for the economic and social development has been further enhanced. The overall development in science and technology in Henan has reached the advanced level in central and western regions in China.

Over the past five years, a total of 106 national science and technology awards have been received by Henan, including State Science and Technology Advancement Award (4 special class and 7 first class), filling the gap in the award list with Natural Science Awards, Enterprise Technology Innovation Project Award, Innovation Team Award and other awards. There have been 94,669 patent applications in 2016 in Henan, and the authorized amount has reached 49,145, 2.2 times and 1.8 times of those in 2012 respectively. The average number of in-force patents per 10,000 people reached 2.4 in 2016, 2.7 times as many as that in 2012. In 2016, the registered volume of technical contracts in the province reached nearly 6 billion yuan (US$ 911.4 million), with a year-on-year growth of 30%. The growth rate has exceeded the national average for the first time in the past 10 years. In the same year, Henan ranked fifth among all the provinces, municipalities and autonomous regions in the number of awarded projects in State Science and Technology Award. Breakthroughs have been achieved in a number of major technologies, and research and development of products such as intelligent robots, high-end heavy mining equipment, etc. There are also a series of scientific and technological achievements with significant influence nationwide, such as the super-sized cross-section rectangular shield machine, the high-pressure VSC-HVDC equipment with high capacity, the new wheat variety "Aikang 58", the split influenza virus A subtype H1N1 vaccine, as well as a new-round replacement of major varieties of food crops and so on. The large amount of achievements in innovation has effectively promoted the transformation and upgrading of related industries.

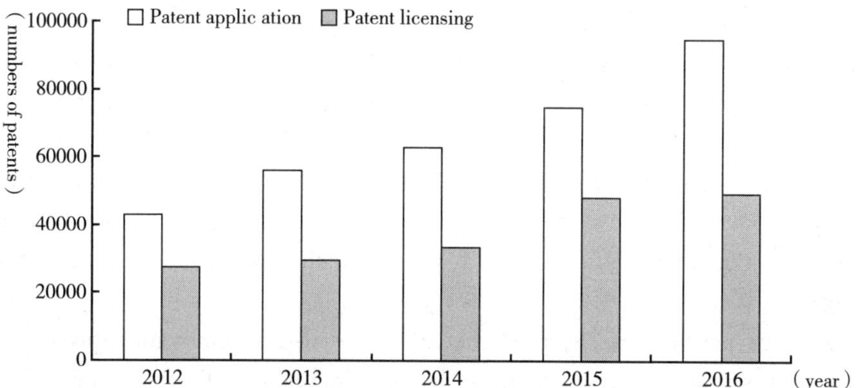

Figure 3 Numbers of patent applications and patent licensing in Henan from 2012 to 2016

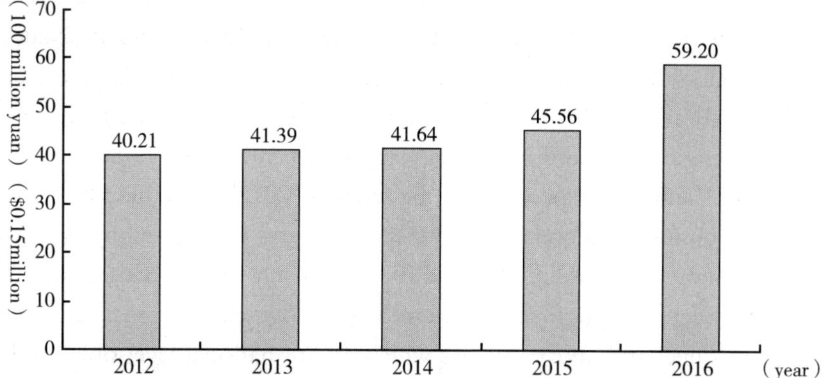

Figure 4 Volume of technological contract transactions in Henan from 2012 to 2016

5. The Significant Acceleration in the Construction of Innovation Platforms

Innovation platforms is an important way to gather innovative elements, integrate resources and effectively enhance the capacity for innovation. Henan has insisted on viewing building platforms for scientific and technological innovation as the basis of implementing the innovation-driven development strategy. Superior resources in the whole province have been integrated for supporting and guiding enterprises to enhance innovation. Investments have been increased to create a favorable policy environment for constructing innovation platforms in the province. Remarkable results have been achieved and a positive role has been played in driving scientific and technological innovation in the province.

Over the past five years, a number of national innovation platforms have been settled in Henan, such as some national high-tech zones and national key laboratories. There are 8 newly-settled national key laboratories, making a total of 14. Major efforts have been made to develop high-tech zones, adding 3 more to the province. The document "Opinions of Henan Provincial Government on Promoting the Development of High-tech Zones" has been published to encourage high-tech zones to start a new undertaking, which has further improved the quality and standard of high-tech zone development in the province.

Over the past five years, a number of national-level innovation platforms have been settled in Henan, such as National Technology Transfer Zhengzhou Center, Modern Agricultural Science and Technology Demonstration Area at Central Plains, National Patent Examination Cooperation Center Henan, National Demonstration Province of Rural Research and Development, National Pilot Province of Intellectual Property. Zhengzhou, Luoyang and Nanyang have been approved as national pilot cities of innovation. By 2016, there have been 10 national engineering and technology research centers and 1,080 provincial ones, adding 1 and 510 respectively to the totals of 2012. There have been 1,072 enterprise technology centers at provincial-level and above, among which 84 are national-level ones, adding 237 and 25 respectively to the totals from 2012. There have been 459 engineering laboratories (engineering research centers) at provincial-level and above, among which 42 are national-level ones, adding 268 and 20 respectively to the totals at 2012. The construction of innovation platforms in the province has been significantly accelerated. These have been the main platforms for enterprises to carry out innovative activities, and also the major carriers for enterprises to enhance innovation capacity. The platforms have been well-developed in many industries and thus have possessed a fairly large scale, which has made them the mainstay in promoting the innovation-driven development in the province.

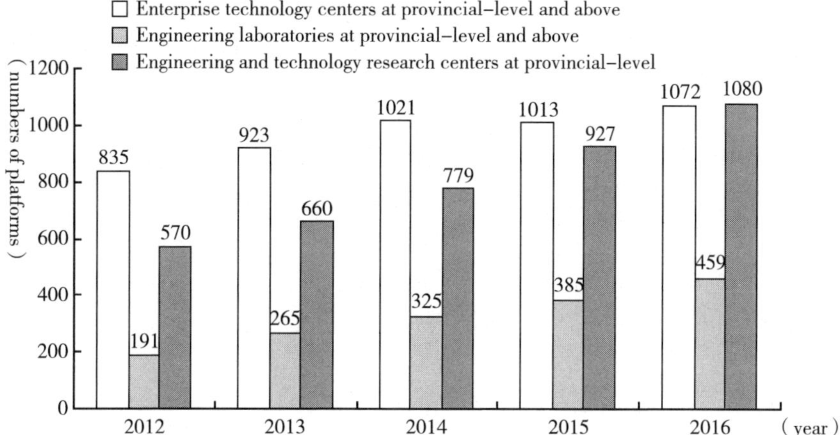

Figure 5 Numbers of major research and development platforms at provincial-level and above in Henan from 2012 to 2016

6. The Rapid Development of the High-tech Industries

High-tech industries are the strategic and guiding industry of the national economy, while high-tech enterprises are the pioneer in leading enterprise innovation and accelerating scientific and technological innovation in the province. Henan, as a province with a large population, diversified industries and abundant labor resource, has adhered consistently to viewing high technology as the primary productive force in promoting economic and social development in the province. Over the past five years, under the principle of "making the overall plan, highlighting the focus, strengthening the investment and forming the industry", Henan has sticked to the guideline of putting equal emphasis on the high-tech industry development and the use of high-tech in the transformation of traditional industries, as well as equal emphasis on the introduction of domestic high technology and R&D innovation. Major efforts have been made to realize commercialization and industrialization of high-tech achievements. A number of industries with technological and market advantages at home have been developed, providing a firmer basis for the economic transformation and development of the province.

Over the past five years, a series of effective measures have been adopted in Henan to promote the development of high-tech industries and enterprises. Innovative products, which have been developed in the province, including intelligent welding robots, and the IE4 ultra efficient three-phase asynchronous motor, have been at the leading level in the world. The key technology of visible light communication technology has supplemented the technological field of indoor high-speed wireless communication in China, which may promote Henan to quickly acquire a dominant position in future industry competition. Innovation capacity in the intelligent energy-saving technology and key components of automobiles and shield equipment of cross-ocean tunnel has been significantly improved, with world-leading industrial competitiveness. The super hard materials account for more than 60%, high temperature functional materials account for more than 50%, UHV transmission equipment account for more than 40% and new energy buses account for more than 30% of the national market respectively. High-tech industries in the province have been developing rapidly. The added value of high-tech industries above the designated scale in the province has exceeded 600 billion yuan (US$ 9.11 billion) in 2016, with a substantial increase from 17.7% in 2012 to 34.9% in terms of the proportion in the added value of all industries of the designated scale. Between 2008 and 2016 there have been 409 newly-developed high-tech enterprises. The number of high-tech enterprises within the period of validity has reached 1,664. The number of high-tech enterprises in Zhengzhou, Luoyang, Xinxiang rank top three among the cities in Henan, accounting for 55.2% of the province's total number, effectively supporting the development of Zheng-Luo-Xin National Innovation Demonstration Area. In 2016, the total income of high-tech enterprises in the province has achieved 547.56 billion yuan (US$ 83.19 billion), driving the growth rate of added value of designated-scale high-tech industries in the province to 14.7%. There have been 16,590 patent applications and 11,285 authorized patents in high-tech enterprises in the province, accounting for 34% and 42.9% of the total of enterprises in the province respectively. High-tech enterprises in Henan have entered a stage of accelerated development.

7. The Impressive Opening-up and Cooperation in Science and Technology

With opening-up and cooperation in science and technology as an important strategy to improve economic and technological competitiveness, Henan has actively adopted various approaches to broaden the channels for opening-up in science and technology to attract and integrate scientific and technological resources at home and abroad. The ability to undertake technology transfer and application of scientific and technological achievements has been constantly enhanced, utilizing external scientific and technological resources to serve the economic development in the province.

Over the past five years, Henan has engaged in active cooperation with ministries, strengthening cooperation with national ministries, the Chinese Academy of Sciences, National Natural Science Foundation of China, and striving for support for scientific and technological innovation in Henan from the relevant ministries. Consultation mechanism has been established between Henan provincial government and the Ministry of Science and Technology as well as State Intellectual Property Office. National Technology Transfer Zhengzhou Center, the Henan CAS Scientific and Technological Achievements Transfer and Transformation Center have been settled in Henan. A number of high-level research and development institutes, such as Institute of Process Engineering and Institute of Automation, Chinese Academy of Sciences, have established branches in Henan. A number of scientific and technological exchange and cooperation platforms have been built through the cooperation, forming stable opening up and cooperation mechanism and carrying out extensive cooperation in terms of technological achievements, talents, scientific and technological condition.

Over the past five years, Henan has continued to strengthen domestic cooperation in science and technology and successfully hosted a series of opening up and cooperation activities in science and technology, such as introduction meeting of Zheng-Luo-Xin National Innovation Demonstration Area in Beijing, Sino-US Cooperation Fair on Scientific and Technological Projects, and "Science and Technology Driving Regional Economic Development". The provincial government has signed strategic cooperation agreements on scientific and technological cooperation with well-known domestic innovation entities such as Tsinghua University, Zhejiang University, China Electronics Technology Group Corporation to introduce or co-build a large number of research and development institutions and technology transfer centers. A comprehensive transformation and transfer service platform for scientific and technological achievements has been formed in Henan, promoting the settlement of a number of high-tech projects with good economic and social benefits in the province. At the same time, increased cooperation has been made with Zhongguancun Technology Park; Zhongguancun Science and Technology Industrial Parks have been established in Nanyang and Jiaozuo. The scientific and technological opening up activities has become an important window for science and technology in Henan to connect with the nation and the world.

Over the past five years, Henan has continued to strengthen the international cooperation in science and technology; the cooperation has been set up with more than 50 countries and regions including the United States, Great Britain, Israel, and Russia. A large number of technology exchange activities have been carried out, such as the China (Zhengzhou) International Conference on Innovation and International Technology Transfer, with a series of cooperation agreements being signed in artificial intelligence, data science, modern agriculture and other fields. A number of powerful enterprises in Henan such as CITIC Heavy Industries Co., Ltd. and YTO Group Corporation have made acquisition of overseas companies and set up overseas research and development centers.

8. The Prosperity in Mass Entrepreneurship and Innovation

Since the 18th CPC National Congress, Henan has accelerated the implementation of innovation-driven development strategy, actively adapting to the new normal of economic development and building a public service platform, in order to promote mass entrepreneurship and innovation and to stimulate market vitality and social creativity to the full. A favorable environment has been formed where government encourages entrepreneurship and innovation, society supports them and labourers endeavor for them, which has become a significant engine for the transformation and upgrading of economy in Henan under the new normal.

Over the past five years, by implementing innovation and entrepreneurship as the way to lead projects at the Central Plains, Henan has been constantly

improving the policy system of innovation and entrepreneurship, creating a favorable atmosphere to encourage innovation and entrepreneurship at all stages. The provincial government and the Ministry of Science and Technology have jointly launched the implementation of the activity "innovation and entrepreneurship leading the Central Plains", in which Luoyang has been approved as a demonstration city of small and micro enterprises innovation base. CITIC Heavy Industries and Henan Hanwei Electronics Co. Ltd. have been approved as the first batch of national professional public creative spaces.

Over the past five years, the development of innovation and entrepreneurship platforms has been strengthened. 324 various innovation and entrepreneurship platforms at provincial-level and above have been built, such as high-tech business incubators, university science parks, public creative spaces, agricultural and rural creative spaces, 78 of which are at national level and have covered all the municipalities in Henan. The enterprise development project "Little Giants in Science and Technology" has been implemented to make major efforts in the development of small and medium high-tech enterprises. The number of small and medium high-tech enterprises in the province has exceeded 15,000, of which 356 have been developed by the project.

Over the past five years, the investment and financing system of mass entrepreneurship and innovation has been continuously improved. Loan investments for high-tech enterprises have been actively carried out. 6 cooperative banks including Henan Provincial Branch of ICBC have signed strategic cooperation agreements with the province on scientific and technological finance, who are to provide credit support of 172 billion yuan (US$ 26.13 billion) for small and medium high-tech enterprises in the province, 17 billion yuan (US$ 2.59 billion) of which is from the loans specifically assigned for high-tech projects. Venture capital funds for scientific and technological innovation have been established, with the first round of funding reaching 500 million yuan (US$ 75.95 million). The focus has been on small and micro high-tech enterprises in innovation and entrepreneurship incubators at or above the provincial level, and on scientific and technological enterprises at start-up stage led by high-level talents such as the "Thousand Talents Program" launched by the nation and the "Hundred Talents Program" by the province. Social capital has been actively guided to invest in innovation and entrepreneurship; the project "Thousand Eagles Spreading Their Wings" has been launched together with China Merchants

Bank, which has provided nearly 7 billion yuan (US$ 1.06 billion) line of credit for small and medium high-tech enterprises in the province.

9. The Continuous Growth of the Scientific and Technological Talent Team

Talents hold the key to innovation. First-class innovative talents means the dominance in scientific and technological innovation. Since the 18th CPC National Congress, government departments at all levels in Henan have focused on the strategy of innovation-driven development and fully implemented the policies for intellectuals by the central government, creating a social custom of respecting talents and appreciating talents. The incentive mechanism of introducing, nurturing, cultivating and using talents has been enhanced, providing them with stimulation, career, payment and opportunities. Scientific and technological talents have been gathered to achieve new breakthroughs in the construction of innovative talents team of science and technology.

Over the past five years, Henan has continued to implement the projects of developing high-tech innovative talent teams at a high level, cultivating 32 "Central Plains Scholars", 161 outstanding talents, 136 outstanding youths and 321 provincial innovative teams in science and technology since 2012. Efforts have been boosted to introduce talents and implement the project of introducing high-level scientific and technological talents. First-class innovative talents of science and technology at home and abroad and their team such as "Thousand Talents Program" have been actively introduced; 174 new academician workstations have been established. Cooperation with the National Natural Science Foundation of China has been extended to promote the signing of the second joint fund agreement with the provincial government, which has raised the annual joint fund of 50 million yuan (US$ 7.60 million) in the first phase to 100 million yuan (US$ 15.19 million). Consequently, 500 million yuan (US$ 75.95 million) has been co-invested on the cultivation of scientific and technological talents and natural science research in the province. Resources have been integrated to set up the Natural Science Foundation of Henan Province, using the evaluation results of the National Natural Science Foundation — Henan Joint Foundation to select the projects which have not been funded and most experts agreed to subsidize and provide support for them. It has aimed to help local scientific and technological talents in Henan accelerate their growth. In 2016, Henan has been selected by the Ministry of Science and Technology into the Innovative Talent Promotion Program and 12 people have been selected in the "National High-level Talents Special Supporting Program" launched by the Organization Department of the Central Committee of the CPC. 5 "Central Plains Scholars", 25 outstanding talents and 25 outstanding youths have been cultivated; 19 new academician workstations have been established, to which 20 academicians and more than 450 team members have been attracted. At present, there are 125 innovation and entrepreneurship incubation platforms at the provincial-level or above in Henan, covering all 18 municipalities and 21 high-tech zones in the province. A large number of returned overseas talents have been introduced, and the system of special commissioners in science and technology has been fully implemented with more than 10,000 commissioners active in the workplaces. Henan has formed a rich pool of innovative talents at all levels to further play the role of talents, in order to provide a strong support for accelerating innovation-driven development.

10. The Outstanding Achievements in the Strategy of Building A Province which is Strong on Intellectual Property

Since the 18th CPC National Congress, the Central Committee of the Communist Party of China with Comrade Xi Jinping at its core has made innovation the primary driving force in development, and put in place the intellectual property system as the basic guarantee and important support for stimulating innovation. An action plan of national intellectual property strategy has been put forward and implemented in efforts to build a nation which is strong on intellectual property. Henan has increased efforts to implement intellectual property strategy in order to strengthen the development of intellectual property system and comprehensively improve the ability of intellectual property management, so that the role of intellectual property in economic and social development of the province has become increasingly prominent.

Over the past five years, the development of intellectual property in Henan has been taken to a new level. In order to speed up the building of a pilot province which is strong on intellectual property, the joint meeting system of implementation of intellectual property strategy in Henan has been established. Research has to be made to issue the documents "Implementation Plan of Constructing a Pilot Province Supported by Strong Intellectual Property in Henan Province" and

"Opinions of the People's Government of Henan Province on Accelerating the Construction of a Province which is Strong on Intellectual Property under the New Situation". The capacity for intellectual property creation has been significantly enhanced; the provincial government has set up a patent award, with 45 patents approved for national patent awards in China. Efforts in intellectual property protection have been strengthened; Zhengzhou Creative Industry Intellectual Property Rights Center has been established to investigate and prosecute a number of violations of intellectual property rights, which has formed an effective deterrent for patent infringement and counterfeiting. The management capacity of intellectual property has been significantly enhanced. 9 municipalities in the province have been approved as the national pilot cities of intellectual property, with the number ranking the top among provinces in central China. The foundation of intellectual property has become increasingly solid. Patent Examination Cooperation Center of the Patent Office (SIPO) Henan has been founded and put into use. Remarkable accomplishments have been made in the construction of National Intellectual Property and Creative Industry Pilot Park, National Intellectual Property Service Industry Cluster Development Demonstration Area and National Patent Navigation (Superhard Materials) Industry Development Experimental Zone. The number of qualified patent agents in 2016 was 2.2 times as many as that in 2012.

11. The Further Advancement in the Reform and Innovation of Science and Technology Institutions

At the Third Plenary Session of the 18th Party Central Committee in 2013, "Decision of the Central Committee of the Communist Party of China on Some Major Issues Concerning Comprehensively Deepening the Reform" has been deliberated and approved. Particular emphasis has been put on promoting institutional reform for scientific and technological development. Sound system and mechanism should be established to encourage the original innovation, integrated innovation and secondary innovation; market-oriented mechanism of the technological innovation should be improved and the collaborative innovation mechanism based on industry-university-research cooperation should be established. Henan has worked scrupulously to ensure compliance with the Central Committee of the Party, and further promoted the reform of science and technology institutions.

Over the past five years, Henan has continued to promote the provincial science and technology financing program and financial management reform, formulated and adopted policies to further improve the financial management of provincial funded research projects, and put forward a series of policies for the "free-up and incentive" of the innovation subjects and scientific research personnel, so that scientific research funds can be better used for the creative activities of human beings. The transfer and transformation of scientific and technological achievements has been continuously accelerated and the document "Implementation Plan of Henan Province on Promoting the Transfer and Transformation of Scientific and Technological Achievements" has been formulated; for example, in 2016, the income of scientific and technological achievements transformation by Henan Academy of Agricultural Sciences was nearly 20 million yuan (US$ 3.04 million). The effect of incentive policy on achievement transformation has become increasingly prominent. The reform of science and technology incentives has been continuously intensified. The provincial government has issued a provincial matching bonus policy for the national science and technology award; high awards have been given to national awarded projects in which Henan occupied the leading position, which has been 10 times as much as the national award bonus standard. The opening and sharing of major scientific research infrastructure and large-scale scientific research equipment has been promoted. The document "Opinions on Implementation of the Promotion of Major Scientific Research Infrastructure and Large Scientific Research Equipment Opening to the Public" has been formulated. Sharing service platform of scientific research facilities and equipment at provincial level has been put into service, opening and sharing more than 1,000 sets of equipment. In 2016, Henan was one of the five provinces (cities) that have been commended by the State Council for "improving the local conditions of scientific research, optimizing the environment for scientific and technological innovation, promoting the transfer and transformation of scientific and technological achievements and better implementing the major policies of national science and technology reform and development".

II New Opportunities in the Innovation-driven Development of Science and Technology in Henan Province

In the new developing period, the conditions in Henan, in China and in the

world are all undergoing profound changes; the new round of technological revolution and the industrial transformation has brought hints of revolutionary breakthroughs concerning important scientific problems and the key technologies, which has led to the integration and group breakthrough of key technologies, and accelerated the economic restructuring and industrial transformation and upgrading. New situation, new opportunities, new demands and new challenges have emerged for the innovation-driven development of science and technology in Henan.

1. New Opportunities in the International Scientific and Technological Innovation

Another climax of competition is taking place in the innovation field around the globe. In the new century, the world has entered a period with great development and changes; especially after the outbreak of the financial crisis in 2008, countries had to improve the ability of technological innovation as the core strategy to reshape the national competitiveness: The US has issued "American Innovation Strategy"; the EU has launched "Create An Innovative Europe"; Germany has enacted "Implementation Proposals of Industry 4.0 Strategic Plan"; Japan and South Korea have proposed new growth strategy; Russia, India, Brazil and other emerging economies have also launched the innovation-driven development strategy. Innovation and entrepreneurship are developing at a fast pace worldwide. The decisive significance of innovation capacity in the global economic situation and the international balance of power has become more prominent, and increasingly a significant symbol of the comprehensive national power competition. The new round of technological revolution and industrial transformation characterized by low-carbon, information and intelligence has emerged with the tide. The boundaries among the basic research, applied research, technology development and industrialization in the traditional sense have become increasingly blurred. Scientific and technological innovation has integrated more closely with financial capital and business models; technological upgrading and scientific and technological achievements transformation have become more convenient; the pace of industrial upgrading has increased. Interaction and integration among information technology, biotechnology, new materials technology and others frequently has boosted new industries, with cloud computing, big data, mobile Internet and other new application fields being expanded. Major technological breakthroughs in many areas and large-scale industrialization are being widely carried out. It is noteworthy that in many emerging areas in the current round of scientific and technological revolution and industrial transformation, China and the developed countries are basically at the same starting line, which is a rare opportunity for China's development. Henan has a good foundation for development of technological advantages in the high-end equipment manufacturing, electronic information, new materials, bio-medicine and other strategic emerging industries, who, consequently, should take the initiative to assume the sacred mission endowed by the nation of accelerating the pace of innovation-driven development, participating more actively and seizing the dominant position of scientific and technological innovation and industrial development in the world, in order to make due contributions to build China into a science and technology giant.

2. New Opportunities in the Domestic Scientific and Technological Innovation

Domestically, China has been in a stage where scientific and technological innovation leads comprehensive innovation. Since the 18th CPC National Congress, the Central Committee of the Communist Party of China and the State Council have attached increasingly greater importance to scientific and technological progress and innovation. The concept of innovation-driven development has been put forward and "Outline of the National Strategy on Innovation-driven Development" has been promulgated to implement the innovation-driven development strategy, with a lot of relevant investments and reforms carried out in China. After years of efforts, China's innovation capacity has been greatly enhanced, scientific and technological strength has been greatly improved and reform of science and technology institutions has been deepened; besides, transformation of scientific and technological application has been accelerated, the industrial cycle of scientific and technological achievements has been greatly shortened, and the enthusiasm and creativity of scientific and technological workers has been further developed. As a result, scientific and technological innovation capacity in China has shown a strong momentum, with scientific and technological development entering a new era of tracking, paralleling and leading; China has become a science and technology giant with great influence around the world. But with the new normal in China's economy—

the slowdown in economic growth, making difficult structural adjustments and absorbing the effects of previous economic stimulus policies, it is extremely urgent to speed up shift of growth pattern from extensive growth focusing on scale and growth rate to intensive growth focusing on the quality and benefit, with scientific and technological innovation as a new engine to lead the new normal. At the National Science, Technology and Innovation Conference, Conference of Academicians of the CAS and the CAE, and the 9th National Conference of CAST in 2016, General Secretary Xi Jinping has elaborated on the strategic thought of promoting scientific and technological innovation at the new historical starting point, which has called for the construction of a science and technology giant in the world and indicated that China has entered a new stage of comprehensive innovation led by scientific and technological innovation. The new era calls for establishing the concept of innovation-driven development, fully implementing innovation-driven development strategy, adhering to scientific and technological innovation and institutional innovation, and getting rid of all the constraints and obstacles of creative thinking. Innovation must be promoted comprehensively; science and technology must play a good supporting and leading role in economy; efforts must be boosted to strengthen areas of weakness in order to solve prominent problems on original innovation and transformation of scientific and technological achievements; the development trend of mass innovation must be conformed to, so as to further emancipate the vitality, and fully realize mass entrepreneurship and innovation. It can be said that innovation has become the primary driving force of development. Innovation-driven development strategy is a national strategy based on an overall picture of the globe and focusing on the key with a holistic plan, rather than a short-term, local strategy; scientific and technological innovation has truly occupied a central place in China's development. At the same time, China has also been at the stage with rapid flow of domestic innovation elements and division of regional advantages in innovation elements. The developed regions such as Beijing, Guangdong, Jiangsu, Shanghai and Zhejiang have become the areas rich in innovation elements, which has placed growing difficulty for Henan to attract and gather innovation elements. Under such circumstance, Henan is required to further emancipate the mind to accelerate the full integration of chains among innovation, industry, talents, policies, capital and service, and give play to the first-mover effect, integration effect, overflow effect, demonstration effect and driving effect formed by comprehensive innovation, which was led by scientific and technological innovation, so as to achieve a new leap in the scientific and technological innovation in Henan.

3. New Opportunities in the Scientific and Technological Innovation in Henan

Henan has entered a critical stage in the construction of a new model of scientific and technological innovation in the central and western regions of China. "Understanding, adapting to and leading the new normal has become the fundamental theme for current and future economic development in China." Along with the nation, Henan has enthusiastically embraced the new normal of economic development. Henan is actively researching and actively developing new driving forces for economic growth due to the weakening of the cost advantages of land, labor force, capital and other factors of production, in conjunction with the problems caused by insufficient domestic demand, the weakening export-driven effect, as well as the unsustainable low-level development model based on resource and energy consumption, quantity based expansion along with low cost competition. Meanwhile, Henan is in the transition from mid-term industrialization to the later period, and is at the significant stage where the competitive advantage shifts from low cost products to capital and technology products. It is more urgent than ever for Henan to adapt to and lead the new normal and further promote the new driving forces; while the traditional driving forces represented by traditional industries and high energy-consuming industries are still very strong, the new driving forces led by new technology, new industry type and new model demand further development. In the short term, the new forces are not strong enough to face the downward sales and production from the traditional industries. In addition, from the perspective of regional competition, the basic situation of Henan — large population, poor foundation, weak base, uneven development — has not fundamentally changed; per capita GDP, disposable income of urban and rural residents along with other major economic indicators are about only 80% of the national average. Science and technology are the most active and revolutionary factors in economic and social development. Innovation-driven development is a way of resource allocation, an endogenous development model, and a higher level economic growth mode. Henan has an urgent need to give positive attention to the research and development of scientific and technological innovation and use the innovations as the economic growth point and the driving force of industries, in order to achieve the transformation of driving forces in the economic development, and to promote economic development to shift from the past "factor- and investment-driven pattern" to "innovation-driven and endogenous growth pattern". Therefore, the 10th Congress of the Henan Provincial Committee of the CPC has put forward the strategy of striving to build a new model of scientific and technological innovation in the central and western regions of China. The economic quality and development benefit should be improved by enhancing the platforms, expanding the community of innovators, speeding up open innovation, strengthening institutional and other reforms. The main problems and major contradictions in the economic and social development should be solved through more efficient development, in order to broaden the space for development, promote the economic and social development in the province by leaps and bounds in a more powerful way, and provide a strong driving force for building an economically strong province.

In the face of the new situation and tasks, Henan must adopt a broader vision and assume stronger responsibility to aim high. It must firmly implement the core strategy of innovation-driven development, actively explore the new model of economic and social development driven by innovation in underdeveloped areas in the central and western regions, and build a new model of scientific and technological innovation in the central and western regions of China, so as to make due contributions to building China into a science and technology giant in the world.

III The Future Prospects of the Innovation-driven Development of Science and Technology in Henan Province

Science and technology kindles human civilization and progress, and innovation is the backbone of national rejuvenation. Now, at the new starting point, the target of the Central Plains rising to a more prosperous and powerful region is closer to us than in any other historical period. In the future, the policy of "innovating independently, focusing on leapfrog development, supporting the development and leading to the future" must be adhered to, in order to take the initiative to lead the new normal of economic development. Taking in-depth implementation of innovation-driven development strategy as the main line and supply-side structural reform as the fundamental point, more efforts should be exerted to build a new pattern of regional innovation-driven development, enhance the technological innovation capacity of the industries, strengthen the basic foundation of innovation-driven development, promote open innovation, boost mass entrepreneurship and innovation, and foster the reform of the science and technology institutions, hence building a new model of scientific and technological innovation in the central and western regions of China, as well as provide more powerful support for building an economically stronger province and promote the Central Plains to give more outstanding performance in the realization of the Chinese Dream of national rejuvenation.

1. Building Zheng-Luo-Xin National Innovation Demonstration Area

Based on the target of building "one center and four areas", efforts should be exerted to build Zheng-Luo-Xin National Innovation Demonstration Area and foster innovative growth poles with core competitiveness that play their role, promoting the across-the-board improvements in the innovation level of the province. Reforming systems and mechanisms should be accelerated. The status of piloting and pioneering endowed by the state should be made full use of, while focusing on the incentives of scientific and technological achievements distribution, the introduction and cultivation of innovative talents and intellectual property protection to accelerate the reform of the system and mechanism. At the same time, the coordinated development of Zhengzhou, Luoyang and Xinxiang should be accelerated with "three cities, three areas and major zones" as the main structure. On this basis, by building "one area and major zones", the influence of the Area on facilitating the development of more surrounding areas should be expanded, in order to form an integrated development pattern of innovation through exploring and promoting the eligible surrounding areas under the co-construction with the Area. Industry support should be strengthened. Zhengzhou focuses on the development of intelligent terminals, shield equipment, superhard materials, new energy vehicles, trenchless technology, intelligent instrument and control systems, visible light communications, information security, Internet of Things, Beidou Navigation System and remote sensing, creating high-end equipment manufacturing and a new generation of information technology industrial cluster with significant domestic influence. Luoyang focuses on the development of industrial robots, complete sets of intelligent equipment, high-end metal materials, new green

refractories, etc., creating a center for research, development and manufacturing of intelligent equipment and new material innovation. Xinxiang focuses on the development of batteries powered by new energy and its materials, bio-pharmacy, biochemical products, etc., to establish an innovation center for batteries powered by new energy and its materials and bio-medical industry cluster. Zheng-Luo-Xin National Innovation Demonstration Area should be built as an important platform for reform and innovation in Henan, the key for industrial upgrading, and demonstration area for innovation and entrepreneurship.

2. Highlighting the Prominent Position of Innovators

The core of enhancing the economic competitiveness of Henan must be firmly grasped. The province should improve the capacity for industrial innovation with major breakthroughs in common key technologies as leading elements and group innovation in key areas of technology as support. Various kinds of innovators are the foundation and the core of building a modern innovation system and implementing innovation-driven development, whose innovation capacity should be enhanced through policy guidance and financial support. Enterprises' position as major innovators and their leading role in innovation should be strengthened. The projects of cultivating leading enterprises in innovation should be implemented, selecting a number of backbone innovative enterprises centering on the leading and pillar industries, which are to be support in the implementation of major science and technology programs, industrial innovation alliance construction, high-level platform construction and talent, technology gathering and so on. As a result, a number of leading enterprises in innovation will be cultivated with international advanced level of technology and international competitiveness. The development of medium, small and micro enterprises should be guided to be "specialized, precisely managed, distinctive and innovative" in order to cultivate a group of "little giants" in science and technology. The vitality of innovation in institutions of higher learning and scientific research institutions should be stimulated. The adjustment of the discipline construction and research direction of colleges and universities should be accelerated. Reforms should be implemented in the evaluation mechanism of scientific research performance in colleges and universities to guide the scientific research personnel to join the main battlefield of economic and social development. The reform of scientific research institutes should be further explored and developed, and modern institutions system should be established to make significant moves to develop new research and development institutions and motivate scientific and technological personnel for innovation. The vitality of scientific and technological innovation lies in promoting and serving development, so it is necessary to turn innovation achievements into real industrial activities. The innovation chains should be developed, centering on the industrial chains. In the manufacturing industries, a number of major science and technology projects should be implemented by breakthroughs in the key technologies which constrain the transformation and upgrading of traditional industries, and in the core technologies which support the development of strategic emerging industries. Biological resources, mineral resources, recycling economy and other chains of processing industries should be opened up to accelerate the transformation of manufacturing industries towards the clustering, intelligent and in-service types. In the service industries, the scientific and technological research and development, as well as the application should be strengthened in the modern logistics, modern finance, e-commerce and other areas; information technology should be used to enhance commerce and trade, transportation and other traditional service industries. In modern agriculture, research should identify and tackle key problems in upgrading the low- and medium-yield cropland, breeding new crop varieties, comprehensive high yields, intensive processing of agricultural products, modern storage and transportation, as well as other aspects, in order to enhance the technological level of the planting industry, animal husbandry and processing industry for agricultural products.

3. Integrating Various Kinds of Innovation Elements

Platforms are the foundation of the scientific and technological innovation activities. The platform system of scientific and technological innovation in the province should be further enhanced to gather innovation elements and provide infrastructure for more efficient scientific and technological innovation activities. A number of industry-oriented key industry research institutes and engineering and technology research centers should be built based on the situations in Henan, with focus on competitive industries and strategic emerging industries, relying on key enterprises with advanced technology and better scientific research conditions; research of technological problems and new product development should be conducted according to the needs of enterprises. Relying on key institutions of higher learning, scientific research institutions and qualified enterprises and institutions, the construction of key laboratories, engineering laboratories, colleges and universities, key laboratories should be strengthened, in order to improve the original innovation capacity of research and development platforms. The policy guidance and macro-control of government in the integration of science and technology resources should be fully implemented, focusing on building sharing platforms of science and technology resources, technology transfer service platforms, as well as science and technology project management platforms, in order to build a public service platform system of science and technology with specialized characteristics. The function of science and technology public service platforms should be enhanced, and the operation mechanism should be further invigorated to improve the operation quality and level of science and technology platforms. The function of science and technology service platforms should be strengthened, highlighting its service for the enterprises, the government policies and the regional economic development, and carrying out targeted service activities. Platforms for the industrialization of scientific and technological innovations should be set up. Great efforts should be exerted to promote the construction and development of science and technology incubators, supporting and encouraging all kinds of market entities to participate in the investment, construction and management of incubators, and promoting the "specialized, precise, in-depth" incubating capacity covering the full cycle and whole industrial chain in an all-round way. Policies to attract investments should be enhanced by building a pool of investment attraction projects centering on the new generation of information technology, biological and new medicine, new materials, new energy, energy saving and environmental protection along with other emerging industries, shifting the science and technology incubation platform into a base gathering technology entrepreneurship and high-end talents. The gathering of various types of resources and factors to innovation platforms should be accelerated through continuous enhancement of the function of platforms, so that they can play a better role in driving the development of their surrounding areas, and promote the extension of scientific and technological innovation from individual research units to innovation chains and then to a broader scale.

4. Implementing the Strategy with the Development of Talents as the Priority

Innovation-driven development is essentially talent-driven, so people should be motivated and investment in people should be increased in order to retain talents and provide continuous power for development. Henan has entered a new stage of innovation-driven development and accelerated modernization, in which talents should be viewed as the primary resource for development and continuous efforts should be made to develop innovative talent teams. Researchers should be gathered for the need of major industries and key fields. Relying on key disciplines, scientific research bases, major scientific research and engineering projects, the project of building high-level innovative talent teams in science and technology should be further implemented, which strives to cultivate a cadre of leading talents in science and technology, engineers and high-level innovation teams. Emphasis should be put on cultivating front-line innovation researchers, as well as young science and technology researchers, so as to support their innovation and entrepreneurship. Systems and policies that are conducive to the work of researchers should be enhanced. The reward mechanism determined by the factor market such as knowledge, technology and management should be improved; the scientific and technological achievements, intellectual property ownership and benefit-sharing mechanism should be enhanced to increase the benefit ratio of the development teams and major inventors; the title evaluation methods for scientific and technological talents should be modified to promote the effective connection between evaluation and employment of science and technology researchers. Meanwhile, the leading function of employing entities in professional title evaluation should be highlighted; a reasonable definition and decentralization of the evaluation authority can promote the independent evaluation by colleges and universities, enterprises and research institutes. All types of enterprises should be encouraged to motivate science and technology research through stock rights, stock options, dividends and other incentives. The two-way flow mechanism of scientific research talents should be established and improved, as well as the cooperation mechanism and exchange platform between scientific and technological personnel and enterprises, in order to encourage and support researchers of institutes and universities to work part-time in the enterprises or start business upon demission. The cultivation of skilled researchers should be accelerated. The projects of revitalizing skills nationwide and implementing vocational education in the crucial period should be further promoted, with establishment and improvement of docking mechanism between skill training and industrial development, so as to train a number of "great country craftsmen" and "elite blue collars" and comprehensively improve the skill quality of workers. Therefore, a large number of high-quality skilled personnel will be provided for scientific, technological innovation, and industrial development and more efforts should be made to build-high-level teams in high-tech innovation on a large scale, with reasonable structure and excellent quality.

5. Promoting Mass Entrepreneurship and Innovation

At present, sharing economy has been growing rapidly worldwide, with modes of entrepreneurship and innovation based on the Internet booming and crowd-innovation, crowd-sourcing, crowd-support, crowd-funding and other supporting platforms for mass entrepreneurship and innovation developing rapidly. New models and new types of business continue to emerge, while online and offline integration accelerates, producing a broad and profound impact on production methods, lifestyles, governance patterns. This opportunity should be firmly grasped to accelerate the formation of support systems for innovation and entrepreneurship, with the gathering of entrepreneurial skills, diversified incubation platforms, smooth financing channels, improved service functions, efficient operation modes and significant demonstration effects; thus, a good environment for innovation and entrepreneurship can be created to fully stimulate the vitality of the whole society. Development of innovation and entrepreneurship incubation platforms should be accelerated. Complementary advantages of traditional incubators in infrastructure and new entrepreneur service agencies in the professional services should be given full attention, so that integration can be achieved between traditional incubators and the new entrepreneur service agencies. Diversified entities should be encouraged and supported to rely on the traditional incubators to develop maker space, startup cafe, innovation workshop and other new incubation models, so as to coordinate the establishment of the complete incubation chain of "crowd innovation space - incubator - accelerator", and to create a number of unique demonstration areas of innovation and entrepreneurship. The investment and financing system for innovation and entrepreneurship should be improved. The project of science and technology finance should be implemented to guide the chain of entrepreneurship and innovation with capital chain, guide and support financial institutions to implement product and service innovation, conduct intellectual property pledge loans, equity pledge loans and other businesses, accelerate the development of angel investment, venture investment and other venture capital investment, develop entity crowd-funding, equity crowd-funding and other new financing models, cultivate venture capital investment and capital market, build science and technology finance service system, as well as establish a good situation in which various types of financial tools support innovation and entrepreneurship. A good environment for innovation and entrepreneurship should be created. "A week for mass entrepreneurship and innovation activities" should be established to strengthen policy advocacy and demonstrate the achievements of innovation. All kinds of incubation platforms should be supported to hold venture competitions, investment road shows, venture salons, entrepreneurial lectures, entrepreneurial training camp and other activities. The propaganda of innovation and entrepreneurship should be enhanced, innovative and entrepreneurial knowledge be popularized, and successful experiences be promoted, in order to accelerate the formation of the social atmosphere where everyone advocates innovation, everyone desires innovation and everyone is capable of innovation.

6. Promoting Open Innovation

Under the circumstance of globalization, information sharing and network development, the innovation elements are more open and mobile, which requires "introducing in" and "stepping out", in order to be actively integrated into the global innovation network. The transfer and transformation of technology must be accelerated. The opportunity of accelerating the flow of innovative resources should be seized, in order to give full attention to location, transportation, market, human resources and other advantages in Henan; targeted policies should be introduced to promote the transfer of advanced technology and talents from other provinces to Henan. The cultivation of technology transfer institutions must be accelerated. With the National Technology Transfer Zhengzhou Center, and Patent Examination Cooperation Center of the Patent Office, SIPO, Henan as the basis, a number of technology transfer institutions should be gathered and cultivated with technical integration and management, technology brokers, as well as technology investment and financing services. The interaction and cooperation should be enhanced, introducing of a number of well-known institutions of higher learning, research institutes, research and development institutions of large enterprises at home and abroad, as well as domestic and overseas high-end, professional, market-oriented technical services institutions. Diversified investors should be encouraged and guided to build various types of regional comprehensive technology transfer institutions, industry, or professional technology transfer institutions. The development and cooperation of science and technology should be strengthened. Active efforts should be made to obtain national innovation resources. The innovation cooperation mechanism with the Ministry of Science and Technology, the Ministry of Education, the State Intellectual Property Office, the National Natural Science Foundation, etc. should be improved, and the ministry-office-province conference among the three should be actively promoted, in order to drive the distribution of national scientific and technological resources in Henan. Qualified enterprises and scientific research institutions should be encouraged to "step out" to form innovation network. Key enterprises should be supported to absorb local scientific and technological resources through the establishment of overseas research and development centers, joint ventures, equity participation, etc., in order to enhance the operation capacity of overseas technology patent. International cooperation and exchanges in science and technology should be strengthened, and the strategic cooperation agreements signed with Beijing, Shanghai and other developed areas, as well as well-known institutions of higher learning and scientific research institutions should be actively implemented. The cooperation with countries along the "the Belt and Road", the United States, Europe, Japan, Korea and Israel should be promoted, with introduction of overseas key technologies and research and development teams to enhance the innovation level in science and technology. The integration of military and civilian science and technology should be promoted. The coordination mechanism of science and technology innovation in the military and civilian areas should be established and improved, and the interaction among science and technology departments, military colleges and universities in Henan, as well as military enterprises should be promoted to strengthen the connection in scientific and technological development strategy, planning, tasks, and policies. In the basic, frontier and exploratory areas, the scientific research system with organic coordination between military and civilian scientific research forces should be formed, while in the application, supporting, service-oriented areas, the scientific research pattern of military and civilian interaction with enterprises as the mainstay should be formed.

7. Developing the Reform of Science and Technology System

Breakthroughs in scientific and technological innovation require not only the "hardware" support such as infrastructure, but also the "software" protection such as systems and mechanisms. The decisive role of the market allocation of innovative resources and the guiding role of the government should be given full and better attention to, in order to build the systems and mechanisms adjusted to innovation-driven development. The evaluation-guided mechanism should be enhanced. Reforms should be made in the project evaluation and evaluation of achievements, with the focus shifting from the number of research achievements to the quality, the value based on originality and practical contribution, so as to switch the cycle of writing papers to gain professional titles to the market- and benefit-oriented style. Scientific researchers should be facilitated to write papers about the products, conduct projects in the enterprises and reap achievements in the industries. The market-oriented mechanism for technological innovation should be established. The innovation mechanism of enterprise-led industrial technology should be improved, and a high-level, normalized enterprise technology innovation dialogue and consultation system should be established, in order to expand the influence of enterprises in the government innovation decision-making, and promote enterprises to become the decision-making subject of technological innovation. The collaborative innovation mechanism among industries, universities, research institutions and application should be improved. Scientific and technological projects with definite market orientation should be implemented, which are led by enterprises, guided by the government, and joined by colleges, universities and research institutes, so that enterprises are encouraged to become the main of technological innovation. A policy system conforming to the international rules should be established and improved to support the procurement of innovative products and services, so as to promote enterprises to become the mainstay of technological innovation transformation. The incentive policies of achievement transformation should be enhanced. The reform of science and technology achievement transformation should be deepened, improving the equity and dividend incentive methods of scientific and technological talents to increase their proportion in the income sharing of transformation, enhancing the incentive reward of service invention and management system of total payroll, boosting the dispute arbitration and legal relief system of service invention, improving the mechanism of technology transfer in institutes of higher learning and scientific research institutions, exploring the management system of intangible assets in institutions, formulating the immunity policies of transfer of state-owned shares of technology, strengthening the expansion of scientific and technological achievements in the way of licensing, as well as encouraging the technology transfer by transference, buying shares, etc.. Reforms of scientific and technological management system should be launched. The reform on the management of the provincial financial plan for science and technology (special projects, funds, etc.) should be deepened, improving the formation mechanism and implementation mechanism of the planned projects, exploring and the implementing the joint meeting system of science and technology plan and fund management, establishing a mechanism which manages scientific research projects by professional institutions, enhancing investing methods of financial fund, as well as increasing the effectiveness of scientific research projects. The scientific and technological decision-making consulting, innovation survey, scientific and technological reporting and other basic systems should be established and improved to speed up the opening and sharing of resources. The reform of science and technology evaluation system should be deepened, improving the criteria for classified evaluation, in order to encourage and support innovation evaluation by the third party.

References:

[1] CPC Henan Provincial Committee. "Work Report at the 10th Henan Provincial Party Congress".

[2] Zhang Zhancang, Wan Shiwei. *Report on Economic Development of Henan Province (2017)* [M]. Social Sciences Academic Press (China), 2017-4.

[3] Gu Jianquan. *Research on the Implementation of Innovation-driven Development Strategy in Henan Province* [M]. Social Sciences Academic Press (China), 2015-12.

[4] The State Council. "Implementation Plan on the Construction of Zheng-Luo-Xin National Innovation Demonstration Area".

[5] Department of Science and Technology of Henan Province. "The 13th Five-year Plan of Scientific and Technological Innovation in Henan Province".

[6] Wei Quanzhong. "Reflections on the Strategy of 'Innovation-driven' Development" [N]. *People's Daily*. 2014-11-20.

[7] Yuan Jinxing. "Accelerating the Integration into the Global Innovation Network"[N]. *Henan Daily*. 2017-5-30.

[8] Yuan Jinxing. "Reflections and Recommendations on Accelerating Mass Entrepreneurship and Innovation in Henan Province"[J]. *Innovation and Technology*, 2016(10).

B.6 Report on Henan Tourism Development

Research Team of Henan Academy of Social Sciences

Abstract: In 2016, Henan's tourism economy continued to develop, leading to a significant improvement. Tourism products were constantly innovating. The tourism market was deepened in the three-dimensional marketing endeavors. Agriculture tourism and rural tourism development grew rapidly. The targeted poverty alleviation by developing tourism achieved remarkable results. The quality of tourism services improved significantly. Industrial space expanded in the whole field.

Although notable progress has been made in tourism development, there are still some problems. For example, the brand construction of sightseeing agriculture tourism lags behind. The refined and effective supply of tourism products is insufficient. The catalytic activity of industrial chain is not strong. There is still great room for improvement in operation management system and so on. Therefore, we must comply with requirements of the central and the provincial party committee in accordance with the development objectives of Henan "13th Five-Year Plan". We must focus on cultivating and implementing high-end tourist marketing strategy, creating "The Silk Road Tourism Belt along the Yellow River", promoting quality tourist routes, cultivating tourism centers in Henan, and tourism trends in the future.

Keywords: Tourism Development; Higher Refinement in Tourism Product; The Silk Road Tourism Belt Along the Yellow River; Henan Province

The overall development goal of the "13th Five-Year Plan" is to build Henan into an innovative pioneer of Chinese historic and cultural tourism, a pilot of ecological and civilized tourism, a model of targeted poverty alleviation by rural tourism, a top tourist destination at home and abroad, and to establish an initial position of a great tourism province that is moderately prosperous in all respects.

In 2016, tourism system all over the province conscientiously implemented the work plan of the National Tourism Bureau, and the Provincial Party Committee and the provincial government, adhering to the synchronization of concept change and structural adjustment, attaching equal importance to investment and consumption as the driving force, sticking to hardware improvement and software upgrade simultaneously, trying to refine travel products, expanding tourist markets, providing better services, doing beautiful theme images, and having high comprehensive benefits. The main indicators of tourism industry all over the province maintained a fast growth and the transformation and upgrading of tourism industry made new progress.

I Great Achievements in Henan Tourism Development

1. Steady Development of Henan's Tourism Economy with a Significant Leading Role

In 2016, as shown in Figure 1,Henan received 583 million visitors at home and abroad throughout the year, with tourism revenue of 576.4 billion yuan (US$87.09 billion), up by 12.37% and 14.47% respectively over the same period, with a growth rate higher than the national average.

In 2016, Henan tourism industry stepped up efforts to attract 122.19 billion yuan(US$18.46billion) investment and had already invested 53.06 billion yuan(US$8.02billion). In 2016, 2.06 million people were directly employed in the tourism industry in Henan. Efforts of the tourism industry in improving the living standards of the people and lifting them out of poverty continued to deliver results.

The tourism industry played an important role in the construction of "Prosperous Henan, Civilized Henan, Safe Henan and Beautiful Henan" and served as an important engine for a "Prosperous Henan", an important means of a "Civilized Henan", an important support for a "Safe Henan", and an important carrier for a "Beautiful Henan".

The development of tourism has led to the great development and prosperity of Henan culture, which has played an important role in broadcasting the culture of the Central Plains and promoting the image of Henan.

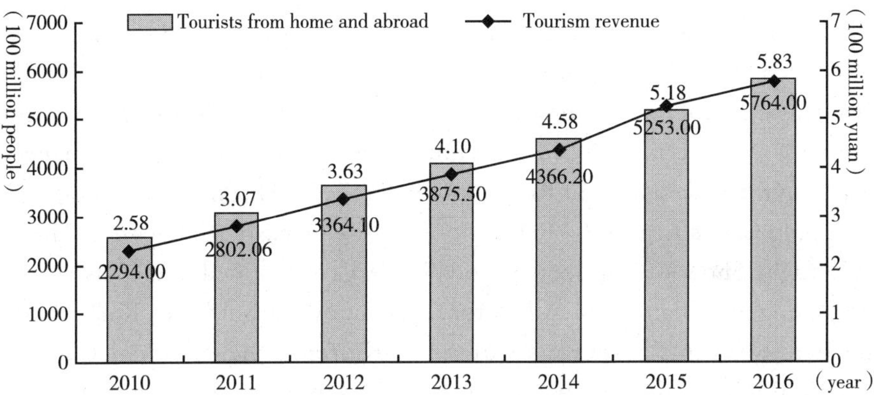

Figure 1 The total revenue and the number of tourists received from home and abroad in Henan in recent years

Data source: The Tourism Administration of Henan Province.

2. Persistent Development and Innovation of Tourism Products with Bright Spots

Efforts were made to intensify structural supply reforms of tourism product. We continued to enrich the mountain resort, cultural experience, tourism performing art, health preservation, outdoor sports and other new forms of tourism, further stretching the industrial chain and expanding the product system. As is shown in Figure 2, by 2015, there are 385 A-class tourist attractions all over the province, including 12 5A-class ones and 134 4A-class ones. Yaoshan Hot Spring Tourist Resort was rated as a national tourist resort by the National Tourism Administration, and five tourist attractions were rated as the national demonstration regions of ecological tourism by the National Tourism Administration and the National Ministry of Environmental Protection.

We have vigorously developed new tourism models, and accelerated transformation from traditional sightseeing to modern leisure and experience tourism. The province has added more than 10 large hot spring resorts, more than 10 ski resorts, more than 20 theme parks, and more than 30 rafting places. The root-kin cultural famous tourism brands, such as the Memorial Ceremony in honor of Yellow Emperor at his birthplace in Xinzheng and temple fairs at the Taihao Mausoleum in Huaiyang, are carried out with new ideas each time. While promoting the fine performing arts like "Shaolin Zen Music Ritual" and "Song Dynasty - the Dreamlike Glory, the Ancient Capital", we have introduced a number of excellent tourist performances including the new "Kung-fu Revelation: 9 Scrolls", "The World of Luoyang", "Sui-Tang Circus Legend", "Return to the Song Dynasty a Thousand Times" and "Light Show of the Iron Pagoda". We have planned and constructed the Zhengzhou Fantawild Adventure, the Luoyang Sui-Tang Relics Park, the Jianye Seven-Prosperous Corner in Kaifeng, the National Cultural and Ecological Tourist Demonstration Site in Zhuxian Town, the Hot Spring Health Resort in Sanmenxia, and the Ice and Snow Cultural Sports Park in Luanchuan, forming a unique tourist product system with Henan characteristics. After the Jiaozuo Phenomena, Luanchuan Model and Xixia Experience, innovation-driven development models, including 5A Songxian, the Kaifeng culture-business-tourism integration and the Smart Longmen, have aroused widespread interest throughout the nation. At the same time, three years plan of the third round of Henan and Taiwan tourism industry determine the 2017-2019 promotion theme in Taiwan—"Depth of New Henan and New discovery", and plan three products of the new rhyme of slow life of the ancient capital, the beautiful scenery of Taihang mountain, and the homesickness for old village and old town. "The new rhyme of slow life of the ancient capital" focuses on the opening of the urban life, alley and Hutong, royal river nightscape, golden night market, the charm of Luoyang's palace and Xuchang's flower sea romance and cycling which brings consumers a new leisure experience of the ancient capital of Taiwan; "the beautiful scenery of Taihang mountain" is a key part of the Henan section of the Taihang Mountains, introducing Taihang Mountain's "steep" and "spectacular" features, appealing to young people in Taiwan; "the homesickness for old village and old town " focuses on deep excavation of the ancient town of Jun porcelain, Shanzhou folk houses and Luoyang Weipo village of traditional ancient village charm, which enriches cultural charm and unique flavor of Henan tourism.

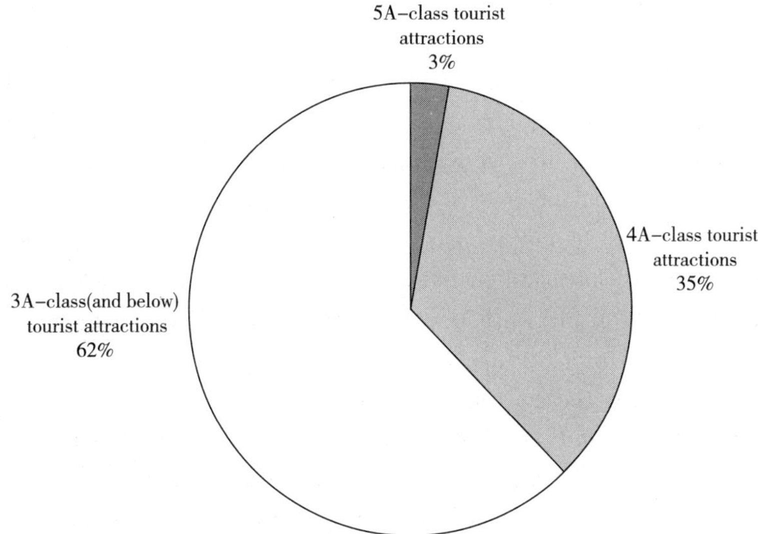

Figure 2 The classification of tourist attractions in Henan

Data source: The Tourism Administration of Henan Province.

3. Deep Expansion of Tourism Market with Remarkable Achievements

With the economy and society stepping into a period of transformation and upgrading, the various factors affecting the development of tourism are intertwined. And there are more external uncertainties. Facing these challenges, Henan tourism continued to expand the depth of the tourism market to reap remarkable achievements.

First, Henan province successfully hosted International Mayor's Forum on Tourism-Zhengzhou, China 2016. National Tourism Bureau Director Li Jinzao spoke highly of the "International Mayor's Forum on Tourism-Zhengzhou, China 2016" as an important platform to deepen our cooperation with the international tourism organization. Henan province has successfully held four sessions in eight years. Second, to continue to enhance the brand influence of "Home in Henan" and focus on accurately promoting the domestic tourist market. Henan have carried out a series of activities such as being spokespersons for "Home in Henan", "Tour Henan by High-speed Railway", hundreds of We-Media giving interviews to "Home in Henan" and the theme promotion in Hong Kong, Macao and Taiwan markets, and travel agencies paying a visit to Henan, to further enhance the "Home in Henan" brand connotation. Third, we regarded "Henan - the birth place of China's history" as the overall image of the brand and vigorously explored the inbound tourism market. We comprehensively promoted Henan key tourism products as well as tourist routes and encouraged the development of inbound tourism. The holding of International Mayor's Forum on Tourism-Zhengzhou, China 2016, Sanmenxia International Yellow River Tourism Festival, "the same root and origin" Henan Taiwan Tourism Summit Forum, Chinese Yuntai Mountain International Tourism Festival, Anyang Air Sports culture and Tourism Festival, Xuchang Cultural Tourism Week and some other events effectively have enhanced the Henan tourism influence and attraction at home and abroad.

4. Significant Improvement in Tourism Services with Demonstration Pilot Projects

Henan actively promoted tourism standardization to improve tourism services and tourist attractions. Luoyang, Huaiyang County, Xixia County, Yuntai Mountain, Chaya Mountain, Taihao Mausoleum and Baligou have become demonstration units of the National Tourism Standardization; The Administration Bureau of Yuntai Mountain Scenic Spot was rated as "The National Benchmark for Quality Tourism Services" by the General Administration of Quality Supervision, Inspection and Quarantine and the National Tourism Administration. Zhengzhou and Jiaozuo have been selected as the pilot of "The National All-for-one Tourism Demonstration Area". On the whole, Henan's capability to provide informed tourism services for tourists was further enhanced. Luoyang and Zhengzhou were rated as national pilot cities of smart tourism, and "Yuntai Mountain Service Standards: Digital Application Standards of Scenic Areas" has become the national standard. In addition, a number of tourist attractions focused on the promotion of civilized tourism by carrying out activities including "civilized tourism in Henan", "civilized travel, rational consumption", "a quality tour with you" and "be a civilized tourist", which continued to push forward the public promotion of civilized tourism. With the emphasis on roads, parking lots, traffic signs, tourist service centers and toilets, the construction of tourist infrastructure has been strengthened and the accessibility of public services and the accessibility of the roads have been continuously improved. A total of 995 new tourist toilets have been built throughout the year, and 364 toilets have been renovated. We actively introduced volunteers into tourism, and encouraged volunteers to play their part in the construction of a civilized tourist environment. We kept a record of uncivilized behavior of some tourists, and meted out penalties, so as to foster a habit of civilized tourism for tourists and tourism practitioners, and to gradually make civilized tours a fashion. At the same time, Henan province also strengthened public promotion and education efforts for outbound tourists to avoid uncivilized behavior.

II New Features of Henan Tourism Development

1. Rapid Development of Agricultural Tourism and Rural Tourism

In recent years, Henan province has given full play to the strong correlation between tourism and other industries, and has vigorously promoted the integration of and interaction between tourism and agriculture. In combination with the beautiful countryside construction, Henan emphasizes the equal importance of development, regulation and promotion, and vigorously develops tourism products including leisure vacation, pastoral tourism, health preservation and old-age care, creative agriculture and farming experience, relying on resources like beautiful rural sceneries, traditional villages and folk culture. The tourism-benefit-people project, "Hundreds of Villages and Thousands of Households", is included in the ten livelihood projects by Henan Provincial Party Committee and the Provincial Government. Henan province will increase policy supports for tourism and innovate development mechanisms so as to comprehensively enhance the quality and service level of rural tourism, thereby promoting rural economic development, restructuring agriculture and increasing farmers' income. At present, Henan province has cultivated a number of highly popular brands of "beautiful rural tourism", with characteristics and styles of Henan, of the Central Plains, and of the times. The Cherry Valley Village of Erqi District in Zhengzhou is rated as one of the first 20 rural tourism bases by the National Tourism Administration; Chongdugou Village of Luanchuan County and Haotang Village of Xinyang became national models of rural tourism development. The province has altogether set up 11 demonstration counties and 21 demonstration sites for national leisure agriculture and rural tourism, 37 model villages for Chinese rural tourism, 40 model households, 400 golden farmhouse resorts and 400 foregoers who become rich by rural tourism. The province will maintain the policy to make tourism a reliable support for Henan's rural tourism and beautiful countryside construction.

2. Rapid Extension of the All-for-one Industrial Space

In 2016, Henan implemented all-for-one tourism to enhance the tourism supply capacity. In accordance with the requirements of the National Tourism Bureau, we created a favorable atmosphere for the development of all-for-one tourism in the whole society. First, issue comprehensive documents and development planning for Henan tourism in the "Thirteenth Five-Year Plan" to speed all-for-one tourism and to enhance quality and efficiency. Successively, Zhengzhou and Jiaozuo have been selected for the first batch and the second batch of "The National All-for-one Tourism Demonstration Area". Second, strengthen the supporting role of major projects. In 2016, there were 607 tourism projects under construction, the total investment and actual investment on which are 589.454 billion yuan (US$89.07 billion)and 57.47 billion yuan(US$8.68 billion) respectively, a year-on-year growth of 18%, higher than the province's fixed asset investment growth of 3.4%. Tourism investment in the province was 155.26 billion yuan (US$23.46 billion), with an increase of 27%. At present, the concept of region-based tourism has sprung up across the province, which can be seen in the transformation from construction and management of separate tourist sites and attractions to coordinate development of comprehensive destinations, the breakdown of institutional and management barriers of tourist sites and attractions, the integration of regulations and public services, and the coverage of tourism supervision and control; in the transformation from ticket economy to industrial economy; in the transformation from the closed self-circulation to an open mode of integrated "tourism plus" development; in the transformation from the separate operation and harvest of tourism enterprises to the joint construction and sharing of the whole society; in the transformation from the non-official security management within scenic spots and areas to the governance by law; in the transformation from management and regulation of individual departments to that of the Party and the government, so as to form the new development pattern of full coverage, full penetration and full time/space for the region-based tourism.

3. Outstanding Achievements in Targeted Poverty Alleviation by Developing Tourism

Poverty alleviation is a major political task and the livelihood project is to build a well-off society in an all-round way in Henan. Most of the main poverty-stricken areas in Henan lie in the "three mountains and the Yellow River beach" areas with relatively abundant tourism resources, a special advantage that can serve as the foundation of aid-the-poor tourism. In order to ensure the poverty alleviation of one million people and 10 poverty-stricken counties, Henan will take tourism as an efficient means of poverty alleviation, and increase farmers' income by vigorously developing rural tourism. In 2016, through the efforts to promote tourism and poverty alleviation, around the poverty alleviation, we implemented "the project of aid-the-poor tourism with the help of hundreds of masters and agronomists, thousands of entrepreneurs and media professionals, and ten thousands of business founders and volunteers" to mobilize multi-force participation in tourism poverty alleviation. We vigorously carried out tourism project that benefit the people, implemented the poverty alleviation program of tourism, and improved the comprehensive contribution of tourism industry. Aid-the-poor tourism is the "hematopoietic type" of poverty alleviation with great potential, good effects, widespread influence and comprehensive benefits, which is an effective way for poverty alleviation in poor areas and an important way for poor people to get rid of poverty and become better off. The "three mountains and the Yellow River beach" areas are not only the key target of Henan poverty alleviation, but also endowed with relatively rich tourist resources; it is a task we are faced with to make good use of tourism in rural poverty alleviation, and to expand the coverage of aid-the-poor tourism in a reasonable and orderly way. In recent years, governments at all levels in Henan have increased their investment in aid-the-poor tourism, and promoted key environmental remediation, the infrastructure construction of road traffic, water and electricity supply, parking lots, toilets, and sanitation, as well as the construction of other supporting facilities of emergency rescue, signs and marks, leisure facilities, network communications and tourist services for villages through aid-the-poor tourism. We have carried out tourism twinning by organizing large-scale tourism enterprises, travel agencies, hotels and restaurants, tourist sites and attractions, and tourism departments in universities to implement one-on-one help targeted at national key rural villages. By various means including publicity and promotion, organizing tourist sources, attracting investment, home-delivery teaching, labor services and supply of agricultural and sideline products, we strive to help the poor in key villages to increase their income; by implementing "the project of aid-the-poor tourism with the help of hundreds of masters and agronomists, thousands of entrepreneurs and media professionals, and ten thousands of business founders and volunteers", we will make the tourism industry an important force for poverty alleviation.

4. The High Level of Tourism Informatization and Intelligence

The influence of knowledge economy and information technology in the tourism industry is increasingly obvious and profound, "Internet plus" tourism and network publicity has been widely used. The role of the province or regional tourism network information center is becoming more and more obvious. The high-tech content of tourism products is increasing, the demand for high-quality talents is increasing day by day, and the talent competition is becoming more and more intense. At present, new means of information dissemination including micro-blog, WeChat, E-business flagship stores, official websites, and APPs are emerging. OTA (online travel agency), SNS (social networking services) and SEO (search engine optimization) all play certain roles in tourism marketing. In recent years, the WeChat marketing is gaining popularity. WeChat tourism marketing is a quick informative experience, enabling tourists to gain access to information about tourist attractions, weather conditions, hotels, local cuisines, etc. even without leaving their houses. Before travelling, tourists simply need to follow a public account about the tourist attraction they want to go to, and it will provide them with tourist services including electronic tickets, service information, guidance on catering and entertainment, remote reservation, self-guide tour and auto-push of messages. At the same time, tourists can post their own travel needs through mobile phones, and then tourism providers will offer personalized travel services for them through certain assisting APPs. There is no doubt that the development of WeChat tourism in Henan province will make a huge difference for the tourism industry, which will go through another round of growth because of WeChat tourism. In 2016, WeChat tourism marketing in Henan province attracted more and more attention. WeChat tourism marketing of all tourist attractions and tourism bureaus of counties and cities is becoming increasingly popular. WeChat has become a marketing tool that enjoys the most attention from Henan tourism industry because of its many advantages such as powerful social functions, real relationship chains and word-of-mouth communication. The application of WeChat to tourism lies in a large number of fashionable users, consumers familiar with WeChat, and word-of-mouth marketing as the method to attract customers. It has effectively boosted the informed and intelligent development of Henan's tourism industry.

Ⅲ Problems of Tourism Development in Henan

Henan has made remarkable achievements in tourism development, but it still faces some insurmountable problems. For example, as there are more natural landscapes than cultural ones, sightseeing is still the main form of tourism, while holiday tourism is still in the early stage of development. Overseas tourists mainly visit cultural landscapes while tourists from within Henan province mainly visit natural landscapes. There are more and more individual tourists while tourist groups are relatively decreasing. Our tourism services mainly meet low-level and middle-level demands, and standardization and specialization are not sufficient. Most scenic spots are ticket revenue-based, and a large tourism development pattern has not yet formed. With the development of the world economy and the improvement of people's living standards, people's consumption ideas for tourism will change greatly. The diversified tourism demands and the diversification trend of tourism will be formed. The traditional tourism and entertainment methods can not meet the needs of tourists. With the progress in transportation, in particular the rapid development of aviation technology, the average transportation cost is decreasing year by year, and distance will gradually be no restriction on tourism. With more leisure time, long-distance tours are possible for more and more people. And the demand for personalized tourism has become a new situation for the development of tourism in Henan.

1. Mass Sightseeing Agriculture and Backward Brand-based Construction

The development of tourism resources in Henan has made great achievements, but many of them are quantity growth-based. While there is a wide spread of tourism agriculture, and rural tourism, economic gains are low and brand building lags behind. There is a lack of image promotion and brand marketing, product popularity is not high and the tourism image is not clear enough. The tourist sites and attractions lack an awareness of product integration and marketing integration, and the government has not exerted its coordination function very well. It has become the weakest link in the overall development of the tourism industry. Tourism talents basically meet the needs of tourism development, but the talent structure needs to be optimized, and there is a lack of incentive and training mechanism, as well as a lack of professional talents in some aspects. There are other problems: emphasizing projects but ignoring the overall quality, and attaching importance to material resources but neglecting non-material resources; some tourism zones are apt to deviate from their native culture, and move towards modernization, homogenization and assimilation, without any clear differentiation; emphasizing investment but ignoring management; the management system and software construction have become weakness of the tourist industry. The consciousness of big tourism is not strong, the construction of the environment is weak, exploitation is in disorder and fragmentation, lack of coordination between the branches and pieces, lack of coordination among the scenic spots and regions.

2. Insufficient Effective Supplies of Tourism Products, and Small Scale International Market

The new normal of Chinese economy has brought Henan opportunities to develop its tourism industry as well as impacts and challenges. At present, the development of tourism in Henan is mainly sightseeing tourism. The development of high value-added and comprehensive products such as leisure vacation, special tourism and urban tourism is slow, and the primary problem of tourism products is prominent. Relatively speaking, Henan province has more regular sightseeing spots than comprehensive and compound tourism products. Tourism elements are not coordinately allocated, and industry clusters and collective functions not cultivated. Leisure facilities that can meet market demands are relatively limited, with incomplete infrastructure and low-level construction. In general, effective supplies of tourism are insufficient, resulting in too much outflow of tourists, demands and consumption. At present, the tourism market development in Henan province is not mature, segment market structure is imbalanced, regional tourist market concentration is high, the potential tourism market is insufficient; the scale of international tourism market is too small; domestic tourists mainly come from within Henan province, fewer from other parts of China. The development of the tourism market in the three city groups in Inner Bohai, Yangtze River Delta and Pearl River is slow. And well-known brands and leading enterprises with international influence are inadequate. The current international economy struggles to recover and the international tourism growth slows down. China as a whole is under pressure of environmental pollution, and major tourism cities in Henan suffer from heavy smog. In addition, economies in these cities are far from developed, tourism products are of a low level, and service facilities cannot meet requirements. These disadvantages, coupled with lack of direct international flights, result in great difficulties in developing inbound tourist markets.

3. Insufficient Tourism Industrial Chains, and Weak Catalytic Drive

At present, 76% of Henan tourism revenue rely on entrance tickets, much more than average national level.The average price of tickets ranked fourth in the country, and tourism consumption ranked second in the country. In Henan, tickets take up about 40%, food and accommodation another 40% and transportation 15%, but shopping and entertainment jointly take up only about 5%. Especially for some regional sources of tourists and scenic spots featuring one-day tours, no accommodation is needed, which gives ticket sales a greater percentage up to over 50%.This expenditure structure is different from that in areas with a developed tourism industry, where ticket sales take up only a very small percentage of tourism income. The ratio of ticket sales to income from other elements is 1:4.2. Now, in the world, a more advanced practice is to cancel entrance tickets, and promote the concept of the "Grand Tour", especially the development of the tourism industry through tourism consumption generated by the flow of tourist elements, commodity sales and the development and organization of related industries within tourist attractions, so as to promote tourism of the whole region and related economic development. Henan tourism industry chain is short, and the driving and catalytic role of the tourism industry is not enough. The investment subject of tourism is single, degree of market operation is low; the level of international tourist income is unbalanced with the status of resource province; the development of high value added products like tourist shopping, tourist recreation, distinctive food and so on is inadequate; the overall management level of tourist business is not high, tourism industry average profit is obviously lower than societal industry. At present, in Henan province, major industrial elements in tourism are not sufficiently cultivated. The allocation of elements including "food, accommodation, transportation, traveling, shopping and entertainment" is unbalanced, and new elements including "business, health, culture, leisure, delight, adventure" need to be explored. Most tourist attractions only focus on "inviting" tourists instead of trying to make them "stay". Most scenic areas do not have tour lines and lack entertainment facilities. Tourist service centers need to be improved and the industrial chain of tourism needs further integration, the catalytic drive is weak.

4. Backward Tourism Management System, and Inefficient Operating Mechanism

For a long time, Henan tourism industry has been affected by institutional constraints and management fragmentation, rendering tourism resources and interests completely in the hands of separate departments. The ownership, management and right to use are bound together, causing mutual restrictions among departments without systematic coordination. This has seriously affected the establishment of a systematic tourism market and the integration of regional tourism resources and hindered the development of tourism resources so much that many resources with development potential have been poorly developed, maintained and operated, and some resources are simply not developed at all. All tourism resources are state-owned, but managed by local departments, which results in serious local and industrial protectionism. Some local governments and industrial management departments use various means to promote local protectionism for narrowly-focused, partial and short-term economic interests. In the process of exploring tourism resources, property rights and conflicts between local and departmental interests lead to disorderly competition, insufficient cooperation and communication between regions and departments, which further results in a lack of industrial chains. Hence it is impossible to establish overall competitive advantages of regional tourism industry. The development of tourist attractions tends to focus on their own operations without overall coordination and organic correlation between each other. For example, Kaifeng City is one of the seven ancient capitals in China. The Song culture is a competitive resource of Henan with nation-wide reputation, which calls for large-scale and organized development so as to make good use of the overall advantages of resources. However, although various attractions in the city focus on the Song culture, the Millennium City Park, Prefecture of Kaifeng, Longting, Memorial Temple of Lord Bao, Tianbo Yang Fu and the Imperial Street all operate in isolation, featuring small scales, different operating levels, decentralized management, and a lack of mutual cooperation. All these factors seriously influence and restrict the whole presentation of the original image of the ancient capital of the Song Dynasty. The uniqueness of resources cannot be changed into the uniqueness of products and the advantages of the resources cannot be changed into economic advantages.

IV Suggestions on Accelerating the Development of Tourism in Henan Province

In accordance with requirements of the "13th Five-Year Plan" of Henan Tourism Development, in order to improve the development of Henan tourism, we need to focus on the "The Four-Pronged Comprehensive Strategy", three national strategic plannings in Henan province, and the construction of a "prosperous Henan, civilized Henan, safe Henan and beautiful Henan"; adhere to five development concepts of "innovation, coordination, eco-friendliness, opening up, sharing"; adapt to the new normal of economy, and speed up innovation-driven structural reform on the supply side, push tourism exploration to shift from quantity expansion to equal stress on both quantity and quality; push tourism products to shift from sightseeing to an integration of sightseeing, leisure tours and vacation tours; push tourism services to shift from popularization to high-quality, personalization and standardization, make efforts to build famous tourism brands, to promote integration of tourism and other industries, to implement targeted poverty alleviation by the tourism industry, and to optimize market environment; promote the sustainable and sound development of Henan tourism industry, and develop Henan into a great tourism province that is moderately prosperous in all respects.

1. Implementation of High-end Tourist Marketing with the Flagship of "Home in Henan"

First, we should cooperate initiatively with publicity, radio and television, culture and other departments, as well as integrate tourism promotion into the whole province's publicity campaign. Second, build media linkage, regional cooperation platform. Third, carry out activities such as being spokespersons for " Home in Henan", "tour Henan by high-speed railway", hundreds of We-Media giving interviews to "Home in Henan" and a series of theme promotion in Hong Kong, Macao and Taiwan markets, travelling agencies paying visits to Henan, to further enhance the "Home in Henan" brand. We need to establish a study base actively, attracting more Hong Kong, Macao and Taiwan youth to study in Henan. And, fourth, actively prepare for the 2018 China (Zhengzhou) International Tourism City Mayors Forum, hold well the 2017 Asia Pacific Tourism Association of Adventure Tourism Fair and Henan Luoyang Adventure Travel and Equipment Expo, increase the observation point of observation station in Henan of sustainable development of the international tourism organization of the United Nations, play a good display function on the platform for the tourism image in Henan. Fifth, we should launch Henan inbound tourism product promotion and channel construction work in the main tourist market of the Asia Pacific region, North America and Europe, relying on foreign mainstream media and industry channels, to establish a global destination marketing system. To actively participate in the 2017 China-Denmark tourism year, the China- Kazakhstan tourism year and the China-ASEAN tourism cooperation year organized by the National Tourism administration. Sixth is to do a good job of tourism product upgrading, integrate to create, bundle to promote Henan Kung Fu, Dynasty Street and South Taihang, Funiu Mountain Dynasty, Dabie Mountain ECO tour etc series of theme tourism products, to create an international brand with distinctive characteristics, suitable for international tourists cognitive habits and fine lines. Seventh, work with departments concerned, and actively strive for schemes such as the 72-hours transit without visa, departure tax refund, to provide convenient inbound tourism conditions, increasing the scale of inbound tourism. Eighth, build "Henan Tourism News island", build a new pattern of tourism promotion with various tourism official website, the headline number, micro-blog, WeChat, mobile phone newspaper and the mainstream media as the core, with the sharing of the province's tourism system, with a joint participation of a variety of media and social public, and to enhance the promotion of tourism publicity.

2. Create A Tour Belt of Silk Road along the Yellow River and Promote the High-quality Travel Routes

According to the position of Henan province in the national strategy of "the Belt and Road Initiative", relying on the cultural presentation along the Luoyang-Zhengzhou-Kaifeng route, tourism service system should be further improved. We should make good use of advantages of the route in position and transportation, choose appropriate locations along the route and build them into international centers for cultural exchanges and tourists distribution along the Silk Road Economic Belt. At the same time, international tourist trains should be planned and established as soon as possible on the basis of road freight transport along the Silk Road Economic Belt. In the future, tourism trains from Zhengzhou to European countries will pass Urumqi and then Central Asia all the way to Hamburg, Germany, and cover 105 cities in 20 countries in Central Asia and Europe. This is not only a colorful tourism route, but also a cultural exchange route between the east and the west. In addition, Zhengzhou airport has launched more than 180 flights, covering the world's major economies except those in Africa. All these efforts provide precious opportunities for cultural exchanges and tourism. What's worth mentioning is that the overall style of a city is an important part of "the Belt and Road Initiative" tourism, but most cities only pay attention to classic tourist attractions rather than the overall tourism atmosphere, which leads to a sharp contrast between tourist attractions and the city style. Without the whole city as a background, tourist attractions seem isolated and cut off. At the same time, a tourism industry based on several scattered attractions greatly reduces the charm and competitive edge of tourism of a city. Culture is a reflection of a nation's soft power, and the culture of the Central Plains is the origin of the Oriental culture and the core of the Chinese culture. In the future competition against the background of globalization in 21st century, we will not possess enough competitiveness if we cannot reach a certain level of civilization. This refers to economic civilization, political civilization, social civilization as well as ecological civilization put forward by the Eighteenth National Congress of the CPC. Henan province is one of the inheritance and innovation areas of the Chinese culture. It is an important task in the "13th Five-Year Plan" of Henan province to give full play to take advantages of ancient culture and civilization, and demonstrate the cultural brand of the Central Plains civilization along the Silk Road Economic Belt. It is imperative to build international centers for cultural exchanges and tourist distribution.

At present, it is necessary to focus on the promotion of the five tourist routes, and the first one is exploring the origin of China. Zhengzhou (Shaolin Temple, The Centre of Heaven and Earth) - Luoyang (Longmen Grottoes, White Horse Temple) - Kaifeng (the Millennium City Park,) - Anyang (Yin Xu). The second is a journey of ancient capital culture. Anyang (The ancient capital of the Shang Dynasty) - Gongyi (The northern Song Dynasty imperial mausoleum) - Luoyang (Ancient city), Zhengzhou (Central Plains merchants, the ancient capital city of Zheng and Han ruins)-Xuchang (The Cao ancient capital city) - Kaifeng(Ancient capital of Song city) - Shangqiu (ancient city, ancient cultural tourism industry park -Bengbu (Daming Cultural Industrial Park).The third is a journey of Buddhist cultural.Zhengzhou (Shaolin Temple, Zhongyue Temple) - Luoyang (The buddhist cultural park of White Horse Temple, the hometown of Xuan Zang) - Kaifeng (Daxiangguo Temple) - Zhoukou (Taiqing palace in Luyi County).The fourth is a journey of root-kin culture.Anyang(The mausoleums of Zhuanxu and Diku) - Puyang (The cemetery of Zhanghui) - Xinxiang (luwang tomb) - Gongyi (Song Mausoleum Park) - Zhengzhou (the hometown of Huang Di)-Shangqiu (The tomb of Suihuang)- Zhoukou (Taihao Mausoleum in Fu Xi scenic spot). The fifth is a journey of Kongfu culture.Zhengzhou (Shaolin Temple, Songshan, Dengfeng) - Jiaozuo (Tai Chi Temple in Chen village) - Xingtai (the former residence of Yang Luchan, the former residence of Wu Yuxiang).

3. Enhance the Consciousness of Tourism Innovation and Improve Industry Informatization

Innovation is an important propeller for tourism development. In accordance with requirements of the "13th Five-Year Plan" of Henan Tourism Development, focus on the "The Four-Pronged Comprehensive Strategy", three national strategic plannings in Henan province, and the construction of a "prosperous Henan, civilized Henan, safe Henan and beautiful Henan"; adhere to five development concepts of "innovation, coordination, eco-friendliness, opening up, sharing"; adapt to the new normal of economy, and speed up innovation-driven structural reform on the supply side. First, we should attach importance to tourism education and various forms of tourism personnel training, establish innovative incentive mechanisms, strengthen the guidance of tourism innovation, organize tourism research and development, and vigorously promote tourism academic research and application research. Second, we should create conditions for the transformation of tourism scientific and technological achievements with the premise of concept innovation, and actively use advanced technology to transform and arm the tourism industry. Third, promote the innovation and development of mechanism innovation, product innovation, management innovation, marketing innovation, the establishment of the province's tourism service, tourism development mode with Henan characteristics, to promote the development of the tourism industry in innovation. Continue to enrich the mountain resort, cultural experience, tourism, performing arts, health, outdoor sports and other new forms of tourism, further stretching the industrial chain, expanding product system. Fourth, innovate the construction mode of tourism informatizaiton, promote the synchronous integration of provinces and cities, and develop intelligent tourism. To implement tourism informatization, we must improve the level of industry intelligence. We will carry out the "Internet Plus government services" model, offer online administrative approvals for scenic spots, hotels, and travel agencies, set up online offices instead of brick-and-mortar offices for administrative approvals and public services. We will continue to build the monitoring platform of tourism industry, and improve public services for tourism information.

4. Focus on the Cultivation of Henan's Tourist Centers and Continue to Promote the Brand of "Divine Mountain of Zhongyue"

The leading strategy is to give full play to the demonstration effect of flagship tourism products, expand product influence, improve product competitiveness and production capability, and provide more market opportunities for other tourism products in the province. Therefore, in the province and regions we must carefully select, and strongly build the leading scenic spots, increase construction efforts, display at a high level the cultural content, and comprehensively enhance the level of construction and cultural quality. We should strengthen tourism publicity, enhance the image of tourism, and create attractive and influential flagship products to promote the development of tourism in the province and all regions. Now in Henan province, there is still no leading tourist attraction that is world famous and able to function as a tourism engine. Therefore, the whole province should coordinate its efforts, centering on the Greater Songshan Mountain Tourism Area to make a package of Shaolin Temple, Longmen Grottoes and other key tourist attractions within the Greater Songshan Mountain area, to build a leading brand of Henan tourism resources and to make Songshan Mountain "the Holy mountain of China", thereby driving Henan province toward its goal to become a great tourism province. At the same time, we should also actively support Dengfeng in its efforts to build an international tourist destination featuring the Chinese Shaolin Kungfu and continue to promote the construction of Dengfeng as "the capital of Kungfu in the world".

5. Follow the Trend of Future Tourism and Build Leisure and Health Tourist Resorts

At present, Henan tourism is converting from sightseeing tourism to leisure and health tourism. In order to adapt to this trend, we should vigorously promote the construction of leisure tourist resorts near mountains, hot springs, forests and lakes, and health tourist resorts related to traditional Chinese medicine. To meet tourists' needs of wellbeing, physical fitness, health care and health preservation, five health tourism products including Tai Chi regimen, Shaolin Zen and Wu medical regimen, hot springs regimen, traditional Chinese medicine regimen, and Taoism regimen will be launched. The health tourism modes of medical healthcare, hot springs, sports fitness, and Taoism regimen should be correlated with sightseeing and leisure tourism modes and demonstration bases of national health tourism should be set up in Henan province. First, we should speed up efforts to level up the quality of current vacation resorts and expand their scales, complete and intensify their leisure function, and explore unique leisure and vacation projects. In the meantime, we should also focus on protection of ecological environment and natural and cultural landscapes, realizing harmony of artificial buildings and natural landscapes. We should accelerate the construction of south Taihang Mountain tourist resort in Xinxiang, and actively promote the development of tourism products such as leisure tours in mountainous areas, summer vacation, fashion and health tours, thereby building the south Taihang Mountain tourist resort into a famous one at home and abroad, integrating sightseeing, leisure, and other functions. As for Funiu Mountain, we should highlight its ecosystem integrity, biodiversity and unique geological structure, and build it into a world biosphere reserve, a world geological park and a national mountain tourism resort with worldwide influences. We should also regard as driving forces Baiyun Mountain and Chongdugou Ravine in Luoyang, Laojieling Ridge in Nanyang, Yaoshan Mountain in Pingdingshan and Chaya Mountain in Zhumadian, and vigorously develop unique tourism products such as hot springs healthcare, fitness tours, summer vacation on the basis of sightseeing and mountainous leisure tours, thereby forging the Funiu Mountain tourism attraction as a first-class tourist resort for mountainous leisure tours in China. Second, we need to promote the integrated development of Henan tourism industry and traditional Chinese medicine, strengthen the innovation of tourism products related to traditional Chinese medicine, and the opening up and sharing of medical resources, and promote international exchanges and cooperation in traditional Chinese medicine health tours, so as to make the culture of Henan traditional Chinese medicine go international via tourism. Third, we should encourage the development of multi-level and diversified elderly tourism products. In order to adapt to an ageing society and improve the tourist market for senior citizens, in places with good ecological environment, pleasant climate and convenient transportation, we should develop a batch of health tour bases for the elderly that feature leisure vacation, farming experience and rehabilitation recuperation. We should regulate the elderly tourism services, develop old-age support in different places, time-share vacation, etc. The construction of barrier-free facilities for the elderly should be completed in tourist attractions, and enterprises should be encouraged to launch some incentives for elderly tourists such as discounts or free of charge. Norms of personalized tourism service should be established according to needs of the elderly to solve their worries and arouse the enthusiasm of the elderly to travel.

V Outlook for Development of Henan Tourism in 2017

In 2017, Henan tourism will be guided by (the development philosophy of) innovation, coordination, eco-friendliness, opening up, sharing, oriented by adjusting the structure, advancing reform, and benefiting the people, regarded to improve the quality and efficiency of tourism industry development and continue to expand tourism investment and consumption, speed up the structural reform of tourism structural supply reforms, and promote the organic integration of various resources, industrial integration and development, social co-construction and sharing, to build an all-for-one tourism pattern. According to "Several Opinions of the General Office of the State Council on Further Promoting Tourism Investment and Consumption", and documents by the provincial Party committee and provincial government on transformation and upgrading of traditional industries, under the guidance of the provincial "working group for tourism transformation and upgrading", and in accordance with "Work Plan to promote transformation and upgrading of tourism industry" formulated by the Provincial Bureau of Tourism, we should promote the continuous growth of tourism investment and consumption, deepen the comprehensive reform of tourism, promote the development of the whole world tourism, and realize the transformation and upgrading of the tourism industry. Tourism resources, in particular, are rich in northern Henan, and some resources are peculiar to the local area, which will be a good foundation of transformation and upgrading. We should carefully grasp the current tourism development opportunities, and actively adapt to the needs of tourists, and effectively realize the transformation and upgrading of the tourism industry. In terms of upgrading, we should create more tourism products, improve the quality of tourism products, enhance the level of tourism services and better meet the needs of tourists; in terms of transformation, we should speed up the transition from ticket economy to industrial economy, by stretching the industrial chain, to form three-dimensional income, and improve income levels; we should actively expand markets in other provinces, as well as overseas markets, make abundant the supply of tourism products, improve food, accommodation, transportation, travel, shopping and entertainment etc, further enhance the overall level of consumption and improve the tourism comprehensive income, so as to promote the sustainable and sound development of the province's economy and society, and to improve the people's happiness index.

References:

[1] Xu Shaoli. "Thoughts and Strategies of Coordinated Development of Tourism in Central Plains Economic Zone"[J]. *IEEE Spectrum*,2013,6.

[2] Feng Dexian. "Study on the Development of Tourism Industrialization in Henan Province" [J]. *Areal Research and Development* 2005,03:57-62.

[3] lv Lianqin. "Problems and Countermeasures of Mountain Tourism Development in Henan Province" [J]. *Areal Research and Development* 2006,03:60-64.

[4] Zhao Zongbiao. "Study on the Development of Revolutionary Tourism in Henan Province"[J]. *Areal Research and Development* 2006,05:76-79.

[5] Zhang Chunxiang. "Strategic Thinking on the Development of Cultural Tourism Industry in Henan Province"[J]. *Journal of Xinyang Teachers College* (Philosophy and Social Science Edition) 2006,06:76-79.

[6] Shan Jianxin. "Research on Shaolin Wushu Cultural Tourism Development in Henan Province" [D]. Central China Normal University, 2008.

[7] Shi Benlin, Zhang Hongna, Meng Deyou, Li Hongzhong. "Regional Disparity and Polarization Pattern of Inbound Tourism Economy in Henan Province"[J]. *Areal Research and Development.* 2011,02:128-132+160.

[8] He Xinnian. "Characteristics and Development of Cultural Tourism Resources in Henan Province" [J]. *Academic Journal of Zhongzhou* 2004,01:21-23.

[9] He Zhen. "Study on the Influence Factors of Tourism Income — Taking Henan as an Example" [J]. *On Economic Problems*.2009,08:121-122.

[10] Li Gengxiang. "'Tourism Province' strategy and Henan cultural tourism industry"[J]. *Journal of North China Institute*,2010,01:49-54.

B.7
Report on Urban Development of Henan Province

Research Team of Henan Academy of Social Sciences

Abstract: From 2012 to 2016, with the city cluster as the main form, Henan has given full play to the guiding role of planning, promoted the development of city-industry integration, and optimized the spatial layout of urbanization, accelerating the process of urbanization with its quality improved. However, there are still issues surrounding the urbanization of Henan, for example, the overall level of urbanization still lags behind, the driving force of major cities is weak and the overall carrying capacity of cities and towns needs to be improved. The State Council approved the "The Development Planning of City Cluster in Central Regions", which marked Henan province as having entered the city cluster era. It also required that we should make full use of the historic opportunity, that is, the central government is adopting more scientific guidelines and initiatives in promoting the new urbanization and urban development. We should give full play to the active role of the market, improve the operation and coordination mechanism as well as other integrated measures, promote the integration of city clusters in central regions, and release the huge potential of domestic demand in the new urbanization, in order to provide strong and lasting impetus for the healthy and sustainable development of the economy.

Keywords: City Cluster in Central Regions; New Urbanization; Urban Development

I Practices and Achievements in the New Urbanization with City Cluster in Central Regions Playing the Leading Role in Henan Province

In 2016, "The Development Planning of City Cluster in Central Regions" won approval of the State Council. It marked that the city cluster in central regions officially entered the rank of the seven major city cluster in China, and became another national strategic plan undertaken by Henan province. With the integration of city cluster in central regions as the lead, Henan province has attached great importance to new urbanization, top-level design and planning to build core growth area and optimize the urban spatial layout, actively promoted the differentiated development of cities concerned, adhered to the priority of integrated transportation and promoted connectivity. With these measures, regional cooperation has been accelerated and remarkable results have been achieved, with the quality of urbanization improved and the urbanization rate increased from 42.43% in 2012 to 48.5% in 2016, an increase of 6.07 points, creating a new prospect for development.

1. Major Practices

We have given full play to the leading role of planning. We have drawn up a sound development planning of city cluster in central regions, specifying strategic positioning, development path and the main goal, and have formed a clear development concept of building "one core, four axes and four zones", pointing out the direction and providing important strategic support for sustainable and healthy development of Henan urbanization. The CPC Henan Provincial Committee and Henan Provincial Government have always put new urbanization high on the list of priorities as it concerns the overall economic and social development, and continued to improve the guidelines and initiatives of development, with the quality and level of urbanization rapidly promoted. The "13th Five-Year Plan on Economic and Social Development in Henan Province" clearly stated that we should "accelerate the integrated development of city cluster in central regions, give full play to the role of new urbanization in promoting the development of the whole region, accelerate the formation of new relations between urban and rural areas, promote equal exchange of urban and rural elements, rational allocation and equal access to basic public services, and realize the goal of common prosperity and coordinated development of urban and rural areas." The "13th Five-Year Plan on Housing and Urban-Rural Development in Henan Province" has put forward the idea of optimizing the pattern and forms of urbanization, highlighting the city cluster as the main form, tapping the full potential of major cities to drive the development of their surrounding areas, with center-oriented development, differentiated development, coordinated development as basic principles, accelerating the integration of transportation, industry links, service sharing, and coordinated development of ecology and landscape, in order to establish the modern urban system characterized by coordinated development of large, small and medium-sized cities as well as small towns.

To guide urban and rural planning in a more scientific way, Henan province has studied and formulated guidelines for planning of the demonstration zone of urban-rural integration, guidelines for planning of the county-level city, guidelines for planning of the key town, guidelines for urban design and other guidance documents. Centering on the development of the spatial pattern of "one core, four axes and four zones", we have actively carried out the construction of clusters of cities and towns in the shape of the Chinese character "米". We have essentially completed the pilot project of demarcating boundary for urban development in Zhengzhou, finished the overall planning for cities of Xuchang, Xinyang, Puyang and Shangqiu, and won the approval of the State Council for the overall planning of Anyang and Pingdingshan. We have finished the overall planning for 30 counties (cities) and the planning of building the new countryside for 27 pilot counties (cities), and steadily promoted the development of 109 model towns and 112 model villages. To accelerate the development of the regional ecological network of "four zones and three belts", we have completed the overall planning for the scenic spots, including the Yellow River, Huaiyuan in Tongbai county, and Baiyun Mountain, to provide a green, low-carbon and efficient industrial system and the spatial pattern for the development of the new urbanization. We have actively promoted the planning and construction of carriers. The revision of the spatial and regulatory planning of certain industry clusters has been launched. We have also adjusted planning for 19 central business districts and business districts with unique characteristics, which will cover an area of 33.3 square kilometers. The area of public green space and the length of roads and water pipes have increased by more than 20% compared with the same period last year.

We have strengthened the development of core areas. The "Development Planning of City Cluster in Central Regions" has stated clearly that, we should take the Zhengzhou metropolitan area as an important starting point to enhance the core competitiveness of the city clusters. Through consolidating the status of Zhengzhou as the door in opening up and its central position in national allocation of resources, enhancing its function as a transportation hub, attracting high-end industry, improving comprehensive service, and promoting the integration of Zhengzhou and the neighboring cities, we should build the Zhengzhou metropolitan area into a core area that can drive the development of the surrounding areas, and extend its influence to the whole nation, with connection to the world. The 10th CPC Congress of Henan province has also proposed that we should promote the integration of Zhengzhou and the neighboring cities, enhance the in-depth integration of Zhengzhou and Kaifeng, accelerate the integration of Zhengzhou and Xinxiang, Zhengzhou and Xuchang, together with Zhengzhou and Jiaozuo, build the combined metropolitan area, and enhance Zhengzhou's driving force for the entire province. In order to build a powerful engine of development, we have intensified our efforts to implement the strategy of tapping the full potential of major cities to drive the development of their surrounding areas. We have promoted the formation of the combined conglomeration of the metropolitan area covering Zhengzhou and the neighboring cities. We have further promoted the combined development of the regional major cities. With these measures, Zhengzhou's status as the regional center in our country has been further strengthened. With Zhengzhou metropolitan area as the core, we have sped up the development of the spatial pattern of "one core, four axes and four zones", which can drive the development of the whole province and certain cities in the neighbouring provinces, with the strength of city cluster in central regions growing and the overall competitiveness of central region's economic zone greatly enhanced. In 2015, the urban population in Zhengzhou metropolitan area was over 16.29 million, among which permanent urban residents in the central area of Zhengzhou City reached 9.56 million, and the urban built-up area of the central city was 443.04 square kilometers.

With the goal of building Zhengzhou into the national center city being put forward, and the development of Zhengzhou Airport Economy Zone, Zheng-Luo-Xin National Innovation Demonstration Zone, as well as China (Henan) Pilot Free Trade Zone, and Cross-Border E-Commerce Pilot Zone being carried out, we have gradually formulated the idea that "the development of transportation hub drives the development of logistics, the development of logistics drives the development of industry clusters, and the development of industry clusters drives the development of city clusters". At present, a three-dimensional transportation network of railway, highway, and aviation emerged in Zhengzhou, where Beijing-Guangzhou railway, Lanzhou-Lianyungang Railway, Beijing-Guangzhou high-speed railway and Xuzhou-Lanzhou high-speed railway meet, forming the "double cross" intersection of national railways. With the acceleration of the preliminary work for the construction of high-speed railways from Zhengzhou to Chongqing, Hefei, Ji'nan, Taiyuan and other cities as well as the construction of inter-city railways from Zhengzhou to Kaifeng, Jiaozuo, Zhengzhou airport and other places, the high-speed railway network in the shape of the Chinese character " 米 " with Zhengzhou at its core and the inter-city railway network of city cluster in central regions are taking shape. The civil aviation transportation system and airline network which combine trunk aircraft and feeder aircraft, center on freight, and highlight transit have emerged. The convenient transportation system is not only the premise and basic condition for the formation of the Zhengzhou metropolitan area, an important starting point for city cluster in central regions to lead the new urbanization in Zhengzhou metropolitan area, but also an important support for the formation of urban spatial pattern.

We have optimized the urban spatial layout. First, we have established a network spatial pattern of "one core, four axes and four zones". In accordance with the basic principles of taping the full potential of major cities to drive the development of other cities, developing economic axis, upgrading the node cities, integrating neighbouring cities, promoting the reasonable division of work, complementary functions, and collaborative development of large, small and medium-sized cities as well as small towns, we have taken concerted effort in working out "The Development Planning of City Cluster in Central Regions". We have established the integrated transportation system in the shape of the Chinese character " 米 ", with Zhengzhou metropolitan area at its core and with the support of the economic axis of Lanzhou-Lianyungang, Beijing-

Guangzhou, Ji'nan-Zhengzhou-Chongqing, Taiyuan-Zhengzhou-Hefei. We have developed the spatial pattern of "one core, four axes and four zones", including the demonstration zone of cross regional collaborative development in the north, the demonstration zone of undertaking industrial transfer in the east, the demonstration zone of transformation and innovation in the west, and the high-efficiency ecological economic zone in the south. As a result, the coordinated urban and rural development has been further promoted. Second, we have continued to enhance the driving force of regional central cities. We have accelerated the transformation of Luoyang, the old industrial base, promoted the development of Kaifeng as the new sub-center city, and promoted the development of the Kaifeng-Zhengzhou Airport Economic Belt, Zhengzhou and Kaifeng Industry-University-Research Demonstration Zone, and the Ecological Zone along the Yellow River, enhancing the coordinated development of Zhengzhou and Kaifeng and upgrading their integration. Third, we have continued to promote the combined development of other regional central cities and coordinated the development of demonstration zone of integrated urban and rural development as well as upgrading of old towns in the city. Xuchang, Puyang, Luohe, Anyang and Pingdingshan have successively completed the overall planning for the combined development of major cities. We have strived to strengthen the development of infrastructure and public service systems, guide the sound distribution of industries and optimize the industrial division of labor and layout between the central areas and other areas. Last, we have continued to improve the development of villages and towns, and actively cultivated and developed small towns with local characteristics. We have studied and drafted the guidance for development of small towns with local characteristics. Four towns, namely, Zhaobao town in Wenxian county, Shenhou town in Yuzhou city, Taiping town in Xixia county, and Zhugou town in Queshan county have been listed in the batch of National Small Towns with Local Characteristics. We have strived to protect and develop traditional settlements, and studied and issued the "Opinions on Conservation and Development of Traditional Villages". We have secured 208 million yuan (US$ 31.5 million) from the central and provincial special funds. And 25 villages have been included in the fourth batch of Chinese Traditional Villages List.

We have strived to promote the differentiated development of cities. In the process of coordination and integration among city clusters, each city should, based on its connection with the regional central city, study and adjust its own development for a proper position among the city cluster, especially its industrial orientation, thus actively promoting differentiated development of city clusters. In an effort to develop into the National Central City, Zhengzhou has continued to strengthen its roles as the logistics and business center, comprehensive transportation hub, the modern service center and the door of opening up in the central and western regions. Zhengzhou has enhanced its driving force at home and resource integration capability abroad, promoted the integration of Kaifeng, Xinxiang, Jiaozuo, and Xuchang, built a modern metropolis, promoted the coordinated development of Luoyang, Pingdingshan, Luohe, Jiyuan and other cities, and formed the core area of the development of the city cluster. Luoyang has been oriented as the sub-center city in the city cluster in central regions, an important national base of advanced manufacturing industry, national historical and cultural city, famous tourist city and the major node city in the Economic Corridor in the new Eurasian Continental Bridge. Anyang has been oriented to become the regional center of Henan, Shanxi and Hebei provinces, the new industrial base, regional node city of national transportation and logistics, the national historical and cultural city. Nanyang has strived to develop new energy and equipment manufacturing industry and become the national model city of efficient ecological economy. Shangqiu aimed to become the regional center of Henan, Jiangsu and Anhui provinces, and an important regional transportation hub and logistics center. Focusing on the development of central cities, we have strived to develop small cities, so that county-level cities would become an important link between urban and rural areas. We have given full play to their positive role in promoting urban and rural exchange of goods and materials, development of agricultural commodity and the development of township enterprises, so that county-level cities became an important node of urban and rural interaction in the city clusters.

We have given priority to the development of integrated transportation. We have actively promoted the construction of transport infrastructure, continued to upgrade the level of interconnection and modernization, and accelerated the development of a network of infrastructure with sound distribution, complete functions and high efficiency. To maintain an unimpeded international transportation channel, we have intensified the role of Zhengzhou Airport Economy Zone as the door of opening up, positively opened new routes, increased the number of flights, and established the "double hub" of aviation and railroad logistics home and abroad. To fully integrate into the "The Belt and Road Initiative", and enhance the driving force of the main node cities along the Silk Road, namely, Zhengzhou and Luoyang, we have actively promoted the connectivity of transportation, information communication, and the platform of open ports, and opened Zhengzhou-Europe train ferries with multiple exit ports, multi-line operation, multi suppliers and permanent go-and-return pattern. In the construction of integrated transportation corridor, we have put in full swing the development of high-speed railway network in the shape of the Chinese character " 米 ", accelerated the construction of Zhengzhou-Hefei high-speed railway, Zhengzhou-Ji'nan high-speed railway, and channels along the railway, and formed the great channel to contact the outside world with Beijing-Guangzhou railway, Lanzhou-Lianyungang railway, Beijing-Zhuhai expressway, and Lianhuo expressway as the main framework. To complete the inter-city network between the city clusters, we have strived to build the Zhengzhou metropolitan transportation network, vigorously developed rail transportation, established various express trains, including Zhengzhou-Airport Economy Zone, Airport Economy Zone-Kaifeng, Airport Economy Zone-Xuchang, Zhengzhou-Xinxiang, and Zhengzhou-Kaifeng, and compound fast lanes connecting central cities, central city and the neighboring cities, and small towns. At the same time, we should speed up the construction of urban and rural roads, increase road density, complete the local highway network, achieve the goal of "highway available in every county, asphalt road and bus available in every village", and thus we can further enhance the capacity of regional transportation of city cluster in central regions.

We have accelerated regional cooperation. With the continuous expansion of population, economic scale and the framework of the city, and the development of highways, inter-city rails and other convenient transportation infrastructure, Zhengzhou has become more and more closely connected with the neighboring cities like Xinxiang, Jiaozuo, Kaifeng, Xuchang and other distant regions. With the Zhengzhou-Kaifeng integration being thoroughly carried out, Henan province Development and Reform Commission, Zhengzhou Municipal Government, and Kaifeng Municipal Government have signed the "Framework Agreement on Further Acceleration of the Development of Zhengzhou-Kaifeng Integration". According to the "Agreement", the three parties would establish a joint meeting system, with director of the Provincial Development and Reform Commission and the mayors of the two cities present. Zhengzhou and Kaifeng would also establish and improve an integration system to carry out practical cooperation in seven aspects to jointly promote their integration. With the completion of Zhengzhou-Kaifeng expressway and Zhengzhou-Kaifeng inter-city railway, Zhengzhou-Kaifeng integration has entered the fast lane. And the Zhengzhou-Xinxiang integration has entered a better era. To seek new development strength, Xinxiang has strived to be integrated into Zhengzhou development. In accordance with the guideline of "taking the advantage of developing Zhengzhou Airport Economy Zone, building Zhengzhou metropolitan area through joint efforts, undertaking great responsibilities, and formulating concerted effort", the "three zones and one belt" has become the frontier of Xinxiang's integration with Zhengzhou. In recent years, 1/4 of the industrial transfer projects undertaken by Xinxiang are from Zhengzhou, most of which were in the "three zones and one belt" area, namely, Pingyuan Demonstration Zone in Xinxiang, Yuanyang Industry Cluster Zone, Kangcun Special Zone and the belt area connecting them. Ever since its foundation in 2010, the Pingyuan Demonstration Zone has been branded with the mark of Zhengzhou-Xinxiang integration, such as support of Zhengzhou, coordinated development, and complementary advantages, and it has become an important link of the Zhengzhou-Xinxiang integration. Relying on the industry cluster area, Yuanyang county has undertaken the industries transferred from Zhengzhou in a clustering manner. Among the 175 industrial projects in Yuanyang Industry Cluster Area, 135 have been transferred from Zhengzhou. Zhengzhou-Jiaozuo integration has continued to be accelerated. With the completion of Zhengyun highway (Zhengzhou-Yuntai Mountain), the operation of Zhengzhou-Jiaozuo inter-city railway and the construction of the Yellow River Bridge along the South extension of Yingbin Road, Zhengzhou and Jiaozuo were more closely linked. Integration is being enhanced in the flow of labor, logistics, information, in the coordinated development of economy of Zhengzhou and Jiaozuo, in infrastructure construction and the industrial space layout. Wuzhi county, as the forefront of Jiaozuo's integration with Zhengzhou, has been fully integrated into the "economic circle within 15 minutes' drive" of Zhengzhou. In industry, seizing opportunity of transformation in Zhengzhou and enterprise relocation, Wuzhi has introduced a number of key projects covering abrasives, mechanical equipment and auto parts. In education, Wuzhi has successfully attracted Huanghe Jiaotong University to settle in Wuzhi. Its neighboring Wenxian county has also took an active part in its integration with Zhengzhou. In 2016 Wenxian county and Jinshui district in Zhengzhou successfully signed the "Cooperation Framework of the Enclave Economy Projects", which was an important measure to solve the bottleneck issue in their development. The integration of Zhengzhou and Xuchang has been carried out in a vigorous manner. With the continuous expansion of Zhengzhou to the east and the south, Zhengzhou's driving force to Xuchang has been significantly enhanced. To promote its spatial integration with Zhengzhou, Xuchang, relying on the National Highway 107, has planned the Xuchang-Changge Urban and Rural Coordination Pilot Zone, which was located between Beijing-Guangzhou railway and Beijing-Zhuhai expressway. To facilitate the Zhengzhou Airport Economy Zone, Xuchang has planned the establishment of a special zone with an area of 150 square kilometers. Transportation between the two cities has also been gradually intensified.

2. Achievements Gained

The level of new urbanization has continued to be improved. Focusing on active and steady advancement of new urbanization that puts people's interests in the first place, we have insisted on attaching great importance to new urbanization as it concerns the overall economic and social development, and continued to improve the guidelines and initiatives of development, with the quality and level of urbanization rapidly promoted. From 2012 to 2016, the total population of Henan province has increased from 105.43 million to 107.8814 million, an increase of 2.45 million, 61.2% of which are in urban areas. By 2016, permanent urban residents have accounted for 57.35% of population in Henan, a 4.78 points increase from the end of 2012 and an average annual increase of 1.2%. Population covered by the urbanization has increased from 44.7339 million to 46.2322 million, an increase of 1.5 million, driving the huge demand for investment and consumption (Figure 1). We have intensified our efforts to implement the strategy of tapping the full potential of major cities to drive the development of their surrounding areas. With the strength of the city cluster in central regions improved, it has become one of the three major city clusters in central and western regions whose development have been given priority by the central government. The development of Zhengzhou Airport Economy Zone has been put in full swing, strengthening its status as the regional center in China. The in-depth development of the integration of Zhengzhou and Kaifeng has been further promoted with integrated telecom and financial services. The driving force of central cities has been enhanced, the combined development has been further promoted, and the carrying capacity of counties has continued to increase. By the end of 2015, the number of cities with an urban population of more than 200, 000 has reached 39, and the number of designated towns has reached 1,103. The new pattern, highlighting city cluster and coordinating development of large, small and medium-sized cities as well as small towns, has taken shape. During the "12th Five-Year" period, the implementation of the overall planning of Zhengzhou, Luoyang, Xinxiang, Luohe, Zhumadian, Jiyuan and other cities have won approval. A new round of revision of the overall planning in 10 counties (cities) and 60 counties, county-level cities has been completed. The system planning of 78 county (city, district) level villages and towns has been submitted for approval. The revision of the overall planning in 782 villages and towns has been completed. We have completed the formulation of the planning for historical and cultural cities, towns, villages, traditional settlements, and the scenic spots, further improving the scientific review and effective implementation of planning. For the successful completion of the objectives and tasks, great efforts have been made to redevelop run-down areas, carry out centralized supervision, and crack the bottleneck of funds. "Guiding Opinions on Accelerating the Monetized Resettlement of Shantytown Area" has been issued as guidance for local government to improve the rate of monetary settlement through a variety of ways, such as government purchase of commercial housing, group purchase of commercial housing, and direct monetary compensation. By the end of October 2016, the number of monetized resettlements has reached 122,000 units (households), accounting for 31.4% of the total. We have accelerated renovation of dilapidated houses in rural areas, actively carried out on-site supervision and inspection, and established systems like ranking notification system, monthly reporting system, and interview systems. By the end of October 2016, the operating rate has reached 80.6%, with a 45.2% completion rate. We have launched the "Project of Quality Improvement in Urban Construction" and approved the "Opinions on Implementation of Project of Quality Improvement in Urban Construction", according to which, the number of the first batch of counties (cities) to implement the project was 31, with 2,940 planned projects and a total investment of 430 billion yuan (US $ 65.2 billion).

The development pattern of the regional center has been further optimized. As the sub-center city of city cluster in central regions, Luoyang has witnessed a new

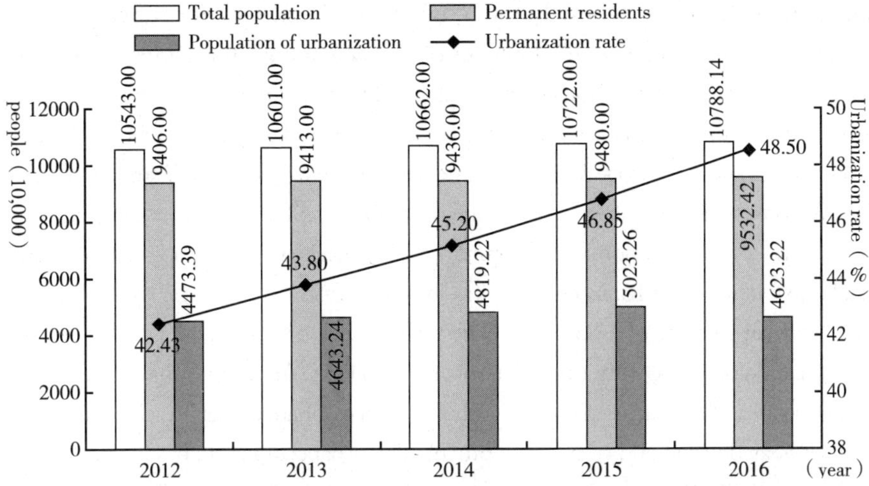

Figure 1 Total population, permanent residents, population of urbanization and urbanization rate of Henan province from 2012-2016

Data source: *Henan Statistical Yearbook (2016)*, *China Statistical Yearbook (2016)*, *Statistical Communique of National Economic and Social Development in Henan in 2016*, websites of National Bureau of Statistics of the People's Republic of China.

situation in the urban and rural integration, and has been listed as one of the first pilot cities of new urbanization in China. The urbanization rate of Luoyang has increased from 47.93% in 2012 to 54.35% in 2016, an increase of 6.42 points. The Core Area and the Yibin New District have taken shape, with a built-up area of 69 square kilometers. Luoyang has been included in the first batch of the National Pilot Smart City. The development of a number of new districts in counties has made great progress, and the development of cultural towns with local characteristics, scenic towns and industrial towns have shown vigorous dynamism. Remarkable achievements have been made in the development of the new countryside in Luoyang, and therefore it has been listed as the model city for improving the rural living environment in Henan. As the regional center located at the bordering area of Henan, Shanxi and Hebei provinces, Anyang has continued to strengthen the leading role of the new urbanization and increase investment in infrastructure. With constant improvement of city function, the overall carrying capacity has been greatly enhanced. The urbanization rate has increased from 42.43% in 2012 to 53.78% in 2016, an increase of 11.35 points. With the completion of Linzhou-Changzhi expressway, Beijing-Guangzhou high-speed railway, and Anyang section of the Shanxi-Henan-

Shandong railway, the railway hub of "two vertical and one horizontal axis" has been basically formed. The development of Anyang airport, the express loop in the northwest, and Anyang section of the Linzhou-Ruzhou expressway have been actively promoted. As the regional center of the bordering area of Henan, Hubei and Shaanxi provinces, Nanyang has vigorously implemented the "two wheel drive" strategy, tapping the full potential of core areas to drive the development of their surrounding areas and promoting county's economic development. With accelerated development of urban-rural integration, the urbanization rate has increased from 34.85% in 2012 to 43.7% in 2016, with an increase of 8.85 points. The built-up area of the central area has reached 120 square kilometers, with a population of 1.2 million. As the regional center of the bordering area of Henan, Jiangsu and Anhui provinces, Shangqiu has accelerated its pace of coordinated urban and rural development. The urbanization rate has increased from 40.2% in 2012 to 49% in 2016, an increase of 8.8 points in five years. The driving force of the city center has been significantly promoted. Urban and rural infrastructure and public facilities have been inter-linked, jointly built and shared. With the completion of the Shangqiu-Zhoukou expressway and Shangqiu-Dengfeng expressway, Zhengzhou-Xuzhou high-speed railway, and Shangqiu-Hefei-Hangzhou high-speed railway, the comprehensive transportation hub has taken shape, including high-speed railway, airports, expressways, and water transportation. Thus, after Zhengzhou, Shangqiu has become another transportation hub of high-speed railway (Figure 2).

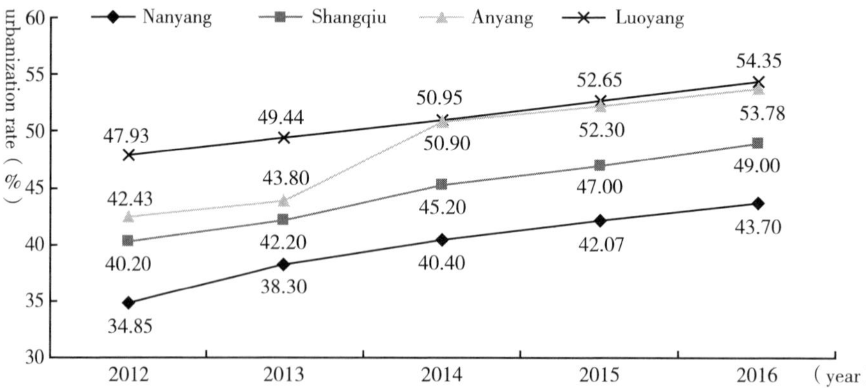

Figure 2 Urbanization rate in Luoyang, Anyang, Nanyang and Shangqiu from 2012 to 2016

Data source: *Henan Statistical Yearbook (2016)*, *China Statistical Yearbook (2016)*, "2017 Luoyang Report on the Work of the Government", "2017 Anyang Report on the Work of the Government", "2017 Nanyang Report on the Work of the Government", "2017 Shangqiu Report on the Work of the Government".

The management of urban and rural development has been put in full swing. With the implementation of the three-year action plan of urban and rural development and promotion of the expansion and improvement of urban development, there has been significant improvement in the overall carrying capacity and capacity to prevent and mitigate disasters of cities and towns. During the "12th Five-Year" period, the actual investment in construction of urban infrastructure in Henan province has reached 1005.699 billion yuan (US $ 152.4 billion). By 2016, the daily processing capacity of city sewage treatment plant has reached 148.23 million cubic meters, with an increase of 26.3% compared with the end of 2012. The rate of pollution-free disposal for urban household solid waste has reached 95%, with an increase of 10.2 points. The ratio of green space has reached 36.4%, with an increase of 0.7 points. We have built 48 water supply plants to support the South-to-North water diversion, and the popularity rate of urban public water supply and gas has reached 93.38% and 90% respectively. Central heating area has reached 227.24 million square meters. By January 12, 2017, Zhengzhou Metro Line 1 (26.2km for Phase 1 and 15.1 km for Phase 2), Line 2 (20.65 km for Phase 1), and suburban line (31.7 km for Phase 1) have been put into operation, with the total mileage of 93.65 km. We have actively expanded the green space and improved its function, improving quality of urban environment. By the end of 2016, the per capita green area in urban parks has reached 10 square meters, and the number of gardens has ranked third in the country. Xuchang has won the title of National Water-Saving City. Changyuan and two other counties have been included in the list of National Garden County. Zhulin town and two other towns have won the title of National Garden Township for the first time. Comprehensive improvement of villages and renovation of dilapidated houses in rural areas have been promoted, with treatment of rural household solid waste and sewage coordinated. As a result, the quality of urban and rural living environment has been notably improved. During the "12th Five-Year" period, the cumulative funding to support 1.2378 million farmers with the renovation of dilapidated houses has reached 9.503 billion yuan (US$ 1.4 billion). We have strengthened the comprehensive improvement of urban environment, with urban refinement management level continuing to improve. The pilot construction of Sponge City and the urban utility tunnels have been launched and achieved initial results, with Hebi City included in the first batch of national pilot Sponge City. By the end of 2016, digital urban management system has covered most cities. Xuchang and Luoyang have been awarded the "China Habitat Environment Award" and "2014 Excellent Award of China Geographic Information Society" respectively for their digital urban management systems. Zhengzhou and the other ten cities (districts) have been included in the National Pilot Smart City (District, Town). We have actively carried out the pilot demonstration of development of the livable countryside, and developed landscape tourist town (village) with its own characteristics. A total of 7 villages and towns have been listed as the Model of Livable Town and Village, and 19 villages have been included in the list of Chinese Traditional Villages.

The interconnected system of infrastructure network has taken shape. From 2012 to 2016, the actual investment in construction of urban infrastructure in Henan province has reached 2191.555 billion yuan (US $ 332.1 billion), with an average growth of 20.38% (Figure 3). The railway mileage has increased from 98 thousand kilometers to 1,240 thousand kilometers. And the mileage of the high-speed railway has increased from less than 10 thousand kilometers to more than 22 thousand kilometers, ranking first in the world. Highway mileage has increased from 4.24 million kilometers to 4.7 million kilometers, among which the mileage of the expressway has increased from 96 thousand kilometers to 131 thousand kilometers, ranking first in the world. The scheduled flight mileage has increased from 3.28 million kilometers to 6.35 million kilometers. The modern and efficient urban rail transit has developed rapidly. By the end of 2016, the urban rail transit line has covered 4,153 kilometers, and the number of cities with operating routes has reached 30. Zhengzhou's status as the modern integrated transportation hub has been consolidated. On the one hand, the construction of Zhengzhou Airport Economy Zone, railway port, highway port, freight station and Logistics Park has been accelerated. The construction of the International Cargo Transportation Center in the north cargo area in Xinzheng International Airport in Zhengzhou, Distribution Center of Air Express Public Service, Wholesale Trading Center of Imported Cold Chain Food, Logistics Center of Cross-Border Electronic Commerce, Collecting and Distributing Center of Logistics, Industrial Park of SF Electronic Commerce, Processing Center of Chinese Postal Air Mail, and logistics bases in Putian, Xuedian, and Guan Yu Temple has been initiated. On the other hand, the function of the three passenger transportation hubs, namely, Zhengzhou

Railway Station, Zhengzhoudong Railway Station, and Zhengzhou Xinzheng International Airport has continued to improve, the project of the first CAT II-operating runway and the auxiliary projects matching the function of double terminals have been completed. The function of Zhengzhouxi Railway Station has been enhanced. Construction of Zhengzhounan Railway Station and Long-distance Passenger South Station, North Station in Zhengzhou Airport Economy Zone and other projects of road transport station have been launched. The layout of the entrance to expressway in Zhengzhou metropolitan area has continued to be optimized. The construction of the second phase of airport-Xihua expressway and eastward reconstruction of National Highway 107 has been completed. The expressway network of "two vertical and three horizontal axis" and the road network of "four vertical and four horizontal axis" in Zhengzhou Airport Economy Zone have been further improved. The function of the regional hub has continued to be strengthened. Construction of feeder route airport, general airport, high-speed railway station, inter-city railway station, port and road transport hub station and other facilities have been launched. Reconstruction and upgrading of the Luoyang Railway Station, Luoyang Longmen high-speed railway station have been implemented. The construction of Zhoukou, Luohe, Shangqiu, Xinyang and other important regional ports has been accelerated. The development of inter-city transportation has continued to be accelerated. Focusing on the development of rail transportation, we have strengthened connection between cities, forming an inter-city transportation network with rail transportation, expressways and fast track as the main framework. The construction of the intercity railway from Xinzheng Airport to Zhengzhounan Railway Station has been launched. The construction of the inter-city railway from Lankao to Heze, from Zhengzhounan Railway Station to Dengfeng to Luoyang, from Jiaozuo to Jiyuan to Luoyang and inter-city railway extension line from Zhengzhou to Kaifeng has been accelerated. Zhengzhou Metro Line 1 and Line 2 have been completed and put into operation, with the construction of Zhengzhou Metro Line 3, Line 4 and Line 5 accelerated. The construction of Luoyang urban rail transit has been launched.

The pattern of urban differentiated development has emerged. Zhengzhou, the core of city cluster in central regions, has taken an active role in the establishment of a modern industrial system with strength, local characteristics and core

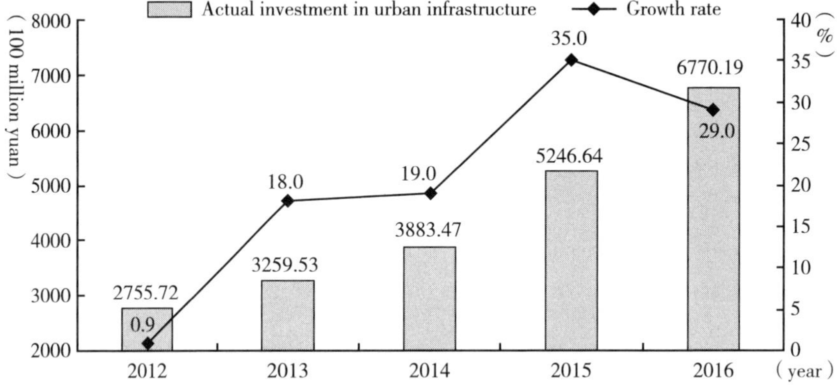

Figure 3 The actual investment in urban infrastructure and its growth rate in Henan province from 2012 to 2016

Data source: *Henan Statistical Yearbook (2016)*, *China Statistical Yearbook (2016)*.

competitiveness. Focusing on the service industry, with high-end manufacturing as support and technological innovation as the driving force, Zhengzhou has greatly enhanced its role in promoting the developoment of neighbouring cities. Luoyang has focused on the five pillar industries of equipment manufacturing, namely, large sets of equipment, agricultural machinery, construction machinery, transportation equipment, as well as the bearings and basic components, providing industrial support for the development of city clusters in central regions. Xuchang has focused on labor intensive industry, with power equipment, tobacco, diamond, hair products, etc. as its pillar industries. Jiaozuo has further highlighted regional advanced manufacturing base, covering intelligent manufacturing, biological medicine, new energy and new materials. To meet the requirement of extended industrial chains and interdepended industries, with the industrial agglomeration area as the carrier, Jiaozuo has taken the initiative to integrate with Zhengzhou and accelerated the industry cooperation, interconnectivity of infrastructure, development and sharing of public service with Zhengzhou. Kaifeng has taken the advantage of its agricultural products and tourism. The pillar industries of Xinxiang are textile, electronics, electrical appliances, machinery, chemical industry, medicine, and construction materials. The pillar industries of Pingdingshan cover coal, machinery, electric power, chemical industry, tobacco, and textile. The pillar industries in Luohe are food, textile, papermaking, leather footwear, chemicals, and machinery, while in Jiyuan they are electricity and aluminum. The development priority of different cities has varied greatly and complemented each other, which functions as the advantage of city clusters in central regions, and conducive to the establishment of a reasonable division of labor, complementary development, and the formation of concerted effort in cooperation.

II Problems and Their Causes in New Urbanization of Henan with City Cluster in Central Regions Playing the Leading Role

In 2016, Henan province has steadily promoted the development of new urbanization. We have promoted an orderly settling down of rural migrant workers through deepening reforms of the household registration system and implementation of the residence permit system. We have continued to improve the urban and rural planning system, accelerated the construction of the demonstration zone of urban and rural integration, and made great effort to improve the overall carrying capacity of cities and towns. As one of the "four cards", the development of new urbanization has promoted the sustainable and healthy development of the economy in Henan province. Despite the achievement, in the process of the development of urbanization, there have been old problems and new contradictions, of which the causes should be analyzed and solutions found.

1. Problems Remaining

The overall level of urbanization still lags behind. In recent years, with the accelerated development of urbanization in Henan, the urbanization rate of the permanent residents reached 48.5% in 2016, with an increase of 1.65 points from 2015. However, despite the narrowing gap, it still lags far behind the national average. In 2016, the national rate of urbanization was 57.35%, nearly 10 points higher than that in Henan province (Figure 4). According to Hollis Chenery (H.Chenery) and others' (1988) Development Model, once the per capita GDP reaches US$400, the corresponding urbanization rate would be 49%. In 2015, however, the per capita GDP in Henan was 39122.6 yuan (US$ 5927.7), so with a comparable income level of US$400, the urbanization level in Henan province was significantly lower than expected.

From the perspective of regional difference, in 2015, the urbanization rate of the core development zone of city cluster in central regions (Zhengzhou, Kaifeng, Luoyang, Pingdingshan, Xinxiang, Jiaozuo, Xuchang, Luohe, Jiyuan, Hebi, Shangqiu, and Zhoukou) was 51.08%, and the urbanization rate of the neighboring cities (Anyang, Puyang, Sanmenxia, Nanyang, Xinyang, and Zhumadian) was 43.60%, presenting a sharp regional difference, with Zhoukou and Zhumadian lagging far behind. From the perspective of industrialization level, the level of urbanization lagged behind the level of industrialization in Henan province. From the urbanization level and industrialization level of Henan Province from 1998 to 2016, as well as the deviation coefficient of the two, we could see clearly that the urbanization of Henan has lagged behind industrialization and its development trend. Based on international experience, if the level of urbanization is higher than the level of industrialization, and the deviation coefficient is positive and increasing, then the level of urbanization is much higher than the level of industrialization. But the situation in Henan has been the opposite. From 1978 to 2015, the deviation coefficient has remained negative, indicating that the level of urbanization in Henan has lagged behind the level of industrial development. However, it could be observed that the deviation coefficient of urbanization rate and industrialization rate has been decreasing year by year, from -0.68 in 1978 to -0.11 in 2015. The situation of urbanization lagging behind industrialization has been improving ever since. In 2016, the urbanization rate of Henan province exceeded the rate of industrialization, but that doesn't mean the level of urbanization has reached the level of industrialization. Generally speaking, a sound ratio of urbanization rate and industrialization rate is in the range of 1.4-2.5. In 2016 with the ratio at 1.02, the level of urbanization still remained below the level of industrialization (Table 1). From the perspective of non-agriculturalization level, the level of urbanization also lagged behind the level of non-agriculturalization in Henan province. The process of urbanization is also the process of non-agriculturalization, the process of which can be completed in the city and in the countryside. If rapid development of non-agriculturalization in rural areas is observed, and the rate of non-agricultural employment far exceeds the rate of urban population employment, it could be defined as "under urbanization". In this paper, the level of non-agriculturalization is measured

by the non-agricultural employment ratio (the ratio of employed population in secondary and tertiary industry over the total employed population). From 1978 to 2014, in terms of the connection between the level of urbanization and the level of non-agriculturalization in Henan, it is clear that the level of urbanization in Henan has been lagging behind the rate of non-agricultural employment, indicating the level of urbanization in Henan has lagged behind the level of non-agriculturalization. On the whole, starting from 1978, the rate of non-agriculturalization has been higher than the rate of urbanization in Henan, with their gap expanding year by year. From 1987 to 1997, it has remained stable with the ratio of non-agricultural employment rate/ urbanization rate fluctuated at around 2. In 1997, with the acceleration of urbanization, the gap between non-agriculturalization and urbanization started to shrink year by year. In 2014, with the ratio of non-agricultural employment rate/ urbanization rate at 1.31, the level of urbanization in Henan was still lagging behind the level of non-agriculturalization (Table 2).

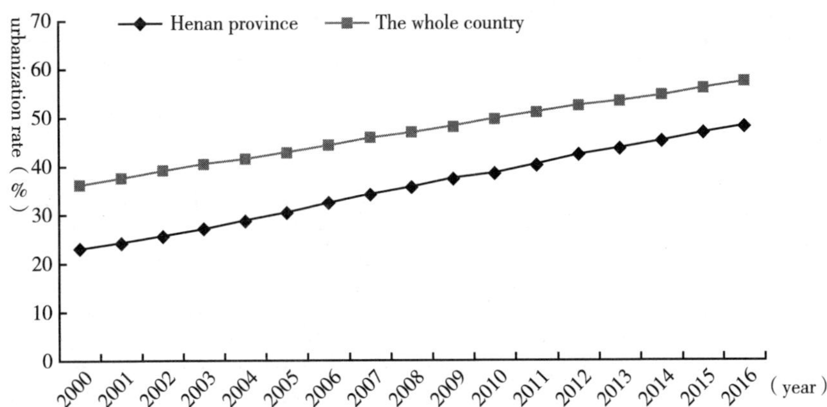

Figure 4 Comparison of the urbanization rate of Henan province and the whole country from 2000 to 2016

Data source: *Henan Statistical Yearbook (2016)*, *China Statistical Yearbook (2016)*, "2017 Henan Report on the Work of the Government", websites of Henan Bureau of Statistics and the National Bureau of Statistics.

Table 1 Relation between the level of urbanization and the level of industrialization from 1978 to 2016 in Henan province

Year	Urbanization rate (%)	Industrialization rate (%)	Deviation coefficient (%)
1978	13.6	42.6	-0.68
1980	14.0	41.2	-0.66
1982	14.4	39.0	-0.63
1984	14.7	36.8	-0.60
1986	15.0	40.2	-0.63
1988	15.3	40.0	-0.62
1990	15.5	35.5	-0.56
1992	16.2	42.6	-0.62
1994	16.8	47.8	-0.65
1996	18.4	46.2	-0.60
1998	20.8	45.0	-0.54
2000	23.2	45.4	-0.49
2002	25.8	45.9	-0.44
2004	28.9	48.9	-0.41
2006	32.5	53.8	-0.40
2008	36.0	55.9	-0.36
2010	38.8	55.5	-0.30
2012	42.4	53.7	-0.21
2014	45.2	51.0	-0.11
2016	48.5	47.4	0.02

Note: The rate of industrialization is calculated as the percentage of the output value of the secondary industry in GDP, and the deviation coefficient is calculated as the urbanization rate / industrialization rate minus 1.

Data source: *Henan Statistical Yearbook (2016)*, *China Statistical Yearbook (2016)*.

Table 2 Urbanization level and non-agriculturalization level in Henan province from 1978 to 2014

Year	Urbanization rate (%)	Non-agricultural employment rate (%)	Non-agricultural employment rate/ urbanization rate (%)
1978	13.6	19.4	1.42
1980	14.0	18.8	1.34
1982	14.4	19.6	1.36
1984	14.7	23.0	1.56
1986	15.0	28.5	1.90
1988	15.3	32.4	2.12
1990	15.5	30.7	1.98
1992	16.2	31.8	1.96
1994	16.8	35.6	2.11
1996	18.4	39.2	2.13
1998	20.8	41.1	1.97
2000	23.2	36.0	1.55
2002	25.8	38.5	1.49
2004	28.9	41.9	1.45
2006	32.5	46.7	1.44
2008	36.0	51.2	1.42
2010	38.8	55.1	1.42
2012	42.4	58.2	1.37
2014	45.2	59.3	1.31

Data source: *Henan Statistical Yearbook (2016).*

The operation efficiency of the city clusters was in need of further improvement. In 2015, the total GDP of city cluster in central regions reached 5.56 trillion yuan (US$ 0.8 trillion), preceded by city clusters in Changjiang River Delta, Pearl River Delta, and Beijing-Tianjin-Hebe, ranking the fourth in the country. However, in 2015, the total GDP of city cluster in Changjiang

River Delta was 13.55 trillion yuan (US$ 2.1 trillion), indicating a big gap of the overall economic strength between city clusters in central regions and the Changjiang River Delta. The development of city cluster in central regions still rely on the expansion of space, without effective collaborating and coordinated development, thus the overall efficiency is low. Despite their individual characteristics and good industrial base for industrial development, there are still problems surrounding the development of city cluster in central regions, like the lack of a sound and scientific division of city function and orientation, serious industrial structure convergence and homogeneous competition, the weak industrial chain, and the lack of concerted effort in industrial agglomeration and industrial division. Due to close location, comparable resources, and similar development orientation, cities have been competing for the development of the same industry or even the same type of products, causing duplicate industrial organization and product homogeneity. Different regions and industrial parks have been competing to attract investment, with inter-city competition overriding cooperation, and this has weakened the coordinated development of city cluster in central regions. For example, in the "13th Five-Year" Planning, many cities and counties were in pursuit of the integration with the Electronic Information Industrial Park in Zhengzhou Airport Economy Zone, for the development of electronic information industry. The regional cooperation among city cluster in central regions is still on the surface, without essential cooperation. Despite the benefits of the win-win cooperation and the internal demand for cooperation, local protection and repeated construction still prevail with the competition pressure. From the above, it is safe to conclude that city cluster in central regions is largely a spatial notion, with no close economic connection, integrated and optimized internal resources, nor highlighted agglomeration of economic benefit.

The driving capacity of core cities is still weak. From the experience of the development of city clusters in the world, the relationship between the core city and the surrounding areas is integration with the surrounding areas before driving the development of the surrounding areas. Within city clusters, with dominant resources gathered into the core city, metropolitan areas, megalopolis, super cities, other spatial patterns emerge and develop as the pioneers of the regional development. And the core city begins to drive the development of the surrounding regions, promoting the core city and the surrounding regions to form a positive interaction with mutual influence, interdependence, and interaction. Therefore, to a great extent, the development level of the core city determine the overall development level of city clusters. The competition between city clusters is manifested as the competition between the core cities. As the core city of city cluster in central regions, Zhengzhou, weak in economic and comprehensive strength, is inferior in its position as the primate city. In accordance with international standards, population of the primate city should account for more than 10% of the population of the region, and the total economic output should account for no less than 30% of the economic output of the region. In 2015, permanent residents in Zhengzhou accounted for 10.1% of the permanent residents in the province, and the population in Zhengzhou accounted for 6% of the population in city cluster in central regions. In 2016, the GDP of Zhengzhou accounted for 19.9% of the provincial GDP, while the proportion of Chengdu, Wuhan, Shenyang, and Xi'an all exceeded 30%. The reason why Nanjing, Hangzhou, Qingdao, Xiamen account for less than 20% of their provincial GDP is that these cities are not the only core city in their provinces. For example, the economic centers of Jiangsu Province are Suzhou, Nanjing and Wuxi. The economic centers of Zhejiang province are Hangzhou and Ningbo. The economic centers of Shandong province are Qingdao and Ji'nan. The economic centers of Fujian province are Fuzhou and Xiamen. In these regions, double core cities and multiple core cities, as the regional economic center, drive regional development, and therefore their position as the primate city is inevitably weakened. The four cities with high primacy ratio, namely, Chengdu, Wuhan, Shenyang, and Xi'an, like Zhengzhou, are the only core city in their provinces, outshine other cities with their significant contribution to, and great driving force for, the economic development in the whole province. These cities would be defined as the "strong core". However, Zhengzhou, as the only core city in the province and low in its position as the primate city, demonstrate limited force in driving the development of the neighboring regions, low efficiency in inter-city transfer and expansion of industrial chain, and limited correlation with the neighboring cities. Therefore it would be defined as the "weak core" (Table 3).

Table 3 General economic condition of central cities in China in 2016

City	GDP (100 million yuan)	GDP Ranking	GDP / Provincial GDP
Tianjin	17855.39	1	—
Chongqing	17558.76	2	—
Shenyang	6782.0	9	30.8
Nanjing	10503.0	6	13.8
Wuhan	11912.6	4	36.9
Chengdu	12170.2	3	37.2
Xi'an	6257.2	10	32.6
Hangzhou	11010.5	5	23.7
Qingdao	10011.3	7	14.9
Zhengzhou	7994.2	8	19.9
Xiamen	3737.0	11	13.1

Data source: *Henan Statistical Yearbook (2016).*

The modern urban system is in need of further improvement. On the one hand, the driving capacity of large cities is insufficient. In the city cluster in central regions, there was one national center city and no sub-provincial city. Classified according to the population of permanent urban residents, Zhengzhou is the only megacity, that is, city with the population of permanent urban residents exceeding 5 million. Twelve cities, namely, Luoyang, Xuchang, Xinxiang, Pingdingshan, Jiaozuo, Anyang, Nanyang, Shangqiu, Handan, Fuyang, Bengbu are classified as large cities, with the population of permanent urban residents between 1 million to 5 million. Seventeen cities are classified as medium-sized cities, with the population of permanent urban residents between 0.5 million to 1 million. In contrast, in the city cluster in the Changjiang River Delta, four cities are classified as the sub-provincial city and above, including three national central cities and one global city. In this region, Shanghai is the megacity behemoth, and Nanjing, Hangzhou and Suzhou are megacities. In the city cluster in the Pearl River Delta, there are three sub-provincial cities, one National Central City and two global cities. Among them, Guangzhou and Shenzhen are megacity

behemoths, and Dongguan, Shantou and Foshan are megacities. Compared with other city clusters, the city cluster in central regions, with limited number of megacities and weak economic contribution to the whole province and the whole region, is weak in its overall economic strength. In the city cluster in the Changjiang River Delta in 2016, cities with GDP more than 1000 billion yuan (US$ 151.5 billion) included Shanghai, Suzhou, Hangzhou, and Nanjing. Cities with the GDP between 800 billion to 1000 billion yuan (US$ 121.2 billion to 151.5 billion) were Wuxi, and Ningbo. Cities with the GDP more than 500 billion yuan (US$ 75.8 billion) included a total of 9 Cities. In the city cluster in the Pearl River Delta, in 2016, cities with GDP more than 1000 billion yuan (US$ 151.5 billion) were Guangzhou and Shenzhen. Cities with GDP between 500 billion to 1000 billion yuan (US$75.8 billion to 151.5 billion) were Foshan and Dongguan. Cities with GDP more than 500 billion yuan (US$ 75.8 billion) included a total of four cities. In the city cluster in central regions, the only city with GDP more than 500 billion yuan (US$ 75.8 billion) is Zhengzhou (Figure 5). On the other hand, the population carrying capacity of small and medium-sized cities is insufficient. First, the size of urban center in other cities is small. For example, the total population of Zhoukou is more than 10 million, and the total population of Zhumadian exceeds 9 million. However, the population of the urban center

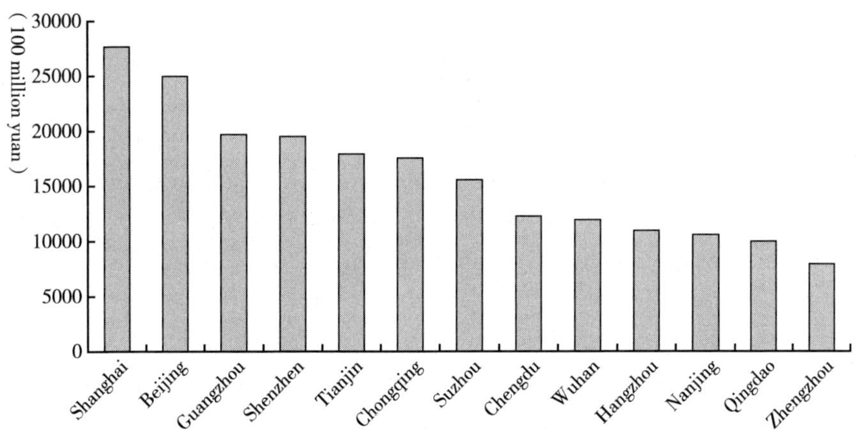

Figure 5 Rankings of Zhengzhou and cities with the GDP exceeding trillion yuan ($ 0.2 trillion) in 2016

Data source: *Henan Statistical Yearbook (2016).*

is less than 1 million in the two cities. With weak economic strength, it is difficult for these cities to drive the development of the neighboring regions. Second, the population carrying capacity of cities is insufficient. Except for Zhengzhou, the population of other cities is all outflowing. Third, with a small size and insufficient development of infrastructure and public service, it is difficult for counties and towns to play their role of attracting and carrying population.

There are growing constraints from resources and environment. In recent years, Henan province has made conscientious efforts to promote environmental protection. However, with the rapid advancement of urbanization, there exist problems like continuing expansion of urban area and agglomeration of urban population. There is no fundamental change to the growing constraints of resources and environment, worsening environmental pollution, and ecosystem degradation. The carrying capacity of urban resources and environment have reached or is close to the upper limit, but the the quality of the environment has not improved obviously. There is a large gap between the improvement of urban environment and people's expectation. With further acceleration of urbanization in Henan province, there would be no fundamental change to the unsound structure of industry and energy in the short term, and there would be more constraints from resources and environment in the future. In 2016, air pollution was still heavy in Henan province. The extent and length of the dense haze pollution has caused serious influence on production and people's lives. In 2016, in the monthly ranking of air quality in cities, the air quality in Xinyang was still the best. According to the monthly ranking of air quality, air quality in Xinyang, Zhoukou, and Nanyang were the best, while air quality in Anyang, Xinxiang, Zhengzhou, Jiaozuo, and Hebi were the worst, among which Anyang was the last in the ranking for six times. The advancement of new urbanization is constrained by land and space as well as the carrying capacity of resources and environment. As the main form to promote new urbanization in Henan, the city cluster should dissolve the pressure on environmental resources and achieve balanced regional development through its agglomeration effect (Table 4).

Table 4 Ranking of urban air quality in Henan province (comprehensive index method) from January to December in 2016

	January	February	March	April	May	June	July	August	September	October	November	December
Zhengzhou	13	12	13	17	18	17	14	16	16	14	12	14
Kaifeng	9	4	4	11	4	3	5	6	10	9	10	10
Luoyang	18	11	7	14	17	12	13	8	14	16	15	13
Pingdingshan	7	5	5	5	5	7	11	17	15	8	11	8
Anyang	14	17	18	16	7	16	17	18	18	18	18	18
Hebi	10	16	16	7	9	14	16	5	11	15	16	17
Xinxiang	16	18	17	15	12	13	12	14	17	17	13	15
Jiaozuo	17	6	15	18	11	18	18	10	7	11	17	16
Puyang	8	15	10	10	3	4	10	3	12	12	8	12
Xuchang	6	8	8	8	10	9	4	9	13	7	7	11
Luohe	12	9	11	12	14	10	6	15	9	10	6	9
Sanmenxia	11	3	12	6	13	8	8	13	4	6	9	4
Nanyang	2	2	2	3	6	6	7	7	3	3	3	2
Shangqiu	4	14	6	13	16	11	9	4	1	4	2	3
Xinyang	1	1	1	1	1	1	1	1	2	1	1	1
Zhoukou	3	13	3	2	2	2	2	2	5	2	4	5
Zhumadian	5	10	9	4	8	5	3	11	6	5	5	6
Jiyuan	15	7	14	9	15	15	15	12	8	13	14	7

Data source: The website of Department of Environmental Protection of Henan province.

2. Analysis of the Causes

The carrying capacity of small and medium-sized cities is insufficient. Speeding up the development of small and medium-sized cities is not only the main way to optimize the size and structure of cities and towns, but also an inevitable requirement for promoting new urbanization. However, in urban development, with resources allocated according to the administrative level, more resources are inclined toward the center regions of Zhengzhou, Luoyang and other big cities and provincial cities. The years of shortage of government budget for the development of central cities and small towns has led to various problems. Among them are lack of industrial support, low carrying capacity of industry and employment and backward infrastructure, such as water, power, gas, and central heating, lack of public services such as education, health care, housing, and social welfare, as well as urgent need of improvement of city functions. As a result, county towns and small towns failed to play their due role in bringing in rural workers and promoting the development of rural areas. Take the municipal public facilities as an example, in recent years, in counties in Henan province, great achievements have been made in areas like water supply, gas supply, area of paved roads per capita, green area per capita, green coverage of built-up area per capita, and garbage disposal rate. Yet compared with the national average and the provincial average level, there is still a wide gap. So is the situation in towns and villages, with the gas supply rate in particular far below the national average. In larger cities in Henan province, job opportunities, capacity of attracting factors of production and life convenience have attracted such a large number of people, causing the so-called "urban maladies", including traffic congestion, housing difficulties, great population pressure, worsening air pollution and inadequate public services. While small and medium-sized cities, without sufficient capacity to support industry and absorb employment, are slow in development, resulting in unbalanced development of the urban system in Henan province.

Innovation in key areas needs to be intensified. The institutional obstacles restricting the acceleration of new urbanization has not yet been eradicated, such as the settling down of rural migrant workers, the urban planning, the establishment of small cities, the reform of super towns, and the urban management system. Among them, transfer of the rural population to urban areas, the development of small and medium-sized cities, and the development of new cities are the focuses of contradictions, the intersection of old and new systems and mechanisms, and the key point of reform. First, the urban-rural dual structure has not been eliminated yet. In 2016 the central government issued the "Plan of the Settling Down of the 100 million Non-Native Permanent Residents". However, accompanying the household registration system is a series of institutional barriers, including employment, medical care, education, and pension. As a result, migrant rural residents are unable to enjoy the equal public services and social security that the urban residents enjoy. Second, there is no substantial policy concerning land reform. The role of current innovations of the land system is limited. Third, the adjustment of administrative districts fail to meet the need of new urbanization. The spatial scope of most counties has broken through their domains. Problems like decentralized management of villages and towns, as well as the city and town sharing the same administrative center have not been fundamentally resolved. Fourth, reform of investment and financing system of the urban public facilities is in urgent need of breakthrough. Finance below the county level could hardly afford the huge amount of capital required for urban public infrastructure construction, as it is unlikely to support large-scale infrastructure construction simply by relying on bank loans.

Coordination among provinces is difficult. The city cluster in central regions covers five provinces and thirty cities, with a large scope and a wide area. Due to the different provinces and administrative relations, it is difficult to coordinate between provinces. The main body of the city cluster in central regions is Henan province, only with some counties in the other four provinces involved. As a result, other cities and provinces would take a "free ride" seeking for significant benefits and would lose motivation of cooperation for the absence of immediate benefits. They may hold that the development of city cluster in central regions is mainly the development of Henan province and has little to do with themselves and therefore, they would show little motivation and enthusiasm. Cities in the city cluster in central regions have their own thoughts on development. Generally speaking, they tend to look at problems from the perspective of regional development, with little overall development concept or consciousness, which would cause various problems such as regional administrative barriers, market segmentation, similar function and industrial structure, and redundant construction between cities, as well as lack of effective cooperation on cross-regional traffic infrastructure construction, reasonable utilization of water resources, and the joint protection of the ecological environment. It has greatly hindered the healthy development of the city cluster in central regions.

"The last mile" problem in infrastructure remains unresolved. In recent years, Henan airlines, high-speed rail, subway, expressway and other transportation infrastructure have developed rapidly, but the problem of "the last mile" has restricted the efficiency of the transportation network. First, in air transportation, with the national strategy being pushed forward, the driving force of Zhengzhou Airport Economy Zone is further enhanced, while the development of supporting facilities in cities of the cluster lag behind. For example, the reason why the high-speed railway from Zhengzhoudong Station to Xinzheng International Airport fails to play its due role is the lack of seamless transfer between the high-speed railway station and the airport terminal. It would take a long time to transfer to the high-speed railway station. The extension of Metro

Line 2 to the airport line has greatly enhanced the convenience for passengers to reach the airport, but how to achieve seamless transfer remains to be solved. On the other hand, the construction of the extension of Metro Line 2 to the airport line would weaken the role of the high-speed railway from Zhengzhoudong to Xinzheng International Airport. Therefore, how to make better use of this high-speed railway and provide direct access to the airport through high-speed railway from cities in the city cluster in central regions also remain for future discussion. Second, the inter-city railway has greatly shortened the commuting time between cities. However, difficulties in getting to the station and transferring to the destination have restrained the convenience of urban railway. In some circumstances, it would take more time to reach the railway station than commute between two cities. Problems like how to achieve seamless transfer between subway and inter-city railway to allow convenient access to and out of inter-city railway station remain to be solved. With the operation of the Zhengzhou Metro Line 2 and construction of other Metro lines, Zhengzhou will usher in the Metro times. However, due to lack of early planning, the "last mile" problem gravely undermine the convenience of the subway, such as the inadequate number of subway interchange stations, lack of connection with the surrounding shopping malls and underground facilities, and the long distance between the interchange station and bus stations. Third, inadequate number of highway entrances and exits undermine the convenience and efficiency of highways, owing to the long distance connecting the highway and other roads as well as the crowdedness of vehicles in the entrance and exit.

The role of market orientation is not fully developed. In the early phase of urbanization, we relied mainly on the leading role of the government, which had brought about a series of problems while promoting the rapid development of urbanization in Henan. Under the GDP oriented assessment system, there appeared the so-called "enclosure movement" in some regions, that is, the excessive expansion of urban areas and promotion of infrastructure construction. Under such circumstances, the land urbanization developed faster than the population urbanization, with "empty city" and "ghost town" emerging. At the same time, the simplistic mode of urban development and various misconceptions, including an emphasis on construction over management, expansion over restructuring, investment over potentials have resulted in the low resource utilization efficiency and land output rate. In all, urbanization has been developing fast but with low quality. Only by giving full play to the role of the market as the main body can we solve the problems caused by government-led urbanization, improve the allocation efficiency of urban resources, enhance involvement of market participants and promote social equity.

Ⅲ Analysis of Current Situation of New Urbanization in Henan Province with City Cluster in Central Regions Playing the Leading Role

At present, highlighting city cluster in central regions as the main form is the objective requirement of a scientific promotion of new urbanization in central regions. The State Council approval of "The Development Planning of City Cluster in Central Regions" indicates that the development of the city cluster in central regions into a national city cluster has more definite guideline, clearer direction and more pragmatic measures. Development strategy of the city cluster, together with a series of policies and measures issued by the central and the provincial governments will release huge comprehensive effect, promoting the coordinated development of the speed and quality of Henan urbanization, and facilitating the innovation and development in Henan urban transformation.

1. Opportunities and Favorable Conditions

The strategy of urban development of the central government becomes clearer and more definite. "Opinions of the CPC Central Committee and the State Council on Further Strengthening the Development and Management of City Planning" was officially released, which was the "schedule" and the "road map" to promote urban development in the "13th Five-Year" period, or even further into the future. It specified and clarified the general guideline for urban development in Henan from five aspects. In the aspect of urban development concept, it emphasized the importance of understanding, respecting and complying with the law of urban development, corrected the guideline for urban development, and required that development must take into account and integrate economy, industry, space and society. In the aspect of urban development direction, it highlighted respect for people and nature, promoted people-oriented new urbanization, as well as human-based planning, development and management. At the same time, it focused on the re-ecologicalization to make the city more natural and more ecological friendly. In the aspect of the urban development blueprint, it stressed the need to shape city features, guard city memory, carry out a systematic development of urban planning with less randomness and blindness in decision-making, as well as prevent and eradicate the phenomenon of cities losing their identities and individual characteristics. In the aspect of the main form of promoting urbanization, it highlighted city cluster in central regions as the main form, relying on the dot-line-field network of urban spatial pattern with infrastructure network, changing the development mode of focusing on a single city, and enhancing the driving force for regional development. In the aspect of systematicness of urban work, it insisted on intensive development, restriction on total volume, limit for capacity, revitalizing the stock, optimizing increments, and improving the quality. It strived to improve the conservation and economical utilization of urban land, water, and ecological resources, as well as optimize the structure of urban land use. More resources tilted to improve production and the living environment of the city residents, so as to strengthen sustainable development and develop a livable city. The "Opinions" provided a clearer goal and guideline for urban development, pointed out the direction and focus of urban development in Henan. It was in accordance with the principles of goal orientation and problem orientation. It started from issues that people were most concerned about and the most urgent in development, promoting the development of urban transformation.

The "Development Planning of City Cluster in Central Regions" has been approved. At the end of 2016, the State Council approved the "Development Planning of City Cluster in Central Regions", which was submitted by the National Development and Reform Commission. So far, the city cluster in central regions has become the fifth approved National City Cluster that covers different provincial administrative regions following the city cluster of the middle reaches of Changjiang River, the city cluster of the Changjiang River Delta, the city cluster of Chengdu and Chongqing, as well as the city cluster of Ha'erbin and Changchun. The approval mark the formation of two major growth blocks in the central region of China, i.e. the city cluster in the middle reaches of the Changjiang River and the city cluster in central regions. The city cluster in central regions will play its role of agglomeration and driving development in an area bordering Beijing, Wuhan, Ji'nan, and Xi'an, with a 500 km radius. Through the promotion of the connection of infrastructure,

皮书系列

2018年

智 库 成 果 出 版 与 传 播 平 台

社会科学文献出版社
SOCIAL SCIENCES ACADEMIC PRESS (CHINA)

社长致辞

蓦然回首，皮书的专业化历程已经走过了二十年。20年来从一个出版社的学术产品名称到媒体热词再到智库成果研创及传播平台，皮书以专业化为主线，进行了系列化、市场化、品牌化、数字化、国际化、平台化的运作，实现了跨越式的发展。特别是在党的十八大以后，以习近平总书记为核心的党中央高度重视新型智库建设，皮书也迎来了长足的发展，总品种达到600余种，经过专业评审机制、淘汰机制遴选，目前，每年稳定出版近400个品种。“皮书”已经成为中国新型智库建设的抓手，成为国际国内社会各界快速、便捷地了解真实中国的最佳窗口。

20年孜孜以求，“皮书”始终将自己的研究视野与经济社会发展中的前沿热点问题紧密相连。600个研究领域，3万多位分布于800余个研究机构的专家学者参与了研创写作。皮书数据库中共收录了15万篇专业报告，50余万张数据图表，合计30亿字，每年报告下载量近80万次。皮书为中国学术与社会发展实践的结合提供了一个激荡智力、传播思想的入口，皮书作者们用学术的话语、客观翔实的数据谱写出了中国故事壮丽的篇章。

20年跬步千里，“皮书”始终将自己的发展与时代赋予的使命与责任紧紧相连。每年百余场新闻发布会，10万余次中外媒体报道，中、英、俄、日、韩等12个语种共同出版。皮书所具有的凝聚力正在形成一种无形的力量，吸引着社会各界关注中国的发展，参与中国的发展，它是我们向世界传递中国声音、总结中国经验、争取中国国际话语权最主要的平台。

皮书这一系列成就的取得，得益于中国改革开放的伟大时代，离不开来自中国社会科学院、新闻出版广电总局、全国哲学社会科学规划办公室等主管部门的大力支持和帮助，也离不开皮书研创者和出版者的共同努力。他们与皮书的故事创造了皮书的历史，他们对皮书的拳拳之心将继续谱写皮书的未来！

现在，“皮书”品牌已经进入了快速成长的青壮年时期。全方位进行规范化管理，树立中国的学术出版标准；不断提升皮书的内容质量和影响力，搭建起中国智库产品和智库建设的交流服务平台和国际传播平台；发布各类皮书指数，并使之成为中国指数，让中国智库的声音响彻世界舞台，为人类的发展做出中国的贡献——这是皮书未来发展的图景。作为“皮书”这个概念的提出者，“皮书”从一般图书到系列图书和品牌图书，最终成为智库研究和社会科学应用对策研究的知识服务和成果推广平台这整个过程的操盘者，我相信，这也是每一位皮书人执着追求的目标。

“当代中国正经历着我国历史上最为广泛而深刻的社会变革，也正在进行着人类历史上最为宏大而独特的实践创新。这种前无古人的伟大实践，必将给理论创造、学术繁荣提供强大动力和广阔空间。”

在这个需要思想而且一定能够产生思想的时代，皮书的研创出版一定能创造出新的更大的辉煌！

社会科学文献出版社社长

中国社会学会秘书长

2017年11月

社会科学文献出版社简介

社会科学文献出版社（以下简称“社科文献出版社”）成立于1985年，是直属于中国社会科学院的人文社会科学学术出版机构。成立至今，社科文献出版社始终依托中国社会科学院和国内外人文社会科学界丰厚的学术出版和专家学者资源，坚持“创社科经典，出传世文献”的出版理念、“权威、前沿、原创”的产品定位以及学术成果和智库成果出版的专业化、数字化、国际化、市场化的经营道路。

社科文献出版社是中国新闻出版业转型与文化体制改革的先行者。积极探索文化体制改革的先进方向和现代企业经营决策机制，社科文献出版社先后荣获“全国文化体制改革工作先进单位”、中国出版政府奖·先进出版单位奖，中国社会科学院先进集体、全国科普工作先进集体等荣誉称号。多人次荣获“第十届韬奋出版奖”“全国新闻出版行业领军人才”“数字出版先进人物”“北京市新闻出版广电行业领军人才”等称号。

社科文献出版社是中国人文社会科学学术出版的大社名社，也是以皮书为代表的智库成果出版的专业强社。年出版图书2000余种，其中皮书400余种，出版新书字数5.5亿字，承印与发行中国社科院院属期刊72种，先后创立了皮书系列、列国志、中国史话、社科文献学术译库、社科文献学术文库、甲骨文书系等一大批既有学术影响又有市场价值的品牌，确立了在社会学、近代史、苏东问题研究等专业学科及领域出版的领先地位。图书多次荣获中国出版政府奖、“三个一百”原创图书出版工程、“五个‘一’工程奖”、“大众喜爱的50种图书”等奖项，在中央国家机关“强素质·做表率”读书活动中，入选图书品种数位居各大出版社之首。

社科文献出版社是中国学术出版规范与标准的倡议者与制定者，代表全国50多家出版社发起实施学术著作出版规范的倡议，承担学术著作规范国家标准的起草工作，率先编撰完成《皮书手册》对皮书品牌进行规范化管理，并在此基础上推出中国版芝加哥手册——《社科文献出版社学术出版手册》。

社科文献出版社是中国数字出版的引领者，拥有皮书数据库、列国志数据库、“一带一路”数据库、减贫数据库、集刊数据库等4大产品线11个数据库产品，机构用户达1300余家，海外用户百余家，荣获“数字出版转型示范单位”“新闻出版标准化先进单位”“专业数字内容资源知识服务模式试点企业标准化示范单位”等称号。

社科文献出版社是中国学术出版走出去的践行者。社科文献出版社海外图书出版与学术合作业务遍及全球40余个国家和地区，并于2016年成立俄罗斯分社，累计输出图书500余种，涉及近20个语种，累计获得国家社科基金中华学术外译项目资助76种、“丝路书香工程”项目资助60种、中国图书对外推广计划项目资助71种以及经典中国国际出版工程资助28种，被五部委联合认定为“2015-2016年度国家文化出口重点企业”。

如今，社科文献出版社完全靠自身积累拥有固定资产3.6亿元，年收入3亿元，设置了七大出版分社、六大专业部门，成立了皮书研究院和博士后科研工作站，培养了一支近400人的高素质与高效率的编辑、出版、营销和国际推广队伍，为未来成为学术出版的大社、名社、强社，成为文化体制改革与文化企业转型发展的排头兵奠定了坚实的基础。

宏观经济类

经济蓝皮书

2018 年中国经济形势分析与预测

李平 / 主编　2017 年 12 月出版　定价：89.00 元

◆　本书为总理基金项目，由著名经济学家李扬领衔，联合中国社会科学院等数十家科研机构、国家部委和高等院校的专家共同撰写，系统分析了 2017 年的中国经济形势并预测 2018 年中国经济运行情况。

城市蓝皮书

中国城市发展报告 No.11

潘家华　单菁菁 / 主编　2018 年 9 月出版　估价：99.00 元

◆　本书是由中国社会科学院城市发展与环境研究中心编著的，多角度、全方位地立体展示了中国城市的发展状况，并对中国城市的未来发展提出了许多建议。该书有强烈的时代感，对中国城市发展实践有重要的参考价值。

人口与劳动绿皮书

中国人口与劳动问题报告 No.19

张车伟 / 主编　2018 年 10 月出版　估价：99.00 元

◆　本书为中国社会科学院人口与劳动经济研究所主编的年度报告，对当前中国人口与劳动形势做了比较全面和系统的深入讨论，为研究中国人口与劳动问题提供了一个专业性的视角。

中国省域竞争力蓝皮书

中国省域经济综合竞争力发展报告（2017 ~ 2018）

李建平　李闽榕　高燕京 / 主编　2018 年 5 月出版　估价：198.00 元

◆　本书融多学科的理论为一体，深入追踪研究了省域经济发展与中国国家竞争力的内在关系，为提升中国省域经济综合竞争力提供有价值的决策依据。

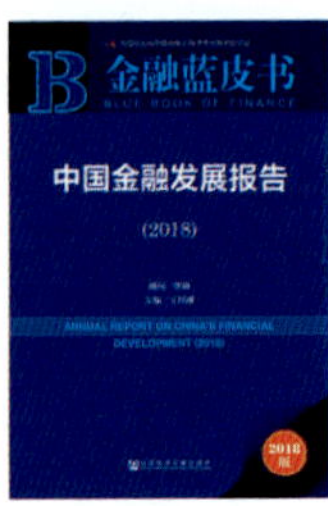

金融蓝皮书

中国金融发展报告（2018）

王国刚 / 主编　2018 年 2 月出版　估价：99.00 元

◆　本书由中国社会科学院金融研究所组织编写，概括和分析了 2017 年中国金融发展和运行中的各方面情况，研讨和评论了 2017 年发生的主要金融事件，有利于读者了解掌握 2017 年中国的金融状况，把握 2018 年中国金融的走势。

区域经济类

京津冀蓝皮书

京津冀发展报告（2018）

祝合良　叶堂林　张贵祥 / 等著　2018 年 6 月出版　估价：99.00 元

◆　本书遵循问题导向与目标导向相结合、统计数据分析与大数据分析相结合、纵向分析和长期监测与结构分析和综合监测相结合等原则，对京津冀协同发展新形势与新进展进行测度与评价。

社会政法类

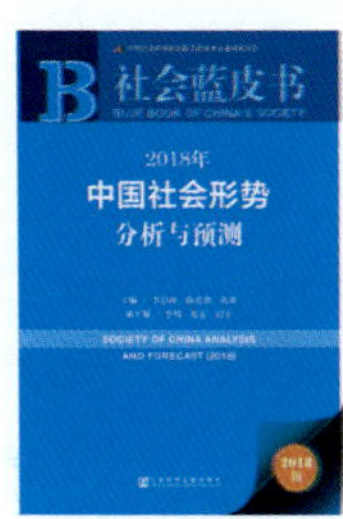

社会蓝皮书

2018年中国社会形势分析与预测

李培林　陈光金　张翼 / 主编　2017年12月出版　定价：89.00元

◆　本书由中国社会科学院社会学研究所组织研究机构专家、高校学者和政府研究人员撰写，聚焦当下社会热点，对2017年中国社会发展的各个方面内容进行了权威解读，同时对2018年社会形势发展趋势进行了预测。

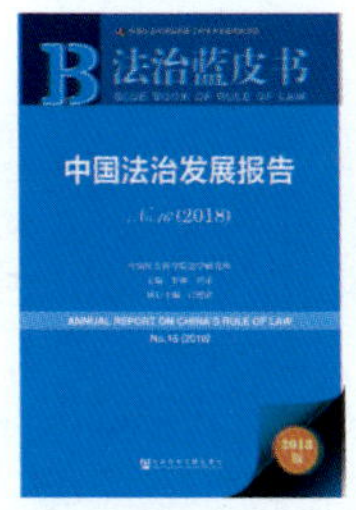

法治蓝皮书

中国法治发展报告 No.16（2018）

李林　田禾 / 主编　2018年3月出版　估价：118.00元

◆　本年度法治蓝皮书回顾总结了2017年度中国法治发展取得的成就和存在的不足，对中国政府、司法、检务透明度进行了跟踪调研，并对2018年中国法治发展形势进行了预测和展望。

教育蓝皮书

中国教育发展报告（2018）

杨东平 / 主编　2018年4月出版　估价：99.00元

◆　本书重点关注了2017年教育领域的热点，资料翔实，分析有据，既有专题研究，又有实践案例，从多角度对2017年教育改革和实践进行了分析和研究。

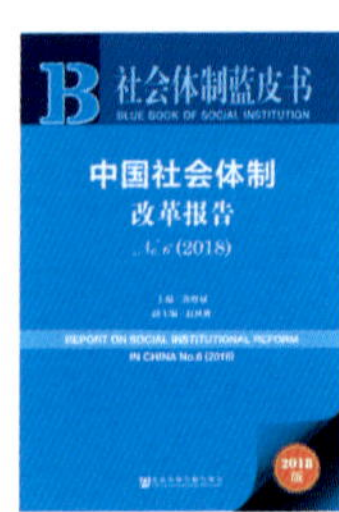

社会体制蓝皮书

中国社会体制改革报告 No.6（2018）

龚维斌 / 主编　2018 年 3 月出版　估价：99.00 元

◆　本书由国家行政学院社会治理研究中心和北京师范大学中国社会管理研究院共同组织编写，主要对 2017 年社会体制改革情况进行回顾和总结，对 2018 年的改革走向进行分析，提出相关政策建议。

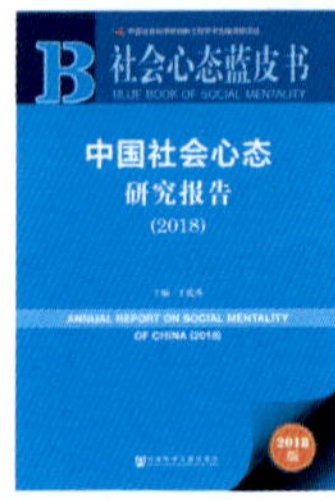

社会心态蓝皮书

中国社会心态研究报告（2018）

王俊秀　杨宜音 / 主编　2018 年 12 月出版　估价：99.00 元

◆　本书是中国社会科学院社会学研究所社会心理研究中心“社会心态蓝皮书课题组”的年度研究成果，运用社会心理学、社会学、经济学、传播学等多种学科的方法进行了调查和研究，对于目前中国社会心态状况有较广泛和深入的揭示。

华侨华人蓝皮书

华侨华人研究报告（2018）

贾益民 / 主编　2018 年 1 月出版　估价：139.00 元

◆　本书关注华侨华人生产与生活的方方面面。华侨华人是中国建设 21 世纪海上丝绸之路的重要中介者、推动者和参与者。本书旨在全面调研华侨华人，提供最新涉侨动态、理论研究成果和政策建议。

民族发展蓝皮书

中国民族发展报告（2018）

王延中 / 主编　2018 年 10 月出版　估价：188.00 元

◆　本书从民族学人类学视角，研究近年来少数民族和民族地区的发展情况，展示民族地区经济、政治、文化、社会和生态文明“五位一体”建设取得的辉煌成就和面临的困难挑战，为深刻理解中央民族工作会议精神、加快民族地区全面建成小康社会进程提供了实证材料。

产业经济类

房地产蓝皮书

中国房地产发展报告 No.15（2018）

李春华　王业强 / 主编　2018 年 5 月出版　估价：99.00 元

◆　2018 年《房地产蓝皮书》持续追踪中国房地产市场最新动态，深度剖析市场热点，展望 2018 年发展趋势，积极谋划应对策略。对 2017 年房地产市场的发展态势进行全面、综合的分析。

新能源汽车蓝皮书

中国新能源汽车产业发展报告（2018）

中国汽车技术研究中心　日产（中国）投资有限公司
东风汽车有限公司 / 编著　2018 年 8 月出版　估价：99.00 元

◆　本书对中国 2017 年新能源汽车产业发展进行了全面系统的分析，并介绍了国外的发展经验。有助于相关机构、行业和社会公众等了解中国新能源汽车产业发展的最新动态，为政府部门出台新能源汽车产业相关政策法规、企业制定相关战略规划，提供必要的借鉴和参考。

行业及其他类

旅游绿皮书

2017 ~ 2018 年中国旅游发展分析与预测

中国社会科学院旅游研究中心 / 编　2018 年 2 月出版　估价：99.00 元

◆　本书从政策、产业、市场、社会等多个角度勾画出 2017 年中国旅游发展全貌，剖析了其中的热点和核心问题，并就未来发展作出预测。

民营医院蓝皮书

中国民营医院发展报告（2018）

薛晓林 / 主编　2018 年 1 月出版　估价：99.00 元

◆　本书在梳理国家对社会办医的各种利好政策的前提下，对我国民营医疗发展现状、我国民营医院竞争力进行了分析，并结合我国医疗体制改革对民营医院的发展趋势、发展策略、战略规划等方面进行了预估。

会展蓝皮书

中外会展业动态评估研究报告（2018）

张敏 / 主编　2018 年 12 月出版　估价：99.00 元

◆　本书回顾了2017年的会展业发展动态，结合“供给侧改革”、“互联网 +”、“绿色经济”的新形势分析了我国展会的行业现状，并介绍了国外的发展经验，有助于行业和社会了解最新的展会业动态。

中国上市公司蓝皮书

中国上市公司发展报告（2018）

张平　王宏淼 / 主编　2018 年 9 月出版　估价：99.00 元

◆　本书由中国社会科学院上市公司研究中心组织编写的，着力于全面、真实、客观反映当前中国上市公司财务状况和价值评估的综合性年度报告。本书详尽分析了 2017 年中国上市公司情况，特别是现实中暴露出的制度性、基础性问题，并对资本市场改革进行了探讨。

工业和信息化蓝皮书

人工智能发展报告（2017 ~ 2018）

尹丽波 / 主编　2018 年 6 月出版　估价：99.00 元

◆　本书国家工业信息安全发展研究中心在对 2017 年全球人工智能技术和产业进行全面跟踪研究基础上形成的研究报告。该报告内容翔实、视角独特，具有较强的产业发展前瞻性和预测性，可为相关主管部门、行业协会、企业等全面了解人工智能发展形势以及进行科学决策提供参考。

国际问题与全球治理类

世界经济黄皮书

2018 年世界经济形势分析与预测

张宇燕 / 主编　2018 年 1 月出版　估价：99.00 元

◆　本书由中国社会科学院世界经济与政治研究所的研究团队撰写，分总论、国别与地区、专题、热点、世界经济统计与预测等五个部分，对 2018 年世界经济形势进行了分析。

国际城市蓝皮书

国际城市发展报告（2018）

屠启宇 / 主编　2018 年 2 月出版　估价：99.00 元

◆　本书作者以上海社会科学院从事国际城市研究的学者团队为核心，汇集同济大学、华东师范大学、复旦大学、上海交通大学、南京大学、浙江大学相关城市研究专业学者。立足动态跟踪介绍国际城市发展时间中，最新出现的重大战略、重大理念、重大项目、重大报告和最佳案例。

非洲黄皮书

非洲发展报告 No.20（2017 ~ 2018）

张宏明 / 主编　2018 年 7 月出版　估价：99.00 元

◆　本书是由中国社会科学院西亚非洲研究所组织编撰的非洲形势年度报告，比较全面、系统地分析了 2017 年非洲政治形势和热点问题，探讨了非洲经济形势和市场走向，剖析了大国对非洲关系的新动向；此外，还介绍了国内非洲研究的新成果。

国别类

美国蓝皮书

美国研究报告（2018）

郑秉文　黄平 / 主编　2018 年 5 月出版　估价：99.00 元

◆　本书是由中国社会科学院美国研究所主持完成的研究成果，它回顾了美国 2017 年的经济、政治形势与外交战略，对美国内政外交发生的重大事件及重要政策进行了较为全面的回顾和梳理。

德国蓝皮书

德国发展报告（2018）

郑春荣 / 主编　2018 年 6 月出版　估价：99.00 元

◆　本报告由同济大学德国研究所组织编撰，由该领域的专家学者对德国的政治、经济、社会文化、外交等方面的形势发展情况，进行全面的阐述与分析。

俄罗斯黄皮书

俄罗斯发展报告（2018）

李永全 / 编著　2018 年 6 月出版　估价：99.00 元

◆　本书系统介绍了 2017 年俄罗斯经济政治情况，并对 2016 年该地区发生的焦点、热点问题进行了分析与回顾；在此基础上，对该地区 2018 年的发展前景进行了预测。

文化传媒类

新媒体蓝皮书

中国新媒体发展报告 No.9（2018）

唐绪军 / 主编　2018 年 6 月出版　估价：99.00 元

◆　本书是由中国社会科学院新闻与传播研究所组织编写的关于新媒体发展的最新年度报告，旨在全面分析中国新媒体的发展现状，解读新媒体的发展趋势，探析新媒体的深刻影响。

移动互联网蓝皮书

中国移动互联网发展报告（2018）

余清楚 / 主编　2018 年 6 月出版　估价：99.00 元

◆　本书着眼于对 2017 年度中国移动互联网的发展情况做深入解析，对未来发展趋势进行预测，力求从不同视角、不同层面全面剖析中国移动互联网发展的现状、年度突破及热点趋势等。

文化蓝皮书

中国文化消费需求景气评价报告（2018）

王亚南 / 主编　2018 年 2 月出版　估价：99.00 元

◆　本书首创全国文化发展量化检测评价体系，也是至今全国唯一的文化民生量化检测评价体系，对于检验全国及各地 " 以人民为中心 " 的文化发展具有首创意义。

地方发展类

北京蓝皮书

北京经济发展报告（2017 ~ 2018）

杨松 / 主编　2018 年 6 月出版　估价：99.00 元

◆　本书对 2017 年北京市经济发展的整体形势进行了系统性的分析与回顾，并对 2018 年经济形势走势进行了预测与研判，聚焦北京市经济社会发展中的全局性、战略性和关键领域的重点问题，运用定量和定性分析相结合的方法，对北京市经济社会发展的现状、问题、成因进行了深入分析，提出了可操作性的对策建议。

温州蓝皮书

2018 年温州经济社会形势分析与预测

蒋儒标　王春光　金浩 / 主编　2018 年 4 月出版　估价：99.00 元

◆　本书是中共温州市委党校和中国社会科学院社会学研究所合作推出的第十一本温州蓝皮书，由来自党校、政府部门、科研机构、高校的专家、学者共同撰写的 2017 年温州区域发展形势的最新研究成果。

黑龙江蓝皮书

黑龙江社会发展报告（2018）

王爱丽 / 主编　2018 年 6 月出版　估价：99.00 元

◆　本书以千份随机抽样问卷调查和专题研究为依据，运用社会学理论框架和分析方法，从专家和学者的独特视角，对 2017 年黑龙江省关系民生的问题进行广泛的调研与分析，并对 2017 年黑龙江省诸多社会热点和焦点问题进行了有益的探索。这些研究不仅可以为政府部门更加全面深入了解省情、科学制定决策提供智力支持，同时也可以为广大读者认识、了解、关注黑龙江社会发展提供理性思考。

宏观经济类

城市蓝皮书
中国城市发展报告（No.11）
著(编)者：潘家华 单菁菁
2018年9月出版 / 估价：99.00元
PSN B-2007-091-1/1

城乡一体化蓝皮书
中国城乡一体化发展报告（2018）
著(编)者：付崇兰
2018年9月出版 / 估价：99.00元
PSN B-2011-226-1/2

城镇化蓝皮书
中国新型城镇化健康发展报告（2018）
著(编)者：张占斌
2018年8月出版 / 估价：99.00元
PSN B-2014-396-1/1

创新蓝皮书
创新型国家建设报告（2018～2019）
著(编)者：詹正茂
2018年12月出版 / 估价：99.00元
PSN B-2009-140-1/1

低碳发展蓝皮书
中国低碳发展报告（2018）
著(编)者：张希良 齐晔
2018年6月出版 / 估价：99.00元
PSN B-2011-223-1/1

低碳经济蓝皮书
中国低碳经济发展报告（2018）
著(编)者：薛进军 赵忠秀
2018年11月出版 / 估价：99.00元
PSN B-2011-194-1/1

发展和改革蓝皮书
中国经济发展和体制改革报告No.9
著(编)者：邹东涛 王再文
2018年1月出版 / 估价：99.00元
PSN B-2008-122-1/1

国家创新蓝皮书
中国创新发展报告（2017）
著(编)者：陈劲　2018年3月出版 / 估价：99.00元
PSN B-2014-370-1/1

金融蓝皮书
中国金融发展报告（2018）
著(编)者：王国刚
2018年2月出版 / 估价：99.00元
PSN B-2004-031-1/7

经济蓝皮书
2018年中国经济形势分析与预测
著(编)者：李平　2017年12月出版 / 定价：89.00元
PSN B-1996-001-1/1

经济蓝皮书春季号
2018年中国经济前景分析
著(编)者：李扬　2018年5月出版 / 估价：99.00元
PSN B-1999-008-1/1

经济蓝皮书夏季号
中国经济增长报告（2017～2018）
著(编)者：李扬　2018年9月出版 / 估价：99.00元
PSN B-2010-176-1/1

经济信息绿皮书
中国与世界经济发展报告（2018）
著(编)者：杜平
2017年12月出版 / 估价：99.00元
PSN G-2003-023-1/1

农村绿皮书
中国农村经济形势分析与预测（2017～2018）
著(编)者：魏后凯 黄秉信
2018年4月出版 / 估价：99.00元
PSN G-1998-003-1/1

人口与劳动绿皮书
中国人口与劳动问题报告No.19
著(编)者：张车伟　2018年11月出版 / 估价：99.00元
PSN G-2000-012-1/1

新型城镇化蓝皮书
新型城镇化发展报告（2017）
著(编)者：李伟 宋敏 沈体雁
2018年3月出版 / 估价：99.00元
PSN B-2005-038-1/1

中国省域竞争力蓝皮书
中国省域经济综合竞争力发展报告（2016～2017）
著(编)者：李建平 李闽榕 高燕京
2018年2月出版 / 估价：198.00元
PSN B-2007-088-1/1

中小城市绿皮书
中国中小城市发展报告（2018）
著(编)者：中国城市经济学会中小城市经济发展委员会
中国城镇化促进会中小城市发展委员会
《中国中小城市发展报告》编纂委员会
中小城市发展战略研究院
2018年11月出版 / 估价：128.00元
PSN G-2010-161-1/1

区域经济类

东北蓝皮书
中国东北地区发展报告（2018）
著(编)者：姜晓秋　2018年11月出版 / 估价：99.00元
PSN B-2006-067-1/1

金融蓝皮书
中国金融中心发展报告（2017～2018）
著(编)者：王力 黄育华　2018年11月出版 / 估价：99.00元
PSN B-2011-186-6/7

京津冀蓝皮书
京津冀发展报告（2018）
著(编)者：祝合良 叶堂林 张贵祥
2018年6月出版 / 估价：99.00元
PSN B-2012-262-1/1

西北蓝皮书
中国西北发展报告（2018）
著(编)者：任宗哲 白宽犁 王建康
2018年4月出版 / 估价：99.00元
PSN B-2012-261-1/1

西部蓝皮书
中国西部发展报告（2018）
著(编)者：璋勇 任保平　2018年8月出版 / 估价：99.00元
PSN B-2005-039-1/1

长江经济带产业蓝皮书
长江经济带产业发展报告（2018）
著(编)者：吴传清　2018年11月出版 / 估价：128.00元
PSN B-2017-666-1/1

长江经济带蓝皮书
长江经济带发展报告（2017～2018）
著(编)者：王振　2018年11月出版 / 估价：99.00元
PSN B-2016-575-1/1

长江中游城市群蓝皮书
长江中游城市群新型城镇化与产业协同发展报告（2018）
著(编)者：杨刚强　2018年11月出版 / 估价：99.00元
PSN B-2016-578-1/1

长三角蓝皮书
2017年创新融合发展的长三角
著(编)者：刘飞跃　2018年3月出版 / 估价：99.00元
PSN B-2005-038-1/1

长株潭城市群蓝皮书
长株潭城市群发展报告（2017）
著(编)者：张萍 朱有志　2018年1月出版 / 估价：99.00元
PSN B-2008-109-1/1

中部竞争力蓝皮书
中国中部经济社会竞争力报告（2018）
著(编)者：教育部人文社会科学重点研究基地南昌大学中国中部经济社会发展研究中心
2018年12月出版 / 估价：99.00元
PSN B-2012-276-1/1

中部蓝皮书
中国中部地区发展报告（2018）
著(编)者：宋亚平　2018年12月出版 / 估价：99.00元
PSN B-2007-089-1/1

区域蓝皮书
中国区域经济发展报告（2017～2018）
著(编)者：赵弘　2018年5月出版 / 估价：99.00元
PSN B-2004-034-1/1

中三角蓝皮书
长江中游城市群发展报告（2018）
著(编)者：秦尊文　2018年9月出版 / 估价：99.00元
PSN B-2014-417-1/1

中原蓝皮书
中原经济区发展报告（2018）
著(编)者：李英杰　2018年6月出版 / 估价：99.00元
PSN B-2011-192-1/1

珠三角流通蓝皮书
珠三角商圈发展研究报告（2018）
著(编)者：王先庆 林至颖　2018年7月出版 / 估价：99.00元
PSN B-2012-292-1/1

社会政法类

北京蓝皮书
中国社区发展报告（2017～2018）
著(编)者：于燕燕　2018年9月出版 / 估价：99.00元
PSN B-2007-083-5/8

殡葬绿皮书
中国殡葬事业发展报告（2017～2018）
著(编)者：李伯森　2018年4月出版 / 估价：158.00元
PSN G-2010-180-1/1

城市管理蓝皮书
中国城市管理报告（2017-2018）
著(编)者：刘林 刘承水　2018年5月出版 / 估价：158.00元
PSN B-2013-336-1/1

城市生活质量蓝皮书
中国城市生活质量报告（2017）
著(编)者：张连城 张平 杨春学 郎丽华
2018年2月出版 / 估价：99.00元
PSN B-2013-326-1/1

城市政府能力蓝皮书
中国城市政府公共服务能力评估报告（2018）
著(编)者：何艳玲　2018年4月出版 / 估价：99.00元
PSN B-2013-338-1/1

创业蓝皮书
中国创业发展研究报告（2017~2018）
著(编)者：黄群慧 赵卫星 钟宏武
2018年11月出版 / 估价：99.00元
PSN B-2016-577-1/1

慈善蓝皮书
中国慈善发展报告（2018）
著(编)者：杨团　2018年6月出版 / 估价：99.00元
PSN B-2009-142-1/1

党建蓝皮书
党的建设研究报告No.2（2018）
著(编)者：崔建民 陈东平　2018年1月出版 / 估价：99.00元
PSN B-2016-523-1/1

地方法治蓝皮书
中国地方法治发展报告No.3（2018）
著(编)者：李林 田禾　2018年3月出版 / 估价：118.00元
PSN B-2015-442-1/1

电子政务蓝皮书
中国电子政务发展报告（2018）
著(编)者：李季　2018年8月出版 / 估价：99.00元
PSN B-2003-022-1/1

法治蓝皮书
中国法治发展报告No.16（2018）
著(编)者：吕艳滨　2018年3月出版 / 估价：118.00元
PSN B-2004-027-1/3

法治蓝皮书
中国法院信息化发展报告 No.2（2018）
著(编)者：李林 田禾　2018年2月出版 / 估价：108.00元
PSN B-2017-604-3/3

法治政府蓝皮书
中国法治政府发展报告（2018）
著(编)者：中国政法大学法治政府研究院
2018年4月出版 / 估价：99.00元
PSN B-2015-502-1/2

法治政府蓝皮书
中国法治政府评估报告（2018）
著(编)者：中国政法大学法治政府研究院
2018年9月出版 / 估价：168.00元
PSN B-2016-576-2/2

反腐倡廉蓝皮书
中国反腐倡廉建设报告 No.8
著(编)者：张英伟　2018年12月出版 / 估价：99.00元
PSN B-2012-259-1/1

扶贫蓝皮书
中国扶贫开发报告（2018）
著(编)者：李培林 魏后凯　2018年12月出版 / 估价：128.00元
PSN B-2016-599-1/1

妇女发展蓝皮书
中国妇女发展报告 No.6
著(编)者：王金玲　2018年9月出版 / 估价：158.00元
PSN B-2006-069-1/1

妇女教育蓝皮书
中国妇女教育发展报告 No.3
著(编)者：张李玺　2018年10月出版 / 估价：99.00元
PSN B-2008-121-1/1

妇女绿皮书
2018年：中国性别平等与妇女发展报告
著(编)者：谭琳　2018年12月出版 / 估价：99.00元
PSN G-2006-073-1/1

公共安全蓝皮书
中国城市公共安全发展报告（2017~2018）
著(编)者：黄育华 杨文明 赵建辉
2018年6月出版 / 估价：99.00元
PSN B-2017-628-1/1

公共服务蓝皮书
中国城市基本公共服务力评价（2018）
著(编)者：钟君 刘志昌 吴正杲
2018年12月出版 / 估价：99.00元
PSN B-2011-214-1/1

公民科学素质蓝皮书
中国公民科学素质报告（2017~2018）
著(编)者：李群 陈雄 马宗文
2018年1月出版 / 估价：99.00元
PSN B-2014-379-1/1

公益蓝皮书
中国公益慈善发展报告（2016）
著(编)者：朱健刚 胡小军　2018年2月出版 / 估价：99.00元
PSN B-2012-283-1/1

国际人才蓝皮书
中国国际移民报告（2018）
著(编)者：王辉耀　2018年2月出版 / 估价：99.00元
PSN B-2012-304-3/4

国际人才蓝皮书
中国留学发展报告（2018）No.7
著(编)者：王辉耀 苗绿　2018年12月出版 / 估价：99.00元
PSN B-2012-244-2/4

海洋社会蓝皮书
中国海洋社会发展报告（2017）
著(编)者：崔凤 宋宁而　2018年3月出版 / 估价：99.00元
PSN B-2015-478-1/1

行政改革蓝皮书
中国行政体制改革报告No.7（2018）
著(编)者：魏礼群　2018年6月出版 / 估价：99.00元
PSN B-2011-231-1/1

华侨华人蓝皮书
华侨华人研究报告（2017）
著(编)者：贾益民　2018年1月出版 / 估价：139.00元
PSN B-2011-204-1/1

环境竞争力绿皮书
中国省域环境竞争力发展报告（2018）
著(编)者：李建平 李闽榕 王金南
2018年11月出版 / 估价：198.00元
PSN G-2010-165-1/1

环境绿皮书
中国环境发展报告（2017～2018）
著(编)者：李波 2018年4月出版 / 估价：99.00元
PSN G-2006-048-1/1

家庭蓝皮书
中国"创建幸福家庭活动"评估报告（2018）
著(编)者：国务院发展研究中心"创建幸福家庭活动评估"课题组
2018年12月出版 / 估价：99.00元
PSN B-2015-508-1/1

健康城市蓝皮书
中国健康城市建设研究报告（2018）
著(编)者：王鸿春 盛继洪 2018年12月出版 / 估价：99.00元
PSN B-2016-564-2/2

健康中国蓝皮书
社区首诊与健康中国分析报告（2018）
著(编)者：高和荣 杨叔禹 姜杰
2018年4月出版 / 估价：99.00元
PSN B-2017-611-1/1

教师蓝皮书
中国中小学教师发展报告（2017）
著(编)者：曾晓东 鱼霞 2018年6月出版 / 估价：99.00元
PSN B-2012-289-1/1

教育扶贫蓝皮书
中国教育扶贫报告（2018）
著(编)者：司树杰 王文静 李兴洲
2018年12月出版 / 估价：99.00元
PSN B-2016-590-1/1

教育蓝皮书
中国教育发展报告（2018）
著(编)者：杨东平 2018年4月出版 / 估价：99.00元
PSN B-2006-047-1/1

金融法治建设蓝皮书
中国金融法治建设年度报告（2015～2016）
著(编)者：朱小黄 2018年6月出版 / 估价：99.00元
PSN B-2017-633-1/1

京津冀教育蓝皮书
京津冀教育发展研究报告（2017～2018）
著(编)者：方中雄 2018年4月出版 / 估价：99.00元
PSN B-2017-608-1/1

就业蓝皮书
2018年中国本科生就业报告
著(编)者：麦可思研究院 2018年6月出版 / 估价：99.00元
PSN B-2009-146-1/2

就业蓝皮书
2018年中国高职高专生就业报告
著(编)者：麦可思研究院 2018年6月出版 / 估价：99.00元
PSN B-2015-472-2/2

科学教育蓝皮书
中国科学教育发展报告（2018）
著(编)者：王康友 2018年10月出版 / 估价：99.00元
PSN B-2015-487-1/1

劳动保障蓝皮书
中国劳动保障发展报告（2018）
著(编)者：刘燕斌 2018年9月出版 / 估价：158.00元
PSN B-2014-415-1/1

老龄蓝皮书
中国老年宜居环境发展报告（2017）
著(编)者：党俊武 周燕珉 2018年1月出版 / 估价：99.00元
PSN B-2013-320-1/1

连片特困区蓝皮书
中国连片特困区发展报告（2017～2018）
著(编)者：游俊 冷志明 丁建军
2018年4月出版 / 估价：99.00元
PSN B-2013-321-1/1

流动儿童蓝皮书
中国流动儿童教育发展报告（2017）
著(编)者：杨东平 2018年1月出版 / 估价：99.00元
PSN B-2017-600-1/1

民调蓝皮书
中国民生调查报告（2018）
著(编)者：谢耘耕 2018年12月出版 / 估价：99.00元
PSN B-2014-398-1/1

民族发展蓝皮书
中国民族发展报告（2018）
著(编)者：王延中 2018年10月出版 / 估价：188.00元
PSN B-2006-070-1/1

女性生活蓝皮书
中国女性生活状况报告No.12（2018）
著(编)者：韩湘景 2018年7月出版 / 估价：99.00元
PSN B-2006-071-1/1

汽车社会蓝皮书
中国汽车社会发展报告（2017～2018）
著(编)者：王俊秀 2018年1月出版 / 估价：99.00元
PSN B-2011-224-1/1

青年蓝皮书
中国青年发展报告（2018）No.3
著(编)者：廉思 2018年4月出版 / 估价：99.00元
PSN B-2013-333-1/1

青少年蓝皮书
中国未成年人互联网运用报告（2017～2018）
著(编)者：季为民 李文革 沈杰
2018年11月出版 / 估价：99.00元
PSN B-2010-156-1/1

人权蓝皮书
中国人权事业发展报告No.8（2018）
著(编)者：李君如　2018年9月出版 / 估价：99.00元
PSN B-2011-215-1/1

社会保障绿皮书
中国社会保障发展报告No.9（2018）
著(编)者：王延中　2018年1月出版 / 估价：99.00元
PSN G-2001-014-1/1

社会风险评估蓝皮书
风险评估与危机预警报告（2017～2018）
著(编)者：唐钧　2018年8月出版 / 估价：99.00元
PSN B-2012-293-1/1

社会工作蓝皮书
中国社会工作发展报告（2016~2017）
著(编)者：民政部社会工作研究中心
2018年8月出版 / 估价：99.00元
PSN B-2009-141-1/1

社会管理蓝皮书
中国社会管理创新报告No.6
著(编)者：连玉明　2018年11月出版 / 估价：99.00元
PSN B-2012-300-1/1

社会蓝皮书
2018年中国社会形势分析与预测
著(编)者：李培林 陈光金 张翼
2017年12月出版 / 定价：89.00元
PSN B-1998-002-1/1

社会体制蓝皮书
中国社会体制改革报告No.6（2018）
著(编)者：龚维斌　2018年3月出版 / 估价：99.00元
PSN B-2013-330-1/1

社会心态蓝皮书
中国社会心态研究报告（2018）
著(编)者：王俊秀　2018年12月出版 / 估价：99.00元
PSN B-2011-199-1/1

社会组织蓝皮书
中国社会组织报告（2017-2018）
著(编)者：黄晓勇　2018年1月出版 / 估价：99.00元
PSN B-2008-118-1/2

社会组织蓝皮书
中国社会组织评估发展报告（2018）
著(编)者：徐家良　2018年12月出版 / 估价：99.00元
PSN B-2013-366-2/2

生态城市绿皮书
中国生态城市建设发展报告（2018）
著(编)者：刘举科 孙伟平 胡文臻
2018年9月出版 / 估价：158.00元
PSN G-2012-269-1/1

生态文明绿皮书
中国省域生态文明建设评价报告（ECI 2018）
著(编)者：严耕　2018年12月出版 / 估价：99.00元
PSN G-2010-170-1/1

退休生活蓝皮书
中国城市居民退休生活质量指数报告（2017）
著(编)者：杨一帆　2018年5月出版 / 估价：99.00元
PSN B-2017-618-1/1

危机管理蓝皮书
中国危机管理报告（2018）
著(编)者：文学国 范正青
2018年8月出版 / 估价：99.00元
PSN B-2010-171-1/1

学会蓝皮书
2018年中国学会发展报告
著(编)者：麦可思研究院
2018年12月出版 / 估价：99.00元
PSN B-2016-597-1/1

医改蓝皮书
中国医药卫生体制改革报告（2017～2018）
著(编)者：文学国 房志武
2018年11月出版 / 估价：99.00元
PSN B-2014-432-1/1

应急管理蓝皮书
中国应急管理报告（2018）
著(编)者：宋英华　2018年9月出版 / 估价：99.00元
PSN B-2016-562-1/1

政府绩效评估蓝皮书
中国地方政府绩效评估报告 No.2
著(编)者：贠杰　2018年12月出版 / 估价：99.00元
PSN B-2017-672-1/1

政治参与蓝皮书
中国政治参与报告（2018）
著(编)者：房宁　2018年8月出版 / 估价：128.00元
PSN B-2011-200-1/1

政治文化蓝皮书
中国政治文化报告（2018）
著(编)者：邢元敏 魏大鹏 龚克
2018年8月出版 / 估价：128.00元
PSN B-2017-615-1/1

中国传统村落蓝皮书
中国传统村落保护现状报告（2018）
著(编)者：胡彬彬 李向军 王晓波
2018年12月出版 / 估价：99.00元
PSN B-2017-663-1/1

中国农村妇女发展蓝皮书
农村流动女性城市生活发展报告（2018）
著(编)者：谢丽华　2018年12月出版 / 估价：99.00元
PSN B-2014-434-1/1

宗教蓝皮书
中国宗教报告（2017）
著(编)者：邱永辉　2018年8月出版 / 估价：99.00元
PSN B-2008-117-1/1

产业经济类

保健蓝皮书
中国保健服务产业发展报告 No.2
著(编)者：中国保健协会　　中共中央党校
2018年7月出版 / 估价：198.00元
PSN B-2012-272-3/3

保健蓝皮书
中国保健食品产业发展报告 No.2
著(编)者：中国保健协会
中国社会科学院食品药品产业发展与监管研究中心
2018年8月出版 / 估价：198.00元
PSN B-2012-271-2/3

保健蓝皮书
中国保健用品产业发展报告 No.2
著(编)者：中国保健协会
国务院国有资产监督管理委员会研究中心
2018年3月出版 / 估价：198.00元
PSN B-2012-270-1/3

保险蓝皮书
中国保险业竞争力报告（2018）
著(编)者：保监会　　2018年12月出版 / 估价：99.00元
PSN B-2013-311-1/1

冰雪蓝皮书
中国冰上运动产业发展报告（2018）
著(编)者：孙承华 杨占武 刘戈 张鸿俊
2018年9月出版 / 估价：99.00元
PSN B-2017-648-3/3

冰雪蓝皮书
中国滑雪产业发展报告（2018）
著(编)者：孙承华 伍斌 魏庆华 张鸿俊
2018年9月出版 / 估价：99.00元
PSN B-2016-559-1/3

餐饮产业蓝皮书
中国餐饮产业发展报告（2018）
著(编)者：邢颖
2018年6月出版 / 估价：99.00元
PSN B-2009-151-1/1

茶业蓝皮书
中国茶产业发展报告（2018）
著(编)者：杨江帆 李闽榕
2018年10月出版 / 估价：99.00元
PSN B-2010-164-1/1

产业安全蓝皮书
中国文化产业安全报告（2018）
著(编)者：北京印刷学院文化产业安全研究院
2018年12月出版 / 估价：99.00元
PSN B-2014-378-12/14

产业安全蓝皮书
中国新媒体产业安全报告（2016～2017）
著(编)者：肖丽　　2018年6月出版 / 估价：99.00元
PSN B-2015-500-14/14

产业安全蓝皮书
中国出版传媒产业安全报告（2017～2018）
著(编)者：北京印刷学院文化产业安全研究院
2018年3月出版 / 估价：99.00元
PSN B-2014-384-13/14

产业蓝皮书
中国产业竞争力报告（2018）No.8
著(编)者：张其仔　　2018年12月出版 / 估价：168.00元
PSN B-2010-175-1/1

动力电池蓝皮书
中国新能源汽车动力电池产业发展报告（2018）
著(编)者：中国汽车技术研究中心
2018年8月出版 / 估价：99.00元
PSN B-2017-639-1/1

杜仲产业绿皮书
中国杜仲橡胶资源与产业发展报告（2017～2018）
著(编)者：杜红岩 胡文臻 俞锐
2018年1月出版 / 估价：99.00元
PSN G-2013-350-1/1

房地产蓝皮书
中国房地产发展报告No.15（2018）
著(编)者：李春华 王业强
2018年5月出版 / 估价：99.00元
PSN B-2004-028-1/1

服务外包蓝皮书
中国服务外包产业发展报告（2017～2018）
著(编)者：王晓红 刘德军
2018年6月出版 / 估价：99.00元
PSN B-2013-331-2/2

服务外包蓝皮书
中国服务外包竞争力报告（2017～2018）
著(编)者：刘春生 王力 黄育华
2018年12月出版 / 估价：99.00元
PSN B-2011-216-1/2

工业和信息化蓝皮书
世界信息技术产业发展报告（2017～2018）
著(编)者：尹丽波　　2018年6月出版 / 估价：99.00元
PSN B-2015-449-2/6

工业和信息化蓝皮书
战略性新兴产业发展报告（2017～2018）
著(编)者：尹丽波　　2018年6月出版 / 估价：99.00元
PSN B-2015-450-3/6

客车蓝皮书
中国客车产业发展报告（2017～2018）
著(编)者：姚蔚　　2018年10月出版 / 估价：99.00元
PSN B-2013-361-1/1

流通蓝皮书
中国商业发展报告（2018～2019）
著(编)者：王雪峰 林诗慧
2018年7月出版 / 估价：99.00元
PSN B-2009-152-1/2

能源蓝皮书
中国能源发展报告（2018）
著(编)者：崔民选 王军生 陈义和
2018年12月出版 / 估价：99.00元
PSN B-2006-049-1/1

农产品流通蓝皮书
中国农产品流通产业发展报告（2017）
著(编)者：贾敬敦 张东科 张玉玺 张鹏毅 周伟
2018年1月出版 / 估价：99.00元
PSN B-2012-288-1/1

汽车工业蓝皮书
中国汽车工业发展年度报告（2018）
著(编)者：中国汽车工业协会
中国汽车技术研究中心
丰田汽车公司
2018年5月出版 / 估价：168.00元
PSN B-2015-463-1/2

汽车工业蓝皮书
中国汽车零部件产业发展报告（2017～2018）
著(编)者：中国汽车工业协会
中国汽车工程研究院深圳市沃特玛电池有限公司
2018年9月出版 / 估价：99.00元
PSN B-2016-515-2/2

汽车蓝皮书
中国汽车产业发展报告（2018）
著(编)者：中国汽车工程学会
大众汽车集团（中国）
2018年11月出版 / 估价：99.00元
PSN B-2008-124-1/1

世界茶业蓝皮书
世界茶业发展报告（2018）
著(编)者：李闽榕 冯廷佺
2018年5月出版 / 估价：168.00元
PSN B-2017-619-1/1

世界能源蓝皮书
世界能源发展报告（2018）
著(编)者：黄晓勇　　2018年6月出版 / 估价：168.00元
PSN B-2013-349-1/1

体育蓝皮书
国家体育产业基地发展报告（2016～2017）
著(编)者：李颖川　　2018年4月出版 / 估价：168.00元
PSN B-2017-609-5/5

体育蓝皮书
中国体育产业发展报告（2018）
著(编)者：阮伟 钟秉枢
2018年12月出版 / 估价：99.00元
PSN B-2010-179-1/5

文化金融蓝皮书
中国文化金融发展报告（2018）
著(编)者：杨涛 金巍
2018年5月出版 / 估价：99.00元
PSN B-2017-610-1/1

新能源汽车蓝皮书
中国新能源汽车产业发展报告（2018）
著(编)者：中国汽车技术研究中心
日产（中国）投资有限公司
东风汽车有限公司
2018年8月出版 / 估价：99.00元
PSN B-2013-347-1/1

薏仁米产业蓝皮书
中国薏仁米产业发展报告No.2（2018）
著(编)者：李发耀 石明　秦礼康
2018年8月出版 / 估价：99.00元
PSN B-2017-645-1/1

邮轮绿皮书
中国邮轮产业发展报告（2018）
著(编)者：汪泓　　2018年10月出版 / 估价：99.00元
PSN G-2014-419-1/1

智能养老蓝皮书
中国智能养老产业发展报告（2018）
著(编)者：朱勇　　2018年10月出版 / 估价：99.00元
PSN B-2015-488-1/1

中国节能汽车蓝皮书
中国节能汽车发展报告（2017～2018）
著(编)者：中国汽车工程研究院股份有限公司
2018年9月出版 / 估价：99.00元
PSN B-2016-565-1/1

中国陶瓷产业蓝皮书
中国陶瓷产业发展报告（2018）
著(编)者：左和平 黄速建
2018年10月出版 / 估价：99.00元
PSN B-2016-573-1/1

装备制造业蓝皮书
中国装备制造业发展报告（2018）
著(编)者：徐东华　　2018年12月出版 / 估价：118.00元
PSN B-2015-505-1/1

行业及其他类

"三农"互联网金融蓝皮书
中国"三农"互联网金融发展报告（2018）
著(编)者：李勇坚 王弢
2018年8月出版 / 估价：99.00元
PSN B-2016-560-1/1

SUV蓝皮书
中国SUV市场发展报告（2017~2018）
著(编)者：靳军 2018年9月出版 / 估价：99.00元
PSN B-2016-571-1/1

冰雪蓝皮书
中国冬季奥运会发展报告（2018）
著(编)者：孙承华 伍斌 魏庆华 张鸿俊
2018年9月出版 / 估价：99.00元
PSN B-2017-647-2/3

彩票蓝皮书
中国彩票发展报告（2018）
著(编)者：益彩基金 2018年4月出版 / 估价：99.00元
PSN B-2015-462-1/1

测绘地理信息蓝皮书
测绘地理信息供给侧结构性改革研究报告（2018）
著(编)者：库热西·买合苏提
2018年12月出版 / 估价：168.00元
PSN B-2009-145-1/1

产权市场蓝皮书
中国产权市场发展报告（2017）
著(编)者：曹和平 2018年5月出版 / 估价：99.00元
PSN B-2009-147-1/1

城投蓝皮书
中国城投行业发展报告（2018）
著(编)者：华景斌
2018年11月出版 / 估价：300.00元
PSN B-2016-514-1/1

大数据蓝皮书
中国大数据发展报告（No.2）
著(编)者：连玉明 2018年5月出版 / 估价：99.00元
PSN B-2017-620-1/1

大数据应用蓝皮书
中国大数据应用发展报告No.2（2018）
著(编)者：陈军君 2018年8月出版 / 估价：99.00元
PSN B-2017-644-1/1

对外投资与风险蓝皮书
中国对外直接投资与国家风险报告（2018）
著(编)者：中债资信评估有限责任公司
中国社会科学院世界经济与政治研究所
2018年4月出版 / 估价：189.00元
PSN B-2017-606-1/1

工业和信息化蓝皮书
人工智能发展报告（2017~2018）
著(编)者：尹丽波 2018年6月出版 / 估价：99.00元
PSN B-2015-448-1/6

工业和信息化蓝皮书
世界智慧城市发展报告（2017~2018）
著(编)者：尹丽波 2018年6月出版 / 估价：99.00元
PSN B-2017-624-6/6

工业和信息化蓝皮书
世界网络安全发展报告（2017~2018）
著(编)者：尹丽波 2018年6月出版 / 估价：99.00元
PSN B-2015-452-5/6

工业和信息化蓝皮书
世界信息化发展报告（2017~2018）
著(编)者：尹丽波 2018年6月出版 / 估价：99.00元
PSN B-2015-451-4/6

工业设计蓝皮书
中国工业设计发展报告（2018）
著(编)者：王晓红 于炜 张立群 2018年9月出版 / 估价：168.00元
PSN B-2014-420-1/1

公共关系蓝皮书
中国公共关系发展报告（2018）
著(编)者：柳斌杰 2018年11月出版 / 估价：99.00元
PSN B-2016-579-1/1

管理蓝皮书
中国管理发展报告（2018）
著(编)者：张晓东 2018年10月出版 / 估价：99.00元
PSN B-2014-416-1/1

海关发展蓝皮书
中国海关发展前沿报告（2018）
著(编)者：干春晖 2018年6月出版 / 估价：99.00元
PSN B-2017-616-1/1

互联网医疗蓝皮书
中国互联网健康医疗发展报告（2018）
著(编)者：芮晓武 2018年6月出版 / 估价：99.00元
PSN B-2016-567-1/1

黄金市场蓝皮书
中国商业银行黄金业务发展报告（2017~2018）
著(编)者：平安银行 2018年3月出版 / 估价：99.00元
PSN B-2016-524-1/1

会展蓝皮书
中外会展业动态评估研究报告（2018）
著(编)者：张敏 任中峰 聂鑫焱 牛盼强
2018年12月出版 / 估价：99.00元
PSN B-2013-327-1/1

基金会蓝皮书
中国基金会发展报告（2017~2018）
著(编)者：中国基金会发展报告课题组
2018年4月出版 / 估价：99.00元
PSN B-2013-368-1/1

基金会绿皮书
中国基金会发展独立研究报告（2018）
著(编)者：基金会中心网 中央民族大学基金会研究中心
2018年6月出版 / 估价：99.00元
PSN G-2011-213-1/1

基金会透明度蓝皮书
中国基金会透明度发展研究报告（2018）
著(编)者：基金会中心网
清华大学廉政与治理研究中心
2018年9月出版 / 估价：99.00元
PSN B-2013-339-1/1

建筑装饰蓝皮书
中国建筑装饰行业发展报告（2018）
著(编)者：葛道顺 刘晓一
2018年10月出版 / 估价：198.00元
PSN B-2016-553-1/1

金融监管蓝皮书
中国金融监管报告（2018）
著(编)者：胡滨　2018年5月出版 / 估价：99.00元
PSN B-2012-281-1/1

金融蓝皮书
中国互联网金融行业分析与评估（2018～2019）
著(编)者：黄国平 伍旭川　2018年12月出版 / 估价：99.00元
PSN B-2016-585-7/7

金融科技蓝皮书
中国金融科技发展报告（2018）
著(编)者：李扬 孙国峰　2018年10月出版 / 估价：99.00元
PSN B-2014-374-1/1

金融信息服务蓝皮书
中国金融信息服务发展报告（2018）
著(编)者：李平　2018年5月出版 / 估价：99.00元
PSN B-2017-621-1/1

京津冀金融蓝皮书
京津冀金融发展报告（2018）
著(编)者：王爱俭 王璟怡　2018年10月出版 / 估价：99.00元
PSN B-2016-527-1/1

科普蓝皮书
国家科普能力发展报告（2018）
著(编)者：王康友　2018年5月出版 / 估价：138.00元
PSN B-2017-632-4/4

科普蓝皮书
中国基层科普发展报告（2017～2018）
著(编)者：赵立新 陈玲　2018年9月出版 / 估价：99.00元
PSN B-2016-568-3/4

科普蓝皮书
中国科普基础设施发展报告（2017～2018）
著(编)者：任福君　2018年6月出版 / 估价：99.00元
PSN B-2010-174-1/3

科普蓝皮书
中国科普人才发展报告（2017～2018）
著(编)者：郑念 任嵘嵘　2018年7月出版 / 估价：99.00元
PSN B-2016-512-2/4

科普能力蓝皮书
中国科普能力评价报告（2018～2019）
著(编)者：李富强 李群　2018年8月出版 / 估价：99.00元
PSN B-2016-555-1/1

临空经济蓝皮书
中国临空经济发展报告（2018）
著(编)者：连玉明　2018年9月出版 / 估价：99.00元
PSN B-2014-421-1/1

旅游安全蓝皮书
中国旅游安全报告（2018）
著(编)者：郑向敏 谢朝武　2018年5月出版 / 估价：158.00元
PSN B-2012-280-1/1

旅游绿皮书
2017～2018年中国旅游发展分析与预测
著(编)者：宋瑞　2018年2月出版 / 估价：99.00元
PSN G-2002-018-1/1

煤炭蓝皮书
中国煤炭工业发展报告（2018）
著(编)者：岳福斌　2018年12月出版 / 估价：99.00元
PSN B-2008-123-1/1

民营企业社会责任蓝皮书
中国民营企业社会责任报告（2018）
著(编)者：中华全国工商业联合会
2018年12月出版 / 估价：99.00元
PSN B-2015-510-1/1

民营医院蓝皮书
中国民营医院发展报告（2017）
著(编)者：薛晓林　2018年1月出版 / 估价：99.00元
PSN B-2012-299-1/1

闽商蓝皮书
闽商发展报告（2018）
著(编)者：李闽榕 王日根 林琛
2018年12月出版 / 估价：99.00元
PSN B-2012-298-1/1

农业应对气候变化蓝皮书
中国农业气象灾害及其灾损评估报告（No.3）
著(编)者：矫梅燕　2018年1月出版 / 估价：118.00元
PSN B-2014-413-1/1

品牌蓝皮书
中国品牌战略发展报告（2018）
著(编)者：汪同三　2018年10月出版 / 估价：99.00元
PSN B-2016-580-1/1

企业扶贫蓝皮书
中国企业扶贫研究报告（2018）
著(编)者：钟宏武　2018年12月出版 / 估价：99.00元
PSN B-2016-593-1/1

企业公益蓝皮书
中国企业公益研究报告（2018）
著(编)者：钟宏武 汪杰 黄晓娟
2018年12月出版 / 估价：99.00元
PSN B-2015-501-1/1

企业国际化蓝皮书
中国企业全球化报告（2018）
著(编)者：王辉耀 苗绿　2018年11月出版 / 估价：99.00元
PSN B-2014-427-1/1

企业蓝皮书
中国企业绿色发展报告No.2（2018）
著(编)者：李红玉 朱光辉
2018年8月出版 / 估价：99.00元
PSN B-2015-481-2/2

企业社会责任蓝皮书
中资企业海外社会责任研究报告（2017~2018）
著(编)者：钟宏武 叶柳红 张蒽
2018年1月出版 / 估价：99.00元
PSN B-2017-603-2/2

企业社会责任蓝皮书
中国企业社会责任研究报告（2018）
著(编)者：黄群慧 钟宏武 张蒽 汪杰
2018年11月出版 / 估价：99.00元
PSN B-2009-149-1/2

汽车安全蓝皮书
中国汽车安全发展报告（2018）
著(编)者：中国汽车技术研究中心
2018年8月出版 / 估价：99.00元
PSN B-2014-385-1/1

汽车电子商务蓝皮书
中国汽车电子商务发展报告（2018）
著(编)者：中华全国工商业联合会汽车经销商商会
北方工业大学
北京易观智库网络科技有限公司
2018年10月出版 / 估价：158.00元
PSN B-2015-485-1/1

汽车知识产权蓝皮书
中国汽车产业知识产权发展报告（2018）
著(编)者：中国汽车工程研究院股份有限公司
中国汽车工程学会
重庆长安汽车股份有限公司
2018年12月出版 / 估价：99.00元
PSN B-2016-594-1/1

青少年体育蓝皮书
中国青少年体育发展报告（2017）
著(编)者：刘扶民 杨桦 2018年1月出版 / 估价：99.00元
PSN B-2015-482-1/1

区块链蓝皮书
中国区块链发展报告（2018）
著(编)者：李伟 2018年9月出版 / 估价：99.00元
PSN B-2017-649-1/1

群众体育蓝皮书
中国群众体育发展报告（2017）
著(编)者：刘国永 戴健 2018年5月出版 / 估价：99.00元
PSN B-2014-411-1/3

群众体育蓝皮书
中国社会体育指导员发展报告（2018）
著(编)者：刘国永 王欢 2018年4月出版 / 估价：99.00元
PSN B-2016-520-3/3

人力资源蓝皮书
中国人力资源发展报告（2018）
著(编)者：余兴安 2018年11月出版 / 估价：99.00元
PSN B-2012-287-1/1

融资租赁蓝皮书
中国融资租赁业发展报告（2017~2018）
著(编)者：李光荣 王力 2018年8月出版 / 估价：99.00元
PSN B-2015-443-1/1

商会蓝皮书
中国商会发展报告No.5（2017）
著(编)者：王钦敏 2018年7月出版 / 估价：99.00元
PSN B-2008-125-1/1

商务中心区蓝皮书
中国商务中心区发展报告No.4（2017~2018）
著(编)者：李国红 单菁菁 2018年9月出版 / 估价：99.00元
PSN B-2015-444-1/1

设计产业蓝皮书
中国创新设计发展报告（2018）
著(编)者：王晓红 张立群 于炜
2018年11月出版 / 估价：99.00元
PSN B-2016-581-2/2

社会责任管理蓝皮书
中国上市公司社会责任能力成熟度报告No.4（2018）
著(编)者：肖红军 王晓光 李伟阳
2018年12月出版 / 估价：99.00元
PSN B-2015-507-2/2

社会责任管理蓝皮书
中国企业公众透明度报告No.4（2017~2018）
著(编)者：黄速建 熊梦 王晓光 肖红军
2018年4月出版 / 估价：99.00元
PSN B-2015-440-1/2

食品药品蓝皮书
食品药品安全与监管政策研究报告（2016~2017）
著(编)者：唐民皓 2018年6月出版 / 估价：99.00元
PSN B-2009-129-1/1

输血服务蓝皮书
中国输血行业发展报告（2018）
著(编)者：孙俊 2018年12月出版 / 估价：99.00元
PSN B-2016-582-1/1

水利风景区蓝皮书
中国水利风景区发展报告（2018）
著(编)者：董建文 兰思仁
2018年10月出版 / 估价：99.00元
PSN B-2015-480-1/1

私募市场蓝皮书
中国私募股权市场发展报告（2017~2018）
著(编)者：曹和平 2018年12月出版 / 估价：99.00元
PSN B-2010-162-1/1

碳排放权交易蓝皮书
中国碳排放权交易报告（2018）
著(编)者：孙永平 2018年11月出版 / 估价：99.00元
PSN B-2017-652-1/1

碳市场蓝皮书
中国碳市场报告（2018）
著(编)者：定金彪 2018年11月出版 / 估价：99.00元
PSN B-2014-430-1/1

体育蓝皮书
中国公共体育服务发展报告（2018）
著(编)者：戴健　　2018年12月出版 / 估价：99.00元
PSN B-2013-367-2/5

土地市场蓝皮书
中国农村土地市场发展报告（2017～2018）
著(编)者：李光荣　　2018年3月出版 / 估价：99.00元
PSN B-2016-526-1/1

土地整治蓝皮书
中国土地整治发展研究报告（No.5）
著(编)者：国土资源部土地整治中心
2018年7月出版 / 估价：99.00元
PSN B-2014-401-1/1

土地政策蓝皮书
中国土地政策研究报告（2018）
著(编)者：高延利 李宪文　　2017年12月出版 / 估价：99.00元
PSN B-2015-506-1/1

网络空间安全蓝皮书
中国网络空间安全发展报告（2018）
著(编)者：惠志斌 覃庆玲
2018年11月出版 / 估价：99.00元
PSN B-2015-466-1/1

文化志愿服务蓝皮书
中国文化志愿服务发展报告（2018）
著(编)者：张永新 良警宇　　2018年11月出版 / 估价：128.00元
PSN B-2016-596-1/1

西部金融蓝皮书
中国西部金融发展报告（2017～2018）
著(编)者：李忠民　　2018年8月出版 / 估价：99.00元
PSN B-2010-160-1/1

协会商会蓝皮书
中国行业协会商会发展报告（2017）
著(编)者：景朝阳 李勇　　2018年4月出版 / 估价：99.00元
PSN B-2015-461-1/1

新三板蓝皮书
中国新三板市场发展报告（2018）
著(编)者：王力　　2018年8月出版 / 估价：99.00元
PSN B-2016-533-1/1

信托市场蓝皮书
中国信托业市场报告（2017～2018）
著(编)者：用益金融信托研究院
2018年1月出版 / 估价：198.00元
PSN B-2014-371-1/1

信息化蓝皮书
中国信息化形势分析与预测（2017～2018）
著(编)者：周宏仁　　2018年8月出版 / 估价：99.00元
PSN B-2010-168-1/1

信用蓝皮书
中国信用发展报告（2017～2018）
著(编)者：章政 田侃　　2018年4月出版 / 估价：99.00元
PSN B-2013-328-1/1

休闲绿皮书
2017～2018年中国休闲发展报告
著(编)者：宋瑞　　2018年7月出版 / 估价：99.00元
PSN G-2010-158-1/1

休闲体育蓝皮书
中国休闲体育发展报告（2017～2018）
著(编)者：李相如 钟秉枢
2018年10月出版 / 估价：99.00元
PSN B-2016-516-1/1

养老金融蓝皮书
中国养老金融发展报告（2018）
著(编)者：董克用 姚余栋
2018年9月出版 / 估价：99.00元
PSN B-2016-583-1/1

遥感监测绿皮书
中国可持续发展遥感监测报告（2017）
著(编)者：顾行发 汪克强 潘教峰 李闽榕 徐东华 王琦安
2018年6月出版 / 估价：298.00元
PSN B-2017-629-1/1

药品流通蓝皮书
中国药品流通行业发展报告（2018）
著(编)者：佘鲁林 温再兴
2018年7月出版 / 估价：198.00元
PSN B-2014-429-1/1

医疗器械蓝皮书
中国医疗器械行业发展报告（2018）
著(编)者：王宝亭 耿鸿武
2018年10月出版 / 估价：99.00元
PSN B-2017-661-1/1

医院蓝皮书
中国医院竞争力报告（2018）
著(编)者：庄一强 曾益新　　2018年3月出版 / 估价：118.00元
PSN B-2016-528-1/1

瑜伽蓝皮书
中国瑜伽业发展报告（2017~2018）
著(编)者：张永建 徐华锋 朱泰余
2018年6月出版 / 估价：198.00元
PSN B-2017-625-1/1

债券市场蓝皮书
中国债券市场发展报告（2017～2018）
著(编)者：杨农　　2018年10月出版 / 估价：99.00元
PSN B-2016-572-1/1

志愿服务蓝皮书
中国志愿服务发展报告（2018）
著(编)者：中国志愿服务联合会
2018年11月出版 / 估价：99.00元
PSN B-2017-664-1/1

中国上市公司蓝皮书
中国上市公司发展报告（2018）
著(编)者：张鹏 张平 黄胤英
2018年9月出版 / 估价：99.00元
PSN B-2014-414-1/1

中国新三板蓝皮书
中国新三板创新与发展报告（2018）
著(编)者：刘平安 闻召林
2018年8月出版 / 估价：158.00元
PSN B-2017-638-1/1

中医文化蓝皮书
北京中医药文化传播发展报告（2018）
著(编)者：毛嘉陵 2018年5月出版 / 估价：99.00元
PSN B-2015-468-1/2

中医文化蓝皮书
中国中医药文化传播发展报告（2018）
著(编)者：毛嘉陵 2018年7月出版 / 估价：99.00元
PSN B-2016-584-2/2

中医药蓝皮书
北京中医药知识产权发展报告No.2
著(编)者：汪洪 屠志涛 2018年4月出版 / 估价：168.00元
PSN B-2017-602-1/1

资本市场蓝皮书
中国场外交易市场发展报告（2016～2017）
著(编)者：高峦 2018年3月出版 / 估价：99.00元
PSN B-2009-153-1/1

资产管理蓝皮书
中国资产管理行业发展报告（2018）
著(编)者：郑智 2018年7月出版 / 估价：99.00元
PSN B-2014-407-2/2

资产证券化蓝皮书
中国资产证券化发展报告（2018）
著(编)者：纪志宏 2018年11月出版 / 估价：99.00元
PSN B-2017-660-1/1

自贸区蓝皮书
中国自贸区发展报告（2018）
著(编)者：王力 黄育华 2018年6月出版 / 估价：99.00元
PSN B-2016-558-1/1

国际问题与全球治理类

“一带一路”跨境通道蓝皮书
“一带一路”跨境通道建设研究报告（2018）
著(编)者：郭业洲 2018年8月出版 / 估价：99.00元
PSN B-2016-557-1/1

“一带一路”蓝皮书
“一带一路”建设发展报告（2018）
著(编)者：王晓泉 2018年6月出版 / 估价：99.00元
PSN B-2016-552-1/1

“一带一路”投资安全蓝皮书
中国“一带一路”投资与安全研究报告（2017～2018）
著(编)者：邹统钎 梁昊光 2018年4月出版 / 估价：99.00元
PSN B-2017-612-1/1

“一带一路”文化交流蓝皮书
中阿文化交流发展报告（2017）
著(编)者：王辉 2018年9月出版 / 估价：99.00元
PSN B-2017-655-1/1

G20国家创新竞争力黄皮书
二十国集团（G20）国家创新竞争力发展报告（2017～2018）
著(编)者：李建平 李闽榕 赵新力 周天勇
2018年7月出版 / 估价：168.00元
PSN Y-2011-229-1/1

阿拉伯黄皮书
阿拉伯发展报告（2016～2017）
著(编)者：罗林 2018年3月出版 / 估价：99.00元
PSN Y-2014-381-1/1

北部湾蓝皮书
泛北部湾合作发展报告（2017～2018）
著(编)者：吕余生 2018年12月出版 / 估价：99.00元
PSN B-2008-114-1/1

北极蓝皮书
北极地区发展报告（2017）
著(编)者：刘惠荣 2018年7月出版 / 估价：99.00元
PSN B-2017-634-1/1

大洋洲蓝皮书
大洋洲发展报告（2017～2018）
著(编)者：喻常森 2018年10月出版 / 估价：99.00元
PSN B-2013-341-1/1

东北亚区域合作蓝皮书
2017年“一带一路”倡议与东北亚区域合作
著(编)者：刘亚政 金美花
2018年5月出版 / 估价：99.00元
PSN B-2017-631-1/1

东盟黄皮书
东盟发展报告（2017）
著(编)者：杨晓强 庄国土
2018年3月出版 / 估价：99.00元
PSN Y-2012-303-1/1

东南亚蓝皮书
东南亚地区发展报告（2017～2018）
著(编)者：王勤 2018年12月出版 / 估价：99.00元
PSN B-2012-240-1/1

非洲黄皮书
非洲发展报告No.20（2017～2018）
著(编)者：张宏明 2018年7月出版 / 估价：99.00元
PSN Y-2012-239-1/1

非传统安全蓝皮书
中国非传统安全研究报告（2017～2018）
著(编)者：潇枫 罗中枢 2018年8月出版 / 估价：99.00元
PSN B-2012-273-1/1

国际安全蓝皮书
中国国际安全研究报告（2018）
著(编)者：刘慧　2018年7月出版 / 估价：99.00元
PSN B-2016-521-1/1

国际城市蓝皮书
国际城市发展报告（2018）
著(编)者：屠启宇　2018年2月出版 / 估价：99.00元
PSN B-2012-260-1/1

国际形势黄皮书
全球政治与安全报告（2018）
著(编)者：张宇燕　2018年1月出版 / 估价：99.00元
PSN Y-2001-016-1/1

公共外交蓝皮书
中国公共外交发展报告（2018）
著(编)者：赵启正 雷蔚真　2018年4月出版 / 估价：99.00元
PSN B-2015-457-1/1

金砖国家黄皮书
金砖国家综合创新竞争力发展报告（2018）
著(编)者：赵新力 李闽榕 黄茂兴
2018年8月出版 / 估价：128.00元
PSN Y-2017-643-1/1

拉美黄皮书
拉丁美洲和加勒比发展报告（2017～2018）
著(编)者：袁东振　2018年6月出版 / 估价：99.00元
PSN Y-1999-007-1/1

澜湄合作蓝皮书
澜沧江-湄公河合作发展报告（2018）
著(编)者：刘稚　2018年9月出版 / 估价：99.00元
PSN B-2011-196-1/1

欧洲蓝皮书
欧洲发展报告（2017～2018）
著(编)者：黄平 周弘 程卫东
2018年6月出版 / 估价：99.00元
PSN B-1999-009-1/1

葡语国家蓝皮书
葡语国家发展报告（2016～2017）
著(编)者：王成安 张敏 刘金兰
2018年4月出版 / 估价：99.00元
PSN B-2015-503-1/2

葡语国家蓝皮书
中国与葡语国家关系发展报告·巴西（2016）
著(编)者：张曙光　2018年8月出版 / 估价：99.00元
PSN B-2016-563-2/2

气候变化绿皮书
应对气候变化报告（2018）
著(编)者：王伟光 郑国光　2018年11月出版 / 估价：99.00元
PSN G-2009-144-1/1

全球环境竞争力绿皮书
全球环境竞争力报告（2018）
著(编)者：李建平 李闽榕 王金南
2018年12月出版 / 估价：198.00元
PSN G-2013-363-1/1

全球信息社会蓝皮书
全球信息社会发展报告（2018）
著(编)者：丁波涛 唐涛　2018年10月出版 / 估价：99.00元
PSN B-2017-665-1/1

日本经济蓝皮书
日本经济与中日经贸关系研究报告（2018）
著(编)者：张季风　2018年6月出版 / 估价：99.00元
PSN B-2008-102-1/1

上海合作组织黄皮书
上海合作组织发展报告（2018）
著(编)者：李进峰　2018年6月出版 / 估价：99.00元
PSN Y-2009-130-1/1

世界创新竞争力黄皮书
世界创新竞争力发展报告（2017）
著(编)者：李建平 李闽榕 赵新力
2018年1月出版 / 估价：168.00元
PSN Y-2013-318-1/1

世界经济黄皮书
2018年世界经济形势分析与预测
著(编)者：张宇燕　2018年1月出版 / 估价：99.00元
PSN Y-1999-006-1/1

丝绸之路蓝皮书
丝绸之路经济带发展报告（2018）
著(编)者：任宗哲 白宽犁 谷孟宾
2018年1月出版 / 估价：99.00元
PSN B-2014-410-1/1

新兴经济体蓝皮书
金砖国家发展报告（2018）
著(编)者：林跃勤 周文　2018年8月出版 / 估价：99.00元
PSN B-2011-195-1/1

亚太蓝皮书
亚太地区发展报告（2018）
著(编)者：李向阳　2018年5月出版 / 估价：99.00元
PSN B-2001-015-1/1

印度洋地区蓝皮书
印度洋地区发展报告（2018）
著(编)者：汪戎　2018年6月出版 / 估价：99.00元
PSN B-2013-334-1/1

渝新欧蓝皮书
渝新欧沿线国家发展报告（2018）
著(编)者：杨柏 黄森　2018年6月出版 / 估价：99.00元
PSN B-2017-626-1/1

中阿蓝皮书
中国-阿拉伯国家经贸发展报告（2018）
著(编)者：张廉 段庆林 王林聪 杨巧红
2018年12月出版 / 估价：99.00元
PSN B-2016-598-1/1

中东黄皮书
中东发展报告No.20（2017～2018）
著(编)者：杨光　2018年10月出版 / 估价：99.00元
PSN Y-1998-004-1/1

中亚黄皮书
中亚国家发展报告（2018）
著(编)者：孙力　2018年6月出版 / 估价：99.00元
PSN Y-2012-238-1/1

国别类

澳大利亚蓝皮书
澳大利亚发展报告（2017-2018）
著(编)者：孙有中 韩锋 2018年12月出版 / 估价：99.00元
PSN B-2016-587-1/1

巴西黄皮书
巴西发展报告（2017）
著(编)者：刘国枝 2018年5月出版 / 估价：99.00元
PSN Y-2017-614-1/1

德国蓝皮书
德国发展报告（2018）
著(编)者：郑春荣 2018年6月出版 / 估价：99.00元
PSN B-2012-278-1/1

俄罗斯黄皮书
俄罗斯发展报告（2018）
著(编)者：李永全 2018年6月出版 / 估价：99.00元
PSN Y-2006-061-1/1

韩国蓝皮书
韩国发展报告（2017）
著(编)者：牛林杰 刘宝全 2018年5月出版 / 估价：99.00元
PSN B-2010-155-1/1

加拿大蓝皮书
加拿大发展报告（2018）
著(编)者：唐小松 2018年9月出版 / 估价：99.00元
PSN B-2014-389-1/1

美国蓝皮书
美国研究报告（2018）
著(编)者：郑秉文 黄平 2018年5月出版 / 估价：99.00元
PSN B-2011-210-1/1

缅甸蓝皮书
缅甸国情报告（2017）
著(编)者：孔鹏 杨祥章 2018年1月出版 / 估价：99.00元
PSN B-2013-343-1/1

日本蓝皮书
日本研究报告（2018）
著(编)者：杨伯江 2018年6月出版 / 估价：99.00元
PSN B-2002-020-1/1

土耳其蓝皮书
土耳其发展报告（2018）
著(编)者：郭长刚 刘义 2018年9月出版 / 估价：99.00元
PSN B-2014-412-1/1

伊朗蓝皮书
伊朗发展报告（2017～2018）
著(编)者：冀开运 2018年10月 / 估价：99.00元
PSN B-2016-574-1/1

以色列蓝皮书
以色列发展报告（2018）
著(编)者：张倩红 2018年8月出版 / 估价：99.00元
PSN B-2015-483-1/1

印度蓝皮书
印度国情报告（2017）
著(编)者：吕昭义 2018年4月出版 / 估价：99.00元
PSN B-2012-241-1/1

英国蓝皮书
英国发展报告（2017～2018）
著(编)者：王展鹏 2018年12月出版 / 估价：99.00元
PSN B-2015-486-1/1

越南蓝皮书
越南国情报告（2018）
著(编)者：谢林城 2018年1月出版 / 估价：99.00元
PSN B-2006-056-1/1

泰国蓝皮书
泰国研究报告（2018）
著(编)者：庄国土 张禹东 刘文正
2018年10月出版 / 估价：99.00元
PSN B-2016-556-1/1

文化传媒类

“三农”舆情蓝皮书
中国“三农”网络舆情报告（2017～2018）
著(编)者：农业部信息中心
2018年6月出版 / 估价：99.00元
PSN B-2017-640-1/1

传媒竞争力蓝皮书
中国传媒国际竞争力研究报告（2018）
著(编)者：李本乾 刘强 王大可
2018年8月出版 / 估价：99.00元
PSN B-2013-356-1/1

传媒蓝皮书
中国传媒产业发展报告（2018）
著(编)者：崔保国 2018年5月出版 / 估价：99.00元
PSN B-2005-035-1/1

传媒投资蓝皮书
中国传媒投资发展报告（2018）
著(编)者：张向东 谭云明
2018年6月出版 / 估价：148.00元
PSN B-2015-474-1/1

非物质文化遗产蓝皮书
中国非物质文化遗产发展报告（2018）
著(编)者：陈平　2018年5月出版 / 估价：128.00元
PSN B-2015-469-1/2

非物质文化遗产蓝皮书
中国非物质文化遗产保护发展报告（2018）
著(编)者：宋俊华　2018年10月出版 / 估价：128.00元
PSN B-2016-586-2/2

广电蓝皮书
中国广播电影电视发展报告（2018）
著(编)者：国家新闻出版广电总局发展研究中心
2018年7月出版 / 估价：99.00元
PSN B-2006-072-1/1

广告主蓝皮书
中国广告主营销传播趋势报告No.9
著(编)者：黄升民 杜国清 邵华冬 等
2018年10月出版 / 估价：158.00元
PSN B-2005-041-1/1

国际传播蓝皮书
中国国际传播发展报告（2018）
著(编)者：胡正荣 李继东 姬德强
2018年12月出版 / 估价：99.00元
PSN B-2014-408-1/1

国家形象蓝皮书
中国国家形象传播报告（2017）
著(编)者：张昆　2018年3月出版 / 估价：128.00元
PSN B-2017-605-1/1

互联网治理蓝皮书
中国网络社会治理研究报告（2018）
著(编)者：罗昕 支庭荣
2018年9月出版 / 估价：118.00元
PSN B-2017-653-1/1

纪录片蓝皮书
中国纪录片发展报告（2018）
著(编)者：何苏六　2018年10月出版 / 估价：99.00元
PSN B-2011-222-1/1

科学传播蓝皮书
中国科学传播报告（2016~2017）
著(编)者：詹正茂　2018年6月出版 / 估价：99.00元
PSN B-2008-120-1/1

两岸创意经济蓝皮书
两岸创意经济研究报告（2018）
著(编)者：罗昌智 董泽平
2018年10月出版 / 估价：99.00元
PSN B-2014-437-1/1

媒介与女性蓝皮书
中国媒介与女性发展报告（2017～2018）
著(编)者：刘利群　2018年5月出版 / 估价：99.00元
PSN B-2013-345-1/1

媒体融合蓝皮书
中国媒体融合发展报告（2017）
著(编)者：梅宁华 支庭荣　2018年1月出版 / 估价：99.00元
PSN B-2015-479-1/1

全球传媒蓝皮书
全球传媒发展报告（2017～2018）
著(编)者：胡正荣 李继东　2018年6月出版 / 估价：99.00元
PSN B-2012-237-1/1

少数民族非遗蓝皮书
中国少数民族非物质文化遗产发展报告（2018）
著(编)者：肖远平（彝） 柴立（满）
2018年10月出版 / 估价：118.00元
PSN B-2015-467-1/1

视听新媒体蓝皮书
中国视听新媒体发展报告（2018）
著(编)者：国家新闻出版广电总局发展研究中心
2018年7月出版 / 估价：118.00元
PSN B-2011-184-1/1

数字娱乐产业蓝皮书
中国动画产业发展报告（2018）
著(编)者：孙立军 孙平 牛兴侦
2018年10月出版 / 估价：99.00元
PSN B-2011-198-1/2

数字娱乐产业蓝皮书
中国游戏产业发展报告（2018）
著(编)者：孙立军 刘跃军
2018年10月出版 / 估价：99.00元
PSN B-2017-662-2/2

文化创新蓝皮书
中国文化创新报告（2017·No.8）
著(编)者：傅才武　2018年4月出版 / 估价：99.00元
PSN B-2009-143-1/1

文化建设蓝皮书
中国文化发展报告（2018）
著(编)者：江畅 孙伟平 戴茂堂
2018年5月出版 / 估价：99.00元
PSN B-2014-392-1/1

文化科技蓝皮书
文化科技创新发展报告（2018）
著(编)者：于平 李凤亮　2018年10月出版 / 估价：99.00元
PSN B-2013-342-1/1

文化蓝皮书
中国公共文化服务发展报告（2017~2018）
著(编)者：刘新成 张永新 张旭
2018年12月出版 / 估价：99.00元
PSN B-2007-093-2/10

文化蓝皮书
中国少数民族文化发展报告（2017～2018）
著(编)者：武翠英 张晓明 任乌晶
2018年9月出版 / 估价：99.00元
PSN B-2013-369-9/10

文化蓝皮书
中国文化产业供需协调检测报告（2018）
著(编)者：王亚南　2018年2月出版 / 估价：99.00元
PSN B-2013-323-8/10

文化蓝皮书
中国文化消费需求景气评价报告（2018）
著(编)者：王亚南　2018年2月出版 / 估价：99.00元
PSN B-2011-236-4/10

文化蓝皮书
中国公共文化投入增长测评报告（2018）
著(编)者：王亚南　2018年2月出版 / 估价：99.00元
PSN B-2014-435-10/10

文化品牌蓝皮书
中国文化品牌发展报告（2018）
著(编)者：欧阳友权　2018年5月出版 / 估价：99.00元
PSN B-2012-277-1/1

文化遗产蓝皮书
中国文化遗产事业发展报告（2017～2018）
著(编)者：苏杨 张颖岚 卓杰 白海峰 陈晨 陈叙图
2018年8月出版 / 估价：99.00元
PSN B-2008-119-1/1

文学蓝皮书
中国文情报告（2017～2018）
著(编)者：白烨　2018年5月出版 / 估价：99.00元
PSN B-2011-221-1/1

新媒体蓝皮书
中国新媒体发展报告No.9（2018）
著(编)者：唐绪军　2018年7月出版 / 估价：99.00元
PSN B-2010-169-1/1

新媒体社会责任蓝皮书
中国新媒体社会责任研究报告（2018）
著(编)者：钟瑛　2018年12月出版 / 估价：99.00元
PSN B-2014-423-1/1

移动互联网蓝皮书
中国移动互联网发展报告（2018）
著(编)者：余清楚　2018年6月出版 / 估价：99.00元
PSN B-2012-282-1/1

影视蓝皮书
中国影视产业发展报告（2018）
著(编)者：司若 陈鹏 陈锐　2018年4月出版 / 估价：99.00元
PSN B-2016-529-1/1

舆情蓝皮书
中国社会舆情与危机管理报告（2018）
著(编)者：谢耘耕　2018年9月出版 / 估价：138.00元
PSN B-2011-235-1/1

地方发展类-经济

澳门蓝皮书
澳门经济社会发展报告（2017～2018）
著(编)者：吴志良 郝雨凡　2018年7月出版 / 估价：99.00元
PSN B-2009-138-1/1

澳门绿皮书
澳门旅游休闲发展报告（2017～2018）
著(编)者：郝雨凡 林广志　2018年5月出版 / 估价：99.00元
PSN G-2017-617-1/1

北京蓝皮书
北京经济发展报告（2017～2018）
著(编)者：杨松　2018年6月出版 / 估价：99.00元
PSN B-2006-054-2/8

北京旅游绿皮书
北京旅游发展报告（2018）
著(编)者：北京旅游学会
2018年7月出版 / 估价：99.00元
PSN G-2012-301-1/1

北京体育蓝皮书
北京体育产业发展报告（2017～2018）
著(编)者：钟秉枢 陈杰 杨铁黎
2018年9月出版 / 估价：99.00元
PSN B-2015-475-1/1

滨海金融蓝皮书
滨海新区金融发展报告（2017）
著(编)者：王爱俭 李向前　2018年4月出版 / 估价：99.00元
PSN B-2014-424-1/1

城乡一体化蓝皮书
北京城乡一体化发展报告（2017～2018）
著(编)者：吴宝新 张宝秀 黄序
2018年5月出版 / 估价：99.00元
PSN B-2012-258-2/2

非公有制企业社会责任蓝皮书
北京非公有制企业社会责任报告（2018）
著(编)者：宋贵伦 冯培　2018年6月出版 / 估价：99.00元
PSN B-2017-613-1/1

福建旅游蓝皮书
福建省旅游产业发展现状研究（2017~2018）
著(编)者：陈敏华 黄远水
2018年12月出版 / 估价：128.00元
PSN B-2016-591-1/1

福建自贸区蓝皮书
中国(福建)自由贸易试验区发展报告(2017~2018)
著(编)者：黄茂兴　2018年4月出版 / 估价：118.00元
PSN B-2016-531-1/1

甘肃蓝皮书
甘肃经济发展分析与预测（2018）
著(编)者：安文华 罗哲　2018年1月出版 / 估价：99.00元
PSN B-2013-312-1/6

甘肃蓝皮书
甘肃商贸流通发展报告（2018）
著(编)者：张应华 王福生 王晓芳
2018年1月出版 / 估价：99.00元
PSN B-2016-522-6/6

甘肃蓝皮书
甘肃县域和农村发展报告（2018）
著(编)者：朱智文 包东红 王建兵
2018年1月出版 / 估价：99.00元
PSN B-2013-316-5/6

甘肃农业科技绿皮书
甘肃农业科技发展研究报告（2018）
著(编)者：魏胜文 乔德华 张东伟
2018年12月出版 / 估价：198.00元
PSN B-2016-592-1/1

巩义蓝皮书
巩义经济社会发展报告（2018）
著(编)者：丁同民 朱军　2018年4月出版 / 估价：99.00元
PSN B-2016-532-1/1

广东外经贸蓝皮书
广东对外经济贸易发展研究报告（2017～2018）
著(编)者：陈万灵　2018年6月出版 / 估价：99.00元
PSN B-2012-286-1/1

广西北部湾经济区蓝皮书
广西北部湾经济区开放开发报告（2017～2018）
著(编)者：广西壮族自治区北部湾经济区和东盟开放合作办公室
广西社会科学院
广西北部湾发展研究院
2018年2月出版 / 估价：99.00元
PSN B-2010-181-1/1

广州蓝皮书
广州城市国际化发展报告（2018）
著(编)者：张跃国　2018年8月出版 / 估价：99.00元
PSN B-2012-246-11/14

广州蓝皮书
中国广州城市建设与管理发展报告（2018）
著(编)者：张其学 陈小钢 王宏伟　2018年8月出版 / 估价：99.00元
PSN B-2007-087-4/14

广州蓝皮书
广州创新型城市发展报告（2018）
著(编)者：尹涛　2018年6月出版 / 估价：99.00元
PSN B-2012-247-12/14

广州蓝皮书
广州经济发展报告（2018）
著(编)者：张跃国 尹涛　2018年7月出版 / 估价：99.00元
PSN B-2005-040-1/14

广州蓝皮书
2018年中国广州经济形势分析与预测
著(编)者：魏明海 谢博能 李华
2018年6月出版 / 估价：99.00元
PSN B-2011-185-9/14

广州蓝皮书
中国广州科技创新发展报告（2018）
著(编)者：于欣伟 陈爽 邓佑满　2018年8月出版 / 估价：99.00元
PSN B-2006-065-2/14

广州蓝皮书
广州农村发展报告（2018）
著(编)者：朱名宏　2018年7月出版 / 估价：99.00元
PSN B-2010-167-8/14

广州蓝皮书
广州汽车产业发展报告（2018）
著(编)者：杨再高 冯兴亚　2018年7月出版 / 估价：99.00元
PSN B-2006-066-3/14

广州蓝皮书
广州商贸业发展报告（2018）
著(编)者：张跃国 陈杰 荀振英
2018年7月出版 / 估价：99.00元
PSN B-2012-245-10/14

贵阳蓝皮书
贵阳城市创新发展报告No.3（白云篇）
著(编)者：连玉明　2018年5月出版 / 估价：99.00元
PSN B-2015-491-3/10

贵阳蓝皮书
贵阳城市创新发展报告No.3（观山湖篇）
著(编)者：连玉明　2018年5月出版 / 估价：99.00元
PSN B-2015-497-9/10

贵阳蓝皮书
贵阳城市创新发展报告No.3（花溪篇）
著(编)者：连玉明　2018年5月出版 / 估价：99.00元
PSN B-2015-490-2/10

贵阳蓝皮书
贵阳城市创新发展报告No.3（开阳篇）
著(编)者：连玉明　2018年5月出版 / 估价：99.00元
PSN B-2015-492-4/10

贵阳蓝皮书
贵阳城市创新发展报告No.3（南明篇）
著(编)者：连玉明　2018年5月出版 / 估价：99.00元
PSN B-2015-496-8/10

贵阳蓝皮书
贵阳城市创新发展报告No.3（清镇篇）
著(编)者：连玉明　2018年5月出版 / 估价：99.00元
PSN B-2015-489-1/10

贵阳蓝皮书
贵阳城市创新发展报告No.3（乌当篇）
著(编)者：连玉明　2018年5月出版 / 估价：99.00元
PSN B-2015-495-7/10

贵阳蓝皮书
贵阳城市创新发展报告No.3（息烽篇）
著(编)者：连玉明　2018年5月出版 / 估价：99.00元
PSN B-2015-493-5/10

贵阳蓝皮书
贵阳城市创新发展报告No.3（修文篇）
著(编)者：连玉明　2018年5月出版 / 估价：99.00元
PSN B-2015-494-6/10

贵阳蓝皮书
贵阳城市创新发展报告No.3（云岩篇）
著(编)者：连玉明　2018年5月出版 / 估价：99.00元
PSN B-2015-498-10/10

贵州房地产蓝皮书
贵州房地产发展报告No.5（2018）
著(编)者：武廷方　2018年7月出版 / 估价：99.00元
PSN B-2014-426-1/1

贵州蓝皮书
贵州册亨经济社会发展报告（2018）
著(编)者：黄德林　2018年3月出版 / 估价：99.00元
PSN B-2016-525-8/9

贵州蓝皮书
贵州地理标志产业发展报告（2018）
著(编)者：李发耀 黄其松　2018年8月出版 / 估价：99.00元
PSN B-2017-646-10/10

贵州蓝皮书
贵安新区发展报告（2017~2018）
著(编)者：马长青 吴大华　2018年6月出版 / 估价：99.00元
PSN B-2015-459-4/10

贵州蓝皮书
贵州国家级开放创新平台发展报告（2017~2018）
著(编)者：申晓庆 吴大华 季泓
2018年11月出版 / 估价：99.00元
PSN B-2016-518-7/10

贵州蓝皮书
贵州国有企业社会责任发展报告（2017~2018）
著(编)者：郭丽　2018年12月出版 / 估价：99.00元
PSN B-2015-511-6/10

贵州蓝皮书
贵州民航业发展报告（2017）
著(编)者：申振东 吴大华　2018年1月出版 / 估价：99.00元
PSN B-2015-471-5/10

贵州蓝皮书
贵州民营经济发展报告（2017）
著(编)者：杨静 吴大华　2018年3月出版 / 估价：99.00元
PSN B-2016-530-9/9

杭州都市圈蓝皮书
杭州都市圈发展报告（2018）
著(编)者：沈翔 戚建国　2018年5月出版 / 估价：128.00元
PSN B-2012-302-1/1

河北经济蓝皮书
河北省经济发展报告（2018）
著(编)者：马树强 金浩 张贵　2018年4月出版 / 估价：99.00元
PSN B-2014-380-1/1

河北蓝皮书
河北经济社会发展报告（2018）
著(编)者：康振海　2018年1月出版 / 估价：99.00元
PSN B-2014-372-1/3

河北蓝皮书
京津冀协同发展报告（2018）
著(编)者：陈璐　2018年1月出版 / 估价：99.00元
PSN B-2017-601-2/3

河南经济蓝皮书
2018年河南经济形势分析与预测
著(编)者：王世炎　2018年3月出版 / 估价：99.00元
PSN B-2007-086-1/1

河南蓝皮书
河南城市发展报告（2018）
著(编)者：张占仓 王建国　2018年5月出版 / 估价：99.00元
PSN B-2009-131-3/9

河南蓝皮书
河南工业发展报告（2018）
著(编)者：张占仓　2018年5月出版 / 估价：99.00元
PSN B-2013-317-5/9

河南蓝皮书
河南金融发展报告（2018）
著(编)者：喻新安 谷建全
2018年6月出版 / 估价：99.00元
PSN B-2014-390-7/9

河南蓝皮书
河南经济发展报告（2018）
著(编)者：张占仓 完世伟
2018年4月出版 / 估价：99.00元
PSN B-2010-157-4/9

河南蓝皮书
河南能源发展报告（2018）
著(编)者：国网河南省电力公司经济技术研究院
河南省社会科学院
2018年3月出版 / 估价：99.00元
PSN B-2017-607-9/9

河南商务蓝皮书
河南商务发展报告（2018）
著(编)者：焦锦淼 穆荣国　2018年5月出版 / 估价：99.00元
PSN B-2014-399-1/1

河南双创蓝皮书
河南创新创业发展报告（2018）
著(编)者：喻新安 杨雪梅　2018年8月出版 / 估价：99.00元
PSN B-2017-641-1/1

黑龙江蓝皮书
黑龙江经济发展报告（2018）
著(编)者：朱宇　2018年1月出版 / 估价：99.00元
PSN B-2011-190-2/2

湖南城市蓝皮书
区域城市群整合
著(编)者：童中贤 韩未名　2018年12月出版 / 估价：99.00元
PSN B-2006-064-1/1

湖南蓝皮书
湖南城乡一体化发展报告（2018）
著(编)者：陈文胜 王文强 陆福兴
2018年8月出版 / 估价：99.00元
PSN B-2015-477-8/8

湖南蓝皮书
2018年湖南电子政务发展报告
著(编)者：梁志峰　2018年5月出版 / 估价：128.00元
PSN B-2014-394-6/8

湖南蓝皮书
2018年湖南经济发展报告
著(编)者：卞鹰　2018年5月出版 / 估价：128.00元
PSN B-2011-207-2/8

湖南蓝皮书
2016年湖南经济展望
著(编)者：梁志峰　2018年5月出版 / 估价：128.00元
PSN B-2011-206-1/8

湖南蓝皮书
2018年湖南县域经济社会发展报告
著(编)者：梁志峰　2018年5月出版 / 估价：128.00元
PSN B-2014-395-7/8

湖南县域绿皮书
湖南县域发展报告（No.5）
著(编)者：袁准 周小毛 黎仁寅
2018年3月出版 / 估价：99.00元
PSN G-2012-274-1/1

沪港蓝皮书
沪港发展报告（2018）
著(编)者：尤安山　2018年9月出版 / 估价：99.00元
PSN B-2013-362-1/1

吉林蓝皮书
2018年吉林经济社会形势分析与预测
著(编)者：邵汉明　2017年12月出版 / 估价：99.00元
PSN B-2013-319-1/1

吉林省城市竞争力蓝皮书
吉林省城市竞争力报告（2018~2019）
著(编)者：崔岳春 张磊　2018年12月出版 / 估价：99.00元
PSN B-2016-513-1/1

济源蓝皮书
济源经济社会发展报告（2018）
著(编)者：喻新安　2018年4月出版 / 估价：99.00元
PSN B-2014-387-1/1

江苏蓝皮书
2018年江苏经济发展分析与展望
著(编)者：王庆五 吴先满　2018年7月出版 / 估价：128.00元
PSN B-2017-635-1/3

江西蓝皮书
江西经济社会发展报告（2018）
著(编)者：陈石俊 龚建文　2018年10月出版 / 估价：128.00元
PSN B-2015-484-1/2

江西蓝皮书
江西设区市发展报告（2018）
著(编)者：姜玮 梁勇　2018年10月出版 / 估价：99.00元
PSN B-2016-517-2/2

经济特区蓝皮书
中国经济特区发展报告（2017）
著(编)者：陶一桃　2018年1月出版 / 估价：99.00元
PSN B-2009-139-1/1

辽宁蓝皮书
2018年辽宁经济社会形势分析与预测
著(编)者：梁启东 魏红江　2018年6月出版 / 估价：99.00元
PSN B-2006-053-1/1

民族经济蓝皮书
中国民族地区经济发展报告（2018）
著(编)者：李曦辉　2018年7月出版 / 估价：99.00元
PSN B-2017-630-1/1

南宁蓝皮书
南宁经济发展报告（2018）
著(编)者：胡建华　2018年9月出版 / 估价：99.00元
PSN B-2016-569-2/3

浦东新区蓝皮书
上海浦东经济发展报告（2018）
著(编)者：沈开艳 周奇　2018年2月出版 / 估价：99.00元
PSN B-2011-225-1/1

青海蓝皮书
2018年青海经济社会形势分析与预测
著(编)者：陈玮　2017年12月出版 / 估价：99.00元
PSN B-2012-275-1/2

山东蓝皮书
山东经济形势分析与预测（2018）
著(编)者：李广杰　2018年7月出版 / 估价：99.00元
PSN B-2014-404-1/5

山东蓝皮书
山东省普惠金融发展报告（2018）
著(编)者：齐鲁财富网
2018年9月出版 / 估价：99.00元
PSN B2017-676-5/5

山西蓝皮书
山西资源型经济转型发展报告（2018）
著(编)者：李志强　2018年7月出版 / 估价：99.00元
PSN B-2011-197-1/1

陕西蓝皮书
陕西经济发展报告（2018）
著(编)者：任宗哲 白宽犁 裴成荣
2018年1月出版 / 估价：99.00元
PSN B-2009-135-1/6

陕西蓝皮书
陕西精准脱贫研究报告（2018）
著(编)者：任宗哲 白宽犁 王建康
2018年6月出版 / 估价：99.00元
PSN B-2017-623-6/6

上海蓝皮书
上海经济发展报告（2018）
著(编)者：沈开艳
2018年2月出版 / 估价：99.00元
PSN B-2006-057-1/7

上海蓝皮书
上海资源环境发展报告（2018）
著(编)者：周冯琦 汤庆合
2018年2月出版 / 估价：99.00元
PSN B-2006-060-4/7

上饶蓝皮书
上饶发展报告（2016~2017）
著(编)者：廖其志　2018年3月出版 / 估价：128.00元
PSN B-2014-377-1/1

深圳蓝皮书
深圳经济发展报告（2018）
著(编)者：张骁儒　2018年6月出版 / 估价：99.00元
PSN B-2008-112-3/7

四川蓝皮书
四川城镇化发展报告（2018）
著(编)者：侯水平 陈炜
2018年4月出版 / 估价：99.00元
PSN B-2015-456-7/7

四川蓝皮书
2018年四川经济形势分析与预测
著(编)者：杨钢　2018年1月出版 / 估价：99.00元
PSN B-2007-098-2/7

四川蓝皮书
四川企业社会责任研究报告（2017～2018）
著(编)者：侯水平 盛毅　2018年5月出版 / 估价：99.00元
PSN B-2014-386-4/7

四川蓝皮书
四川生态建设报告（2018）
著(编)者：李晟之　2018年5月出版 / 估价：99.00元
PSN B-2015-455-6/7

体育蓝皮书
上海体育产业发展报告（2017~2018）
著(编)者：张林 黄海燕　2018年10月出版 / 估价：99.00元
PSN B-2015-454-4/5

体育蓝皮书
长三角地区体育产业发展报告（2017～2018）
著(编)者：张林　2018年4月出版 / 估价：99.00元
PSN B-2015-453-3/5

天津金融蓝皮书
天津金融发展报告（2018）
著(编)者：王爱俭 孔德昌　2018年3月出版 / 估价：99.00元
PSN B-2014-418-1/1

图们江区域合作蓝皮书
图们江区域合作发展报告（2018）
著(编)者：李铁　2018年6月出版 / 估价：99.00元
PSN B-2015-464-1/1

温州蓝皮书
2018年温州经济社会形势分析与预测
著(编)者：蒋儒标 王春光 金浩
2018年4月出版 / 估价：99.00元
PSN B-2008-105-1/1

西咸新区蓝皮书
西咸新区发展报告（2018）
著(编)者：李扬 王军
2018年6月出版 / 估价：99.00元
PSN B-2016-534-1/1

修武蓝皮书
修武经济社会发展报告（2018）
著(编)者：张占仓 袁凯声
2018年10月出版 / 估价：99.00元
PSN B-2017-651-1/1

偃师蓝皮书
偃师经济社会发展报告（2018）
著(编)者：张占仓 袁凯声 何武周
2018年7月出版 / 估价：99.00元
PSN B-2017-627-1/1

扬州蓝皮书
扬州经济社会发展报告（2018）
著(编)者：陈扬
2018年12月出版 / 估价：108.00元
PSN B-2011-191-1/1

长垣蓝皮书
长垣经济社会发展报告（2018）
著(编)者：张占仓 袁凯声 秦保建
2018年10月出版 / 估价：99.00元
PSN B-2017-654-1/1

遵义蓝皮书
遵义发展报告（2018）
著(编)者：邓彦 曾征 龚永育
2018年9月出版 / 估价：99.00元
PSN B-2014-433-1/1

地方发展类-社会

安徽蓝皮书
安徽社会发展报告（2018）
著(编)者：程桦　2018年4月出版 / 估价：99.00元
PSN B-2013-325-1/1

安徽社会建设蓝皮书
安徽社会建设分析报告（2017～2018）
著(编)者：黄家海 蔡宪
2018年11月出版 / 估价：99.00元
PSN B-2013-322-1/1

北京蓝皮书
北京公共服务发展报告（2017～2018）
著(编)者：施昌奎　2018年3月出版 / 估价：99.00元
PSN B-2008-103-7/8

北京蓝皮书
北京社会发展报告（2017～2018）
著(编)者：李伟东
2018年7月出版 / 估价：99.00元
PSN B-2006-055-3/8

北京蓝皮书
北京社会治理发展报告（2017～2018）
著(编)者：殷星辰　2018年7月出版 / 估价：99.00元
PSN B-2014-391-8/8

北京律师蓝皮书
北京律师发展报告 No.3（2018）
著(编)者：王隽　2018年12月出版 / 估价：99.00元
PSN B-2011-217-1/1

北京人才蓝皮书
北京人才发展报告（2018）
著(编)者：敏华　　2018年12月出版 / 估价：128.00元
PSN B-2011-201-1/1

北京社会心态蓝皮书
北京社会心态分析报告（2017~2018）
北京市社会心理服务促进中心
2018年10月出版 / 估价：99.00元
PSN B-2014-422-1/1

北京社会组织管理蓝皮书
北京社会组织发展与管理（2018）
著(编)者：黄江松
2018年4月出版 / 估价：99.00元
PSN B-2015-446-1/1

北京养老产业蓝皮书
北京居家养老发展报告（2018）
著(编)者：陆杰华　周明明
2018年8月出版 / 估价：99.00元
PSN B-2015-465-1/1

法治蓝皮书
四川依法治省年度报告No.4（2018）
著(编)者：李林　杨天宗　田禾
2018年3月出版 / 估价：118.00元
PSN B-2015-447-2/3

福建妇女发展蓝皮书
福建省妇女发展报告（2018）
著(编)者：刘群英　　2018年11月出版 / 估价：99.00元
PSN B-2011-220-1/1

甘肃蓝皮书
甘肃社会发展分析与预测（2018）
著(编)者：安文华　包晓霞　谢增虎
2018年1月出版 / 估价：99.00元
PSN B-2013-313-2/6

广东蓝皮书
广东全面深化改革研究报告（2018）
著(编)者：周林生　涂成林
2018年12月出版 / 估价：99.00元
PSN B-2015-504-3/3

广东蓝皮书
广东社会工作发展报告（2018）
著(编)者：罗观翠　　2018年6月出版 / 估价：99.00元
PSN B-2014-402-2/3

广州蓝皮书
广州青年发展报告（2018）
著(编)者：徐柳　张强
2018年8月出版 / 估价：99.00元
PSN B-2013-352-13/14

广州蓝皮书
广州社会保障发展报告（2018）
著(编)者：张跃国　　2018年8月出版 / 估价：99.00元
PSN B-2014-425-14/14

广州蓝皮书
2018年中国广州社会形势分析与预测
著(编)者：张强　郭志勇　何镜清
2018年6月出版 / 估价：99.00元
PSN B-2008-110-5/14

贵州蓝皮书
贵州法治发展报告（2018）
著(编)者：吴大华　　2018年5月出版 / 估价：99.00元
PSN B-2012-254-2/10

贵州蓝皮书
贵州人才发展报告（2017）
著(编)者：于杰　吴大华
2018年9月出版 / 估价：99.00元
PSN B-2014-382-3/10

贵州蓝皮书
贵州社会发展报告（2018）
著(编)者：王兴骥　　2018年4月出版 / 估价：99.00元
PSN B-2010-166-1/10

杭州蓝皮书
杭州妇女发展报告（2018）
著(编)者：魏颖　　2018年10月出版 / 估价：99.00元
PSN B-2014-403-1/1

河北蓝皮书
河北法治发展报告（2018）
著(编)者：康振海　　2018年6月出版 / 估价：99.00元
PSN B-2017-622-3/3

河北食品药品安全蓝皮书
河北食品药品安全研究报告（2018）
著(编)者：丁锦霞　　2018年10月出版 / 估价：99.00元
PSN B-2015-473-1/1

河南蓝皮书
河南法治发展报告（2018）
著(编)者：张林海　　2018年7月出版 / 估价：99.00元
PSN B-2014-376-6/9

河南蓝皮书
2018年河南社会形势分析与预测
著(编)者：牛苏林　　2018年5月出版 / 估价：99.00元
PSN B-2005-043-1/9

河南民办教育蓝皮书
河南民办教育发展报告（2018）
著(编)者：胡大白　　2018年9月出版 / 估价：99.00元
PSN B-2017-642-1/1

黑龙江蓝皮书
黑龙江社会发展报告（2018）
著(编)者：谢宝禄　　2018年1月出版 / 估价：99.00元
PSN B-2011-189-1/2

湖南蓝皮书
2018年湖南两型社会与生态文明建设报告
著(编)者：卞鹰　　2018年5月出版 / 估价：128.00元
PSN B-2011-208-3/8

湖南蓝皮书
2018年湖南社会发展报告
著(编)者：卞鹰　　2018年5月出版 / 估价：128.00元
PSN B-2014-393-5/8

健康城市蓝皮书
北京健康城市建设研究报告（2018）
著(编)者：王鸿春　盛继洪　　2018年9月出版 / 估价：99.00元
PSN B-2015-460-1/2

江苏法治蓝皮书
江苏法治发展报告No.6（2017）
著(编)者：蔡道通 龚廷泰 2018年8月出版 / 估价：99.00元
PSN B-2012-290-1/1

江苏蓝皮书
2018年江苏社会发展分析与展望
著(编)者：王庆五 刘旺洪 2018年8月出版 / 估价：128.00元
PSN B-2017-636-2/3

南宁蓝皮书
南宁法治发展报告（2018）
著(编)者：杨维超 2018年12月出版 / 估价：99.00元
PSN B-2015-509-1/3

南宁蓝皮书
南宁社会发展报告（2018）
著(编)者：胡建华 2018年10月出版 / 估价：99.00元
PSN B-2016-570-3/3

内蒙古蓝皮书
内蒙古反腐倡廉建设报告 No.2
著(编)者：张志华 2018年6月出版 / 估价：99.00元
PSN B-2013-365-1/1

青海蓝皮书
2018年青海人才发展报告
著(编)者：王宇燕 2018年9月出版 / 估价：99.00元
PSN B-2017-650-2/2

青海生态文明建设蓝皮书
青海生态文明建设报告（2018）
著(编)者：张西明 高华 2018年12月出版 / 估价：99.00元
PSN B-2016-595-1/1

人口与健康蓝皮书
深圳人口与健康发展报告（2018）
著(编)者：陆杰华 傅崇辉 2018年11月出版 / 估价：99.00元
PSN B-2011-228-1/1

山东蓝皮书
山东社会形势分析与预测（2018）
著(编)者：李善峰 2018年6月出版 / 估价：99.00元
PSN B-2014-405-2/5

陕西蓝皮书
陕西社会发展报告（2018）
著(编)者：任宗哲 白宽犁 牛昉 2018年1月出版 / 估价：99.00元
PSN B-2009-136-2/6

上海蓝皮书
上海法治发展报告（2018）
著(编)者：叶必丰 2018年9月出版 / 估价：99.00元
PSN B-2012-296-6/7

上海蓝皮书
上海社会发展报告（2018）
著(编)者：杨雄 周海旺
2018年2月出版 / 估价：99.00元
PSN B-2006-058-2/7

社会建设蓝皮书
2018年北京社会建设分析报告
著(编)者：宋贵伦 冯虹 2018年9月出版 / 估价：99.00元
PSN B-2010-173-1/1

深圳蓝皮书
深圳法治发展报告（2018）
著(编)者：张骁儒 2018年6月出版 / 估价：99.00元
PSN B-2015-470-6/7

深圳蓝皮书
深圳劳动关系发展报告（2018）
著(编)者：汤庭芬 2018年8月出版 / 估价：99.00元
PSN B-2007-097-2/7

深圳蓝皮书
深圳社会治理与发展报告（2018）
著(编)者：张骁儒 2018年6月出版 / 估价：99.00元
PSN B-2008-113-4/7

生态安全绿皮书
甘肃国家生态安全屏障建设发展报告（2018）
著(编)者：刘举科 喜文华
2018年10月出版 / 估价：99.00元
PSN G-2017-659-1/1

顺义社会建设蓝皮书
北京市顺义区社会建设发展报告（2018）
著(编)者：王学武 2018年9月出版 / 估价：99.00元
PSN B-2017-658-1/1

四川蓝皮书
四川法治发展报告（2018）
著(编)者：郑泰安 2018年1月出版 / 估价：99.00元
PSN B-2015-441-5/7

四川蓝皮书
四川社会发展报告（2018）
著(编)者：李羚 2018年6月出版 / 估价：99.00元
PSN B-2008-127-3/7

云南社会治理蓝皮书
云南社会治理年度报告（2017）
著(编)者：晏雄 韩全芳
2018年5月出版 / 估价：99.00元
PSN B-2017-667-1/1

地方发展类-文化

北京传媒蓝皮书
北京新闻出版广电发展报告（2017~2018）
著(编)者：王志 2018年11月出版 / 估价：99.00元
PSN B-2016-588-1/1

北京蓝皮书
北京文化发展报告（2017~2018）
著(编)者：李建盛 2018年5月出版 / 估价：99.00元
PSN B-2007-082-4/8

创意城市蓝皮书
北京文化创意产业发展报告（2018）
著(编)者：郭万超 张京成　2018年12月出版 / 估价：99.00元
PSN B-2012-263-1/7

创意城市蓝皮书
天津文化创意产业发展报告（2017～2018）
著(编)者：谢思全　2018年6月出版 / 估价：99.00元
PSN B-2016-536-7/7

创意城市蓝皮书
武汉文化创意产业发展报告（2018）
著(编)者：黄永林 陈汉桥　2018年12月出版 / 估价：99.00元
PSN B-2013-354-4/7

创意上海蓝皮书
上海文化创意产业发展报告（2017～2018）
著(编)者：王慧敏 王兴全　2018年8月出版 / 估价：99.00元
PSN B-2016-561-1/1

非物质文化遗产蓝皮书
广州市非物质文化遗产保护发展报告（2018）
著(编)者：宋俊华　2018年12月出版 / 估价：99.00元
PSN B-2016-589-1/1

甘肃蓝皮书
甘肃文化发展分析与预测（2018）
著(编)者：王俊莲 周小华　2018年1月出版 / 估价：99.00元
PSN B-2013-314-3/6

甘肃蓝皮书
甘肃舆情分析与预测（2018）
著(编)者：陈双梅 张谦元　2018年1月出版 / 估价：99.00元
PSN B-2013-315-4/6

广州蓝皮书
中国广州文化发展报告（2018）
著(编)者：屈哨兵 陆志强　2018年6月出版 / 估价：99.00元
PSN B-2009-134-7/14

广州蓝皮书
广州文化创意产业发展报告（2018）
著(编)者：徐咏虹　2018年7月出版 / 估价：99.00元
PSN B-2008-111-6/14

海淀蓝皮书
海淀区文化和科技融合发展报告（2018）
著(编)者：陈名杰 孟景伟　2018年5月出版 / 估价：99.00元
PSN B-2013-329-1/1

河南蓝皮书
河南文化发展报告（2018）
著(编)者：卫绍生　2018年7月出版 / 估价：99.00元
PSN B-2008-106-2/9

湖北文化产业蓝皮书
湖北省文化产业发展报告（2018）
著(编)者：黄晓华　2018年9月出版 / 估价：99.00元
PSN B-2017-656-1/1

湖北文化蓝皮书
湖北文化发展报告（2017~2018）
著(编)者：湖北大学高等人文研究院
中华文化发展湖北省协同创新中心
2018年10月出版 / 估价：99.00元
PSN B-2016-566-1/1

江苏蓝皮书
2018年江苏文化发展分析与展望
著(编)者：王庆五 樊和平　2018年9月出版 / 估价：128.00元
PSN B-2017-637-3/3

江西文化蓝皮书
江西非物质文化遗产发展报告（2018）
著(编)者：张圣才 傅安平　2018年12月出版 / 估价：128.00元
PSN B-2015-499-1/1

洛阳蓝皮书
洛阳文化发展报告（2018）
著(编)者：刘福兴 陈启明　2018年7月出版 / 估价：99.00元
PSN B-2015-476-1/1

南京蓝皮书
南京文化发展报告（2018）
著(编)者：中共南京市委宣传部
2018年12月出版 / 估价：99.00元
PSN B-2014-439-1/1

宁波文化蓝皮书
宁波“一人一艺”全民艺术普及发展报告（2017）
著(编)者：张爱琴　2018年11月出版 / 估价：128.00元
PSN B-2017-668-1/1

山东蓝皮书
山东文化发展报告（2018）
著(编)者：涂可国　2018年5月出版 / 估价：99.00元
PSN B-2014-406-3/5

陕西蓝皮书
陕西文化发展报告（2018）
著(编)者：任宗哲 白宽犁 王长寿
2018年1月出版 / 估价：99.00元
PSN B-2009-137-3/6

上海蓝皮书
上海传媒发展报告（2018）
著(编)者：强荧 焦雨虹　2018年2月出版 / 估价：99.00元
PSN B-2012-295-5/7

上海蓝皮书
上海文学发展报告（2018）
著(编)者：陈圣来　2018年6月出版 / 估价：99.00元
PSN B-2012-297-7/7

上海蓝皮书
上海文化发展报告（2018）
著(编)者：荣跃明　2018年2月出版 / 估价：99.00元
PSN B-2006-059-3/7

深圳蓝皮书
深圳文化发展报告（2018）
著(编)者：张骁儒　2018年7月出版 / 估价：99.00元
PSN B-2016-554-7/7

四川蓝皮书
四川文化产业发展报告（2018）
著(编)者：向宝云 张立伟　2018年4月出版 / 估价：99.00元
PSN B-2006-074-1/7

郑州蓝皮书
2018年郑州文化发展报告
著(编)者：王哲　2018年9月出版 / 估价：99.00元
PSN B-2008-107-1/1

皮书起源

“皮书”起源于十七、十八世纪的英国，主要指官方或社会组织正式发表的重要文件或报告，多以“白皮书”命名。在中国，“皮书”这一概念被社会广泛接受，并被成功运作、发展成为一种全新的出版形态，则源于中国社会科学院社会科学文献出版社。

皮书定义

皮书是对中国与世界发展状况和热点问题进行年度监测，以专业的角度、专家的视野和实证研究方法，针对某一领域或区域现状与发展态势展开分析和预测，具备原创性、实证性、专业性、连续性、前沿性、时效性等特点的公开出版物，由一系列权威研究报告组成。

皮书作者

皮书系列的作者以中国社会科学院、著名高校、地方社会科学院的研究人员为主，多为国内一流研究机构的权威专家学者，他们的看法和观点代表了学界对中国与世界的现实和未来最高水平的解读与分析。

皮书荣誉

皮书系列已成为社会科学文献出版社的著名图书品牌和中国社会科学院的知名学术品牌。2016 年，皮书系列正式列入“十三五”国家重点出版规划项目；2013~2018 年，重点皮书列入中国社会科学院承担的国家哲学社会科学创新工程项目；2018 年，59 种院外皮书使用“中国社会科学院创新工程学术出版项目”标识。

中国皮书网

（网址：www.pishu.cn）

发布皮书研创资讯，传播皮书精彩内容
引领皮书出版潮流，打造皮书服务平台

栏目设置

关于皮书：何谓皮书、皮书分类、皮书大事记、皮书荣誉、皮书出版第一人、皮书编辑部

最新资讯：通知公告、新闻动态、媒体聚焦、网站专题、视频直播、下载专区

皮书研创：皮书规范、皮书选题、皮书出版、皮书研究、研创团队

皮书评奖评价：指标体系、皮书评价、皮书评奖

互动专区：皮书说、社科数托邦、皮书微博、留言板

所获荣誉

2008 年、2011 年，中国皮书网均在全国新闻出版业网站荣誉评选中获得“最具商业价值网站”称号；

2012 年，获得“出版业网站百强”称号。

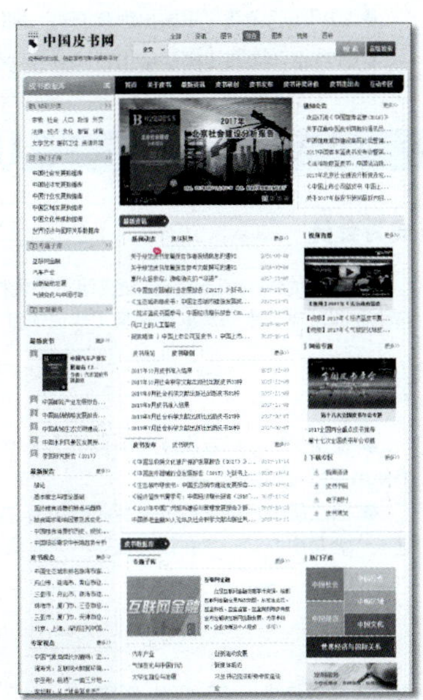

网库合一

2014 年，中国皮书网与皮书数据库端口合一，实现资源共享。

更多信息请登录

皮书数据库
http：//www.pishu.com.cn

中国皮书网
http：//www.pishu.cn

皮书微博
http：//weibo.com/pishu

皮书微信“皮书说”

请到当当、亚马逊、京东或各地书店购买，也可办理邮购

咨询/邮购电话：010-59367028　59367070

邮　　箱：duzhe@ssap.cn

邮购地址：北京市西城区北三环中路甲29号院3号楼
华龙大厦13层读者服务中心

邮　　编：100029

银行户名：社会科学文献出版社

开户银行：中国工商银行北京北太平庄支行

账　　号：0200010019200365434

the city cluster in central regions will deepen the division and cooperation of the industrial system, strengthen management and protection of the ecological environment, promote the development and sharing of public services, promote the coordinated development of urban and rural areas, and accelerate the process of industrialization, urbanization, informationization, greening and agricultural modernization in city cluster in the central region as well as the whole central and western regions. The approval is conducive to promoting the role of the city cluster in central regions as the main platform of the new urbanization in Henan and the neighboring provinces. Such a platform will contribute to the acceleration of a clear functional positioning of each city, promotion of the scientific and reasonable division of labor, strengthening of the cooperation between cities, and mutual sharing of development.

Zhengzhou has entered the group of National Central City. The "Plan on Promotion of the Rise of the Central Region in the 13th Five-Year Period" clearly supported two cities in the central region, that is, Wuhan and Zhengzhou to develop into National Central City. According to the "Plan", Zhengzhou has no other choice but to enhance its role of agglomeration and driving development, and accelerate the construction of the international modern comprehensive transportation hub, the door of opening up in the central-west, important national base of advanced manufacturing industry, international logistics center, regional modern financial center, center for innovation and entrepreneurship in central region with international competitiveness, heritage and innovation center of Chinese history and civilization. All of which would significantly enhance the driving force of the Zhengzhou as the National Center City, improve the urban system, enhance the supplying capacity of public service, and promote the urbanization of Henan towards better quality and a higher level.

The effects of national strategies multiply. By the end of December 2016, Henan has been the home of seven national strategic planning, including planning of "the Core Area of Food Production", "Central Plain Economic Zone", "Zhengzhou Airport Economy Zone", "Zheng-Luo-Xin National Innovation Demonstration Area", "China (Henan) Free Trade Zone", "Pilot Zone for National Big Data", and "City Cluster in Central Regions". Among them, Zhengzhou, Luoyang, Xinxiang, Kaifeng and other large and medium-sized cities are not only the strategic support for multiple national strategic planning, but also the growth pole promoting the development of Central Plain Economic

Zone, and enhancing the driving capacity of the city cluster in central regions. Such multiplied effects is conductive for cities in Henan to making full use of the opportunities of pilot implementation of national strategy, to form systematic advantage of reform and innovation, thus providing a favorable atmosphere and opportunity for the development of the supply-side reform of urban development.

Urbanization demonstrates great potential for development. In 2016, permanent urban residents accounted for 46.85% of the population in Henan. In the recent five years, about two million rural residents have migrated to the city every year, making it the fastest developing period in the promotion of urbanization. However, the urbanization rate of permanent urban residents in Henan is still lower than the national average by 9 points and 5 points lower than the average level in the central region. In the urbanization rate of urban residents with a household registration, the proportion of urban residents with a household registration is 20% below the proportion of permanent urban residents. We are facing serious problem of such "semi-urbanization". It can be said that there is no fundamental change to the crux of the economic and social development of Henan, that is, the low urbanization quality. However, it could be understood from another side. Under the new normal, the urbanization in Henan will have some common traits with other cities in China. For example, the development concept will change from "city oriented" to "people-oriented", the development pattern will change from extensive to intensive, and the urban management will change from allocation in accordance with administrative level to allocation in accordance with population size. On the other hand, urbanization in Henan has its own characteristics in areas like the growth rate and industrial restructuring. For example, urbanization in Henan will maintain a relatively rapid pace and a large scale, especially certain cities in Huang-Huai area have greater space for the development of urbanization. The urbanization rate of Henan would maintain a certain growth rate, narrowing the gap with the national average. The great potential for development of urbanization has also provided sufficient space for the supply-side reform of urban development.

2. Challenges and Unfavorable Conditions

The carrying capacity of cities and towns is low. During the rapid development of urbanization, there are obvious weak points in the supporting capacity of urban infrastructure and supplying capacity of public service in Henan. In the aspect of the interconnection level of infrastructure, we are in urgent need of solving the "last mile" problem, especially traffic congestion, poor convergence and transfer inconvenience in intercity transportation. In the aspect of internal infrastructure, the urban road area per capita and green area per capita in 2016 were lower than the national level. As the capital city of Henan province, Zhengzhou was the only city in the province with an inflowing population from 2011 to 2015. 37% of the inflowing population from other provinces and 60% of the floating population from within Henan moved to Zhengzhou. The inflowing population to Zhengzhou has reached 1.85 million in the past five years, only 10,000 less than Shenzhen, and rank seventh among the national large and medium-sized cities. The huge inflowing population has brought lasting innovation vitality and maintained the demographic dividend. However, it has also caused acute problems like traffic congestion, soaring housing prices, environmental degradation and management inefficiency. From the comparison of indicators including the number of permanent urban residents, built-up area per capita, area of paved roads per capita, green area per capita, and number of hospital beds per 10,000 (person) with Beijing, Wuhan, Changsha, Shanghai, Taiyuan, and Chengdu, Zhengzhou is in serious overload stage. At the same time, during the "12th Five-Year" period, the new urban population agglomerated in 106 counties (cities) in Henan accounted for 74% of the new urban population in the province, which had become the main force in the urbanization in Henan and played an important role in promoting the new urbanization. However, with huge population and low starting point for development, the level of infrastructure in county level cities in Henan, such as water supply, gas supply, pipeline density in built-up area, ratio of green space is significantly lower than the national average. The investment in the municipal public facilities construction in 106 counties (cities) account for less than 20% of the total amount. In the aspect of the supplying capacity of city public service, there are still widespread problems of weak industrial support, relatively few employment opportunities, low level of planning and development, simplistic urban management, lack of prominent cultural characteristics, poor ecological environment, and inferior overall competitiveness. They have seriously affected the urbanization of migrant rural workers in the province. In addition, the growth of the number of permanent urban residents in central areas in Luoyang, Xinxiang, Jiaozuo, Kaifeng, Nanyang and other cities is slow, with limited capacity in bringing in rural workers and weak overall carrying capacity.

The gap in investment and financing still exist. With the acceleration of new urbanization and the expansion of urban population and industrial scale, there is more demand for urban infrastructure and public service facilities as well as more urgent need to make up for the deficiency in urban development. For Henan urban development, the gap in investment and financing is mainly manifested in three aspects: first, the capital needs for infrastructure construction. This part of the capital needs include the construction of urban roads, bridges, tunnels and other transportation facilities, as well as water, electricity, gas, heat and other types of pipe network, with the updating and maintenance of all the facilities mentioned above. Second, the capital needs for utility service, mainly covering the layout and construction of public facilities of environmental sanitation, urban security, water supply and drainage, electricity, gas, heat, cultural and sports sites, postal communications, and so on. Third, the capital needs for public service, mainly covering basic urban public service facilities, including employment, pension, housing, health care, medical care, and schools. According to the data of the relevant government agencies and research institutions, for each migrant rural worker, there should be about 150,000 yuan (US$ 22,727.3) invested in infrastructure and public services. During the "13th Five-Year Plan" period, the total number of new rural residents with nonagricultural employment is expected to reach 1.5 million, so the capital needed is estimated at 200 billion yuan at least (US$ 30.3 billion). And there would be a huge funding gap. As the system and mechanism of investment and financing is immature in Henan, government financial investment is the main source of urban construction funds, with land sale revenue as the main guarantee. The funds were mainly operated by the government, with the risk borne by the government. In the background of reducing the number of unsold homes in real estate industry, it is out of the question to rely on land sale revenue to support the sustained investment in urban construction. Henan has vigorously promoted the application of PPP model in urban infrastructure and municipal utilities sector, especially in urban road traffic, sewage treatment, pollution-free disposal of urban household solid waste, landscaping, low-income housing, sports facilities, health care, pension services, and other projects. However, for the majority of small and medium-sized cities, the promotion of the PPP project still could not ease the demand for fund.

Polarization of cities still prevails. In the process of urbanization, the migration of rural population is expected to be a process of gradient transfer, that is, the population of villages and towns moving to small towns and county-level cities, and the population of small and medium-sized cities moving to large and medium cities. However, currently in Henan, in addition to population in many third-tier and forth-tier cities, rural population mostly flow directly to big cities such as Zhengzhou, causing population explosion in Zhengzhou and population outflowing in third-tier and forth-tier cities. According to the index of population increase and its growth rate from the research data in China Business News, from 2012 to 2015, like Tianjin, Beijing, Shenzhen, and Wuhan, Zhengzhou was also included in the team of high population increment and growth rate. At the same time, the total number of rural residents migrating to county level cities is larger than that of Luoyang, Xinxiang, Jiaozuo and other third or fourth tier cities and small towns, with the coordinated development of large, medium and small cities yet to be formed. The root of the problem lies in the fact that under current economic, social, and political system, with Zhengzhou as the capital city of Henan province, the administrative power enhances the advantage of resource agglomeration in core cities. Public resources are overly concentrated in large cities, causing polarization in cities and exerting fundamental influence on the flow of the population. Due to low expense incurred from the transfer to urban areas, rural population could enter the secondary industry and tertiary industry, and in the meanwhile attend to their rural homestead and farmland covered by contract. As a result, a large proportion of them choose to transfer to nearby county level cities. Under the pressure from both ends, the central area in cities can hardly play their due role in attracting rural population into cities or reverse the trend of their population moving to Zhengzhou. It is foreseeable that the "new economy", which is represented by the Internet, high-tech, and high-end manufacturing, still demonstrates good development trend in the new normal, which will mainly exist in the first and second tier cities with high-end population resources and predominant education resources. Nevertheless, the "old economy", with bulk stock and resources as the core, will mainly exist in the third and fourth tier cities, including coal, steel, aluminum and other industries. At the same time, some small and medium-sized towns with their ecological livability, convenient transportation, and collected capital, also take the initiative in the new economic development and become the carrier to attract inflows of population. Under the new normal of economy, we should respect the objective

law of economic development, remain sensitive to the huge pressure from the development of central areas in cities, realize the urgent need to promote structural reforms in the innovation of resource allocation system, the supply of public services and other aspects, and promote the formation of the modern, scientific and sound urban system in Henan.

Institutional obstacles still exist. The deficiency in system and mechanism of urban planning, development, and management have led to low efficiency of urban development and low quality of urbanization, which are manifested in three aspects. First, the price mechanism of urban construction land needs to be improved. The unsound price mechanism of urban construction land has caused the imbalance of urban land use structure. For instance, the mechanism of the price ratio between industrial land and residential land is yet to be established. The majority of the urban construction land is intended for industrial use, while the ratio of residential land, transportation land, and green land is relatively low, which directly affect the efficiency of urban operating, and constitutes an important factor in the high housing price. At the same time, without a unified urban and rural land market mechanism, the rural collective construction land cannot share equal rights with the state-owned land, such as entering the market with equal conditions, price and rights. As a result, rural migrant workers are unable to get the capital needed for settlement in the city from the land profit, affecting the stability of cities and the improvement of the quality of urbanization. In industrial cities like Luoyang, Hebi, Jiaozuo, Pingdingshan, Anyang, and Xinxiang, with the deepening of the adjustment of industrial structure and the implementation of the policy of "suppressing the second industry and developing the tertiary industry" in central areas, some industrial enterprises fail to fully transform into the urban industry. As a result, without in-depth integration and re-development of the idle industrial land, the land utilization is inefficient. Second, the housing support mechanism is in need of improvement. Housing has dual attributes, namely, residence and investment. However, for a long time, the goal oriented mechanism to "guarantee of people's livelihood and growth" is not established, and the idea that "housing is meant for residing, not for speculation" is not deep rooted in urban management departments, resulting in the failure to meet diversified and multi-level demand of housing. Besides, there is no real and effective statistical data concerning the total area, total units and vacancy rate of urban housing. Also, the supply of residential land is not allocated in accordance with rural population absorbed into cities. Therefore, residential land in big cities such as Zhengzhou is inadequate while at the same time, residential land pile up in excess in central areas in some cities and most counties, resulting in a waste of resources. Third, improvement is needed in the mechanism of human resources flow. At present, Zhengzhou, as well as certain counties, has an inflowing population, and enjoys a demographic dividend, while Pingdingshan, Hebi, Anyang, Sanmenxia and other resource-based cities should learn from the lessons of cities in the northeast, accelerate the development of transformation and upgrading, and focus on the continuous development of industry as well as the cultivation of demographic dividend. In the process of population flow, the mechanisms of compensation for expenses incurred from the transfer of the rural population to urban areas and financial transfer payment in large and medium cities have not been fully established.

The constraint of the "two non-sacrifices" still plays its part. The development of the city cluster in central regions with the Central Plains Economic Zone as the basis determines that the development of the city cluster in central regions should be in accordance with the special situation of the Central Plains Economic Zone and follow certain common guidelines defined by the development of the Central Plains Economic Zone. The "Guiding Opinions of the State Council on Speeding up the Development of Central Plains Economic Zone in Henan Province" pointed out that, "to actively explore the coordinated development of the 'new industrialization, new urbanization and agricultural modernization' without sacrificing the interest of agriculture and the environment is the core task in the development of the Central Plains Economic Zone." Therefore, in the development of the city cluster in central regions, we should reflect on crucial issues like how to correctly handle the relationship between the Central Plains Economic Zone and the city cluster in central regions, how to properly coordinate the development of the city cluster and economic zones, how to better promote the new agricultural modernization with the new urbanization and industrialization. We are in urgent need of actively promoting the in-depth integration of informationization and industrialization, positive interaction of industrialization and urbanization, coordination of urbanization and agricultural modernization in accordance with the local circumstances and national strategic requirements. We should carry out the coordinated development of the "four modernizations".

IV Suggestions on New Urbanization in Henan Province with City Cluster in Central Regions Playing the Leading Role

As a newly emerged city cluster, compared with other more developed city clusters, the city cluster in central regions is fraught with problems and deficiencies in the development. To accelerate the development of the city cluster in central regions and give full play to the leading role of new urbanization, we need to further understand the law of development of the city cluster, rely on its strength, make full use of the existing opportunities, and build a core area that is comparable to the city cluster in the middle reach of Changjiang River and drives the development of the central region as well as a new space to support the development of the national economy.

1. Giving Full Play to the Leading Role of the Market

Let the market play the decisive role. Affected by planned economy system and GDP oriented cadre evaluation system, the idea of administrative region economy prevails among cities in the city cluster in central regions and there are widespread administrative barriers hindering the regional economic integration. The cultivation and development of the city cluster requires allocation of resource factors and free flow of resource factors in the whole region, as well as freedom in choosing industrial layout for all kinds of economic entities, all of which depend on the unified and open market system as the guarantee. Covering thirty cities in five provinces, the new city cluster in central regions is facing a most challenging issue of how to handle the relationship between government and the market, allowing the market to allocate resource in accordance with the economic law in the region, to solve the issue of population flow and to enable people to choose where to settle down. We should reduce administrative intervention by government in every city, eliminate administrative barriers, fully play the decisive role of the market in resource allocation, and achieve the optimal allocation of infrastructure, industrial layout, public services, and ecological construction among cities in the city cluster, bringing out the full potential of the city cluster.

We should establish the mechanism for the integration of markets. Focusing on core factors that have restricted the development of integration, such as people, land, and money, etc., we should strive to establish a unified market of talents, land, finance and other factors, and promote the optimization of all kinds of elements in accordance with the laws of the market economy within the city cluster. We should actively improve the level of human resources services through information tools, accelerate the development of integrated and various professional human resources market, and promote free flow and efficient allocation of talent resources within the city cluster. We should thoroughly carry out decisions of the central government, continue to promote reforms of the rural land contract right, land use right, and collective income distribution right, explore the means for rural collective construction land to enter the market, and accelerate the establishment of a unified urban and rural construction land market. Relying on the Zhongyuan Bank, the Zhengzhou Futures Exchange and other financial institutions, we should develop the trading platform of public resources in the city cluster in central regions, and promote the development of financial, futures, bonds, property rights transactions and other markets. Relying on the traffic advantage in central regions, we should promote the development of big market, big circulation, and big logistics, accelerate the upgrading and transformation of the consumer goods market, production market, and agricultural products market, and establish an integrated commodity market in the city cluster in central regions.

2. Improving the Coordination Mechanism

We should establish an authoritative coordination mechanism for the operation of the city cluster. The long-standing administrative region economy has exerted great influence on city clusters of cross-administrative regions. We can hardly form a stable and productive relationship of cooperation by relying on one single municipal government, as the operation and coordination of the city cluster has to rely on higher levels of government or authority beyond single municipal government. The city cluster in central regions covers thirty cities in five provinces, namely, Henan, Hebei, Shanxi, Anhui and Shandong. Therefore the central government should take the lead in setting up institutions with statutory power to coordinate routine work. We should delegate appropriate authority to the coordinating organizations to ensure their authority and efficiency. We should speed up the formulation of relevant organizational agreements, systems and laws for efficient operation of the city cluster, so that the coordination institutions have the laws to abide by. In addition, we should speed up the establishment and promotion of provincial consultation mechanism and working mechanism, launch annual promotion meetings by making good use of major investment platforms and festivals, establish city alliances, and carry out the implementation of unified planning of major facilities, coordinated layout of major projects, and coordinated promotion of major reforms.

We should establish industrial and inter-city coordination organizations. With the deepening of specialization and division of labor, conflicts of interests between cities are inevitable. As a useful supplement to the government's authoritative coordination mechanism, coordination among industries becomes more and more important. Through a variety of industrial coordination organizations, we can effectively coordinate conflicts of interests between cities, reduce transaction costs, and promote the settlement of inter-city issues. It is far from enough for the city cluster in central regions, an inter-provincial city cluster, to rely on the regional coordination organization. We are in great need of setting up all kinds of industrial coordination organizations. Through the coordination of various industrial organizations, we can deal with issues like industrial layout and environmental protection in the trans-administrative regions, and promote cooperation and exchange between the government, enterprises and civil organization. The industrial coordination organizations could be official, semi-official and private, so as to form the new management mode of the city cluster, with the integration of governmental organization and non-governmental organization, the combination of multi participation, and expression of the will of all parties.

We should establish a mechanism for coordinating interests across regions. The efficient operation of the city cluster relies heavily on the proper management of the relationship between the cities and to find the balance of interests among cities. At present, we should establish a benefit sharing mechanism which will facilitate the cooperation of the city cluster as soon as possible. With inter-region distribution mechanism of tax benefit as the core, we should include headquarter economy, corporate mergers and acquisitions, cooperation and development of projects, cooperation and development of parks, enclave economy, enterprise relocation, investment in the scope of cooperation of the city cluster. In this way, we can achieve the goal of efficient use of resources in the city cluster, mutual opening of regional markets, and agglomeration of competitive industries.

In addition, we should actively explore inter-city and inter-provincial interests compensation mechanism. Through standardizing the financial transfer payment system, establishing the compensation system and setting up special funds for coordinated development of cities, we should compensate for the loss of interests during the coordinated development to neighboring cities.

3. Promoting the Optimization of Spatial Layout

We should establish a network spatial pattern of "one core, four axes and four zones". A strong core city is crucial to the formation and cultivation of a city cluster. With the development of Zhengzhou Airport Economy Zone, Zheng-Luo-Xin National Innovation Demonstration Zone, China (Henan) Pilot Free Trade Zone and Cross-Border E-Commerce Pilot Zone being carried out, we should strive to enhance Zhengzhou's role as the logistics and business center, comprehensive transportation hub, as well as the modern service center and the door of opening up in the mid-east, accelerate its development as the regional center and build a powerful engine for development. We should promote the integration between Zhengzhou and neighboring cities like Kaifeng, Xinxiang, Jiaozuo, Xuchang, and develop modern metropolitan areas. Relying on integrated transport network in the shape of the Chinese character " 米 ", we should enhance the driving capacity of cities along network, build economic axes of the "Main Development Axis Stretching in the Direction of Long Hai Railway", the "Development Axis Stretching in the Direction of Jingguang Railway", the "Ji'nan - Zhengzhou - Chongqing Development Axis" and the "Taiyuan - Zhengzhou - Hefei Development Axis". We should innovate institutional mechanism, break the limitation of administrative zone economy, promote coordinated development of inter-provincial cities, and cultivate demonstration zone of cross regional collaborative development in the north, the demonstration zone of undertaking industrial transfer in the east, the demonstration zone of transformation and innovation in the west, as well as the high-efficiency ecological economic zone in the south.

We should improve the urban and rural planning system. Relying on the central area in Zhengzhou, Zhengzhou Airport Economy Zone and other carriers, we should strengthen its role as the transportation and logistics hub, and build the core area of Zhengzhou metropolitan area. We should speed up the development of integrated transportation network, promote the joint development of

Kaifeng, Xinxiang, Jiaozuo, Xuchang and the central area of Zhengzhou, and form a metropolitan space system that is networked, combined and intensive. We should promote the coordinated development of cities in northwest Henan and Luoyang, further enhance the status of Luoyang as the sub-center city, and build a new regional economic growth pole. With Changzhi, Handan, Liaocheng, Anyang, Bengbu, Fuyang, Shangqiu and Nanyang as the focuses, we should actively optimize the urban form, enhance the carrying capacity and driving capacity, and build regional centers. We should support three types of cities to develop into important node cities in the city cluster, namely, Luohe, Jiyuan and other cities with a better industrial base, cities used to be traditional cultivated regions, like Zhoukou City, Xinyang, Zhumadian, Heze, Yuncheng, as well as resource-based cities, including Pingdingshan, Hebi, Puyang, Sanmenxia, Suzhou, Huaibei, Bozhou, Xingtai, and Jincheng. We will select small towns with superior location, good foundation and great potential to develop industries with local characteristics, inherit traditional culture, strengthen ecological environment protection, and build towns with local characteristics.

We should coordinate the distribution of population with development priority zones. With the urbanization of the "three types of the '100 million people'" as the focus, we will continue to deepen the reform of the household registration system, carry out implementation of "Notice on Fiscal Support for Providing Services to Rural Migrants", and accelerate the transfer of agricultural population and their settlement in cities. It clearly identifies the responsibility of local government, especially government of cities with an inflowing population as the main body for the transfer of rural population to urban areas, and encourages rural population with the ability and willingness for stable employment and living in cities to move with their entire family. In accordance with the planning of the development priority zones, we will actively guide the population to concentrate in key development regions, enhance the industrial agglomeration capacity of key development regions, improve the comprehensive function of the core region of urbanization, optimize living environment, and promote the agglomeration of population and industry in key development regions. We should promote an orderly withdrawal of population from key ecological function areas. With protection and restoration of the ecological environment as well as providing ecological products as the primary tasks, we should strive to reduce the proportion of population of key ecological function areas in total population and relieve the pressure of population on the ecological environment.

4. Deepening the Industrial Division and Labor Cooperation

We should cultivate competitive industrial clusters. Relying on the existing industrial base and comparative advantage of each city, we will promote industrial division and cooperation, guide the development of industrial clusters, and jointly build a modern industrial system with complementary advantages, close cooperation, as well as integrated development. We will promote the integration of information technology of the new generation and manufacturing technology, enhance the basic manufacturing capacities and innovation capacities, and strive to build industry cluster of electronic information and high-end equipment manufacturing. With cold chain food, flour products, meat products, snack foods, beverages, oils and fats, fruits and vegetables as the focuses, we will build a number of well-known green food industrial clusters. We will intensify our efforts to transform and upgrade traditional pillar industries, such as iron and steel, metallurgy, chemical, building materials, and raw materials, eliminate excess manufacturing capacity, and build industrial cluster of high-quality raw materials. We will give full play to the scientific and technological innovation as well as leading role of Zheng-Luo-Xin National Innovation Demonstration Zone, and accelerate the cultivation of new industrial clusters like biological medicine, robotics, new energy, and new materials. With the promotion of industrial transformation and upgrading as well as improvement of the efficiency of division as the lead, and with modern logistics, modern finance, modern trade, cultural tourism, and health care as the key focus areas, we will strive to accelerate the development of modern service industry. Focusing on the development of the national grain production area, we will strengthen and promote our status as the national important grain production base. In the meantime we will speed up the adjustment of agricultural structure, promote the integrated development of the first, second and tertiary industries in rural areas, foster a number of leading enterprises of agricultural industrialization, and develop modern agricultural clusters.

We should carry out an orderly undertaking of industrial transfer. At present, the selective undertaking of industrial transfer is still an important way to speed up the industrial transformation and upgrading of the city cluster in central regions. We should rely on our own advantages, innovate new models and new paths to undertake industrial transfer, actively undertake domestic and foreign advanced industries which are in accordance with the green development concept and direction of industrial development, and promote industrial transformation and upgrading of the city cluster. We will establish the inter-regional integration mechanism of industrial transfers, rely on carriers like industrial agglomeration zones, central business districts, and special customs supervision zones, and set up a number of transfer platforms for high-end industry, so as to enhance the undertaking capacity and attraction. We should actively go out and attract investment from the economically developed areas both at home and abroad, and promptly carry out a series of high-level industrial transfer activities. What's more, we should strengthen the management of undertaking industrial transfer, strengthen the environmental impact assessment and review of energy assessment of the industrial transfer projects, guide local positioning in accordance with local development priority, optimize the industrial development environment, and cultivate new economic growth point.

We should improve the mechanism of industrial coordinated development. As the city cluster in central regions is an organic whole, the coordinated development of industries between different cities essential and directly affects the overall strength of the region. Under the guidance of "The Development Planning of City Cluster in Central Regions", we should speed up the formulation of industrial development plan for each city and strengthen the guidance to the industrial development of the city cluster. From the perspective of the reconstruction of the industrial chains, the linkage mechanism between the upstream and downstream of the regional industrial chain should be established to promote the rational distribution of industrial increments and orderly adjustment of the stock. We will set up a guiding fund for the development of key industries in the city cluster in central regions, and support the development of industries and projects in line with the planning direction. We will speed up the transformation and upgrading of existing industrial agglomeration zones and central business districts, and form a regional agglomeration highland of production factors. We will encourage cooperation in building industrial parks with domestic and foreign strategic investors through joint investment and cooperation projects, technical support, resource complementary, etc.. We will also encourage Sanmenxia, Shangqiu, Hebi and other inter-provincial border cities to carry out cooperation in building industrial parks. Therefore, we can optimize the allocation of resources, and enhance regional economic growth.

5. Strengthening the Economical and Intensive Utilization of Resources

We should strengthen the economical and intensive utilization of land resource. Land resource is the most precious natural resource and material wealth. The economical and intensive utilization of land resources is the strategic choice of the new urbanization, and the basic policy for the development of ecological civilization. We will carry out the most stringent land conservation system, vigorously promote the conservation and intensive use of land, and accelerate the transformation of land utilization mode and the mode of economic development, to provide a solid guarantee for the development of the city cluster in central regions. We will carry out implementation of the control system of the total amount of urban and rural construction land, promote re-development of urban and industrial underused land, revitalize the stock of construction land, and curb the excessive development of land resources. We will carry out strict authorization of all kinds of urban land for new construction, allocate land utilization index in accordance with the flow of population during urbanization, increase urban new construction land, strengthen our control of urban and rural construction land in counties and small and medium-sized cities with limited inflowing population or out flowing population. We will reinforce the control of land use, promote the multi-functional and comprehensive development of construction land within the city, strictly control the speed and scale of industrial land and rural collective construction land, and strictly observe the minimum amount of arable land.

We will comprehensively promote the development of water-saving society. We will carry out implementation of the most stringent water resource management system, and strengthen the "dual control" of the total amount and intensity of water resource consumption in the process of urbanization. We will carry out the implementation of the most stringent water management system, and adhere to the principle of taking the carrying capacity and ecological environment of water resource as the rigid constraints for industrial and urban development. We will include an index system of water resource development, utilization and conservation into the evaluation system of local economic and social development, reinforcing rigid constraints of water ecological environment.

We will carry out implementation of the national water conservation action plan, speed up water-saving transformation of key industries, such as thermal power, petrochemical, steel, paper making and chemical industries, speed up the construction of urban water supply network and popularize new water-saving technologies and efficient water-saving products. We will carry out projects including the utilization of rainwater resources and reclaimed water, and accelerate the utilization of unconventional water resources. We will actively carry out the evaluation of the carrying capacity of water resources, and reinforce rigid constraints over the carrying capacity of water resources. We will enhance the demonstration of sustainable utilization of water resources in the process of economic and social development planning, urban overall planning and the construction of major projects.

We will strengthen the economical utilization of mineral resources. Mineral resources are the important material basis of economic and social development as well as the elements of the ecological environment. We should stick to conservation priority and strengthen the concept of "conservation is economy", placing priority on conservation. We should adhere to the principle of "development in conservation and conservation in development", supporting the sustained development of economic and social development with the least consumption of mineral resources. We should strengthen the planning and control of mineral resources, strictly implement zoning management, total quantity control and mining access system, and coordinate the development and utilization of mineral resources in the region. We will vigorously develop and promote the application of advanced and applicable technology to speed up the pace of transformation of technique and technology of mining enterprises. We will actively promote the development experience of national and provincial green mine, vigorously implement a demonstration project of the conservation and comprehensive utilization of mineral resources, the protection and reservation project of mineral resources, improve the recovery rate, concentration recovery ratio and comprehensive utilization rate, to provide support for the sustainable development of a city cluster in central regions.

6. Speeding up Interconnection and Intercommunication of Infrastructure

We will speed up the construction of integrated transportation network. We will enhance the function of airports in Zhengzhou, Luoyang, Nanyang, Yuncheng, Handan, Fuyang, and Changzhi, carry out orderly construction of airports in Xinyang, Shangqiu, Xingtai, Heze, Liaocheng, Anyang, Bengbu, Bozhou, Suzhou, and Lushan, expand domestic routes and regional routes in the city cluster, and optimize the route network to establish an efficient and convenient air transportation network. We will accelerate the development of high-speed railway network in the shape of the Chinese character "米", actively promote the construction of trunk freight railway with "six vertical and four horizontal axes", in order to promote the development of feeder railway and local railway and establish a network of modern railway transportation. We will speed up the construction of the inter-city railways from Zhengzhou airport to Zhengzhounan Station, from Zhengzhounan Station to Dengfeng to Luoyang, from Jiaozuo to Jiyuan to Luoyang, and the extension line of inter-city railway from Zhengzhou to Kaifeng. We will carry out orderly development of inter-city railways from Xinxiang to Jiaozuo, Hefei to Bengbu to Suzhou to Huaibei, and Xuzhou to Huaibei to Suzhou to Fuyang. We will speed up the development of waterways of Huaihe and Shaying River, and open up a water transportation channel from inland central regions to East China. We will vigorously develop intelligent transportation, and promote the innovation, integration and application of Internet of Things, cloud computing, big data and other modern information technology in the field of transportation, so as to improve the level of transportation services.

We will speed up the construction of efficient and extensive information system network. In order to achieve the goal of global connectivity, intelligent perception, data openness and integration of applications, we will promote the evolution and upgrading as well as advanced layout of information infrastructure. With Zhengzhou playing the leading role as the national backbone joint point of the Internet, we will effectively dredge the network traffic between Henan, Shandong, Shanxi, Anhui and other provinces. We will actively promote upgrading of inter-city backbone networks and regional networks, and optimize the network structure of information and communication. We will support Zhengzhou, Luoyang, Handan and other cities to carry out pilot development of 5G network, achieve the goal of wireless LAN covering main public places, and build a "wireless" city cluster. Focusing on promoting the construction of a national large data hub in Zhengzhou and Luoyang, we will establish a unified platform for data exchange and sharing in the city cluster, establish a unified standard, open data port, develop an integrated public application platform, and build a smart city cluster.

We will improve the modern energy support system. We will vigorously promote the structural reform of the energy supply side, and accelerate the development of clean, low-carbon, safe and efficient modern energy supply system. We will actively dissolve the overcapacity in coal industry and carry out strict control of the new capacity. We will carry out an orderly development of alternative mines in the coal bases in central Shanxi and East Shanxi construction with the scale of coal production controlled. We will limit the scale of coal production in west Shandong, central Hebei, Henan, and Huainan-Huaibei. We will coordinate the construction of power supply in the city cluster, and carry out orderly planning and construction of efficient clean coal-fired thermal power units and cogeneration units. We will enhance the capacity of safe accommodation of electricity from Xinjiang and the capacity of inter-province power exchange, and strengthen our role as the national power network hub. Relying on the national natural gas pipeline, we will carry out the distribution and development of supporting branch lines to improve the capacity of introducing natural gas from the northwest, natural gas imported from coastal cities, and coal gas from west Neimenggu, achieving the goal of providing gas supply and central heating in all cities and some key counties (cities).

We will build water conservancy infrastructure. We will establish the guarantee system for water resources, improve the capacity of water supply, and strengthen safety guarantee of water resource. We will coordinate efforts to promote the construction of key water sources projects, water resources allocation projects, emergency standby water sources projects and network interconnection projects. We will intensify our efforts in the utilization of urban regeneration water and improve the capacity of urban drinking water supply. We will steadily push forward the construction of water diversion projects across the river, enhance the capacity of allocation of water resources and promote water conservation in urban and rural areas. We will focus on promoting the development of water diversion projects, including Yellow River to Baiyangdian water diversion, Changjiang River to Huai River water diversion, Huai River to north water diversion, Yellow River to Xiaolangdi Dam water transfer, etc.. Surrounding the large and medium-sized irrigation areas on northern and southern bank of Xiaolangdi Dam, we will carry out in-depth implementation of transformation and construction of large and medium-sized irrigation areas. We will build a cooperation platform for water conservancy, improve the coordination mechanism of upstream and downstream, and form a management mechanism for joint protection, development and utilization of water resources.

7. Striving to Narrow the Gap in Public Services

We will promote sharing of high quality educational resources in the region. We should coordinate and optimize the education resources in the region, encourage various forms of education cooperation, speed up the training of human resources, in order to provide a strong intellectual support for the development of the city cluster in central regions. We should strengthen exchanges and cooperation between universities in the city cluster in central regions and well-known universities at home and abroad, support the construction of high-level Chinese-foreign cooperative universities, and encourage the establishment of Chinese-foreign cooperative education institutions. We will speed up the the development of first-class universities and first-class disciplines, and support development of a number of universities and disciplines entering the first class in China. We will explore the new mode of "Internet Plus Education", encourage the use of digital education resources in primary and middle schools, and expand the coverage of quality education. Education policy should be formulated according to local conditions to ensure equal schooling for the children living with the rural migrant workers in cities. We will actively innovate personnel training mechanism, and encourage development of innovative and strategic alliances between universities, vocational colleges, research institutes, and enterprises, to jointly cultivate high-level innovative talents.

We will strengthen cooperation and exchange of medical and health resources. In order to achieve the goal of serving the development of "healthy central regions", we will actively optimize the layout of medical and health institutions, improve the medical service system with joint efforts and complement to each other, and promote the cross-regional flow of medical resources to the grassroots clinics. We will support the cross-regional coordination and establishment of branch offices in Henan Provincial People's Hospital and the First Affiliated Hospital of Zhengzhou University and other large hospitals to realize the sharing of regional high quality medical resources. We will strengthen cooperation of regional medical institutions and joint training of personnel, and carry out joint tackling of complicated diseases and joint consultation of major diseases. We will jointly promote reform of the health system, strengthen inter-regional cooperation, accelerate the development of basic medical and health care system, establish and improve the basic medical and health system, such as diagnosis and classification system, modern hospital management system, medical insurance system, drug supply security system, and comprehensive supervision system, etc. We will promote the sound development of "Internet Plus Medical and Health Care". We will accelerate the development of informationization of medical and health care, achieve information sharing and business collaboration of medical services at all levels, medical security, and public health services, and build a healthy central region with joint efforts.

We will promote coordination of social securities. We will carry out the implementation of the national insurance registration scheme, improve the coverage rate of social security for rural workers for the self-employed workers, migrant workers and other groups, and achieve full coverage of people in the region. We will promote the social security mode of "Internet Plus", establish a social security information network covering both urban and rural areas, accelerate the remote settlement of basic medical insurance, and implement the direct settlement of hospitalization expenses for inter-provincial retirees, achieving the goal of "one card settles all" for social security. We will strengthen the integration of regional pension insurance, old age welfare and other systems, further simplify the inter-regional transfer of pension insurance and other procedures, and gradually implement the provincial coordination of employment injury insurance. We will strengthen the cooperation of emergency management, build food and drug safety monitoring and control network, and improve joint prevention and control mechanism of public health emergencies. We will actively carry out transformation governance of social assistance, and establish inter-provincial information system of social assistance. We will establish and improve the integration mechanism of comprehensive management, prevention and control of social security, promote transformation of social management from a single city to a city cluster, and form a full coverage of the social management and service network.

8. Carrying out An All-Round Deepening of Comprehensive Coordinated Reform

We will deepen structural and mechanism reforms. We will straighten out relationship between government and the market, and accelerate the implementation of decentralization, delegating power and strengthening regulation as well as optimization of services. We will accelerate the transformation of government functions, promote reforms of the administrative examination and approval, management fees, education, investment, and strive to solve the major issues that are interdisciplinary, cross sectoral, and cross level in order to speed up the formation of a unified regional market. We should speed up the establishment of the information sharing mechanism of enterprise credit within the city cluster, and realize the sharing of government information, such as unified social credit code, enterprise registration, tax payment, contract performance, product quality supervision and so on. We should vigorously promote the cooperation mode of government and social capital (PPP) in the key areas, such as cross regional infrastructure construction, ecological environment protection and public services, so as to stimulate the vitality of social capital to the greatest extent. We will establish a cross regional investment, regional gross domestic product, tax and other benefits sharing mechanism to promote industrial division of labor, industrial integration, and co-construction of various parks in city cluster.

We will establish a mechanism to share the expenses incurred from the transfer of the rural population to urban areas. The urbanization level of city cluster in central regions is not high, while the number of the rural population to transfer to cities is huge, presenting an arduous task. As a result, the establishment of a sound sharing mechanism of the expenses incurred from the transfer of the rural population to urban areas is of particular importance. The government will carry out the organization of a scientific calculation of the expenses incurred from the transfer of the rural population to urban areas. The calculation will be conducted by a team of experts to establish a sound mechanism to share the expenses with the participation of governments, enterprises, and individuals. We will establish a mechanism of linking financial transfer payment to the transfer of rural population, improve the transfer payment system from national and provincial finance to cities and counties (cities), and gradually realize the goal of estimating the allocation of financial funds in accordance with permanent residence, in order to strengthen the capability of financial security of local government with an inflowing population to provide basic public service. We will carry out the implementation of corporate responsibility. Relevant enterprises should increase investment in training, pay employee pension, medical, work injury, unemployment and other social insurance and housing fund for transferred rural population with a formal labor relation according to the law, and carry out the implementation of "equal pay for equal work" for migrant workers. In addition, the population transferred to cities should undertake relevant social insurance fees according to the regulations, and actively participate in vocational education and skills training to enhance their ability of self-development and integration into the city.

We should establish a diversified and sustainable investment and financing mechanisms for urbanization. It is of vital importance to establish a sustainable and diversified investment and financing mechanism to solve the problem of funding in the development of the city cluster in central region and the new urbanization. Taking the urbanization of the city cluster in central region and the government financial situation into consideration, we should make comprehensive use of local government bonds, policy financial instruments, asset securitization and other initiatives, and broaden the financing channels through establishment of government guide funds, PPP mode, government purchase and a variety of other ways. We will play the leading role in the use of government investment. The new government construction funds goes first to projects in areas with more migrated workers, such as reconstruction of village in the city, construction of utility tunnels, and development of integrated zones. We will strengthen coordination and integration of policy financial institutions, and provide financial support to construction projects of infrastructure in cities with more migrated workers. We will actively promote the market reform of development of urbanization infrastructure, establish and improve the franchise system, pricing mechanism, terms of financial subsidies, and the government supervision mechanism that are market friendly. We will guide social capital to participate in the construction and operation of urban public facilities, improve the supplying capacity of city infrastructure, and provide a wide range of financial support for the development of the city cluster in central regions.

References:

[1] Liu Zhenfeng, Xue Dongqian. Temporal-Spatial Evolution of Economic Strength Disparity for Cities above Prefecture Level [J]. *Henan Science*. 2015. No. 3.

[2] Liu Zhenfan, Zhan Guohui, Li Xiangdong. Analysis of Problems and Causes of Investment and Financing System in Prefecture Cities in China [J]. *Assets and Finances in Administration and Institution*. 2014. No. 28.

[3] Fang Huizhen, Dong Ruoyu. The Promotion of the New Urbanization from Supply Side Structural Reform under the New Normal [J]. *Journal of the Party School of Tianjin Committee of the CPC*. 2016. No. 4.

[4] Li Quanqing. Predicament and Solutions of the New Urbanization under Supply Side Structural Reform [J]. *Truth Seeking*. 2016. No. 11.

[5] Chen Xiuying. New Model of Regional Economic Special Structure in Informational Society: The Twofold Carriers of Cities and Region [J]. *China Soft Science*. 2009. No. 3.

[6] Yang Dongyuan. Thinking on the Comprehensive Transportation Planning of City Cluster in Changjiang River Delta – Target, Task and Theory [J]. *Traffic and Transportation*. 2016. No. 4.

[7] Ning Yuemin. On the Development and Construction of China's City Cluster [J]. *Regional Economic Review*. 2016. No. 1.

[8] Fang Chuanglin. The Need of Integrated Mechanism for the Development of City Cluster in Changjiang River Economic Belt [J]. *The New Chongqing*. 2016. No. 2.

[9] Sun Binding, Ding Song. Is Big City Beneficial to the Economic Growth of the Small City? - Evidence from City Cluster in the Changjiang River Delta [J]. *Geographical Research*. 2016. No. 9.

[10] Zhou Zheng, Du Lizhu, Zhang Yi. Research on Development Strategy of City Cluster in Ha'erbin and Changchun under the New Normal [J]. *Urban Studies*, 2016. No. 6.

[11] Zhang Zhenzhen. The Countermeasures for the Sustainable Development of City Cluster in the Middle Reach of Changjiang River [J]. *China Soft Science*, 2016. No. 11.

[12] Qi jie, Zhang Guixiang. Research on Comprehensive Carrying Capacity of Transportation: Taking Beijing-Tianjin-Hebei Urban Agglomeration as an Example [J]. *Ecological Economy*. 2016. No. 4.

[13] Zhang Xiusheng, Wang Peng. Economic Development under the New Normal and Industrial Structure Optimization [J]. *On Economic Problems*. 2015. No. 4.

[14] Wei Jie, Zhang Lin. Industrial Structure Adjustment and the Related Reform under the New Normal [J]. *Economic Review*. 2015. No. 6.

[15] Li Wei, Liu He, Lu Zhongyuan, Long Guoqiang. Re-Manufacturization Strategy of Developed Countries and the Influence on China [J]. *Management World*. 2013. No. 2.

B.8 Henan Agricultural and Rural Development Report

Research Team of the Institute of Agricultural Development, Henan Academy of Social Sciences

Abstract: At present, the agricultural and rural development in Henan province is at a critical stage of transition and transformation. It is not only in the period of fast development, but also in a state of profound transformation. From 2012 to 2016, agriculture and rural areas in Henan province maintained good development momentum. Food crop production increased steadily, and farmers' income grew rapidly; the farmland circulation was accelerated, and new types of agricultural business entities developed rapidly. In 2017, although the various traditional and non-traditional challenges were increasingly prominent, favorable conditions were gradually accumulated. Under the promotion of structural reform of the supply side in agriculture, the output of major agricultural products would increase steadily, and the supply had an accelerated transformation from quantitative growth to quality upgrading, and innovation of agricultural business entities and integration of urban and rural development would be further accelerated.

Keywords: Structural Reform of the Agricultural Supply Side; Modern Agriculture; Income of Farmers; Adjustment of Agricultural Structure; Henan Province

I The Analysis of Henan Agricultural and Rural Development

1. Accelerating the Adjustment of Agricultural Structure

Since 2012, the grain production capacity in Henan has been rising steadily and achieved great success, as shown in Table 1. In terms of the overall situation, the year 2015 was a turning point when the summer grain production exceeded 70 billion jin, which demonstrated that the summer grain production in Henan province completed a great leap from the medium-to-high yielding to stably high.

Table 1 Total output of grain and its growth in Henan province from 2012 to 2016

Unit:100 million *jin*

Year	Grain yield (100 million Jin)			Year-on-year growth rate (%)		
	Total output	Summer grain	Autumn grain	Total output	Summer grain	Autumn grain
2012	1127.72	637.2	490.52	19.22	10.9	8.32
2013	1142.74	647.04	495.7	15.02	9.84	5.18
2014	1154.46	667.8	486.66	11.72	20.76	-9.04
2015	1213.42	702.36	511.06	58.96	34.56	24.4
2016	1189.32	695.36	493.96	-24.1	-7	-17.1

Data source: China's Economic and Social Development Statistical Database (cnki.net).

From 2012 to 2016, the total grain output in Henan increased steadily. From a further analysis of the continuous data (Figure 1), a distinct characteristic can be seen: the growth of the summer grain production had been bigger than that of the autumn grain production. It was a result of the government's incentive policies on wheat production on the one hand, and the rapid development of food processing industry in Henan on the other.

The cultivation area of Henan province over the years from 2012 to 2016 was shown in Table 2. The cultivation area of summer grain held steady at more than 80 million acres with a steady annual increase; the cultivation area of autumn grain increased with fluctuation, and currently it held steady at more than 70 million acres. In 2016, among the four major grain varieties of autumn grain production in Henan province, the cultivation area of maize reduced by 8.6%, that of soybean soared by 123.4%, and that of rice and sweet potato increased respectively by 7.5% and 4.5%. At present, the comprehensive mechanization

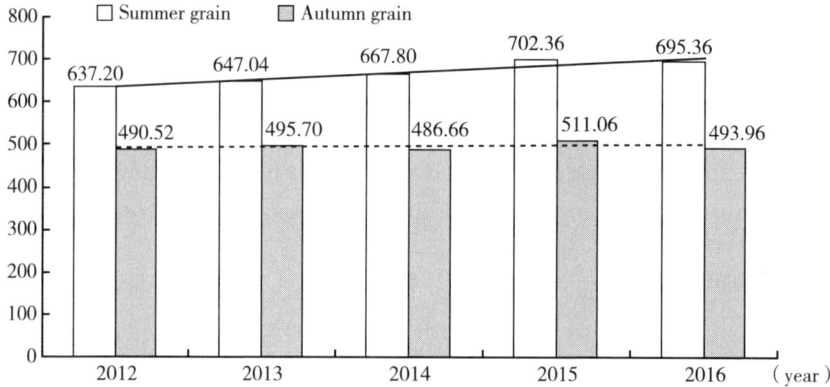

Figure 1 Total grain output in Henan province from 2012 to 2016

level of farming of the main crops was close to 80.6% of all farmland in Henan, the area ploughed, harrowed and sown by machines exceeded 90%, and comprehensive utilization rate of straw reached 87%, which laid a good foundation for promoting transformation and upgrading of agriculture, as well as the construction of modern agricultural province.

The total grain output in Henan decreased in 2016 by 2%, 2.41 billion jin less than that in 2015.There were two main reasons for this.

Firstly, the main reason was the impact of natural disasters. In 2016, summer grain production in Henan suffered from multiple disasters, such as low temperature and weak light before winter, frost damage in winter, an attack of wheat scab heavier than previous years and a wide range of continuous rainfall during harvest time. In the process of autumn grain production, some areas encountered adverse weather conditions such as extremely heavy rainfall and continuous high temperature. In 2016, summer grain output was 69.536 billion jin, reduced by 0.7 billion jin compared with that in 2015 and by 1% in production rate, but the output continues to rank first in the country and was still the second highest in history.

Secondly, it was also due to the adjustment in planting structure. In 2016, autumn cultivation area in Henan is 71.9073 million mu, 315 thousand mu less than the previous year, of which the corn planting area is 49.7529 million mu, 405,000 mu less than the previous year. The main reason is that Henan actively promotes the structural reform of the supply side in agriculture, reducing the planting area of corn while increasing the cultivation area of quality peanut.

Table 2　Total grain output and its growth in Henan province (2012-2016 years)

Unit: million acres

Year	Summer sown area			Autumn sown area		
	Total area	Increase	Increase (%)	Total area	Increase	Year-on-year growth rate (%)
2012	8050	20	0.25	6928	171	2.53
2013	8090	40	0.50	7033	105	1.50
2014	8150	60	0.74	7165	132	1.88
2015	8179	29	0.36	7222	57	0.80
2016	8239	60	0.70	7191	-32	-0.44

Data source: China's Economic and Social Development Statistical Database (cnki.net).

As to the structure of animal husbandry production shown in Table 3, in 2016 the total production of pork, beef, mutton and fowl in Henan was 6.825 million tons, with an increase of 226 thousand tons and a growth rate of 3.4% compared with that in 2012; the total egg production was 4.225 million tons, with an increase of 183 thousand tons and a growth rate of 4.5% compared with that in 2012; the total milk production was 3.268 million tons, with an increase of 107 thousand tons and a growth rate of 3.4% compared with that in 2012.

Table 3　Total output of livestock products and its growth in Henan province from 2012 to 2016

Unit: 10 thousand tons

Year	Grain yield			Year-on-year growth rate		
	Pigs, cattle, sheep and poultry meat	Eggs	Milk	Pigs, cattle, sheep and poultry meat	Eggs	Milk
2012	659.9	404.2	316.1	35.3	13.7	9.5
2013	681.8	410.2	316.4	21.9	6.0	0.3
2014	703.5	404.0	332.0	21.7	-6.2	15.6
2015	696.5	410.0	342.2	-7.0	6.0	10.2
2016	682.5	422.5	326.8	-14.0	12.5	-15.4

Data source: Statistical Annals of Henan Province in 2016, Statistical Network of Henan Province.

From 2012 to 2016, the development of animal husbandry was relatively steady on the whole, as is shown in Figure 2.

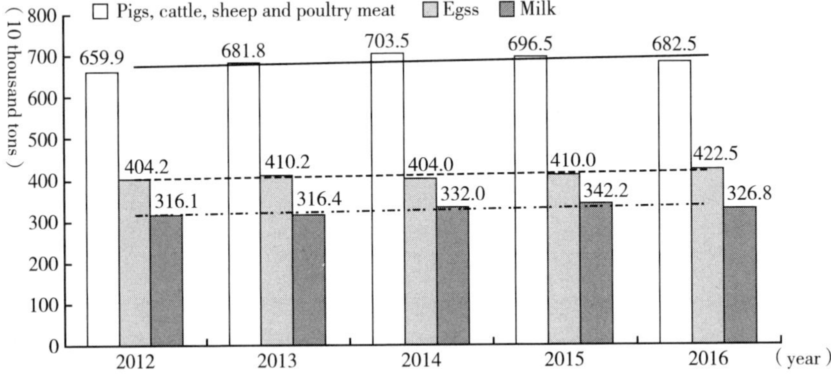

Figure 2 The total output of animal husbandry in Henan province from 2012 to 2016

2. The Improvement of Balance between Supply and Demand of Grain

On the whole, the food crop production in Henan province had been increasing for 12 consecutive years until 2016, when there was a reduction in production. However, it was still a bumper harvest with a second-high yielding in history. The growth in food crop production results in a simultaneous increase in yielding capacity, grain storage and import quantum in grain supply. This was mainly because of the fact that after the Chinese economy entered a new normal, the demands in the grain market became diverse. At present grain production in Henan could not meet the new requirements of the upgrading consumption structure in variety and quality, leading to a mismatch between grain supply and demand and a situation in grain supply and demand featuring an overall balance and a structural shortage. Customs statistics showed that, although Henan boasts of the highest wheat production in China, it still imported nearly 40 thousand tons of wheat in the first half of 2016. In fact, during the same period China as a whole imported 1.77535 million tons of wheat, with year-on-year growth rate of 27.3%.Due to the high production cost and the limited number of high-quality wheat varieties in Henan, the domestic prices of wheat were higher than the international ones, and the needs of food processing enterprises were hard to meet, leading to the simultaneous increase in yielding capacity, grain storage and import quantum. In order to solve this problem, promotion of the structural reform on the supply side in agriculture should be further accelerated.

3. Structural Adjustment of Agricultural Regional Layout

Due to the different natural conditions, resources and potentials in agricultural function expansion of different places in Henan, its agricultural development features a regional pattern made up of areas for urban agriculture, high-efficient agriculture of appropriate scale and ecological agriculture. With the further expansion of agricultural function and the further integration of industries in the future, the agricultural development of the whole province would, based on this regional pattern, further promote the leading function of regional agriculture and the development of dominant industry, optimizing the regional pattern and the industrial layout while taking into account of the carrying capacity of the resources and the environment and regional comparative advantage.

Huang Huaihai Plain and Nanyang Basin: areas for high-efficient agriculture of appropriate scale. There were rich and high-quality agricultural resources in these areas, advantageous conditions for agricultural development, advanced agricultural development level and a great potential for future development, which make it an important area of agricultural production. The goal of development was to realize the seamless joint of standardized agricultural production and the industrial chain of fine and further processing, focusing on enhancing the industrialization of bulk agricultural production, to expand the depth of product processing and the use of resources and to strengthen the production function of basic agricultural products, attaching great importance in developing 95 major grain producing counties, 51 counties specializing in cotton production, 40 counties specializing in oil production, 69 counties specializing in production of live pigs, 52 counties specializing in milk production, 30 counties specializing in production of table poultry, 20 counties specializing in production of egg-laying poultry, 15 counties specializing in waterfowl production, we should attract fine processing capacity of grain, oil, meat, poultry, fodder, wine-making, cotton spinning to congregate in this area, so as to construct core region for steady grain production, guaranteed region for bulk agricultural and animal products supply, demonstrated area for industrialized development as well as demonstrated area for coordinated development of industry and agriculture modernization.

The hilly and mountainous regions in southern, western and northern Henan province: areas for green ecological agriculture. These areas had fine ecological environment, which was suitable to further develop green agriculture according to the ecological rule and standards for green agricultural products, highlighting the regional characteristics and advantages of these agricultural products which bring in more wealth, constructing a key area for coordinated development of agricultural modernization and ecological environment had become the focus of the regional development. The main focus would be on the development of beef cattle, mutton sheep and other herbivorous animal husbandry and the production of fruit, Chinese herbal medicine, tea, edible fungi, tobacco, silk and other advantageous agricultural products, as well as the production of green oil and grain. We should pay attention to standardized production bases that produce high-quality fruits, Chinese medicinal herbs, tea, etc., and eco-agriculture demonstration zones so as to cultivate a number of reputable green agricultural products. We should speed up the integration of production and processing bases with well-known logistics companies and networks at home and abroad, promoting the exportation of characteristic agricultural products, in order to achieve a win-win situation of agricultural efficiency and ecological construction.

Outskirts of major cities: areas for urban agriculture. We should expand the derivative services of agriculture, and promote city-serving agriculture with functions of sightseeing, leisure, tourism, ecology, demonstration of science and technology so as to realize the coordinated promotion of urbanization and agricultural modernization. A stratified development was carried out for urban agriculture based on the orientation of city development: in the urban area, the main goal would be to optimize the environment, improve ecology, beautify the city and serve the city. And the main focus was on the development of urban landscape agriculture, agricultural exhibition, forest park landscape. On the outskirts of the city, great importance would be attached to the function of production, ecological development and leisure life, green vegetables, high-end flower seedlings and other precision agriculture, combined with innovation and transformation in agricultural science and technology, constructing agricultural hi-tech demonstration parks and developing recreational agricultural parks with services of self collection, leisure and entertainment.

4. Further Refinement of Rural Industrial System

Henan province was among the leading provinces where industrialized agricultural management and leading agricultural enterprises first began to develope. The formulation of "Company Plus Farmers" first appeared in Xinyang, Henan. Since 2012, the processing industry of agricultural products in Henan had developed rapidly. There had been an obvious transformation from rough processing to fine and further processing. A large number of unique local agricultural products had been processed in this way. Among them, the food processing industry had grown into the province's largest pillar industry, and a batch of brands became well-known both at home and abroad, of which Shuanghui, Sanquan, Sinian, and Baixiang had become persuasive illustrations of the achievements made in the industrialization in Henan. The output value of the food industry in this agricultural province exceeded 1 trillion yuan for the first time in 2015, ranking second in China. The rapid development of food industry and agricultural industrialization had made Henan a "granary" and "kitchen" of China. From 2012 to 2016, the number of processing enterprises of agricultural products above designated size in Henan province went from 6532 to 7670, an increase of 1138. In 2016, agricultural processing enterprises offered job opportunities to 2.25 million people and their total revenue exceeded 2.2 trillion yuan. Since 2012, Henan had given priority to the development of agricultural industrialization clusters. At the end of 2016, there were altogether 207 agricultural industrialization clusters, covering 11 industries and more than 50 sub-industries in agriculture. Six major industrial chains featuring wheat, soybean, oil, meat processing, dairy industries had already come into being. Meanwhile, with the extensive application of the Internet+ model, e-commerce also flourished in rural areas. In Henan there were 21 national level demonstration counties in the project of E-commerce into the Countryside, and another 27 provincial-level ones.

Agricultural economic model in Henan province had been rapidly shifted from the original isolated production to an organic integration with the second and third industries. They were closely related, and integrated, and formed a complete industrial chain which promoted the integration, optimization and recombination of resources, elements, technologies and markets in rural areas. The comprehensive benefits of agriculture were greatly improved. That helped 11.47 million rural households and offered job opportunities for 1.405 million farmers. The per capita income in the industry was 23,856 yuan. There were totally 15,000 business entities of agricultural tourism with 316,300 employees and business revenue of 11.17 billion yuan.

5. Moderate Rise in Prices of Agricultural Products

Details of the Consumer Price Index(CPI) and Food Consumption Price Index(FCPI) from 2012 to 2016 were shown in Table 4. During the five years, the CPI experienced some fluctuations, but it was relatively stable on the whole. In contrast, the FCPI fluctuated greatly. Affected by the fluctuations of food prices, the FCPI made a good start in 2013 but kept going down in the following years until 2016 when it gradually returned where it used to be in 2012, as is shown in Figure 3.

Table 4 Consumer price index and food consumption index in Henan province from 2012 to 2016

Year	Consumer price index	Food consumption index
2012	102.5	103.6
2013	102.9	105.6
2014	101.9	102.6
2015	101.3	101.8
2016	101.9	103.2

Data source: Statistical annals of Henan province.

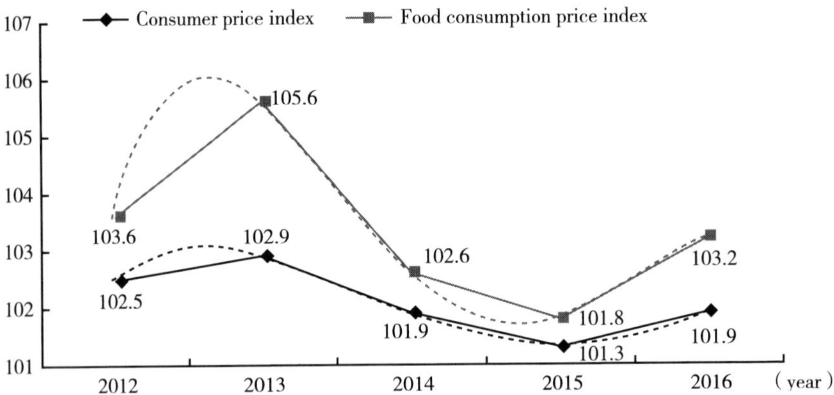

Figure 3 The year-on-year variation tendency of consumer price and food consumption price index from 2012 to 2016

As is shown in Table 5, in terms of different agricultural products, the CPI of grain barely fluctuated, and kept declining after a slight increase in 2012. The great impact on the FCPI came from prices of eggs, table poultry and related products, and fresh vegetables. As is shown in Figure 4, the change of prices in fresh vegetables and meat followed the same trend though with different amplitude of variation. The price of eggs began to fall in 2015 after a sharp rise in 2013 and 2014.

Table 5 Consumer price index of major agricultural products in Henan province from 2012 to 2016

Year	Grain	Fresh vegetables	Table poultry and relevant products	Eggs
2012	104.1	115.1	99.4	94.4
2013	106.6	110.3	104.8	104.4
2014	105.2	94.9	98.8	114.4
2015	102.9	107.3	103.5	85.5
2016	100.1	111.3	112.8	95.6

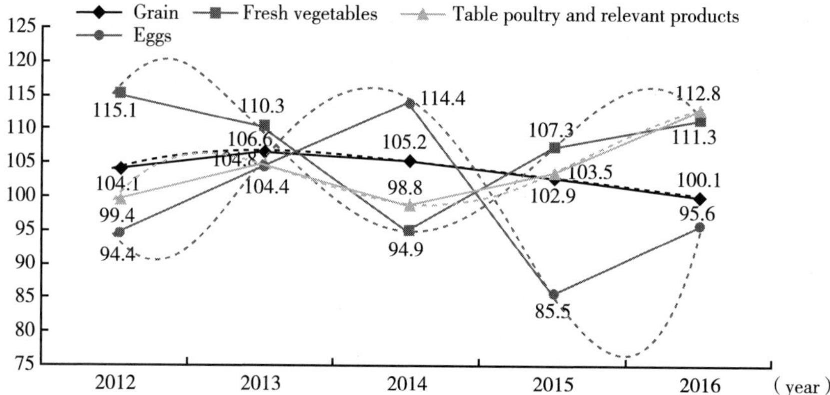

Figure 4 The trend of consumption price of main agricultural products in Henan province from 2012 to 2016

6. Stable Development in Agriculture and Rural Area

There was a steady growth of agricultural production. The years from 2012 to 2016 witnessed a generally stable and moderate growth in the gross value of production of the primary industry and the total output value of agriculture, forestry, animal husbandry and fishery in Henan province, as is shown in Table 6. According to the national industry classification and the classification standard of three industries adopted in 2014, the annual growth rate of primary industry in Henan and the total output value of agriculture, forestry, animal husbandry and fishery had been more than 4% ever since.

Table 6 Primary industry and the total output value of agriculture, forestry, animal husbandry and fishery in Henan province

Year	Primary industry	Agriculture, forestry, animal husbandry and fishery	Primary industry	Agriculture, forestry, animal husbandry and fishery
	Output value (unit: 100 million yuan)		Year-on-year increase (%)	
2012	3772.31	-	4.5	-
2013	4058.98	-	4.3	-
2014	4160.01	4261.54	4.0	4.2
2015	4209.56	4348.41	4.4	4.4
2016	4286.30	4440.05	4.2	4.4

Data source: *Henan Statistical Yearbook 2016.*

Farmers' income continued to grow at a high speed. As is shown in Table 7, from 2012 to 2016, the per capita disposable income of rural residents and per capita consumer spending kept growing at a steady high speed, with an increase of more than 7% in the per capita disposable income of farmers, in line with the trend in agricultural development and grain output.

Table 7 Per capita disposable income and per capita consumption expenditure of rural residents in Henan province

Unit: yuan

Year	Per capita disposable income			Per capita consumption expenditure		
	Income	Increase (%)	Actual increase (%)	Consumption	Increase (%)	Actual increase (%)
2012	7524.94	13.9	11.3	5032.14	16.5	13.8
2013	8475.34	12.6	9.5	5627.73	11.8	8.7
2014	9416.10	11.1	9.4	6438.12	14.4	12.6
2015	10853.00	8.9	7.6	7887.00	8.4	7.1
2016	11696.74	-	7.8	8586.59	-	8.9

Data Source: *Henan Statistical Yearbook 2016.*

II Basic Experience in Agricultural Development in Henan Province

We steadily improved the comprehensive production capacity of agriculture. As a province with the largest wheat production in China, Henan province earnestly implemented the food crop production strategy based on farmland management and technological application, sped up the cultivation of high-standard farmland, and improved grain production capacity. The whole province focused on the cultivation of high-standard farmland, strengthening the construction and maintenance of field engineering projects. We continuously improved the ability of agricultural disaster prevention and disaster resistance, aggregating project funds and sped up technological follow-up so as to raise the standard of construction and management. By 2016, Henan province had had 53.57 million mu of high-standard farmland, completing 84.1% of the goal; in 2016 another 2.6 million mu of farmland added to the total number by way of restoration and improvement of effective irrigation, which further strengthened its comprehensive grain production capacity. The protection and promotion of the quality of cultivated land had been actively carried out, through returning straw to the farmland, increasing the application of organic fertilizer, green manure cultivation, sub-soiling and other measures, and the productivity of land has greatly improved. Under the circumstances of adjustment and optimization of planting structure as well as reduction of grain planting area, in 2016, Henan's total grain output reached 118.932 billion jin, marking the 11th consecutive year with a total output over 100 billion jin as well as the second highest in history. The province's total purchase of wheat amounted to 33.6 billion jin, with a year-on-year increase of 4.5 billion jin.

We continued to change the mode of agricultural development. Henan actively implemented the subsidy program for the popularization mechanism of basic agricultural technology, sending the agro-technology technicians to the grass-level units, innovating and promoting service models. Each technician had connection with at least 3 township (district) stations for agricultural technology popularization. And the responsibility system on the service of science and technology should be implemented, promoting the normalization of services provided by thousands of scientific and technical personnel for thousands of villages. We built a model of agricultural science and technology innovation and popularization, and improved the pertinence and timeliness of the cultivation of new professional farmers. Township(district) station construction was combined with the implementation of the project of information entering villages and households in order to promote the informationization of services of technology popularization, and make them a major platform to provide information and technical services for farmers.

At the same time, for the purpose of high-yield, efficient, high-quality and green grain production, we strived to make technological breakthrough, and select and popularize a batch of new grain varieties and new technologies. We promoted high-yield, efficient and green food production packages, popularized related production technologies, and promoted the combination of improved grain varieties and advanced technologies and the integration of agricultural machinery and skills, so that the content of science and technology in grain production continued to improve. The coverage rate of improved varieties of food crops like wheat and corn reached 98%, machine harvest rate of corn 75%, machine sowing rate of wheat more than 96%. Technical measures such as deep ploughing, deep scarification and straw returning, soil testing, formula fertilization and integrated pest control had been widely applied, agricultural machinery integrated with agricultural skills, which significantly improved the level of scientific and technological content in grain production. Affected by many factors such as decreased profit from grain planting, farmers had become increasingly unwilling to invest capital and labor. In order to stabilize grain production, on the one hand, Henan province had strictly implemented the minimum purchase price policy for wheat and rice, stabilizing the income expectation of grain farmers; on the other hand, it made full use of incentive funds for counties with a high grain yield. Through a series of measures, including high standard crop fields, the policy of supporting agriculture and benefiting farmers, we should stimulate the internal dynamism of grain production to secure a steady grain production capacity.

We vigorously promoted the structural reform of the supply side in agriculture. In the face of the new economic norm, Henan actively promoted structural reforms of agricultural supply side, speeding up the fostering of new momentum in agriculture and rural development, changing the mode of agricultural development, in order to fundamentally correct mismatches in supply and demand structure and distortions of factor allocation. In November 2016, Henan Provincial Government and Provincial Committee of CPC proposed to focus on the development of high-quality wheat, high quality peanut, high quality grassland animal husbandry, high-quality forestry and fruit, promoting regional distribution, large-scale operation, standardization of production and development of industrialization under the guidance of overall planning. Centering on the “Four Advantages and Four Modernizations”, we attached importance to the connection between production and marketing, and adopted the order form-based production mode, and established an organic mechanism of integrated interests chain among the large agricultural products acquisition and processing enterprises, farmers cooperatives and farmers to ensure the interests of farmers. The funds of current projects like the integration of the three industries, industrial clusters, structural adjustment, straw comprehensive utilization, and subsidies of agricultural support and protection went primarily to "regionalized agricultural pattern, systematic expansion of agricultural business, standardized production and industrialized development" and "the development of high-quality wheat, peanut, livestock and fruit". We switched from the development model in the past that blindly pursued output to a new model which emphasized both quantity and efficiency, both production and ecology.

III The Outlook of Agricultural Development in Henan Province

In 2017, profound changes have been taking place in the international environment, and the domestic economy has entered a new normal featuring shifting growth, structural optimization and momentum conversion. Henan agricultural and rural development is prepared with a solid foundation and strategic opportunities, and also faced with bottlenecks and challenges posed by the urgent need for breakthrough and transformation. But on the whole, the advantages outweigh disadvantages and there is still large room for further development of Henan agriculture and rural areas, and of itself as a major agricultural province.

1. Favorable Conditions

The environment of agricultural and rural development has been further optimized. Since 2010, a series of national strategic plans and platforms in Henan have been approved, including the construction of Central Plains Economic Region, Zhengzhou Airport Economy Zone, Central Henan Urban Agglomeration, National Central City Zhengzhou, Self-dependent Innovation Demonstration Areas of Zhengzhou, Luoyang and Xinxiang City, China (Henan) Pilot Free Trade Zone, comprehensive testing zone of international electronic commerce, comprehensive testing zone of national massive data, which suggested a situation of added favorable national strategies. Henan is also a core region for national grain production, which would be helpful for it to gain more preferential policies from the central government for agricultural and rural development so as to solve a series of problems such as difficulties in grain production increase, unreasonable agricultural structure and hysteric urbanization, to plan as a whole all the tasks involved in agricultural modernization and to make up for the under-development of rural areas and agriculture. Speeding up the integration into Maritime Silk Road Initiative (the Belt and Road Initiative) would help Henan make full use of the advantages of Zhengzhou Airport Economy Zone and China (Henan) Pilot Free Trade Zone to further open to the outside and accelerate the pace of "going global" for agricultural products.

At present, Henan is pushing forward the construction of a province with advanced manufacturing, pillar service industry, modern agriculture and strong Internet economy, namely, "A Province with Four Mighty Industries". It will also further promote the five synchronization, and ultimately achieve the ultimate goal of a well-developed Henan. At the same time, with the changes in consumption structure and the rise of consumption level of urban and rural residents, the huge potential in the consumption of multilevel, diversified and personalized agricultural products and services is becoming prominent, which will give more room for development to advantageous agricultural products, such as organic, green, pollution-free food and vegetables, fruits, flowers, herbs and the like. In addition, the deep integration of tourism, entertainment, education and culture, health preserving, and agriculture will also provide a capacious value-added space for the expansion of agricultural function and the extension of value chain.

Structural reform of the agricultural supply side will stimulate the potential and vitality of agricultural and rural development. Currently, the reforms in rural areas have been in full swing, helping to revitalize rural asset resources, stimulate development potential, and release vitality and momentum. The reform of the property right system in rural areas has been deepening, and the registration and certification of ownership of rural collective construction land has basically been completed. Rural property rights trading centers have been set up in Zhengzhou, Xinxiang, Xinyang, Jiyuan, Lankao, Hebi, Puyang, etc. Nine county-level cities like Dengzhou and Changge have been approved as pilot cities for the rural contracted land management rights mortgage, and Huaxian and Lankao had been approved as pilot counties for rural housing property rights mortgage. Changyuan had been approved as a pilot county for the collective construction land entering market, and for the reform of land acquisition system. Clarity of rural property rights would be beneficial to the rational allocation of rural resources, expanding farmers' property income and building long-term effective mechanism for farmers' income growth. The innovation of rural finance is speeding up, and the construction of a financial reform pilot area had been launched in the Central Plains Economic Region, which would be beneficial to crack the bottleneck for funds shortage that had plagued the agricultural development in Henan province for a long time.

Currently, a new round of technological revolution is gaining momentum. Internet-related thinking is infiltrating in all respects of life. The application of new technologies such as big data, cloud computing, and the Internet of Goods is just unfolding, creating new modes of production, business models and growth opportunities. New modes of production and forms of business are constantly emerging. For example, new business forms such as crowd-funding have infiltrated into traditional sectors such as agriculture and new agricultural business models, such as Chu Orange (the brand name of an orange planted in Yunnan province, named after Chu Shijian, a famous farmer entrepreneur), Liu Kiwi (the brand name of a kiwi planted in Sichuan province, named after Liu Chuanzhi, the chairman of Lenovo) and Jutudi (a program launched by Taobao for private transaction of idle land on the Internet), by using Internet as a channel to organize farmers without regional restrictions, have provided opportunities for traditional major grain-producing areas to catch up with and surpass those developed areas. Internet technology has realized the transparency in the whole process of agricultural production from the fields to the table and it is helpful for the implementation of precision in agriculture, controlling the quality of agricultural products, improving the competitiveness of Henan province in the market of agricultural products. It has become an important way of agricultural growth. Internet is more conducive to promote the integrated development of the primary, secondary and tertiary industries in rural areas and promote transformation and upgrading of agriculture.

2. Unfavorable Factors

In recent years, the modern agriculture construction in Henan province has been accelerated, maintaining the good momentum of grain production and income increase, but at the same time various risks and structural contradictions have been accumulated and there are some glaring problems to be solved.

The decrease of agricultural resources and the deterioration of the ecological environment are becoming increasingly prominent. The province's agricultural resources are congenitally deficient, and the per capita cultivated land and fresh water resources are only 4/5 and 1/5 of the national average and 1/4 and 1/20 of the world average respectively. In recent years, great achievements have been made in the development of agriculture, but a heavy price has also been paid. On the one hand, the usage of chemical synthesis such as chemical fertilizers, pesticides and agricultural plastic film is increasing greatly year by year, the "high input" in agricultural production and operation not only is a waste of resources, intensifying the constraints of resources and environment and making the land increasingly barren, but also brings serious pollution. A series of problems like pollution of agricultural resources, deterioration of the quality of the cultivated land and groundwater overdraft, have become increasingly prominent. In addition to this, the pollution of industrial and domestic waste also makes rural environmental problems increasingly serious, leading to frequent occurrence of safety issues of agricultural products and food; on the other hand, with more rigid requirements of whole society on the quality and safety of the ecological environment and agricultural products, the task of ensuring food safety was arduous and difficult.

Agricultural comparative benefits are low, and the problem of agricultural products price inversion at home and abroad is becoming increasingly prominent. At present, the relationship between supply and demand of agricultural products has begun to change into the pattern featuring a balance of the total amount and a structural shortage. On the one hand, a large number of agricultural products are in surplus and unsalable; on the other hand, a good many emerging agricultural needs are not met, and the lacking in some grain varieties can only be made up by imports. As a major agricultural province, Henan has an agriculture industry that is large in scale but not strong in competitiveness, and ample agricultural products that is not of high quality.The development of high-quality, diversified and specialized agricultural products is still lagging behind, and their quality and safety level still need to be improved, because they cannot meet the changing requirements of urban and rural residents' consumption of agricultural products.

On the one hand, the cost of agricultural production has been on the rise in recent years. With the rising prices of raw materials and primary energy, the production cost and prices of major agricultural production materials such as chemical fertilizers, pesticides, seeds etc. are also increasing. Meanwhile, with the acceleration of industrialization and urbanization, the cost and prices of land and workforce also keep rising. Under the combined effect of these factors, the cost of agricultural production has been rising continuously. However, the price of agricultural products stays at low ebb, leading to low efficiency in agricultural production. On the other hand, the inversion of prices of international and domestic agricultural products results in a continuous increase of imports. The high costs and the low prices are nibbling together at the space for agricultural development. The pattern of low comparative benefits of agriculture is difficult to change fundamentally in a short term, and it is difficult for grain production, with a high starting point, to achieve stable growth in production.

With the migration of a large number of young and middle-aged labor force, the problems of "who will cultivate land" and "how to cultivate land" are becoming more prominent. Although rural land circulation is being accelerated, the number of small-scale farmers has not been greatly reduced, and small-scale farming and sideline farming still play a dominate role. Part-time farming has increasingly made farming a part-time job for many farmers, who pursue a high yield only by expanding the cultivation areas. This will have a negative influence on food supply and food security. In this case, the new types of agricultural business entities become the white hope to replace small farmers as the main producers of future commodity grain.But in recent years, with the decline of agricultural profits, especially profits in grain, the enthusiasm of new agricultural business entities such as professional farmers has been thwarted, and the cultivation has become more difficult. The system of socialized agricultural service is not perfect, the degree of agricultural organization is relatively low, and there is still obvious contradiction between small-scale production and the big market.

3. The Outlook of Future Development

In 2017, despite the various traditional and non-traditional challenges, the favorable conditions are being accumulated, and the agricultural and rural development in the province would still win more space for improvement. The overall situation would suggest a trend of "steady increase in production, expanding profits in income, transformation of approaches and promotion of integration". The quality and efficiency of the agricultural supply system would be remarkably improved, farmers' life would reach a relatively comfortable standard of living, and the agricultural ecological environment would improve gradually. The level of technical equipment would be remarkably improved, and the development of moderate scale management of various forms of agriculture would speed up.

With the effect of the comprehensive measures for promoting the construction of core region for grain production, the areas of high standard farmland would continue to increase, the building of irrigation and water conservancy facilities would be strengthened, and effective irrigation area would increase dramatically, which would help to enhance the ability of disaster prevention and reduction and maintain a steady growth in output of major agricultural products.We would speed up the development of quality specified strong gluten and weak gluten wheat; maintain a sufficient supply of cottonseed oil, vegetables and fruits, meat, milk, aquatic products and other agricultural products, and try to make the supply structure of major agricultural products more reasonable. The processing and transformation rate of agricultural products would exceed 60%. More than 60% of the farmers in the province would benefit directly from the development of industrial integration. At the same time, capabilities of quality and safety supervision of agricultural products, as well as disease prevention and control of animal and plant increased significantly. The modern agriculture industry system would be constructed, forming a development pattern of orchestrating grain crops, economic crops and forage crops, forming a development pattern featuring the combination of farming, forestry, animal husbandry and fishery, the integration of planting, breeding and processing, and the coordination of the first, second and tertiary industries, Significant achievements would be made in the production of high quality wheat, peanuts, livestock, fruits and vegetables, as well as localized agricultural layout, standardized production and industrialized development.

Farmers' income would keep increasing. with the implementation of a series of national strategic planning and platform construction, under the driving forces of reform, opening up and innovation, risk resistance ability of economic development would increase significantly, which would promote farmers' income to play the role of the initiative of farmers income increasing continuously. As another major source of income of farmers, household income would also benefit and keep increasing. Meanwhile, with the change of the mode of agricultural development, especially with the acceleration of industrial integration, the application of technologies such as Internet of Things, cloud computing and big data would further increase in agriculture. Agriculture itself and its integration with the second and tertiary industries would be further accelerated; agricultural industrialization clusters and urban eco-agriculture would develop further; agricultural e-commerce, network marketing and other new formats and models would be further enriched; rural financial services would be further expanded, the process of sending agricultural entity market off to the network and the realization of virtual market would speed up.

The integration of urban and rural development would be further accelerated. In 2017, the confirmation, registration and certification of the contractual management right of all rural land in Henan would be completed, and circulation of the rural land management rights and the moderate scale management of agriculture would be further accelerated. With the establishment of equal employment system for the urban and rural laborers, we would further explore the implementation of the reform of the household registration system and residence permission system, and the equalization of systems and mechanisms of the basic public services for urban and rural residents, the protection of the original rights and interests of the transferred population, employment security, housing security, educational guarantee for the accompanying children, social security and the cost sharing mechanism of citizens. The urbanization of rural migrant workers and the integration of urban development and rural development would be further pushed forward.

IV Suggestions on Promoting the Construction of Henan Province as A Major Modern Agricultural Province

At present, Henan has reached the critical period of accelerating its transformation and upgrading. The mode of agricultural production, the employment mode of rural labor force, the relationship between urban and rural areas, and the rural lifestyle have been undergoing profound changes. We must seize new opportunities to make good use of the current favorable conditions and boost the structural reforms of the agricultural supply side, to accelerate the transformation of agricultural development mode, and to promote agricultural transformation and upgrading. We must increase the intensity of innovation drive with the transformation of the modes of agricultural development as its core, so as to actively guide the development of various forms of moderate scale business. We must construct modern agricultural management system, production system and industrial system, to promote the transformation of agricultural development modes and achieve substantial results as soon as possible. We would do our utmost to keep the steady development of agriculture and continuous increase of farmers' income, exploring a new road for the development of modern agriculture that emphasizes production efficiency, products safety, resource saving and environment coexistence and making great efforts to create a new situation of the construction of Henan province as a major modern agricultural province.

1. Intensifying the Construction of Agricultural Infrastructure

To speed up agricultural transformation and upgrading, it would be essential to optimize infrastructure. Agricultural infrastructure construction should be taken as an important part of agricultural development, and agricultural production capacity and disaster prevention and reduction capability should be effectively improved.

Firstly, we should push forward the construction of farmland water conservancy and other infrastructure construction. We should keep on promoting the construction of major irrigation projects, accelerating the construction of a drought emergency water supply project and flood prevention and control projects, and improving the ability of disaster prevention and reduction in agriculture in an all-round way. We should focus on the improvement of the conditions of irrigation and water conservancy, promoting the construction of farmland water conservancy projects on a large scale. Advanced water-saving irrigation technology should be actively applied to improve irrigation efficiency and the comprehensive production ability and disaster prevention and reduction ability of agriculture. Advanced water-saving irrigation technology should be actively applied to improve irrigation efficiency, the comprehensive production ability, and disaster prevention and reduction ability in agricultural production.

Secondly, we should enhance the capacity of grain output constantly. We should hold firmly onto the food crop production strategy based on farmland management and technological application and steadily improve the comprehensive grain production capacity. Under the guidance of the plan to build Henan into a core region for grain production, we should speed up the construction of high standard crops fields of Super Large Plowland, attaching equal importance to its construction and improvement. It is also important for us to implement of the "Henan High Standard Crops Fields Protection Ordinance", carrying our special protection for high standard crops fields as permanent farmland and ensuring the usage and benefits of high standard crops fields in the long run.

2. Accelerating the Adjustment of Agricultural Structure

Firstly, we ought to lay heavy stress on the structural reform of the agricultural supply side and to adjust and optimize the structure of agriculture. According to the diverse needs of the market, the focus of agricultural production has switched from the development of regular agricultural products of large quantities to that of high-quality wheat, peanut, grassland animal husbandry, forestry and fruits. We should develop superior quality products with obvious characteristics and high added value. As to wheat, great emphasis should be laid on the development of high quality strong gluten and high quality weak gluten wheat. As to peanuts, we should focus on the development of high quality peanut oil and oleic acid peanuts and edible peanuts; as to grassland animal husbandry, we should focus on the development of high quality cows and beef cattle. As to high-quality forestry and fruits, we should focus on the development of brand-name varieties, expanding the proportion of high-end, high-quality fruit varieties. We should strengthen variety improvement of high-quality agricultural products and the research, development and popularization of new crop varieties, and speed up the upgrading of crop varieties, in order to push forward the agricultural supply from medium-low level to medium-high level. As for the production of specialized grain, livestock and poultry products, forest products, oil and fruits and vegetables and other high-quality distinctive agricultural products, we should switch from the original pattern of decentralized management, extensive management, low-end processing to the layout of regionalization, large-scale operation, production standardization, and development industrialization. It would be necessary to establish strict management system of agricultural input, to vigorously carry out the standardization of agricultural production and to actively develop agricultural products certified as "Pollution-free Agricultural Products, Green Food, Organic Agricultural Products" and "Geographical Indications of Agricultural Products". We should protect the ecological environment of the raw material production bases for those famous brand products, and strengthen the source control, process administration and quality inspection, so as to establish a supervision system capable of tracing the quality and safety along the whole production chain of agricultural products.

Secondly, we should work under the guidance of the concept of greater agriculture, explore all kinds of agricultural resources in a reasonable way, speed up the development of agriculture with high efficiency and unique characteristics, and provide consumers with rich varieties of agricultural products. We should vigorously promote "One Famous Product per Village" and "One Famous Industry per Town", accelerating the aggregation of competitive products and industries in dominant areas. We should positively promote the planting of some woody or aquatic food crops like Chinese chestnuts, red jujubes, walnuts and lotus roots. We should promote concentration of vegetable planting and speed up the large-scale development of quality vegetables that are famous, pollution-free and standardized. We should build core regions for flowers and gardening production and production bases of high quality tea, fruits, edible fungus and Chinese herbal medicines. We should strengthen the marketing and promotion of famous agricultural products and step up efforts to protect related intellectual property rights, and speed up the development of agricultural products of geographical indication.

Thirdly, we should actively coordinate farming and animal husbandry, and intensify the development of circular agriculture. We should work at building a farming structure that balances grain production and fodder production and combines agriculture and animal husbandry, capable of circular development. In view of local conditions, we should cultivate fodder corn and silage corn, actively develop the planting of high-quality forage grasses such as alfalfa and speed up the construction of modern fodder grass industry. We should explore the crop rotation, fallow of cultivated land and the subsidy system for planting high quality forage grasses to promote the coordinated development of grain crops, cash crops, forage grasses and animal husbandry. As for arable land on the plain, especially major grain-producing areas, we should optimize the structure of planting industry and its varieties under the premise of guaranteeing grain safety. In those areas we can also carry out the rotation of food crops and forage grasses and plant corn that can be used as both food and fodder. We should explore the full potential of straw which can be used as fodder. It is also necessary to digest and utilize the surplus stock of stale grain and vigorously develop animal husbandry. In the hilly region, we should speed up the construction of artificial or half-artificial grassland, actively support the improvement of grassland, improve the livestock carrying capacity of the grassland and promote balance between grassland and livestock.

We should promote the transformation and upgrading of large-scale animal husbandry and the structural adjustment of fishery farming. Around the key leading enterprises and counties with large-scale animal husbandry, development of competitive animal by-products concentrated area and the processing industry of animal by-products should be sped up. The development of the ecological farming in the form of a pasture should be encouraged. That is to build "fertile farmland in the air", "fertile farmland underwater" and "economy in the forest". According to local conditions, we can promote technologies such as fish farming in the paddy fields or in the vegetable fields. With microbial resource industry as the starting point, we should speed up the development of the three-dimensional agriculture composing plants, animals and microbes.

3. Strengthening the Protection of Agricultural Resources and Environment

Firstly, we should go all out to break the bottleneck in the protection of agricultural resources and environment. We should specify as soon as possible the red line for ecological protection and construct ecological security barrier. Focusing on the improvement of the regional environmental quality of the Yellow River basin, we would strengthen the prevention and control of agricultural defused pollution and carry out comprehensive environmental improvement in full swing. We should seek to apply for national pilot projects of agricultural resources recuperation, fully implement the subsidies for upgrading soil organic matter, and give energetic support to the popularization of conservation tillage. We should establish a natural ecological environment protection mechanism and an agricultural ecological compensation mechanism which are beneficial to agricultural production increase and improve the subsidy reward system for farmland ecological protection and ecological agricultural production, in order to realize the sustainable development of agriculture.

Secondly, we should carry out pollution-free production mode. In accordance with the requirements of "reduction, reuse and recycling" and the principle of integration, coordination, recycling and regeneration, we should plan and organize agricultural production in a systemic and reasonable way, establish according to local conditions industrial cycle systems featuring inter-industry interdependence as well as efficient utilization of products, intermediate products and waste exchange, and actively guide the construction of internal recycling systems, agricultural internal recycling systems and the family cycle systems of farmers. We would support the development models of livestock–biogas–fruit, livestock–biogas–grain, livestock–biogas–vegetables and other farming and animal husbandry combined cycle development model, and promote the closed circulation and comprehensive utilization of processing link waste in agricultural processing parks. We would also vigorously promote agricultural resource conservation, and step up efforts in conservation-oriented agricultural technology innovations like land saving, water saving, fertilizer saving, seeds saving, etc., and actively support the research and development, improvement and popularization of agricultural technology of straw returning to field, promoting the comprehensive utilization of straw returning. We would promote straw returning, straw raising livestock, straw gasification, and popularize the use of straw fertilizer, energy, raw materials, feed, base material, to boost the development of modern agriculture to the environment-friendly direction. We should adapt to the needs of urban and rural residents for a livable eco-environment, and actively improve the living conditions in rural areas, so as to speed up the construction of beautiful countryside and improve the quality of human settlements.

Thirdly, we should step up efforts on ecological protection. The overall protection, systematic restoration and comprehensive treatment of the landscape, forest and farmland Lake should be promoted; the project of returning farmland to forests, protecting natural forests and forests along the Yangtze River in Huaihe should be sped up; the construction of ecological system in mountainous areas, reconstruction and expansion of farmland shelter-belt system and construction of ecological corridor network should be accelerated, the construction of ecological security barriers should be sped up, and the damaged ecological environment should be gradually repaired.

4. Promoting the Integrated Development of the Primary, Secondary and Tertiary Industries

Firstly, we should accelerate the cultivation of new agricultural management entities. Great importance should be attached to the cultivation of new agricultural business entities and service entities, as well as active guidance in the development of various forms of moderate scale business. On the one hand, we should speed up efforts

to cultivate new agricultural business entities, such as family farms, professional farmers, farmers' cooperatives, agricultural industrialization, and leading enterprises etc. by way of improving fiscal and credit insurance policies, in order to give full play to their leading function in modern agriculture. On the other hand, new types of agricultural service entities, such as rural supply and marketing cooperatives, farmers' cooperatives, etc., should be supported to provide small-scale farmers in rural areas with professional scale services, such as contract farming, cooperative farming, and land trust, and to provide socialized services for the agricultural industry. Many kinds of scale business modes, such as land circulation, land trust (semi-trust), the pooling of land etc., should be formed to enable farmers to get increasingly involved in participation and sharing.

Secondly, we should strengthen the processing industry of agricultural products,, build a batch of high-quality and efficient modern agricultural industrial clusters that covers all parts of the production chain and of industrial circulation, foster a number of processing enterprises, and build a batch of Henan agricultural brands that are famous home and abroad. We would implement the "Giant Dragon Project", build "giant" agricultural leading enterprises that are as well-known as "Shuanghui". We should provide these large-scale leading enterprises with the most favorable policies and the greatest support in order to further promote their coordination, listing, financing, and integration into giant enterprise groups, and encourage them to exert their agglomerating and spin-off effects, in order to step up their competitive edge in domestic and international markets. We should continue to promote the plan to build leading enterprises, and focus on supporting large-scale leading enterprises with a good foundation and a strong spin-off effect. We should implement the strategy to promote spin-off effects of famous brands by providing more financial input and subsidies to help enterprises step up efforts on its promotion, so as to enhance the popularity, reputation and market share of Henan agricultural products and to build a number of preponderant brands of agricultural production.

Thirdly, we should refine the rural leisure tourism industry. We should further promote the strategic adjustment of agricultural industrial structure and make good use of the value of the countryside in ecological recreation, tourism, culture and education via the construction of a number of scenic towns and villages with historical, cultural, regional, ethnic characteristics, and the exploration of diversified and distinctive rural tourism and recreation products, including leisure vacation, pastoral tourism, health preserving and elderly care, creative agriculture and farming experience, handicraft. We should make it a new pillar industry for the prosperity of the rural areas and affluence of farmers.

Fourthly, we should promote the Internet plus agriculture pattern. We should implement the three-year plan of Internet plus modern agriculture, build the agricultural big data center, and accelerate the promotion of horticultural crops, breeding, quality and safety traceability applications in the field of Internet of things. We should vigorously develop the "Internet plus agriculture" pattern by encouraging the development of e-commerce industry parks, the implementation of "Thousand Villages" project of Alibaba, the "Thousand Counties Prairie Fire" project of JD.com and "The Most Beautiful Village" project of Su'ning, and promoting the interconnection of business, supply and marketing, postal service, and e-commerce. We should actively foster a group of new modern modes that combines "planting, breeding and sale" to enhance the competitiveness of agricultural products. Large electronic commerce platforms should be encouraged to serve farmers and rural areas, gradually forming a two-way circulation pattern featuring the fusion of online and offline businesses, and the flows of agricultural products to cities and of capital and commodities to the countryside.

Fifthly, we should boost the integration of urban and rural development. The mechanism of the integration of urban and rural development should be highlighted and improved to promote the permanent urban residency of migrant farmers. The binary structural system of rural and urban areas should be eliminated, and migrant workers should be entitled to rights and obligations equal to those of urban residents. We should also enhance the urbanization rate of permanent residents. The residence permission system should be popularized, the basic public services mechanism that is connected with residence should be established and improved, and we should strive to achieve a complete coverage of the basic public services for permanent residents. The mechanism should be explored and established to orderly transfer rural residents into cities proper or in their vicinity. We should speed up the development of small-and-medium-sized cities and small towns with unique characteristics to enhance the capacity to accommodate eligible rural workers. The balanced configuration of rural and urban public resources should be promoted and the focus of the development of social undertakings should be put on rural areas and the towns that have the capacity to accommodate more eligible rural workers. We should extend urban public services to the countryside, and make good use of the spin-off effect of new urbanization on agricultural modernization. We should spare no efforts in guiding urban modern production factors toward agriculture and rural areas. The intensity of the balanced transference and payment of central government budget should be increased to promote equalization of basic public services in the urban and rural areas.

5. Perfecting the Innovation and Service System of Agricultural Science and Technology

Firstly, we should further deepen the reform in the management of agricultural scientific researches. It is important to strengthen the innovation system of agricultural science and technology, deepen the reform of management system for scientific researches of agriculture, improve the mechanism of cooperative innovation and promote the close combination of industries, colleges and research institutes and of agriculture, science and education.

Secondly, we should step up the construction of agricultural science and technology platforms. We should develope market-oriented agricultural science and technology, achievements transformation, and industry incubation institutions, and establish industrial science and technology innovation centers and strategic alliances of industrial technology innovation. We would actively promote the construction of national-level innovation platform in fields of wheat, peanut, grain processing, frozen food, etc. and strive to reach new heights of modern agricultural innovation.

Thirdly, we should speed up popularization and application of agricultural technology. We should constantly improve the agricultural technology popularization system to meet the needs of modern agriculture, provide accurate support for those non-profit and profit-oriented service agencies to popularize agricultural technology on community level. Through improving promotion system of agricultural technology and skill and vocational trainings for farmers, a qualified team of high-quality farmers would be brought up to adapt to the development of modern agriculture. We should establish and perfect the market competition mechanism for agricultural technology popularization paid for by governments, exploring multi channels to solve the problems that often occur at the last step of agricultural technology popularization. We should speed up the commercialization of research findings and the development of modern crop seeds industry. We should vigorously promote the integration of seed breeding, nursery and promotion. High-quality crop varieties that require less water and energy and are diseases-preventing, highly adaptive and high-yielding should be cultivated and popularized. That would speed up the upgrading of new species of the main food crops. We should accelerate the mechanization of the whole production process of major crops and enhance the level of comprehensive mechanization of cultivation and harvest.

6. Further Deepening of the Rural Reform

First, the structural reform of the agricultural supply side should be rapidly boosted. Agricultural resources should be rationally allocated according to changes in the market and in demands. Effective supplies of agricultural products such as high-quality wheat, characteristic cash crops, etc. should be expanded. The concept of "Greater Food" should be established. We should accelerate structural adjustment of planting and greater agriculture, and explore more agricultural resources in a rational way in order to provide more kinds of agricultural products and to meet the increasingly diversified demands of urban and rural residents for food consumption. The strategy of food safety should be implemented to improve the quality and safety of agricultural products. We should alsopromote the standardized production and brand management to meet the needs of the upgrading of the consumption structure of the whole society.

Second, the reform of rural property rights system should be deepened. At present, the crucial part of the rural reform is to implement confirmation, registration and certification of the contractual management rights of rural land. The division of ownership, contract rights and management rights should be improved and the specific provisions of the unchanging long-term rural land contracting relations should be clarified. We should encourage farmers to solve the problem of fragmented farmland by means of exchanging related rights before they are finalized at the registration. The confirmation, registration and certification of the rural collective construction land and the cartilage that has the integration of houses and land should be accelerated. The construction of property rights trading market should be sped up, and the capitalization and flow of rural assets and resources should be promoted. Pilot work should be actively carried out, such as financing by the mortgage of contractual management right, the collection of rural farmland, the collective construction land for business entering the market, etc.. The equal exchange of rural and urban production factors and the balanced configuration of public resources should be promoted.

Third, more financial resources should be guided toward rural areas. We should encourage financial institutions to open more county-level branches and to delegate approval power to lower levels. We should carry on with the pilot projects of mortgage of land management right and housing property right, and enlarge in rural areas the scope of effective mortgage properties so that farmers can successfully apply for loans at a less cost. We should establish a rural financial service system that is multi-level, wide-ranging and sustainable. Rural finance that benefits all should be developed and the financing cost should be reduced. The policy financing, cooperative financing, commercial financing and other new financial institutions should be guided to develop collaboratively and complement each other, so that the chain of the rural financial service would be activated in all respects. We would continue to strengthen the responsibility of the policy financial institutions to serve agriculture, rural areas, and farmers, and financial resources should be guided towards agriculture, rural areas, and farmers. Commercial financial institutions should be encouraged to expand business related to "agriculture, rural areas and farmers"; cooperative finance should be encouraged to develop, the credit cooperative pilots should be popularized in famers' cooperatives, and risks prevention and solving mechanism should be improved. Compensation mechanisms should be explored to reduce the risks of mortgage of farmers' rights. The disposal of the mortgaged property should be improved to reduce the risks of financial loans. A sound system of agricultural insurance should be established, the agricultural insurance coverage should be expanded, and insurance varieties should be increased to improve the level of risk guarantee and enhance the risk resistance ability of the agricultural production.

7. To Win the Battle of Poverty Alleviation in Rural Areas

Firstly, measures should be taken in all respects for targeted poverty aid and targeted poverty alleviation. Focusing on the poverty aid and development of those concentrated destitute areas and the old revolutionary base areas around "three mountains and the Yellow River floodplain", the strategic deployment of "Three Fives" should be fully implemented. We should adhere to "Five Ways", that is, "transferring, aiding, moving, maintaining and saving". We should vigorously implement "Five Steps" of poverty alleviation, that is, by knowledge and skills, cooperation, financial policies, infrastructure construction, and housing project. We should strengthen "Five Guarantees", that is the responsibility of party committees and governments at all levels, the role of party organizations at community levels as fighting forts, social forces, the duty of sectors to support and serve poverty alleviation, and assessment mechanism. Measures should be taken according to local conditions and policies should be made according to different household and individual conditions.

Secondly, the work mechanism of targeted poverty alleviation should be established and improved. The big data management mechanism should be established and the big data platform should be built to realize the precise management of targeted poverty alleviation. The accurate recognition and exit mechanism should be further improved and implemented to ensure that the poverty alleviation is indeed targeted, and we should take precautions against deception, falsification, and the manipulation of numbers in poverty alleviation. Management and supervision mechanism of poverty alleviation projects and funds should be improved. On the platform of poverty alleviation planning and major projects, we should explore the integration of funds involved in agriculture, financial capital, and social capital at county levels to fight for poverty alleviation.

Thirdly, the responsibility system of poverty alleviation should be improved. We should improve the assessment procedures of poverty alleviation work and the third-party assessment system. Besides, we would also put great emphasis on responsibilities shouldered by different persons in charge in order for them to work in a coordinated way.

Fourthly, adequate attention should be paid to poverty alleviation via development of industries, which is the fundamental way route for poverty alleviation. We should attach great importance to secured employment of poverty-stricken populations, and the exploration of more job opportunities by expanding the capacity of industrial zones, rural tourism, and ecological construction projects for more labor force.

Fifthly, the endogenous power should be further stimulated. We should step up efforts to find, summarize and promote good examples in the fight against poverty, and kindle and enhance in poverty-stricken populations a strong will to fight off poverty via their hardworking. We should also invite them to participate more in every step of poverty alleviation projects.

References

[1] *China Statistical Yearbook 2016*, China Statistics Web, http://free.xiaze.com/nianjian/zgtjnj2016/.

[2] Henan Provincial Bureau of Statistics. *Henan Statistical Yearbook 2016*[M]. Beijing: China Statistics Press, Sep. 2016.

[3] Wheat Producing Cost per Mu and Profitability in Henan Province from 2010 to 2016. Statistical Network of Henan Province.

[4] China's Economic and Social Development Statistical Database, cnki.net.

[5] *Statistical Annals of Henan Province in 2016*, Statistical Network of Henan Province.

[6] CPC Henan Provincial Committee, Government of Henan Province. Opinions on the Implementation of New Concept of Development to Speed up the Modernization of Agriculture and Realize the Goal of the Overall Well-off Society [N]. *Henan Daily*, Jan. 18th, 2016.

[7] CPC Henan Provincial Committee, Government of Henan Province. Implementation Opinions on the Further Promotion of Structural Reform of the Agricultural Supply Aspect and Speeding up the Fostering of New Motive Power in Agriculture [N]. *Henan Daily*, Feb. 21st, 2017.

[8] Wu Haifeng, Chen Mingxing. *Research on the New Leap Forward of Henan Provinces Agriculture: Report on the Development of Agricultural and Rural Areas in Henan 2015* [M]. Social Science Literature Press, 2015.

[9] Chen Runer. Accelerating the Adjustment of Agricultural Structure and Improving the Efficiency of Product Supply[N]. *Henan Daily*, Sep. 22nd, 2016.

[10] Liu Xinmin. Reflection on the Structural Reform of the Agricultural Supply Aspect. [J]. *Rural Area·Agriculture·Farmers* (Version B), 11th, 2016.

[11] Han Changfu. Accelerating the Transformation of Agricultural Development Mode Unswervingly [J]. *Qiushi*. 2010(10).

[12] Han Changfu. Promoting the Healthy Development of Land Circulation and scale Management [N]. *Farmers Daily*, Oct 20th, 2014.

[13] Zhang Hongyu. New Agricultural Management Entities: Current Situation and Development [J].*China Farmers' Cooperatives*, 2014(10).

[14] Du Zhixiong. The Theoretical Reflection on the Reform of Basic Agricultural Management System in China [J]. *Theoretical Investigation*, 2013(4).

[15] The Ministry of Agriculture. Guidance on Further Adjusting and Optimizing Agricultural Structure [N]. *Farmers Daily*, Feb 12th, 2015.

B.9

Report on Social Development of Henan Province

Research Team of Henan Academy of Social Sciences

Abstract: 2016 was the first year of the "Thirteenth Five-year Planning" period of Henan, during which the Tenth CPC Congress of Henan was held and the Central Plains was in a new historical moment of its development, marking the coming period of enriching the people and strengthening the province as well as building an all-round well-off society. During this year, the priorities were focused on strengthening the supply-side structural reform for improving the quality and efficiency of the supply system, striking the balance for notable achievements in the economy, the reform, industry restructuring, well-being of people and risk prevention. We extended the reforms and opening up in all areas, put forth effort to shore up areas of weakness, and accelerated the development for all residents so as to obtain steady development of the province's economy and continuous improvement of people's living standard. But at the same time, a series of problems and difficulties in the development became increasingly prominent. For instance, we met with the following problems: ever-increasingly limited resources, polluted environment, the task of poverty alleviation made even tougher with its impending deadline, less employment opportunities for a large working population, the increasingly prominent employment structural contradictions. Besides, the income growth of Henan urban and rural residents' lagged behind its economic growth, with a widening gap compared with the national level; the aging population exerted a negative impact on economic and social development; the rapid urbanization brought a series of social problems and there was a long way to go to achieve the people's urbanization. 2017 is the year scheduled to go further with the Thirteenth Five-year Plan and to fully implement the policies formulated by the Tenth CPC Congress of Henan for accelerating the common development. We always put the well-being of people and common development in the first place by taking targeted measures of poverty alleviation. In addition to this, the major tasks ahead for us also include fixing properly the problems arising from the new-type urbanization, intensifying the social construction and the social governance, promoting the ecological construction of a beautiful and green Henan, and enhancing the basic public services, which would be decisive for building the all-round well-being and comprehensive development of Henan province.

Keywords: Social Governance; Well-off Society; Targeted Measures in Poverty Alleviation; Shared Development

I An Analysis of the Social Development and Characteristics of Henan in 2016

2016 was the first year of the Thirteenth Five-year Planning period and the final countdown of building a moderately all-round well-off society, during which the Tenth CPC Congress of Henan was held and the Central Plains stood on a new historical starting point for its development, marking the period of enriching the people and strengthening the province as well as building an all-round well-off society. During this year, the priorities were given to strengthening the supply-side structural reform. Over the past year, under the leadership of the Henan Provincial Government and Provincial Committee of CPC, we formulated and implemented the development strategies featured by innovation, coordination, environment-friendliness, openness and benefit sharing, strengthened the supply-side structural reform, comprehensively deepened the reform and opening up, and developed the innovation-driven economy so as to achieve a steady rise and good momentum in Henan's economy. With the official approval of the establishment of China (Zhengzhou) Pilot Region for the Cross-border E-commerce, the State-level Zhengzhou-Luoyang-Xinxiang Demonstration Zone for Independent Innovation and China (Henan) Free Trade Pilot Area, the total number of state-level planning zones of the strategic importance went up to six in Henan province, which would effectively speed up economic and social development, the structural optimization and upgrading in the province. In general, we witnessed the progresses in the comprehensive economic strength, urbanization, innovation and people's living standards in 2016, which took a solid step forward in achieving the good start formulated in the Thirteenth Five-year Planning and building the all-round well-off society in the Central Plains.

1. Steady Progress in National Economic Growth

With the polarization in world economy and the domestic economic slowdown intertwined with the structural problems, the Henan Provincial Government and Provincial Committee of CPC, according to the general trend of development, fully implemented the six national strategic planning schemes of the Core Areas of Grain Production, the Central Plains Economic Zone, Zhengzhou Airport Economic Comprehensive Experiment (Zhengzhou), China (Zhengzhou) Pilot Region for Cross-border E-commerce, the State-level Zhengzhou-Luoyang-Xinxiang Demonstration Zone for Independent Innovation and China (Henan) Free Trade Pilot Area. On the one hand, the economy maintained a rapid growth and the size of GDP continued to expand; on the other hand, the economic structure was continuously optimized, leading to a remarkably transformed economic development mode and a continuously improved quality of economic development. In 2016, the province's economy generally maintained the steady progress and achieved a good start for the Thirteenth Five-year. According to the data released by Provincial Bureau of Statistics, the GDP in Henan province reached 4,010,600,000,000 yuan, an increase of 8.1% over the previous year. The growth rate was 1.4 percentage points higher than the national average, ranking the fifth among all the provinces. Firstly, there was a steady growth in the agricultural production in Henan province, with a total grain output of 118.932 billion jin in 2016, while the animal husbandry production also grew steadily. The industrial production saw a steady growth as well. The added value

of industrial enterprises above designated size increased by 8.0%, 2.0 percentage points higher than the national average. From the perspective of the growth trend, the growth rate started to rise steadily from 7.5% in January and February, and has stayed at 8.0% since June, which indicated that the enterprises achieved better performance following the downturn. From January to November, the profit of industrial enterprises above designated size totaled 462.086 billion Yuan, increased by 6.0% over the previous year. The service industry quickened up its growth, with the added value accounting for 41.9% of GDP in the province and its share increased by 1.7 percentage points over the previous year. Secondly, the quality of economic development continued to improve with new achievements in optimization, transformation and upgrading of its structure. In recent years, we saw the optimization and upgrading of industrial structure from the fact that the tertiary industry accounted for the increasing share of gross national product in Henan(Figure 1).

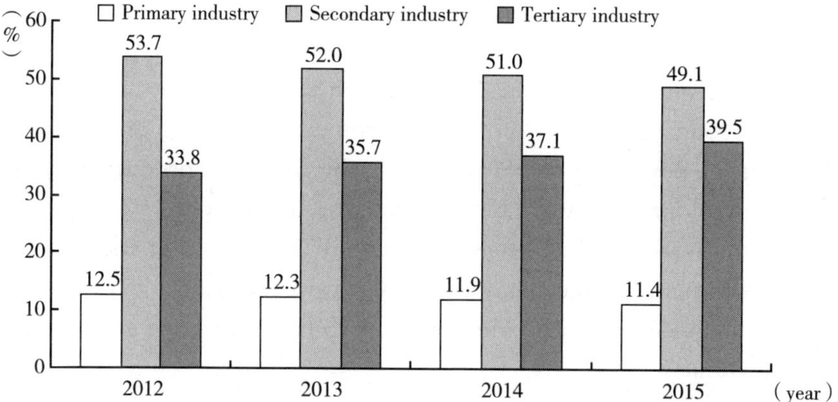

Figure 1　Schematic diagram of three industries in Henan province from 2012 to 2015

Data source: Henan Statistical Yearbook from 2012 to 2015.

In 2016, the added value of the primary industry was 428.63 billion yuan, an increase of 4.2% over the same period of last year; the added value of the secondary industry was 1905.544 billion yuan, an increase of 7.5% over the same period of last year. Of the added value of the tertiary industry was 168.1827 billion yuan, an increase of 9.9% year on year, which contributed 49.3% of the

GDP growth and continued to be the major driving force of economic growth. On one hand, the industrial production structure was continuously optimized, with the high-growth manufacturing industry developing rapidly and accounting for a larger share. More and more mid-to-high-end industries took shape. The equipment manufacturing industry in Henan province increased by 12.7%, 4.7 percentage points higher than the industrial growth rate in the province, accounting for 16.6% of the province's value of industrial output and increased by 0.6 percentage points year on year. The structure of the traditional industries was further optimized and the technical content continued to be improved, which indicated that the transformation and upgrading witnessed a continuous growth. On the other hand, the demand structure was improving. Firstly, the investment structure continued to optimize. The province's investment in service industry increased by 17.1%, 3.4 percentage points higher than that in fixed asset and 8.2 percentage points higher than the industrial investment growth. The investment in service industries accounted for 48.5% of the province's total investment, an increase of 1.4 percentage points year on year. For the industrial investment, the investment in the equipment manufacturing industry increased by 9.4%, 3.6 percentage points higher than in the manufacturing. The investment in the equipment manufacturing industry accounted for 25.5% of that in the manufacturing, an increase of 0.8 percentage point year on year. Secondly, the consumer products witnessed growing development rate. The sales volume of computers and ancillary products increased by 49.2%, together with a 37.3% growth in sales of sports and entertainment products and a 32.0% growth for electronic publications and audio and video products, which were much higher than the growth rate of enterprises (units).

2. Continuous Growth in Financial Investment for People's Well-being

In recent years, Henan province saw continuous growth in financial investment for people's well-being in an effort to solve the problem of insufficient investment in people's livelihood and to promote the development of various social undertakings. In 2016, the fiscal spending for people's well-being in the province reached 578.88 billion yuan, accounting for up to 77.6% of the total fiscal expenditure, 0.2 percentage points higher than that in 2015. 113.19

billion yuan went to the key projects for people's well-being and another 134.83 billion yuan was invested in education with a year-on-year growth rate of 6.1%. We set the same benchmark quota for compulsory education of urban and rural areas according to the "Two-Free and One-Subsidy" Education policies, with improved education-funding mechanism for general high schools. The expenditure in providing the social security and employment opportunities reached 106.92 billion yuan, with the year-on-year growth rate of 13%. The minimum monthly per capita subsidies for living allowance in the urban and rural area were raised to no less than 240 yuan and 132 yuan respectively. Henan raised the standard to 4,000 yuan a year for the disadvantaged persons living in social welfare homes in rural areas to enjoy the minimum living standards for food, clothing, medical care, housing and burial expenses offered by the government, and 3,000 yuan for those living in their own houses in the rural areas. The expenditure on the medical and health and family planning reached 77.59 billion yuan, increased by 8.1% year on year. We carried forward and implemented the reform of the expenditure approval mechanism for the province-level hospitals, with the allotted fees determined by the medical services, quality and patients' satisfaction to promote their level of medical services. The expenditure on the public culture service reached 3.54 billion yuan, increased by 10.3% over the previous year. We extended implementation of projects in favor of the general public, encouraging the museums, memorials, art galleries, public libraries, and cultural centers (stations) to provide free access. The expenditure on housing security reached 26.63 billion yuan, increased by 2.5% over the previous year. We spent a total of 51.6 billion yuan on the renovation of shanty areas and the construction of 369,000 apartments. The expenditure on the public security reached 35.79 billion yuan, increasing by 18.8% over the previous year. We extended the reform of safeguard mechanism for the political and legal affairs by vigorously supporting peace and stability by providing legal aid, community-level correction and judicial relief for disadvantaged groups provided when the general public campaigned with letters and visits. We intensified the efforts in the enforcement of the laws concerning safety supervision of food and drug safety. The designated funds for poverty alleviation reached 4.1 billion yuan, increased by 37% over the previous year. A number of poverty alleviation projects were smoothly carried forward, including those at village level achieved by industrial development or relocating villagers, guided on spot by a major secretary sent directly by the provincial government.

3. The Rapid Rise in Urbanization Level

In recent years, the urbanization in Henan has been accelerating. In 2016, the residents in urban areas reached 48.5% of its whole population, increased by 1.65 percentage points year on year, 10.8 percentage points higher than that of 37.7% in 2010.The growth rate was much greater than the national average of 6.2%, showing that significant achievements had been made in transferring the agricultural population in the urban area and the trend towards the urbanization was very obvious (Figure 2). Generally speaking, the urbanization rate of the population in Henan province maintained an average annual growth rate of about 1.5 percentage points. In November 2014, the Henan provincial government promulgated "The Proposals on Deepening the Reform of the Household Registration System", calling for the establishment of a unified household registration system for urban and rural areas, which meant that the distinction between agricultural residence registration and non-agricultural residence registration was eliminated, and that agricultural residence registration had been upgraded to be household registration. The introduction of this measure marked the official ending of the dual and separated household management model and clearing the way for the urbanization of the population in the rural area.

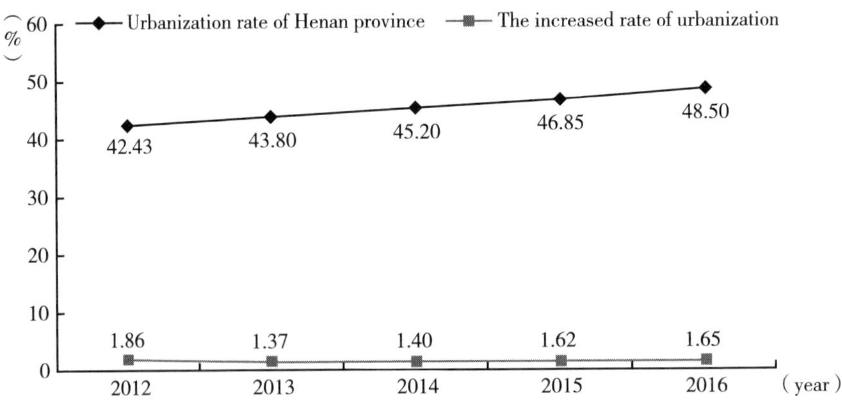

Figure 2 The urbanization rate of Henan province and its growth from 2012 to 2016

Data source: Henan Statistical Yearbook for the Corresponding Years.

In October 2016, we introduced "Major Tasks for Promoting the New-style Urbanization in Henan Province in 2016", providing the careful planning and detailed measures of the six major tasks of urbanization including the transfer of agricultural population in the urban area, the construction of the metropolitan area of the Central Plains, the development of the small and medium-sized cities and feature towns, capacity building of the urban area, the integration of the urban and rural areas and reforms in these important fields, to surely lay a solid foundation for the new-style urbanization in Henan province during the "Thirteenth Five-year Planning" period. In December 2016, we promulgated and fully implemented "Measures for Implementation of Residence Permit in Henan Province". The residence permits were shown to be worthwhile in that the holder can be covered with six basic public services including services in education, employment, health care, culture, sports, legal services, other basic public services provided by the State and Henan province, and nine conveniences including conveniences for handling entry and exit documents, changing and re-applying for resident identity cards, driver's license, the registration of vocational qualification examinations, applications for professional qualifications and childbirth services. It can also provide cross-regional subsidies without restrictions on household registration and let the holders who were more than 60 years old to enjoy free transport. The implementation of this system can benefit about 5.2 million of the floating population so as to further promote the urbanization of population in Henan.

4. The Continuous Rise in Education Modernization

In 2016, Henan continued to adhere to the policies of giving the priority to the development of education, its focus on people-orientedness, reform and innovation, promotion of fairness, improvement system systems, quality and services so as to retain the coordination and high-quality development of all levels of educational institutions.

Firstly, the funding in the education continued to grow. In 2016, the fiscal expenditure on education reached 134.83 billion yuan, increased by 6.1% over the previous year and by 22% over the year of 2012 (Figure 3).

Secondly, pre-school education witnessed rapid development and the enrolment rate in pre-schools increased significantly. Henan province vigorously promoted the development of pre-school education, and strived to improve the level of pre-school education and the quality of the teaching and education. As a result, the early-stage of

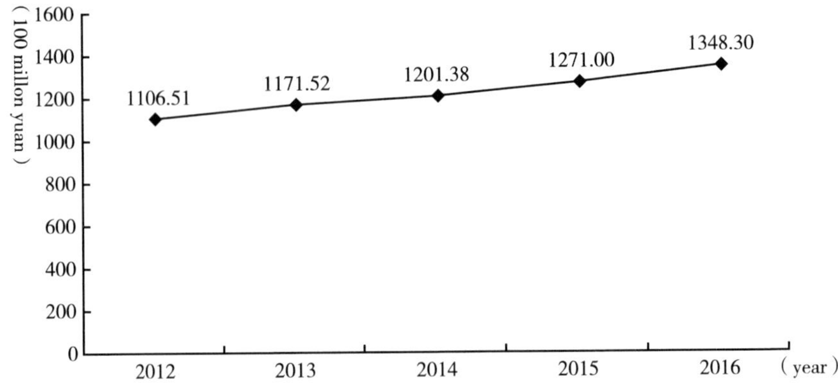

Figure 3 Diagram for Education Funding in Henan Province

Data source: Henan Statistical Yearbook for the corresponding years.

the pre-school education network took shape, featuring the overall coverage of urban and rural areas, rational layout and qualified conditions. The number of pre-school institutions and staff steadily increased (Figure 4). In 2016, the gross enrolment rate for three years prior to pre-school reached 83.2% of all eligible children, 30.4 points higher than that of 52.8% in 2010, which shows the popularity of pre-school education has greatly improved (Figure 5). In 2016, there were 2,266 newly built, reconstructed and expanded kindergartens, providing additional education for 180,000 children and relieving the difficulty in receiving the preschool education.

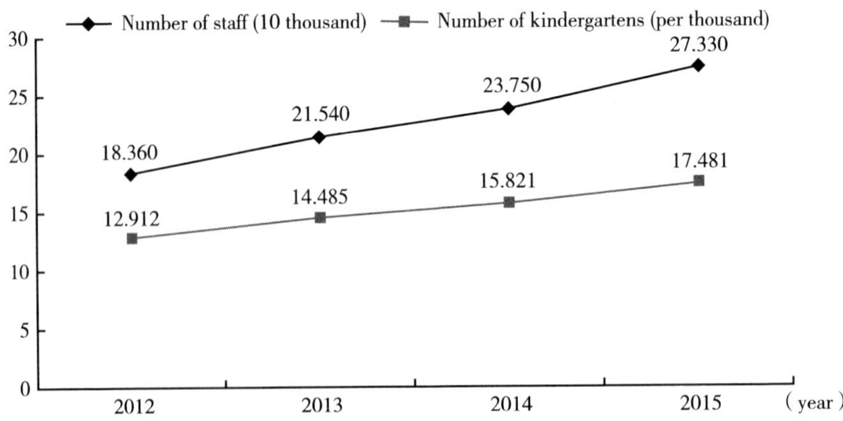

Figure 4 The Development of the Pre-school Education of Henan

Data source: Prepared according to Statistical Bulletin on the Education Development in Henan Province for the corresponding years.

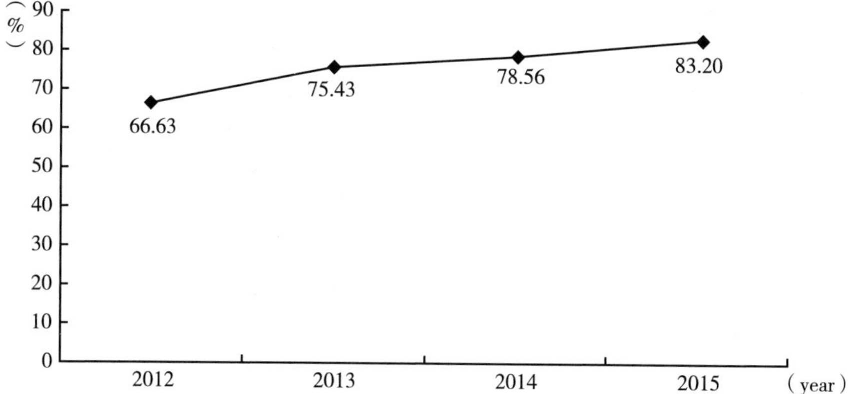

Figure 5 The universal level of the pre-school education of Henan province

Data source: Prepared according to Statistical Bulletin on the Education Development in Henan province for the corresponding years.

Thirdly, we improved the basic conditions of compulsory education in poor areas and focused on the quality and fairness in education. At the beginning of 2016, Henan Education Department held a work conference on improving the basic conditions of compulsory education in poor areas and the province's education, pointing out that the priorities of education development in 2016 in Henan was to promote the basic conditions of compulsory education in poor areas, that was, to shore up the shortness, making improvements in schools, instruments, equipment, living facilities and faculties so as to fully standardize education in the compulsory stage. This work was proved to be fruitful. By the end of October 2016, there was a total of accumulated investment of 15.955 billion yuan improving the basic conditions of compulsory education in poor areas including constructing school buildings and outdoor sports facilities for 4,897 schools in the compulsory education, and providing the living facilities, desks and chairs, computers, and teaching equipment, books, etc.. The work done outperformed the scheduled annual tasks in 2016.

Fourthly, high school education witnessed further popularity and smooth development while the secondary vocational education saw the connotative development. In 2016, the gross enrollment rate for high school reached 90.40% of all eligible adolescents. As for the vocational education, more attention was paid to the connotative development and the enhancement of their own quality. In 2016, double-qualified full-time teachers in the secondary vocational education-were 1.7 percentage points higher than that in 2012. The share of the qualified full-time teachers increased by 2.5 percentage points and the share of the full-time teachers with a master's degree and above increased by 2.5 percentage points.

Fifthly, the gross enrollment rate of higher education continued to rise rapidly, and the quality of higher education was further improved. The level of popularization of higher education was gradually improved, and the gross enrollment rate of higher education was steadily increased to 38.8% of all eligible high school graduates in 2016. In 2016, the general admission rate of college entrance examinations reached 83% of all participants. The higher education in Henan was in smooth transformation from popularization to universalization. The significant achievement was made in the high-level higher education in Henan. In 2016, there were 27 institutions offering the postgraduate training programs, fifty-five of which belonged to the primary discipline doctoral programs.

In October 2016, Henan promulgated the "Comprehensive Education Reform Program of Henan Province", which outlined the main objectives and main measures of the comprehensive reform of education in Henan province by the end of 2020, providing detailed plans for many areas of school-running, management, examination and enrollment systems, personnel training models, resource allocation and others. According to the "Comprehensive Education Reform Program of Henan Province", there would be no oversized classes in the primary and the junior high schools in the urban areas of Henan. The proportion rate for choosing top schools for compulsory education would be within 10% of all students admitted. The allocated students enrolled in the high-quality high schools would account for more than 50% of all students in high school, with more students being gradually selected from the less-developed junior high schools. We would improve the decision-making power of colleges and universities to enable them to set up their own specialties. In 2020, the examination and enrollment model featured by classified tests, all-round evaluation and various ways for candidates' enrolment would come into being.

5. The Rapidly Expanded Coverage of Social Security

In recent years, Henan has witnessed rapid development of social security characterized by greater coverage and significantly increased level of care.

Firstly, the social insurance system was further improved and the coverage continued to expand. With the constantly improved social security system, more and more people were covered by the social security system in the province, which increasingly benefited those who can now have access to the minimum standard of living. By the end of 2016, 17.4998 million people had been covered by the urban employee pension insurance program, among which 13.2344 million were insured and 4.2654 million were retired. There were 48.9374 million covered by the pension insurance program for the urban and rural residents and 12.2734 million covered by the basic medical insurance scheme in urban areas, including 8.8274 million employees and 3.4460 million retired people. There were 11.3340 million covered by basic medical insurance for the residents living in urban areas, 7.8807 million covered by the unemployment insurance scheme. There were 8.7697 million people covered by the workplace injury insurance scheme, and 6.4680 million covered by the childbirth insurance scheme. The variety of pension insurances for the insured staff can be linked up from place to place and from the one scheme to another. In 2016, the basic annuities of the retirees had been increased by 6.5% on average. The subsidy per capita for the people covered by the employee health care schemes and the new rural cooperative medical system was raised to 420 yuan per head. In the country we took the lead in the implementation of the overall planning and speedy clearance of the new rural cooperative medical insurance and the critical illness insurance for urban residents at the provincial level, effectively alleviating the poverty caused by illnesses.

Secondly, the level of social assistance continued to improve. In recent years, the social assistance of the urban and rural areas in Henan witnessed rapid development, with the new type of assistance system generally established featuring the wide-coverage of all people in the urban and rural areas, the well-developed system and mutual link-up (Table 1). The level of relief was also rising, and in 2016 the governments in Henan province provided the low-income persons covered by the minimum living standard with the supplementary subsidies of 240 yuan per month for one person in urban area while the minimum living standard in the countryside was 132 yuan per month for one person. Henan provided 4,000 yuan a year for the people living in dire poverty in the social welfare home, and 3,000 yuan a year for the persons living in their own hometowns.

Figure 1 The development of social assistance in urban and rural areas in Henan province

Year	The security pension for minimum living standard for the people living in the urban area (100 million yuan)	The security pension for minimum living standard for the people living in the rural area (100 million yuan)	The number of people living in the urban area provided with the minimum living standard (10 thousand)	The number of people living in the rural area provided with the minimum living standard (10 thousand)	Pension for medical aid for people living in the urban and rural area (100 million yuan)	The number of people provided with the medical aid (10 thousand times)
2012	31.02	42.47	133.44	372.29	6.49	107.03
2013	36.63	53.26	131.05	389.83	9.44	107.96
2014	31.97	49.47	118.90	395.26	7.13	74.33
2015	31.70	55.80	107.86	393.25	7.13	69.86
2016	28.38	57.46	82.12	327.76	-	-

Data source: Prepared according to the Data from *Henan Statistical Yearbook*.

Thirdly, a basic old-age care service system was gradually established, and its mode of the social elderly care service saw the continuous improvement. Based on the characteristics of the aging of Henan population and the direction of development, Henan actively explored the old-age service model suitable for its own conditions, and generally established the home-based, community-based and institution-supported system for the old-age service. In 2016, Henan continued to improve the basic pension level for retirees. With more than 200 million yuan from the financial budget, we established a pension service system for people living in urban and rural areas, and attempted to have the pilot program of the old-age care service combined with the health care, which can accommodate 22,000 persons.

6. Targeted Poverty Alleviation Paid off Generally

Poverty alleviation was one of the major and difficult issues for building the well-off society in the "13th Five-Year Plan" period for Henan. Henan identified the backward area of Dabie Mountain, Funiu Mountain, Taihang Mountains and the Beach Area of the Yellow River as the key areas for poverty alleviation in the new stage, and adhered to the policies of regional development combined with targeted poverty alleviation. The measures for improving employment, optimizing the industrial structure of poverty-stricken areas, relocating the poverty–stricken population and regarding the whole village as an important platform for poverty alleviation would be adopted. Meanwhile, we provided the poverty–stricken population with the minimum living standard and medical assistance, enhanced ecological construction and environmental protection so as to vigorously implement poverty alleviation.

Firstly, we strengthened the top-level design for building the relatively complete poverty-alleviation polices. In the first place, we strengthened the leadership and identifying it as the top priority and the major political task for the well-being of the general public, with general secretary of Henan Provincial Committee of CPC and governor of Henan as the team leaders and the cadres at all levels who made the pledge. We sent the excellent leaders from the provincial organs to 53 poverty–stricken counties as the members of the Standing Committee of CPC and the vice chiefs of the counties in charge of poverty alleviation. To strengthen the poverty alleviation leadership, the major leaders of the CPC committee and government at the prefecture-level cities and county level acted as the local team leaders. When it was time to elect a new committee, the deputy secretary would be appointed to the township in charge of the work of poverty alleviation so that the efforts were strengthened at the grass-root frontier for poverty alleviation.

In the second place, the system for the poverty alleviation was becoming better developed. Henan Provincial Government and Henan Provincial Committee of CPC introduced "Proposals for Success in Poverty Alleviation" and the "Important Policies and Measures for Implementing Proposals for Success in Poverty Alleviation formulated by Henan Provincial Government and Henan Provincial Committee of CPC", which answered the questions of "who would be supported, who would take charge, how to alleviate the poverty and how to withdraw from the poverty alleviation". We developed the fifteen policies for the targeted poverty alleviation and the more complete poverty policy system came into being.

In the third place, we established and improved the three major mechanisms for poverty alleviation and the assistance system. Henan Provincial Government and Henan Provincial Committee of CPC formulated the "Implementation Scheme for Alleviating the Poverty in the Poverty–stricken Counties Led by Provincial Leaders and Units", clarifying that the 37 provincial leaders would be in charge of alleviating the poverty in the 38 state-level poverty–stricken counties, the 15 province-level working units would be in charge of alleviating the poverty in the 15 province-level poverty–stricken counties until these counties were completely derived of poverty. Such measures were also adopted for the leaders and departments to work at prefecture level and county level cities for poverty-stricken townships, villages and households respectively, which acted as the strong impetus for the poverty alleviation. We also normalized a supervision mechanism. Henan Provincial Government and Henan Provincial Committee of CPC issued the notice on carrying out the supervision on poverty alleviation of poverty–stricken Area, clarifying that the ten heads of the provincial departments would be the leaders of the ten supervisory teams for providing the five-year supervision upon the province's poverty alleviation. Such measures were also adopted for the leaders at prefecture level and county level cities for supervision and inspection so that a total of nearly 700 supervisory groups were established for widespread uninterrupted supervision and inspection. We also strengthened the assessment mechanisms for poverty alleviation. Henan Provincial Government and Henan Provincial Committee of CPC issued "Assessment and Evaluation for Poverty Alleviation and the Economic and Social Development in the Poverty-stricken Counties in Henan Province", which pointed out that the poverty alleviation accounted for 60% of the assessment results and the economic and social development accounted for 40%. We would conduct self-assessment at the county level, the first-time assessment at the municipal-level and the re-assessment at the provincial level, and introduce third-party assessment. All the measures would be adopted annually for the rigorous assessment of the 53 poverty-stricken counties in Henan province and the results on a scale of A, B, C, D would be publicized so as to play a leading role for the work. We also put forward the "Assessment Approach for Poverty Alleviation in Henan Province", covering the four indexes of the effectiveness of poverty reduction, precision identification of poverty, providing precise assistance for the poverty-stricken population and poverty alleviation. We conducted annual assessment of the poverty alleviation led by the governments and committees of CPC. It also pointed out that 40%, 30% and 30% of the results of the precision identification of poverty and the precision assistance for the poverty-stricken population should be determined by the daily supervision, annual assessment and third party assessment respectively.

Secondly, our tasks were aimed at the six major fields for vigorously implementing the targeted poverty alleviation. According to the unified deployment of Henan Provincial Government and Henan Provincial Committee of CPC, we issued the cards and established the archives for the poverty-stricken population in preparation for further inspection and examination, which aimed to ensure that all the poverty-stricken population or household should be covered by the program. As the basic standard for the poverty-stricken population, the annual net income of 2,855 yuan per capita will be applied for indentification of such-farmers. We would ensure that the poverty-stricken population could be provided with basic living conditions of food and clothing, along with housing, medical care and the compulsory education. We would adopt the six steps of visiting, observation, calculation, comparison, discussion and final determination for choosing the candidates for the aid recipients. These procedures would be strictly implemented with great care. We would choose the candidates for the aid recipients by the four steps of the farmers' application, the villagers' assessment, selection by CPC Village Committee and Villager Administrative Commission as well as the approval of the township government. The final list of the selected poverty-stricken population must come together with the signatures of the first secretary of CPC Party Committee of poor village or the village team leader, the cadre in charge of the village sent from the upper-level working unit, village committee director, chief of CPC Party Committee, secretary of CPC Party Committee, township chief and township secretary. The strictly implemented measures and the "looking-back" or the reassessment policies are to ensure the accurate identification and full coverage of the poverty-stricken population and areas, laying a solid foundation for the identified policies.

Then, in accordance with the specific situation of the poverty-stricken population and areas, we implemented the Five-package Project, that is, a number of poverty-stricken population were pulled out of poverty either by improving agricultural production or by transferring the labor forces, providing labor services through intermediary organizations, developing local industries, encouraging groups of people to be locally flexibly employed, supporting the start-up of their own businesses, and developing public-interest positions. At the end of September of 2016, the province had assisted a total of 423,000 people out of poverty by transferring labor services. On the other hand, we eliminated poverty by developing local industries. According to the local conditions, Henan Provincial Government and Henan Provincial Committee of CPC led the local governments to adjust the measures to differing conditions to select the industries for assisting them out of poverty. At the end of September of 2016, the province had assisted a total of 606,000 people out of poverty by developing local industries. The poverty was alleviated by relocating poverty-stricken population in other places. If a local place did not have its own way of supporting its own inhabitants, the poverty-stricken population were encouraged to move to other places based on the supporting policies formulated by the government, farmers' own will, financial subsidies, and the county-level and municipal-level government solely responsible for the assigned task until it was fulfilled. In 2016, the province invested 3.985 billion yuan for the construction of 349 resettlement sites accommodating 97,400 people. Poverty was alleviated by offering ecological compensation. We formulated "Proposals for Poverty Alleviation by Promoting the Development of Forestry", "Work Program for Poverty Alleviation by Promoting Forestry Science and Technology in Henan Province" and "Planning for Poverty Alleviation by Promoting the Development of Forestry during the Thirteenth Five-Year". We created a position of ecological rangers who would help to alleviate the poverty in his or her whole family. Such position would be firstly given to poorer people with more family members. In 2016, a total of 100 million yuan financial fund for special purposes was set up and there would be 100,000 positions in the province, which would help to assist 360,000 poverty-stricken populations out of poverty. The poverty was alleviated by developing ecology, afforesting, tending of woods, reconstructing the degraded shelter belts, restoring the ecosystem of the places where the relocated poverty-stricken population in other places previously lived and breeding high-quality seedlings and better seeds. Such forestry ecological engineering projects were of great importance and funded by the program of government procurement of public services, which would encourage the poverty-stricken population to get paid by improving the ecological environment and constructing the green bank for the poor areas so as to lay a solid foundation for the long-term stability and poverty alleviation in the region. Poverty was alleviated by developing local education. We issued the cards and established the archives for the students in the poverty-stricken families in preparation for financial support. Starting from the fall semester of 2016, we offered subsidies for the students in the poverty-stricken families who had been registered in the archives and offered with the cards so as to prevent them from becoming dropouts from schooling. We vigorously improved the school conditions in poor areas by investing 24.556 billion yuan in the 53 poverty-stricken counties during the "Thirteenth Five-year Planning" period. We implemented the Rural Teacher Support Program in poor areas by recruiting no less than 8,000 specially contracted teachers each year, encouraging the qualified local students to apply for such posts who would be given priority over other job applicants under the same conditions. By the social security, insurance and other poverty alleviation measures can we provide the poverty-stricken population the minimum living standard so as to guarantee their basic livelihood. For example, we integrated the rural minimum living security system into the poverty alleviation policies effectively, and the government in Henan province provided the low-income persons covered by the minimum living standard with the supplementary subsidies of 132 yuan per month per head increased from 127 yuan, and an annual 2,960 yuan per head increased from 2600 yuan. We offered the financial subsidy to the poverty-stricken population who couldn't pay for the new rural cooperative medical care, and more medical assistance was offered to those who couldn't still afford medical expenses even after the coverage of serious illness insurance. By the end of September 2016, the province had provided the basic social security to a poverty-stricken population of 3.56 million and special assistance to another 48, 000 who fell into poverty due to sudden disasters or illnesses.

Lastly, the standard for the identification of the poverty-stricken population was firmly established, which would be the basis for drawing the roadmap of the targeted poverty alleviation. Henan Provincial Government and Henan Provincial Committee of CPC formulated the "Measures for Poverty Alleviation in Henan Province", which clearly stated the poverty exit mechanism that applied strict, standardized and transparent criteria, procedures and verification methods to deregister from the poverty alleviation list on all households, villages, and counties that have been lifted out of poverty. In strict accordance with the procedures of the investigation and inspection, the verification and approval, announcement to the public and elimination of deregistering from the poverty alleviation list, we would strictly implement the poverty-free acceptance and ensure that the achievements can be convincing and recognized by the general public. We clarified the timeline and roadmap for the poverty alleviation. According to Rolling Plan for Deregistering the Identified and Registered Poverty-stricken Population from the Poverty Alleviation List formulated by Henan Provincial Government and Henan Provincial Committee of CPC, Lankao County and Huaxian County was deregistered from the poverty alleviation list at the end of 2016. For each year from 2017 to 2019, there would respectively be ten, twenty-eight and thirteen poverty-stricken counties deregistered from the poverty alleviation list, with 11 million, 10 million, 900,000, 700,000, 600,000 poverty-stricken residents lifted out of poverty for each year from 2016 to 2020. Each prefecture-level city and county would formulate such rolling plans tailored to each individual in each poverty-stricken village. A buffer period would be established in order to avoid possible comebacks of poverty while efforts of its alleviation progressed forward. Immediately after the identified and registered poverty-stricken population, villages and counties deregistered from the poverty alleviation list, the existing poverty alleviation policies and related supports in the state-level and province-level should remain unchanged for a while before the supporting mechanism is finally dismantled. At the same time, we would still give a specified reward to the deregistered counties so as to form a positive incentive for others.

Thirdly, we should improve the responsibility system so as to unite all forces for poverty alleviation. Above all, we would strictly fulfill our duties. In accordance with the work mechanism for alleviating poverty featured by the general co-ordination by the central government, the overall responsibility taken by Henan Provincial Government and Henan Provincial Committee of CPC, and implementation taken by the county-level government, the government and Committee of CPC of the provincially administered municipality would link the upper provincial government and the county-level government for coordination in the region, supervision and examination in an effort to deregister the poverty-stricken counties from the poverty alleviation list on time. The government and Committee of CPC of the poverty-stricken counties should be fully responsible for the implementation of the policies, with the CPC secretary and county magistrate as the first responsible officials. The relevant departments of provincial units, municipality and county assumed the responsibility for their specific fields. The first secretary of CPC Party committee of poor village or the village team leader, under the leadership of the county-level government and Committee of CPC, should be responsible for their villages. Thus, everyone must bear their own responsibility for the tasks to fulfill.

Then, we made the best of policies and made good use of governmental fiscal funds. The investment of the special finance funds for poverty alleviation at all administrative levels totaled 5.907 billion yuan, increased by 36% over the previous year, 1.242 billion yuan of which came from the provincial finance fund, increase by 49% over the previous year, and 1.834 billion yuan of which came from the finance funds from the prefecture-level cities or counties, increased by 27% over the previous year. The additional government bonds for poverty alleviation reached 3.485 billion yuan for poverty alleviation projects. The central government proposed that the pilot project for the integration of the agricultural–related fund would begin in no less than one-third of the state-level poverty-stricken counties this year. Henan province enacted "Implementation Approach for the Integration of the Agricultural –related Fund in Henan Province", aiming at carrying it out in all poverty-stricken counties in the province at one time. One the basis of 61 integrated funds from the 20 categories specified by the central government, we clarified the 28 integrated funds from the 13 categories, with the annual integrated funds of 17.2 billion yuan. We strengthened management of government funds for poverty alleviation, putting the funds concerning the poverty alleviation like the local government bonds, targeted construction funds, policy-related benefits, the loan for the national development, the loan provided by the policy-oriented financial institutions and the donated funds under the supervision so as to achieve full coverage of supervision. The priority should be given to the role played by the financial and insurance policies. In coordination with the various financial institutions, we encouraged them to introduce preferential policies for poverty-stricken areas and people, and encouraged the China Development Bank to provide loans of 50 billion yuan for poverty alleviation in Henan. Rapid steps were taken to establish the Puhui Financial Testing Area in Lankao County and Fiscal and Financial Testing Area in Huaxian County. We established the risk compensation mechanism for micro-credit for poverty alleviation in an attempt to explore the insurance model and financial products for poverty alleviation, and seize the opportunity for enterprises in the state-level poverty-stricken county to go public with IPO without queuing up. The good use of all kinds of financial means according to the policies could help lift them out of the poverty. We should implement the policies concerning the land for construction purposes. As for the county-level or above projects included in the poverty alleviation planning, we could make sure that the land can be approved and supplied to them. According to the policies on linking the increase in land used for urban construction with the decrease in land used for rural construction, we actively encouraged the introduction of an index adjusting mechanism that can organically connect to the farmland occupation-compensation system. The proceeds can then be used for poverty alleviation and development.

Lastly, we made a concerted effort, and encouraged the units like the CPC party and government organs, the non-governmental organizations, state-owned enterprises, institutions of higher learning, the scientific research institutes and others to take the lead in the fixed-point poverty alleviation which should be their political duties. On June 21, 2016, the national leadership of the other political parties held the conferences on the democratic supervision of the poverty alleviation. The Henan government further encouraged the other political parties and prominent citizens of non-party affiliation to actively serve the overall situation of tackling poverty, and organized the democratic parties to inspect and supervise the poverty alleviation in province-governed municipalities of Pingdingshan, Xinxiang, Puyang, Nanyang, Shangqiu, Xinyang where the tasks for poverty alleviation were rather tough. To carry out the program of "One Thousand Enterprises Help One Thousand Villages to Alleviate Poverty", the private enterprises were encouraged to provide poverty alleviation aid to the designated sister counties and villages. Before and after the Poverty Alleviation Day this year, the opening ceremony for establishing the Provincial Poverty Alleviation Foundation, the package donating ceremony and the public welfare program of Final Campaign over the Poverty Relief, the publicity theme of Striving to Become Well-off were launched, aiming at extensively mobilizing the forces in all fields to fight against poverty.

7. The Continuous Expansion for the Employment of the Urban and Rural Residents

Giving full play to the forces in all fields and the comprehensive policies, Henan province achieved stable performance in providing job opportunities while securing progress by vigorously implementing the employment-oriented strategies and the more active employment policies. In 2016, there was a total of 1. 45 million new jobs created in cities and towns, and there had been a total of 0.62 million transferred rural workers employed. With the employment structure further optimized and the transformation and upgrading of Henan's industrial structure, the small and micro enterprises from the rapidly-expanded tertiary industry mainly benefiting from the government reform dividends became the main source for employment. The number of practitioners in the primary

industry was declining year by year, while the number of practitioners in the second industry declined yearly from 2013 when the employment peak took place, and the number of the practitioners in the tertiary industry showed a steady upward growth (Figure 6).

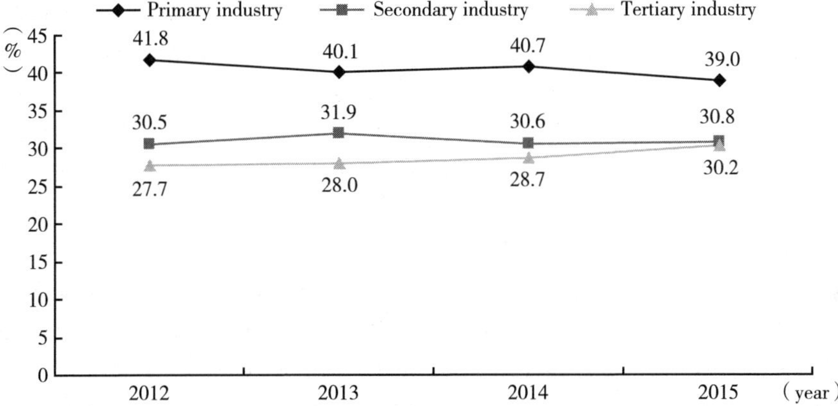

Figure 6 Variation diagrams of the practitioners of the three major industry in Henan province

Data source: Henan Statistical Yearbook over the years.

In 2016, Henan saw the steady progress in employment, the main employment indicators better than expected. Firstly, in 2016, there was a total of 1. 45 million new jobs created in cities and towns, accounting for 145.1% of the expected annual target increased by 0.7 percentage points over the previous year, which reached the historical height since the Twelfth Five-Year. For many years, the new jobs created annually in cities and towns reached more than 1.4 million, accounting for 1/10 of that in China, which not only helped to maintain the stability in employment in Henan province, but also made a contribution to the stability for the overall employment of the country. With the outperformed indicators of employment and the indicators of new empolyment better than expected, the registered unemployment rate in the urban area was 3%, much lower than the expected 4.5% set at the beginning of the year.

Secondly, the situation for the employment of special groups stayed basically stable. We resolved the excess capacity of the coal and steel industry and dealt with the difficulties in the development of enterprises by providing the enterprises in financial straits with unemployment insurance while the jobs should be kept for the workers. We encouraged people into pre-retirement, or to transfer to other positions, the compensated termination of labor relations so as to ensure the steady progress with the replacement of the workers. At the end of 2016, the province settled the surplus employees totaling 58,581, accounting for 91.2% of the required 64,200 with 5.7 percentage points higher than the national average. We tried to help all groups of people with job hunting difficulties by improving employment services and assistance. A total of 488,000 unemployed people gained re-employment in the province, accounting for 137.2% of the annual objective. 191,900 people with job hunting difficulties were employed, accounting for 159.9% of the annual objective. At the same time, we actively eliminated "zero-employment families" by providing welfare contributions to meet the basic needs of those in difficulties securing employment.

Thirdly, we saw an increase of the migrant labor forces in the rural returning home to find jobs and start businesses. The newly transferred migrant workers found jobs in the province. In 2011, the migrant workers transferring in Henan province outnumbered those in other places. In recent years, the number of employed in the province was increasing year by year. From the scale of the transferred employees, there had been a total of 28.76 million transferred workers in the province by the end of 2016, increased by 2.2% over the previous year, 17.09 million of which accounted for 59.42% of the total and were employed in Henan province, increased by 1% yearly. In particular, 90.3% of the 62,000 rural laborers newly transferred gained employment in Henan province in 2016, for the first time exceeding 90% of the total. Greater progress was also made in the employment of poverty-stricken people in rural areas. We vigorously promoted the employment of poverty-stricken people on purpose of lifting them out of poverty by providing a variety of channels like the official registration, providing skills training for free and broadening the channels of employment and others.

Fourthly, we encouraged entrepreneurship and innovation, which resulted in remarkable achievements because the startup businesses became the greatest strength for employment. In 2016, there were 230 incubation bases in a variety of industries, 125 province-level innovation platforms and 24 nation-level platforms. The entrepreneurship and innovation acted as the driving forces for improving employment. In 2016, the province granted guaranteed loans of 12.992 billion yuan in support of entrepreneurship by implementing the Special Program of Improving Entrepreneurship, with the cumulative total amount of 86.122 billion yuan ranking first in the country. We trained 253,200 people for business startups, and helped 147,000 people to succeed in starting up businesses which provided 435,000 jobs, accounting for 30% of newly increased jobs in the urban areas. We encouraged the returning migrant workers into start up businesses on a broad scale, and 155,200 newly arrived migrant workers responded to it and start up businesses, an increase of 25.6%, which provided jobs for 1,293,700 rural workers in the urban areas.

8. The Relatively Rapid Income Increase of Urban and Rural Residents

In 2016, to improve the income level of urban and rural residents and to improve the living standard were the important development goals for Henan to build a moderately prosperous society. A variety of measures such as improving the personal income for employees and retirees, providing the employment opportunities, encouraging the entrepreneurship, helping groups in difficulties and other initiatives were applied and resulted in a steady improvement of income and living standards of the urban and rural residents.

Firstly, the income of urban and rural residents witnessed sustained growth and the income of the rural residents grew faster than that of the urban residents. In 2016, the disposable income per capita of the residents in Henan province reached 18,443.08 yuan, increased by 7.7% over the previous year and accounting for 77.4% of the national average income. The disposable income per capita of the residents habitually living in urban areas reached 27,232.92 yuan, increased by 6.5% over that in the previous year and accounting for 81.0% of the national average income. The disposable income per capita of the residents habitually living in rural areas reached 11,696.74 yuan, increased by 7.8% over the previous year and accounting for 94.6% of the national average income. The income of the rural residents grew faster than that of the urban residents (Figure 7).

Secondly, the consumer price index was kept relatively stable and people's living standards continued to improve. In recent years, the prices for the household witnessed the slight drop year by year and the consumer price index was kept relatively stable. The prices for the household spending in urban area and the prices in rural area were increased by 1.9% and 2.0% respectively over those in the previous year in 2016, with an average growth rate of 1.9% (Figure 8).

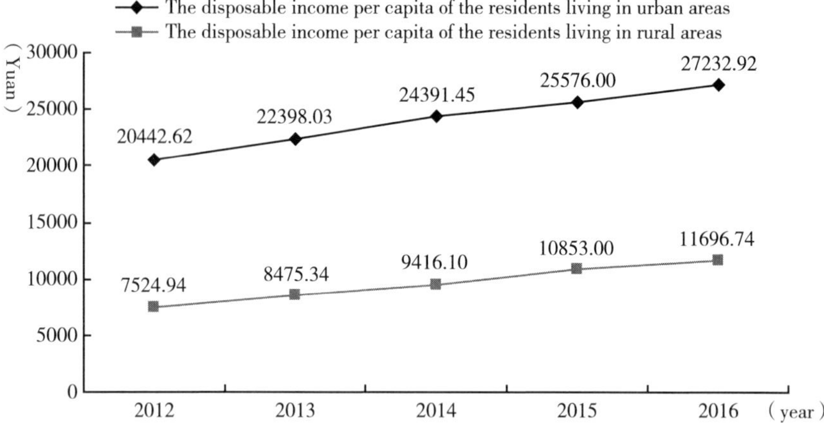

Figure 7 Variation diagram of income increase of urban and rural residents

Data source: Henan Statistical Yearbook over the years, Statistical Bulletin on the National Economy and Social Development in Henan province in 2015.

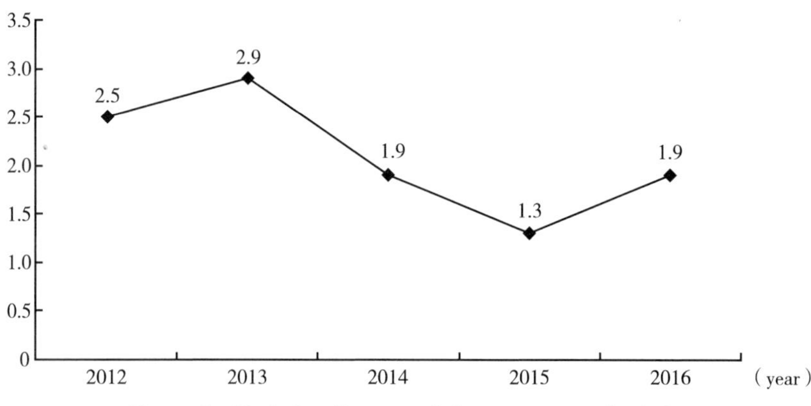

Figure 8 Variation diagram of the consumer price index

Data source: Henan Statistical Yearbook over the years, Statistical Bulletin on the National Economy and Social Development in Henan province.

With the significantly increased consumption level in the urban and rural area, Engel coefficient continuously fell down, indicating that people's livelihood went up in terms of its quantity and quality (Figure 9). From the Engel coefficient, it can be said that the urban and rural residents were kept fed and clothed in Henan, and moved forward to the moderately well-off and then to the well-off in an all-round way.

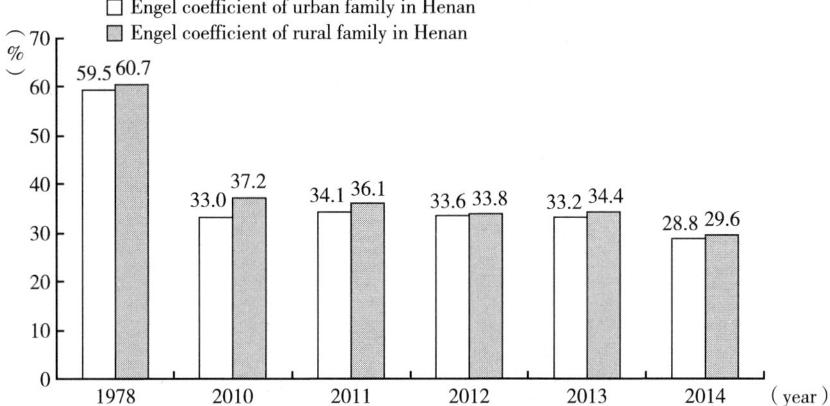

Figure 9 Variation diagram of engel coefficients for the residents in urban and rural area

Data source: Henan Statistical Yearbook over the years.

9. To Deepen the Reform on Medical and Health Service

In 2016, we fostered the coordinated reforms on medical treatment, health care and medication, and launched a series of major measures to develop and improve the medical and health system, which resulted in the rapid development of health care and the continuous improvement of the health status of the residents in urban and rural area, safeguarding the economic and social development in the province.

Firstly, we intensified the efforts of constructing the medical and health institutions in counties and townships. In 2016, 21 county-level hospitals, 133 township-level hospitals, 23 maternal and child health care institutions, 15 centers for disease control and prevention and 35 county-level hospitals specializing in the certain fields were either constructed or improved.

Secondly, we further improved the health care system for the general public, and further improved the level of basic medical insurance. In 2015, the people covered by the employee health care scheme, basic medical insurance system for urban residents and the new rural cooperative medical system accounted for more than 95% of the total population. In 2015, the basic standard of the public health service for the urban and rural residents increased from 40 yuan per capita to 45 yuan per capita. The subsidy per capita for the people covered by the employee health care schemes and the new rural cooperative medical system was raised from 380 yuan to 420 yuan. The insured persons for the employee health care schemes and the medical care schemes for the urban residents can be rewarded with 80% and 75% re-payment for hospitalization respectively. We further raised the level of funding for serious illness and the proportion of payment. In November 2016, the provincial government examined and approved the "Opinions on the Providing the Supplementary Medical Insurance for the Seriously-ill People in Straitened Circumstances (Trial)", which marked that the supplementary medical insurance system could fully cover all the seriously-ill people in straitened circumstances in the province, who can be at most rewarded with 90% re-payment for hospitalization. As a result, the multi-level medical security insurances including the basic medical security, the serious illness insurance, the supplementary medical insurance for the serious illness, medical assistance, charity relief and so on were formed so that the people suffering from the serious illnesses can get timely and effective treatment without worrying about the payment which would be likely to put them into financial difficulties.

Thirdly, we made the full use of advanced information technology "Internet +" and allied technologies, which can help to spread the high-quality medical resources to the grassroots level. The province implemented the people-benefit projects aiming at putting the medical resources to the grassroots level by means of "Internet + medical health", using the completed telemedicine network for improving the pathological processing system in the 118 county-level remote medical centers. Such technologies helped to train 200,000 persons, providing the collective medical consultation for 20,000 patients and providing one on one consultation services for 50,000 people. At present, the Smart Healthcare Program has been adopted for many hospitals around the province. Taking the remote medical care of No. 1 Affiliated Hospital of Zhengzhou University for example, it covered more than 130 hospitals in 107 counties (cities, districts) in the province following many years of construction, and gained access to the hospitals in Sichuan, Xinjiang and other provinces. The remote medicare centre could provide services such as online booking, remote consultation, graphics and text information transmission, which can greatly save human and material resources of the hospitals so as to improve the diagnosis and treatment of the grass-level hospitals. In addition, Zhengzhou Yihe Hospital as well as the hospitals in Luohe, Jiaozuo, Nanyang and other cities witnessed the great progress in smart medicare, which can surely offer more benefits to many patients.

Fourthly, remarkable achievements were made in the medical and health services. In the first place, the basic public health services were increasingly becoming widespread. In 2016, we invested a total of 77.59 billion yuan by the Provincial Department of Finance for promoting health care and family planning, increased by 8.1% over the previous year. The per capita spending on basic public health was increased to 45 yuan, which helped to provide 47 items of basic public health service in 13 categories for free for the urban and rural residents. There were a cumulative total of 94.953 million electronic health files, accounting for 92.2% of population in Henan. At the end of 2015, there were 71,397 hospitals (including village-level clinics) that can accommodate 489,600 patients, increased by 49% over the year of 2010. There were 519,800 health technicians (including technicians in village-level clinics), increased by 39% over the year of 2010.

In the second place, we took effective measures for the prevention and control of the major diseases. The nation-level immunization program was implemented steadily, with 31.232 million people inoculated with vaccines of Class 1, 96.8% of children from 0 to 6 years old getting vaccinated so that the province was polio-free. The prevention and control of tuberculosis witnessed orderly progress, and so did that of AIDS, thrombocytopenia syndrome with fever, and the foot and mouth disease. The steady progress was made for controlling and treating patients with the severe mental disorders.

In the third place, remarkable achievements were made in both maternal and child health care. By the end of 2015, 9.021 million children from 0 to 6 years old and 1,784,000 pregnant and lying-in women were provided with health care services. The rate for the neonatal disease screening and the free-of-charge premarital check-up rate reached 80% and 74.8% respectively. The free-of-charge prenatal test basically covers all the urban and rural residents.

In the fourth place, the supervision on health and food safety was carried out effectively. We continued to fight against illegal medical practice and promote lawful licensed practicing of medical services. The major indexes such as the supervision coverage and the number of handled cases ranked among the best, and there were more public health-supervision demonstration areas and the coverage rate of food monitoring was in excess of 93%. With the seven local standards on food safety publicized, we were able to strictly check the food in terms of its safety and source.

10. The Continuous Improvement of Social Governance and Its Modernization Level

After the 18th CPC National Congress was held, Henan attached great importance to the social governance and its innovation based on the provincial situation so that the social governance and its modernization level were improved from many aspects.

Firstly, we achieved steady progress in upholding law and order in Henan and the overall situation of public security continued to improve smoothly. To begin with, we made full use of modern science and technology to construct an all embracing three-dimensional prevention and control system. We carried out the campaign of "the Year of Upholding Law and Order by Adopting Video Surveillance" in an encompassing way, with the video surveillance platforms fully completed in the prefecture-level cities, counties and townships where the total number of monitoring sites reached more than 330,000 covering the major roads and areas, 90% of the villages and communities. In recent years, the Political and Legal Affairs Committee of the provincial CPC Committee coordinated with the Provincial Committee for Comprehensive Management of Public Security to disintegrate the tasks for the social security prevention and control in detail and to deploy in an all-round way. As a result, we established the mechanism for combating organized crime, abduction, illegal buying and selling of firearms, robbery, stealing, prostitution and whoring, gambling, drug trafficking on a regular basis. We aimed at crushing criminal activities endangering people's lives and property with the iron fists, and established patrol teams in the prefecture-level cities, counties and townships. There were 94,000 full-time patrol members in the province, with an average of 15 or more for one township.

Next, we strengthened the infrastructure construction in terms of safeguarding the peace at the grass-roots level. The management system in upholding law and order at the grass-roots level, the system of resolving contradiction and disagreement, the social security prevention and control system and the comprehensive service management system should be established so that there were enough personnel, money and regulations for safeguarding the law and order at the grass-roots level. The nearly 50% of the grassroots units and 80% of the villages and the communities in the province witnessed less incidences of criminal offense, resulting in good order, social stability and satisfaction from the general public. The coverage for safeguarding law and order at the grass-roots level continued to expand. From small increments to great abundance, and the overall orderliness was based on the peace at the grass-roots level.

In the third place, we paid attention to the special groups for providing a sense of safety not only for the settled people with the comparatively steady jobs but also for the migrating population whose needs of safety were even much higher. Henan province attached a greater importance to providing service and management for the migrating population. In order to strengthen the service and management of these special groups, we set up community correction agencies in all prefecture-level cities, and 89.9% of the counties, county-level cities and districts, with the community correction centers built in 68 counties, county-level cities and districts, and with community correction information management platforms built in 17 prefecture-level cities and 152 counties, county-level cities and districts. We vigorously took the problem-addressing actions for safeguarding law and order in school campuses and the surrounding areas, with a total of 5,840 security guard posts around the campuses and 8,815 posts for protecting students built in primary and secondary schools in the cities. The coverage rate of "Safety Campus Program" reached 100%.

Secondly, we witnessed fast growing social organizations in terms of quantity and size. The number of social organizations in Henan also maintained rapid growth year by year. The number of social organizations in Henan was 20,970 in 2012, 22,983 in 2013, 27,238 in 2014, and 29,207 in 2015. In 2015, the number of social organizations in Henan province ranked first in the six provinces in central China (Table 2). From the perspective of the growth rate of social organizations, the number of social organizations in Henan province was generally increasing starting from 2012 although the growth rate was moderate in 2015 (Table 3).

Table 2 Overview of the social organizations in six provinces in central China in 2015

Unit: Entity

Province	Social organizations	Private Non – enterprise organization	Foundations	Total
Henan	11728	17365	114	29207
Hunan	13188	14272	222	27682
Hubei	12086	15179	106	27371
Anhui	12527	11841	95	24463
Jiangxi	8235	7034	50	15319
Shanxi	6396	5773	67	12236

Data source: Statistical Yearbook from the Provinces over Years.

Table 3 Quantity of the social organizations in Henan province and the growth rate

Unit: Entities, %

Year	Social Organizations			Total	Year-on-year growth rate
	Social groups	Private non – enterprise organizations	Foundations		
2012	10915	9978	77	20970	7.4
2013	10817	12068	98	22983	9.6
2014	11158	15976	104	27238	18.5
2015	11728	17365	114	29207	7.2

Data source: Statistical Yearbook from the provinces over years.

Thirdly, we gradually improved the multi-level mechanisms for safeguarding legal rights according to the law and for resolving contradictions and disputes, which helped to significantly resolve social contradictions. In recent years, focusing on the solution of practical problems and aiming at maintaining social stability, Henan took many steps for tackling difficulties to resolve a large number of social contradictions and disputes, which created a harmonious and stable social environment conducive to the leap-forward socio-economic development of the province. With 11,000 mediators for labor disputes, 13,000 supervisors for the fulfillment of labor laws and 205,800 full-time and part-time mediators, and 771 professional people's mediation committees, we had resolved 1,081,300 disputes successfully, accounting for 97% of the total. As a result, almost all disputes can be solved in the grass-root levels of the villages, townships and counties, and almost no disputes were handed over to the upper-level governments. By expanding the people's mediation organizations in terms of categories, we established the wide-ranging network for contradictory dispute investigation and warning in the whole society so as to promote the construction of the professional mediation organizations covering many fields. Depending on the platforms in the counties, townships, villages and the different fields, we could have the one-stop resolution of the contradictions and disputes. In addition, we pooled the social forces by, for example, inviting a third party, to participate in the reconciliation of contradictions and disputes together. The reconciliation of contradictions and disputes was brought into the overall planning of the economic and social development of the 18 prefecture-level cities, the ten counties or county-level cities under the direct leadership of the provincial government as well as the 148 counties or county-level cities. We found 220,380 disputes in many fields, with 211,527 resolved, accounting for 95.9% of the total.

II The Major Problems of Social Development in Henan Province in 2016

1. The Serious Environmental Pollution

In recent years, the environmental pollution, especially air pollution was gaining more and more people's attention. In spite of progress in environmental protection in the province, we were still faced with grave difficulties. The situations like the restriction of resources upon the environmental protection, the serious environmental pollution and the ecosystem degradation were not fundamentally improved, with the carrying capacity of natural resources close to the upper limit and no indication for the improvement of environment. There was a large gap between the improvement of environmental quality and the expectations of the people. At the same time, the industrialization, urbanization and agricultural modernization of Henan were still in full swing coupled with the ineffective implementation of environmental protection, the weak law enforcement and inadequate capability at the grass-roots levels so that it was difficult to fundamentally change the heavy industry-based structure and the unreasonable energy structure in the short term. The pressure and challenges were great for us. To achieve the overall improvement of environment required the concerted efforts of the relevant departments at all levels and the participation of the whole society to fight against pollution. In 2014 and in 2015, the eighteen prefecture-level cities of Henan province witnessed 183 days of fairly good air quality, accounting for 50.2% of a year. In 2015, the air in the seventeen prefecture-level cities was moderately polluted in general except for the Xinyang City where the air was mildly polluted. In the first half of 2016, the days of fairly good air quality in the eighteen prefecture-level cities of Henan province accounted for only 46.8% of the year (85 days). There were 109 days of fairly good air quality or higher than 60% in Xinyang, and more than 72 days of fairly good air quality or higher than 40% in Hebi, Kaifeng, Zhoukou, Jiyuan, Zuchang, Anyang, Puyang, Nanyang, Pingdingshan, Jiaozuo, Sanmenxia, Luohe and Luoyang, and less than 72 days of fairly good air quality or less than 40% in Xinxiang, Shangqiu and Zhengzhou. In particular, Zhengzhou was ranked one of the top ten severely polluted cities in Henan by the Ministry of Environmental Protection of China, which not only tainted the image of Zhengzhou and reduced its core competitiveness, but also posed a seriously negative impact on the rise of central China in Henan and the development of Zhengzhou as a central city in China. In 2016, the annual average concentration of PM10 was 128 micrograms per cubic meters, a 5.2% drop over the previous year while the annual average concentration of PM2.5 was 73 micrograms per cubic meters, a 8.8% drop over the previous year. There were 196 days of fairly good air quality, increased by thirteen days over the previous year. Despite better performance than that in 2015 generally, the air was still in serious pollution and the haze during the New Year days of the solar calendar once again reminded us that there was a long way to go in environmental protection in Henan.

2. The Tough Work for Poverty Alleviation

Henan province was one of the six provinces in China with a poverty-stricken population of over 5 million. For Henan, poverty became the biggest roadblock in building the relatively well-off society. It can also be said that once poverty was eliminated, we can lay a solid foundation in building the relatively well-off society. In spite of the remarkable performance achieved for the poverty alleviation during the 12th Five-Year in Henan province, the fight against poverty was still the most arduous task ahead for us in the 13th Five-Year planning period. As one of the provinces with so heavy tasks for the poverty alleviation in China, there were 53 poverty-stricken counties, including the 38 state-level poverty-stricken counties and 15 province-level poverty-stricken counties. By the end of 2015, there were 6,492 poverty-stricken villages and 4.3 million poverty-stricken people. The poverty-stricken population in the backward area of Dabie Mountain, Funiu Mountain, Taihang Mountain and the Beach Area of the Yellow River accounted for 71% of the total in Henan province, which would be the major areas for poverty alleviation in the new stage. There were 44 poverty-stricken counties located in the Dabie Mountain, Funiu Mountain, Taihang Mountain, taking up 83% of the total number of poor counties in the province. The 13th Five-Year Planning of Henan clearly put forward that all the poverty-stricken counties defined by the current national standard should have been deregistered from the list by 2020 so as to lift out of poverty all the stricken population in the backward area of Dabie Mountain, Funiu Mountain, Taihang Mountain and the Beach Area

of the Yellow River. It can be said that due to the time limit and the heavy tasks, we should regard the poverty alleviation as the top priority to achieve the social development of Henan. The following major problems must be resolved for poverty alleviation.

Firstly, poverty-stricken areas suffered from a slowly growing economy, leading to a widening gap compared with the average level of the provincial economy. In the case of the regional poverty-stricken areas, the Dabie Mountains and the Funiu Mountain area as shown in Figure 10 and Figure 11, it can be seen that

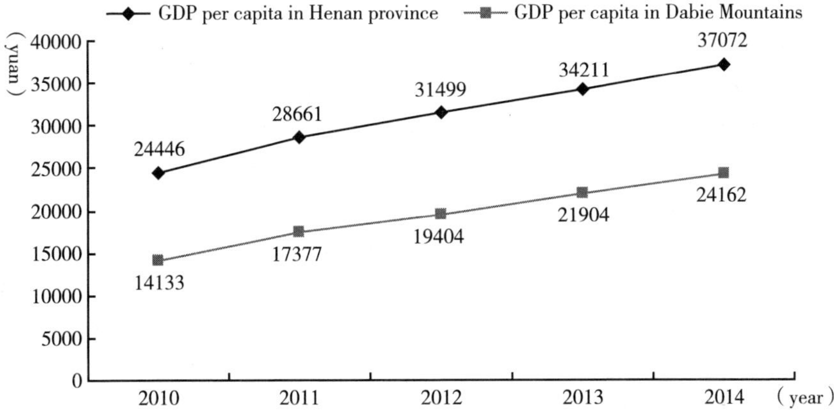

Figure 10 Per capita GDP growth of Dabie Mountains

Data source: Henan Statistical Yearbook of the corresponding years.

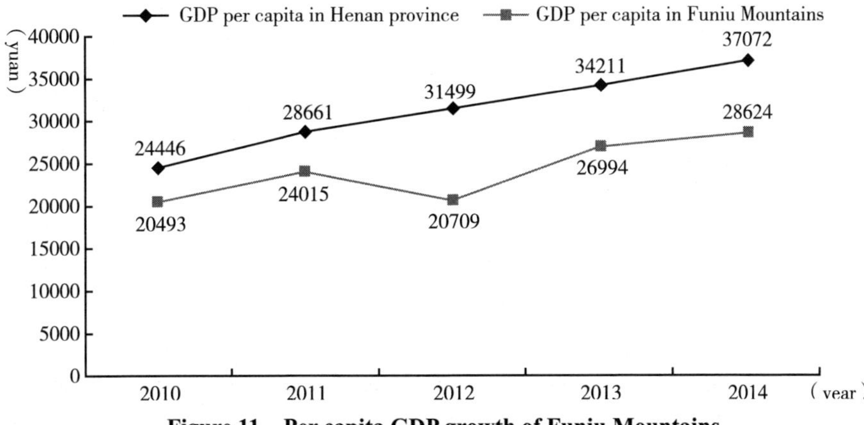

Figure 11 Per capita GDP growth of Funiu Mountains

Data source: Henan Statistical Yearbook of the corresponding years.

the economic development of the Funiu Mountain area was less stable and the per capita GDP in 2012 witnessed the V-shaped decline. In the long run, the gap of per capita GDP between the areas of Funiu Mountain and the other places was still widening. In 2010, the per capita GDP of the Funiu Mountain area is 83.83% of the province's average level, and it went on shrinking to only 77.21% of the province's average in 2014, with the gap widened by 6.62 percentage points. The per capita GDP of the Dabie Mountain area maintained the stable growth generally, with the gap between narrowed. In 2010, the per capita GDP of the Dabie Mountain area is 57.81% of the province's average level and it went up to 65.18% of the province's average in 2014, with the gap narrowed by 7.37 percentage points. However, compared with the Funiu mountain area, the Dabie Mountains region was more underdeveloped with much lower foundation, facing more difficulties if the poverty was to be alleviated as expected. Therefore, it was more urgent to speed up the economic development in the region.

Secondly, there was the widening income gap between the members in different regions, and the relative poverty was still serious. The gap between the per capita income of people in urban area and the people in rural area was increasingly widening in general from 2,780.44 yuan in 2000 to 15,536.18 yuan in 2016. In rural areas, we can also see the widening gap. The per capita net income of farmers in poverty-stricken areas in 2011 was 82.43% of the per capita net income of farmers in other places of the province, increased only by 0.82 percentage points compared with 83.25% in 2014, but the exact income was reduced by 417.53 yuan. The income gap of the people in different rural areas cannot be ignored.

Thirdly, there was a serious shortage of investment in poverty alleviation. In recent years, with the continuous improvement of the financial revenue of the nation and the province, we witnessed the significantly increased investment for poverty alleviation year after year in spite of the fact that the investment was not enough. In 2016, the general budget for the public expenditure in the province totaled 615.88 billion yuan, with the actual spending of 745.66 billion yuan, 4.1 billion yuan of which was raised for poverty alleviation accounting for only 0.5% of total actual expenditure. Moreover, due to their location disadvantages, the poverty-stricken areas always featured the less fiscal revenue and the underdeveloped collective economy so that the spending on the poverty alleviation was limited.

Fourthly, the concerted efforts for the poverty alleviation had not yet fully formed. As a result of the inner gene of the market economy system, the factors of production would be always pooled to the well-developed areas while much less to the poverty-stricken areas. What was more, coupled with the less policy-based mechanisms for the poverty alleviation, the area had to endure increasing impoverishment and long-lasting debility. In the recent years, Henan province had continuously been promoting the implementation of the preferential policies for the farmers, and introduced a variety of investment channels to the poverty-stricken areas so as to turn around the uneven distribution of resources to some extent although the concerted efforts, the coordination and overall planning should be improved. Therefore, we must establish an effective management system for the improvement of capabilities to create the different mechanisms suited for the different area so as to achieve the poverty alleviation in all around way.

3. The Increasing Structural Contradictions of Employment

With the steady and rapid development of Henan's economy, the employment in Henan maintained the generally steady growth. There are more job opportunities in cities and towns in our province year by year, and we saw the continuous expansion of employment. There was a total of 1. 451 million new jobs created in cities and towns, accounting for 145.1% of the annual target and increased by up to 0.7 percentage points over the previous year. There were a total of 480,200 people once out of job getting reemployed and 191,900 people with job hunting difficulties were reemployed, accounting for 137.2% and 159.94% of the annual target respectively. The registered urban unemployment rate was less than 3%. There was no "zero-employment family". However, the supply and demand of the talents in job market became increasingly unmatched. During the first half of 2016, the jobs provided by the companies at the job fairs in the province reached 861,000 while the registered job applicants reached 844,000, with the ratio of supply and demand reaching 1.02. However, the achieved rate remained lower than 30%. There were more than three positions provided for one high-end talent. According to the data collected, 111 enterprises provided 3205 technical posts in the first half of the year in Henan province, but only with 923 actually recruited and accounting only for 28.8% of the required. Therefore, the current employment situation in Henan was becoming more and more complex and the employment contradiction became increasingly intense which became the primary contradiction in the field. The structural contradiction of employment had a negative impact on the following several aspects.

Firstly, it would hinder the development of the employment scale. Due to the impact of economic restructuring, the talents for the emerging industries were in the short supply while the large number of low-end laborers got unemployed due to the fact that the enterprises in some traditional industries and labor-intensive industries had to lay off the low-end laborers under the pressure of eliminating the backward production capacity and upgrading the industrial structure. Most of them were less skilled and could not maintain the jobs for a much longer period, which would inevitably affect the expansion of employment. The strategic emerging industries were starting to take off in Henan province, and could bring more job opportunities. However, due to the lack of high-quality professionals and skilled personnel, there was the serious shortage of the high-level and the middle-level talents in the employment structure, to some extent restricting the employment development in the new industries.

Secondly, it negatively impacted the improvement of the employment quality. To begin with, the structural contradictions led to the imbalance between supply and demand in the job fairs, raised the threshold of entrepreneurship and restricted the entrepreneurial environment which brought the startup entrepreneur more difficulties. Next, the structural contradictions affected the improvement of the quality of employment, and it became very difficult for some university graduates and skilled workers to achieve self-worth in their own work so that they became less and less eager to further improve themselves. Among them, under the background of the structural contradiction of employment, the difficulty for the college graduates to seek the employment opportunities was becoming greater so that there was a wide gap between the actual performance and the expectation value. With the relatively weak competitiveness in the job market, some university graduates can only get employed in some low-end industries. As the result, some graduates willingly got unemployed because they were not qualified for the high-end jobs and unwilling to apply for the low-end jobs. Naturally, it was difficult to obtain the continuous improvement of themselves in terms of their competitiveness on the job market. In the third place, the structural contradictions affected the implementation of labor standards, which weakened the role played by the job seekers in general in the

job market. On the other hand, some enterprises had to lower the standards for recruiting workers, thus further affecting the improvement of the quality of employment.

Thirdly, it could negatively impact the economic restructuring and industrial restructuring. As the biggest bottleneck, the severe shortage of the high-quality talents could hinder the development of emerging industries. Especially the structural contradictions of employment directly affected the industrial and economic restructuring. The traditional industries attach the importance to the number of laborers rather than their quality while the emerging industries need a lot of high-quality talents especially the technology-intensive industries, which sets an even higher standard for the workforce, and provides the direction of reform for the current education system and training model. Therefore, the top priority for solving the structural contradiction in Henan province should be given to providing more talents for the emerging industry and replacing of the laborers in the traditional industries.

4. The Arduous Task of Achieving the People-oriented New-style Urbanization

With the rapid development of urbanization in Henan in recent years, the rate of urbanization of the residents reached 48.5% in 2016, increased by 1.65 points over the previous year, 11.2 percentage points higher than the national average of 37.3% in 2010. With not enough supporting constructions corresponding to the urbanization in Henan, the level was significantly lower than the national average in terms of the infrastructure construction whether in urban area, in the prefecture-level cities and county-level cities, or in townships. In the course of the rapid development of urbanization, Henan is confronted with a series of problems and contradictions like the imbalance between the urbanization of people and of the land, the unsynchronized pace between the agricultural modernization and the urbanization, insufficient carrying capacity in urban area, the unsynchronized pace between the urbanization and the management, the uneven level between the well-developed Zhengzhou and the other less developed cities, the imbalance of urbanization in different cities as well as many other problems, which further hindered the process of urbanization and were manifested in the following aspects in 2016.

Firstly, the housing prices of the central cities soared once again. The soaring prices of the central cities, with Zhengzhou in particular, triggered a new round of formulating the house purchase quota policies and hindered the advancement of people's urbanization. At the end of 2015, the housing prices of Henan were heated up and rose rapidly especially in Zhengzhou under the policy of "selling out the unsold apartments and houses" proposed by the central government. The growth rate of the housing prices of Zhengzhou was much higher than that of most cities nationwide. Such phenomenon was clearly contrary to the original intention of the central and provincial government, which was intended to cut the overcapacity of production in the real estate. On the one hand, we attempted to sell out the unsold apartments and houses which had been constructed during the craze for real estate. On the other hand, we encouraged a large number of migrant workers from the rural area to be citizenized. But for various reasons, it resulted in the unexpected consequences, leading to the soaring house prices in large and medium cities on the one hand and the difficulty of selling the overstocked apartments and houses in the small and medium-sized towns or cities. Take Zhengzhou, a city known for the soaring housing prices, for example, in order to curb the rising prices, we reformulated the new-round house purchase quota policies after three years in September 2016 and further upgraded the purchase quota policies in December. These policies helped to curb the rising of housing prices but prevented the migrant workers buying their own apartments. What's more, the high prices and the correspondingly rising rental greatly raised the living costs of the migrant workers, which was bound to hinder the people's urbanization. Due to the dissatisfaction and living instability resulting from the great impossibilities to have the comfortable housing, it would bring the new potential risks for the social governance in the cities.

Secondly, the difficulty for the social governance was increasing. The large-scale demolition of the villages-in-city can lead to the improvement of the urban environment and the more supplies for land while the migrant workers would be more easily separated and marginalized, which would add more difficulties for the social governance. Take Zhengzhou for example, the villages-in-city in the planned urban area, the shantytowns located outside of the Fourth-ring Road and within the planned urban area as well as areas 3 kilometers around it were expected to be demolished by the end of 2016. The villages-in-city of Zhengzhou would be history, which would increase the difficulties of up to one million of migrant workers in Zhengzhou trying to find their own position in the city. The living cost and the high housing prices made them more alienated from the city's atmosphere but also prevented them from taking roots in the city, which would bring the new potential risks for the social governance in the cities.

Thirdly, the seriously troubled construction of new rural communities hurt the vital interests of farmers. In recent years, undue emphasis was placed on the quantity and speed in the construction of new rural communities in Henan, which led to the waste of a lot of arable land and an enormous sum of money that the people could not afford. According to the statistics of the relevant departments, the construction of 1,366 new rural communities came to a stop, resulting in a direct loss of more than 600 billion yuan. According to the investigation conducted by Xinhua News Agency, to build the new rural communities, the government supported the construction by exempting the general charge, introducing more flexible policies, providing the appropriate incentives and offering land for free, with the advance-fund provided by the real estate developers. Once some communities were uncompleted and some were unsold, the government at a higher level evaded the responsibilities to that at a lower level, and in the end the village administration forced the villagers to buy the apartments. In this way, the construction projects of new rural communities not only failed to achieve the initial purpose of improving the living environment and the quality of life of farmers, but wasted lots of arable land instead of releasing the land resources for intensive development. It was rather thought-provoking for all. Undoubtedly, the pace of the urbanization would be quickened with the rapid development of economy and society. The economic development, especially the development in the rural area, must be kept under the control of its own rules, its own laws and rhythm. It would result in the counterproductive effects simply in the pursuit of speed and efficiency regardless of living habits, cultural traditions and material interests of the villagers.

In a word, negligence of the intrinsic rules in development and the people oriented principle, and the overemphasis on speed, efficiency and political achievements alone are reasons why the problems arose in the process of urbanization in Henan. Only by making efforts to avoid and correct such practices, to draw lessons and to take the people-oriented measures, complying with the law and cultural traditions for the economic and social development, can we carry on the task of urbanization.

5. The Growth Rate of the Income of Urban and Rural Residents Lower than the Economic Growth Rate

Firstly, the farmers' income grew faster than that of the urban residents. As a large agricultural province and the state-level grain production zone in China, Henan was offered with preferential policies and financial supports in the agricultural industry so that the farmers' income grew faster than that of the urban residents. This was the case in 2016. The disposable income per capita of the residents in Henan province reached 18,443.08 Yuan, increased by 7.7% over the previous year. According to the analysis of the places of the residence, the per capita disposable income of the urban residents reached 27,232.92 yuan, increased by 6.5% over the previous year. The disposable income per capita of the rural residents reached 11,696.74 yuan, increased by 7.8% over the previous year. During the Twelfth Five-Year Planning period, the per capita disposable income of urban residents in Henan Province was increased by 10.6% annually, and the per capita net income of rural residents increased by 13.2%. It can be seen that in 2016, the income growth rate of urban and rural residents decreased greatly, with 4.1 percentage points and 5.4 percentage points in reduction for the urban and rural residents respectively. This also showed that due to the slow-down economic growth, Henan's economic development also witnessed the downturn due to the overall quality in 2016.

Secondly, the income growth of urban and rural residents was lower than the growth rate of the gross national product. In 2016, the GDP growth rate of Henan province was 8.1%, but the income growth of the province's residents was only 7.7%. In addition, maintaining a relatively high growth rate in 2016, the GDP growth rate in Henan was 1.4 percentage points higher than the national average. However, the gap between the income of urban and rural residents in Henan and that of the national average was widening (Figure 12). In particular, the income of the rural residents saw a drastic decline compared with the corresponding national average, decreasing by 11.34%. This also showed that the quality of Henan's economic development needed to be improved because the rapid economic development did not bring tangible benefits to people. The overall income level of urban and rural residents in Henan was still lower than the national average level, and the pace of the income growth of urban and rural residents could not keep up with the growth rate of the economic development, which made it a big challenge in the economic and social development of Henan.

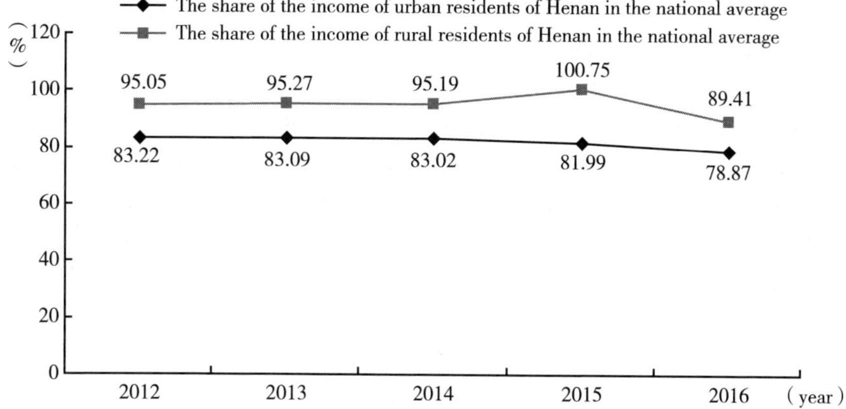

Figure 12 The variation figure for the share of the income of urban and rural residents of Henan in the national average

Data source: Henan Statistical Yearbook, Communique of National Economic and Social Development in Henan, China Statistical Yearbook, Communique of National Economic and Social Development in China.

6. The Ever-prominent Problems Arising from the Irrational Population Structure and Aging

As the most populous province in China, Henan had a registered population of 107.22 million by the end of 2015, which means that of every 100 Chinese, there is one coming from Henan. With such a large population, Henan province was in the prime of demographic dividend for a long period, which could contribute to the economic and social development. However, a series of gradually accumulating problems arising from the irrational population structure began to take shape.

Firstly, the per capita level would be lower than the national average for the economic and social index due to the large population. In recent years, Henan's economic and social development maintained the momentum, with the national GDP ranking fifth in the country and the growth rate higher than the national average. Such achievements ranked much higher than those of other provinces. However, the per capita income and per capita GDP were in the lower reaches, much lower than the national average. Take 2015 for example, the GDP in the province totaled 3701.025 billion yuan, ranking fifth in the country while the per capita disposable income in the province was 17125 yuan, 77.96% of the national average of 19,281 yuan. In 2015, the per capita GDP in Henan province ranked No.22 among the 31 provinces and regions.

Secondly, the population in Henan province was increasingly aging and the social burden became heavier and heavier. In 2015 for the permanent residents, the populations of children aged between 0 and 14 years old, working people aged between 15 and 64 years old, as well as the elderly aged 65 and above were 20.15 million, 65.55 million and 9.13 million respectively, accounting for 21.22%, 69.15% and 9.63% of habitual residents correspondingly. Compared with those in 2010, the children's population increased by 1.22%, and the population aged 65 years and older increased by 1.27% with the net increased population of 1.27 million. However, the working population decreased by 1.49%. The changes in the population structure sped up population aging and added to the social burden. According to international standards, it is an aging one when the population aged 65 years and above took up more than 7% of the total population of a society. That's to say, since 2000, Henan province has entered the phase of aging society, with an increasing elderly population year by year. The total population dependency ratio (the ratio of non-working population to the working one) was 44.61%, increased by 3.05% compared with that in 2010. It reached the lowest level in 2008 before it rose continuously for seven years. At the same time, a large number of working-age population migrated to other provinces hunting for jobs or starting up their businesses because Henan is a province of out-migration, which made the situation even more serious. With the elderly population increasing, the proportion of working population fell down year by year after it reached the highest in 2008 and the total number of the working-age population reached 68.21 million in 2009. Currently, the working-age population now dropped to less than 66 million and was on the decrease year by year, which also brought a lot of adverse effects for Henan's economic and social development.

Thirdly, the quality of the population was not high. The transformation from the province of large population to the province of abundant human resources cannot be done at one go. By the end of 2015, there were 6.39 million population with university or college degrees, 13.94 million with senior high school degrees, 38.06 million people with junior high school degrees and 23.55 million people with the primary level of education (including all kinds of school graduates, undergraduate students and on-campus students). The proportion of the population with the primary and secondary education in Henan reached the average level of the whole country. However, the population with the university education (college and above) was 6.39 million, its ratio to the whole population in Henan amounting only to half of the national average. This also showed that in spite of comparatively better performance in the basic education, Henan still lagged behind the domestic average level in higher education and the quality of its population needed to be improved.

III Basic Situation and Policy Suggestions of Social Development in Henan in 2017

1. An Analysis of Basic Situation

Firstly, we would fully implement policies of the Tenth CPC Congress of Henan and deal with the higher requirements raised by acceleration of inclusive development. From the perspective of the strategic overall situation of Henan, the Tenth CPC Congress of Henan made a comprehensive planning and deployment of the social development and the improvement of the people's wellbeing. In implementing the overall layout of the "Five-in-one" and "Four-pronged Comprehensive Strategies", we would further strengthen the important position of social development. The Tenth CPC Congress of Henan put forward the overall objectives of building the moderately well-off society in all-around way and promoting the development of the Central Plains. It proposed many new ideas, deployment and requirements aiming at improving the social development and people's livelihood in Part Six, and reaffirmed adherence to the people-oriented development so as to solemnly strengthen the people's sense of gain, and to spread the reform and development results to all the people in the more equitable way, which could be done in the following five aspects according to the report: to develop the socialist democracy for fully mobilizing the people, to strengthen the leading role of culture to gather strong spiritual strength; to win the fight against poverty and to build the moderately well-off society in all-around way for every single one; to improve the people's livelihood and sense of happiness, to effectively improve the ecological environment and to construct the beautiful home with a blue sky and unpolluted water. In terms of improving people's livelihood, the report also elaborated on the planned development of employment sector to which priorities are to be given, of education sector that satisfies people, and of sound construction of the Central Plains. Regarding the social development and improvement of the people's livelihood as the starting point, the Tenth CPC Congress of Henan set the higher requirements for acceleration of inclusive development, which indicated the direction for the social development in the Thirteenth Five-year Planning. To regard the social development in Henan as the important goals and tasks, we aimed at the vigorous promotion of the poverty alleviation and people's livelihood, focusing on holding onto the bottom line and highlighting the major fields, constant improving public services and their sharing level, and solving the problems concerned most to people so as to let the achievements of reform to benefit everyone.

Secondly, the strategies for many state-level development zones in Henan would be conducive to the improvement its economic status in the nation and the preferential policies would surely bring Henan bonuses for its development. Since the introduction to the reform and opening up, the nation implemented the strategies like "East China Taking the Lead in Development", "Development of West China", "Revitalization of Northeast China" and "Rise of Central China", and proposed planslike "the Belt and Road Initiative", "Coordinated development for the Beijing-Tianjin-Hebei region", "Yangtze River Economic Belt" during the "13th Five-Year Planing" period based on the overall strategy of regional development. The vertical economic belt along the coastal area and the horizontal economic belt along the Yangtze River took shape, and the urban agglomerations became the major platform for grouping of the population and industries. The adjustment of national regional development strategy meant that we would pay more attention to the coordinated development in China's different regions in the future. By cultivating some central growth poles for promoting regional synergistic development can we work out enough space for the medium-to-high-speed growth of the economy. At the same time, implementing the new development strategies for different regions was also a process of re-shuffling and reshaping relations for regional development. It was a wise choice for local governments to base their development and regional policies on their own advantages, to cultivate the core growth pole and the growth zone. Currently, Henan was offered with the development strategies like "Region of Grain Production in China", "Zhongyuan Economic Zone", "Zhengzhou Comprehensive Experimental Zone for Airport –based Economy", "China (Henan) Free Trade Experimental Zone",

"China (Zhengzhou) Cross-border E-Commerce Integrated Experimental Zone", "Zheng-Luoyang-Xinxiang National Independent Innovation Demonstration Zone", which would become the strong impetus for promoting the economic and social development in Henan and then pick up the pace for the structural optimization. With the implementation of the six state-level strategies, the overall position of Henan in the country would be significantly improved and the advantages for the its own location in Central China would be given the full play so as to speed up the revitalization of the Central Plains with Henan in particular. In 2017, we would adopt a variety of effective initiatives to cultivate and give full play to the advantages of this province located in Central China, which would not only play a decisive role in the future development but also have a profound impact on the rise the Central Plains. In short, Henan should further develop its own advantages, and seize the major opportunities for the gradient transfer of the industries and the supports of the national government concerning the "Rise of Central China" in 2017. On the one hand, we should actively promote the transformation and upgrading of the traditional industries in Henan by vigorously developing the high-tech industries and other emerging industries. By this way, we can race to be the highland for the future development, and improve the overall quality and the size of the economy as well as the competitiveness, making Henan's cake bigger; on the other hand, we should promote the inclusive development and construction of people's livelihood, and reform the income distribution system so as to heighten comprehensively people's sense of gain, distributing Henan's cake in a good way.

Thirdly, the acceleration of new urbanization could serve as an impetus to the social development of Henan. As an important way to build the well-off society in an all-round way, the new urbanization was also important for expanding the domestic demand. In 2017, we would pay more attention to the connotative development of urbanization and vigorously promote the new urbanization. With the people-centered happiness as the ultimate goal, the new urbanization, quality-oriented and of a high level, should be integrated with the new industrialization, informationization and agricultural modernization, which would not be achieved at the cost of the environment and resources. At present, in spite of the weakening driving force of urbanization in some places, e.g. the aging of rural population, the limited resources for the agricultural production, the unsustainable development of land urbanization, the narrowing income gap between urban and rural residents, etc., there were other driving forces that would play an important role in the process. To begin with, the differences for basic public facilities and services between the urban and rural areas would be an important and significant factor in promoting further development of the new urbanization, which would continuously improve the municipal construction of the public facilities and services. The increasing supply of basic public services in cities and towns can result in the agglomeration of the larger population and the stronger absorptive capacity in return, with more and more people continuing to migrate and move to the cities and towns at all levels. Next, the relocation of the whole family was also an important driving force to promote the urbanization. The migration of China's population was gradually shifting from migrant-vendor style to the family-based style, and we could see that the relocation and movement of whole family would be the long-term trend in the future and an important driving force of the urbanization. According to the *New Urbanization Planning in Henan Province (2014-2020)*, the urbanization rate of the resident population would have reached about 56% by 2020, with eleven million more rural residents moving out. The urbanization rate of the registered population would have reached about 40%. The improvement of the urbanization rates of the resident population and the registered population would enhance the economic and social development, which would further activate and stimulate the economic and social development of Henan. This can be understood in two aspects: In the first place, The urbanization was an important source for driving the economic growth mainly by offering the supply and demand. From the supply side, the urbanization promoted the upgrading of industrial structure. With the advance of urbanization, the labor force of the first industry with low productivity was shifted to the more productive second and third industries, which could promote the upgrading of industrial structure. At the same time, urbanization promoted the spatial clustering of population and economic activities, which would facilitate the mutual use of technological and financial resources so as to increase productivity. On the demand side, on the one hand, the urbanization brings much higher labor productivity through the transfer of the labor forces from the agricultural industries in a large scale, and thereby could increase the income of rural residents and would encourage a large number of the rural residents to be the urban residents, which in turn would promote the demand for consumption. On the other hand, the urbanization would stimulate investment and create huge demands for housing, transportation, energy, education, landscaping, the urban security systems and other infrastructures as the shifting population pores into the cities, which would drive the rapid growth of investment and could fully support the stable and rapid social development during the "Thirteenth Five-year Plann" period. In the second place, the urbanization was also an important way to solve the problems related to the agricultural industry, rural areas and farmers, and could fully support the coordinated development in the region. As an important starting point for expanding domestic demand and promoting industrial transformation and upgrading, the urbanization was of the great historical and practical significance for building a well-off society in an all-round way, accelerating the pace for Henan to enter the first phalanx in terms of its comprehensive strengths in China and promoting the Rise of the Central China. Acceleration of urbanization could promote the stable growth of the economy, the social fairness and justice and stability, and meet the needs to improve the well-being of the people.

At present, the level of urbanization in Henan was lower than the national average, which showed that while we would take on the heavier tasks in achieving the national average level on the one hand, we still had large room for the new-type urbanization in Henan that would bring us the great potential and strong driving force on the other hand. Compared with the developed areas, Henan had considerable potential in urbanization. At present, we should change the old-style overspreading urbanization, reform the urbanization-based supporting system by integrating the urban-rural areas rather than segmenting the urban-rural areas, change from the hierarchical urbanization to the more homogeneous urbanization, restrain land urbanization and promote the people's urbanization. On the basis of the residents' actual conditions and the urban-rural system, we would improve the population density in urban areas, enhance the agglomerating effect of the city and the capital of human resources so as to reshape urban industrial competitiveness. Only in this way can the urbanization produce agglomerating effect and scale economies effect, which could effectively improve the efficiency of economic and social development.

Fourthly, the tasks were arduous for achieving the shared development for all people with the widening income gap between urban and rural residents. To begin with, the overall income level of Henan urban and rural residents was low, whether in terms of its percentage of per capita GDP of the whole country or in terms of its comparison with the national average level. The Tenth CPC Congress of Henan clearly stated that one of the future tasks is to "enhance people's sense of gain in the decisive fight for an all-round well-off society and a better future for the Central Plains". In recent years, the total economic output of Henan province ranked fifth in the country and the growth rate was among the highest; however, the level of per capita income was not satisfactory. The tasks were arduous for achieving the shared economic development for all people. In 2016, the per capita disposable income of urban residents and that of rural residents in Henan province were only 81% and 94.6% of the national average level respectively. The size of economy was out of line with the per capita disposable income, which reflected that Henan had a large population, and the economy development was of low quality, with over-dependence on investment and trade, and an irrational industrial structure, leading to the disproportion of the economic growth rate to the income growth rate. Therefore, we witnessed the limited achievements for the shared development.

Next, the income gap for the people in different regions and industries was widening and the level of the shared development needed to be improved. The income gap for the people in urban and rural areas in Henan province was narrowing in recent years. In 2012, the per capita income of rural residents was only 37% of the per capita income of urban residents and the percentage reached 43% by 2016, but the gap in terms of absolute amount was widening, increasing by 2618.5 yuan from 2012 to 2016 (Table 4).

Table 4 Income gap for the people in urban and rural areas in Henan province

Year	The per capita income of urban residents (yuan)	The per capita income of rural residents (yuan)	Absolute income difference between the urban residents and rural residents (yuan)	The ratio of the disposable income per capita of rural residents to the disposable income per capita of urban residents
2012	20442.62	7524.94	12917.68	0.37
2013	22398.03	8475.34	13922.69	0.38
2014	24391.45	9416.1	14975.35	0.39
2015	25576.00	10853.00	14723.00	0.42
2016	27232.92	11696.74	15536.18	0.43

Data source: Statistical Bulletin on the National Economy and Social Development in Henan Province from 2012 to 2016.

Judging from the different cities, we can see that the income per capita of the urban residents employed in the non-private sector in Zhengzhou reached 52,376 yuan, the highest level in the province while its counterpart in Hebi was 39,187 yuan, the lowest in the province, only 75% of Zhengzhou's per capita income. Judging in terms of different industries, we can see that the income per capita in the banking industry reached as high as 74,441 yuan in 2015 while the income per capita in the accommodation and catering industry was 33,854 yuan, the lowest in all industries, with a gap of 40,587 yuan compared with the highest. Judging in terms of individual income, we can see that there were many low-income people in Henan province. Sixty percent of the population in the province lived on an income lower than the provincial average level, and 40% of the population lived on an income that was lower than 75% of the provincial average level. Besides, there were also many poverty-stricken areas and a large poverty-stricken population. In Henan, nearly six million people in more than 8,100 villages of fifty-three counties were poverty-stricken, which made Henan province one of the six provinces with more than five million poverty-stricken people in China. The tasks for the poverty alleviation were also arduous. These are all great challenges for us to improve the people's livelihood and the shared development for all in 2017.

Fifthly, the innovation-driven strategy would enhance the endogenous power of Henan's economic and social development. Since "the Twelfth Five-Year plan" period, China had actively explored and transformed the economic growth from the factor-driven and investment-driven mode to the innovation-driven mode. The 18th National Congress of the Communist Party of China made it clear that it was necessary to implement innovation-driven development strategy. The Thirteenth Five-Year plann of Henan province put forward that we should regard the innovation as the starting point of economy development, including innovations in science and technologies, institutions, management, culture innovation, etc.. To speed up efforts in cultivating the new impetus and competitive advantage, we could shift the driving force from production factors to innovation. The Tenth CPC Congress of Henan clearly stated that the top priority should be given to the innovation, and the scientific and technological innovation provides strategic support for raising the productive forces and boosting the overall industrial development, fully releasing the dividends of market-oriented reforms and human capital, and we should attach importance to infrastructure construction and create the new supply and demand so as to improve the quality and efficiency of development. According to the proposals formulated in the Tenth CPC Congress of Henan, we should let the new concept guide the development, speed up industrial transformation and upgrading, and vigorously implement the innovation-driven development so as to create new pillar industries for development. It was clear that the implementation of the innovation-driven strategy and the up-bringing of the new pillar industries would be major tasks for Henan's economic and social development in 2017, which would also bring a series of new changes and growth as well.

To begin with, we would speed up the reform of the institutional mechanism and implement the comprehensive supplementary reform, resolve the deep-seated contradictions in major fields and steps, and build the mechanism conducive to the scientific development, which would provide a powerful driving force for the economic and social development in Henan. At the same time, we would strive to meet the increasing material and spiritual needs of people by providing more public services of high quality, more cultural products of various kinds, more complete social governance and more secure living environment, which would also drive the economic and social development in Henan.

Next, the innovation-driven strategy can help Henan overtake at the corner and take the favorable positions in the domestic and international competitions in the new round of technology and industrial revolution. With the improved innovation environment and abilities, especially the breakthroughs and the cross-integration of key technologies, the innovation-driven strategy would gradually narrow the overall technical gaps between Henan and the developed provinces, and would enable us to take the leading positions domestically and internationally in some high-tech industries, which would lay a solid foundation for building Henan into an innovative province well-developed in scientific-technologies.

In the third place, the innovation-driven development can greatly improve the status of industrial specialization. Through the accelerated accumulation of innovative elements and the faster-growing ability to innovate, the advantages created by the innovation would gradually make up for the rising labor costs so as to transform industries in Henan with comparative advantages from labor-intensive ones to technology-and knowledge-intensive ones, which would push Henan upstream along the industry chain.

In the fourth place, the innovation, a result of accumulation of knowledge, could continuously enhance the economic growth by providing the quality human capital. As the essence of innovation, the talents were playing the decisive role. Therefore, we would take a series of effective measures to create a fair environment to stimulate innovation, to establish a market-oriented mechanism for the technological innovation and to improve the transformation of scientific research achievements in order to improve the human capital, stimulate the entrepreneurship and enterprises' motive for innovation, which would transform the technological achievements to the real productive forces so as to fundamentally transform and upgrade the mode of economic development in Henan.

In the fifth place, the innovation in the field of production can enhance the product quality, product variety and the supply of products in the market; the innovation in transaction and transportation could reduce the costs so as to strike a balance at higher yield level; the paradigm-shifting innovation could help to create a new market, which would have an important impact on the economic and social development.

Sixthly, we would continue to stimulate the vitality of social development and release new reform dividends by deepening the reform in an all-round way. In recent years, Henan witnessed the important progress in the administrative system reform and the government functions, which could be seen in the fact that a total of more than 180 administrative approval and the non-administrative licensing matters were transferred to lower-level governments while only 394 approval and licensing matters were kept at the provincial-level administrations. With the further deepened reform in the investment system, the great progress had been achieved in the reforms of interest rate liberalization, of pricing, and of monopoly industries, together with a new phase in implementing the rule of law and comprehensive strengthening of Party discipline. Such initiatives stimulated Henan's economic and social development. To begin with, the reform of the economic and administrative systems would enhance the vitality of the market players by purifying the market environment and regulating the governmental behavior, which would further mobilize all parties, and enhance the social innovation so as to provide a solid foundation for quality economic development. Under the effect of reforms during the 12th Five-year plan period and in 2016, the vitality and production capacity of the enterprises in Henan were greatly enhanced, and the number of unprofitable and debt-laden enterprises decreased significantly due to rational judgments made by enterprises and market clearing. In 2017, such situation would be further improved. Next, the political system reform would further strengthen the constraints and supervision of the power so as to promote the rule of law. In order to build the market-oriented economy, remove its obstacles and release new dividends brought by the reform, we would vigorously transform the government functions, improve the government services and its administrative capabilities; we would further strengthen the constraints and supervision of the political power so as to promote the rule of law; and we would deepen the reform of the judicial system and abolish the System of Indoctrination through Labor, which would lay a solid foundation for the rule of law in the nation. What's more, the social system reform would effectively help to improve the people's livelihood and social fairness and justice. The reform of the distribution system, the pay system and the pension system would further improve the income distribution structure and the social security system so that the social system would be more equitable and sustainable.

2. Policy Recommendations

Firstly, we would always give the top priority to the improvement of people's livelihood and the shared social development. We should put people's interests first during the reform and development, and always adhere to the people-oriented principles so as to promote the shared development and people's sense of gain. Regarding the improvement of people's livelihood and the shared social development as the foundation of social progress, we would spare no efforts to improve the mechanism, shore up areas of weakness, and stick to our ethics and principles so as to continuously improve people's living standards. We would emphasize on the improvement of people's livelihood when assessing government officials, prioritizing indicators for safety, health and basic security of people. To speed up the reform of the income distribution system, we would strive to make the residents' income grow at the same pace with the economic development, and the income of residents at the same pace with the improvement in productivity; and we should raise the share of the residents' income of the national revenue and proportion of payment in the primary income distribution. Efforts will be made to establish and improve the wage growth mechanism and wage payment security to ensure that the wages of workers would be raised together with the increase in economic growth and corporate profits. We would complete the mechanism for regular pay raises and the mechanism for guaranteeing payments to make sure that wages of corporate employees rise as the economy and the corporate profits grow. We would also complete the mechanism for regular pay raises for employees working in the CPC and government organs so as to gradually narrow the gap with the national average level and to improve the wages in the whole society. We would implement more vigorous policies of entrepreneurship and employment, paying special attention to the employment of major groups and the changes in the employment situation. The relevant policies should be prepared to stabilize and increase employment opportunities. To speed up the construction of basic public service system, we would make sure that the equalization of basic public services regarding people's livelihood be realized in different aspects at the same pace. As for the well being of people, we should further improve the mechanism for steady pay raises, and continuously provide more public services especially for the socially disadvantaged groups in rural areas and poverty-stricken areas. By these ways, we could promote the balanced allocation of resources, public services, the development opportunities and the educational resources so as to comprehensively promote the population quality.

Secondly, we should make regulations on the basis of the actual reality so as to realize targeted poverty alleviation. It is the second year into the countdown of comprehensive poverty alleviation. The tasks in poverty alleviation were rather arduous in Henan and we should establish long-term mechanisms and adopt a variety of ways to eliminate poverty in balanced and sustainable manners.

To begin with, we must give full play to our institutional advantages, and improve the patterns for poverty alleviation at the provincial level, prefecture level, county level, township level and village level. First of all, we must specify the responsibilities of the top leaders of CPC committee and the governments, and CPC committees and governments at all levels should succeed in carrying out the assignments and act as the party of prime responsibility, taking poverty alleviation as the top task and the most important project for people's well-being in 2017. They should take the leadership and the subordinates at the lower level should follow them so as to give full play to the institutional advantages for pooling all poverty alleviation efforts, which would improve the five-level patterns for poverty alleviation. Then, we should specify the main responsibility of poverty-stricken counties. To be deregistered from the poverty alleviation list should be the major task, and should be an increasingly important index for assessment of the effectiveness of poverty alleviation in poverty-stricken counties. Performance in poverty alleviation would be the overriding factor in accessing administrative work in poverty-stricken counties. We would constantly improve the mechanism for deregistering from the poverty alleviation list and the evaluation mechanism for the special indexes. The performance for the poverty alleviation would be the important basis for us to offer the rewards or penalties for leaders of local CPC committees and governments in the poverty-stricken counties or regions, which would stimulate the leaders at the grass-roots level. Next, we must further encourage the relevant governmental sectors to perform the duties, further clarify their responsibilities and obligations and improve their sense of responsibilities. A variety of working mechanisms like the poverty alleviation aid to the designated sister regions provided by the relevant units, eradicating poverty with science and technology, personnel training in poverty relief and the poverty alleviation provided by the non-governmental units would be further established.

In the second place, we should regard the poverty alleviation as our guiding principle and implement strategies for targeted poverty alleviation. In accordance with the requirements of "Six Targets", referring to the selection of the targeted poverty-stricken population, the targeted poverty-eradication projects, the targeted uses for the funds, the targeted poverty eradication measures, the targeted personnel for the targeted villages and the targeted achievements, we should fully implement the targeted poverty alleviation policies formulated by the Central Government. First of all, we should accurately identify the targeted poverty-stricken population and make sure that the poverty-alleviation funds indeed end up in the hands of every poverty-stricken household. The scope of poverty alleviation work cannot be randomly expanded and no poverty-stricken county should be allowed to manipulate its status simply to claim funds; the poverty-alleviation funds should be used fair and square. Then, the targeted poverty alleviation measures should be taken and we should sum up the lessons learned in poverty alleviation, and apply different measures according to different situations, including offering the development opportunities, relocating the poverty-stricken population, improving the education and training level, constructing the infrastructure, providing the low-interest loans, arranging the projects in the poverty-stricken areas, etc.. Next, we must accurately formulate the road map and timetable for poverty reduction. We must not let the poverty-stricken population and the poverty-stricken areas fall behind in the process of building the well-off society. We must not leave them alone.

In the third place, we must increase the investment of human capital in the poverty-stricken areas and eradicate the root of the poverty. Capacity cultivation should be put into the first place and the enhancement of the self-development capacity of the poverty-stricken population should play the important role so as to improve the endogenous power and development vitality for the poverty-stricken population and the poverty-stricken areas. Emphasis should be put on increasing investment of human capital in the poverty-stricken areas and expanding supporting networks of the social capitals for individuals, so that the targeted poverty-stricken people can really benefit. We should focus on the development of education (especially distance education) in poor areas, and encourage college graduates to teach in remote rural areas so as to provide the equal opportunities to education and other development for children in poor families, which could prevent poverty from being inherited. We should also gradually change some traditional customs in poverty-stricken areas that are backward, telling people to be content and poor.

Thirdly, we would further strengthen the social construction and innovate the ways of the social governance. To promote and to modernize the systems for the national social governance has been fully integrated into the future planning of China's economic and social development, and has become the country's major strategy for the long-term stability. The improved positions of the social governance were particularly important for achieving scientific development in such a populous province.

First of all, we should further improve the pattern of social governance, and pay more attention to the role of the social organizations. The government should play a leading role in encouraging and supporting all sectors of society to participate in the governance, and strive for a benign interaction among administration of the government, self-regulation of the society and self-governance of the residents. On the one hand, the government should speed up the transformation of its own functions from the economic field to that of social public services. There would be more space for social organizations to function once the government delegates power to lower levels. On the other hand, we should give full play to the social organizations in social governance.

In the second place, we should timely prevent and tackle the social conflicts at their roots. To begin with, we should be fully prepared by establishing the risk analysis and assessment mechanisms for major issues, which would be the necessary procedures in government decision-making when it comes to major projects and policies concerning the interests of the people. Then, we would establish the grass-roots mediation system based on mediation by people, coupled with the administrative mediation and judicial mediation so as to strive to resolve the contradictions and disputes before they further escalate. Next, we should improve the petition mechanism. We should explore the possibility of petition agency system in an attempt to build a three-level platform and four-level networks in counties or county-level districts, which would bring convenience for people to protect their legitimate rights.

In the third place, we should pay attention to the blind spots and weak links in social governance. To begin with, we should further strengthen the management of floating populations; establish a sound dynamic management mechanism so as to cover all of the actual population. People migrating to Henan would be managed and served by governments of their residential areas, which would help them integrate into the local communities. Then, we would strengthen the supervision over food safety, safety production and public security to further improve the level of urban security. Next, virtual society management would be stepped up by establishing an integrated on- and off-line management system, and improving the mechanism to guide the public opinions online, so that we could respond to the social concerns on time. In addition, the service and management would be improved for the villages-in-city and rural-urban interface. These are weak links in the chain of social governance, so we would provide the social service and strengthen the management in time so as to effectively respond to problems, which would improve the social management in all round ways.

Fourthly, we should properly solve the prominent problems arising from the new urbanization. As an agricultural and populous province in China, Henan, whose urbanization rate was 8.85 percentage points lower than the national average, should actively and steadily promote the healthy development of new urbanization and properly solve the problems arising from the process, which would be of great and far-reaching significance.

First of all, we must properly handle the emerging problems arising from the construction of the new rural community. The "Twelfth Five-year Plan" of Henan and the report of the Ninth CPC Congress of Henan regarded the construction of the new rural community as the starting point of integrated urban and rural development as well as the terminal of the five-level urbanization. However, it was proved by years of practice that this plan went beyond the current development stage of Henan according to and against Henan's developmental realities. Therefore, it was inappropriate to carry out in a comprehensive way the construction of the new rural community in the process of new urbanization. To begin with, it was not in line with the guidelines and policies of the Central Committee of the Communist Party of China. In 2013, the State Council and the Central Committee of the Communist Party of China formulated its No. 1 Document, namely *Opinions on Accelerating the Development of Modern Agriculture and Further Enhancing the Development Vitality of Rural Area*, which made it clear that as for the relocation of rural settlements and the withdrawal of villages, we must respect farmers' own free will and the decision made by villagers' conference. We do not advocate or encourage splitting and merging of villages and construction of large-scale residential communities for farmers outside the urban planning area; we must not force the farmers to move or live in buildings. These statements in the No. 1 Document were specifically directed to problems in reality. Then, it went well beyond the current development stage of Henan due to its deviation from the actual situation in Henan province. On the one hand, there were indeed many areas well-developed in terms of economic conditions, public infrastructure or the secondary or the tertiary industries, which could be directly incorporated into the urban area or be regarded as terminals of the urbanization system. On the other hand, the economic and industrial conditions in many areas were not yet mature enough, so new rural communities can be regarded as a transitional form between urban and rural areas but not a part of the urban system. There were still some underdeveloped areas far from being mature enough to be integrated into the urban system, hence better to maintain their original rural patterns. Therefore, it was not appropriate to directly incorporate the new rural community into the urban area, because it deviated from the actual situation of Henan province. If we were to carry on with this process, it would mean that we were actually looking for a single cure-all solution to diverse problems in practice. Besides, the construction of the new rural community was a rather complex project, covering in a series of issues including the switch from rural institutions to urban ones, restructuring the collective assets, the circulation of rural land, funding for construction, farmers' employment, social security, community management, the exercise of the farmers' rights, etc..

With no breakthroughs in dealing with the institutional roadblocks and practical problems, the construction of the new rural community would be a heavy burden for the local economy and hence difficult to go on. Next, it was not in the long-term interests of farmers. According to the Decision of the Third Plenary Sessions of the 18th CPC Central Committee Required for Speeding up the Reform of Some Major Issues, we should ensure rural households' usufruct of their homestead, and improve the rural homestead system through reform. We will select several pilot areas to steadily and prudently push forward the mortgage, guarantee and transfer of farmers' residential property rights, and expand the channels for farmers to increase their property income. Once the farmers' homesteads were collected for the construction of the new rural communities, they could not increase the property revenue by building more houses. Therefore, such an approach was neither in line with the guidelines and policies of the Central Committee of the Communist Party of China nor in the interests of farmers, which would lead to hidden risks of social instability.

The new-type urbanization was a process of the long-term natural development, rather than the simple relocation of farmers and the changes in the living environment. As an important indicator for the quality of the construction of new urbanization, how to properly handle the farmers' transferred land, employment, social security and other issues could ensure that the farmers are indeed willing to move in, get employed and become wealthy. If the long-term benefits of residents in the community cannot be safeguarded, a number of social contradictions would break out in new rural communities in a few years.

In the second place, we must properly improve the people's urbanization, the primary task of which was to urbanize the permanent resident population according to the principles formulated in the Central Work Conference on Urbanization. To single out and tackle the principal contradictions arising from the people's urbanization would indicate the direction for future urbanization efforts. In 2016, China's urbanization rate reached 57.35%, with an urban population of 790 million, a world average level. However, the urbanization of the people transferred from rural areas was relatively slow, the household registration rate was a low 37%, indicating that more than 200 million migrant workers and their accompanying family members were in a semi-urbanization situation (about more than 12 million migrant workers still on the waitlist of citizenship), and that they cannot enjoy the same basic public services in education, employment, pension, affordable housing and other aspects as the urban residents do. In a word, the urbanization of such groups lagged far behind. They were no longer rural residents but had yet to integrate into the city, situated somewhere between the country and the city, making the original dual structure a ternary one. Therefore, the central government has made a primary task the urbanization of these 200 million migrant workers and their accompanying family members. Due to historical reasons and the limited financial resources, we should deal with the problems step by step.

In the third place, we should preferentially provide enough employment opportunities for the migrant population. The people would go to places where there are employment opportunities, which in turn appear where there are industries. This is a natural or endogenous type of urbanization. Therefore, we would see that in spite of the implementation of conditional restrictions that big cities put on the household registration, house-purchase, school education for their children for migrant workers, farmers continue to pour into cities due to the high productivity and the high-level resource allocation in urban area. The city was in essence where the population and industries gathered for development; the greater productivity and the high-level resource allocation, the greater attraction of the big cities. Therefore, we must promote the farmers' full re-employment as our priority in the new urbanization.

The prerequisite for urbanization was to deal with farmers' re-employment, and it would be meaningless to change their living places if we don't change their production mode. Urbanization is the result of industrialization and modernization as well as the development of the service industries. In the process of industrialization in the West, the western urbanization followed a three-level mode of large and medium-sized cities plus satellite cities, where a lot of industries would settle. We would achieve the industrial agglomeration effect in large and medium-sized cities, the size and speed of which should not be determined by administrative orders. There was still a lot of work to do to let people live in peace and enjoy one's work in the cities. To achieve the economies of scale and agglomeration effect in many industries played an important role in the urbanization, that is, we should bring many industries in a region. The urbanization should be the result of no other than industrialization. Without industrial development, the rural population would have no employment opportunities once they came to the cities, which would make urbanization a burden for the society and the economy. Therefore, despite the opportunities for the investment and the enhanced competitiveness brought about by the urbanization which would be called as the new engine of economic growth, we could not try to help the shoots grow by pulling them upward, but should base it on the level of the economic and industrial development. Once the industrialization outpaced the urbanization and the economic development laid a solid foundation, urbanization would come its own way.

To solve the problems arising from the urbanization, we must adhere to the industry-led and the market-led policies by developing the industries and markets rather than just expanding the urban areas, which would be based on the industrial expansion and upgrading. First of all, we should promote the development of the industrial parks and the agglomeration areas where a lot of job opportunities would be created. In the second place, we should vigorously develop the modern service industry and create employment opportunities. In the third place, we should use the training platforms like "Sunshine Project" and "Rain and Dew Project" to improve the education of the farmers so as to prepare them for job hunting.

Fifthly, we should vigorously promote ecological construction by building a beautiful and green Henan. In 2016, the serious smog haunted every inhabitant in Henan. The environmental pollution in Henan was a serious problem for the further economic and social development in Henan. It became the most urgent task to vigorously bring the environmental pollution under control and to make mountains green and waters clear again in Henan, which became a project that benefits all people.

First of all, we must vigorously promote the comprehensive improvement of urban environment by further improving the sewage treatment facilities, and the rate of garbage harmless treatment and sewage treatment in the cities. The strict control over air pollution should be strengthened and the environmental access system for motor vehicles must be implemented. Measures should also be adopted to avoid the dust pollution during the transportation and construction, and to control noises created in the catering and entertainment service industries. We encouraged the low-carbon lifestyle and sped up the pace of constructing the energy-saving buildings.

In the second place, we must vigorously promote the comprehensive improvement of the rural environment by setting the higher environment-protecting access standards for the industrial projects and by preventing the backward production capacity from transferring to the rural areas. We should improve the ecological environment in the rural area and prevent the pollution caused by pesticides, fertilizers, plastic sheeting and poultry manure and other sources.

In the third place, we must strengthen the energy saving and emission reduction. The top priorities should be given to the management of water and energy resources. The quantity, quality and its disposal of water should be under the strict control and we should strictly control the consumed quantity and emission of energy as well. We encouraged the organic combination of the effective investment expansion and the elimination of the backward production capacity. The environmental standards and the differential power and water prices should be adopted so as to force the enterprises to upgrade their technology and production, which would be conducive to get rid of pollution from the start.

In the fourth place, we would further improve the ecological environment of Henan by preserving and restoring the environment of mountains, waters, forests and the farming land. The ecological networks covering the "Four Areas and Three Zones" and the ecological corridors along the old course of the Yellow River in Ming and Qing Dynasties would be constructed. With such measures, we intended to improve the forestation as well as the ecological environment of wetland, rivers, farmland and urban areas so as to build a barrier against ecological deterioration.

Sixthly, we would further increase the supply of the basic public services and improve the quality on the basis of equalization. With the rapid development of economy and society, the basic public service in Henan witnessed the development by leaps and bounds, covering fields like employment, education, medical care and others. An all-round and multi-field basic public service system was established. However, a series of issues like the difficulty and the high cost of getting medical services, the craze for top schools and the over-sized classes increasingly stood out. As an urgent issue that needed to be faced with in social construction in 2017, further improvement of the basic public services on the basis of equalization was decisive for us to offer the people fairer and easier people-oriented services.

First of all, we must promote the coordinated development of education. The priority should be given to the development via comprehensively deepening the reform in the field of education, and promoting the fairness and services in education. As for the elementary education, we should improve its wide coverage for the well-being of the people by constructing the hardware including the school buildings, equipment and others on the one hand, with no gap left between the level of cities and of the countryside, and by upgrading the software and achieving the balanced development of the required resources. A series of measures would be taken to encourage teachers to regularly shift to other schools, to get regular training and improve the teachers' salary so as to effectively stabilize and improve quality of teachers in the urban and rural area. We would speed up to construct the modern vocational education system by promoting the in-depth integration of schools and enterprises so as to encourage the vocational schools and the industrial association and the enterprises to jointly cultivate high-quality technicians and technical personnel. We should optimize the structure of higher education; establish the classified management and guidance systems for universities so as to improve the overall quality of higher education. We would improve the education service of schools and optimize the allocation of educational resources in urban and rural areas. The school principals and teachers in the compulsory education should take part in the regular exchange program, and we would encourage the teachers in the urban area to teach in the rural area so as to promote the balanced development of the compulsory education. In this way, we could narrow the gap between different schools, between urban areas and rural area as well as between different regions.

In the second place, we must effectively improve the health of all people. In view of actual conditions like the increasingly aging population and the increasing health consumption, we would systematically promote the development of the health industries and service system in medical treatment, health care, pension, medicine and insurance in accordance with the medical and health system reform and health insurance system. The public health services and the funding standards for the per capita basic public health services would be improved and we would continue to implement the health service projects for the basic security and the major public security in the nation. The measures for the prevention and control of major diseases would be strengthened and the prevention and control of the chronic diseases and major diseases would be of great importance by adhering to prevention combined with the treatment according to the policies for building the Heath Central Plains. We would consolidate and improve the basic drug system, and orderly expand the implementation of essential medicine system, deepen the comprehensive reform of the health care institutions at the grass-root levels, accelerate the reform of the public hospitals at the county level, abolish the compensation system for the medical cost through medicine-selling profits and rationalize the medical prices so as to establish the scientific compensation mechanism. We would give priorities to the local and grassroots levels by a variety of means like the overall hosting, two-way referral and forming medical consortium. The close cooperation would be strengthened between the third-class hospitals and the county-level hospitals and the health care clinics at the grass-root levels. We would also improve the hierarchical diagnosis and treatment model so as to promote the vertical flow of quality medical resources. Gradually, we can achieve the immediate diagnosis in the hospitals at the grass-root levels, graded diagnosis and treatment, two-way referral, the divided treatments for the acute-care and chronic diseases. We should promote the development of health services, encourage the establishment of the privately operated hospitals so as to form the non-profit medical institutions-centered system supplemented by the profit-oriented private hospitals.

In the third place, as for the construction of the affordable housing, we would establish the system based on the market distribution combined with the governmental protection, and actively develop affordable housing for leasing and establish the strict system for the applications, approval and introduction of the low-rent housing. We would dynamically manage both the low-rent housing and its applicants. The standards for applying the low-rent housing should be determined reasonably and fairly so as to gradually expand the coverage of low-rent housing to include not only the lowest income applicants but also low-income ones. We would make sure that all applicants eligible for such affordable housing must be covered by the system. The monetary subsidies combined with the provision of affordable housing for leasing purposes should be adopted. To ensure that people can really get benefits, we would adopt the balanced and reasonable mechanisms for the shantytown development, villages-in-city renovation, capital security, project responsibility, supervision and inspection as well as the fair and reasonable distribution of the new housing. In accordance with the principle of "raising funds from more sources and concentrating on major issues", we would fully respect the living habits, customs and affordability of farmers, and encourage the farmers to improve their housing and constantly quicken the pace of rural housing construction for effectively improving the standards and quality for housing construction in rural area.

References:

[1] Chen Runer. 2017 Henan Provincial Government Work Report [N]. *Henan Daily*, February 22, 2017.

[2] Xie Fuzhan. 2016 Henan Provincial Government Work Report [N]. *Henan Daily*, February 4, 2016.

[3] Henan Provincial Government. The Thirteenth Five-year Planning of the National Economic and Social Development of Henan Province [N]. *Henan Daily*, May 18, 2016.

[4] Henan Provincial Bureau of Statistics. A Solid Start of the Province's Economic Development in 2016, http://www.ha.stats.gov.cn, the website of Henan Provincial Bureau of Statistics, January 22, 2017.

[5] Henan Provincial Bureau of Statistics. 2015 Bulletin of the Sample Survey of Population in Henan Province, http://www.ha.stats.gov.cn, the website of Henan Provincial Bureau of Statistics, June 14, 2016.

[6] Zhou Qingsha. The Review of the Integrated Management and Peace-keeping in Recent Years in Henan Province Construction [N]. *Henan Daily*, June 24, 2016.

[7] Liu Ruichao. The Report of the Environmental Status of Henan Province in the First Half of the Year, What about Your Hometown? [N]. *Henan Daily*, August 13, 2016.

[8] Li Xiaojian, Zhang Jintao. *The Advisory Proposals Set for the Coordinated Development of the Three Modernizations in the Central Plains Economic Zone* [M]. Social Science Literature Publishing House, 2016.

[9] Gu Jianquan. *The Research on the Implementation of the Innovation-driven Development Strategies in Henan* [M]. Social Science Literature Publishing House, 2016.

[10] Wan Shiwei. *The Research on Building the All-round Well-off Society in Henan* [M]. Social Science Literature Publishing House, 2017.

[11] Zhang Kan, Feng Qinglin. *The Research on the Social Development of Henan during the Thirteenth-five Year Planning Period* [M]. Henan People's Publishing House, 2017.

[12] Zhang Baofeng and others. *The Theory and Practice on Building the All-round Well-off Society in Henan* [M]. Social Science Literature Publishing House, 2016.

[13] Wei Yiming, Zhang Zhancang. *The Research on Sino- Britain Strategic Cooperation in Response to the Belt and Road Initiative* [M]. Social Science Literature Publishing House,

2016.

[14] Wei Yiming, Ding Tongmin. *The Research on Maintaining the Harmonious Social Order* [M]. China Legal Publishing House, 2015.

[15] Tu Xiaoyu. *The Research on the Social Integration of the Contemporary China* [M]. Henan People's Publishing House, 2016.

[16] Geng Mingzhai, Li Yanyan. *The Road to Achieve Modernization in Central Plains Economic Zone* [M]. People's Publishing House, 2012.

B.10 Report on Henan Cultural Development

Research Team of Henan Academy of Social Sciences

Abstract: During the period of the "Twelfth Five-year Plan", the cultural construction in Henan province has been moving forward rapidly: the tenth Provincial Congress of Party Representatives put forward the new target to speed up the construction of the national important cultural highland, issued and carried out the construction plan on the inheritance and innovation zones of Chinese civilization; the establishment of public cultural service system demonstration areas (projects) has been actively promoted, and the level of public cultural service has been continuously improved; the protection of cultural heritages has achieved remarkable results, and 16 historical and cultural heritages were included in the special planning on the preservation of large national sites in the "13th Five-year Plan". The construction of the intangible cultural heritage database has been well arranged in Henan province; the development of the cultural industries made new breakthroughs. The construction of a batch of provincial-level cultural industry demonstration zones, bases, and projects has been carrying forward, and the added value of culture and related industries maintains a growth rate of more than 12%; in the process of cultural exchanges with foreign countries, the Henan cultural soft power and influence has been strengthened constantly, so the cultural construction of Henan province stands at a new historical starting point. But relatively low per capita GDP restricts the overall investment of the cultural construction in Henan province, and the effective integration, protection and use of the cultural resources is yet lacking. The development of small and medium-sized cultural enterprises is still struggling, and the cultural creative talents are still in short supply. The subjective and objective factors, such as insufficient innovation ability of cultural industries, restrict the development of Henan cultural construction in different degrees. In 2017, in the face of quite severe development situation, Henan should adjust the concept of development, innovate the mode of development, optimize the development environment and perfect the development mechanism with great efforts, in order to prepare firm foundation for achieving a new goal at a new historical starting point.

Keywords: Cultural Highland; The New Starting Point; Development Trend

During the period of the "Twelfth Five-year Plan", Henan province has been implementing thoroughly the important policies of cultural development issued by the central government since the 18th National Congress of the CPC (the Communist Party of China), promoting the construction of culture. The Henan Provincial Party Committee introduced *Suggestions for Promoting Socialist Literature and Art* and *Plans for Inheritance* and *Innovation Zones of Chinese Civilization*, and put forward the development goals to "construct the national important cultural highland". Driven by a series of major polices concerning the overall situation of the cultural development, the cultural construction in Henan province has stood at a new starting point, and is speeding up. The "two benefits" are being promoted, and the leading and supporting role of culture has been strengthened, which presents a steady trend towards good development.

I The Basic Situation of Cultural Construction in Henan Province in 2016

1. Henan Cultural Construction Standing at a New Historical Starting Point

The year of 2016 was the beginning year of the "13th Five-year Plan", and it is also the key year to comprehensively deepen reform. Xie fuzhan, Secretary of provincial Party Committee in Henan province, put forward the goal of "speeding up the construction of the national important cultural highland" in the tenth party congress report. After the two periodic goals— "accelerating to step over from a big province rich in different types of public resources of history and culture to a strong cultural province" put forward by the 8th CPC Henan Provincial Party Congress and "speeding up the construction of a strong cultural province" put forward by the 9th CPC Henan Provincial Party Congress, Henan provincial party committee put forward this new goal on Henan cultural development during the "13th Five-year Plan", which marks the Henan cultural construction is standing at a new historical starting point. This goal is based on the vigorous promotion of civilization construction in Henan province, the constant increase of the provincial people's civilization quality, springing up of the high-quality cultural products constantly, the gradual perfection of the public culture service system, the development and growth of the cultural industry, and the escalating influence of the central plains culture. It is consistent with the goal of the national culture construction during the "13th Five-year Plan". It is also the intrinsic requirement for the construction of the inheritance and innovation zones of the Chinese civilization and the necessary condition for building a moderately prosperous society in all respects in Henan Province, which will have far-reaching influence on Henan cultural construction in the future.

The construction of the inheritance and innovation area of Chinese civilization, is a major cultural mission that Henan province, as a historical and cultural core area, must take, and is also the key for "building national important cultural heights". In September 2016, the Henan Provincial Government and Provincial Committee of CPC issued *Notice on Printing and Distributing the Plan about the Construction of the Inheritance and Innovation Area of Chinese Civilization*, which defines the guiding thought, basic principles, strategic positioning and development goals of construction of the inheritance and innovation area of Chinese civilization, and confirms to carry out five major projects, which are the construction of the cultural shrine of the same ancestor of the global Chinese, the construction of demonstration bases for Chinese cultural heritage protection and inheritance, the construction of national important cultural industry base, the construction of the new heights of modern cultural innovation and development, and the construction of the important bases for "Chinese culture going out".

All these have provided necessary policy guarantee for the construction of the inheritance and innovation area of Chinese civilization.

Table 1 Five major projects and key items of the construction of the inheritance and innovation zones of Chinese civilization

	Major projects	Key items
Major projects and key items of the construction of the inheritance and innovation zones of Chinese civilization	1. The construction of the cultural shrine of the same ancestor of the global Chinese	1. Songshan Forum 2. Cultural Garden of Chinese Surnames
	2. The construction of the demonstration bases of the Chinese cultural heritage protection and inheritance	1. Central China Folk Culture Museum 2. Central China Culture Museum 3. Central China Ancient Folk House Exhibition Park
	3. The construction of the national important cultural industry bases	1. Central New Film Chinese Cultural Industry Park 2. Central China International Culture Wisdom Port in Zhengzhou 3.The Innovation Demonstration Zone of Zhengzhou Modern Cultural Industries 4. Kaifeng Core Exhibition Area of Ancient Capital Culture in the Song Dynasty 5.The Area for Experiencing Cultural Tourism in Yin Relics in Anyang 6. The Demonstration Area of Experiencing Acrobatics in Puyang City 7.The Core Exhibition and Experience Area for Culture in the Three Kingdoms Period in Xuchang 8. Tongbai--- Red (Revolution) Tourism Area of Dabieshan Mountain
	4. The construction of the new heights of modern cultural innovation and development	1. Key Project of the Cultural Facilities 2.The Five Major Projects of the Humanistic Spirit in Central China 3.The Eight Major Projects of Internet Communication on Socialist Core Values 4. Cultural Complex project 5. Omnimedia Matrix of Dahe Newspaper 6.The Platform for Omnimedia Digital Resource Aggregation and Delivery
	5.The construction of the important bases for Chinese culture "going out"	1. Yu Opera Festival 2. Cross-Strait Heluo Culture and Yu Opera Development Forum 3.The Export Bases for Cultural Products and Services in Central China

The development goal established in the Construction Plan is "to finish basically the major items listed in this plan, and make the inheritance and innovation areas of Chinese civilization begin to take shape by 2020. Chinese history and civilization will receive effective protection and inheritance. The construction of socialist core values will be deeply promoted. The degree of social civilization and the citizens' moral quality will be generally improved. The power and vitality of cultural reform and development of the cultural industries will be significantly enhanced. The cultural industries will be developed and expanded further, and the system of cultural industries will be improved. The high-quality literature and art works will be constantly emerging, and modern public cultural service system will be established and perfected. The cultural market system will be developed soundly to improve the image of Henan province remarkably. Henan will become the major regional cultural center all over the whole country, and go in advance among all central and western regions in the construction of socialist cultural power." This development goal has the internal consistency with the development goal established by the tenth party congress of Henan province, which is to accelerate the construction of the national important cultural highland. At present, Henan province has launched recommendations and promotion for relevant projects, and the construction of the inheritance and innovation zone of the Chinese civilization is entering the substantive stages of implementation.

The remarkable achievements of cultural construction provided basic support for speeding up the construction of the important national cultural highland. The construction of public cultural service network in Henan province has solid foundation and has achieved remarkable results: two demonstration areas of the construction of the national public cultural service system have been built; one demonstration area of the construction of the national public cultural service system is waiting for inspection and acceptance;12 demonstration areas of the construction of the provincial public cultural service system and 12 demonstration projects of the public cultural service are being established. In the cultural industries, Henan province has been making great efforts to make superior cultural industry parks more extensive, make key cultural enterprises stronger, support small and medium-sized cultural enterprises, cultivate new cultural enterprises, improve the technological content of the cultural enterprises, continue to promote the construction of the provincial cultural industry demonstration parks, bases, and projects, significantly enhance the scale of the cultural industry and cultural industry benefits, and constantly increase the strength of the cultural industries, so growth rate of the added value of the cultural and related industries is faster, and the development of cultural industries achieves a new breakthrough. All of these built a solid foundation for the national cultural highland.

The six national strategies provided strong policy support for the construction of cultural highland. Henan province has six national strategic advantages: the core area of the national grain production, the Central China Economic Zone, Zhengzhou Airport Economy Zone, the Zheng-Luo-Xin National Autonomous Innovation Demonstration Zone, Chinese (Zhengzhou) Comprehensive Test Zone for the Cross-border E-commerce, Chinese (Henan) Free Trade Zone, which not only provide policy support for the economic development of Henan province, but also for accelerating the construction of an important national cultural center in Henan province.

2. Public Cultural Service Continuously Improved

The public cultural infrastructure has been escalating. In 2016, Henan province continued to increase investment and policy support in public cultural construction, strive to improve the technological content of public cultural infrastructure, strengthen the construction of software, and continuously improve service capabilities. Firstly, we continued to implement cultural benefitting-people projects deeply, open the public cultural service facilities for free, such as museums, libraries and so on, and actively build the demonstration areas (projects) of the public cultural service system, and took more initiatives to promote standardization and equalization of the basic public cultural service. Now we received periodical achievements in all aspects. Some cultural projects preceded orderly, such as The Erlitou Xia Dynasty Historic Site Museum in Yanshi City, the Central Plains Archaeological Museum, the New Theaters of the Provincial Art Troupes. Puyang City Library, Shangqiu City Museum and other major cultural facilities had been built up and opened one by one. Secondly, we continued to support the art troupes' performances and fine art creation, and to strengthen the protection of cultural relics, cultural heritages, and traditional villages. Thirdly, a large number of new sports projects for farmers and sports construction projects in villages and towns have been built throughout Henan province. At present, there are totally 158 public libraries, 205 cultural centers, 171 artistic performance organizations, 283 museums including 15 new private museums, 358 units of the national key cultural relics protection, and 113 projects listed into the national intangible cultural heritage. The coverage rate of the broadcast population is 98.43%. The coverage rate of the television population is 98.64%, and there are 10.6889 million cable television users. All year round, the total number of periodical publications is 88 million copies, the total number of published books is 239 million copies, and about 1.945 billion copies of newspaper are printed. By the end of the year, there have been totally 177 comprehensive archives, and 4.7278 million archives among all kinds of files have been opened. The construction of the digitization, informatization and networking of the provincial libraries has basically been completed.

Since 2012, the construction of the public cultural infrastructures in Henan province has been continuously improved, and the indicators have been steadily increasing. By 2016, all the goals set by the government had been basically achieved.

The establishment of the demonstration zones (projects) of the public cultural service system has been steadily promoted. The construction of the basic public cultural service system is an important component of cultural construction, and it is also an important part of adhering to the "five major development concepts" and promoting local governments to continuously improve the public cultural

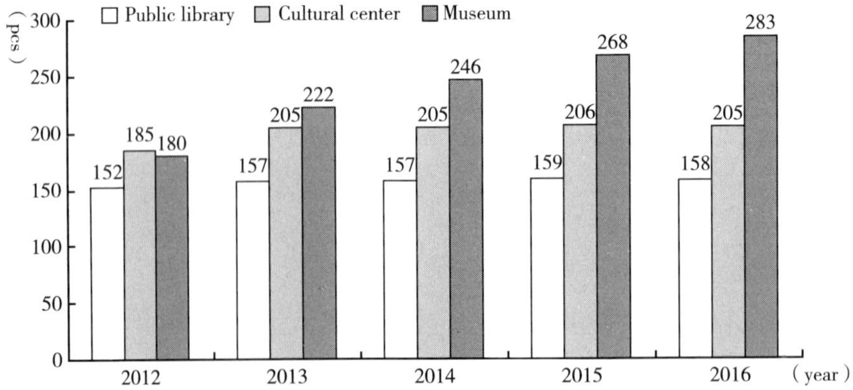

Figure 1 The construction of public cultural infrastructures in Henan province during 2012~2016

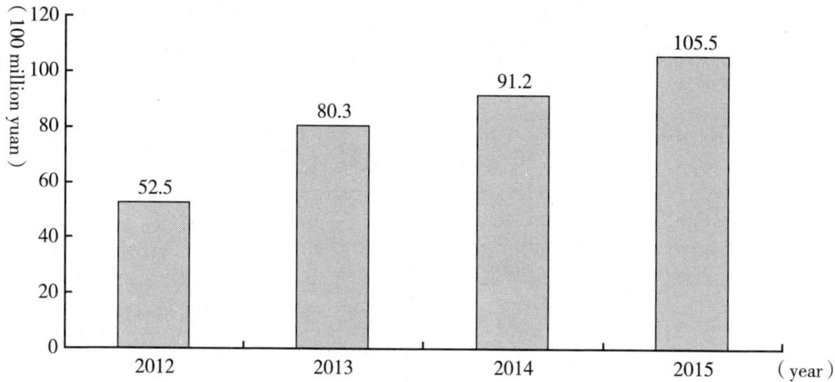

Figure 2　The expenditure of culture, sports and media in the public budget in Henan province during 2012~2015

service. In November 2015, in order to implement the policies of the 18th National Congress of the CPC and the 3rd, 4th, 5th Plenary Sessions of the 18th CPC Central Committee, Henan Provincial Party Committee and Government announced *Suggestions for Accelerating the Construction of Modern Public Cultural Service System*, and issued *Implementation Standards of the Basic Public Cultural Services in Henan Province*. Thus the construction of modern public cultural service system has entered into the accelerating stage. In April 2016, the Provincial Party Committee and Government held the conference to push the construction of the modern public cultural service system in Zhengzhou City. In June, three cities in Henan province obtained qualifications for the establishment of the demonstration areas of the national public cultural service system in Henan province, and six province-governed municipalities obtained qualifications for the establishment of the demonstration projects of the national public cultural service system. In September, the Provincial Party Committee and Government held on-the-spot meeting about the construction of the basic public cultural service system in Yongcheng City. The provincial government office also issued some policy documents, such as "the implementation suggestion for doing well the work of government procurement of public cultural services, "the implementation plan for promoting the construction of basic comprehensive cultural service centers", and set up special funds for the government purchasing public cultural service, which provided strong support from the two aspects of capital and technology. Now, there are four batches, a total of 48 demonstration zones and projects of the construction of the public cultural service system being established (Table 2).

Table 2 The list of the provincial demonstration areas (projects) of the public cultural service system in Henan

Selected time	Batches	Demonstration areas	Demonstration projects
December 2014	First batch (2014)	Huaiyang county Yongcheng Linzhou city Jianxi district of Luoyang city Gongyi Jiefang District of Jiaozuo city	1 Kaifeng city: happy weekend 2. Xinyang city: publicity of folk dance in southern Henan province 3. Hebi city: qishui parent-child story paradise 4. Anyang city: "321" public cultural co-construction 5. Huojia county: union auditorium 6. Pingdingshan city: cultural living room
December 2014	Second batch (2015)	Yancheng district of Luohe city Lankao county Xichuan county Lingbao county Nanle county Wugang city	1. Luohe city: "happy Luohe" 2. Xihua county: old area, new network 3. Jiyuan city: cultural auditorium 4. Zhengzhou city: international street dance competition 5. Jiaozuo city: firefly reading program 6. Sanmenxia city: impression of the swan city
February 2016	Third batch (2015)	Xinzheng city Laocheng district of Luoyang Xixia county Minquan county Huaibin county Xiping county	1. Pingdingshan: "jasmine fragrance" music concert in the eagle city 2. Hebi city: "Qishui garden" cultural construction project 3. Xinyang city: grid one-stop community culture construction in Shihe district 4. Jiaozuo: culture super market for common people 5. Zhengzhou: pastoral erqi cultural volunteer service in Erqi district 6. Ruzhou city: "internet plus local culture" project
June 2016	Fourth batch (2016)	Chanhe district of Luoyang city Xingyang Heshan district of Hebi city Fangcheng county Puyang county Tangyin county	Zhengzhou: "Tian Zhong" pulpit Sanmenxia city: the folk culture garden of the underground cave dwelling in Shanzhou district Kaifeng: hui culture micro pavilion Hebi city: "ten-hundred-thousand mass culture promotion project" in Shancheng district Anyang: cultural stage Yuanyang county: cultural benefitting-people information platform

In the process of establishing the demonstration areas (projects) of the public cultural service system, these cities and counties, relying on local geographical and cultural advantages, open up their own ways with local characteristics, which provides a realistic basis for comprehensive upgrading of the construction of the public cultural service system in Henan province. In August 2016, in the process of the project inspection and acceptance for the second batch of the demonstration areas (projects) of the national public cultural service system, Luoyang City was highly evaluated by the Ministry of Culture, because among the 72 acceptance indexes, 90% reached excellent and 100% reached standard. Luoyang City, with the reputation of the ancient capital of thirteen dynasties, has been persisting in the way of innovation and development, and actively exploring the deep integration of the traditional media and new media, the traditional cultural resources and modern service system, the traditional culture brands and modern concepts of industry. In respect of the supply of cultural services, cultural management system, cultural operation mechanism, the construction of talent teams, and the participation of all social circles, Luoyang City has formed its own characteristics in the construction of the public cultural service system, which provides reference experience for other provincial cities in Henan province.

The cultural projects for the public are constantly wonderful. The Finance Department of Henan province and seven other departments jointly issued the Implementation Plan of the Construction of the Public Cultural Service System in Poverty-stricken Areas during the Period of the "13th Five-Year Plan", have vigorously promoted the precise culture poverty alleviation, and actively strived for the central financial support to distribute the cultural facilities in value of 31.6 million yuan for the 38 national poverty-stricken counties, 1580 village cultural activity rooms, and 48 mobile library vans for the provincial poverty counties and 20 mobile culture service vehicles for the provincial poverty-stricken counties. Various types of cultural activities have been carried out consistently all over the province, such as "Opera into Campuses", "Sending the Stage Art to Farmers", "Farm Forum", "the Lecture Hall of Sinology in the Central Plains", "Knowledge Forum", "Happy Central Plains", "Cultural Stage in the Central Plains" and "Rural Projection Room", which let more and more people enjoy rich and colorful cultures. Taking Xinyang City as an example. In the first 10 months of 2016, 108 rural film projection teams had been dispatched, and 29,068 public welfare films had been projected, including 4,341 scientific and educational films, which had benefited 2,384 administrative villages, and 3.97 million people watched the films. All these provided leisure and entertainment for the farmers, popularized science, and improved the awareness of people. In this series of cultural activities, "the Lecture Hall of Sinology in the Central Plains" is particularly prominent. It has been carried out for ten years, and more than one hundred thousand people have studies on the spot, which has not only improved people's cultural and spiritual taste, but also helped people enhance the common understanding of values, so as to make a contribution to the construction of the Central Plains Economic Zone. National reading activities are vivid and dramatic. Some reading activities have enhanced the reading atmosphere in Henan province, such as "National Reading Month", "Children's Classic Reading Contest", "Autumn Poetry", "Poetry Festival", "Tang and Song Poetry Recitation". Anti-corruption and promoting integrity was an important part of cultural activities in Henan in 2016. In 2016, Henan Opera School launched the great work—Yu opera *Zhang Boxing*, part of "the trilogy of the incorrupt government culture". The previous two works are *Family Portrait* and *Bao Shizhao*. The Trilogy has been put on nearly 400 shows, and praised unanimously by the audience. In addition, the number of some play shows were added, such as *the Story of the Red Lantern, Jiao Yulu, Shi Laihe, the Village Head Li Tiancheng, Teen Heroine Liu Hulan*, *Yan Zhenchang*, and the film —*The Medal Carved in the Millstone* was also released.

The original fine works of art and literature had a good harvest. In 2016, taking the ideas of General Secretary Xi Jinping's speech at the symposium and the opinions of the CPC Central Committee on prosperity and development of socialist literature and art as guide, the Henan literature and art circles researched, formulated and implemented the Plan on Five Major Projects of Central China Humanistic Spirit, adhering to the socialist core values, and following the people-centered creative direction. They have been taking the creation and production of outstanding works as the central task, and have been launching a large number of original fine works of art and literature. As far as the opera, films and television are concerned, more than 70 plays (programs) have been launched, such as the Henan Yu Opera "*Zhang Boxing*", modern drama "*Jiao Yulu*", opera "*Cai Wenji*", dance drama "*Guan Yu*". Among them, *Jiao Yulu* won "Wenhua Award" in the Eleventh Chinese Art Festival, and Jia Wenlong, its leading actor, also won the "Wenhua Performance Award", which achieved the sixth straight Championship in the Chinese Art Festival and the fifth successive "Wenhua Award"; the opera "*Cai Wenji*" won the silver award during the Fifth literature and art joint performance of the National Minority; drama "*Jiao Yulu*", Henan Yu opera "*Chongdugou*", and Qu opera "the *Medicine Fragrance*" were also selected in the annual Fine project of the Central Plains Art Creation in 2016. At the beginning of December, the following films won the second prize and third prize respectively during the selection and discussion of the documentary films whose theme is "the Fifth Season of Humanistic China. Red Memory". The films are *The Eternity Of Jiao Yulu* produced by Henna Film Group, *Those Stories in Jinggangshan* produced by Henan Zhengzhou Education TV Station, *The Story of a Sharpshooter during the Anti-Japanese War* produced by Henan Energy and Chemical Industry Group, "*the Power of Faith—the Historical Apocalypse of the Revolutionary Struggle in Dabieshan Mountains* produced by Henan Xinyang Radio and Television Station. The movie —*Yang Jingyu*, with the theme of revolution and the military, co-produced by Henan Songxun Culture Communication Co., Ltd. and the August First Film Studio of PLA won four big prizes: the Best Film Award of the fourteenth Russian Military Film Festival, the Best Actor Award, the Candidate Prize in the twelfth session of the Sino-American international film festival and the New Actor Award. Three dimensional action film—*Escape Route*, whose production took three years by Henan (Zhoukou) Sanchuan Film Co., Ltd won three big prizes— the Best Movie, the Best Director and the Best Music Creation in the third San Francisco International New Concept Film Festival, which created a new Chinese film record. Micro film — *The Beautiful China in My Heart*, won the top prize in the13th Academy Award of Advertising Festival of Chinese College Students. *Light Life, My Mother in White Hair*, and *Hello! Mr. Tree* won big prizes in the First Central China Micro Film Festival. In addition, Xi Tongfa's *the Question and Answer of a Bird*, and Feng Jie's *Nine Pieces of Roof Tiles* were among the new outstanding works in 2016. The original Peking opera *the Ramayana* produced by Henan Peking Opera Art Center won the Best Famous Star Award, the Best Organization Award and three gold medals for performance in the third Vietnam International Experimental Drama Festival. The screenplay—*Going Home in Spring Festival* written by Cuidu, a young director of Henan origin was the first screenplay taking the female and highway as theme, which was titled "the Potential Screenplay" during the collection of excellent screenplays named "Xia Yan Cup" in 2016. As for literature creation, many excellent works won the second Du Fu Literature Prize, such as Li Tiancen's *the Human Relations*, Zhao Yu's *Our Spiritual Life*, Cheng Taoguang's *the Crane in Bule Sky—Liu Yuxi*, Gao Jinguang's *the Breath in the World*, and Wu Yuancheng's *the Character of the Flowers and Trees.* It is worth mentioning that the original network novel— *Back to Song Dynasty* written by Liu Fenghui (Gengxin) won the Network Literature Award, which is the first time that a young writer from Henan won the laurel. In respect of book publishing, *Fighting the beast --Nian*, the picture book published by Petrel Publishing House owned by the Central Publishing Media Group and *the Series of Books on the Famous Persons' Family Tradition* published by the Elephant Press were selected into One Hundred Outstanding Publications recommended to teenagers by State Administration of Press, Publication, Radio, Film and Television of the People's Republic of China (SAPPRFT) in 2016. *Series of books on introduction of famous Henan artists* published by the Elephant Press won the Excellence Award of Henan Publicity Promotion. A total of six works won awards: *The Major Department of Chinese Characters, Collections of Tingyun Pavilion* (a book of collections containing models of engraving calligraphy for learners to copy), *the Principle and Technology of Large-array Digital Aerial Photography, Twelve tone poems of Feng, Ya, Song, Xiaomei Learning Plays* and *Revolution of Publishing* respectively won the National Book Award, the Audio and Video Electronic Publication Award, and the Excellent Research Paper Award, the most in its history. In the selection of the twenty-fifth "Golden Bull Cup" excellent art books, Henan Art Publishing House won eight awards of four kinds, among which *the Calligraphy of the Republic of China* won the gold medal; *the Correction of the Complete Works on Chinese Tea* published by Zhongzhou Ancient Books Publishing House won the first prize of national ancient books collection.

3. Cultural Industries Continuing to Develop and Becoming Stronger

In 2016, we achieved new breakthroughs in Henan cultural industries. The added value of culture and related industries maintained a growth rate of over 12%, of which the expenditure of provincial finance in culture, sports and media has increased significantly over the previous year. The industries of culture, sports and entertainment completed 54.766 billion yuan in fixed assets investment, an increase of 47.6% over the previous year. Six enterprises, incuding Dengfeng E Po Shaolin Wushu Culture Expo Co., Ltd., and two projects, including China Shaolin Dacheng (Berlin) Health Center, were selected in the list of key enterprises and key items of national culture export in 2015-2016.

In 2015, the added value of the cultural and related industry in Henan province was more than 111.187 billion yuan for the first time, an increase of 12.9% yearly, of which the legal entities realized 100.551 billion yuan added value, an increase of 12.8% yearly, the growth rate of which was significantly higher than the Gross Domestic Product (GDP), accounting for more than 3% of GDP. There are more than 52,000 legal entities of the cultural and related industries all over the whole province, an increase of 35.71% over the previous year, among whom there are 7,410 enterprises for cultural manufacturing, with the year-on-year growth of 34%, accounting for 14.2% of the total number of the legal entities in the whole province; there are 8,853 enterprises for cultural wholesale and retail, with the year-on-year growth of 66.7%, accounting for 17% of the total number of corporate units all over Henan province; there are 35,840 enterprises for cultural services, with the year-on-year growth of 30.1%, accounting for up to 68.8% of the total number.

There are more than 2,718 cultural and related enterprises above the designated size, an increase of 542 over the previous year, ranking the seventh in the whole country, the first among the six central provinces. Among them, the number of cultural manufacturing enterprises are 1,006, 7.2% higher over the previous year, the number of units ranking the seventh in the whole country and the second among six central provinces; the number of cultural services enterprises has reached 1,072, with an increase of 15.3%, ranking the fifth in the whole country and the first among the six central provinces; there are 640 cultural wholesale and retail enterprises, with an increase of 57.4%, ranking the seventh in the whole country and the first among six central provinces.

In Henan province, the number of enterprises of culture and related industries above designated size has steadily increased. Since 2013, it has increased by more than 18% for three consecutive years.

The enterprises of culture and related industries above designated size have owned 286.757 billion yuan assets, 17.9% higher over the previous year. Among them, the assets of cultural manufacturing enterprises have reached 160.84 billion yuan, 11.2% higher over the previous year; the wholesale and retail cultural enterprises have owned 22.66 billion yuan assets, 3% higher than the previous year; cultural services enterprises have owned 104.607 billion yuan assets, with an increase of 34.5% over the previous year. The cultural and related industrial enterprises achieved an operating income of 317.969 billion yuan, with an increase of 16% over the previous year, ranking the eighth in the whole country and the second in the six central provinces. The operating income of the cultural manufacturing enterprises has reached 243.112 billion yuan. The wholesale and retail cultural enterprises have realized an operating income of 39.723 billion

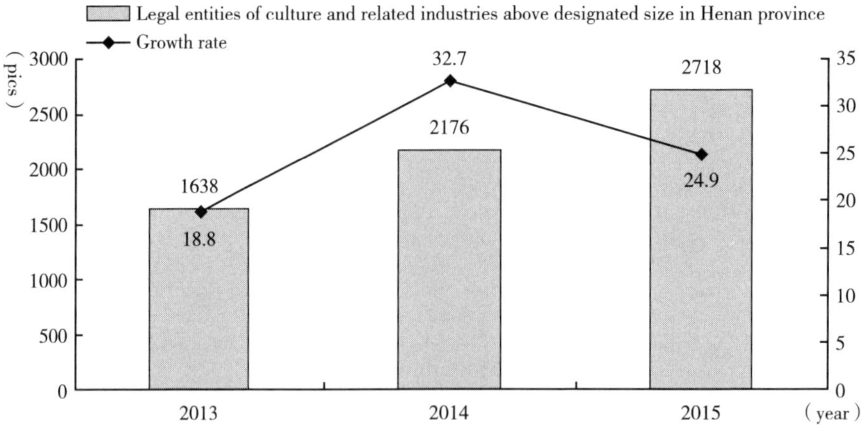

Figure 3 Information of the legal entities of culture and related industries above designated size in Henan province from 2013 to 2015

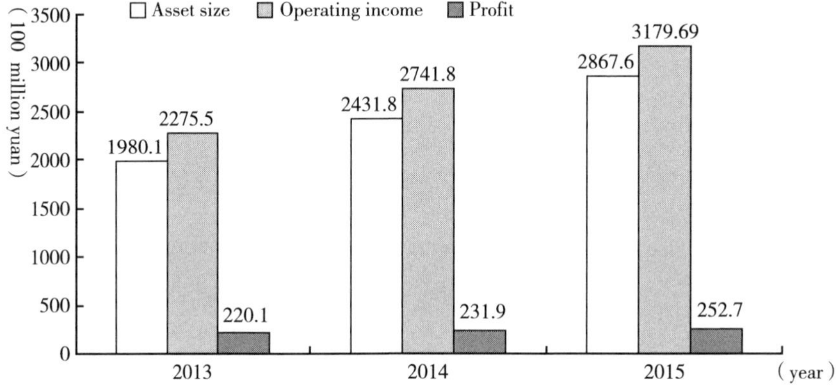

Figure 4 The development of the legal entities of culture and related industries above designated size in Henan province from 2013 to 2015

yuan. The operating income of the cultural service enterprises has reached 35.133 billion yuan. The growth of them is 14.2%, 14.3%, and 32% over the previous year respectively. By the end of 2015, the total assets of cultural industries in Henan province had reached 499.582 billion yuan, with an increase of 21.1% over the previous year; its annual operating income was 401.745 billion yuan, with an increase of 17.2% over the previous year. The number of the industry practitioners had reached 1.85 million, with an increase of nearly 110 thousand over the previous year, rising as high as 9.8%.

Table 3 The amount, growth rate and proportion of cultural enterprises in Henan in 2015

The number, growth rate and proportion of cultural enterprises in Henan in 2015			
Related categories	Cultural manufacturing industry	Cultural retail business	Cultural service industry
Number	7410	8853	35840
Growth rate (%)	34.00	66.70	30.10
The proportion (%)	14.20	17.00	68.80

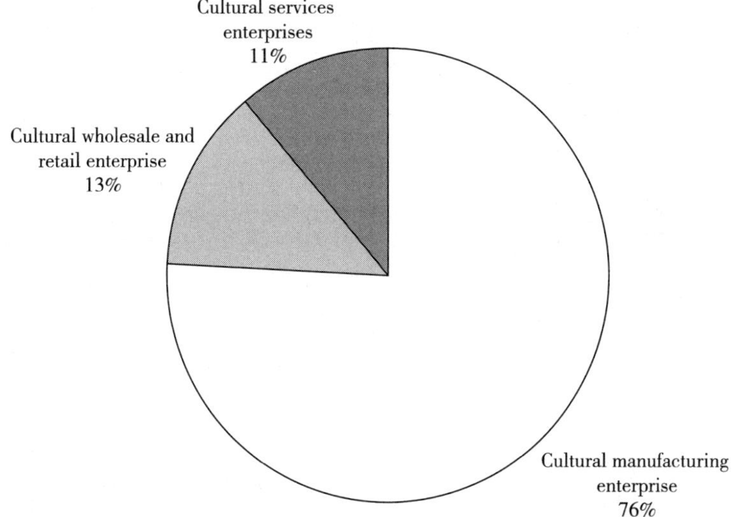

Figure 5 The proportion of the operating income of the cultural enterprises above designated size in Henan in 2015

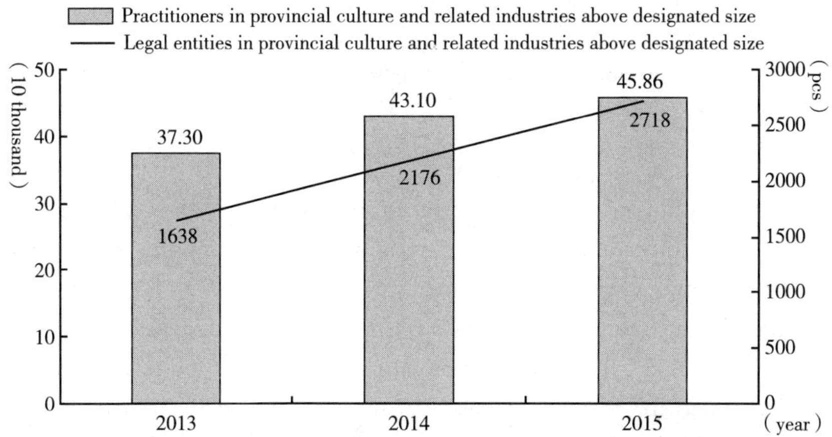

Figure 6 Information form of legal entities and practitioners in provincial culture and related industries above designated size

According to the increase of the added value of the cultural and related industries in municipalities administered provincially, in 2015, the top three municipalities were Zhengzhou City, Xuchang City and Nanyang City, with the added value of 28 billion yuan, 12 billion and 9 billion respectively. The proportion in GDP of the added value of the cultural industry in Xuchang City is the highest, and the proportion is 5.7%. There are 11 provincial municipalities whose growth of the added value was more than 10%. The operating situation of the cultural industries has been continuing to be improved.

Since 2012, the development of cultural industries in Henan province is very fast, the investment in fixed assets is very active, and the amount of investment and the corresponding increase are very obvious:

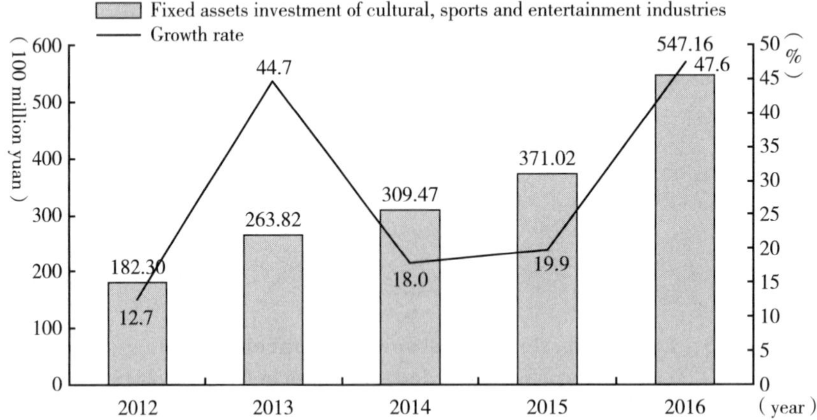

Figure 7 The status of fixed assets investment of cultural, sports and entertainment industries in Henan province during 2012-2016

Corresponding to the fixed assets investment in culture, sports and entertainment industries, the consumption intention and capacity of residents have also been improved, while the corresponding consumption price index is also increasing or decreasing at the same time.

The traditional culture industry had a good momentum of development. There were more than 458.6 thousand practitioners in the cultural and related industries above designated size throughout the year, an increase of 6.5% over the previous year. Among all practitioners, there are 34.9 thousand people engaged in the cultural creativity and design services, 23.9 thousand people engaged in news

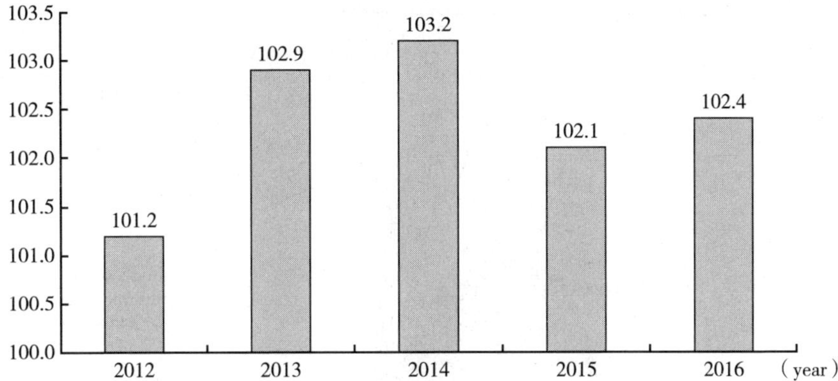

Figure 8 The consumption price index for entertainment, education, cultural goods and services in Henan province during 2012-2016

publishing services, 12 thousand people engaged in culture and art services, 11.5 thousand people engaged in cultural information transmission services, 6.5 thousand people engaged in the production of cultural special equipment, and 4.5 thousand people engaged in the radio, film and television service, with an increase of 22.1%, -5.6%, 30.1%, 14.4%, 9%, and 36.9% respectively. According to categories, the annual revenue of the cultural goods production reached 117.83 billion yuan; the production of arts and crafts reached 95.6 billion yuan; the auxiliary production of the cultural production reached 52.858 billion yuan; the annual revenue of the news publishing services reached 11.958 billion yuan; the annual revenue of the radio, film and television service reached 1.545 billion yuan; respectively, the growth of them is 7.5%, 21.6%, 19.2%, 2.8%, and 41.7% over the previous year, and all kinds of indexes have been steadily growing.

In 2016, the development of the publishing industry in Henan showed steady rise and promotion in key work, and remarkable progress in transformation and upgrading. Taking the Central Plains Publishing Group as an example. In recent years, based on the traditional publishing industry, it has been actively implementing the digitization and informatization of the content, resources, printing and publishing, and promoting industrial restructuring and upgrading. At present, the Omnimedia Digital Processing Group of Central China Publishing & Media Group has established multiple databases, and with the help of "the Belt and Road Initiative", digital content has been sold at home and abroad. In 2015, the total assets of the group were close to 13.7 billion yuan, the operating income was

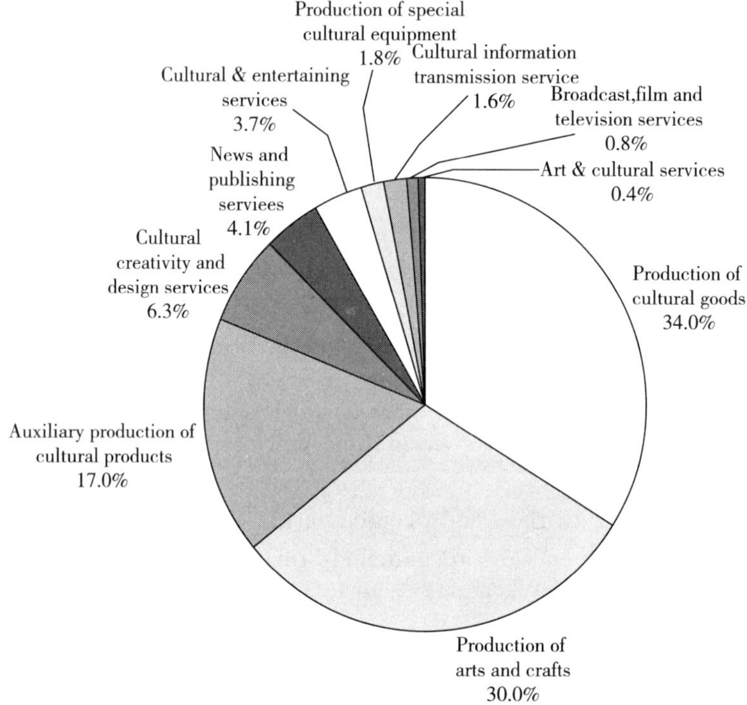

Figure 9　The proportion of the operating income of various cultural industries in Henan province in 2005

12.622 billion yuan, and the annual profit income was 649 million yuan. In 2016, depending on the strong industry capacity and stable growth, the group was listed in the eighth national 30 top cultural enterprises and the second session of the key cultural enterprises in Henan province, so it has become the only cultural enterprise in Henan province that has been selected as one of the 500 top service industries, which has highlighted its comprehensive strength and social influence among similar national industries and in the field of cultural industries in Henan province.

The new cultural industries have developed rapidly. In 2015, the revenue of the cultural creativity and design reached 17.221 billion yuan, and that of the cultural information transmission service reached 4.581 billion yuan, with respective growth rates of 39% and 50.8%. In the ten categories of cultural industries, the added value of the assets of the cultural and creative enterprises is the most, with the annual growth of 8.23 billion yuan, and that of the design services enterprises reached 4.463 billion yuan, ranking the third. Affected by the

"Internet plus" policy, the revenue growth rate of the enterprises in the cultural information transmission service is as high as 34.4%. In 2015, the profit of the cultural and creative industry reached 1.6 billion yuan, with an increase of 14.7%; the annual profit of the cultural information transmission services was 345 million yuan, with an increase of 32%. In order to promote the healthy and rapid development of emerging cultural industries, the People's Government of Henan province and the Culture Department of Henan Province have printed and distributed *the regulations about further supporting the development of cultural enterprises* and *several opinions on vigorously promoting the cultural and financial cooperation, the development of the specific cultural industry of the small and micro enterprises* and *the notice on printing and distributing implementation plan for the "Internet plus"*, which provided the highly targeted and strong operational solutions to solve financing difficulties and the shortage of talents in the small and micro enterprises. At the same time, we should increase efforts to support the emerging cultural industries and carry out the corresponding financial and tax credits. In April 2016, in order to promote the transformation from the advantages of cultural resources to the advantages of cultural development in Henan province, the Finance Department of Henan province issued 2016 annual project funds for the cultural industries to provide the main support for 30 items including the "Double Tens" projects (10 key cultural industry zones and 10 key cultural enterprises) named by the People's Government of Henan Province, the cultural industry projects with outstanding social benefits and the integration projects of the traditional media and emerging media, and for 43 projects of the new cultural industries which are related with digital creativity such as animation, network game, software design, computer special effects, digital media and film and television works. Among these annual project funds, there are 50 million yuan as the cultural industry project subsidies and 50 million yuan for supporting the new cultural industries. In the same year, Henan province received a total of 77.8 million yuan from the central special funds for the development of the cultural industries, part of which will be inclined to support the small and micro enterprises, not to make perfection still more perfect but offer timely help or support. In 2016, the People's Government Office of Henan province issued a number of policies to support the development of cultural enterprises and the transformation of for-profit cultural institutions from public undertakings into enterprises, which implements tax relief for the whole industrial chain engaged in film production and distribution, and support the film and television production industry at the stage of development. The provincial cultural work focuses in 2016 proposed to promote cultural transformation and upgrading, accelerate cultural integration of science and technology, and increase the related use of cloud computing, big data in cultural industries.

"Double Tens" projects of the cultural industries have been continuously promoted. In April 2016, the directory selected in the second "Double Tens" projects of the culture industries in Henan province was announced. There are six cultural industry parks selected as the key parks of the second "Double Tens" projects: Zhengzhou International Cultural and Creative Industry Park, Kaifeng Ancient Capital of Song Dynasty Cultural Industry Park, Xuchang Jun Porcelain Cultural and Creative Industry Park, Luohe Kaiyuan Cultural Industry Park in Yuanhui District, Zhenping County (Shifosi Town) Jade Cultural Industry Park, and Ruzhou Ru Porcelain E-commerce Industrial Park. There are 10 cultural enterprises selected into the key cultural enterprises in the second "Double Tens" projects: Zhengzhou Huaqiang Culture &Technology Co., Ltd., Kaifeng Millennium City Park Co., Ltd., Luoyang Daily Newspaper Group, Henan Acrobatics Group Co., Ltd., Xiangcheng Ruyang Liu Writing Brush Industry Co., Ltd., Xiping County Tangxi Sword Industry Co., Ltd., Henan Daily Newspaper Group Co., Ltd., Central Publishing & Media Investment Holding Group Co., Ltd., Henan Cable TV Network Group Co., Ltd., and Henan Culture, Film and TV Group Co., Ltd.

New progress has been made in the cultural and technological innovation projects. In order to promote the integration of culture, science and technology, the Science and Technology Department of Henan province launched the implementation plan on Henan culture, science and technology innovation projects in 2014. In April 2016, the Henan provincial Party Committee Publicity Department and the Henan provincial Science and Technology Department jointly organized selection of the first batch of demonstration bases for culture, science and technology integration, through procedures of application, recommendation, expert review and field investigation. In the end, six units were selected as the first batch of demonstration bases, including Kaifeng Ancient Capital of Song Dynasty Cultural Industry Park, Luoyang Hi-tech Industrial Development Zone, Puyang International Acrobatics Cultural Park, Nanyang Eco-industrial Park, Ruzhou City Ru Porcelain E-commerce Park, Yuzhou City

Cultural Reform and Development Zone.

The promotion platform of Henan cultural industries has been increasingly mature. In May 2016, Henan province organized a delegation to participate in the 12 ICIF (International Cultural Industries Fair) in China (Shenzhen), showing the modern cultural and creative products with the central plains culture characteristics, such as Wu Zetian's Gold Jian (the slips for writing), and the Central Plains Stone Rubbings. In addition, Henan has also taken an active part in the important cultural industries fairs at home and abroad, such as the great Sino-Russian cultural fair, and the exhibition of the arts and crafts in Taiwan, to enhance social awareness of Henan's cultural industries and cultural products. Luoyang Peony Cultural Festival is a famous cultural festival in Henan province. In 2016, the 34th China Luoyang Peony Cultural Festival received more than 600 merchants from all over the world. The total amount of contracts was up to 51.81 billion yuan. The third Central Plains (Hebi) Fair held in October 2016 has developed into the largest exhibition platform for cultural products in the Central Plains. There were 138 projects signed during the period, with an increase of 68.29% over the previous session; the total amount of all signed contracts reached nearly 9.9 billion yuan, with an increase of 13.71%. The amount of the spot transaction reached about 315.7 million yuan, with an increase of 29.10%. The most signed categories are animation projects. There are 23 projects, with the total amount of 628.92 million yuan. The growth rate of performance and art projects was highest. There were 13 signed projects, with the amount of 258.43 million yuan. The growth rate reached 36.30%. There were 14 projects involving cultural cooperation between the two sides of the Straits, with 204 exhibitors, which was the most ever.

4. Protection of Cultural Heritages Carried out Smoothly

In 2016, we achieved remarkable results in protecting the cultural heritages in Henan province. In the notice issued by State Administration of Cultural Heritage on printing and distributing the "13th Five-year Plan" about the major site preservation, there were 16 historic cultural heritages selected into this special plan, such as the Erlitou Site, the Shang Town Relics in Yanshi City, the Site of the Han-Wei Period Capital in Luoyang City, and Yin Dynasty Relics. Tai Chi Hall Relics from Han and Wei dynasties in Luoyang City was selected into the national top 10 archaeological discoveries in 2016. Since 2003, there have been major archaeological discoveries being selected for 14 successive years in

Henan province. In 2016, the following projects were selected into "five major archaeological discoveries" in Henan province: the site of Xuchang Man in the Paleolithic Age in Lingjing, Xuyang Cemeteries of Eastern Zhou Dynasty in Yichuan County of Luoyang City, the No.8 tomb of the site of Chengyang City during the Warring States Period in Xinyang, Tai Chi Hall Relics from Han and Wei dynasties in Luoyang City, tombs from Tang and Song dynasties in the eastern district of Gongyi City. In 2016, Henan province announced the seventh batch of units of the cultural relics protection, and a total of 327 units were selected, including 59 important historical sites and buildings of modern times, 149 ancient buildings, eight cave temples and stone carvings, 86 ancient relics, 26 ancient tombs, and one other unit.

In aspect of the protection of intangible cultural heritage, preparation, data acquisition and training for the construction projects of intangible cultural heritage database in Henan province has been basically completed; the related facilities have been basically established; data collection work is in good order and well arranged. Through the ongoing rescue and protection projects, traditional art projects among representative projects at all levels of intangible cultural heritage have been investigated, registered and established. Significant progress has been made in the study of cultural relics in Henan province. The key techniques for the swelling recovery of dried shrinked wooden culture relics developed by the Relics and Archaeology Institute of Henan province won the second prize of the Cultural Relics Protection Science and Technology Innovation Award in the "12th Five-Year Plan", which is a major breakthrough in the development of science and technology of cultural relics in Henan province, being the first of its kind in China. Henan Museum and Zhejiang Museum of Natural History co-sponsored the exhibition named "Life. Transcending — Animal Images in the Central Plains Cultural Relics", which won the Excellence Award of in the 13th Top Ten museum displays and exhibitions in China; Henan Cultural Relics Bureau won "the Best Organization Award" in the seventh exposition of museum and related products and technology; Henan Museum won "the Best Show Award". The complete volume of the portrait stones of Han Dynasty in Nanyang City compiled by Nanyang Portrait of Han Dynasty won the National Art Book Award.

5. Remarkable Cultural Exchanges with Other Countries

In 2016, Henan province achieved remarkable results in cultural exchanges with foreign countries. In the 4th China Art Festival held in Berlin, Germany, the local cultural performances from Henan province, such as Shaolin Kung Fu, acrobatic performances and folk art exhibitions, were well received; in the 3rd Vietnam International Experimental Drama Festival, the Peking opera--*Ramayana*, produced by Henan Province Peking Opera Art Center, won the Best Star award, three gold medals and two silver medals for performance, as well as best organization and leadership award, which has become the biggest highlight of the whole art festival; in Beijing Exhibition Month of excellent Yu operas, there are 23 sessions of the new and old Yu operas put on the stage in Beijing Chang'an Grand Theater and Mei Lanfang Theater, including "*Cheng Ying Rescues the Orphan*", "*Populous in Desert*" and "*Rainny Hometown*", which gained great success. Henan province successfully held many upscale cultural forums, such as the 5th Session of the Songshan Forum, Cross-strait Zhouyi Cultural Forum in 2016, the 14th Heluo culture seminars, the 10th International Forum on the Culture of the Yellow Emperor. The international cultural exchange activities play a significant role in enhancing Henan cultural influence. In 2016, Henan cultural performances were spread all over the continents of the world, the shows of Kaifeng Acrobatics Troupe in three African countries, Henan Shaolin martial arts groups in Palestine, the Mediterranean and North American, Henan Peking Opera Art Center in the United States and Taiwan, "the Joyful Spring Festival" of Henan Art Troupe in Central Asia, *Kung Fu Poems, Nine Volumes* in France, and a series of tours of *Cheng Ying Rescues the Orphan* in North America, which not only demonstrated the charm of Henan culture, but aroused local people's enthusiasm to learn the culture of Central China. In July 2016, the 4th Shaolin Kung Fu Class for African students sponsored by the Ministry of Culture recruited more than 100 students from over ten African countries. In August, the Henan Acrobatics Group bought the Branson comprehensive art center in the United States and established the acrobatics training and playing base in the United States, which became the base to improve the international competitiveness of Henan acrobatics.

The "going out" of Henan Culture made new progress in 2016. Central China Publishing & Media Group has been preparing to build Central Asia department of the overseas development center of central cultures in Kyrgyzstan, to promote the Central China culture to go out in the digital way. Henan Airport Satellite TV Media Company has been preparing actively to create the only overseas convergence media group, through which Henan province can join "the Belt and Road Initiative". Within only two years, "China African Movie Channel" established by Henan Film &TV Production Group has broadcast for more than 13 thousand hours, and its ratings are very spectacular, which has become a new window for Henan overseas publicity and the new platform for central China culture "going out". On the morning of October 14th, the launching ceremony of Henan Acrobatics Group overseas listing was held in Vancouver City of Canada, which has taken important steps to open up overseas markets. That is another milestone of Henan culture "going out". In the list of the key enterprises and key projects of national cultural exports from 2015 to 2016, a total of six companies and two projects in Henan province were selected, which have become an important carrier for the spread of Henan culture and have enhanced Henan cultural soft power and influence.

Table 4 The key enterprises and key projects of national cultural exports during 2015-2016

Key enterprises and key projects of national cultural exports from 2015 to 2016		
Key enterprises Of cultural exports	1	Central China Media Investment Holding Group Co., Ltd.
	2	Dengfeng E Po Shaolin Kungfu Culture Expo Co.
	3	Gushi Hengda Arts and Crafts Co., Ltd.
	4	Gushi Huayuan Arts and Crafts Co., Ltd.
	5	Huangchuan Yongjiang Feather Products Co., Ltd.
	6	Henan York Information & Technology Co., Ltd
Key items of the cultural exports	1	Dacheng Shaolin (Berlin) health center, affiliated to Dengfeng Dacheng Fitness Co., Ltd.
	2	Henan film and television production group's "China Africa film channel"

II Analysis of the Cultural Development Trend of Henan Province

In 2016, the CPC Henan Provincial Committee and government unswervingly promoted the steady growth, promoted the reform, adjusted the structure and improved people's livelihood. While keeping a good momentum of economic development, Henan province further increased investment for cultural infrastructure, accelerated construction of public cultural service system, and achieved remarkable results, which became a good beginning for cultural construction in the period of "13th Five-Year Plan". Led by the spirit of the 3rd, 4th, 5th, 6th Plenary Sessions of the 18th CPC Central Committee and the 10th Congress of Henan province, the cultural construction in Henan Province has been keeping accordance with the general requirements and the relevant arrangements of the "13th Five-Year Plan" of the central and provincial Party committees, aiming at the new development goal, implementing the new development strategies, promoting the construction of the five major projects about central humanistic spirit, promoting the construction of public cultural service system to a higher level, constantly improving the cultural market system and cultural industry system, promoting the rapid growth of the high-growth cultural industries, promoting the proportion of cultural industries in the national economy, and further enhancing the spread and influence of Central China culture. The construction of inheritance and innovation zones of Chinese history and civilization received significant results.

1. Cultural Policies Leading Henan's Cultural Construction into a Fast Development Period

In 2016, according to the spirit of the Party Central Committee, Henan province intensively issued a series of policies and measures to promote cultural reform, development and implementation. The cultural construction in Henan entered into a fast developing period. At the beginning of 2016, Premier Li Keqiang mentioned the new ten-year plan for the rise of Central China in the government work report; in December 23, 2016, the instructions on submitting the "13th Five-Year Plan" (Draft) for promoting the rise of the central region, which was presented by the National Development and Reform Commission (NDRC), was officially approved by the State Council. The State Council made it clear that the People's Government of Shanxi, Anhui, Jiangxi, Henan, Hubei and Hunan provinces must deepen the understanding of the importance and urgency of the rise of the central region, become more aware of the need to uphold political integrity, keep in mind the bigger picture, follow the CPC as the core of the Chinese leadership, act consistently with CPC Central Committee policy, link up the major projects, major items, major policies and the main task of reform with local economic and social development, work hard for deployment, improve the promotion mechanism, strengthen policy guarantees, and decompose and implement various tasks, so as to ensure the target tasks listed in the Plan to be finished in time. On December 6, 2016, the State Administration of Cultural Heritage, the National Development and Reform Commission, the Ministry of Science and Technology and other ministries issued the three-year action plan of "Internet plus Chinese civilization", in which the three-year development goals and four major tasks were put forward. That is to establish the sharing system of the antique information, to basically form the rules of the authorized management and protection of intellectual property rights by the end of 2019, to promote the opening and sharing of the antique information, to arouse the enthusiasm of the Museums to make good use of cultural relics resources, to stimulate the vitality of enterprise innovation, to perfect the supporting system of the development of industries, to make new contributions to meet people's multi-level, diverse spiritual and cultural needs, and to promote the cultural prosperity and economic and social development. In the same month, the Ministry of Science and Technology, the Ministry of Culture and the State Administration of Cultural Heritage jointly issued the plan for the protection of national cultural heritages and technology innovation of the public cultural service during the "13th Five-Year Plan", in which the general idea, the main development target, and major tasks and important measures were defined. Thus, it provided the policy basis for implementing the spirit of all documents of the CPC Central Committee and the State Council on scientific and technological innovation, cultural relics protection, the construction of modern public cultural service system, strengthening the protection and inheritance of cultural heritage and constantly improving the ability of public cultural services during the period of the "13th Five-Year Plan". In December 2016, 19 ministries and commissions including the Ministry of Housing, the NDRC, National Health and Family Planning Commission of the People's Republic of China, the Ministry of Education and other ministries jointly completed the establishment of the national urban system planning, and in addition to four cosmopolis of Beijing, Guangzhou, Shanghai, and Shenzhen, selected 11 National Center Cities: Tianjin, Chongqing, Shenyang, Nanjing, Wuhan, Chengdu, Xi'an, Hangzhou, Qingdao, Zhengzhou, and Xiamen, and defined their missions.

From the current situation of Henan's development, Henan is located in the center of China. It has the strategic position of "linking the east and the west, connecting the south and the north, and influencing all directions". It is also the leader and hub of the rise of the central region, and there is no doubt about its geographical advantages. In December 2015, the new proposal on formulating the "13th Five-Year Plan" for the national economic and social development in Henan province brought forward clear development goals of the cultural construction. These goals are that "public cultural service system must be basically completed, the construction of inheritance and innovation zones of Chinese historic civilization must make remarkable achievements, and the cultural industries must become a pillar industry of the national economy". In October 2016, the CPC Henan Provincial Party Committee and the Government printed and distributed the plan for the construction of inheritance and innovation zones of Chinese historic civilization, which defined the development goal and implementation method of the construction of the inheritance and innovation zones of Chinese historic civilization. On October 31st, Xie Fuzhan, the provincial party secretary, gave a report entitled "*Thoroughly Implement the New Concept, New Ideas and New Strategies of the Party Central Committee Governing, Strive for Winning the Overall Well-off to Make Central China More Colorful*" in the tenth Henan provincial Congress of Communist Party, in which some development goals were put forward: Henan province should transform from "one of four major provinces" to "one of four stronger provinces", and should accelerate the construction of an important national cultural highland and so on. These statements fit in with the new concepts, new ideas and strategies of the Party Central Committee, and fit in with the actual development of Henan Province, which was playing a huge role in promoting the cultural construction in Henan province. The "13th Five-Year Plan" for the science and technology innovation of Henan province issued in November defined the target of the science and technology innovation of Henan province, the ideas and measures of the innovation-driven development, and the every concrete work of science and technology. The Plan can be called the construction drawings of Henan implementation of innovation-driven development. As one of the key cities and the leading city rising from Central China, Zhengzhou has a new development opportunity, and the cultural construction in Henan province will develop at top speed with the rise of Central China.

2. Differentiated Management Promoting the Construction of Modern Public Cultural Service System

The construction of modern public cultural service system was the important content of Henan cultural construction. In 2016, in order to accelerate the construction of modern public cultural service system, and to further strengthen the government procurement of public cultural service, Henan province promulgated the implementation opinions on government procurement of public cultural services, and allocated 100 million yuan as special funds for the purchase of 21 public cultural services. The special funds were mainly divided into two types: the art development funds and the funds for government procurement of public cultural services, which was set up by the Finance Department of Henan province on the basis of the six previous special funds—"special funds for sending the stage art to farmers", "special funds for provincial art creation", "special funds for awards and subsidies for the county-level public cultural service facilities", and so on, together with an additional sum of 46.68 million yuan. While promoting standardization and equalization of public cultural services, the differentiated management was incorporated into the management objectives. Besides the purchase of public cultural service products, the government fully considered the differences of the service objects in terms of cultural needs, cultural consumption habits and cultural consumption conditions, paid attention to commonness and individuality of management, and solved problems that the single traditional public cultural service content cannot meet the cultural needs of the masses, overall service efficiency is low and the like, so that the construction of modern public cultural service system has become the real cultural livelihood projects.

3. Strengthening Mutual Cooperation and Promoting the Rapid Development of Cultural Industries

In the increasingly fierce competition of the market economy, taking the development mode of the complementary advantages, collaboration, and win-win cooperation is the correct choice for Henan cultural enterprises to survive and develop in adversity. That also promotes the rapid development of cultural industry in Henan province. The practice in two provincially administered municipalities, Kaifeng City and Luoyang City, has typical significance.

Since 2015, relying on the National Cultural Industry Demonstration Zone—the Cultural Industry Park of the ancient capital of Song dynasty, and centering on the goal of building an international cultural tourism city, Kaifeng City first presented the "culture plus" development concept, vigorously implemented the "culture plus tourism", "culture plus exhibition" and other special operations, steadily explored the new mode of the integration development of culture and economy, and has made remarkable achievements. In October 2015, in order to expand the tourism resources and cooperation space in the cities along "the Belt and Road", Kaifeng City, with the theme of new Silk Road, new tourism and new cooperation, proposed sharing of tourism resources, brand cooperation, and interaction of customer sources, and jointly issued *The Declaration of Kaifeng*--Tourism Alliance of cities along "the Belt and Road" with more than 30 cities in 17 provinces, cities, and autonomous regions, such as Shanxi province, Xinjiang Uygur Autonomous Region, Gansu province, which attracted wide attention at home and abroad, and opened the new path for innovative and united development of cultural industry in Henan province. In the first half of 2016, the total number of visitors in cultural tourism in Kaifeng City exceeded 25 million, with a year-on-year growth of 13.7%; the comprehensive income of tourism reached 18.72 billion yuan, with a year-on-year growth of 67.4%, and the cultural tourism industry has become a powerful drive for the development of Kaifeng City.

In recent years, closely centering on the goal of "Four higher levels in economic development, people's life, urbanization and ecological construction, one stronger ability of innovation, taking the lead in building a moderately prosperous society in all respects", taking Chinese civilization inheritance and innovation as the core, relying on abundant historical, cultural and landscape resources, supported by major industrial projects and brands, Luoyang City made effective attempts in key tourism projects, two major festival brands, innovative development ideas, promoting the industry integration, and enhancing tourism services. Since its cultural industry has been maintaining a strong growth, Luoyang City has been named the "Big Tourism City in the World" and "tourist attraction with cultural charm, and characteristic charm", and "well-known international leisure tourist attraction, " "Chinese outstanding tourist city" and "one of the ten top attractive cities in China". On November 17th, 2016, in the presentation about tourist attractions in Luoyang City of China Railway Tourism named "My Hometown in Henan. Old Imperial Capital", Luoyang Municipal Tourism Commission and Chinese Railway Tourism Alliance signed a strategic cooperation agreement to jointly build the high-quality routes of special trains for Luoyang tourism, stating that 50 tourist-dedicated trains will transport a lot of tourists to Luoyang City. On December 18th, Luoyang Cultural Industry Alliance was officially launched, sponsored and established by the Luoyang Cultural Industry Association, together with Luoyang Federation of Industry and Commerce, Luoyang Enterprise Association, Luoyang Association of Social Sciences, Luoyang Association of Returned Overseas Chinese and other units. It aims to integrate resource advantages of all associations, and to start all work with the idea of cross-border integration and united development. Luoyang City will be committed to push the optimization of the industrial layout as a whole, to enhance scientific and technological content and original innovation level, and to foster new cultural forms, which will make great contributions to the development of the agglomeration, conglomeration and scale of Luoyang culture industry. By the end of November of 2016, Luoyang received a total of 109.1655 million visitors, with a year-on-year increase of 9.44%, including 1.927 million inbound visitors, with a year-on-year increase of 14.92%; the total income of tourism was 86.886 billion yuan, with a year-on-year increase of 15.7%, and the cultural tourism industry has become an important part of the national economy.

4. More Colorful Forms and Contents of "Culture Going Out"

In 2016, the Cultural Department of Henan province actively built trading platforms of cultural industry, cultivated the effective carrier to publicize Chinese culture and the culture of Central China, and organized Henan cultural enterprises to participate in important trading activities related with cultural industry at home and abroad, such as the great Sino-Russian cultural fair, the exhibition of arts and crafts in Taiwan, and International Cultural Industries Fair in Shenzhen, encouraged and supported the Yu opera, song and dance, folk music, Kongfu, acrobatics and other cultural products with the cultural elements of central China "going out". In 2017, according to the important development goal on accelerating the construction of cultural center issued by the provincial Party Committee, cultural departments concerned must depend on the five national strategic platforms and numerous provincial exchange platforms to have a joint with major cultural projects proposed by the Cultural Department of China, such as the cultural innovation project, Internet plus cultural action plan, cultural big data engineering etc., give full play to the new advantages of Henan cultural construction, make use of activity carriers such as "Cultural Silk Road in

Central China" to promote the culture of Central China "going out", promote the culture of the Central Plains "going out", and continuously improve the Henan cultural soft power and influence with richer and more colorful forms.

III Constraints on Speeding up the Construction of Important National Cultural Highlands

In 2016, Henan cultural construction made gratifying achievements, but due to the large population, the per capita GDP and financial revenue was lower than the national average level, so the service of public culture still had much room for improvement. Effective integration, protection and utilization of cultural resources was not enough. The core innovation capacity of key cultural industry was insufficient. The development of small and medium-sized cultural enterprises was struggling. The potential advantages of cultural consumption of urban and rural residents were yet fully explored. Compared with other culturally advanced provinces and cities, there were many gaps and restricting factors on accelerating the construction of an important national culture highland.

1. Less Total Investment in Cultural Construction Restricting the Construction of Cultural Heights

Although the per capita GDP isn't the same with per capita income and living standard, it can reflect the investment ability and investment level in per capita income, living standard and social construction of a country or region, so it is often used as an important reference index of per capita income level, consumption level and the level of public cultural services. The economy in Henan has grown higher than the national average in recent years and the total economy has steadily ranked the fifth in the whole country, which shows the situation of "shifting gears without deceleration, increments with the improvement of quality", but the huge population, relatively extensive mode of operation and many uncertain factors affecting the steady economic growth made the development of Henan economy, society and culture complicated and severe, and there is still room for improvement in the urban and rural residents' cultural consumption and the public cultural services. *The Statistical Bulletin on National Economic and Social Development of Henan Province in 2015* issued by the provincial Bureau of Statistics and Henan Survey Group of the National Bureau of Statistics showed that by the end of 2015, the province's total population had been 107.22 million, including 94.8 million permanent resident population, and Henan Province's GDP in the whole year had reached 3.70125 trillion yuan, up 8.3% over the previous year. The added value of the first sector reached 420.956 billion yuan, with an increase of 4.4%; the added value of the second sector reached 1818.936 billion yuan, with an increase of 8%; the added value of the third sector reached 1,461 billion 133 million yuan, with an increase of 10.5%. The rate of the three sectors was 11.4: 49.1: 39.5. In 2015, the per capita GDP in Henan province was 34,939.38 yuan, which was 10.92% less than the national average value, and compared with the national per capita GDP of 39,222.39 yuan, there were still many gaps. During the "13th Five-Year Plan" period,, the most arduous and onerous task of building a well-off society would be in poor rural areas. There were currently 4.3 million poor rural population, accounting for 7.7% of the national poor rural population, and thus the task of combating poverty was very arduous; besides, the regional development level is imbalanced, so it will inevitably have a certain effect on the investment in Henan Province's cultural construction.

2. Insufficient Integration and Exploitation of Cultural Resources

The rich cultural resources in Central China are spectacular. In recent years, the government and the private have been fully aware of the value of this cultural gold mine, so they have invested a lot of manpower, material resources and funds. From the perspective of investment in cultural undertakings, in 2015, the national cultural undertaking cost was 68 billion 297 million yuan, and the per capita cultural undertaking cost was 49.68 yuan, with an increase of 16.5%. The cultural undertaking cost of the cultural units in the eastern region reached 28.787 billion yuan, accounting for 42.1%, increased by 0.5%; that of the cultural units in the central region reached 16.427 billion yuan, accounting for 24.1%, increased by 1.2%; that of cultural units in the western region reached 19.387 billion yuan, accounting for 28.4%, dropped by 0.9%. From the added value of cultural industries, in 2015, the added value of the national cultural industries reached 2.5829 trillion yuan, higher than the GDP growth rate of 2.3% in the same period, accounting for 3.82% of the proportion of GDP; the added value of Henan's cultural industry achieved 111.187 billion yuan, an increase of 12.9% over the previous year, and the proportion of GDP broke 3% for the first time. However, due to various factors, the effective integration, protection and utilization of cultural resources all over Henan province are insufficient, and the input and output are mostly less than the national average level. After all, these phenomena and other problems also need to be investigated deeply and solved properly, such as the inaccurate position of the local cultural development, the imbalanced supply and demand in some areas, the stereotyped local comprehensive cultural centers, the fuzzy geographical and cultural characteristics and the shortage of implementing cultural policies,etc.

3. The Development of Small and Medium-sized Cultural Enterprises Struggling

The small and medium-sized cultural enterprises are important forces to promote the development of cultural industries, and play an irreplaceable role in promoting the sound development of cultural industries. Although the overall development of the national cultural enterprises were basically the same, the development of small and medium-sized cultural enterprises in Henan province was still struggling. By the end of 2015, there have been nearly 50 thousand small and mediumsized cultural enterprises in Henan province, accounting for 97.5% of all operating cultural enterprises, taking in 388 thousand employees. No enterprise can develop without the support of funds and technology, so financing capacity and technological innovation ability is a common bottleneck to restrict the development of small and medium-sized enterprises. Because of the small scale, weak strength, more intangible assets, fewer tangible assets, long construction period, less obvious economic benefits, inefficient communication between cultural products and capital markets, and other factors, the small and medium-sized cultural enterprise in Henan province fell into the "disadvantaged groups", so there are more problems, such as the financing difficulties, expensive financing and slow financing etc., compared with those large-scale cultural enterprises that own bigger size and more investment. The development of the small and medium-sized enterprises has been struggling, which has become a major bottleneck to restrict the rapid development of cultural industries in Henan province. However, the shortage or delay of capital investment has seriously affected the improvement of technological innovation capability of cultural enterprises, which forms a vicious circle. Therefore, it is urgent to improve the investment and financing system of cultural industries, and to provide a strong support for the rapid development of small and medium-sized cultural enterprises with multi-level, wide-range and efficient investment and financing system.

4. High-Level Cultural and Creative Talents in Short Supply

If cultural and creative industries are new challenges, new opportunities and new issues for cultural construction in the new economic era, talents are the decisive factor for the development of cultural industries in a country or region. Since the 18th National Congress of the CPC, promoting the transformation and upgrading of traditional industries and the rapid development of high-tech industries has become the consensus of the central and local governments to adjust the economic structure and change the mode of development. But due to the influence of the incomplete ideas, policies, intellectual property rights protection system and other factors, some problems of Henan cultural and creative industries, such as the weak original ability, lack of strength in enterprises, the relatively more prominent cultural trade deficit etc., were still serious. Ultimately, it was because of the insufficient cultural and creative talent reserve, lack of high-quality and professional versatile talents. The shortage of high-level and versatile cultural and creative talents will become an obstacle to the construction of an important national cultural highland in Henan province.

5. The Cultural Core Industries Lacking Innovation Ability

Among the core elements of the cultural industry, the level of technological innovation is crucial to the cultural core industry. According to *the Rank of the Comprehensive Competitiveness of the Cultural Industries in 31 Provinces, Cities, and Autonomous Regions in China in 2010* exclusively issued by Creative Industry and the Cultural and Creative Net in June 2012, the comprehensive competitiveness of the cultural industries in Henan ranked 12th, which fell into the forefront of the middle level. In the two aspects of "related industries and cultural resources" and "government support and cultural supply factors", the scores of Henan province were higher, ranking fifth and seventh in the country respectively; but in two main factors — "the cultural environment and power" and "the market demand and innovation" which were the core of the development of cultural industries, Henan province relatively fell to the bottom, ranking the 2nd from the bottom and the 20th respectively, which apparently became the weaknesses of Henan culture. Although there were a lot of progress in the past two years, these weaknesses were still the key factors to restrict the development of cultural industry in Henan province. In 2015, the proportion of the added value of Henan culture and related industries in the provincial GDP exceeded 3%. Compared with 3.97%— the proportion of the added value of the national culture and related industries in the national GDP, there are still some gaps; compared with the Korean cultural industries accounting for 20% of its national GDP and American cultural industries accounting for 30% of its national GDP, there was considerable room for development. The reason lies in the insufficient innovation ability of the core cultural industry, the single form of the cultural products, low-level repeated development, art copy and so on. Because of the lack of the consciousness of deeply mining the local resources, the lack of high-quality original cultural products with differentiation and specialization, a large number of cultural resources can't be effectively transformed into the cultural capital, and therefore the industrialization, specialization and innovation consciousness of cultural enterprises need to be enhanced urgently.

IV Measures to Build the Important National Cultural Highland

"Speeding up the Construction of the Important National Cultural Highland" will be one of the "Three Heights" that Henan will strive to build in the next five years. As far as the cultural construction in Henan province during the "13th Five-Year Plan" period is concerned, it is both the direction and path, as well as encouragement and spur. Judging from the objective situation, the development situation faced by Henan province in 2017 is still quite severe, and it has a long way to go to build a cultural highland. To achieve the development goals of accelerating the construction of an important cultural center of the whole country, Henan province must increase innovation in the development concept and pattern, and further optimize the development environment, and mechanism to lay a more solid foundation for achieving new goals in the new historical starting point.

1. Adjusting the Development Concept and Adhering to Culture-Led Development

Accelerating the Construction of an Important National Cultural Highland is the timely response to the new concepts, ideas, and strategies proposed by the CPC on cultural self-confidence. It is the effective measures to spread the profound traditional culture in Central China, to advance and enrich the excellent humanistic spirit in Central China, to build the characteristic cultural symbols of Henan province, and to enhance the overall external image of the Henan province, and it is also another innovation initiative to promote the culture of Central China to go abroad.

First of all, we should further promote the humanistic spirit of Central China. In recent years, Henan has vigorously been promoting the construction of civilization in Henan, continuing to carry forward the Spirit of Jiao Yulu, the Hongqiqu Canal Spirit, the Spirit of Yugong Moving away the Mountains, the Spirit of Diverting the Water from the South to the North (the sprits of great determination and courage) etc., publicizing the Spirit of the Dabieshan Mountain and the Spirit of Diverting Water from the South to the North, which has made the humanistic spirit in Central China gradually deep into the hearts of the people. Jiao Yulu Executive Leadership Academy, Hongqiqu Canal Executive Leadership Academy, Dabieshan Executive Leadership Academy and the Education Base of the Spirit of Yugong Moving away the Mountains, Base of Xinxiang Advanced Group and Base of the Spirit of Diverting the Water from the South to the North are known as "Three Academies and Three Bases" in Henan province. Among them, Dabieshan Executive Leadership Academy pursues the school-running characteristics of "ideal and belief", and advocated the Spirit of the Dabieshan Mountain—sticking to the belief, keeping the whole situation in mind, unity and having the courage to be the vanguard; Hongqiqu Canal Executive Leadership Academy lays stress on the concept of the arduous struggle, and advocated the Hongqiqu Spirit—self-dependence, arduous efforts, solidarity and cooperation, selfless contribution; Jiao Yulu Executive Leadership Academy emphasized "the public servant consciousness of leaders", and advocated the Jiao Yulu Spirit of "loving the people, working hard, scientifically seeking the truth, facing difficulties and selfless dedication". By the March of 2016, the "three Academies" have held 2,380 training sessions for more than 151000 trainees. Advanced individuals and groups have been emerging, such as those figures in "Toughing China" and national moral models etc., and "phenomena of good persons" aroused strong applause in the whole society, all of which cannot come true without socialist core values and the humanistic spirit in Central China.

Secondly, it is necessary to create cultural symbols with Henan characteristics.

Henan province should deeply explore the characteristics of Central China, and cultural resources with Chinese style, strengthen the practical transformation of cultural resources, and make full use of art and modern science and technology to refine the cultural symbols with the characteristics of Central China. We should also attach importance to the important link of literary and artistic creation and production, and grasp the correct orientation from the source. The departments concerned should guide a lot of staff members in literature and art to implement the important spirits of the speech of General Secretary Xi Jinping at the meeting of national publicity and ideological work and the symposium on literature and art work, adhere to the people-centered creative direction, and accelerate the application of new technology and the development of high-tech cultural products, to create more popular cultural products for the masses of people. Henan province should strengthen the construction of cultural and ideological field on the Internet, improve mechanisms for public opinions guidance, optimize the ability and structure of media communication, bring forth new ideas to overseas publicity, cultural exchanges and trade, and build the Chinese opera, calligraphy, literature, character, Chinese folk art forms and other cultural symbols with Central China characteristics to further expand cultural influence of Central China.

Finally, we should continue to enhance the overall overseas image of Henan province. Based on Central China culture, Henan province would advance and enrich the excellent traditional culture in Central China, give full play to publicity, and cultural fields, make good use of the channels and carriers of cultural exchanges and trade with foreign countries, tell the stories of Central China well and spread the sound of Central China, so as to further enhance the cultural image of Henan province. Only by constantly cultivating more cultural images which show the characteristics of Chinese civilization and Central China culture, by preading "spiritual hometown, hometown in Henan", by strengthening a sense of identification and belonging with Central China culture, and by putting the party's new concepts, new ideas, and new strategies into practice, can Henan province further enhance attractiveness and influence of Central China culture, improve its overall image, and promote the construction of cultural highlands.

2. Innovating the Development Mode, and Constantly Improving the Public Cultural Service System

The construction of modern public cultural service system is an important part of cultural construction, reflecting public welfare duties at all government levels in the cultural field. In recent years, Henan province has constantly been deepening the reform of cultural system, continuing to implement the projects— "culture benefits the mass", and increasingly perfecting the public cultural network facilities. But compared with other provinces and cities all over the country, there is still much room for improvement. We should innovate the mode of cultural development, fully redeploy the enthusiasm of social organizations, and form a powerful combination of government, society and individuals to build a modern public cultural service system; as far as the construction of public cultural service system is concerned, it is necessary to pay attention to the hardware construction of the basic network infrastructure, strengthen the management and services to improve the quality and level of public cultural services, and give full play to existing network facilities of public cultural services. We would speed up the construction of the demonstration areas (demonstration projects) of the national and provincial public cultural service system, further perfect the system of public cultural services, and focus on regional coordination and the coordination of urban and rural areas, so as to let the masses share the achievements of cultural construction. We should also speed up building the supply system of public cultural products which is about planning production according to demand, further strengthen the pertinence and effectiveness of government's procurement of public cultural services, and improve the quality and efficiency of public cultural services. At the same time, the performance evaluation mechanism of public cultural services should be established, and the equalization, standardization and facilitation of basic public cultural services should be improved. Henan province will strive to achieve the development goal to establish and perfect a modern system of public cultural services by 2020.

3. Improving the Development Mechanism and Promoting the Cultural Industries in Henan into a New Stage

To promote the cultural industries into a new stage, we must further innovate the development mechanism of cultural industries, optimize the structure of cultural industries, and promote the development of cultural and creative industries and new cultural forms by major cultural projects. Firstly, Henan province will continue to deepen the reform of the cultural system, innovate and perfect the development mechanism of the cultural industry. Starting from policy support, investment and financing system, cultural production, cultivation of the cultural market and the cultural personnel training and other aspects, we will form the development mechanism to adapt to the modern cultural industry system and cultural market system, the innovation ability, the comparative advantage and the business environment of cultural enterprises in Henan province as soon as possible, so as to promote cultural industries in Henan province to the high-end; secondly, it is necessary to perfect the system of cultural industries, straighten out the internal mechanism of traditional industries, characteristic industries and new industries. Led by emerging cultural industries and supported by traditional industries and characteristic industries, the development of traditional industries, characteristic industries and new industries was in a good situation. Henan province has been supporting the key technology, the generic technology and the core technology in the cultural core industries, transforming the traditional cultural industries with new technology and new forms, optimizing characteristic industries, and upgrading new industries. In terms of research and development of products, and cultural business models, we will further improve the development level of cultural industries, enhance the competitiveness of cultural products to build the cultural industry heights with Central China characteristics; finally, we should strengthen the integration and development of cultural industries, modern science and technology, especially the integration and development of high-tech, such as the Internet, digital technology and cloud computing etc., strengthen the integration and development of cultural industries and other industries, especially the integration and development of tourism, leisure, design, experience and other industries, and expand the marginal effect of cultural industries; we will persistently implement major cultural projects, put major industries, major projects and key industrial parks, famous brands and backbone enterprises into practice and pay attention to the details to promote cultural industries in Henan province to make more substantive breakthroughs. During the "13th Five-Year Plan" period, the development of cultural industries in Henan province will be taken to a new level.

4. Optimizing the Development Environment and Speeding up the Construction of Heritage and Innovation Zones of Chinese History and Civilization

The development environment is the concrete embodiment of the degree of mind emancipation in a country or a region, the degree of the market development, the level of the government's managing ability, and it directly affects the prospects and growth potential of local development, so it is the invisible competitiveness and productivity. Centering on the strategic positioning for inheritance and innovation zones of Chinese civilization, *the construction plan of inheritance and innovation zones of Chinese civilization* proposes to focus on implementing the construction of the cultural shrines for global Chinese with the same ancestor, the important national cultural industry bases, the innovation and development projects of new highlands of modern culture, the demonstration bases of Chinese cultural heritage protection, and the important bases of Chinese culture "going out", which provides practical and feasible foundation to build the cultural highlands. During the "13th Five-Year Plan" period, based on rich local cultural resources, guided by the spirit of the 10th Provincial Communist Party Congress, Henan province will fully promote the construction of the five major inheritance and innovation projects of Chinese history and civilization. It is necessary to focus on creating a good environment for culture development, increasing the support in policy, funds, legal system, talents, environment and other aspects, optimizing the policy environment and the ecological environment for supporting the construction of the inheritance and innovation zones of Chinese civilization, cultivating the development environment in favor of building cultural highlands, and creating the market environment and the cultural environment to promote the culture of Central China to "go out". We should also improve communication, guidance, influence, credibility of the mainstream media, thus to promote the construction of the cultural highlands and enhance the influence of Central China culture on the whole country and the world.

References:

[1] The Outline of the 13th Five-year Plan for National Economic and Social Development of the People's Republic of China [Z]. The Xinhua News Agency Report, 2016-03-17

[2] State Administration of Cultural Heritage.the NotiDistributing the 13th Five-year Special Plan about the Major Sites Preservation(issued by SACH No.22 [2016] [Z].2016-10-31.

[3] The State Council's Approval of the 13th Five-year Plan for the Promotion of the Central Region (The National Letter [2016] No. 204) [Z].2016-12-17.

[4] Notice on the Issuance of the Three- Year Plan for "Internet plus Chinese Civilization" (Cultural Relics Letter [2016] No.1944) [Z]. The Website of National Cultural Relics Bureau, 2016-12-06

[5] The Department of Science and Technology, The Department of culture and the State Administration of Cultural Heritage. the Innovation Plan for National Cultural Heritage Protection and Public Cultural Service during the 13th Five-Year Plan [N]. *Chinese Cultural Daily*, 2016-12-14.

[6] The General Office of the CPC Central Committee and the General Office of the State Council. Opinions on Speeding up the Construction of a Modern Public Cultural Service System [Z]. Xinhua Website, 2015-01-15.

[7] The Guidance on Further Strengthening Cultural Relics Work Issued by State Council [Z]. Henan Cultural Network, 2016-03-09.

[8] The Proposal on the Formulation of the 13th Five- year Plan for National Economy and Social Development of Henan Province Issued by Henan Provincial Committee of the CPC [N]. *Henan Daily*, 2016-01-04.

[9] Henan Province Bureau of Statistics and Henan Investigation Team of National Bureau of Statistics. The Statistical Bulletin on Henan National Economic and Social Development in 2015 [N]. Henan Provincial Statistical Network, 2016-02-28

[10] Henan Provincial Government. The Thirteenth Five-year Planning of the National Economic and Social Development of Henan Province [N]. *Henan Daily*, 2016-05-18.

[11] The General Office of the People's Government of Henan Province. The Notice on Some Policies Issued in Henan Province to Support the Development of Cultural Enterprises and Cultural Business Enterprises (Office of Henan Government 2016 No. 98) [Z]. Henan Provincial People's Government Portal Website, 2016-06-14.

[12] The the Full Text of Work Report Given by Xie Fuzhan Announced in Tenth Party Congress of Henan province [N]. *Henan Daily*, 2016-11-07.

[13] The Opinions of Implementation on the Development of Socialist Literature and Art Given by CPC Henan Provincial Committee [N]. *Henan Daily*, 2016-06-14.

[14] The Opinions of Implementation on Further Strengthening the Cultural Relics (Yu Zheng [2016] No. 57) [Z]. Henan Cultural Network, 2016-09-18.

[15] The Notice on Construction Plan about the Inheritance and Innovation Zones of Chinese Civilization Issued by Provincial Committee of the Provincial Government (Henan Province [2016]32) [Z]. Henan Cultural Relics Network, 2016-10-27.

[16] The Recognition Bulletin on Recent Award-winning Films Issued by (Henan) Provincial Press and Publication Bureau of Radio and Television, See the

Documents of Henan Provincial Press and Publication Bureau of Radio and Television (Issued by the office of Yu PPB [2016]455).

[17] The Summary of Cultural Work in the Whole Province during the "12th Five-Year Plan" Periord[Z]. Henan Cultural Network, 2016-01-27.

[18] Henan Province Protecting the Small and Micro Cultural Enterprises [N]. *China Culture* Daily, 2015-12-30.

[19] The Central China Culture Wanting to "Go out" and also "Stay", *Henan Daily*, 2016-10-19.

[20] The 13th Five-Year Plan to Promote the Rise of the Central Region Approved by the State Council [N]. *Henan Daily*, 2016-12-24.

[21] Henan Province Bureau of Statistics and Henan Investigation Team of National Bureau of Statistics. The Statistical Bulletin on Henan National Economic and Social Development in 2016 [N]. Henan Provincial Statistical Network, 2017-03-01.

[22] The Summary of Work in 2016 Given by the Cultural Department of Henan Province [Z]. The Website of the Cultural Department of Henan Province, 2017-04-20.

B.11
Report on Development of Rule of Law in Henan Province

Research Team of Henan Academy of Social Sciences

Abstract: The 18th National Congress of the Communist Party of China started a new journey in the rule of law construction in our country. In the past five years, the rule of law construction in Henan improved steadily with the sustainable development: fields of legislation were pushed forward, law enforcement became stricter, judiciary reform was rolled out, and the rule of law culture became stronger. At the same time, in the face of endless social problems and growing demands of the masses, Henan is shouldering more arduous tasks and greater missions in the rule of law construction: legislative quality needs to be further improved, the rule of law government construction is to be highlighted, the judiciary reform is to be put forward, and people's law-abiding awareness should be normalized. On the way to the rule of law construction, Henan needs to march step by step with perseverance, comprehensiveness, and emphasis. Only when Henan becomes a really strong province under the rule of law, and the cornerstone of the rule of law in the Central Plains is solid and forceful, will our economic and social development stride forward faster.

Keywords: Governing the Province in Accordance with the Law; the Rule of Law Construction; Scientific Legislation; Judiciary Reform; Henan Province

Over the past five years, the rule of law construction in Henan has developed fast with great endeavour, and Henan comprehensively and soundly carried out the policy of governance by law and the judiciary reform step by step. In the past five years, the party committees and governments at all levels in Henan have seriously implemented the strategic thought of governing the country according to the law put forward by the central committee of the party with comrade Xi as the core. With the spirit of "dare to face toughness", Henan reformed with keen determination and took a series of measures to muster the rule of law power escorting Henan's economic and social development, so as to lay the foundation of the rule of law for playing well the "four cards" (Optimization and Upgrading of Industrial Structure; Innovation-driven Development; Infrastructure Construction; New-type Urbanization) and to make the central plains of China more excellent.

I Basic Situation and Main Characteristics of the Rule of Law in Henan since the 18th National Congress of the CPC

Since the 18th National Congress of the CPC, local legislation reform and development in Henan have been more closely linked. Governments' law enforcement in key areas has been more rigorous, judiciary justice has paid more attention to people's livelihood, and rule of law publicity activities have been carried out comprehensively centering on the overall situation. As a result, the atmosphere of the rule of law has been richer, law studies and exchanges with foreign countries have helped each other forward, law research results have been more substantial, and the platform effect of law has been more obvious. Achievements in every field present the tension of the rule of law, which help promote the rule of law construction in Henan to a higher goal.

1. Sticking to Legislation First, and Promoting Comprehensive Provincial Governance by Law

(1) Legislation is Always Centered on Major Issues in the Reform and Development

Over the past five years, we keenly and continuously explored coordinated development of new industrialization, new urbanization, and agricultural modernization in the process of informationization. We prioritize empowering cities with districts to make laws, and legislation survey of undertakings related to people's livelihood. We actively implemented the anti-corruption work deployment from the central and provincial party committee. The standing committee of Provincial People's Congress reviewed and passed work regulations to prevent duty-related crimes. From the above activities, it can be seen that the National People's Congress and its standing committee of Henan province performed duties endowed by the constitution and the law and took scientific development as priority in their work. Our legislation is always centred on the major issues in reform and development, and we actively carry out the legislative work in key areas, and strive to improve the quality of legislation.

In 2013, related departments of Henan People's Congress Standing Committee put forward the *Local Legislation Plan of Henan People's Congress Standing Committee from 2014 to 2018* (Draft) on the basis of opinions from various aspects. Social hot issues were emphasized in legislation taking Henan reality into account. Henan formulated *Regulations on Enterprise Salary Collective Negotiation in Henan Province*, *Regulations on Non-tax Income Management of Henan Government*, *Regulations on Social Emergency Medicine in Zhengzhou City*, *Regulations on Toad Traffic Safety in Luoyang City* (Revised), *Regulations on the Protection of Intangible Cultural Heritage in Henan Province*, *Regulations on Protection of Yuntai Mountain Scenic Spot in Henan Province*, and *Regulations on Reducing Pollutant Discharge in Henan Province*, etc. In 2014, Henan People's Congress Standing Committee passed *Regulations on Civil Transport Airport Management in Henan Province*, *Implementation of Soil and Water Conservation Law of People's Republic in Henan Province, Decisions on Strengthening the Control Work of Tuberculosis Made by Henan People's Congress Standing Committee*, *Fire Control Regulation in Henan* (Revised), *The Population and Family Planning Regulation of Henan Province* (Revised), *Regulations on Decisions on Major Matters of Henan Province People's Congress Standing Committee* (Revised), *Regulations on Conscription Work in Henan Province* (Revised), *Regulations on Statistical Management in Henan Province (Revised)*. Besides these eight pieces of regulations, the Standing Committee also issued other legal resolutions. In 2015, Henan local legislation body initiated the formulation of regulations on the protection of high-standard arable land, clarifying responsibility in land planning, construction, and management of governments at all levels; *Regulations on Development and Application of New Walling Materials in Henan Province* was deliberated and passed to prescribe developing principles, supervision and management of new wall materials; Preliminary examination of *Regulations on Tourism in Henan Province (Revised Draft)* was carried out; Regulations on wetland protection and radiation pollution prevention were formulated with a view to accelerating the "Beautiful Henan Project". In 2016, in order to meet the requirements of reform in the administrative examination and approval system, related content in local rules and regulations were reviewed and cleaned up comprehensively, and relevant provisions in ten laws and regulations, including rules on coal, regulations on metrological supervision and management, and regulations on tobacco monopoly management, were modified. At the same time, in order to continuously promote streamline administration and institute decentralization, and to delegate power and strengthen regulation, administrative examination and approval of coal production licenses, special licenses for tobacco monopoly businesses and imported measuring instruments were subsequently cancelled. Meanwhile, to promote stricter administration according to law, and to make law enforcement standard and fair, legal responsibilities resulting from uncivilized law enforcement was prescribed in the regulations. The provincial standing committee revised the fining threshold set by original regulations, from 30,000 yuan to 50,000 yuan, to solve the problem of low administrative fines, and low cost of law violation. In particular, fine maximum for violation of public safety, personal property safety, ecological environment protection, limited resources development and utilization were raised up to 200,000 yuan. After revision, the deterring and retribution function in laws and regulations was strengthened and the arbitrariness of punishment was also effectively prevented.

(2) Scientific Legislation, and Democratic Legislation were Pushed Forward

Since the Third Plenary Session of the 18th CPC National Congress, Henan People's Congress Standing Committee has continuously perfected legislation systems and mechanisms and made legislative norms more scientific, to improve the quality of legislation and utility. Firstly, the leading role of legislation of National People's Congress was strengthened. In the process of drafting and reviewing the draft regulations, National People's Congress in Henan played an increasingly important role in overall coordination and comprehensive guidance. In the face of some major controversies, Henan People's Congress Standing Committee first fully listened to the opinions of the drafting unit and main related parties of interests, then held director's meetings to study and reach consensus. As for those laws and regulations with complex legal relationships and high social concern, such as *Property Management Regulations*, it's imperative to have strict assessment, public bidding and introduction of draft laws and regulations from a third party, in order to prevent the legalization of departmental interests. Secondly, the research and practice of legislation are reinforced. Taking the legislation of air pollution as an example, in 2014, Henan People's Congress Standing Committee set up a research group to inspect law enforcement of *Air Pollution Prevention Law* and listened to special reports about the prevention and control of air pollution by provincial government and related departments. In this way, the National People's Congress in Henan promoted the implementation of laws, regulations and policies about prevention and control of air pollution all over the province; In 2016, the National People's Congress in Henan held systematic research to revise regulations for the control of air pollution. Thirdly, the orderly participation scope in legislation was further expanded. We continuously completed collection mechanism of public opinions. When soliciting opinions about the draft laws and regulations, we took many effective measures such as holding hearings, forums to encourage the free airing of views, and to listen to different voices. Thus, any draft law and regulation and its explanations must be published on the Internet, and any important draft laws and regulations must be promptly sent to representatives for advice. At the same time, legislative expert database was constantly perfected. Relevant experts and scholars invited actively participated in the modification of draft regulations, further explored and established a service base of local legislation assessment and advice, focusing on recruiting full-time and part-time legislation personnel, so as to strengthen and amplify work power and intellectual support of local legislation.

(3) Prioritizing the Empowerment of Cities with Districts to Make Laws

After the Fourth Plenary Session of the 18th CPC National Congress, Henan actively implemented the legislation empowerment of cities divided into districts, carried out surveys about legislation related to people's livelihood, and set out a timetable for local law-making of 15 cities with districts in two batches. At present, all cities with districts in Henan have local legislative power, which opened a new chapter in Henan's democracy and rule of law. For those cities with districts without experience in legislation, their legislative content and legislative process, are undoubtedly the common focus of the public and municipal leaders. The provincial standing committee realized the importance of this work, so they gave more timely work instructions, tracked down the whole working process, and promoted strict censorship in work procedures, which opened a new page in the legislative work of cities with districts in our province. Firstly, more attention was paid to the legislative training. Two large-scale legislation practical trainings were organized, to explain the spirit of the National People's Congress conference about legislative work and new changes of the legislation law and local legislation technology. Secondly, actively participating in the legislative work in cities with districts. While focusing on the legitimacy issue of the draft laws and regulations made by cities with districts, we gave them guidance on norms of legislative technology, pertinence and operability, to help them improve work ability and the level of legislation as soon as possible. Thirdly, researching and formulating working opinions on the examination and approval of local laws and regulations in cities with districts. Henan People's Congress Standing Committee maintained legality as the working principle, focusing its work on examining whether the laws and regulations submitted for approval conflict with a higher ranking law, and whether they are beyond the legislative power. In 2016, a wide range of laws and regulations appeared in approved cities with districts, covering areas including management of environmental health, protection of history and culture, protection of traditional villages and ecological city construction. The newly formulated laws and regulations not only conform to the spirit of Legislation Law, but also reflect the local characteristics and provide a propelling role in the city's economic and social development in accordance with the law.

At the same time, the National People's Congress and its standing committee of Henan province formulated *Measures for State Functionaries to Pledge Allegiance to Constitution in Henan Province*, which stipulates that after January 1, 2016, all state functionaries, elected or appointed by Provincial People's Congress and its standing committee or by Henan government, Henan People's Court, and Henan People's Procuratorate, need to swear an oath to uphold the Constitution. On the basis of situations of comprehensively deepening reforms in Henan and with the approval of the provincial party committee, the Five-year Plan of legislation by the standing committee was adjusted, and 14 new legislative programs were added. We will work to practically innovate the work of the Provincial People's Congress, strengthen legislation mechanism led by Provincial People's Congress with orderly participation of its representatives and all social parties, and improve work assigned from deliberations of the standing committee members. Our aim is to provide strong systematic supports for comprehensively deepening reforms, by pushing people's congress system to keep pace with the times.

2. Strengthening the Service Tenet, and Taking Thorough Steps to Promote Law-based Government Construction

Since the 18th National Congress of the CPC, governments at all levels in Henan have adhered to the tenet of serving the people, have had a firm grip on the responsibility system of administrative law enforcement and on the construction of a service-oriented administrative law enforcement, and have taken "six changes" as key points, to promote administration by law, so as to strengthen supervision by law, and to improve law-based government construction.

(1) Strictly Implementing the Responsibility System of Administrative Law Enforcement

Since the 18th National Congress of the CPC, governments at all levels in Henan have completed the responsibility system of administrative law enforcement, and have made remarkable achievements in strengthening the management of administrative law enforcement, and in the standardization of administrative law enforcement behavior. The general office of Henan provincial government timely issued *Opinions of the Comprehensive Implementation of the Responsibility System of Administrative Law Enforcement* ([2015] No.42) to ensure the implementation of various measures; *Notice to Build Supervision System of Comprehensive Implementation of the Responsibility System of Administrative Law Enforcement* (Administrative Office by Law ([2015] No.87) was promulgated to ensure full implementation of the responsibility system of the administrative law enforcement relying on a supervision platform. In order to promote the filing and review of major administrative punishments, *Regulations on Filing and Review of Major Administrative Punishments in Henan Province* (Government Order No.168) took effect from July 1, 2015.Administrative punishment discretion in Henan governments at all levels was further standardized. A batch of pilot work on compulsory administrative discretion and administrative licensing discretion was carried out; The revision work of administrative law enforcement documents was carried out, which laid a foundation for further format standardization of administrative law enforcement documents. Administrative organs at all levels conscientiously responded to reports of supervision and complaints about administrative law enforcement, strived to handle cases actively, and investigated problems and traced responsibilities of units and personnel concerned, in strict accordance with *Regulations on*

Responsibility Investigation of Administrative Law Enforcement in Henan Province (Trial Implementation).Taking Xinyang city as an example, the city government issued *Interim Procedures of Supervising Administrative Law Enforcement*, clarifying the specific content, ways and methods to carry out the supervision and inspection of administrative law enforcement, and promoting the routinization of law enforcement supervision and inspection. At the same time, the city took annual inspection of administrative law enforcement certification and its supervision work as an opportunity to establish the city's administrative law enforcement personnel database and paper files, focusing on strengthening dynamic management of main body qualifications in law enforcement.

(2) Continued Progress Made in Service-oriented Administrative Law Enforcement

In 2015, The general office of Henan people's government issued *Notice to Promote Construction of a Service-oriented Administrative Law Enforcement* in 2015 ([2015] No.38).The provincial administrative law enforcement departments focused on promoting service-oriented administrative law enforcement within their own systems. *Notice to Establish Four Work Regulations (Trial Implementation) to Push Ahead Service-oriented Administrative Law Enforcement in Henan* was issued, to build a long-term mechanism of service-oriented administrative law enforcement. In March, the provincial government organized observation activities concerning construction of service-oriented administrative law enforcement for departments concerned, which greatly enhanced their capability and levels of construction of a service-oriented administrative law enforcement system. At the same time, in line with their responsibilities and realities within their own systems, these departments made work plans with detailed measures, and promoted construction of the service-oriented administrative law enforcement in a solid and effective way. On the basis of the development of situation, construction of law-based governments in Henan required strengthening administrative assessment by law. Law-based government construction indicator system and assessment standards were established based on scientific researches, with complete assessing contents, clear assessing procedures and innovated assessing methods, as well as an increased proportion of daily assessment scores. The assessment results will be used effectively as an important content to judge the work of leading groups and leading cadres at all levels and will be taken as part of the performance appraisal indicator system. The usage of assessment results should be normalized.

(3) Gradually Establishing a Long-term Mechanism of Law Enforcement

In July 2016, Henan launched a battle against atmospheric pollution, on the basis of pollution treatment in accordance with the law, and a series of harsh measures were taken to renovate enterprises with heavy pollution and small, scattering businesses with poor sanitation conditions and air pollution in key industries and fields. To achieve the environment law enforcement effect, Henan actively established long-term effective mechanism of environment law enforcement, and formulated accountability mechanism for damage of ecological environment and the ecological compensation mechanism for air quality. At the same time, in terms of comprehensive management of soil and water, Henan did effective work in the construction of forestry, stopped the commercial deforestation comprehensively, and planted 3.21 million acres of forests. So far, we have fostered 4.83 million acres of forest that protect the ecological zone on either side of the main canal for the middle line of the south-to-north water transfer project. In recent years, the management and standardization of the key industries in Henan were further strengthened, and crackdown efforts on illegal violations were maintained. There were not many major and extraordinarily serious accidents, fire accidents, or safety accidents in production. The reform of handling complaints made by letter or in person was pushed forward further. By focusing on the handling of large-scale complaints, the legitimate rights and interests of the public were preserved, and the number of illegal level-skipping complaints obviously reduced.The rule of law publicity and legal aid were further enhanced, and more progress were made in public order management. Through cracking down on illegal and criminal activities and violence, people felt more secure and became more satisfied.

3. Striving to Enhance Judicial Credibility, and Extending Judicial Reform to the Full

The purpose of the rule of law is to achieve freedom, equality and justice. The process of modern rule of law is to a process to maintain equality, freedom, and to carry forward justice. Since the 18th National Congress of the CPC, Henan judicial organs worked closely around the aim of “striving to make the people get justice in every judicial case”, always adhered to principles of judicature for the people, judicial justice, and faithful performance of duties given by the Constitution and laws, gave full play to judicial and legal supervision functions, and made thorough efforts to serve economic and social development in Henan. Judiciary reform in Henan, starting from handling of administrative cases across administrative areas, reform of people's juror system, and quick trial of criminal cases, will be extended to the full.

(1) Actively Implementing Case-filing Register System

As of May 1, 2015, facing the increasing pressure of growing number of cases cases and lack of judges, courts in Henan resolutely implemented instructions from the central government and the Supreme Court, and fully carry out registration system, and open the door to cases. They received complaints and put them on record as long as the law suits were valid. If the materials applicants provide are not complete, we will inform them of all the details once and for all,so that they need not travel back and forth for the rest of the materials. If their cases can't meet the requirements for the filing, a written verdict must be made. It is strictly prohibited to withhold responses or legal documents. These measures, solved some long-hung cases, making people satisfied by giving them convenient ways to file a suit. Over the two years after case-filing register system was implemented, the number of cases the provincial court accepted witnessed a nearly 40% year-on-year growth each year. More than one million cases on average have been put on file annually, and the number of closed cases again has reached a new high.

(2) Pilot Work on Reform of People's Juror System

After the Fourth Plenary Session of the Eighteenth Party Central Committee, Anyang intermediate court, Zhengzhou Zhongyuan district court, Lankao county court and other five courts were determined as pilot units of people's juror system reform by the standing committee of the National People's Congress. Henan court earnestly implemented the reform requirements, and improved the methods of jury selection, shifting from unit recommendation or individual application, to randomly selection of the qualified citizens.Juries was reformed. Jurors no longer heard problems of law applicability, but the facts in cases per se. More people will act as assessors in a law case, and major cases will be trialed by grand collegial jury panel consisting of 3 judges and 4 or 6 assessors. Henan's exploration and reform in the aspect of perfecting people's juror system, make more ordinary people know more about justice, and supervise the operation of justice, and also deepens the judicial democracy, and improves the social credibility of the judicial referees.

(3) Actively Promoting the Reform of Long-Distance Jurisdiction of Administrative Cases.

After the 18th National Congress of the CPC, the Supreme Court summarized experiences from Xinyang, issued the Regulations of Long Distance Jurisdiction of Administrative Cases (Trial Implementation), and fully implemented the reform of long distance jurisdiction of administrative cases across the province. Henan took the lead in realizing administrative cases under the jurisdiction of the court all across the country, and required "folks suing officials" cases be accepted in turn by another court from another city, which was known as the ice-breaking move in the implementation of the central reform "to establish the jurisdiction system of appropriate separation between local cases and administrative divisions. In 2015, the reform of long distance jurisdiction of administrative cases in Henan has achieved initial success. Firstly, the action is to enhance people's confidence in the rule of law. The situation in which people "believe in petition letters but not in the law" has preliminary reversed. There were 22,642 "folks suing officials" cases last year, increasing by 43.8%, compared with the number of 15,746 last year. Folks' winning rate was 27.8%, compared with the earlier 10.2%, which increased by 17.6%. Secondly, it promoted administrative judicial credibility. Lawsuit dropping rate after the first trial increased to 76.6% from 46.7%, and lawsuit dropping rate after the second trial reached 98.5%. The number of petitioners to Beijing decreased by 16.4%, which reduced for the first time in five years. Thirdly, it promoted the administration so that it acted in accordance with the law. The White Book of administrative trial was published, and 600 pieces of judicial suggestions were put forward to warn relevant departments of plugging up loopholes in management, and the standardization of administrative behaviour. Meng Jianzhu, secretary of the designator praised that" Henan did a good job", and Zhou Qiang, Director of the National Supreme Court suggested "summarizing and promoting the practice and experience of Henan Superior Court", Guo Gengmao, Secretary of Provincial Party Committee, instructed that "it is imperative to insist on the reform and keep improving". Central leading group of comprehensively deepening reform specially introduced Henan's experience in the conference of exchanging reforming situation, and People's Daily reported our story for an entire page.

(4) Actively Promoting the Pilot Work in Quick Trials of Criminal Cases

Since the Third Plenary Session of the 18th CPC National Congress, the

Decision on the authorization of the Supreme People's Court, the Supreme People's Procurator ate in Parts of Setting up Pilot Areas about Quick Trial of Criminal Cases (hereinafter referred to as the "Decision") was passed by voters in the standing committee of the National People's Congress, and then 18 cities including Zhengzhou were listed among the first batch of pilot areas. Courts and procurator rates of two levels in Zhengzhou, with active exploration, ice-breaking bravery, and courageous practice, have achieved obvious results. Only in 2015, 1,781 cases suitable to quick trial process were closed in Zhengzhou, accounting for 23.24% of the total number of criminal cases closed during this period, which was 8.24% higher than the average rate of 15% national pilot courts, and making up 44.02% of the cases sentenced to fixed-term under a year during the same period. Zhengzhou people's procurator rate explored the working mode of "1 + 2 + 8" process for quick trial. Pilot spots on quick trial of criminal cases were set up, to shorten the time of handling cases, to improve the efficiency of litigation, and to save a lot of judicial resources.

(5) Carrying Out Many Measures Simultaneously to Overcome Difficulties in Enforcement

Since the Fourth Plenary Session of the Eighteenth Party Central Committee, policemen in courts all over the province worked with dedication. The number of cases judged and executed rose 47.7% and that of execution amounting rose 75.2% (Figure 1) according to a year-on-year comparison, which brought an end to "blank note of law"(some orders of court cannot be executed).

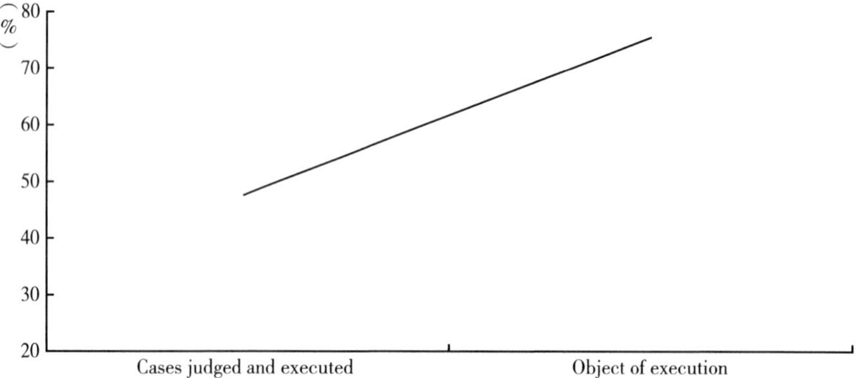

Figure 1 Year-on-year growth rate of numbers of cases judged and execuled and object of execution in 2016 Henan

Firstly, province's courts determine to start a resolute battle. In order to overcome the difficulty of hard execution, the judicial system in Henan made a pledge at every level in office. If the task can't be finished, the director, or executive director of the court should resign, otherwise, he/she will be dismissed by the superior according to organizational procedures. During the process, 2 directors were fired, and positions of 20 incompetent executive directors were changed. In terms of supporting work, more human and financial resources and materials were devoted to the front line, reinforcing 1,575 policemen and more than 3,200 pieces of equipment including police cars, UAVs, law enforcement recorders, individual command systems were added to ensure the team's abilities to win. For example, judges in Zhengzhou Intermediate People's Court spent 22 months, trudged nearly thousands of kilometers across four provinces, and overcame various difficulties, forcing a Fushun bus company in Liaoning province to pay back Yutong Group 280 million yuan as reimbursement. Secondly, legal networks were set across the province, to strengthen joint constraints. In 2016, Henan put more than 417,000 faithless people into the black list, so that they would be faced with limitations in taking public posts, promotion, bidding, government procurement, financing, taking planes and high-speed trains, and leaving or entering the country, etc. For example, a boss in the black list could not buy the return ticket after his Antarctic tour until he paid off his debts; A municipal grain bureau which refused to perform effective judgment, was revoked the title of "Provincial Civilization Unit". Thirdly, good opportunities were taken to give strong punches towards diehard debtors. The province's courts started a "Storm" "Mid-Autumn Thunder", "Midnight Action", "Attack in the Early Morning", to siege diehard debtors, wherever they fled. In 2016, deposits of 15.89 billion yuan, more than 8,000 land cases, and over 43,000 houses were invalidated, 18,327 people were under judicial detention, and 68.248 million yuan was confiscated as fines.1,244 criminals were sentenced, which was three times of that of 2015. More than 56,000 people performed their obligations out of pressure, as a result, the applicants applauded while diehard debtors trembled with fear. Fourthly, striving for support in every way, to converge into powerful forces. In order to provide support for the livelihood of the people, and manifest the justice for the people, the party committees and governments at all levels in Henan focused on difficulties in implementation and execution and tried to mobilize all forces to solve the implementation problems. The representatives witnessed execution, actively participated in the implementation of paragraph, and propped up the spirit of people's court. Media reporters went into the front line, dined with policemen and reported the implementation results in a all-round way. More than 300 press conferences were held, over 100 microfilms completed, more than 1,000 times of live execution on Weibo and WeChat were put online by courts of three levels in Henan, creating a rich atmosphere of condemning dishonesty among people.

4. Rule of Law Publicity Activities Carried Out Comprehensively Centering on the Overall Situation and Richer Atmosphere of the Rule of Law

(1) Carrying out Legal Publicity and Educational Activities Solidly

Since the 18th National Congress of the CPC, Henan has been carrying out all kinds of legal publicity and education theme activities solidly. Taking the leading cadres, civil servants, youth and farmers as the focus of law-popularizing objects, to boost the thorough developments of law publicity among the people. It is important to step up the construction of rule of law culture parks, and squares, adhere to the requirements of "uniqueness of a city, distinctive brands of a county," and put forward the creation and promotion of the rule of law works of literature and art. Rule of law culture activities such as exhibitions and selections of demonstration units were organized. Special pages, columns, and projects relating to law were set up by means of newspapers, radio, television, network, and mobile news media, to strengthen the culture, radiation and influence of rule of law. Taking 2016 as an example, Henan Law Association, provincial Office of Comprehensive Management, and provincial law-popularization office carried out "legal services into grass-root units" activities throughout the province. More than 6,670 rule of law seminars were held in total, more than 6230 times of centralized campaigns were carried out, nearly 15.4 million copies of all kinds of popularization materials were distributed, more than 1,490 thematic theatrical performances were organized, 8,000 legal service windows were established, and nearly 60,000 fixed publicity windows and billboards were made. Legal consultation served nearly 1.6 million person-times (Table 1). At the same time, Henan Law Association, actively organized many experts and scholars and the relevant units, to give advice on the construction of Song Zhai village in Jinshui district of Zhengzhou, and rule of law exhibition pavilion and rule of law culture square in Xinye County of Nanyang city, to contribute to building a platform for the grass-roots level rule of law publicity education.

Table 1 Results of "Legal Services in Grass-root Units" activities

The rule of law seminar	More than 6,670 times
Centralized Publicity Activities	More than 6,230 times
All Kinds of Publicity Materials Given Out	15.4 million (copies)
Theatrical Performance Organized	More than 1,490 times
Legal Services Window Established	8,000
Windows and Fixed Publicity Billboards Created	60,000
People Received Legal Consultation	1.6 million (person-times)

(2) In-depth Learning and Popularization of Constitution and Key Laws and Regulations

Over the past five years, Henan thoroughly studied the conference spirit of the 18th National Congress of the Communist Party of China, and made full use of all kinds of platforms, carriers to put forward popularization and education of law. We studied General Secretary Xi Jinxing's important insights of fully advancing law-based governance, and promoted scientific legislation, strict law enforcement, impartial judiciary, and people's law-abiding awareness, and spread the effects and experience of rule of law construction in Henan. We thoroughly studied and publicized the constitution and the legal system of socialism with Chinese characteristics, improved the mass' awareness of constitution and the rule of law, forming good atmosphere of studying the constitution, abiding by the constitution and upholding the constitution in the whole society. Finally, we actively carried out all kinds of popularization activities about specialized laws. Cities such as Sanmenxia city, Gongyi county strived to improve the whole society's awareness of environmental protection and the concept of environmental protection according to the law by opening environmental publicity columns in the media, making lecture tours about new environmental in key enterprises, and conducting activities of environmental monitoring and public law enforcement. The Provincial Bureau for Letters and Calls insisted on taking May as intensive publicity month of Correspondence and Visitation Regulation, and widely publicized Correspondence and Visitation Regulation and related laws and regulations through various channels and in various fields such as holding press conferences, answering reporters' requests, mobilizing publicity cars, setting up information desks, handing out information cards, organizing knowledge contests, art performances, and rule of law publicity caravans, etc.

(3) Supporting Economic and Social Development

During the past five years, guided by the concept of innovation, harmony, green, opening-up and shared development, Henan centred on "13th Five-Year Plan" for economic and social development, and carried out services for the construction of Zhengzhou airport comprehensive pilot zone, independent innovation demonstration areas in Zhengzhou, Luoyang and Xinxiang, and China free trade zone(Henan). Meanwhile, we provided support for the construction of the Belt and Road, supply-side structural reform, cracked down on illegal fund-raising, promoted environmental protection and other specialized events. We organized lawyers, notaries, grass-root legal service workers, and law-popularization volunteers to make up all kinds of special legal service team, provided counsel for companies, and strove to provide legal consultation and service for the reform of state-owned enterprises, digestion of excessive production capacity, merger and reorganization of enterprises, and for prevention of financial risks, thus improving the precision and efficiency of the law-popularization work. We gave play to organization and coordination, organized lawyers to act as legal advisers and government lawyers. There are 289 lawyer representatives of People's Conferences at all levels, CPPCC members, and perennial legal adviser in 18,000 units, providing efficient legal service of high quality for the legal governance and administration of party committees and governments.

5. Law Studies and Exchanges with Foreign Countries with More Substantial Law Research Results

(1) Increasingly Greater Platform Role of Provincial Law Association

As the platform of law studies and the rule of law publicity, Henan Law Association organized experts and scholars to actively participate in various academic activities held by China Law Society. Awards for Outstanding Organizers and Awards for Outstanding Papers were won in Forum of Rule of Law in China, Youth Forum of Chinese Law Studies, Outstanding Achievement Award of Chinese Law Studies and Dong Biwu Law Achievement Award of Youth. At the same time, to change the present situation of few provincial law institutes with small coverage as soon as possible, and to perfect the research associations, organization system, in May 2015, the provincial Politics and Law committee forwarded *Guidance of Law Institute Construction in Henan*. It clearly put forward opinions that 20 research institutes were to be established in two batches, amounting to more than 30 institutes plus the original 11 ones. Moreover, Provincial Law Association held three propelling meetings, and several coordination meetings, to promote the preparatory work. By the end of 2016, the total number of associations affiliated to Henan Law Research Association had reached 41, which achieved a historic breakthrough.

We actively participated in foreign exchange activities held by China Law Society, and recommended 3 members of our province to visit and exchange ideas in the United States, France and India respectively. Henan Law Association and Institute of Law in Chinese Academy of Social Sciences, International Law Research Institute established a normalized cooperation mechanism by signing a strategic cooperation agreement, so business connection and pragmatic cooperation between the two sides, lending much theoretical and intelligence support to the rule of law construction in Henan. The first legal consulting service centre for Taiwanese businessmen was set up in the Law system across the country, with professional teams providing legal consulting service and case litigation and arbitration agency services for Taiwan businessmen in Henan. They were also involved in the dispute mediation and legal analysis of investment projects for Taiwanese, and received praise from Taiwanese businessmen. At the same time, as the organizer of the "Summit Forum on Henan-Taiwan Economic and Trade Cooperation and the Rule of Law Support", we organized Henan and Taiwan law and legal workers to have academic exchanges on legal issues on cross-strait economic development, economic and trade cooperation, which enhanced the theory support and the rule of law support of economic and trade cooperation between Henan and Taiwan; The Ninth Forum on Rule of Law of Rise of Central China, carefully organized and planned, was a complete success. The forum took the law support of targeted poverty relief in countryside as the theme, and centred on the key work of the party committees and governments; Specialized topic research seminars and lectures were organized. The first Youth Forum on the Rule of Law in Henan set the rule of law support of innovation-driven development as the theme, and the second forum was organized concerning the intellectual property rights and innovated development; The First Rural Forum of Rule of Law in Henan took rural governance under the rule of law as the theme, while the second took "theory and practice of law enforcement mechanism of farmers and land separation" as the theme.

Provincial Law Association, along with Provincial Human Resources and Social

Security Office, held the Second Selection Campaign of Henan Outstanding Young Lawyers in which, a group of outstanding legal talents stood out, creating a rich atmosphere for the rule of Law construction in Henan. Achievements were more productive. We compiled the *Achievements Report*, submitted it to provincial leaders, China Law Society and relevant departments, and got positive feedbacks from the provincial government, which instructed the departments concerned to study and make the best of it. We carefully organized hundreds of reports given by hundreds of famous jurists. Taking 2016 for example, 40 legal law experts selected by Provincial Law Association were organized as a speech team, and held 126 reports in all levels of law association across the entire province. Our main law-popularization brand--"Double Hundred" was absorbed into the seventh five-year plan of law-popularization, and was written in the memo of the provincial party committee. The activity of "Spreading Law Culture among Grass-root Units by young law-popularization volunteers" was carried out in good atmosphere. The Henan Law Association at all levels held the rule of law culture activities, such as the rule of law lectures, knowledge contests, mock trials and so on, to popularize law for cadre at the grass-root level, college students and the community crowd, and provided legal service for over 6.5 million people. In order to expand the scope of law popularization further, Henan Provincial Law Association constructed new comprehensive media service platforms, including "one website, one Wechat account and one headline". Among them, Henan Law Network, the Rule of Law in Central Plains headline and its Wechat account played a leading role, while the overarching framework was formed by websites, headlines and Wechat accounts of law research institutes in all cities and counties in Henan. It is worth mentioning that the headline of "rule of the central plains", won the Special Contribution Award, which is the first prize in the national law system. In addition, *Internal Reference of Henan Rule of Law* compiled by Henan Law Association became an important channel for the leading cadres at all levels to learn law theories and the rule of law practice.

After the 18th National Congress of the CPC, Henan Law Association further completed organization system. Firstly, the party construction of law associations was strengthened at the county level. We attached great importance to the party construction of law associations at the county level, and supervised pushed its implementation within the deadline. Until August 30, 2016, party organizations were set up in law associations of 158 counties (cities/districts).Secondly, the construction of law research association was further strengthened. By the end of 2016, the total number of associations affiliated to Henan Law Research Association had reached 41. Leaders of China Law Society, and relevant experts and scholars were invited to the seminar on law research to train directors and secretaries of research institutes. Thirdly, management of member service was strengthened. So far, the number of individual members in the China Law Society is among the largest across the country, with more than 30,000 members representing a wider coverage of people, and more reasonable age structure. Fourthly, information construction was enhanced. Henan actively explored a new working model of "internet + law", giving full play to the system of "one website, one Wechat account and one headline" of the Provincial Law Association.

(2) Rich Scientific Research Achievements Made by Law Schools of Universities in Henan

Since the 18th National Congress of the CPC, law studies in Henan made diversified achievements. Experts and scholars in all colleges and universities of Henan studied hard on the basis of combination of theory and practice, actively participated in foreign exchange, and played a very important role in law education. Taking 2016 as an example, scientific research activities in law schools of universities in Henan were more abundant, with more substantial scientific research achievements (Table 2).

Table 2 Statistics of scientific research achievements in law schools of universities in Henan, 2016

Scientific research achievements unit	Projects supported by National Social Science Foundation (items)	Provincial Soft science projects (items)	Published (copies)	Chinese Core Journal Criterion of PKU (copies)	Reprint rate and quote rate (times)
Zhengzhou University Law school	2	5	288	28	17
Henan University Law school	2	4	113	17	3
law school of Henan University of Economics and Law	1	4	60	26	10
Henan Normal University Law school	1		41	14	6
Henan University of Technology Law School			37	13	
Zhengzhou Institute of Light Industry Law School	1				
North China University of Water Resources and Electric Power Law School		1	3	2	

Ⅱ Main Problems in Law Construction

Over the past five years, rule of law construction in Henan has been moving forward bravely in difficulty, especially the judiciary reform which has broken through layers of barriers. While significant results were obtained in the rule of law construction, problems inevitably appeared. In this sense, the rule of law construction is always on-going.

1. Insufficient Legislation Talents Reserves and Lagging Legislation

In line with the spirit of the Fourth Plenary Session of the Eighteenth Central Committee, cities with districts in Henan own legislative power. At the same time, with the deepening promotion of the comprehensive work of governing the province in accordance with the law, legislative tasks are becoming greater day by day. However, the problem of weak legislation is becoming more and more serious, in fact, human resources of legislation cannot meet the demand of legislation and legislative requirements. The present situation is that People's Congress in cities with districts have no legislative power (except in Zhengzhou, Luoyang), and thus have no separate legislation manning quotas, and no legislation experience. For provincial People's Congress, there will be more legislation workload, especially the work of legislative guidance, training, record review for cities divided into districts, so this needs sufficient talent reserves to support. At the same time, in terms of legislation, we tend to formulate a law when the situation is mature. Due to the unsteady standard of maturity, it is difficult to determine the relationship between legislation and social development. Thus, legislation inevitably lag behind. If the legislation hasn't caught up with the practice, it is hard to avoid many problems.

2. Inadequate Legal Support for Ecological Environment and the Rule of Law Construction in Finance yet to be improved

At present, the new environmental law has just come into effect, people's awareness of environmental protection is gradually improving, and various environmental problems have reached the point where they must be resolved. In 2014, the department of environmental protection in Henan province and the provincial public security department jointly issued the *Notice on Strengthening Conscientiously the Cohesion Work of Environmental Administrative Law Enforcement and Criminal Justice* and the *Notice on Printing Temporary Provisions of Overseeing Major Crimes of Environmental Pollution*, and established the "3 + 3" joint working mechanisms. "Three systems", refers to contact meeting system, significant environmental pollution cases listed supervisory system, and an environmentally illegal information published in newspaper system; "Three mechanisms", refers to joint investigation mechanism, transferring mechanism for 11 types of environmentally illegal crimes related to public security penalties, and transferring mechanisms for four kinds of illegal crimes of environmental pollution, which formed a good system network of combating environmentally illegal crimes by administrative and criminal forces. The environmental protection, however, is not a one-day business, ecological protection according to law must be carried out in entirety with a long-term mechanism. In general, the rule of law support of Henan ecological environment is still weak and insufficient. Legislative guide stresses on prevention and control of environmental pollution but not on natural resources protection and ecological construction; Law enforcement is strong but it has not become a routine to crackdown on environmental illegal activities; specialized courts for environment protection have been established, but litigation systems for environmental public interests have not been set up or improved. Therefore, Henan must gear up in legislative thinking, and the professionalism of law enforcement and judicial environment, to comprehensively promote the deep integration between ecological civilization and the rule of law civilization.

Finance is the lifeblood of the economy, and the development of financial industry is a barometer of economic development. Rapid and sound social economy is impossible, without a stable financial order. Major financial cases such as illegal fund-raising, illegal public deposits absorption are happening in cities, especially in Zhengzhou, Xinxiang and Kaifeng recently, which resulted in the closing-down of micro, small and medium enterprises because of running bosses, leaving social situation unstable. Therefore, we need to strengthen the rule of law construction and provide law guarantee for the rise of finance in Henan.

3. Legal Advisory System Yet to Be Completed As Soon As Possible

The Third Plenary Session of the 18th CPC National Congress first proposed "to establish legal advisory system all over the country". The Third Plenary Session of the 18th CPC National Congress made the deployment and requirements of legal advisory system construction clearer. By the end of 2016, not all levels of parties and governments across the entire province have established legal advisory system. As for those departments with a legal consultant system, there are also problems about its legal advisers such as low comprehensive quality, and lack of responsibility. Some legal advisers in governments even blindly cater to government leaders in order to continue serving recognized as legal advisers. They were too showy, and ignored the principles of adhering to the facts and law.

4. Grim Situation of Social Public Security

At present, Henan is in a critical period of ascending and transformation faced with prominent problems of unbalanced, uncoordinated and unsustainable development caused especially by increasing economic downward pressure. New contradictions and new problems that are brought about tend to be more intricate and overlapping. Henan is faced with outstanding problems in illegal fundraising, land requisition and demolishing, problematic properties, environmental protection, social insurance, medical care, enterprise reform, terrorist attack, etc. Economic problems may easily trigger social ones. Problems in one place or group easily cross over to many places or groups, and demands from one group spread to other groups. If these small sensitive problems can't be timely resolved, or managed properly, they will trigger bigger one, and become more serious and more wide-spread, threatening social public security.

5. Imbalanced Development of Law Teaching Faculty and Research

Our current strategic layout "comprehensively governing the country according to law" is of great significance to the reform of law education, and the legal science education development and legal talent training in Henan must meet the all-round new requirements on governing the province according to the law. We should change as soon as possible the status quo of small-scale law education, non-standard teaching content, poor teaching practice and students' lack of belief in law in colleges, and comprehensively improve the quality of law students, cultivating legal talents of high quality for the rule of law construction in Henan. Teaching faculty is insufficient in law education, affecting the improvement of law education quality. Construction of law teaching teams in private colleges and vocational colleges is not optimistic and the title structures of law teachers vary widely among different universities, law teachers are lacking in law affairs competence in general and law teaching faculty is not stable, etc. Those problems must be highlighted and solved as soon as possible.

6. Spirit of Law yet to be Carried Forward Further

The spirit of rule of law is the core of law culture, for long it runs in conflict with our traditional culture of man-ruling, and acquaintances society, so it is difficult to reconcile conflicts between them in a short time. At present, there are quite a number of leading cadres who can't uphold the rule of law principle, which breeds the growing department protectionism and local protectionism; large members of the mass lack the concept and consciousness of the rule of law. Once they have disputes, they will not consult a lawyer, but find their acquaintances first. All these phenomena come about, because the authority of the law as a whole has not been established in our society, their faith in law has not yet been built, or has not been strong enough. So we need to further spread and carry forward the spirit of rule of law, invest more efforts in fostering the law culture.

III Prospects, Countermeasures and Suggestions for the Rule of Law Construction in Future Henan

In the past five years, with the guidance of "fully advancing the law-based governance of the country" which was put forward in the Fourth Plenary Session of the Eighteenth CPC Central Committee, centred on the Four-Pronged Comprehensive Strategy (The strategy is to make comprehensive moves to finish building a moderately prosperous society, deepen reform, advance the law-based governance of China, and strengthen Party self-conduct) in Henan. The rule of law construction has made great progress and gained substantial results. For instance, local legislators worked actively, judicial work overcame difficulties, social security comprehensive administration moved forward in the face of odds, and law studies made diversified achievements. However, there is never an end to reforms, and the rule of law construction is always improving. In the future, Henan will build on past achievements; we are to find out and make

up for deficiencies, and to carry out higher quality of multi-aspect, multi-angle and multi-level construction efforts of the rule of law. We are to attach great importance to the law talent team building, work hard to promote judicial system reform, strengthen the airport economic legislation, and bring further prosperity to law studies. We must create a favorable atmosphere for the cultivation of legal thinking and ways of working. Henan's economy and society are to forge ahead further from the new starting point with the driving and supporting power of the law.

Over the past five years, the power of law has brought the progresses, which has warmed our heart. However, there is no stop in reform and development, and there is no end to law construction. In the future, the rule of law construction in Henan, will further increase the people's sense of achievement and move reform forward in an all-around way and in depth.

1. Paying More Attention to Improve the Quality of Legislation

In the future, Henan local legislative work will closely revolve around the urgent needs of economic and social development, attach great importance to the scientific and democratic legislation, and ensure the synchronization of reform and development with high-quality law systems, so that major reform carried out on a legal basis. In the coming years, National People's Congress in Henan plans to revise *Regulations for the Control of Air Pollution*, *Property Management Regulations*, *Energy Saving Regulations* and Administrative Measures for the *Management of Small Food Processing Workshops and Food Vendors*, *Guarantee Act of Minority Rights and Interests*, *Regulations on Vocational Training*, and *Regulations on Reward and Protecting the People Who Take up the Cudgels for a Just Cause*, etc. At the same time, nine regulations such as *Regulations on Poverty Relief and Development*, *Regulations on Emergency Response, and Regulations on Governance of Overloaded Transportation* will be taken as backups, to be reviewed as circumstances permit. 0 regulations applied by cities with districts shall be reviewed and approved. Legislation of 31 regulations including *Measures for the Implementation of Urban and Rural Planning*, *Regulations on Budget Supervision, and Regulations on Promoting the Development of E-commerce* will be surveyed and studies in proper order.

Henan provincial government will seriously implement *Opinions on Strengthening Legislative Work of Government*, and will shoulder the responsibility to standardize and guide the legislative work of governments at lower levels; municipal governments with districts should establish and improve the procedures of drafting and formulating local rules and regulations and standardize the local legislation work, with the legislation work as the focus, from the aspects of strengthening the leadership, institutions and personnel; the Provincial Office of Legislative Affairs is to enhance the guidance of legislative work of governments with rights of local legislation in cities directly under the provincial government and help them in institution establishment and personnel training.

2. Constructing Law-based Governments More Effectively

2017 is the second year since the implementation of *The Guidelines on Building a Law-based Government (2015-2020)*. Henan is to fully implement the guideline and formulate concrete implementation plan, further complete the propulsion mechanism of the construction of law-based government, and insist that the legislation, decision-making, and the execution of the administration of the government should abide by the law. In order to further improve the rule of law qualities and abilities of government workers, and to develop their consciousness and concept of leading law-learning and law-obeying, we should carefully organize law training, and make use of law courses, with the combination of theory and practice, to help them develop habits of handling affairs according to law, and developing the rule of law thinking in deepening reform, promoting development, solving disputes, and maintaining stability. Governments at all levels, administrative organisations should establish legal systems as soon as possible, and give full play to the professional knowledge and the unique advantages of legal advisers, in order to build a "safety network" for the scientific and democratic decision-making. We need to take the rule of law construction as an important standard of evaluating officials in governments at all levels, and to ensure that all governmental activities are on the legal track.

3. Promoting the Judicial Reform More Soundly

In the future, Henan judiciary authorities will continue to carry forward the spirits of "daring to face toughness", work harder to push forward judiciary reform, and strive for the successful completion of various tasks deployed in the Third/Fourth Plenary Session of the 18th CPC National Congress. The reform of personnel quota system will be completed in courts of Henan, fulfilling the minimum requirements of "one judge, one assistant and one clerk" and forming trial execution teams with sufficient assistants. Courts in Henan will complete judiciary responsibility system, promote the normalization of leaders taking the lead in the handling of cases, and guarantee the principal position of judges. Those judges unwilling or afraid to take responsibility and lacking in abilities will be cast out. After the completion of selection work, all Procuratorates will regard implementing the responsibility system as a key task in deepening reform, and will live up to the principle that "the one who handles the case and makes decisions is responsible". Meanwhile, management levels of business units should be reduced, to make it more flat gradually. This year, Supreme People's Procuratorate will further complete the guidance of procurators' power. Henan Procuratorate will organize in-depth researches, with the cooperation and assistance from institutes at all levels, to delimit the authorization scope of procurators more accurately and reasonably, and to promote the establishment of clear and unified powers and responsibilities, orderly supervision, and effective restraining mechanism of procuratorial power. The provincial court will soundly push ahead the reform of internal institutions, streamline department, and reduce the management levels, to ensure more than 85% of the staff enter the trial frontline. We will separate complicated cases and simple cases, and carry out quick trial of small civil cases. We will start the systematic pilot system of "leniency towards confessions" and deepen the pilot work of people's jury system, to alleviate the pressure of too many cases with too few people, with the help of external forces such as the people's mediators, society judges, lawyers, and arbitrator; We will continuously deepen the reform of lawsuit system centred on verdicts, strictly implement the principle of conviction on evidence, increase the number of witnesses testifying in courts, and increase the defence rate of lawyers, making the court the place of safeguarding judiciary justice.

4. More Efforts should be Made to Foster the Law Culture

The rule of law will bring security to the society, while culture will soften people's hearts. In the next few years, the rule of law construction in Henan needs to cultivate the rule of law culture of higher quality, and to guide people to develop the noble beliefs of law in heart and to establish lifestyle based on the rule of law, making the rule of law a behavioral habit. Therefore, we should carry out various forms of activities on law publicity and education, further explore the "Internet + law publicity and education," and create relevant literary and art works with simple language but far-reaching themes, so as to popularize legal knowledge in convenient and efficient ways. We need to guide people to do the right thing in the rule of law society using the rule of law publicity and platforms, and lead people to give up what we are not supposed to do, support what the law encourages, and deny what the law prohibits, so that people can tell what is right from what is wrong, make clear-cut rewards and punishment, and establish the rule of law concept that to obey the law is glorious and to commit crimes is shameful.

All in all, over the past five years, the rule of law construction in Henan has achieved good results. The provincial political organs and law offices safeguarded people's livelihood with strong determination, and gave a hand of legal aids to more people who need it, so that law publicity can disseminate the spirit of law more and more widely, and every progress in the rule of law can be seen by everyone. But at the same time, there are still many problems in the rule of law construction in Henan, which need to be resolved effectively by law. In the next few years, the rule of law construction in Henan will move on with the deepened reforms in society and economy, and provide legal support for the construction of Henan free trade pilot zone, and independent innovation demonstration area in Zhengzhou, Luoyang and Xinxiang, to make contributions to building an all-round well-off society and to the excellence of central plains of China. We will create a better rule of law atmosphere, so that people can live a happy life!

References:

[1] Zhuo Zeyuan. *The Theory of Governing the Country by Law*, Law Press, 2008.

[2] Ding Tongmin, Zhang Linhai, ed.. *The Report on the Development of Rule of Law in Henan (2016)* [M]. Social Sciences Academic Press, 2016.

[3] Gong Pixiang. Regional Development in China under the Rule of Law [J]. *The Law*, 2015 (1).

[4] Han Xu. Six Relations to be Well Dealt with in Governing Provinces According to the Law [J]. *Party Construction in Sichuan Province*, 2014(12).

[5] Ma Changsheng. *Research on Governing Provinces According to the Law* [M]. Hunan People's Publishing House, 2000.

[6] Jiao Fengjun, Research on Legal System Safeguard in Regional Economic Development, Dissertation of Master degree, University of Science and Technology

of China, 2014.

[7] Ding Tongmin, Zhang Linhai, ed.. *The Report on the Development of Rule of Law in Henan (2015)* [M]. Social Sciences Academic Press, 2015.

[8] Zhang Linhai, Li Hongwei, ed.. *Studies of Comprehensive Law-based Governance in Henan* [M]. Social Sciences Academic Press, 2016(12).

[9] *The Five-year Development Plan of the Informatization Construction of the People's Court (2016-2020).*

[10] On Comprehensively Advancing Decisions on Comprehensive Law-based Governance and Certain Major Issue Made by the Central Committee of the Communist Party.

[11] Zhang Linhai, Li Hongwei, ed.. *The Report on the Development of Rule of Law in Henan (2017)* [M]. Social Sciences Academic Press, 2017.

[12] Li Hongwei, How to Grasp the Key of Promoting Comprehensive Law-based Governance Firmly [J]. *Legal Daily*, August 31, 2016.

[13] Li Hongwei. To Win "Three Tough Battles" with the Help of Rule of Law [N]. *Henan Daily*, December 2, 2016.

B.12
Report on the Development of Zhongyuan Bank Co., Ltd.

ZYB Research Group[*]

Abstract: Since the official opening in 2014, under the correct leadership and support of the Henan CPC committees and provincial government, ZYB has pressed forward vigorously and taken the initiative in accordance with the "market-oriented" reform direction, adhered to the characterized development orientation, continued to promote the integration of internal management, strived to resolve the historical burden, speeded up service innovation constantly, prevented financial risks, improved bank's corporate governance, and strengthened internal management and other aspects of deepening reform in the service of the real economy; thereby it has achieved the transformation from scratch to coming into being, from a small scale to a large scale; what's more, it blazes a path of the successful reform via restructuring and reorganizing, adding investment and stakes, and listing in Hong Kong Stock Exchange, and eventually it has become "a leader in Henan Finance Realm".

Keywords: ZYB; A Leader in Henan Finance Realm; The Structural Reform in the Supply Side; IPO and Listing on Stock Markets

---

* Leader: Dou Rongxing;Deputy Head: Wang Jiong;Members: Wang Liubao, Zhang Ke, Wei Zhigang, Yang Tao, Zhao Yun, Liu Ningwei.

To integrate regional financial resources, guard against financial risks, enhance financial support for economic development and explore mixed ownership of economic reform, the CPC Henan Provincial Committee and provincial government has decided to consolidate Kaifeng, Anyang and other 11 city commercial banks and form a modern joint-stock commercial bank in 2013, which operates independently and is self-financing. Approved by the China Banking Regulatory Commission, ZYB was officially opened On December 26, 2014. For more than two years, under the firm leadership of the provincial committee and government, with the help and support of all social sectors, ZYB heads the mission and deepens reform. It has fully carried out both Party building and banking, and promotes the integration of internal management. It has also strived to resolve the disputes such as asset quality, historical burden, actively responds to economic downturn, promoted interest rate liberalization, the impact of the Internet and other financial challenges. Furthermore, it has served the real economy as its mission, adheres to risk prevention and spearheaded the innovation-driven transformation to achieve a stable, healthy and growing development, and has become a financial leader in Henan province. ZYB actively created conditions for the successful listing of Hong Kong on July 19, 2017 and embarked on a new journey of development.

I The Establishment of the Reorganization

1. The Planning and Preparation of the Merger and Reorganization

As the main part of the Central Plains, Henan has always been an important economic and cultural center, especially in recent years. With the implementation of the national strategies on the Core Area of Grain Production, the Central Plains Economic Zone and the Zhengzhou Airport Economic Comprehensive Experimentation Area, the demand for the large-scale, multi-level and diversified financial services is increasing. But for a long time, there has not been any local provincial commercial bank in Henan. On the one hand, it was not commensurate with the province's economic and financial development, and the financial contribution of GDP was far lower than the national average. The former city commercial banks were in a small-scale asset without strong competitiveness and their support of economic and social development was limited; five of which, on the other hand, were burdened with the historical debts that were not dealt with effectively, which might become hidden risks. At the same time, at the starting point of the merger and reorganization nationwide, among 31 provincial administrative regions (excluding Hong Kong, Macao and Taiwan), 25 have formed the national or regional joint-stock commercial banks, and a considerable number of them are based on the integration of the city commercial banks. As we can see, the experience of other provinces has proved that the regional joint-stock commercial banks based on city commercial banks can achieve a balance between the self-development, economic and social development. Therefore, to effectively integrate the local financial resources in Henan province, and to set up a regional joint-stock commercial bank with capital strength and the capability to withstand risks, become an inevitable choice to optimize the allocation of financial resources and promote the economic and social development.

2. The Formation Process of ZYB

As early as 2006, the Henan provincial government began to organize the relevant departments to carry out extensive research on restructuring of city commercial banks. In May 2012, the Provincial Finance Office led the meeting with BOC Zhengzhou Branch, Henan Banking Regulatory Bureau, the Department of Finance, Research Room of the Provincial Government, Henan Development Research Center and other departments to carry out special investigations in Anhui, Hubei, Hunan, Shanxi, Heilongjiang, and to learn from the bank formation experiences of the provinces. The conference on the establishment of a provincial banking, presided by Governor Xie Fuzhan, was held on June 26, 2013. In the conference, Xie was debriefed the related work of the bank formation and its program, and the division of responsibilities and other matters were discussed and enforced. So far, the merger and reorganization plan was basically determined, and the establishment work of ZYB could possibly start.

The provincial government held the ninth executive meeting on August 5, 2013, which *Overall Plan for the Reform and Restructuring of Some City Commercial Banks in Henan Province* was deliberated and passed. It was clearly stated that a provincial institution was to set up on the basis of Kaifeng, Anyang, Hebi, and other 10 city commercial banks and officially launched its reform and reorganization work. On August 9th, Xie Fuzhan held a mobilization meeting for mayors of the 13 cities involved in the plan, arranged for the reform and reorganization work, emphasized the requirements of the five disciplines and reached a common understanding. On the next day, the Provincial Finance Office, BOC Zhengzhou Branch, Henan Banking Regulatory Bureau gave talks to the chairmen of the 13 city banks. On August 21st, Li Ke, the executive vice governor (a sitting member), chaired a meeting for a report on the reorganization work of the reformed banks. Then, the Program of the Reform and Restructuring of Some City Commercial Banks in Henan Province"(Drafted) and the Overall Plan for the Reform and Restructuring of Some City Commercial Banks in Henan Province" (Drafted), were both drafted by the provincial finance office, and a working arrangement for the next phase was made. On December 9th, the committee on the reform and reorganization of city commercial banks was established and its first meeting was held.

On January 15, 2014, the leading group held the bid opening and evaluation meeting on the verification and evaluation of assets. After the comprehensive evaluation given by the bid assessment committee and the final vote of the legal representatives (or authorized voters) from 13 city commercial banks, some accounting firms were selected for the project on capital verification and asset assessment of the banks. Since February 10th, the accounting firms have started to work in 12 city commercial banks, and carried out the verification and evaluation of assets. On June 14th, a symposium was held in Henan by the leading group of the reform and reorganization Committee for some city commercial banks, which explored and discussed the ways to handle the historical debts of 5 city commercial banks. From June 25 to August 4, the second board meetings and general meeting of stockholders of 13 city commercial banks, including Nanyang Bank, Puyang Bank, Xinyang Bank, Xinyang Bank, Anyang Bank, Xuchang Bank, Zhumadian Bank, Kaifeng Bank, Hebi Bank, Sanmenxia Bank, Shangqiu Bank, and Luohe Bank, were held respectively. On August 28th, the 13 banks involved in the reform and reorganization were notified in the *Henan Daily* for a merger and reorganization announcement, which proclaimed the establishment of a joint stock commercial bank through the merger. Later approved by the China Banking Regulatory Commission, ZYB was officially opened on December 26, 2014. Therewith, ZYB was officially opened in December 26, approved by the China Banking Regulatory Commission. On December 18th, ZYB convened the inaugural meeting to elect the first board of directors and the board of supervisors; the first board meetings were followed, and elected the chairman and chief supervisor. ZYB employed a president and other senior managerial personnel. On December 23rd, Henan Banking Regulatory Bureau formally approved the opening of Zhongyuan Bank, and ZYB lawfully obtained its financial business license and the administrative license. On December 26th, ZYB celebrated the opening ceremony, and officially conducted business. Thus, based on the repeated demonstration, and successful experiences (of other provinces), Henan has reformed the banks in accordance with the principles of legalization, market-oriented, "optimization of the allocation of resources without risking the new institutions", and "taking the interests of the municipal government, shareholders, executives, employees into account". It went through four stages, i.e. preparations and mobilization, asset and capital verification, real-value assets and discount on Bonds, and opening preparation and business operation. It lasted a year and four months, and finally ZYB launched into business.

The Reform and reorganization of ZYB has served to highlight the following aspect: Firstly, firmly carry out capital verification and evaluation of assets. The work was based on the principle of "same standard, time, scale". Through the fair and open election of the well-known intermediary institutions, the capital verification and evaluation of assets were carried out independently within the 13 city commercial banks. Therefore, the authority and fairness of the verification and assessment results had a smooth passage through the directors and shareholders of the 13 banks. Secondly, ZYB has innovated the idea of disposal, and thoroughly removed the historical burden. According to the principle of "respecting for history, cost sharing, common disposal by the old and new shareholders and government", using the marketing approach and being convertible to cash offered the severance packages and realized the cash inflows, which was highly praised by CBRC and became a model of domestic banking restructure removing the historical burden. Thirdly, ZYB has completed the target of capital expansion in spite of recession and built a reasonable shareholding structure. Despite the sluggish capital market, ZYB has raised RMB10.398 billion (US$1.57 billion) through two public share offers with a total capital of 5 billion (US$0.76 billion) shares, which greatly enhanced the capital strength; at the same time, the cone-shaped shareholding structure, which followed the basic principles of the multi-party participation, with three levels of shareholders, minority shareholders and leading shareholders, achieved the moderate concentration and effective balance, and further optimized the ownership structure. Fourthly, ZYB has proposed the direction of market-oriented reform. The provincial committee and government have done a better job in implementing the marketing guiding principles and plans after the 18th CPC Central Committee and the Third Plenary Session of the 18th CPC Central Committee and established a market-oriented mechanism. The Ninety-eighth Standing Committee of the Ninth Henan CPC Committee gave a very clear vision for the direction of marketing reform involved in governance structure, market management system, de-administrative and compensation system, and laid a good foundation for the ZYB development and invigorated the company.

II The Reform and Development of ZYB

1. The Strength of the Financial Development has been Further Enhanced

Zhongyuan Bank has achieved development from scratch, from small to large in two years, and the performance brand has been significantly improved. Firstly, the institutional system has been improved. Five branches of Zhengzhou, Luoyang, Jiaozuo, Pingdingshan and Jiyuan have been set up to realize the full coverage of the sub-branches in 18 cities within the province. By the end of July 2017, ZYB has involved 12,000 employees and 426 business establishments. At the end of 2016, Zhongyuan Consumer Finance Company was approved by the China Banking Regulatory Commission. It has nine sub-offices in the rural area within Henan. Secondly, ZYB has the rapid growth in the scale of business. It is currently the largest conglomerate of Henan province. It operates the Legal financial institutions with a total asset amounting to RMB462.4 billion (US$69.87 billion) and doubled over its establishment. The deposit was RMB271.2 billion (US$40.98 billion), with an increase of 67.6% compared with the establishment period. The balance of loans provided by various branches comes to RMB182.5 billion (US$27.58 billion), up 62.8 percent from the first year. Thirdly, ZYB has improved the efficiency of business. In the first seven months in 2017, its net operating income reached RMB 6.58 billion (US$0.99 billion), up 8.9 percent on last year's same period; and registered a net profit of RMB1.92 billion (US$0.29 billion), up 12.4 percent on last year's same period. Fourthly, the total tax revenue of RMB8.139 billion (US$1.23 billion) has been realised since its inception and the quality of assets stably maintained. By the end of July 2017, the total capital adequacy ratio of ZYB was 11.71%, and the NPL ratio was 1.86%. The provision coverage rate was 205%, and all the indicators met the regulatory requirements. Fifthly, the brand has been widely recognized. For three consecutive years, ZYB obtained regulatory 2C level, its main credit rating obtained AAA class, which bumped it up into the list of national good banks. ZYB was entitled "Top Ten City Commercial Banks", and won the awards on" Best Service for Local Economy", "Best Bank Service for Real Economy" and "Henan Financial Outstanding Achievement, by *Financial Times* for two years in a row. In the 1000-global-bank 2017 list published by British Banker, the first tier capital of Zhongyuan Bank ranked 227th in the world, and ranking the thirty-fifth among 126 Chinese banks on the list.

On August 24, 2017, Vice Chairman of China Banking Regulatory Commission (CBRC), Cao Yu, said that ZYB has become a major achievement of the financial reform promoted together by CBRC, the Henan Provincial Party Committee and the provincial government. The reform results were given a well-deserved recognition.

2. The Market Mechanism has Basically Established

In conformity with the requirements of the provincial Party committee, ZYB has been going deeper with the reform, taking enterprises as the main body of the market to promote ZYB to plurality and multi-lever. Based on the capital structure of the former city commercial banks, ZYB actively introduced the strategic investors. After two capital expansions, it has the cone-shaped shareholding structure with three levels of shareholders, minority shareholders and leading shareholders, using capital as the link. It realized the integration between the state-owned and private capitals, and mixed the diversified structure of property right, thereby to ensure the direction of the market, and the stable and healthy development. By the end of August in 2017, ZYB had a paid-up capital of RMB20.075 billion (US$3.03 billion). Among the shareholders, the proportion of state shares and state owned legal person shares accounted for 26.16%, while the proportion of private legal persons, natural persons and H-shares accounted for 73.84%. Secondly, to improve the corporate governance. The establishment of the "three boards and one system", namely the general meeting of shareholders, board of directors, board of supervisors and senior management system, bettered the system of independent directors and external supervisors, developed sound rules of effective checks and balances, and established a good internal governance mechanism. It has formed a modern enterprise system with effective and efficient operation and greatly improved the efficiency of resource allocation. Thirdly, to establish market-oriented employment mechanism. According to the requirements of the professional manager system, we adopted the market-oriented way to select executives. ZYB added the de-administration into the company's articles, abrogated the administrative rank of all cadres, established the fair and competitive mechanism in the matter of selection and appointment, and an effective checking and inspiring system. Thus, it has created a sound mechanism under the basic principles of "recruitment and promotion through open and fair competition, and inducement and payment on the basis of merits".

3. ZYB has Focused on Serving Local Development

ZYB adheres to the status of Henan province, and serves the local economic and social development as the core. Firstly, map out the strategic blueprint. Based on the three major strategies, "characterizing traditional services, sophisticating in innovative breakthrough, and the future bank to lead the future competition", ZYB strengthened the implementation of the strategy through the "Internet finance to the countryside", which increased the financial support for structural adjustments to the local economy, especially for agriculture, rural areas and farmers, and small and micro businesses. ZYB has its roots in Henan and built an integrated nationwide network constantly, to enhance the service capacity of the real economy. It has realized the reorganization from tradition to modern, strived to transfer from "runners" to "winner" in the financial industry and achieved a first-class commercial bank The financial services capability on real economy has promoted significantly. We continue to optimize the credit structure, support our provincial economic transformation and supply side structural reform. The first 7 months of this year, ZYB has provided for the real economy a total amount of RMB176 billion (US$ 26.6 billion). To achieve greater balance in the national strategies, ZYB has traced the provincial progress in pursuing the Belt and Road Initiative and the "Three Zones and Greater Area". We have deepened cooperation with local governments, provincial departments and bureaus, signed a strategic cooperation agreement with 18 local governments, so as to provide financial support for industrial restructuring, state-owned enterprises reform, urban construction and other key areas. To enforce the support on the livelihood security and residents' power consumption, ZYB was approved to launch its own credit cards. Moreover, its Consumer Finance Company provided about RMB2.68

billion (US$0.4 billion) for 720,000 people within the first eight months. Thirdly, ZYB is to channel great energy into developing inclusive finance. To strengthen the policy to support agriculture, 10 pilot township branches were established and more Huinong Service Points were set up in 1,282 villages within the province. It filled the gaps in rural financial services, and achieved the last stage of financial terminal services. By the end of July in 2017, the balance of agriculture-related loans reached RMB50.8 billion (US$ 7.68 billion), with an increase of 8.1 billion (US$1.22 billion) over the beginning of the year, up 19%.To explore financial innovation and products on the poverty alleviation, it took the lead in directing the loans onto the photovoltaic solar industry. ZYB has cooperated with Bangladesh Grameen Bank, which was introducing the international advanced experience, and moved faster to promote the development of contiguous poor areas and helpfully reduced poverty there. To support small and micro businesses, it has also increased loans to 92.4 billion (US$13.96 billion), ranking first all over the province. It has outdone the average increase in loans overall by nearly 40,000 loan accounts, with the acquisition rate of 93.4%.

4. The Risk Control has been Continuously Improved

As a regional major bank in Henan, ZYB adheres to the bottom line of risk, strictly controls the regional financial risks, and maintains financial stability. Firstly, to effectively enhance the capabilities of risk prevention and control. ZYB will build a standardized and sound risk management system for monitoring, forecast-alarm, crisis handling, supervision and accountability, and continuously improve the ability of early identification, early warning and early handling. As a lead bank, ZYB and 5 city commercial banks have joined efforts to establish the liquidity mutual-aid mechanism, and improved the liquidity risk management ability within the region. Secondly, to guard against and reduce financial risks. To promote "reducing the non-performing loans and controlling new loans", we have implemented leadership responsibility, field visits, scheduled supervision, accountability questioning, and taking measures on cleaning, transferring, reorganizing, verifying, to effectively resolve the non-performing assets. ZYB strictly implements the credit management and responsibility system, to ensure the quality of new loans, while the new loan non-performing rate was only 0.42% after its establishment. Thirdly, to carry out internal control construction. ZYB strengthens the long-term mechanism of compliance management, focuses on key systems, key positions and key personnel, and rigidly enforces the system of staff visits. And it also strengthens the audit supervision on compliance and important risks, and adheres to the regulatory accountability. Its tough stance on corruption has been maintained, to conscientiously abide by the laws and principles.

5. ZYB has Optimized the Structure of Qualified Personnel

ZYB has implemented the talent strategy of strengthening the province through vigorously attracting and inviting high ranking technical specialists. It moved fast to make up for the lacking in employees with high academic qualifications and a competitive edge in age, in order to attract high level financial talents. Firstly, by hiring high-level professional personnel. Through the public recruitment and industry introduction, ZYB has invited successively more than 100 high-quality professionals from Tencent, Alibaba, the US Federal Reserve, Citibank, and other well-known Chinese and foreign financial institutions and IT companies. It introduced domestic core business professionals to set up the leading groups of investment banking, direct banking, consumer finance companies. A large number of financial professionals from Beijing, Shanghai, and Guangzhou have taken root in Henan to provide the support for the rapid development. Secondly, by recruiting outstanding graduates. ZYB has recruited a total of more than 2,000 outstanding graduates from the world's top 200 universities and 985 institutions. It has brought in new blood for the healthy and sustainable development of the enterprise. Thirdly, by establishing pyramidal training system. Through the continuous improvement of hierarchical talent training system, i.e., senior managers as captain, middle-ranking officials as helmsman and new staff as sailor, to select the outstanding young reserve cadres to carry out the "special training" program to the rural professional talents team construction. Fourthly, by strengthening the development and utilization of human resources. ZYB has made more efforts on finding other positions within the enterprises for its redundant workers, as well as on the on-the-job training. And we strive to explore the potential of our employees, stimulate their work enthusiasm according to the "people-oriented, performance-oriented" concept, and transfer "surplus labor" to "talented personnel".

6. The Financial Technology has Accelerated A Rational Allocation of Resources

The Internet has changed the mode of banking services and broadened the scope of banking development. ZYB adheres to the commercial banking development "initiated and driven by science and technology" as a breakthrough of the reform directions, and actively explores the transformation and development of data banking and tech banking. Firstly, to consolidate the foundation. At the beginning of the establishment, it started planning technology development and data centralization, and spent 18 months in completing a set of IT infrastructure system group for the city commercial banks to meet the management needs and to support the long-term development. It successfully switched from the old systems to new ones, a record in the banking industry on constructing a great amount of systems at one time and integrating in a shortest time. It laid the foundation for the intensive management to all businesses in banking industry. Secondly, to enhance the security system. Investment in science and technology has increased year by year, and the construction of science and technology infrastructure has been steadily implemented. It set up the information system and disaster recovery system in Zhengzhou and Shanghai, a project named "Two Cities, Three Data Backup Centers", to ensure the normal order of the banking operation. The construction of the science and technology center with an area of 55 mu (3.66 hectares) and a construction area of 160,000 square meters is under construction. Thirdly, to strengthen research and development. ZYB has started the construction of large data platforms and specified the development direction of risk control, precision marketing, customer profiles, and fine management. It has cooperated to innovate the joint application of big data and develop block chain technology with Huawei and Tsinghua University. Fourthly, to involve the application of innovation. With the mobile banking updating constantly, some of its functions are at the cutting edge in the industry. Direct banking, credit card, consumer finance and other fields make full use of big data, artificial intelligence and other technologies to carry out online business applications and automatic approval. It has innovated the mode for the mortgage of housing to individuals, and developed an online financial product "Perpetual Loan". Nowadays, it has provided RMB 12.5 billion (US$ 1.89 billion) in credit funds for 13,000 account holders and won the prize of Best Innovation Project in China's financing industry.

Ⅲ IPO and Listing in Hongkong

Since the very beginning of the establishment, ZYB has made a scientific and rational plan for its development path on the strategic level. It has taken a coordinated approach in the three major tasks, including reorganization and integration, business development and IPO and listing on stock markets. In the second half of 2016, ZYB launched the issuance and listing of IPO in Hongkong with elaborate planning and adequate investigation. Confronted with time-pressured reorganization, historical problems and difficulties, ZYB made a detailed plan for listing, inverted schedule, division of responsibility, promotion and launching.

The main tasks were as follows: Firstly, careful organization of efforts. ZYB carried out a series of investigations and researches, and completed preparatory work before reporting to and exchange opinions with the government and regulatory authorities for their consent and support. Based on these efforts, ZYB set up a leading group with chairman as leader, president and chief supervisor as deputy head, and promoted the listing in Honkong as "Project No. 1". At the same time, it has established efficient collaborative working mechanism, which stands on call on a 24/7 basis to ensure the coordination link between all branches and departments. Secondly, orderly promotion. ZYB has effectively completed the internal decision-making process, and held a general meeting of the shareholders, the board of directors, the board of supervisors, etc. And it has passed the listing motions, and implemented corporate governance procedures according to the law and principles. At the same time, according to the listing requirements and market practices, ZYB has employed sponsors, lawyers, accountants from more than 20 intermediaries through the bidding, to lay the foundation for the standardized and orderly work. Thirdly, consolidation of the foundation. ZYB has been working strictly in accordance with the listing standards when checking the equity with 9,881 shareholders and confirming its ownership of 617 pieces of real estate. At the same time, it has vigorously coordinated and steadily promoted the transfer reduction of state-owned shares, assigned specially assigned person to carry out door-to-door transfers, and pushed forward the signing of the letter of commitment. As a result, 62 state-owned shareholders have rapidly transferred or reduced their shares with the declaration and approval. Fourthly, effective examination and approval. The examination and approval work has been carefully sorted out and carried out at the same time, and was reported on a regular basis to the relevant departments to speed up the approval process. It applied for the administrative license in line with the laws and regulations, and successfully obtained two documents showing support from the provincial government and three documents of approval from the CBRC. The various application materials were well-organized and declared, which in turn were examined and approved by the SASAC of the State Council, and the Non-State-Owned Economy Office and International office of the CSRC. ZYB has sped up the procedures needed for the approval of the listing in Hongkong. Fifth, introduction of high-quality investors. ZYB has organized meetings of analysts, non-deal roadshow, analysts roadshow, management global roadshow, and held press conferences, luncheons for investors and dinners for stock analysts in Hongkong, which all aimed at introducing ZYB to more potential investors. Through a series of solid work, the image of good investment value has been fully displayed, and ZYB successfully attracted a number of international and domestic well-known high-quality investors, such as China Minsheng Investment, China Energy Company (Shanghai), China Create Finance Holdings Group, Keywise Capital, Jane Street, and Millenium.

Through these efforts, ZYB has completed a series of complex investigations and paperwork regarding financial audit, equity ownership, state-owned shares reduction, the law, the business, the third party, etc.. It submitted A1 Application to the Hong Kong Stock Exchange on April 18. The hearing was completed on June 22. The international underwriting agreement was signed on July 11. It received a notice from the Stock Exchange approving the listing of the Bank on July 18. Finally, ZYB was listed on the Stock Exchange of Hong Kong through the issuance of H-shares. It took only 3 months since the submission of A1, which refreshed the record on financial companies listed on the Hong Kong Stock Exchange.

Since listing in the Main Board of the Hong Kong Stock Exchange, ZYB officially became the Ninth listed city commercial banks in China and the third in Henan, with the net proceeds of approximately HK$8.2 billion (US$12.82 billion) (after the exercise of the over-allotment option). So far it is the second largest IPO since the beginning of 2017 and the second largest amount of IPO projects in Henan. Furthermore, ZYB hit a new record from the establishment of operations to achieve the listing within two and a half years and became one of the world's fastest growing financial enterprises achieving a historical leap as a very important milestone. Being Listed in Hongkong has promoted its self-development and served the local economy, which has a profound strategic significance. Through the listing in Hongkong, ZYB has successfully connected the international capital market and established a smooth capital supplementary channel. It helps enhance the capital strength, profitability and anti-risk ability, promoting the standardized management and transparency, raising the market visibility and influence, and also further expanding the "Financial Realm in Henan", for better serving economic and social development in Henan.

IV The Prospects of Development

In the next phase of work, ZYB will earnestly study and implement the guiding principles at the fifth national financial work conference, to achieve the goal of building an all-round well-off society and an outstanding Henan set by the tenth provincial Party Congress, and deepen the reform with new accomplishment, which will be dedicated to the upcoming 19th CPC National Congress.

1. To Adhere to the Development Orientation

Based on the market orientation to serve citizens and small- and micro-enterprises, to support agriculture, countryside and farmers, and to promote regional economic development, ZYB will take its root in Henan and deepen the cooperation with local governments, to increase support for small- and micro- enterprises, and promote the development of "bank for citizens". In order to emphasize rural finance services, and speed up the implementation financial network at the levels of county, township and village, ZYB strives for establishing more than 2,000 service points to benefit farmers. It will do more in implementing targeted poverty reduction, and cultivate the international cooperative project between itself and the Grameen Bank during finishing the building of a society that is moderately prosperous in all respects.

2. To Provide Effective Institutional Safeguard

To implement the provincial decision-making and a series of national strategic deployment in Henan province, the limited resources will be dedicated to fields that ZYB is best at, and located at important parts of the local supply side structural reform, in order to transform the local economy and upgrade the local industrial structure, thereby realizing the high efficiency and high quality of self-operation and the interaction with local economic transformation and upgrading.

3. To Maintain Steadfast Management

In accordance with the work of "reducing the non-performing loans while controlling the new ones", ZYB will actively solve loan issues and offset the debts left by history. It will comprehensively advance the risk management system, and effectively promote the asset quality, and constantly improve the capacity to prevent risks and sustainable development of commercial Banks. It will establish robust long-term mechanisms to proceed with expertise team building in parallel with institutional improvement, operation modes, culture cultivation in enterprises, etc.

4. To Actively Strive for Qualifications

The support will be granted to financial leasing companies, which actively play the important role of financial leasing services in the development of the real economy, and promote steady economic growth, transformation and upgrading. To apply for the independent licensee of direct bank, ZYB will set up an online branch after it applies for an independent license of direct banking and reach a scale of RMB100 billion (US$ 15.11 billion) three years afterwards.

5. To Promote Business Transformation

With the trend of the Internet technology, ZYB will constantly improve the information system, and make a lot of effort to develope mobile banking and online banking under the overall plan and arrangement about team building, financial system, management mechanism, operation mode, and risk management. It will continue to improve the development of mobile banking, investment banking and trading bank, strengthen the Internet financial development research, increase cooperation with the Internet enterprises, thereby seeking the transition from the traditional banks to the future banks and from a "follower" to a "pioneer".

6. To Insist on Leading by Party Building

ZYB will further improve the party's organizational structure, standardize the implementation of the system of "three sessions and one lesson", do a good job in the development and management of Party members, implement the Party inspection mechanism, and improve Party conduct and moral integrity.

It will further consolidate the foundation of party building work, integrate the governance of corporations with policy of being strict in Party discipline, reinforce the its core concept of being "steady and healthy, innovative, enterprising, efficient"; if will activate the exemplary vanguard role of the Party members, shape the staff professional ethics of discipline, hard work, honesty, orderliness, devotion, and responsibility.

The rise of the Central China has brought new opportunities and requirements for the growth of ZYB. It will stand firmly and make great efforts to give stable performances, steer the new normal in economic development, integrate with the development of Henan, seize the strategic opportunities, and build a first-class commercial bank.

✤ 皮书起源 ✤

“皮书”起源于十七、十八世纪的英国，主要指官方或社会组织正式发表的重要文件或报告,多以“白皮书”命名。在中国,“皮书”这一概念被社会广泛接受,并被成功运作、发展成为一种全新的出版形态，则源于中国社会科学院社会科学文献出版社。

✤ 皮书定义 ✤

皮书是对中国与世界发展状况和热点问题进行年度监测，以专业的角度、专家的视野和实证研究方法，针对某一领域或区域现状与发展态势展开分析和预测，具备原创性、实证性、专业性、连续性、前沿性、时效性等特点的公开出版物，由一系列权威研究报告组成。

✤ 皮书作者 ✤

皮书系列的作者以中国社会科学院、著名高校、地方社会科学院的研究人员为主，多为国内一流研究机构的权威专家学者，他们的看法和观点代表了学界对中国与世界的现实和未来最高水平的解读与分析。

✤ 皮书荣誉 ✤

皮书系列已成为社会科学文献出版社的著名图书品牌和中国社会科学院的知名学术品牌。2016 年，皮书系列正式列入“十三五”国家重点出版规划项目；2012~2016 年，重点皮书列入中国社会科学院承担的国家哲学社会科学创新工程项目;2017 年,55 种院外皮书使用“中国社会科学院创新工程学术出版项目”标识。

权威报告·热点资讯·特色资源

皮书数据库

ANNUAL REPORT(YEARBOOK) DATABASE

当代中国与世界发展高端智库平台

所获荣誉

- 2016年，入选“国家‘十三五’电子出版物出版规划骨干工程”
- 2015年，荣获“搜索中国正能量 点赞2015”“创新中国科技创新奖”
- 2013年，荣获“中国出版政府奖·网络出版物奖”提名奖
- 连续多年荣获中国数字出版博览会“数字出版·优秀品牌”奖

WWW.PISHU.COM.CN

成为会员

通过网址www.pishu.com.cn或使用手机扫描二维码进入皮书数据库网站，进行手机号码验证或邮箱验证即可成为皮书数据库会员（建议通过手机号码快速验证注册）。

会员福利

- 使用手机号码首次注册会员可直接获得100元体验金，不需充值即可购买和查看数据库内容（仅限使用手机号码快速注册）。
- 已注册用户购书后可免费获赠100元皮书数据库充值卡。刮开充值卡涂层获取充值密码，登录并进入“会员中心”—“在线充值”—“充值卡充值”，充值成功后即可购买和查看数据库内容。

社会科学文献出版社 SOCIAL SCIENCES ACADEMIC PRESS (CHINA) 皮书系列

卡号：314344772535

密码：

数据库服务热线：400-008-6695

数据库服务QQ：2475522410

数据库服务邮箱：database@ssap.cn

图书销售热线：010-59367070/7028

图书服务QQ：1265056568

图书服务邮箱：duzhe@ssap.cn

S 子库介绍
Sub-Database Introduction

中国经济发展数据库

涵盖宏观经济、农业经济、工业经济、产业经济、财政金融、交通旅游、商业贸易、劳动经济、企业经济、房地产经济、城市经济、区域经济等领域，为用户实时了解经济运行态势、把握经济发展规律、洞察经济形势、做出经济决策提供参考和依据。

中国社会发展数据库

全面整合国内外有关中国社会发展的统计数据、深度分析报告、专家解读和热点资讯构建而成的专业学术数据库。涉及宗教、社会、人口、政治、外交、法律、文化、教育、体育、文学艺术、医药卫生、资源环境等多个领域。

中国行业发展数据库

以中国国民经济行业分类为依据，跟踪分析国民经济各行业市场运行状况和政策导向，提供行业发展最前沿的资讯，为用户投资、从业及各种经济决策提供理论基础和实践指导。内容涵盖农业，能源与矿产业，交通运输业，制造业，金融业，房地产业，租赁和商务服务业，科学研究，环境和公共设施管理，居民服务业，教育，卫生和社会保障，文化、体育和娱乐业等 100 余个行业。

中国区域发展数据库

对特定区域内的经济、社会、文化、法治、资源环境等领域的现状与发展情况进行分析和预测。涵盖中部、西部、东北、西北等地区，长三角、珠三角、黄三角、京津冀、环渤海、合肥经济圈、长株潭城市群、关中—天水经济区、海峡经济区等区域经济体和城市圈，北京、上海、浙江、河南、陕西等 34 个省份及中国台湾地区 。

中国文化传媒数据库

包括文化事业、文化产业、宗教、群众文化、图书馆事业、博物馆事业、档案事业、语言文字、文学、历史地理、新闻传播、广播电视、出版事业、艺术、电影、娱乐等多个子库。

世界经济与国际关系数据库

以皮书系列中涉及世界经济与国际关系的研究成果为基础，全面整合国内外有关世界经济与国际关系的统计数据、深度分析报告、专家解读和热点资讯构建而成的专业学术数据库。包括世界经济、国际政治、世界文化与科技、全球性问题、国际组织与国际法、区域研究等多个子库。

权威·前沿·原创

皮书系列为

“十二五”“十三五”国家重点图书出版规划项目

河南发展报告（2017）

主　编／魏一明　张占仓
副主编／周　立　袁凯声　王承哲

社会科学文献出版社
SOCIAL SCIENCES ACADEMIC PRESS (CHINA)

作者名单

B.1　河南开放发展报告

河南省社会科学院院长　张占仓

B.2　河南经济发展报告

课题组组长：张占仓

课题组成员：完世伟、武文超、袁金星、唐晓旺、王　芳

B.3　河南工业发展报告

课题组组长：张富禄

课题组成员：赵西三、杨志波、宋　歌、刘晓萍、李婧瑗、杨梦洁

B.4　河南金融发展报告

课题组组长：张占仓

课题组成员：完世伟、赵　然、武文超、王　芳、石　涛

B.5　河南科技创新发展报告

河南省社会科学院　袁金星

B.6 河南旅游发展报告

执　笔：许韶立、侯红昌

B.7 河南城镇发展报告

课题组组长：张占仓、王建国

课题组成员：王新涛、左　雯、郭志远、彭俊杰

B.8 河南农业农村发展报告

课题组成员：乔宇锋、生秀东、赵广宇（延安大学）

B.9 河南社会发展报告

课题组组长：牛苏林

执　笔：牛苏林、张侃

B.10 河南文化发展报告

课题组组长：卫绍生

课题组副组长：李立新、杨　波

课题组成员：郭海荣、郭　艳、陈勤娜、田　丹；

执　笔：杨波、郭海荣

B.11 河南法治发展报告

课题组组长：张林海

课题组副组长：李宏伟

课题组成员：祁学瑞、赵新河、王运慧、欧广远、栗　阳、刘　旭、刘　硕、李浩东

执　笔：李宏伟、王运慧

B.12 中原银行股份有限公司发展报告　中原银行课题组

课题组组长：窦荣兴

课题组副组长：王　炯

课题组成员：王留豹、张　克、卫至刚、杨　涛、赵　允、刘宁伟

中文目录和中文摘要

摘　要: 作为传统内陆腹地，河南省在“十二五”时期通过建设郑州航空港国际枢纽，在供给侧提供新的生产要素，促进进出口总额年均增长 32.9%，创造出“对外开放靠蓝天”的新模式。2016 年，河南省多项国家战略获批，战略叠加效应凸显，发展动能提升，全省进出口总额达到 4714.7 亿元，升至全国中西部地区第一位，开放带动效应显著。伴随区域发展模式创新，结合全面融入“一带一路”建设的需要，河南省明确提出建设内陆开放高地的战略目标，并使其成为河南进一步发展的一种战略导向。我们研究认为，要实现这种战略目标，就要毫不动摇地推动中原腹地成为开放发展前沿，毫不动摇地构建双向开放新体系，毫不动摇地提升开放型经济发展水平。促进开放型经济发展，应重点抓好五大战略举措：深度融入国家“一带一路”战略，进一步提升郑州航空港开放发展优势，支持郑州建设国家中心城市，加快推进开放式创新，积极探索以“枢纽经济”为标志的自贸区建设之路。通过全面开放，河南正在从内陆腹地迈向开放发展的前沿，全力打造内陆开放高地优势。

关键词: “一带一路”　郑州航空港　“对外开放靠蓝天”　内陆开放高地　开放型经济

摘　要：党的十八大以来，河南省坚持稳中求进工作总基调，以新发展理念为引领，主动适应经济发展新常态，着力打好“四张牌”，经济实力大幅提升，经济结构持续优化，人民生活稳步改善，一批国家战略落地实施，开放型经济发展活跃，经济社会发展取得了巨大成就。当前，面对国内外复杂的经济形势，河南省将不断深化供给侧结构性改革、实施创新驱动发展战略、积极拉动内需、努力扩大对外开放、有序推进新型城镇化、改善居民生活，实现经济社会可持续发展，正在由经济大省迈向经济强省。

关键词：河南省　供给侧结构性改革　稳中求进　创新驱动

摘　要：2012 年以来，河南抓住国家战略叠加机遇，推进供给侧结构性改革，加快动能转换，工业保持平稳发展。尤其是 2016 年以来，河南工业经济呈现缓中趋稳、企稳回升的总体态势，供给结构明显优化，利润增速稳步走高，先进制造模式加速渗透，工业稳增长成效明显，支撑了全省经济平稳较快发展。展望 2017 年，伴随着我省转型发展攻坚战的全面推进和制造业供给侧结构性改革的持续深入，河南工业将继续保持平稳增长，预计规模以上工业增加值增速同比增长 8.0% 左右，产业产品结构持续优化，五大主导产业和高技术产业继续保持高速增长。

关键词：河南工业　中国制造 2025　转型升级　供给侧结构性改革　先进制造业强省

摘　要：十八大以来，河南省金融行业坚持稳健发展，深化改革创新步伐，金融业发展实力增强，“金融豫军”迅速崛起，服务实体经济能力显著提升，金融扶贫取得突破，金融改革创新亮点不断。展望未来，面对国内外复杂的经济金融形势，河南金融发展的机遇和挑战并存。未来几年，河南省应加大重点领域金融支持、加快多层次资本市场发展、加强薄弱环节金融创新、深化金融改革、突出规范监管、强化风险防范，实现河南金融业继续健康发展。

关键词：金融豫军　供给侧结构性改革　金融创新　河南省

摘　要：岁月更替，斗转星移。五年风雨兼程，波澜壮阔。党的十八大以来，河南深入贯彻落实中央创新驱动发展战略的重大决策部署，推动河南科技事业取得长足发展，以创新驱动经济社会转型发展的宏伟蓝图正在中原大地浓墨重彩地向现实转化，创新已经成为河南“决胜全面小康社会让中原更加出彩”的第一动力。新的历史时期，世情、国情、省情正在经历深刻变化，河南科技创新发展也面临着新形势、新机遇、新要求和新挑战。未来，要继续把创新摆在事关河南发展全局的核心位置，充分发挥科技创新的基础、关键和引领作用，奋力打造中西部科技创新高地，为建设经济强省、促进中原在实现中华民族伟大复兴中国梦的进程中更加出彩提供更多动力支撑。

关键词：科技创新　创新驱动战略　中西部科技创新高地　河南省

摘 要： 2016年河南旅游经济持续发展，带动作用明显提升。旅游产品不断创新，旅游市场在立体营销中深度拓展，农业观光、乡村旅游发展迅猛，旅游精准扶贫工作成绩显著，旅游服务品质水平显著提升，产业空间在全域发展中扩大延伸。虽然旅游发展成绩显著，但仍面临一些阶段性难题，如有观光农业旅游的品牌化建设滞后，旅游产品精细化有效供给不足，产业链条的催化带动性不强，运行管理体制机制仍有较大提升空间等。为此，必须遵照中央和省委的要求，按照河南“十三五”旅游规划的发展目标，重点培育实施高端客源营销策略，打造“沿黄丝路旅游带”，推广精品旅游线路，培养河南的旅游中心和未来旅游趋势。

关键词： 旅游发展　旅游产品精细化　沿黄丝路旅游带　河南省

摘 要： 2012~2016年，河南以城市群为主体形态，充分发挥规划引导作用，推动产城融合发展，优化城镇化空间布局，城镇化进程不断加快，质量不断提升。但是，河南城镇化仍然存在总体水平滞后，中心城市带动力弱、城镇综合承载力弱等问题。国务院批复《中原城市群发展规划》，标志着河南全面进入城市群时代，也要求河南把握好中央推进新型城镇化和城市发展思路、举措更加科学清晰等历史性机遇，采取发挥市场主体作用，完善运行协调机制等综合性措施，推进中原城市群一体化发展，充分释放新型城镇化蕴藏的巨大内需潜力，为经济持续健康发展提供持久强劲动力。

关键词： 中原城市群　新型城镇化　城市发展

摘 要： 当前，河南农业农村发展正处于转折转型的关键阶段，既处于加快发展的机遇期，又处于深刻变革的转型期。从2012年至2016年，河南农业农村发展态势良好，主要农产品产量稳定增长，农民收入持续高增长，农地流转加速，新型农业经营主体发展加快。2017年，尽管各种传统和非传统挑战叠加凸显，但有利条件也在逐步累积，在农业供给侧结构性改革推动下，主要农产品产量将稳定增长，农产品供给将加速从数量增长向质量提升转变，农业业态创新和城乡发展一体化将进一步加快。

关键词： 农业供给侧改革 现代农业 农民收入 农业结构调整 河南省

摘 要： 2016年是河南“十三五”规划的开局之年，也是省十次党代会召开，中原崛起河南振兴富民强省迈出坚实步伐，决胜全面小康、让中原更加出彩站上新的历史起点的关键一年。一年来，河南以加强供给侧结构性改革为抓手，提高供给体系质量和效率，更加注重稳增长、促改革、调结构、强基础、惠民生、防风险综合平衡，全面深化改革开放，着力补齐民生短板，加快推进共享发展，实现了全省经济稳中向好，人民生活水平持续提升的发展态势。但同时，一系列发展中的问题和困难也日益凸显。比如，资源环境约束加剧，大气污染问题日益严重；全面脱贫进入倒计时，扶贫攻坚任务艰巨；就业压力没有根本性缓解，就业结构性矛盾日益凸显；城乡居民收入增速滞后于经济增速，与全国水

平有拉大的趋势；人口老龄化对经济社会发展的负面影响日益显现；快速城镇化带来一系列社会问题，人的城镇化任重道远等。2017年，是河南“十三五”规划走向深入的一年，也是全面贯彻落实省十次党代会精神，加快推进共享发展的关键一年。始终把保障和改善民生、推进共享发展摆在社会发展的优先位置，全面推进精准扶贫精准脱贫，进一步加强社会建设、创新社会治理，妥善解决好新型城镇化进程中的突出问题，大力推进生态建设、打造美丽绿色河南，提升基本公共服务质量，将是河南决胜全面小康、推进社会建设全面发展面临的主要任务。

关键词： 社会治理　小康社会　精准脱贫　共享发展

摘　要：“十二五”时期，河南省文化建设快速推进：省十次党代会提出“加快构筑全国重要的文化高地”新目标，《华夏历史文明传承创新区建设方案》颁布实施；公共文化服务体系示范区（项目）创建工作积极推进，公共文化服务水平不断提升；文化遗产保护工作成效显著，16处历史文化遗产被列入国家大遗址保护“十三五”专项规划，“河南省非物质文化遗产数据库建设工程”有条不紊地进行；文化产业发展实现新的突破，一批省级文化产业示范园区、基地、项目建设持续推进，文化及相关产业增加值仍然保持着12%以上的增长速度；河南文化的软实力和影响力在对外文化交流的过程中不断增强，河南文化建设站在新的历史起点上。但是，相对较低的人均GDP制约着河南文化建设的总体投入，文化资源的有效整合和保护利用尚不到位，中小文化企业发展仍然步履维艰，文化创意人才依然紧缺，文化产业创新能力不足等主客观因素，不同程度地制约着河南文化建设的发展速度。2017年，面对依然相

当严峻的发展形势，河南应在调整发展理念、创新发展模式、优化发展环境、完善发展机制等方面下大功夫、下深功夫、下苦功夫，为在新的历史起点上实现新的奋斗目标打下更加坚实的基础。

关键词： 文化高地　新的起点　发展趋势

摘　要： 党的十八大开启了我国法治建设的新征程，五年来，河南的法治建设在持续发展中得到稳步提升，立法领域有序推进，执法措施更显严格，司法改革全面铺开，法治文化更加浓厚。与此同时，面对层出不穷的社会问题和日益高涨的群众需求，河南的法治建设肩负着更加繁重的任务和伟大的使命，立法质量需要进一步提升，法治政府建设要凸显成效，司法改革要扎实推进，全民守法应该成为一种常态。在法治建设的道路上，河南需要循序渐进，持之以恒，全面出击，重点突破，只有建成真正的法治强省，中原大地的法治基石才能更加坚固有力，经济社会发展才能大步前行。

关键词： 依法治省　法治政府建设　科学立法　司法改革　河南省

摘　要： 2014 年正式开业以来，在河南省委、省政府的正确领导和关心支持下，中原银行迎难而上、主动作为，按照“市场化”改革方向，坚守特色化发展定位，持续推进内部管理整合，努力化解历史包袱，不

断在服务实体经济、加快业务创新，防范金融风险、改善治理结构、加强内部管理等方面深化改革，实现了从无到有、从小到大的转型，走出了一条重组改制、增资扩股、香港上市的成功改革之路，成为“金融豫军”的领头羊。

关键词： 中原银行；金融豫军；供给侧结构性改革；发行上市

法律声明